Grant Invades Tennessee

MODERN WAR STUDIES

GRANT INVADES TENNESSEE

The 1862 Battles for Forts Henry and Donelson

Timothy B. Smith

University Press of Kansas

Published by the University Press of Kansas (Lawrence, Kansas 66045), which was
organized by the Kansas Board of Regents and is operated and funded by Emporia
State University, Fort Hays State University, Kansas State University, Pittsburg State
University, the University of Kansas, and Wichita State University

Library of Congress Cataloging-in-Publication Data

Names: Smith, Timothy B., 1974– author.
Title: Grant invades Tennessee : the 1862 battles for Forts Henry and
Donelson / Timothy B. Smith.
Description: Lawrence : University Press of Kansas, 2016. | Series: Modern
war studies | Includes bibliographical references and index.
Identifiers: LCCN 2016028708 | ISBN 9780700623136 (cloth : alk. paper) |
ISBN 9780700623143 (ebook)
Subjects: LCSH: Fort Henry, Battle of, Tenn., 1862. | Fort Donelson, Battle
of, Tenn., 1862. | Grant, Ulysses S. (Ulysses Simpson),
1822–1885—Military leadership.
Classification: LCC E472.96 .S65 2016 | DDC 973.7/31—dc23
LC record available at https://lccn.loc.gov/2016028708.

British Library Cataloguing-in-Publication Data is available.

Printed in the United States of America

10 9 8 7 6 5 4 3 2 1

The paper used in this publication is recycled and contains 30 percent postconsumer
waste. It is acid free and meets the minimum requirements of the American National
Standard for Permanence of Paper for Printed Library Materials Z39.48–1992.

To God Be the Glory

CONTENTS

CONTENTS

Illustrations follow page 180.

LIST OF MAPS

PREFACE

It was quite the scene, as the two old generals sat and enjoyed each other's company. Veterans had reminisced together many times since the Civil War, but this meeting had more multiple layers of meaning than normal as a dying Ulysses S. Grant visited with one of his oldest friends, Simon Bolivar Buckner. The visit was newsworthy if for no other reason than Grant was a former president of the United States, and the most popular American alive at the time. Buckner was no slouch himself, of course, being a former Confederate general and governor of Kentucky, but Grant was clearly the elder statesman of the two and Buckner came to pay what he knew would be his final respects to the living legend.[1]

Beyond Grant's presidential credentials, the meeting was also significant in other ways. The two were generals before they were politicians, and on opposite sides of the great Civil War that had torn the nation asunder some two and a half decades before. Their meeting together and discussion (Grant writing on scraps of paper because his throat cancer had ended his ability to talk) of the reconciliation even then taking place were certainly noteworthy. Grant noted, "I have witnessed since my last sickness just what I wished to see ever since the war: harmony and good feeling between the sections. I have always contended that if there had been nobody left but the soldiers we should have had peace in a year." The meeting also illustrated the need for old soldiers to write memoirs, preserve battlefields, and give their recollections about what had happened; this generation, with Grant its standard-bearer, was beginning to pass away. Grant was dying, but Buckner was getting old as well. At one point, Grant wrote of Buckner, "you look very natural except that your hair has whitened and you have grown stouter."[2]

The 1885 meeting was fraught with other fascinating contexts as well. The scene harked back to earlier relationships these two had shared. Their days together at West Point had been enjoyable and full of youth, and their service together in Mexico fighting for the United States government was by then a fond memory as well. Grant and Buckner reminisced about those times, Grant even writing a short note to Buckner's new wife: "I knew your husband long before you did. We were at West Point together and served together in the Mexican War."[3]

Significantly, Grant only mentioned a few parts of their association. Not so glorious, for each of them, were other meetings that one or the other obviously remembered less fondly. In fact, their recorded association in the 1850s was when Grant was out of money and a charitable Buckner bailed him out. Apparently neither mentioned their next meeting either, which was certainly their most famous and significant. The two had met again at Dover, Tennessee, in February 1862. By this time, Grant was an up-and-coming Union general while Buckner was the chivalrous expatriated Kentuckian defending one of the key points in the Confederacy. While the Union victory at Fort Donelson won laurels for Grant, Buckner was not totally humiliated. While he faced numerous months in Federal captivity, some of it in solitary confinement, he emerged from the ordeal beloved by his soldiers, whose fate he had chosen to share. Yet no evidence remains that in 1885 the two talked over the Fort Donelson events. The charitable Grant never brought it up, no doubt fearing it would cause Buckner embarrassment. It had to be in the back of their minds, though, as the two sat and visited for one last time. It was, to be sure, a curious meeting of two friends, made more curious and perplexing by the odd happenings of a civil war decades earlier.[4]

The Forts Henry and Donelson campaign certainly affected the Grant and Buckner relationship, but its significance spread even farther. In a real sense, the battle portended a lethal result for Grant because it was there that he switched from a pipe to cigars. Admiring Americans began to send him boxes of the latter when he was shown in the papers calmly smoking one. Even larger ramifications resulted from the February 1862 events, however; much of the reunification and even reconciliation even then discussed by these two elder statesmen had come from those events decades earlier. Thus for many reasons, the Forts Henry and Donelson campaign is rich in significance and consequence.[5]

For all its importance, few major studies of the February 1862 campaign have surfaced through the century and a half since. While there are certainly many books detailing the operations on the twin rivers in 1862, only two stand out as major academic studies. A path-breaking publication by Benjamin Franklin Cooling brought the campaign to the forefront in 1987: *Forts Henry and Donelson: The Key to the Confederate Heartland*. Sixteen years later, in 2003, Kendall D. Gott published *Where the South Lost the War: An Analysis of the Fort Henry-Fort Donelson Campaign, February 1862*. Both are serious academic studies worthy of attention.[6]

Yet while both books are very well done, they approach the fighting from completely different angles and neither fully covers the story. Cooling is interested mostly in context, and as a result takes the broadest possible approach in his examination. Everything is seemingly fair game, and as a result he spends nearly the entire first half of the book on background economics, politics, and society. Likewise, much of the latter part of the book (as well as two additional volumes) is contextual material on what happened in the area after the fighting, including commemorative efforts. While there is certainly validity in this approach, it leaves little room for the coverage of tactical military detail.[7]

Gott's exploration also leaves gaps. He is much more interested in the military action than Cooling, but as a former army officer, Gott seeks to explore the leadership and command relationships involved in the campaign. Like Cooling, Gott rarely goes beyond the brigade and at times even the division level. Thus, the coverage is almost entirely on the top tier of the armies, with little inclusion of the common soldiers' viewpoints or actions.

Each author succeeds admirably in their approach, but the fact remains that there has never been a truly comprehensive tactical treatment of the Forts Henry and Donelson campaign. There is consequently a desperate need for an overall, comprehensive, detailed, and balanced book on the topic. Unlike most other Civil War battles, which have numerous tactical studies causing some socially oriented historians to complain about the lack of context, Forts Henry and Donelson have surprisingly never had that depth of treatment.

In providing a detailed tactical examination, this book will obviously differ from the previous volumes. Since neither academic book on the campaign treats the fighting in great detail, this book will illuminate aspects of the battles never before examined. At the same time, it will steer clear of too many minutiae. This book will also rely on the personal accounts of the soldiers: contemporary primary sources, particularly manuscript material. Popular historians and previous overviews almost by definition do not include such research, but even the two academic works are not definitive in that respect.

Another theme regards overall strategic orientation. This book will completely immerse the reader in the larger picture of the Mississippi Valley campaign, discussing how Forts Henry and Donelson were a part of the larger context of the war in the west. This book will examine how the initial Tennessee River campaign was critical to the ultimate Union victory in the Mississippi Valley, and how Henry and Donelson proved decisive. The book's focus will thus be less on the Cumberland River results of Fort Donelson and the capture of Nashville and more on Forts Henry and Heiman and the Tennessee River line's importance. Despite the large surrender and later emphasis on Fort Donelson, Forts Henry and Heiman and the opening of the Tennessee River were actually more important in the larger Union operational and strategic efforts.

The opening of the Tennessee River could not have been a permanent Union achievement without the neutralization of Fort Donelson, which added many degrees of success with the capture of a Confederate army, the taking of Nashville, and the emergence of Ulysses S. Grant. Still, it was the capture of Fort Henry that actually shook the Confederacy to its core from Richmond to New Orleans. The Confederate retreat from Columbus and Bowling Green, Kentucky, and the famous concentration at Corinth, Mississippi, that resulted in Shiloh all began as a result of Fort Henry's and Fort Heiman's fall, not Fort Donelson's. Additionally, the Federal Cumberland River advance ended at Nashville, and as important as that was, it was the ability to move into the cotton states via the Tennessee River that was much more significant. Contemporary correspondence from Grant, Henry Halleck, and others clearly indicates that taking Fort Donelson and even Nashville was only a temporary detour. They each planned for the Union armies to quickly return again to the main axis of advance on the Tennessee River. Subsequent events bore out this strategy, as the armies moved southward along the Tennessee Valley to Shiloh and eventually Corinth, the climax of the Tennessee River campaign.

This recasting of the focus on Fort Henry rather than on Fort Donelson, part of which is preserved as a national park after all while Fort Henry has been under water for the past seventy years, certainly cuts against the grain of modern scholarship. Even some contemporary viewpoints took this Donelson-centric position; many thought Fort Donelson was the dominant achievement at the time. Henry Halleck opined that "the fall of Columbus, the great 'Gibraltar of the West,' and the taking of New Madrid have followed as consequences of the victory of Fort Donelson, just as Bowling Green &

Nashville were abandoned to Gen. Buell in consequence of the same strategic movements." Similarly, another observer wrote, "in all probability the careful historian will yet decide that in shaping events which step by step wrought the downfall of the Southern coalition, Fort Donelson stands preeminent."[8]

Recent historians have generally taken the same viewpoint, one Tennessean noting long after the war that "when Fort Donelson fell the strategic military key of the Confederacy was taken which unlocked the door to Southern territory from which the South, in spite of the gallant and courageous struggle of her people to form other lines of defense, was never able to recover." Even Bruce Catton declared, "Fort Donelson was not only a beginning; it was one of the most decisive engagements of the entire war, and out of it came the slow, inexorable progression that led to Appomattox."[9]

It is highly likely that each of these writers was including the operations against Fort Henry under the larger title of the Fort Donelson campaign, but it is important to separate the two. Only a few have tried to do so, among them an early biographer of the key Union figure in the all-important Fort Henry victory, Flag Officer Andrew H. Foote. James Mason Hoppin wrote quite correctly in 1874 that

> there were far greater battles during the war, both on land and water, than that sharp fight on the narrow river which resulted in the fall of the earth-work of Fort Henry . . . but there were few battles of more vital importance to the Union arms than this earliest success of the Western flotilla. . . . Fort Henry was the key of the rebel position in the West. . . . By it the first strong rebel line of defense—the spinal column, as it were—was broken. The control of the direct line of railroad which connected the great rebel force of Columbus with that at Bowling Green was secured, a point far in the rear of both of these was seized, and the road was opened for the southward advance of our armies. Bowling Green was soon after evacuated. The desperate battles of Pittsburg Landing, Shiloh, and Corinth were the logical consequence of the capture of Fort Henry, being the struggle on the part of the rebels to establish a new line of defense running from Memphis and Island No. Ten to Pittsburg Landing, on the Tennessee, and Chattanooga.[10]

Obviously, Hopping was eager to emphasize Foote's importance, but in this case he exemplified less hero worship and more truth than most other accounts. It is entirely fitting that the battlefield at Fort Donelson is today partially preserved as a national park, but it is also sad that such an important piece of tangible history as Fort Henry today lies at the bottom of Kentucky Lake, the victim of the Tennessee Valley Authority's flood-control efforts in the 1930s and 1940s. I hope to restore respect for one of the Civil War's most defining sites in this book.

No author writes a book alone, and numerous people, for whom I am very grateful, have aided me in this process. The archivists and workers at the various repositories were all extremely helpful. I have to single out the great people at the Fort Donelson National Battlefield, where a major portion of the research was conducted. Superintendent Brian McCutchen and his staff were great to work with, accommodating my every request, and they definitely made this a much better book by their cheerful aid and help. In particular, Doug Richardson facilitated my research in the park library and proved to be a great sounding board for ideas. Susan Hawkins, Debbie Austin, Mike Manning, and Bobby Hogan helped facilitate my research visits there as well, and Susan was extremely helpful in scanning photographs and providing documents in the park's archives.

Others were also helpful in sorting out what can at times be confusing battle reports and terrain that unfortunately is not fully preserved. In addition to Doug Richardson at the park, who spent a day with me and my dad on the battlefield, others aided my terrain research during my many on-site visits to the battlefields. One particularly enjoyable day was when Superintendent McCutchen, former park historian Jimmy Jobe, Henry and Donelson campaign authority Jim Vaughan, and I (joined later by Ranger Richardson) spent a rainy day sorting out various aspects that were fuzzy or lacking complete understanding. There are still some of those uncertainties that will probably never be fully known, but the knowledge that these men have between them is amazing and I thank them for their willingness to invest some of that in me.

Once the manuscript was completed, these talented historians also agreed to read the finished product. McCutchen, Richardson, Jobe, and Vaughan all made numerous and productive comments on the manuscript, making it much stronger. In addition, Greg Biggs also agreed to read the manuscript and provided many helpful suggestions as well. As always, John F. Marszalek read the manuscript and made it a much better book by his incisive analysis and editing.

Working with the University Press of Kansas has again been a pure joy.

Mike Briggs is one of the best in the business, and Kelly Chrisman Jacques and Mike Kehoe are first-rate and super easy to work with. Copyeditor Robert Demke worked his magic on the prose, for which I am thankful.

I am especially grateful for a generous faculty research grant provided by the University of Tennessee at Martin. These funds allowed me to research at numerous repositories, including in Washington, DC, Carlisle, Pennsylvania, West Point, New York, and Indianapolis, Indiana.

My family is my special safe haven from the world, and anything I do would be worthless without being able to share it with my wife, Kelly, and daughters, Mary Kate and Leah Grace. Leah Grace even enjoyed a special day of research at Fort Donelson on a day off from kindergarten. She made a special friend in Jimmy Jobe, who eagerly showed his grandfather's heart to this newcomer to Fort Donelson. I am also thankful for my parents, George and Miriam Smith, who started it all, and am especially thankful to have them living closer to us now. My dad and I were even able to spend an enjoyable day (despite his attack of kidney stones) at the park at the very beginning of the research.

As always, the most important thing in my life is my God and the salvation provided through Jesus. I join Flag Officer Andrew H. Foote, after the victories on the Tennessee River, in proclaiming thanks to him for all he has done in my life: "Let us thank God from our heart, and say not unto us alone, but unto Thy name, O Lord, belongs the glory."

PROLOGUE

Stewart County, Tennessee, is off the beaten path today, bypassed by modern interstates and other transportation routes across the United States. Because of technological advances of the second industrial revolution, aviation and superhighways have left the rural Tennessee county isolated and almost forgotten. But that is the opposite from the situation in the nineteenth century, when the very different technological advancement of the original industrial revolution created a very different result. Then, the advances of steam power made sure the area was a focus of commerce and transportation in the region. Indeed, the county was squarely in the middle of some of the most heavily traveled corridors of the state and even of the nation.

In the first half of the nineteenth century, Stewart County was very much a major commercial player, mainly because it offered access to two of Tennessee's major internal waterways, the Tennessee and Cumberland rivers. The birth of steam power and its use on steamboats on waterways and railroads on land were vital in bringing Stewart County into prominence. The two rivers offered access to the county, and even visitors traveling to larger metropolitan areas such as Nashville often stopped there when their steamboats needed fuel or provisions. Likewise, the county later housed a major railroad that ran through its borders after 1861, the Memphis, Clarksville, and Louisville. The technological advances of the industrial revolution thus had an important impact even on the seemingly isolated Stewart County.

The first settlers into the area arrived about 1795, prior to statehood, when the land in the more western reaches of the state was filled mainly with the Chickasaw, some of whom were initially hostile to the white intruders. Many of the settlers came laterally from North Carolina, having received large tracts of land as partial repayment for their services in the Revolutionary War. The state legislature created the county in November 1803, naming it after one of the original prominent citizens, Duncan Stewart. Originally it was much larger, but over the next few decades it was whittled down in size by the creation of newer counties.[1]

The county's seat emerged around 1805 and was originally named Monroe, but later it was changed to Dover. It sat along the southern edge of the Cumberland River and soon had a log courthouse and jail. Private businesses such as mills and hotels emerged as well as a brick school. A female academy opened its doors in 1840, and numerous religious denominations built churches. Despite newer buildings over the next few years, the town never really took on a cosmopolitan feel. One unimpressed observer noted in the 1860s that it was still "unknown to fame, meager in population, architecturally poor."[2]

Despite its nearness to two rivers, Stewart County was not a productive agricultural area. There was some cotton farming early on, but it soon became unprofitable. Even so, the county had a respectable cash value of farms, over a million dollars, and contained an assortment of the expected farm animals: horses, mules, oxen, and cattle. There were also many sheep and swine, fostering a good economic trade of wool and bacon. Farmers in 1860 also produced respectable amounts of corn, tobacco, and potatoes, and there was also a lively honey industry. Nevertheless, the county, situated as it was between two large rivers and filled with choppy land in ravines and hills, was not plantation country. The small number of slaves as compared with other Tennessee counties demonstrated that Stewart was not a place of large plantations.[3]

Instead of being an agriculturally dominant society, Stewart County hosted manufacturing. The 1860 census listed establishments in the county such as a cobbler, mills, and leather, liquor, lumber, harness, and shingle businesses, but by far the most prevalent industry was iron. Located on the edge of the iron belt, the hills and hollows of Stewart County were well endowed with ore. The first forge in the county appeared in 1820, the Dover Furnace, and by 1860 there were fourteen furnaces in existence, one (the Cumberland Iron Works) owned by senator and later Constitutional Union presidential candidate John Bell. Slaves worked these forges, and blacksmiths also made their livings off the production. Several bar iron, bloom, and casting operations produced refined goods, but the major production was pig iron.[4]

Iron was a profitable business, but it took capital from rich owners in middle Tennessee to make it work. In 1860, there was more than $621,000 invested in the forges and other infrastructure in the county, and it employed 596 laborers, including seventy women. The annual value of the products

produced was $622,881. The big iron companies also owned subsidiary enti-
ties such as thousands of acres of land on which the iron was mined as well
as charcoal and trees used as fuel for the furnaces.[5]

The nearness to the river was a large factor in making the county a major
iron-producing center; the product could easily be shipped by boat all across
the United States. The emergence of steam power on the river significantly
added to that ability, making the county a haven for iron production and travel
in the nineteenth century. In fact, the rivers were such important thorough-
fares of travel in that day that the Army Corps of Engineers took on the task
of improving inland river channels on the Tennessee and Cumberland rivers
prior to the Civil War. Few realized that the opening of the streams would
play a major role in the naval warfare on those very rivers just a few short
years later.[6]

By 1860, the county's population was 9,896, which included 7,404 whites,
76 "free colored," 2,415 slaves, and but one Native American. Although it
was not a large slave community, Stewart County had racial problems, most
notably an 1856 slave rebellion that the locals quashed mercilessly. Stewart
County was thus not immune from sectional confrontations over slavery and
states' rights, and citizens routinely policed their slaves just like in plantation
areas. Vigilance committees emerged in response to rebellion rumors, and
many slaves were whipped and at least six hanged in the particularly nasty
1856 episode.[7]

By the 1860s, with such racial issues evident, Stewart County joined other
counties in Tennessee in facing the prospects of war. In the first referendum
on secession in February 1861, Stewart County citizens voted heavily in favor of calling a convention. The later vote saw that majority rise, and the
county soon sent many of its favored sons off to the war. They eventually
enlisted in several regiments, most notably the 14th Tennessee and a full five
companies in the 50th Tennessee.[8]

Sadly, that was not the extent of Stewart County's participation in the war.
Because of its geographic location between two major rivers, the interstate
highways of the age, the residents of the county soon found themselves in the
thick of war. The Tennessee and Cumberland rivers figured importantly in
both Union and Confederate strategies. Both sides vied for possession of the
very rivers that had previously given local residents such an economic boost.
Now those rivers, positioned as they were as avenues of invasion into the new
Confederacy, placed Stewart County early on in the very seat of war.

1

"The Keys of the Gate-Way into Her Own Territory"

Had Jefferson Davis been a prophet and able to see into the future, he perhaps would have opposed the move of the Confederate capital to Richmond, Virginia. Having set up a government, established a military, and elected Davis as their provisional president, the Confederate congress soon decided that Montgomery, Alabama, was too small and isolated to serve as the new nation's chief political center. Many factors went into the decision to relocate to Richmond, not the least of which was the wooing of Virginia onto the Confederate side, which came quickly enough in April 1861. Still, the transfer of the seat of government took the expected media and limelight with it, and the Virginia theater garnered most of the attention for the remainder of the war and for numerous decades thereafter. Meanwhile, Federal armies tore the heart out of the South in the west left behind by the politicos of the Confederacy.[1]

Obviously, no one could tell what would happen in the next four years, and there were indeed good reasons to relocate the capital. Nevertheless, the move illustrated in allegorical form the transfer of attention, men, weaponry, money, and indeed the very stakes involved in the growing conflict. With the transfer of Davis and his government to Virginia, the western Confederacy took second billing, and would remain as such for the rest of the war and afterward. Indeed, the Confederacy's top commanders, top weapons, and major army were all seated in what became known as the eastern theater, or the roughly hundred-mile box stretching between the two capitals and the Shenandoah Valley and the sea. For nearly four years the armies battled back and forth across the theater, occasionally spilling over to areas immediately north or south of the capitals themselves, but little was decided as a stalemate grew ever grimmer, taking tens of thousands of lives in increasingly bitter fighting.[2]

The west, in contrast, saw many more critical developments over those four years. The exchange of huge amounts of territory, the critical debasing of Confederate morale, and the deletion of several entire Confederate armies were commonplace beyond the Appalachian Mountains. In terms of successes that created lasting repercussions on winning and losing, the west was far more involved in deciding the Civil War than any other area.[3]

The reasons for the Confederacy's inability to maintain parity in the west and thus produce a similar stalemate were legion. One revolved around the contemporary mentality of sending or keeping the best material, generals, and armies in the vaunted east. Another reason was geography. It has long been asserted that the rivers of Virginia flowed east and west, allowing the Confederate defenders better defensive terrain with which to parry Federal thrusts; the Shenandoah Valley likewise allowed multiple Confederate generals to operate independently. On the other hand, the rivers in the west, such as the Mississippi, Tennessee, and Cumberland, mostly ran north and south, offering broad highways of invasion into the Confederacy.[4]

Perhaps the biggest factor in depriving the South of a chance to match the enemy in the west was the region's sheer size. If the eastern theater primarily covered the eastern half of one state, the west, even if defined only as the area west of the eastern theater to the Mississippi River, conversely covered all or parts of six states, from Kentucky to the Gulf coast. Since the South had a disadvantage in terms of available men, material, and logistical ability, it had a much better chance of defending a relatively narrow corridor of activity in the east than it did the huge swaths of territory in the west.[5]

If the decision to move the capital to Richmond might be considered a bad one, the manner in which the Davis administration chose to defend the west was much worse. In a confederation built upon the concept of states' rights, those individual states saw themselves as nothing less than important cogs in the entire Confederacy. Thus, they wanted to be defended just as much as the others. The Confederate government therefore decided on the unwise policy at the beginning of the war to defend every nook and cranny of the Confederacy, whether threatened or not, thereby leaving the actual vulnerable locations significantly weaker.[6]

Consequently, in the results of a policy born in urban settings amid well-dressed politicians housed comfortably in their metropolitan surroundings, this defective policy was taken advantage of in one of the most remote locations of the western Confederacy, at a small fortification called Fort Henry on the Tennessee River. The Confederacy would be hard pressed to overcome the results.[7]

In the initial stages of the war, the Confederate west was left alone even as the war began to grow more fierce through the spring and summer of 1861. Union forces instead advanced toward northern Virginia and southwestern Missouri that summer. The battles of Bull Run and Wilson's Creek became headline news for a population devoid of any military activity since 1848, and both Union and Confederate society drank in all the information they could obtain about the fighting. Unfortunately, those first battles turned out to be small compared to what lay ahead, but they were nonetheless comparable in size to the major battles in the Revolutionary War, the War of 1812, and even the more recent Mexican War.[8]

Meanwhile, matters remained calm in the crucial area east of the Mississippi River and west of the Appalachian Mountains. Several reasons existed for this lack of fighting, including an almost continual turnover in Federal command, the massive logistical effort needed to operate in the vast area, a similar need to acquire or develop vessels capable of operating along the theater's major rivers, and the all-inclusive fixation on the east. Yet the major reason so little activity developed in the west was the political action of one of the states.[9]

Kentucky had a long history of leadership in US politics. It was the first state west of the Appalachian Mountains to join the Union, and it was thus the leader of other, later states that now numbered over thirty. It had also been the famous Kentucky Resolution, penned anonymously by Thomas Jefferson, that had first begun the concept of nullification and even secession, ideas that ultimately led to the situation in which Kentucky now found itself. The state was also home of the vaunted Henry Clay, who had compromised the nation out of the kind of war it now faced. It was perhaps no accident that the first major crisis comparable to those earlier ones (1820, 1833, 1850) that occurred after his death in 1852 led to war. Clay's shoes had been partially filled by another Kentuckian, one John J. Crittenden, who like Clay had tried to offer a compromise that would not split his nation. That effort failed, and even Crittenden's family split, one son going North and another one South. Even so, the state's major role in national politics could not garner for it any special consideration now, as it sat squarely between the combatants of the growing civil war.[10]

Kentucky exercised its independence by wrangling over how to react to the warlike world around it. Obviously, both Abraham Lincoln and Jefferson Davis, both native Kentuckians themselves, desired to have the state on his side; Kentucky after all contained many men, raw materials, horses, and agricultural products. Either side would benefit from having the state on its side, and it has long been related that Abraham Lincoln stated that he hoped to have God on his side, but he had to have Kentucky. There is no proof Lincoln ever said this, but it does illustrate the importance of the state. A dual government even emerged, with the state sending representatives to the US and Confederate congresses. The paradox of being a slave state but also being a part of the United States tore at Kentuckians, but the commonwealth remained loyal throughout the entire war. Even so, it sent thousands of troops and generals such as John C. Breckinridge and Simon Bolivar Buckner to the Confederacy.[11]

The way Kentucky stayed in the Union was unique, and actually aided the Confederacy in the initial months of the war. Torn in two directions as it was, Kentucky went its own way, declaring itself neutral and asking that each side stay out of its territory. Clearly wanting to remain out of the war and the devastation that would no doubt result, Kentucky's leadership tried a tactic that would not, and could not hope to, succeed. Rarely do any areas remain out of war, especially when they are as influential and, in Kentucky's case, sitting squarely between the belligerents. All the same, Kentucky declared itself neutral, forcefully telling each side to stay away. This stance worked initially, because each side recognized that not respecting Kentucky's neutrality would effectively drive it into the enemy's ranks.[12]

Kentucky thus kept vast amounts of men, supplies, and territory from each side, although undercover and covert enlistment and trading frequently occurred. More importantly, sitting as it did along almost the entire border of the Confederacy from the Mississippi River to the Appalachian Mountains, Kentucky's neutrality effectively shielded the Confederacy, forcing any Union invasion of the South to move around rather than through the state. In effect, Kentucky's neutrality safeguarded perhaps the most vulnerable portion of the Confederacy, its border with the United States in the vast western theater.[13]

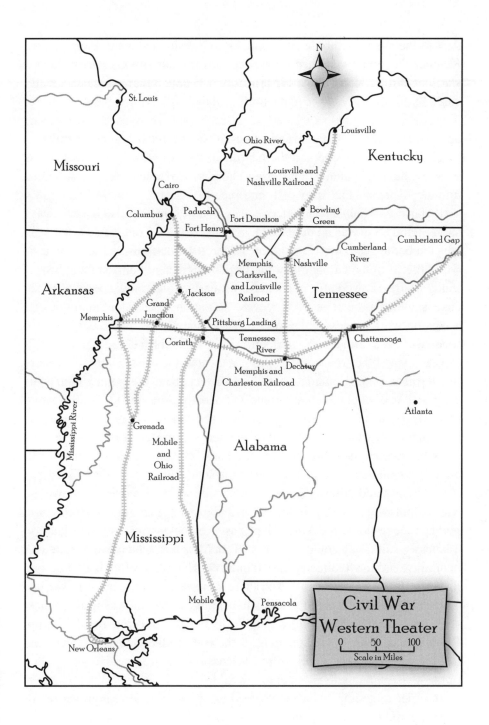

N

St. Louis

Missouri

Cairo

Columbus

Paducah

Fort Donelson

Fort Henry

Ohio River

Louisville

Kentucky

Louisville and
Nashville Railroad

Bowling
Green

Cumberland Gap

Cumberland
River

Arkansas

Memphis,
Clarksville,
and Louisville
Railroad

Nashville

Tennessee

Jackson

Grand
Junction

Memphis

Pittsburg Landing

Corinth

Tennessee
River

Chattanooga

Memphis and
Charleston Railroad

Decatur

Mississippi River

Grenada

Mobile
and
Ohio
Railroad

Alabama

Atlanta

Mississippi

Mobile

Pensacola

New Orleans

Civil War
Western Theater

0   50   100
Scale in Miles

It was the state that bordered Kentucky to the south that most appreciated Kentucky's neutrality. When Tennessee Governor Isham G. Harris led that state out of the Union in June 1861, he found its defense arrangements greatly eased by Kentucky's stance to the north. All the while, Harris worked to form his state's military assets into a potent force, and when he turned his state army over to the Confederate authorities, it became the basis of the army that would defend Tennessee and the heartland: the Army of Tennessee. Harris was so influential that noted historian Thomas Lawrence Connelly has called him the "Father of the Army of Tennessee."[14]

If Harris was bold and productive, he was unfortunately also in some ways short-sighted. He was no doubt a major player in the Confederacy (his state was the border with the United States after all), but almost all his emphasis was targeted in the wrong direction. Depending heavily on Kentucky's neutrality, Harris showed little concern for the eastern and middle portions of the state, shielded as he believed they were. Rather, he focused his attention and forces on west Tennessee. Harris was from that region, Paris, but his main focus was even farther westward, on the Mississippi River itself.[15]

Like many other rivers in the western theater, the Mississippi ran directly into the heart of the Confederacy and was in fact one of the major Union goals espoused in Winfield Scott's famous and debated Anaconda Plan. But while other rivers such as the Tennessee and Cumberland dove southward into the Confederate heartland, those were contained within Kentucky's and Tennessee's borders as they passed through. Thus, movement along those rivers would be tantamount to an invasion of the state. Not so with the Mississippi River; it bordered differing states on each side so that a movement down the Mississippi would not be an official invasion. As a result, the Federals could perhaps move down the Mississippi past Kentucky's territory and land on Tennessee soil. They could also cross from Missouri, which had declared no neutrality, and move directly into Tennessee. Harris therefore had to defend his state on its western flank. And there were larger ramifications. Not just Tennessee was at stake, but perhaps the entire Confederacy as well. Tennessee state general Gideon Pillow insightfully noted that losing the Mississippi River would result in the "opening of the river to the Gulf of Mexico, and isolating all the country west of the Mississippi, destroying the great valley of the Mississippi, with all its untold wealth."[16]

In order to solidify what he deemed to be the critical region, Harris almost ignored other areas of concern in east and middle Tennessee. Kentucky shielded those areas at the moment, but there was no guarantee that matters would remain that way. He had no plans to break Kentucky's neutrality, but Harris could not control the actions of others. Gideon Pillow, who was a Mexican War general and friend of Tennessean James K. Polk, had caused enormous political problems in the 1840s with little military success in return; he could obviously do so again. Then there was the Confederate commander in the west, Leonidas Polk. While Harris certainly had their ear, he could not necessarily dictate their actions and movements. If one of them decided that the ends justified the means of invading Kentucky, then Harris would be left defenseless across much of his border. Much like the situation on the Rio Grande River back in Gideon Pillow's previous war, when a seemingly minor episode was used to vault the United States into war, an inconsequential movement by a minor commander could bring neutrality crashing down and endanger Tennessee. The bottom line was that Harris had far too many intangibles embedded in his west Tennessee focus to leave the rest of his state basically unguarded.[17]

The rest of the state was not happy either. In east Tennessee, Harris operated more as a politician than as a military-minded overseer defending his state. Noted for their Unionism, the east Tennesseans were ripe for rebellion and Harris had to walk a fine line, particularly with late summer elections slated for the state in August 1861 and Harris himself on the ballot for reelection. Although Harris won the election, he lost east Tennessee and immediately after the election unloaded on the section, imprisoning leaders and punishing loyalists for their actions. One Confederate colonel went so far that fall as to write Confederate Secretary of War Judah P. Benjamin, "Tories now quiet, but not convinced. Executions needed." As a result, it was clear that almost the entire eastern third of the state turned flagrantly against Harris and the Confederacy, bringing on years of guerilla and sabotage action. Even worse, Federal officials were also concentrating on the area as a perfect place to foster US support within the Confederacy; Abraham Lincoln himself pushed to begin operations in the area. Harris nevertheless did little over the summer and fall of 1861, even leaving the critical Cumberland Gap relatively exposed and undefended.[18]

The same lack of concern was evident in middle Tennessee with little preparation for the defense of Nashville, that "great Western capital of the Confederacy," as one newspaper described it. One of the key transportation hubs of the northern Confederacy, just a few miles south of the Kentucky border, Nashville sat at the junction of the Cumberland River and the numerous rail lines entering it from the deep South. Its worth in production, storage, and morale to the Confederacy was immense, yet Harris made little effort to defend it.[19]

Not so with west Tennessee, particularly the Mississippi River flank. Harris placed his most valuable assets of men, guns, and supplies facing west along the river, bunching his defenses in one area instead of spacing them out to cover the entire breadth of the state. The result was Tennessee depending on the only thing Americans knew as a first line of land defense—the static fortification. Since the Revolutionary War and certainly the War of 1812 (Fort McHenry's stellar defense of Baltimore being a prime example), Americans had put their trust in earthen and masonry fortifications, spurring a massive generational system of coastal defenses. The threat had always been from the outside, for which these forts were adequately situated, but now that the threat came from within, no fortifications existed to stop an advance down the Mississippi or down the other rivers. Knowing only to defend Tennessee with fixed fortifications, Harris began to establish defenses on the Mississippi River.[20]

Ironically, this was the opposite of the overall Confederate strategy to cover all geographic areas, which would have been a better policy for Harris to utilize in his particular state. Perhaps Davis and Harris should have swapped ideas, with Harris's localized defense being used for the Confederacy and Davis's spread-out format being used for Tennessee itself. Neither Davis nor Harris saw the error of their ways, however, and continued their separate policies. While thousands of troops garrisoned little-threatened locales far to the south, Tennessee's eastern and middle sections lay vulnerable with only the thin Kentucky neutrality protecting them. All the while, Harris concentrated on land fortifications along the Mississippi River. With little time to erect masonry or stone fortifications and even less capability to construct gunboats covered with iron, Harris opted for the next best thing: earthen fortifications. Confederate engineers agreed with this need, Jeremy Gilmer later writing, "there is not plate iron in the whole Confederacy sufficient to protect the hundredth part of the surface of one boat." Railroad iron would have to suffice, but that would make the boats far too heavy for the mostly shallow rivers in the region. "I am forced to the opinion," Gilmer noted, "that the best reliance for defense will be batteries ashore, in combination with such obstructions as may be devised in the channel under the guns of the works."[21]

A series of such forts accordingly emerged along the Mississippi River, with the purpose of blocking any potential Union movement southward: Forts Wright, Pillow, and Randolph on the Chickasaw Bluffs midway along the state's river sector, and Fort Harris a little north of Memphis on another prominent area of high ground. Harris also tried to defend Memphis, that city being a critical supply and logistical rail and river hub. The forts were certainly formidable enough to river traffic, but were limited in that high ground along the river was at a premium and most of the time the river's wide delta precluded fortifications along much of its route. As a consequence, Harris had to defend his state where he could, the first instance south of Kentucky being the Chickasaw Bluffs. Harris also concentrated the majority of his troops along the river to defend against a land attack.[22]

Also left almost completely undefended were the north-south rivers between western and middle Tennessee that shot like arrows into the heartland of the state and the Confederacy. The Tennessee and Cumberland rivers were uniquely positioned for an enemy invasion, yet Harris paid little attention to either of them. And while he would be able to recover from his lapses of judgment concerning eastern and middle Tennessee, a disaster on the twin rivers would be much harder to overcome.[23]

Just as Harris settled into the comfort of having his northern border secured, the unthinkable happened: Kentucky's neutrality collapsed. This development obviously left Tennessee's entire northern border, and more ominously the broader western theater border of the Confederacy itself, open to invasion. Because of Harris's fixation on the Mississippi River, little stood between the Confederate heartland and invading Union armies. There was, as a result, a scramble, to say the least, to establish new defenses.[24]

Shocking as that development was, the manner in which it happened was perhaps even more disgusting. If Harris never considered that Kentucky's shield might fall, he also probably never mulled over the possibility of how that would happen. The fact that the culprit was on his own side was even less palatable.[25]

The actual decision lay on the shoulders of one man, Leonidas Polk. He had attended West Point with Davis, where they became fast friends, and he reaped the rewards of knowing well a president who never forgot his acquaintances, whether they were competent or not. In Polk's case he was not, and frequently throughout the war he demonstrated the fact that he was a much better preacher than general. That stands to reason, since Polk had resigned from the army soon after his graduation from the military academy and had spent the intervening decades in the ministry, rising eventually to the office of Episcopal bishop of Louisiana. His old friend Davis made him a general nevertheless, despite the fact that he had not served in any military save the Lord's army in decades. It just so happened that Polk was put in a place where he, as a novice, could do irreparable damage.[26]

Commanding in western Tennessee, Polk kept an eye on Union activity east of the Mississippi River as well as on the river itself. With a fixation on Columbus, Kentucky, Polk dreamily viewed that locale as the end-all and be-all bastion that would stop any Federal movement along the Mississippi River. Indeed it would, as long as the landward defenses were held, but that posed a problem. As much weaponry would have to go into defending the landward side as it would take to protect the actual river approaches, which were almost impregnable themselves atop the nearly two-hundred-foot-high cliffs. At any rate, Polk saw a major bastion at Columbus as the key to the defense of the Mississippi Valley, and in his hopes of achieving that he began to experience fears that were not there. He grew anxious that the Federals would capture Columbus to deprive the Confederacy of perhaps the best defensive area north of Vicksburg, Mississippi. Polk thus weighed the odds, watching closely Federal movements at nearby Cairo, Illinois, and soon settled on one of the true blunders of the war.[27]

Dismissing Kentucky's neutrality as a political factor secondary to the military importance of Columbus, Polk invaded Kentucky and occupied the bluffs on September 2. In doing so, he made Columbus a bastion that would never be moved by a frontal assault down the Mississippi River. At the same time, and more importantly, he removed the western theater–wide barrier that defended the northern border of the Confederacy, thereby leaving the width of the nation from the Mississippi River to the Appalachian Mountains wide open with little defense. Almost as critical, Polk did not occupy Paducah and Smithland, Kentucky, at the mouths of the nearby Tennessee and Cumberland rivers, which were necessary to keep those rivers from being used to outflank Columbus. Basically, Columbus was no good without adequate defenses at other places.[28]

As expected, Kentucky would from then on be a solid, if partially divided, member of the United States and would send far more troops to Lincoln's armies than to Davis's. More importantly, Federal officials were also quick to move into Kentucky, taking the vast majority of the state into Union hands, including its enormous resources in terms of men, material, horses, and supplies. They captured other strategic locations as well, such as the railroad line running from Louisville to Nashville, parts of eastern Kentucky near the Cumberland Gap, and the mouths of the Tennessee and Cumberland rivers at Paducah and Smithland. One Illinoisan wrote of his arrival at Smithland and described the amazing lack of Confederate defense, stating, "we took possession of the town within an hour from the time we put our foot on shore." Each move set Federal forces not only at defensive areas, erecting large cannon, but also at jumping-off points to invade along natural and manmade transportation routes leading directly into the Confederacy's heartland. Unfortunately for Davis and Harris, most of those routes still lay almost totally unguarded.[29]

As glaring a disaster as Polk's invasion of Kentucky was, there was one bright spot for the Confederacy in that September 1861. The individual many considered as the savior of the South had finally arrived and had taken the helm from novices like Polk and Pillow. Albert Sidney Johnston had been the US Army's Department of the Pacific commander at the outbreak of the war, with headquarters in California. With his adopted state of Texas's secession, he resigned his commission and returned east, planning to offer his services to Jefferson Davis. Theirs was a friendship much like Polk and Davis's, the two having attended Transylvania University in Kentucky and West Point together. The major difference was that Johnston had remained in the military rather than moving to a religious setting, first in Texas and then in the US army, where then Secretary of War Davis appointed him colonel of the new 2nd United States Cavalry. Now that Davis was president of the Confederacy, he once again placed Johnston in a prime leadership position, appointing him as the second-ranking general in the Confederacy and sending him to the expanded western theater that now included everything from the Indian Territory to the Appalachian Mountains. While Davis did Johnston no favor when he appointed him to such a massive department with pitifully few resources and comparatively many more problems, Johnston was fortunately no Polk, and he set seriously to his self-described "chief object," that is, to "shield the valley of the Mississippi from the enemy and assure its safety." He was at least competent, and he had the confidence of western leaders. Perhaps best of all he had the full confidence of Jefferson Davis. The president later declared to doubters, "if *he* is not a general, we had better give up the war, for we have no general." The question remained, however, if even Johnston could lure success out of the mess Leonidas Polk had made in Kentucky.[30]

A mad scramble indeed ensued when news came that Kentucky was no longer neutral and Tennessee's long border with the United States now lay vulnerable at all points. The idea of Federals moving down the Mississippi River or across from Missouri was still plausible, though at least one of those scenarios soon faded away. Polk, despite severe injury from an exploding cannon, worked to make Columbus more and more domineering, effectively ending any chance of enemy movement down the river. Columbus's presence likewise lowered the possibility of a Union army crossing the river from Missouri or Arkansas. Large numbers of boats would be required to transport the troops across the river, so Columbus denied the Federals any river access below Kentucky as well. In fact, Polk was also fortifying and garrisoning areas below Columbus such as New Madrid, Missouri, and he also called on Confederate naval commander George N. Hollins and his fleet of six small gunboats to aid in the defense. Despite a lack of everything needed in arms and supplies, the bishop still showed a bold front: "we nevertheless propose, by God's blessing, to give the best account of our command that we can."[31]

As overall commander, however, Albert Sidney Johnston had to look after Tennessee's larger defense, and work therefore continued on the earthen forts above Memphis, seen as second, third, or fourth lines of defense should something happen to Columbus. But the new situation on the Mississippi River did little to solve the problems along the rest of Tennessee's border, and Johnston had to move quickly to shore up those areas as well. He logically concentrated on the most likely avenues of invasion: the rivers running north and south instead of east and west, as in Virginia. Similarly, a rail line also traveled north and south, the Louisville and Nashville. Added to the new inventions on those transportation routes was the age-old natural byway of the Cumberland Gap in east Tennessee, which offered access to an area already seething with anti-Confederate sentiment. Federal forces could also march into Tennessee on any number of lesser routes, but these were the most conspicuous and dominant. Johnston was wise to identify them as most in need of defense.[32]

The result of this situation was a sectional Confederate, or cordon, defense under Johnston. West of the Mississippi River, a conglomeration of

Confederate units came together under the command of Earl Van Dorn, who eventually joined with Sterling Price and his old Missouri command of Wilson's Creek fame. Those generals were tasked with holding Arkansas, and the primary zone of concern was the southwest Missouri/northwest Arkansas corridor, the same area that had seen the advances earlier in 1861 that had culminated in the Wilson's Creek battle. As important as the trans-Mississippi was, however, it paled in comparison to the heart of the western theater. That was exactly where Johnston placed the bulk of his meager force.[33]

With the bastion at Columbus blocking any travel toward the south, the Mississippi River sector appeared to be safe. Leonidas Polk was tasked with blocking the river traffic as well as providing for land defenses. Polk did a good job, focused as he was on his pet project, although the danger was not so much frontal assault or even capture but, like all other fixed points of defense, the turning movement. Polk would consequently have to be aware of his surroundings, and he and many others worried about a Federal army getting around Columbus and, in Pillow's words, "reducing it by famine."[34]

A Union movement in early November 1861 to his exact area of operation illustrated Polk's need to watch carefully. Federal forces landed on the western side of the Mississippi River in Missouri and moved forward toward a small Confederate camp across from Columbus, thereby sparking the battle at Belmont on November 7. The Federal force achieved initial success but was driven back to their supporting boats by Confederate reinforcements Polk sent across the river. The small affair did not settle much, although it was the baptism of fire for Ulysses S. Grant. It also showed that the Federals were probing and looking for advantages, right to the very defenses of Columbus.[35]

Less action took place at other points, but Johnston nevertheless placed additional assets at the most critical transportation routes into the Confederacy. The next bastion east of Columbus was located at the twin rivers, the Tennessee and Cumberland, the two on parallel routes no more than ten or fifteen miles apart. Obviously, both routes had to be blocked, but the rivers' nearness to one another along the Tennessee state border suggested creating earthen fortifications along both rivers that were in supporting distance of each other. Fortunately, some work had already been done despite Isham Harris's tepid defense of the majority of Tennessee. There had been concern about these rivers early on, and the Tennessee Military and Financial Board quickly began to pay some attention there. "We request that you immediately examine the Tennessee and Cumberland rivers," the board told engineer Adna Anderson in

April 1861. They told him to establish "the proper military defenses on those streams." Surveying and locating likely positions prior to Kentucky's change of sentiment, Harris's officers had no choice but to place the defensive forts on Tennessee soil, thereby severely limiting their effectiveness. All the same, the fortification on the Cumberland River was begun under Anderson as early as May 1861, when Tennessee was still a part of the Union. It was not much of an issue because good high ground near Dover allowed for adequate defense, although there was still talk of moving the fortification to another area such as Lineport, some fifteen miles to the north. Ending the discussion, more work under Tennessee engineer Bushrod Johnson soon commenced at Dover even before the coming of formal secession. The fort itself was on the high ground defending the river, and the water batteries were sunk into the side of the hill above the Cumberland River. The fortification quickly gained the name of Donelson, for one of Tennessee's own generals, Daniel S. Donelson.[36]

Unfortunately for the Tennesseans, there was no high ground sufficient for defense south of the Kentucky border on the east side of the Tennessee River, which was necessary for the two forts to mutually support each other. Engineers consequently chose the best site possible for Fort Henry, named after Gustavus A. Henry—later a Tennessee senator in Richmond. The best that could be had was low ground that was susceptible to flooding. Anderson had picked out a site on high ground five miles to the south near the mouth of Standing Rock Creek, but the location was later changed to Kirkman's Landing, and the 10th Tennessee soon arrived to begin construction in June 1861. The first gun went up in July and was test fired. Officers arriving later were not impressed. One noted, "I was convinced by a glance at its surroundings that extraordinarily bad judgment, or worse, had selected the site for its erection." He later added that "the accidental observation of a water-mark left on a tree caused me to look carefully for this sign above, below, and in the rear of the fort; and my investigation convinced me that we had a more dangerous force to contend with than the Federals,—namely, the river itself." Local citizens confirmed as much, but arriving troops were satisfied. One soldier in the 27th Alabama noted that it "looked formidable to us who had never seen anything like it before," and Gustavus A. Henry himself described his namesake fort as "in fine condition for defense, the work admirably done." Ironically, Henry had no such compliments for nearby Fort Donelson, describing it as "in very bad condition."[37]

With the Mississippi River emphasis, work went slowly at each fort. Held at Fort Henry in September 1861, celebrations commemorating the Mexican War battle at Monterrey, fought fifteen years before, illustrated the lethargic nature of the work and the emphasis on other activities. Colonel Adolphus Heiman of the 10th Tennessee was a veteran of the battle and ordered Captain Jesse Taylor to fire a salute of eleven guns at noon. Citizens of "a pleasure party" had arrived on steamboats for the occasion, and a dress parade was held, followed by an address. The entire regiment was even invited to drink to Heiman. One Tennessean smacked his lips and noted, "I wish our Colonel had fought a battle every day in the year." While celebrations certainly added to morale, it is a wonder that more attention was not paid to preparing the fort for new battles rather than celebrating past victories.[38]

Still, the twin rivers were not the only concern for Johnston. His next major bastion was at Bowling Green, Kentucky, where he utilized the Barren River in his defense of the Louisville and Nashville Railroad. A mere twenty or thirty miles north of the Tennessee border, Bowling Green became the de facto headquarters of the department when Johnston himself chose to make his headquarters there. He frequently used the rail system that connected the town with the rest of his department and surveyed the major sites (although not Forts Henry and Donelson) in the months after he assumed command. Although Johnston was there most of the time, the portion of the army that garrisoned the Bowling Green defenses was as of early December under William J. Hardee, a former US officer known best for authoring *Hardee's Tactics*, the military's latest rendition of tactics, said to be light-infantry tactics to compensate for the emergence of rifling in small arms. Hardee's troops watched perhaps the foremost Federal host that confronted this line, although the frequent change of commanders effectively eroded the Union army's effectiveness. Still, Hardee and Johnston had to hold Bowling Green and its key railroad access to Tennessee but quietly began the fortification of Nashville as well.[39]

The final sector of Johnston's quickly formed four-hundred-mile defensive line guarding Tennessee was positioned to cover the eastern section of the state as well as the critical Cumberland Gap. This small force amazingly contained dual commanders, one of the Crittenden boys from Kentucky, George, and Tennessee politician and editor Felix Zollicoffer. Both had their limitations, Crittenden having a fondness for the bottle and Zollicoffer having poor eyesight as well as training in journalism, not military affairs. Despite their limitations, the two officers watched Federal moves farther and farther into southeastern Kentucky, wondering what they could do in retaliation with such meager forces.[40]

Johnston wondered the same thing. With four hundred miles to cover and with inadequate troops to defend even one of the locations properly, Johnston realized that the enemy could pick and choose and presumably mass his forces at a single area and attack before Johnston could rush in reinforcements. He had to determine where the threat was and respond quickly if he was going to parry the thrust. Obviously, if the enemy moved forward at all points at the same time, nothing could be defended. Johnston gambled on the corresponding naivety and chaos in the Union high command to give him time to build up adequate defenses. He also had some good fortune in interior lines of communication along some of his line, including the critical Memphis, Clarksville, and Louisville Railroad, which ran parallel to the Confederate line from Bowling Green toward the west. Even so, he did not have an enviable position. Some probably thought Jefferson Davis placed too much confidence in Johnston, but the fact was that perhaps no one could emerge victorious from the situation Davis had entrusted to his friend.[41]

The transition from fall to winter of 1861 was an exciting time in the Confederacy as indications of intervention from Great Britain over the *Trent* affair fueled hopes for a quick victory. As time would tell, however, there were significant problems developing, especially in the west and particularly at the twin rivers. Although the Federals as yet had no firm plans to strike at the forts, they would nevertheless become the focal points on this four-hundred-mile-long Confederate defensive line in the west. Amazingly, even as Johnston and his commanders showed concern about strategic operations in the theater, they showed a remarkable lack of concern over the individual forts and the critical rivers they defended.[42]

A new Confederate commander for the forts arriving in late November did not help. Brigadier General Lloyd Tilghman, a Kentuckian from nearby Paducah, had been busily organizing his state's troops into brigades and had worn himself down physically to the point that he was not in good health when he assumed command at Forts Henry and Donelson. "I was not in the best condition," he related, "so late as December 15." What he had to work with was just as weak. Fort Henry had a meager six smoothbore 32-pounders and a 6-inch rifle. At Donelson, Tilghman found "at my disposal six undisciplined companies of infantry, with an unorganized light battery, while a small water battery of two light guns constituted the available river defense." Despite the lack of resources, Tilghman did what he could with what he had, keeping a wary eye to the north for smoke that would indicate a possible Federal river advance.[43]

Several other factors also made these forts more vulnerable than the rest of the line. The garrisons manning them throughout the summer and even into the fall were certainly smaller than the other major bastions on the defensive line. Tilghman worked hard to man his forts, but as the new year approached only a few regiments were stationed there, including the 10th Tennessee and 4th Mississippi at Fort Henry. At Fort Donelson were three regiments, the 30th, 49th, and 50th Tennessee, as well as Maney's Tennessee Battery. Unfortunately, Tilghman was not always well liked even among these few troops. Wesley Dorris of the 30th Tennessee, garrisoning Fort Donelson, wrote: "General Tilman issues orders prohibiting female visitors Gross humaity another is issued from him that no one is be furlowed home dead or alive before the 8th of January 1862." Another 30th Tennessee soldier wrote, "General Thilman is our Brigade officer yet but we want to get rid of him very bad but do not see any chance." As time went on, Tilghman even had troubles with the colonels; George W. Stacker of the 50th Tennessee resigned in protest, leaving the regiment to Cyrus A. Sugg; Colonel John W. Head of the 30th Tennessee threatened to resign as well. Colonel James Bailey of the 49th Tennessee tried to play peacemaker and succeeded in talking Head into staying: "[I] feel that I have done some good in restoring harmony to other regiments here," Bailey wrote his wife.[44]

Other problems continued as well. The forts' static positions likely doomed them to being flanked or turned, as any landward force could encircle them rapidly and starve them out. That could also be done at Columbus and at Bowling Green, but those areas had much larger garrisons, which effectively proved to be mobile armies that could meet threats to the flanks. Perhaps most significant, the twin rivers sat at the junction of two districts or cordons of defense, so there was little coordination as to who actually oversaw them and who was responsible to see that they were developed properly or were reinforced in an emergency. Polk at Columbus had control, but he informed Johnston that "the difficulty of communicating as rapidly as the exigencies of the service required, through the circuitous route to Columbus, made it expedient for him [Tilghman] to place himself in direct communication to the

general headquarters." As a result, command decisions fell to the larger departmental commander Johnston, who at best should not have had to control
smaller entities such as this. Besides, he was far more interested in defending
Bowling Green, where he expected the major attack to fall.[45]

Another part of the problem was the result of not finding enough labor
to work on the forts. Johnston's chief engineer, Jeremy F. Gilmer, was in
charge but the work was actually done under Lieutenant Joseph Dixon. But
Dixon and Tilghman were at odds over a number of issues, including where
to fortify and how to get laborers. Soldiers were deemed one source, but
there was also a need to use slaves, which local planters were not willing to
provide. Then there was the issue of slaves and soldiers working alongside
one another, something white soldiers found unacceptable. Gilmer, in fact,
reported, "I do not think that the labor of troops and slaves can be combined
to any advantage." Another issue developed over unity of command. Gilmer,
Dixon, and a civilian engineer, Charles Hayden, who was a captain in the
Tennessee state army, all worked on the defenses, as did civil engineer T. J.
Glenn, who was building an obstruction across the river. These men received
different orders from the various general officers, particularly Tilghman and
Gideon Pillow, who had been sent to command the Clarksville depot. Gilmer
logically asked Johnston to make him the "channel through which you and all
others engaged in the direction and construction of defenses in the Western
Department shall receive their instructions." He again had to ask for clarification when Tilghman ordered Glenn to cease work on the obstruction in the
Cumberland River and concentrate on the Donelson defenses. Gilmer ordered
Glenn to resume work and complained to Johnston, "it will be impossible for
me to rely upon any work being done properly if each subordinate brigadier-
general be allowed to suspend operations ordered by me."[46]

For all these reasons, work on Forts Henry and Donelson and troop strength
to man them lagged woefully behind the other major defensive positions
on the Confederate line. At Fort Donelson, for instance, work progressed
through the fall and into winter, but it was certainly not with any sense of
urgency. "We have all been enjoying ourselves here and almost doing as we
pleased for near three months," wrote a member of the 49th Tennessee in
November. Dixon only concentrated his efforts there in November, building a "new battery" on the Cumberland River and preparing to place guns
there in late November. The garrison apparently later moved the guns, as
one writer described it, because "our cannon have been put in better position

than they formerly occupied." Dixon also established "a little work" nearer the encampment and placed two cannon there. Still, it was difficult to obtain additional cannon for the forts. Gilmer noted in late November that he was sending "at least one more 32 pounder gun . . . —if possible, two more." He also issued a requisition order later in the month for four 8-inch columbiads and four 32-pounders. All the while, those stationed there were versed in their importance, Albert Sidney Johnston's staff officer Edward W. Munford drilling into H. S. Bedford, commanding some of the artillerymen, the importance of the place: "the Cumberland River cut his rear, and the occupation of Bowling Green was dependent upon the proper guarding of that stream."[47]

Problems also abounded at Fort Henry. In fact, Dixon could do but little at Fort Donelson because he was often ordered to the Tennessee River. Fort Henry was obviously placed too low and was susceptible to flooding, but it was the best-available position when the decision had been made. Now complicating matters further, a new plan to fortify the opposite and much higher bank of the river emerged. On November 20, Dixon was ordered to establish what would become known as Fort Heiman. Tilghman agreed wholeheartedly, writing Johnston that "the absolute necessity of our occupying an eminence on the opposite side of the river from Fort Henry involves not only the erection of a small field work there, with several heavy guns, but also the occupation of an advanced point with a small force, aided by a field battery." Engineer Gilmer was not so sure, writing, "of course, no guns designed for fire upon the river will be placed so high," and characterized the role of Heiman as "to prevent our enemy from occupying ground dangerous to Fort Henry." He noted, "field guns will probably be sufficient for the armament, with proper provision for using the musket and rifle."[48]

Other problems continued as well. The river's rises and falls made construction difficult, and the low level of the gun positions made almost any work futile. Gilmer sent guns there in late November anyway, including four 32-pounders and four additional heavy weapons "with platforms, chassis, and carriages complete, and 50 rounds of ammunition." What Gilmer thought a grand total of fifty rounds would stop is not clear.[49]

Despite the lack of armament, Fort Henry seemed to be the key fortification in Confederate minds. Losing Fort Donelson would be disastrous but it would net the enemy lesser gains than operating on the Tennessee River. Certainly the fate of Nashville stood on Donelson's shoulders, and perhaps so did the fate of Hardee's force north of Nashville and the Cumberland River.

However, the waterway made only a slight bend into the Confederate heartland before curving back east and northward into Kentucky once more. Consequently, a penetration along the Cumberland watershed would definitely reap Federal benefits, but these would be limited when compared to potential operations on the Tennessee River. That waterway made a much deeper curve, all the way into the lower cotton states. Movement along the Tennessee watershed would place Federal troops into the deep South states of Mississippi and Alabama, certainly a more substantial proposition than operations on the Cumberland.[50]

Therein lay the concern for the Confederates, because Fort Henry was in no shape or form capable of withstanding an immediate attack. Many Confederates recognized the situation, including Tilghman, who wrote Johnston in late November: "I have completed a thorough examination of Henry and Donelson and do not admire the aspect of things." He noted that he "must have more heavy guns for both places at once," and he also needed small arms for a thousand unarmed troops. He concluded, "I feel for the first time discouraged, but will not give up." If Tilghman was discouraged, the inhabitants of the Tennessee Valley could only be described as being in a panic. Logically, they were mostly those who had a direct stake in the defense of northern Tennessee. The citizens of Florence, Alabama, and the northern part of the state, for example, were astonished at the lack of defense, knowing full well that besides Fort Henry, there was nothing else between the Federals and them. They wrote letters and even sent delegations to find out just how well defended the rivers were and to lobby for more protection. All Gideon Pillow could tell them in late November: "in regard to the question, Do I consider the Tennessee River safe, I answer unhesitatingly that I do not." He expounded on why: "the work at Fort Henry is as good as we could construct in the time allowed for it and the means at our hands; but we have received but little assistance from any quarter in the construction of the works on the Mississippi, Tennessee, and Cumberland, except from Tennessee, and in guns." He took the opportunity to lecture the Alabamians on the need for that state to help in the preparations, "thus allowing her to hold the keys of the gate-way into her own territory."[51]

Another factor in that lack of help came at the very top spot. Despite being lauded as the west's savior, Johnston was having trouble viewing where his greatest threat lay. He called for additional troops from Alabama, Tennessee, and Mississippi, but these states were unable to send much at all; "the response has not been such as the emergency demands," Johnston reported on Christmas Eve. Governor John J. Pettus of Mississippi provided the most help, but it was only in the form of two small, untrained, and unarmed militia brigades for sixty days. It was certainly not what Johnston was looking for, but he was able to send one of the motley brigades under Reuben Davis to Bowling Green and the other under James L. Alcorn to Camp Beauregard, between Columbus and Fort Henry. This movement allowed Johnston to take John S. Bowen's regular brigade from there to Bowling Green, the place he feared for the most. Johnston also managed to acquire several regiments from Mansfield Lovell defending New Orleans, including the 13th Louisiana and 3rd Mississippi. In one of the best renditions of Davis's geographic defense, Lovell asked that these troops be sent back as soon as the crisis passed, as "we cannot tell at what hour the enemy may appear off the mouth of our rivers and bayous." Other troops were likewise ordered from Virginia under John B. Floyd, including a brigade of four Virginia regiments and the 20th Mississippi.[52]

Besides trying to obtain more men, Johnston displayed a severe lack of concern for the twin rivers, even after the bungling Gideon Pillow on December 11 accurately informed him that the enemy "will use their large water power to capture Fort Henry and pass up and take possession of Tennessee bridge and separate your command and General Polk's." Apparently, this warning did not register in Bowling Green. In addition to the lack of arms, pay, and supplies, and a host of other problems, Johnston just did not recognize the weakest link in his line. In all of Johnston's correspondence from November onward, he always dwelled on the threats to Columbus and Bowling Green and hardly if ever mentioned any concern for Forts Henry or Donelson. In late November, for example, he wrote Benjamin, "we are making every possible effort to meet the force which the enemy will soon array against us, both on this line [Bowling Green] and at Columbus." On Christmas Eve, Johnston wrote that "a decisive battle will probably be fought on this line [Bowling Green]." Historian Benjamin F. Cooling has asserted quite correctly that "it took only ninety days for Albert Sidney Johnston to descend from theater to district commander." Moreover, the disposition of weaponry throughout the department told the same story. At the same time that Tilghman was begging for just four large guns for each fort, Columbus contained 142 guns and the engineer at Fort Pillow on the Mississippi River above Memphis reported that he had fifty-eight 32-pounders at the fort, all but one mounted and ready for action.[53]

So, the stage was set for a major disaster should the Federals capitalize on the weakest link in Johnston's chain. Although few if any knew such operations would eventually develop, all Confederate officers should have at least been cognizant that the possibilities were real and that stricter defensive measures were needed. The Confederate authorities, however, still insisted on a geographical defense of manning entire sections of the South whether threatened or not, leaving the most vulnerable areas less defended. Such tunnel vision was extremely dangerous as the Federals began to work through their own problems and ultimately found perhaps the only man who was willing to capitalize on such a grand opportunity.

2

"You Have No Idea How Much Work Is Required to Improvise"

A foreboding feeling settled over Washington, DC, on New Years Day 1862 as Abraham Lincoln confronted just as many difficult issues, and perhaps even more, than his enemies to the south in Richmond. For any advantages he may have held at the beginning, the US military had pitifully little to show for several months of labor. Those on both sides who had forecasted a three-month war were obviously wrong, and it seemed that the longer the conflict went on, the more the pendulum would swing toward the Confederacy. Essentially, that is the way the United States itself had beaten England twice, by waiting the enemy out and refusing to give in until the British did. As the war dragged on and on, now into a second year, Lincoln had reason to worry.[1]

In some respects, Lincoln had a harder job than Davis. He had a fully functioning political party system that needed to be coordinated and led. Some wanted preservation of the Union, others wanted the abolition of slavery, and still others wanted to let the South go. Lincoln stood in the middle of it all, trying to hold the political system together for the sake of the Union. On the military front, and particularly out west, Lincoln also had additional factors to consider. If Jefferson Davis and Isham Harris and the many other Southern governors could rely on fixed fortifications, whether they were competent or not, Lincoln had to have movable striking potential that could engage at differing spots. As most of the Confederate land fortifications sat on transportation routes such as the various rivers and railways, Lincoln obviously needed mobile armies that could march to and encircle, turn, or cut off those fortifications. Unfortunately, large bodies of men were not accustomed to working together in tandem, and neither were their officers. Armies were

already much larger than those seen in earlier wars, and the commanding generals of this war were primarily lower-level staff and company officers in the
Mexican War, where they did not necessarily concern themselves with large
troop coordination. Consequently, these large bodies of men would have to
be thoroughly trained and given experience to be able to tackle these enemy
defensive fortifications and the garrisons that defended them.[2]

The fact that many of the Confederate fortifications sat on rivers added another degree of difficulty. Not only landward military units would be needed,
but so also would a vast and efficient naval force. Because there had never
been a need for internal naval power, however, all existing naval thinking
pointed toward defending America's external coastal areas. As a result, Lincoln had nothing at the beginning of the war that could operate powerfully on
the western rivers. Naval and army officers had to arm merchant ships while
the lengthy and problem-prone process of building new riverine warships
went on. Then, a similar amount of training and experience would be needed
for these boats to operate efficiently.[3]

Furthermore, if offensive ability gave Lincoln's generals and naval commanders options as to where and when to strike, it also necessitated that they
be able to move large bodies of men, animals, and ships, as well as the supplies that supported all three. The logistical needs of armies even this early in
the war were enormous, as men needed food, shelter, and ammunition, horses
and mules needed oats and fodder, and the riverine vessels and locomotives
needed vast amounts of coal and wood. Just getting to the battlefield in effective shape was an ordeal in and of itself.[4]

Most significantly, Lincoln also faced the need to conquer, although this
fact was not fully realized until later in the war. The South had time on its
side because the longer the war went on, the more the Northern public would
grow weary. It had happened before, so Davis settled on a defensive offensive
mindset, wherein all he had to do was defend his territory, not conquer the
enemy's. So emerged the garrisoning of almost the entire South in a defensive
posture that would only turn offensive on the local operational or even tactical level when a good opportunity presented itself. In essence, Davis could in
all likelihood win the war by not losing it. On the other hand, for him to win
the war, Lincoln had to conquer the South to the point of surrender. Therefore,
Lincoln's military needed that effectiveness, training, and cohesion to operate
in enemy territory against substantial defenders that could occasionally throw
offensive jabs against them. It was a hard task to be sure, and it would take

time. Unfortunately, Lincoln did not want to give his commanders much of the latter.[5]

One of the biggest concerns Lincoln faced was with his commanders. Historians are adept at describing the turnover in command that occurred in the east, where the president sought a competent commander to lead the Army of the Potomac to victory in Virginia. He went through several generals, George B. McClellan twice, but he only found someone who could bring the war to a close after three years of the conflict. In fact, Lincoln also had the same issues out west, and the departments that corresponded to Albert Sidney Johnston's western theater command also saw an almost continual revolving door of commanders in the fall of 1861. To make matters worse, Lincoln initially insisted on dividing the western control, thereby losing all aspects of unity of command.[6]

Lincoln was obviously no trained military theoretician, but common sense dictated that the western command needed to be placed under one general, or else cohesion would be lost if two or more local commanders were not in harmony. In fact, Lincoln would quickly see the error of his ways and eventually place the western command under one general, but throughout 1861 and into March 1862, the area between the Appalachian Mountains and the Mississippi River was divided. As a result, for nearly a year the Union forces in the west produced few positive results.[7]

The westernmost of these districts straddling the Mississippi River saw several changes, some militarily oriented but most the result of politics. The initial commander was the Pathfinder of the West, John C. Fremont, who was put in charge of the Department of the West in July 1861. He was a luminary from the Mexican War, during which he had led expeditions to California and elsewhere. He gained much of his political clout when he married well— Jessie Benton, the vivacious daughter of Missouri's longtime senator Thomas Hart Benton. Fremont proved himself to be such a celebrity that he acquired the 1856 Republican presidential nomination. Fremont was thus a natural fit for the Mississippi River command, or so Lincoln thought. He had military experience, was well known in the Mississippi Valley, and knew how to get things done.[8]

Unfortunately for Lincoln, Fremont was almost too much of a luminary and began to act as if he were the president. In addition, Fremont soon had multiple charges against him, including waste, bribery, and graft. Quarter-master General Montgomery Meigs wrote of some of the minor infractions: "the Department is embarrassed by the action of the commanding general in ordering so many mortar rafts, tugs, and altered boats in addition to those contracted for by this Department." Most troublesome, Fremont also caused a major problem in late 1861 when he declared martial law in Missouri and stated that slaves of rebellious owners were free. Lincoln agreed in prin-ciple, but the timing for such emancipation was far too early in the war. The president, much as with his concerns over Kentucky, feared that such an edict would tip Missouri over to the Confederacy. Lincoln rescinded Fremont's original order and then relieved him, ultimately sending Fremont to a com-mand in Virginia where he tangled unsuccessfully with Stonewall Jackson in the Shenandoah Valley.[9]

To replace the politically overactive Fremont, Lincoln selected a thor-oughly military officer—perhaps the foremost military thinker of the day in America. Henry W. Halleck had translated Jomini and written his own text in 1846, *Elements of Military Art and Science*. He was very much a thinker, even being awarded an honorary membership in the Bay State Literary Institute in Boston during this time. Although Halleck would certainly not be immune to politics in his department, Lincoln figured he would likely have little of the compulsion that Fremont had to think he was superior to the president. Con-sequently, Halleck took command of the Department of the Missouri on No-vember 19, which included Missouri, Iowa, Minnesota, Wisconsin, Illinois, Arkansas, and "that portion of Kentucky west of the Cumberland River."[10]

While Halleck took over operations in the Mississippi Valley, logically directing the armies on both sides of the river, the Department of the Ohio was more problematic. Running from Halleck's domain ending at the Cum-berland River eastward to the mountains, this area also saw a revolving door of commanders. First to command there was Robert Anderson of Fort Sumter fame, taking the position in May 1861. Anderson quickly ran afoul of Lin-coln's desires in the west, but Lincoln had to tread lightly with the national hero. Failing health also played into the decision to change commanders, and Anderson gave way in October.[11]

Replacing him was one of the truly colorful and important characters of the war, William T. Sherman. The Ohioan had made a name for himself as an old army officer and prewar educator in Louisiana. It did not hurt him that his brother John was a powerful US senator and his father-in-law was the influential Whig politician Thomas Ewing. Sherman had commanded a brigade at Bull Run and then took command of the Kentucky department in October, but his tenure was anything but smooth. Always one to speak his mind, Sherman flatly stated that it would take years and several hundred thousand men to clear the Mississippi Valley of Confederates. Newspapers labeled him crazy, and a nervousness bordering on a breakdown did not reassure his superiors. Falsely labeled insane, Sherman nevertheless asked to be relieved of his command in November.[12]

Lincoln finally found an able if lethargic commander for the department in Don Carlos Buell. One of the many lower-level officers who had learned his trade in Mexico with Winfield Scott and Zachary Taylor, Buell served in Virginia early in the war but then took command at Louisville, Kentucky, in November. There, he surveyed the best options for advance into the Confederacy, Lincoln firmly pushing him toward his favored east Tennessee route. Buell balked at the harsh mountainous terrain and desired instead to move overland toward Nashville. Over time, commanding general George B. McClellan firmly explained his and the president's desires, writing, "the object to be gained is to cut the communication between the Mississippi Valley and Eastern Virginia; to protect our Union friends in Tennessee, and re-establish the Government of the Union in the eastern portion of that State." Even so, Buell would have none of it. He saw his first duty as organizing what he considered to be the rabble that he had inherited in his command. He complained that the governor of Ohio, William Dennison, "evidently looks upon all Ohio troops as his army" and that "every colonel and brigadier general has his personal establishment or army." He so wrote McClellan in late November, "without abandoning any line, I am concentrating somewhat for the purpose of organization and outfit." Looking down on his enemy, Buell said that "as for his attacking, though I do not intend to be unprepared for him, yet I should almost as soon expect to see the Army of the Potomac marching up the road." As a result, Buell did little of anything, which would become his trademark throughout his career.[13]

The Union west thus had two commanders instead of the unified command of Johnston's Confederate department. It was a recipe for disaster, if the Confederates could exploit it, but they were weaker and content to remain on the defensive. This command division nevertheless limited and thwarted Federal advances into the Confederacy throughout late 1861 and into early 1862. Halleck and Buell discussed operations with McClellan in Washington, but neither seemed willing to support the other, fearing the other would gain all the glory. Their superior McClellan was in Washington, far away from the western expanses, and his attention was primarily on his other duty, as commander of the Army of the Potomac. The stalled Union armies in the west might have made major gains against such a gaunt Confederate line, but McClellan seemed content to referee between Halleck and Buell and put the majority of his energy into his own Virginia theater. The result was limited movement in the west for the entirety of 1861.[14]

The lethargy actually went deeper than just Halleck and Buell. Subordinates tended to assume the stances of their superiors, and those under Halleck and Buell reflected their timid and careful approach to breaking the Confederate defensive line in the west and then invading the Confederacy. Left practically on their own, these western commanders were loathe to take on any more authority than their timid bosses expected of them. As a result, only small and relatively insignificant engagements occurred in Kentucky and Missouri in the summer and fall of 1861. In reality, the Federals simply gained control of unoccupied portions of Kentucky that lay north of Johnston's main Confederate defensive line, meeting only roving portions of Confederate defenders. The lack of any major engagements demonstrated the lack of will among both Confederate and Union commanders, whether departmental or lower-level district officers, to go out on a limb and attack. Still in the process of organizing their forces, bringing new units into the armies, and gathering supplies, few wanted to embark on a major campaign this early.[15]

While such limited action took place, Lincoln became more and more impatient, looking for someone, anyone, to demonstrate aggressiveness against the enemy.

As Federal army commanders organized their forces and probed the determined if thin Confederate defensive line, they recognized that another factor would be needed in the coming military operations. The western Confederacy was so well endowed with rivers that naval forces would certainly have to play a role in the coming war. The Mississippi River obviously drained two-thirds of the continent, and Iowa and Illinois wheat and corn farmers were just as dependent on the river as Mississippi and Louisiana cotton plantation owners. The river's many tributaries, such as the Ohio, Missouri, and Red rivers, and their numerous tributaries such as the Tennessee and Cumberland

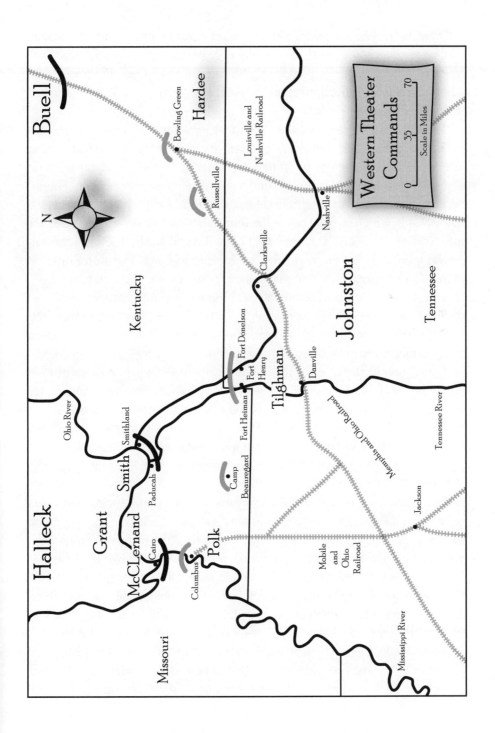

Western Theater Commands

Scale in Miles
0   35   70

Halleck

Buell

Grant

Smith

McCLernand

Hardee

Polk

Tilghman

Johnston

N

Missouri

Kentucky

Tennessee

Ohio River

Smithland

Paducah

Cairo

Columbus

Camp
Beauregard

Fort Heiman

Fort Henry

Fort Donelson

Danville

Clarksville

Russellville

Bowling Green

Nashville

Jackson

Louisville and
Nashville Railroad

Memphis and Ohio Railroad

Tennessee River

Mobile
and
Ohio
Railroad

Mississippi River

rivers in Tennessee, offered far greater reach for steamboats and travelers as well as farmers selling their crops than ever before. Although railroads had by 1860 bonded the nation together with east and west lines, the rivers were still important for intracontinental commerce and travel, particularly west of the Appalachian Mountains.[16]

The railroads quickly became important in terms of shipping men, supplies, and ammunition, but the rivers likewise were important transportation arteries of men and supplies. In fact, as Johnston created his defensive line across the western Confederacy, the primary defenses sat on rivers simply because there was only one railroad that connected with the larger network in the South, which crossed out of the four-hundred-mile defensive perimeter into Northern territory. That was the Louisville and Nashville, and Johnston placed a critical portion of his available force to guard that transportation route. At the same time, three large rivers crossed the same defensive perimeter, forcing the Confederates to establish earthen fortifications to defend the Confederate heartland. As a result, river travel was more important in the western military construct than even railroads, at least in terms of approaches the Federals could use to break Johnston's line.[17]

Consequently, it was clear that naval warfare would play a major role in the future. Both sides therefore began to build gunboats, the South lagging far behind because of a lack of shipyards and factories to produce the machinery needed for these vessels. When the idea emerged of arming these boats with iron, the Confederacy found itself even more limited. Yet, numerous ironclad gunboats were being planned, although it was a slow process as the South had to blaze a trail seldom trod prior to the war.[18]

Just because the majority of the shipyards capable of producing riverboats were along the rivers in the North did not mean that the Union had that much of a head start. It would be early 1862 by the time the Federal war machine was able to put a large fleet of gunboats on the rivers. Meanwhile, the initial burst of naval energy came from Captain John Rogers, who after discussions with naval constructor Samuel Pook somewhat rashly bought three river steamers at Cincinnati and outfitted them with guns. The total price was good, well under the worth of the boats, but times were hard for owners. "After mature reflection and consultation with my friends," wrote Daniel Collier, "I agreed to sell the boat [*Tyler*]. The price I considered under the value, but in view of the condition of affairs at the time I thought it prudent to sell."

Despite the good price, Secretary of the Navy Gideon Welles chastised Rogers, reminding him that the army was the branch with purchasing ability and thus all purchases had to come from them. McClellan soon gave his consent, however, writing Rogers in June to "use your own judgment in carrying out the ends of government. Spare no effort to accomplish the object in view with the least possible delay." With no armor, these vessels soon became known as timberclads because "bulwarks of oak plank 5 inches think" were placed on the sides to enclose the decks, that being, Rogers reported, "[what] I found by experiment a sufficient guard against small arms." The boilers were also dropped into the holds for protection, and "the steam pipes were lowered as far as possible." The decks were also strengthened with beams to support the heavy guns. These three boats, the *Tyler*, *Conestoga*, and the brand new *Lexington*, one inspector calling the latter "a No. 1 boat," carried seven, four, and six guns, respectively, and were in service by June, although the first steamboat, known prior to the transfer as the civilian *A. O. Tyler*, had been fired upon near Vicksburg by excited Mississippi cannoneers immediately after the secession of that state in January 1861. The boat was not hit and ironically went on to be one of the first vessels to combat the Confederacy. Until more formidable gunboats could be had, however, these three carried the war to the enemy on the western rivers that summer and fall.[19]

Rogers also had additional concerns besides fitting the boats for military service. While the army purchased the vessels and had control over them, they were to be armed and crewed by navy men. Rogers therefore had to assemble crews for the ships, which was no easy task with most volunteers going into the army; there was also competition for crews from the Atlantic fleet, Secretary Welles, who was thoroughly preoccupied with the blockade, telling Rogers, "you will, therefore, have to obtain your men from the West." Likewise, Rogers had to have knowledgeable pilots who were familiar with the western rivers: "the management of these engines in the muddy waters of the Mississippi requires a peculiar experience, which it is cheaper to employ than to teach," Rogers wrote. He also had to acquire armament for the gunboats, which he did from army arsenals. The cooperation between the two branches was not always smooth because of so much bureaucracy, but Welles and his counterpart in the War Department, Simon Cameron, tried their best, Welles writing, "nor must the two branches of service become complicated and embarrassed by separate action." Moreover, Rogers soon found defects with the new upgrades on the vessels and had to send the gunboats periodically to shipyards for repair. He wrote in July that the original work on the three "is more like the work of Irish laborers than of mechanics."[20]

Even so, the three boats were in Cairo by mid-August, and Lieutenant Seth Ledyard Phelps soon took command of the flotilla. The boats immediately became engaged, chasing a couple of Confederate vessels near New Madrid, although Phelps wisely called off the chase: "I did not think it advisable to risk encountering batteries at that point with the condition of the gunboats, and therefore turned back." In fact, Phelps frequently challenged enemy positions but rarely if ever got into a firefight that could deny the meager naval arm one of its only assets. Gideon Pillow at Columbus accordingly noted in late November, "the enemy's gunboats came down to-day, made a grand flourish, but did not come within reach of our guns." At times, Phelps and his timberclads also ventured into the Tennessee and Cumberland rivers, one Clarksville newspaper reporting one such incident when three Union sailors were found dead in a cornfield: "it is supposed they were caught stealing corn and shot by some of the citizens who did not recognize their right to depredate upon private property." Phelps particularly investigated the Confederate forts on the twin rivers, taking the *Conestoga* up the Tennessee in mid-October and reporting that he "ascended the Tennessee River to near Fort Henry, where we lay overnight. The next morning I examined the fort carefully at a distance of from 2 to 2 1/2 miles, the rebels not opening fire upon us." He wrongly reported Fort Henry to be "quite an extensive work and armed with heavy guns, mounted en barbette, and garrisoned by a considerable force." He also heard that the enemy was building three ironclads above the fort. On the same voyage, Phelps went up the Cumberland some sixty miles until stopped by a shoal near Eddyville, where the enemy had sunk several coal barges filled with stones. He did find, however, that "it was reported the rebels were building a battery below the town." Phelps delivered all his information to the army commander at Paducah, who sent it up the chain of command. He was unable to find out much more about the forts on later cruises, in December reporting, for example, "I could not verify this report, as the afternoon was rainy and misty when we were there, and at any time it can not be examined without engaging it, as it can only be seen at a distance of 1 mile."[21]

The Union high command was obviously not content with three small wooden boats and set their sights on larger and more powerful vessels. The same ideas were present in Washington, and the result was the collaboration of the army and private officials, mainly Quartermaster General Montgomery Meigs with Samuel Pook and James B. Eads, both well-known maritime designers. They produced was a series of seven ironclad gunboats, known as city-class vessels, carrying the names of cities located on the inland rivers: *St. Louis* (name later changed to the *Baron de Kalb*), *Carondelet*, *Cincinnati*, *Louisville*, *Mound City*, *Pittsburgh*, and *Cairo*. These gunboats had thirteen mounted guns each, three in the bow, four on each side, and two in the stern, plus an added howitzer on the deck to make fourteen in total. Each boat was 175 feet long and fifty-one feet wide, with a 512-ton displacement. A crew of 175 was housed inside a casemate of two-and-a-half-inch-thick iron on the sides and somewhat below the waterline. These were powerful machines, if a little slow, especially against the current of a fast-moving river, and they were not totally indestructible. Not every inch of the boats was covered with iron, because this would have made them far too heavy; only the most critical areas of boilers, engines, and paddle wheels were inside the armored casemate. Significantly, the decks were still wood, which allowed a plunging fire from a higher enemy battery to fire down onto the vessels and cause major damage.[22]

Other boats also became part of this naval force, including two other converted steamboats that John C. Fremont bought while still in command. A much larger Eads-owned vessel became the sixteen-gun ironclad *Benton*, which one naval commander commented was "worth any three of the new gunboats" despite the fact that the boat was slow and needed the engines replaced to provide more power. Likewise, a former snag boat became the five-gun *Essex*. This ironclad, in fact, was the first to enter service in early October and was sent to Paducah to counter the alleged Confederate gunboats being built up the Tennessee River. In addition, some thirty-eight mortar boats towed by steamboats were devised, built to bombard fortifications from far away. A huge array of merchant ships and barges were also rented or otherwise acquired to transport troops, ammunition, supplies, forage, and coal for the fleet. This was all a major undertaking, and it was a slow process. One naval official described the chaos: "the service on the Western rivers was anomalous. The officers of the Navy in charge of the vessels being transferred, for the time being, to act under the general directions of the War Department, with the want of navy-yard facilities, and having but a single navy officer to each vessel, superadded to the want of navy equipments and stores, especially in the ordnance department, rendered the building and equipment of the flotilla a work of almost insuperable difficulty."[23]

The difficulty of building and gathering crews for such a fleet in such a short period of time was indeed mind-boggling. "You have no idea how much work is required to improvise, as we are doing, a navy here, with our limited means," wrote one naval officer. In fact, the timber that would go into the ironclads was still growing in the forests when Eads signed the contracts for the gunboats in August 1861. The agreement called for the boats to be delivered in October, a massive gamble for Eads. He went to work with a will, however, subcontracting with sawmills, rolling mills, and railroads to produce and get the parts to the shipyards where they would be assembled. Even that caused problems, because there was no shipyard that could build all seven boats at one time. As a result, four (*Carondelet*, *St. Louis*, *Louisville*, and *Pittsburg*), plus the overhaul of the *Benton*, were built at Carondelet, Illinois, (just south of St. Louis) and the other three (*Mound City*, *Cincinnati*, and *Cairo*) at Mound City, Illinois. Eads missed his October deadline, but in what was nevertheless a remarkable engineering feat, he began delivery of the seven ironclads in late October and all were receiving their guns and crews over the winter months. It was the birth of the Union naval fleet that would take the war to the Confederate heartland via the rivers.[24]

The gunboats accordingly began to enter service in December 1861 and January 1862, first as stationary bases while still under the contractors. All four from Carondelet (as well as twenty mortar boats) arrived at Cairo by mid-December, though low river stages were a concern. The *St. Louis* and *Essex* were quickly armed and used as defenses at Cairo while all the boats were held for inspection by a five-man board made up of three army officers and two naval officers.[25]

Even though progress was being made on the boats themselves, there was also the problem of command. John Rogers was apparently not the man to lead this effort. He had raised the ire of the Navy Department, and Fremont was not happy with him either, writing fellow Missourian Montgomery Blair in August: "it would subserve the public interest if Commander John Rogers were removed and an officer directed to report to me to have command of the operations on the Mississippi. Show this to President." New faces soon arrived in the west to replace Rogers, who was not happy at all about leaving the scene of his hard work just when it was about to bear fruit. He wrote Welles a scathing letter: "when the plant thus watered and cultivated gives its first prematurely ripe fruit, the crop is turned over to another with cold words." Welles responded that "the Department has received and read with much interest your letter," assuring him that the government had every confidence in him. Despite such assurance, he was transferred elsewhere.[26]

New faces were indeed soon in command. One was Commander Henry Walke, who because of rank soon took command of the three gunboats from Phelps, who reverted to command of just the *Conestoga*. By far, the major new player was Captain Andrew H. Foote, who was then serving at the New York Navy Yard but was promoted and ordered to "take command of the naval operations upon the Western waters, now organizing under the direction of the War Department." That in itself should have alerted Foote to the oddity of the command he was entering, but Welles assured him: "the Western movement is of the greatest importance, and the Department assigns you to this duty, having full confidence in your zeal, fidelity, and judgment." Perhaps with that in mind, Foote assumed command on September 6 and immediately took up for Rogers: "he deserves great credit for what he has done, and his labors have been hard." The highly religious Foote also began, over the course of the next few months, to issue general orders that prohibited drinking, nonobservance of Sunday, and "profane swearing."[27]

Foote had to worry about his own job as well. He informed the Navy Department that he needed to be given flag rank so he could deal equally with high-ranking army officers. "The Army say I rank only with a lieutenant-colonel, and in one instance a colonel ordered a gunboat to go with his regiment on a certain duty." He requested flag rank, writing, "if I am not considered eligible to that position, that an older officer of that rank be sent out immediately and I transferred to serve correspondingly to my rank in the Southern Atlantic Expedition or Atlantic Blockading Squadron." Fortunately for Foote, he was appointed flag officer on November 13, and he immediately began to push to end the delay with Eads's boats. Foote informed Washington in early November, "still the boats are not ready, and I am nervously anxious about them." He also wrote the contractors, "you will use every dispatch in completing the gunboats." Washington was not happy either. "We relied upon the naval constructor who modeled these gunboats," Meigs wrote Foote, "I still hope he has not blundered." Gustavus Fox similarly wrote, "I suppose if they barely float they may do, unless they draw too much water. It will be a blow upon the Navy if they fail."[28]

By late December, the boats were receiving their guns and other equipment, and the only thing left to obtain was crews to man them. In transferring to one of the gunboats, Commander Walke desired to take his crew from a timberclad, but Foote told him such a move would weaken the only veteran ships he had. In fact, by the new year, the crews were all that were still needed, Foote writing Washington: "we had all things in comparative good condition, and only wanted men to begin, if not to complete, the commission of all the gunboats this week or early in the next. . . . Now we are thrown back again for want of men." Moreover, all the problems were not solved once the crews arrived. "It is important that the vessels should be in commission soon," Foote wrote Halleck, "as many preliminary arrangements are necessary to be made, with frequent exercise of great guns, before so many raw recruits will be qualified to perform their part of the work in the flotilla." And this naval delay had larger ramifications. Considering the predominant rivers in the west, the army commanders could not move until the navy was ready.[29]

While most Federal officers showed little desire to make any moves, and the naval forces needed additional time to create an inland navy almost from scratch, one unlikely Union officer was quite willing to take the war to the enemy immediately. The Mississippi River sector in Halleck's command saw the most fighting in the fall of 1861, yielding the only real battle during that period, and it was mainly the result of the aggressiveness of one of Halleck's commanders who was not content to timidly feel his way southward like all the rest. This was a war, after all, and Ulysses S. Grant saw no need to delay action.[30]

Grant was certainly an unknown commodity in the summer and fall of 1861. He had led a difficult life despite his education at West Point. Serving well in the Mexican War, he nevertheless could not survive in the army when, absent from his wife and family, boredom and drinking set in on the isolated western frontier. He returned east but found it difficult to make a living as a civilian. Finally settling in Galena, Illinois, he worked for his father. War revitalized the man foundering in hard times, and he quickly offered his services to the governor of Illinois, who eventually made him colonel of the 21st Illinois. Grant whipped the unruly regiment into shape and soon acquired a brigadier general's star through the efforts of his guardian congressman from Galena, Elihu Washburne. He served briefly in Missouri in the summer but soon took command of the District of Southeastern Missouri under Fremont, the area that also included Illinois east of the Mississippi River. His headquarters was at Cairo at the tip of Illinois where the Ohio and Mississippi rivers joined, an incredibly important strategic point. Outlying posts under his command were at Bird's Point and Cape Girardeau, Missouri, Mound City, Illinois, and Fort Holt, Kentucky. Still, Grant was an unknown; not yet having a brigadier's uniform, he showed up at the post headquarters in civilian clothes and had to reason with the astonished colonel who was then in command to let him take charge. Despite the commander's lack of notoriety, the district sat on important byways, and access to the rivers gave Grant options and opportunity. That was all he needed.[31]

Grant set about transforming his new command into an efficient force. To help him, he began forming his official military family. Grant obviously needed a staff, but he unfortunately chose officers less on merit and more on availability. He accordingly created a lackadaisical staff that would only eventually turn into a professional and competent staff later in the war. In fact, many of these early appointments were gone by the time his staff reached the professional and efficient level. Thinking he needed someone from his old regiment, Grant appointed Clark Lagow. Having known the lawyer William S. Hillyer in St. Louis, he also added him to the staff. Neither proved particularly good at staff work, but another appointment did work. Desiring someone from Galena, Grant appointed John A. Rawlins, who would become a guardian for Grant and would stay with him for the entire war. Grant eventually made an artillery officer, Colonel Joseph D. Webster, his chief of staff. Grant's official family was emerging even this early.[32]

Grant also needed additional numbers of everything, including men, supplies, and arms, but his most basic need was cavalry. "The condition of this command is bad in every particular except discipline," Grant noted, writing that the troops were armed with "the old flint lock repaired" as well as "others of still more inferior quality." Transportation needs were huge as well, as were clothing and other necessary items for the troops. Funds were exhausted and credit was not to be had. Even hospital space at Cairo and Mound City was in need of expansion, especially if fighting emerged any time soon. Most concerning, however, the cavalry were far too few, and those Grant had were poorly armed, some without sword belts or modern weapons. He had eight full cavalry companies who possessed no weapons at all.[33]

Like almost all Federal commanders, Grant also worried that he was terribly outnumbered and would be attacked soon. He wrote Halleck's headquarters at one point stating that if "they [the Confederates] are let alone, they may be induced to act on the offensive if more troops are not sent here soon."

The Confederates indeed soon became bolder, even sending three gunboats to Cairo on one occasion. "Bishop Major-General Polk's three gunboats made a Sunday excursion up to see us this evening," Grant informed Halleck. "Fired five or six shots when within about half a mile of the nearest point of the camp at Fort Holt."[34]

Despite such fears, Grant was quick to go on the offensive and expand his area of command. When Polk captured Columbus and broke Kentucky's neutrality, Grant immediately saw the importance of securing the mouths of the Tennessee and Cumberland rivers. He quickly sent units of his district hurriedly by boat to take control of Paducah, which sat where the Tennessee flowed into the Ohio River. It was a muddy pit, one Federal writing they were "all in mud nearly knee deep." Grant and his troops, with newly arrived Captain Foote along, arrived just in time to take possession of the city, deflecting Confederates who were marching overland from Columbus and were almost at the point of entering the town. Grant noted the many "secession flags flying over the city," but reported that "before I landed, the secession flags had disappeared." He also related, "I landed the troops and took possession of the city without firing a gun." Later, Grant also sent a portion of his command farther up the Ohio to Smithland, where the Cumberland poured into the Ohio River. There, soldiers fanned out to live in "churches and empty houses of which there are plenty," one Federal noted. The writer's company quartered in the Episcopal church, which he described as "a poor barn like sort of thing," but it was much better than living outside in tents. Eventually, on December 23, Grant's district was expanded into the District of Cairo, including southern Illinois, Missouri south of Cape Girardeau, and Kentucky to the Cumberland River, which encompassed the posts Charles F. Smith commanded at Paducah and Smithland.[35]

With the choice pieces of Kentucky carved up between the two sides, matters quieted down for a few weeks as both armies built up strength and watched the other. Grant meanwhile went through administrative changes, including Halleck's arrival. He also began to develop relationships with subordinates in his new, larger district. Among his major subordinates was Illinois politician John A. McClernand, whom Grant would command for two years through some of the most significant battles and campaigns of the Civil War. Their relationship was never warm, probably because of the haughtiness the politician McClernand arrived with; he was already complaining of the lack of Illinoisans in the high command (conveniently forgetting that Lincoln was commander in chief) as well as what he called the "jealousy" of career generals toward "citizen generals" like him. A former Democratic congressman from Illinois appointed specifically by Lincoln to secure the southern reaches of the state politically, McClernand knew he was needed and often took the opportunity to write his old friend Lincoln personally. Since many of the lower counties of Illinois, Ohio, and Indiana were tied economically more to the Ohio River and Kentucky slavery than to the free labor industries farther north, there was some fear that those counties might side with the South early in the war, particularly if Kentucky joined the Confederacy. Accordingly, Lincoln made it a habit of appointing political generals to firm up support in those regions, men such as John A. Logan and McClernand who had major ties to "little Egypt."[36]

McClernand played his role perfectly, but he also brought with him a feeling of importance and being indispensable, which Grant despised. Of course, McClernand chafed at being subordinate to a man like Grant, who had barely provided for his family before the war. McClernand, at the same time, was one of the power players in Congress. Despite their differences, Grant had to deal with him, and McClernand over time actually made a decent general. But for now, he served well if obnoxiously in command of the Cairo area.[37]

Another of Grant's subordinates actually had a greater claim than McClernand to Grant's job. If McClernand complained, it would have been seen as egotistical, but Charles F. Smith had every right to feel upset at serving under Grant. Smith was a very well-respected career officer, having graduated from West Point when Grant was a toddler. Moreover, Smith served as commandant of cadets at the academy when Grant was a student there. Grant himself felt some trepidation at commanding someone who was obviously his superior in time served and perhaps known ability, but the nonegotistical Smith never made an issue of it and served willingly under the upstart Grant. In fact, when confronting the situation in person, Smith told his former cadet, "General, I am now a subordinate. I know a soldier's duty. Pray, feel no awkwardness whatever about our new relations." Whether he saw something in the young brigadier general or was simply following orders to the fullest is not known, but Smith soon became one of Grant's major mentors and friends, even as a subordinate.[38]

Smith was probably not going to get the command anyway, as he was in some trouble for alleged disloyalty stemming from an episode in Paducah in which Lew Wallace disobeyed his orders and wound up getting Smith in trouble in the Northern press. The event not only caused a rift between Smith and Wallace, but it also hurt Smith's standing with the War Department, at one point even threatening his commission. In the midst of campaigning, Grant even had to write to his guardian congressman Elihu Washburne: "get the Senate to reconsider Gen. Smiths Confirmation. There is no doubt of his loyalty and efficiency. We Cant spare him now."[39]

Grant also met other military leaders in the area, including several Confederate officers whom he had known in Mexico. They liked to come from Columbus northward by boat under a flag of truce, and Grant always met them. As would be expected, such good feelings did not last. By November, operations were heating up and Grant took advantage of one of those opportunities that most others missed. When Sterling Price moved northward after the battle at Wilson's Creek into the Missouri River valley, forces from St. Louis moved out to meet him. Grant was called on to dispatch several columns to support the effort, making sure that Price was not reinforced from the Columbus area or anywhere else that his district fronted. Grant sent out two columns, one westward under Colonel Richard J. Oglesby. To demonstrate against Columbus itself and to help protect Oglesby's column, Grant took a column on boats down the river toward the Confederate bastion.[40]

Unlike other commanders of districts, Grant opted to take a large force down the Mississippi River to demonstrate against Columbus, and he soon saw what a positive effect campaigning had on the men. Grant received word of a Confederate camp across the river from Columbus near Belmont and decided en route to attack it. He landed his troops on the western Missouri bank of the river on November 7, out of range of Columbus's guns of course, and then marched southward and attacked the camp. The ensuing battle saw Grant drive the enemy out, but the victorious Federals began to loot, destroying what they could not carry away. Others began to gloat; ever the politician, John A. McClernand made a grand speech. All the while, Polk sent reinforcements across the river and the regrouped Confederates counterattacked. Grant's Federals fell back to their boats, barely getting out in time. Still, the battle had larger ramifications; in a period when no one else was doing much of anything, Grant was not afraid to fight the enemy.[41]

People began to notice as news of this new commander Grant first became known. His first major attempt to do something other than watch the enemy, as so many of the other Union front-line commanders were doing, resulted in positive outcomes. Obviously, the strategic idea of keeping Confederate troops pinned down in Columbus succeeded, allowing other commanders flexibility to deal with other crises. Perhaps more importantly, Grant later noted that this initial fighting created for the troops a "confidence in themselves" that would last, for those units, the entire war. Perhaps too, while Belmont did not go strictly according to plan and could have easily resulted in a major loss, Grant's troops learned to have confidence in their commander. At the least, they learned that no matter how badly things went in battle, Grant was not going to give up.[42]

It was a good lesson for the future.

3

"Too Much Haste Will Ruin Everything"

The year 1861 was proverbial child's play compared with what was coming in 1862. While the battles of the war's initial year were every bit as large as those of the Revolution, War of 1812, or Mexican War, they were only minor compared to those that raged later in the war. Indeed, Wilson's Creek, Belmont, and numerous other battles ranged in size comparable to the famous battles of earlier American history in both numbers engaged and casualties, and Bull Run was greater in both categories. By the end of 1862, however, Bull Run was a minor battle compared to a second encounter fought on that very battlefield as well as other terrible engagements such as Antietam, Shiloh, and Fredericksburg.[1]

Still, as the year turned over, most Americans looked less to the future than they did to the past. Both sides were beginning to feel the effects of the war, especially families who had received word that loved ones had died on faraway battlefields at places they had never heard of before. The wounded and sick themselves suffered severely as well. Even those who made it through the year unscathed were also affected. Many soldiers had joined up thinking they would serve only a few months and then be able to go home. Their families were similarly surprised to realize that the soldiers were in the army long term. In the South, the Union blockade, thin though it was, began to take effect, adding yet another degree of difficulty to war life. The year 1861 had certainly not turned out the way most people expected, and the suffering already experienced in these initial months demonstrated that it was not going to be any easier any time soon.[2]

The two leaders of the belligerent nations did not have such a luxury to look back; they had to look ahead and try to implement policies that would make the war as short as possible so the suffering could stop. But the future looked just as bleak as the past, and neither Jefferson Davis nor Abraham Lincoln could take much comfort in thinking that they were winning. Davis had a host of worries, not the least being the situation in the west. The eastern front was relatively quiet, more so because of Federal inactivity than anything else. The major problem spot was in the western theater, where, despite Albert Sidney Johnston's personal attention, his line was long and the defenders few. Numerous holes existed between Johnston's major garrisons, and even some of those major locations were thinly held. Furthermore, Davis had little hope of additional troops until spring, when new levies would, it was hoped, augment the army's numbers. Yet Johnston needed numbers immediately and sent a staff officer, Colonel St. John R. Liddell, to Richmond. There an enraged Davis thundered in exasperation, "why did General Johnston send you to me for arms and reinforcements, when he must know that I have neither?" Calming down, Davis simply told Liddell, "tell my friend, General Johnston, that I can do nothing for him; that he must rely upon his own resources. . . . May God bless you."[3]

Matters were worse for Lincoln, who had to conquer rather than defend. Few of his commanders wanted to engage the enemy, much less conquer the South, so Lincoln grew increasingly impatient. He told his commanders to advance, but they responded with a hint of lecture in their words that it could not be done now. "It is exceedingly discouraging," Lincoln wrote in the first days of the new year. "As everywhere else, nothing can be done." Lincoln displayed his discouragement when he told his quartermaster general: "the people are impatient; Chase has no money and tells me he can raise no more; the General of the Army has typhoid fever. The bottom is out of the tub. What shall I do?"[4]

January 1862 began with the same timidity on both sides that much of 1861 had witnessed. That was certainly the case in the western theater, where the Confederates were primarily content to hold their ground during the hard winter months. The Federal forces were no more active. A divided command kept most of them disengaged and their common superior was not much help; George McClellan was sick much of the winter. That development left

Lincoln no option but to prod as best as he could, though he realized his shortcomings as a military man and was somewhat hesitant to order specific actions. He read up on military strategy in an effort to be able to get some-thing, anything, done.[5]

Henry Halleck and Don Carlos Buell were the two reasons that the Union war effort in the west stalled. Their divided command left neither of them willing to go forward alone without the other's support, or to support the other and forfeit any possible glory. Worse, the two did not communicate, preferring to go through McClellan, who became sick for several weeks over the new year. Lincoln himself realized the problem but would not, and felt he could not, wait. He sent two dispatches, one to Halleck and one to Buell, on December 31, both stating the same thing. To Halleck, he wrote: "Gen-eral McClellan is sick. Are General Buell and Yourself in concert? When he moves on Bowling Green, what hinders it being re-enforced from Colum-bus? A simultaneous movement by you on Columbus might prevent it." He sent basically the same message to Buell, with the intention of doing what McClellan would not, and now could not, do—to get operations moving in the west. The result was not encouraging. Buell responded, "there is no ar-rangement between General Halleck and myself." Halleck responded, "I have never received a word from General Buell," but added, "I am not ready to co-operate with him. Hope to do so in a few weeks." He lectured the president: "too much haste will ruin everything."[6]

Even as Buell blamed McClellan and Halleck blamed Buell, the two hard-headed generals got the message and reluctantly began to correspond with each other. Halleck declared that he had too few troops to do much of any-thing and compared his task to "a carpenter who is required to build a bridge with a dull ax, a broken saw, and rotten timber." To drive his point home to the uneducated Lincoln, he explained the strategic situation in Jominian terms, clearly thinking Lincoln could not fathom what he was saying: "to operate on exterior lines against an enemy occupying a central position will fail, as it always has failed, in ninety-nine cases out of a hundred. It is condemned by every military authority I have ever read." For his part, Buell responded with a lengthy lecture on what he believed needed to be done. Lincoln responded with some of his common sense, telling the two generals that the key to Union victory was "menacing him with superior forces at different points at the same time, so that we can safely attack one or both if he makes no change; and if he weakens one to strengthen the other, forbear to attack the strengthened one, but seize and hold the weakened one, gaining so much." Lincoln's trained military leaders could not understand this, or if they could, they did not act on it.[7]

Tellingly, the only action that resulted in battle during January occurred because of Confederate offensive movement, not any Federal advances. The small army on Johnston's far right flank in east Tennessee and Kentucky unwisely advanced across the Cumberland River in mid-January and fought a small battle against some of Buell's troops at Mill Springs. The January 19 fight was a disaster for the Confederates. One of the commanders, Felix Zollicoffer, was killed when the nearsighted newspaperman rode toward Federal lines. The overall commander, George Crittenden, did little better; he was drunk. Crittenden's troops conducted a fighting withdrawal to the Cumberland and barely made it across. Despite the escape, Johnston's right flank was crippled and had to withdraw from eastern Kentucky. That left the door wide open for a Federal advance toward the Cumberland Gap; the victorious George H. Thomas wrote Buell that Zollicoffer's forces "are entirely dispersed; they threw away their arms and disbanded, and should we go into East Tennessee now there would be no enemy to encounter." Even so, a lethargic Buell and his subordinate commanders did nothing.[8]

As a result, the only real Union success came not from Federal offensive action but when the Confederates bungled into defeat. An increasingly irritated and impatient Lincoln consequently took action on his own. On January 27, he issued his famous General Orders No. 1, which stated that all Federal forces, east and west, should advance against the enemy on or before February 22, George Washington's birthday. Common sense told Lincoln that the enemy could not withstand a simultaneous advance. He could only hope his commanders would agree and act.[9]

It was a good thing for Albert Sidney Johnston that he faced such a divided Union command, because even as the calendar showed 1862 his defenses were still woefully inadequate, especially on the crucial twin rivers. In fact, just two days into that year, Lloyd Tilghman reported that he still had two thousand unarmed men. "I have not men enough armed at this post [Donelson]," he said, "to man one-half the lines within the fortification, much less to effect anything at points which command my whole work." Still, work was progressing steadily on the fort itself, with the bastion soon to be enclosed and the heavy guns mounted. In addition, the men were now housed in winter quarters of log cabins within the fort proper, "something like 400 good cabins," Tilghman reported. One Confederate excitedly wrote home, "we expect to get into our cabins this week as they are nearly done. I will be glad of it for these tents are very cold." Despite the cold and lack of arms, as well as an outbreak of measles and little pay, the garrison had high morale, the same Confederate writing, "we have been living very high for some time." Another soldier wrote that despite rain and mud, they were living well "in our houses as saucy as pigs." There was plenty of food, and even the guards at the fort had "little houses . . . so now they can stand in them when it is raining and not get wet." The formal presentation of a flag to the 30th Tennessee in early January, attended by citizens of Nashville and Clarksville brought down by the steamboat *General Anderson*, only added to morale.[10]

In order to man the big guns, Tilghman had no choice but to detail a couple of infantry companies from the Fort Donelson garrison. Captains B. G. Bidwell of the 30th Tennessee and T. W. Beaumont of the 50th Tennessee began to instruct their men on the heavy artillery, aided by Dixon and other artillery officers sent by Polk from Columbus, including a future general, Major Alexander P. Stewart. Transitioning from infantry to heavy artillery was quite a leap, and Bidwell wrote, "my company had at that time never drilled in heavy artillery nor knew anything about it, and I myself had never directed my attention to that branch of the service; but, with the assistance [of trained artillerymen] . . . I was enabled to arrive at a tolerable degree of proficiency for myself and company." One of the common soldiers was very proud of his cannon and stated it more bluntly: "I think we would shake an old gun boat right smartly if she would venture up."[11]

To aid in communication within his small command, Tilghman connected both Fort Henry and Fort Donelson with Cumberland City by telegraph, some thirty-five miles of wire in total. He was also able to report that work on Fort Heiman and its outer works was progressing, as were efforts at Fort Henry, stating that "the entire command [is] in a most admirable state of efficiency." Efficiency did not equal numbers, however, and the fort went on high alert when the Federals finally began to show some life in mid-January.[12]

One reason the Federals were so hesitant about moving forward in Halleck's Mississippi River department was because any movement along the rivers needed the support of naval gunboats. McClellan in Virginia, Buell in central Kentucky, and others west of the Mississippi River in Missouri did not need gunboats. Because Halleck's department had so many rivers, however, the need to coordinate operations with the naval arm was great. But Halleck had to wait for the Eads gunboats to come on line before he could move. That was an excruciating wait.[13]

Other matters ate at army-navy effectiveness too. The vessels being built were hybrids: the army paid for them, but Eads built them to navy specifications, and his work was being overseen by naval supervision. When the boats were launched in October 1861 and received by the Federal government some two months later, the army held command over them, but the officers and crews were all navy. Therefore army boats with navy crews and officers were ultimately under army orders. Perhaps the defining feature was that the army paid the crews' salaries, as well as those of the pilots who boarded as civilians to maneuver the ironclads. It was an odd situation and would only be resolved in the fall of 1862 when the boats were completely transferred to the navy for good.[14]

Foote nevertheless continued Rogers's work. He worked through Halleck as the new departmental commander, but he found his real soul mate in Ulysses S. Grant. With Grant in command of the forward area at Cairo and Foote's boats entering the war, it was obvious that geography brought the two together. In fact, they eventually teamed up to convince Halleck of the need to move offensively on the western waters. Yet, little could be done until the boats were actually ready for service. Although most had been delivered to the army in October, there were still numerous tasks required to get them ready for action. They had to be assigned a crew; that crew had to train on the new boats, weaponry had to be added, and the entire lot had to learn to work together. Unfortunately, there was no time for such training in January 1862.[15]

By the new year, only two of the ironclads had joined the three timberclads in service: the *Essex* and the newly commissioned *St. Louis*, one of the city-class boats. The others would not be commissioned until January 16. Frustration reigned in the meantime. Grant wrote late in 1861, "I have been much dissatisfied with the progress upon the gunboats being built at Mound City, and have expressed the fear that the detention upon those being built at Carondelet would prevent their being brought out this winter." Since the Mississippi River typically fell to very low stages in December of each year, the gunboats could potentially be trapped in the upper portions of the river,

particularly those at Carondelet, until the river rose again in the spring. Instead, Grant recommended that the boats be brought to Cairo immediately for
completion, "as soon as practicable," he wrote.[16]

Delay still attended the ironclads even once they reached Cairo. Several
last-minute modifications had to be made, such as "changing the steam drums
to the top of the boilers," Foote informed Washington, "which the trial of the
engines in coming down from St. Louis proved necessary, as they worked water instead of steam, endangering the engines, as well as from the carpenters
having to prepare pilot houses and completing other work." Eads himself had
to travel to Cairo for the inspection process, which was not completed until
mid-January.[17]

Ironically, the finishing of the boats was not the major delay. Crewing the
vessels was more problematic than anyone thought it would be, mainly because the naval pay of eighteen dollars a month was far less than what sailors
were accustomed to making in private service, some thirty dollars a month.
Grant wrote in late January, "men are absolutely necessary before the gunboats, now nearly ready for use, can be used," and Foote estimated in mid-
January that he was one thousand men short. Much of the problem came with
the "master of transportation" in the quartermaster department at Cairo, who
because of his incompetence was "entirely unable to get crews for the necessary boats." By mid-January, Foote had men enough for only a few boats but
opted to divide them equally, placing sixty men on each, far below the needed
number. Another issue developed when the "association of engineers" in St.
Louis began "interfering with men of their calling entering the service of the
United States." In one major example, an engineer or pilot was obtained for
the gunboats, but the association managed to make him quit when it informed
him that they held a mortgage on his property and would foreclose if he went
into Federal service. While pilots were hard to come by, Grant had a plan
for the crews themselves. He notified Halleck that he had quite a few men in
prison for desertion and other crimes, and recommended that "in view of the
difficulty of getting men for the gunboat service, that these men be transferred
to that service; also that authority be given to transfer unruly men hereafter."
Grant indicated that he had spoken with Foote about this arrangement and
that "I believe it meets with his approval." It is hard to imagine the detailed
and religious Foote agreeing fully to take all of Grant's troublemakers as the
backbone of his crews, but then he had few other options at that point.[18]

Crew troubles thus prevented all the boats from being fully in service by
the time February rolled around. Although all seven of the city-class vessels

were commissioned by January 16, despite Foote warning Washington that "some work yet remains to be done before they are fully completed," the government accepted Eads's work even while reminding him of the lateness: "the work on the seven gunboats . . . has been completed according to the terms of the contract with the Government, excepting the time at which they ought to have been finished and delivered at Cairo." Yet because of crew issues, only three of the seven Eads boats made it into service on time, including the *St. Louis*, *Carondelet*, and *Cincinnati*. The older *Essex*, which had been commissioned earliest, was also available, as were the three timberclads that Halleck and his commanders had been depending on for so long. Unfortunately, sailors for the others were not likely forthcoming, Secretary Welles informing Foote in late January not to look for any crewmen from him as "the ships on the Atlantic are waiting for men [as well]," and Fox telling him "there are several ships waiting for crews. You can not expect men from the Navy." Foote consequently had to make do with what he had. He began training, Foote himself teaching young lieutenants to save ammunition in locating ranges: "I am aware of your difficulties in new and undisciplined crew and officers, but make these criticisms rather as indicative of correcting things in the future."[19]

In the meantime, the few boats in service continued to patrol, guard, and explore. Phelps, now back in command of his squadron when Henry Walke took command of one of the new ironclads, was particularly active in gaining vital intelligence on the Cumberland and Tennessee rivers, making another run toward the forts in early January. "Yesterday I ascended the Tennessee River to the State line," he notified Foote, "returning in the night. The water was barely sufficient to float this boat, drawing 5 feet 4 inches, and in coming down we dragged heavily in places." He nonetheless provided valuable knowledge, although he gave the Confederates too much credit for their work. "The rebels are industriously perfecting their means of defense both at Dover and Fort Henry," he wrote, adding that moving up the Cumberland River would "alarm the army at Bowling Green," but alas, "at this time there is no water in the river."[20]

The army needed the navy, and the navy needed men and water sufficient to float. The result was even more waiting.

Even as the work progressed on the naval arm, planning went on regarding where and when to strike. Rumors of Confederate offensives near the twin rivers served to bring attention to that area, one commander reporting, "the inhabitants in the counties east of the Cumberland and bordering on the river are much alarmed and send messages that a force is coming." More importantly, Lincoln's involvement in the process, particularly when McClellan was sick around the new year, caused both Halleck and Buell to prompt each other to set a date for movement. Neither would, and even Lincoln's action of setting a movement date in late February did not garner much attention or results.[21]

During this time, however, there appeared a myriad of options regarding moving on Johnston's defensive line. In central Kentucky, Buell argued with McClellan and even Lincoln about whether to move into east Tennessee or through middle Tennessee to Nashville. Buell stated that a move into east Tennessee was unwise, which prompted McClellan to respond sharply: "you have no idea of the pressure brought to bear here upon the Government for a forward movement. It is so strong that it seems absolutely necessary to make the advance on Eastern Tennessee at once." The defeat of Zollicoffer's Confederates at Mill Springs eliminated Confederate forces from the Cumberland Gap region, yet Buell was still reluctant to move there. As a result, he did nothing except call on Halleck to support him and avoid offering support for any of Halleck's plans.[22]

On the Mississippi Valley front, Halleck likewise chose to delay. He had fewer geographical impediments such as mountains, but he had more territory to cover, including the Missouri side of the river. Both Federals and Confederates recognized that the main idea was to acquire control of the Mississippi River, but the series of defenses along the river at Columbus, the various forts in Tennessee, and even Memphis had to be overcome. It was hoped that excursions from the south via the Gulf of Mexico, also with vast naval support, would capture the lower Mississippi at the same time that Halleck's troops were taking the northern stretches.[23]

Columbus was the obvious problem on the Mississippi. Henry Halleck told McClellan as late as January 20 that "the idea of moving down the Mississippi by steam is, in my opinion, impracticable, or at least premature. It is not a proper line of operations, at least now." Attacking that citadel was more than Halleck believed he could do at the time, even though such waiting only offered Polk the opportunity to make his fortress stronger. In fact, Polk was busy erecting batteries and filling the river with "torpedoes" and stretching a chain across the waterway. It would take massive effort, planning, and numbers to take Columbus by force, if it could be done at all. "Columbus cannot be taken without an immense siege train and a terrible loss of life," Halleck told McClellan. "I have thoroughly studied its defenses; they are very strong." As a result, the idea of bypassing Columbus and taking a site lower on the river, perhaps New Madrid, continued to crop up as an option. The hope was that if river travel was interdicted south of Columbus, it would cut Polk off and he would have to evacuate Columbus.[24]

Over time, a better idea emerged, one that would set in motion the campaign on the twin rivers. Because of Polk's fixation on Columbus, he left other points in his district vulnerable. "A much more feasible plan is to move up the Cumberland and Tennessee," Halleck wrote in late January. "This would turn Columbus and force the abandonment of Bowling Green." Federal commanders were beginning to realize that the movement did not necessarily have to be down the Mississippi River itself. A parallel river system would work just as well, and the Tennessee River and its valley were positioned perfectly for such an operation. Better yet, operations on the Tennessee instead of the Mississippi River would confront fewer obstacles such as Columbus and would allow access to the heart of the Confederacy's rail system, not just the terminuses of the several lines where they ended at the Mississippi River.[25]

The Tennessee River flowed from eastern Tennessee in a bowl through northern Alabama and Mississippi into a northern orientation before emptying into the Ohio River at Paducah. The Federals already held the Kentucky city "under strict martial law," as one Iowan reported it, because of Grant's quick work back in September. Consequently, Federal forces could move southward along the Tennessee instead of the Mississippi, netting the same amount of territory but facing infinitely fewer defenses. Once in southwestern Tennessee and northern Mississippi and Alabama, where the river curved eastward in its bowl, the Federals had only a twenty or so mile leap over land to one of the Confederacy's critical railroad hubs, Corinth, Mississippi. Such a move would clearly threaten the railroads, and the citizens of the cotton states complained to Richmond, "it is only 18 miles from the Big Bend of the Tennessee to their [railroads] junction at Corinth." Even better, Corinth was south of Memphis, and its capture would effectively outflank that city, allowing operations to continue southward through Mississippi or to leap back westward to the Mississippi River and its valley, where few defensible areas existed north of Vicksburg.[26]

Accordingly, a movement down the Tennessee River would, at the least, cut the Memphis, Clarksville, and Louisville Railroad that Johnston depended on for interior lines of communication on at least a portion of his line. If the move was successful, it would also outflank Columbus, the various Harris-built forts, and Memphis, netting huge amounts of territory and river miles as well as breaking one of the true rail hubs of the western Confederacy at Corinth. Additionally, breaking the Confederate line at the Tennessee River would also outflank Nashville, certainly if the operation included action on the Cumberland River, which formed a much more shallow bowl but obviously controlled access to Nashville. If Nashville were outflanked by Federals moving to the Corinth area, then Johnston's army at Bowling Green would likewise be outflanked and perhaps even caught within the bowl of at least one of the parallel flowing Cumberland or Tennessee rivers. Hence, it was not without exaggeration when Halleck began arguing, "this line of the Cumberland or Tennessee is the great central line of the Western theater of the war."[27]

It is not clear who saw this possibility first, although the initial recorded mention of it came as early as November 20, 1861, when an engineer, Colonel Charles Whittlesey, wrote Halleck: "will you allow me to suggest the consideration of a great movement by land and water up the Cumberland and Tennessee Rivers?" Whittlesey went on to explain his thinking, writing that such a move would "allow of water transportation half way to Nashville" and was "the most passable route into Tennessee." More importantly in the larger strategic sense, Whittlesey argued that such a move would indeed turn both Columbus and Johnston's position at Bowling Green: "would it not necessitate the evacuation of Columbus by threatening their railway communication" and "would it not necessitate the retreat of General Buckner [Hardee] by threatening his railway lines?"[28]

An even more forceful recommendation came from Flag Officer Foote in early December. In writing to Secretary Welles, Foote reported, "I have suggested to General Halleck that I should, in the course of two or three weeks, when we get our men, proceed up the Tennessee River with two or three of our gunboats and a regiment of soldiers, for the purpose of destroying the rebel boats and a battery which now renders Paducah more valuable than any other point." He noted, "the general approvingly refers me to General Smith, commanding at Paducah." Others were also thinking strongly of a Tennessee-Cumberland river campaign. Phelps reported to Foote how a winter campaign would work: "unlike the Ohio, the Cumberland and Tennessee rivers rarely freeze over. An old pilot informs me that in thirty-one years living upon its banks he has seen the Cumberland frozen over but four times, and steamers at times have laid by several weeks, unable to pass up the Ohio on account of ice, while boats were daily plying upon the Cumberland and Tennessee. Nor does the Tennessee fall to low stage like the Ohio in midwinter."[29]

Even Don Carlos Buell wrote as early as November 27, 1861, that in combination with his eventual move toward Bowling Green, there should be a "movement of two flotilla columns up the Tennessee and Cumberland, so as at least to land and unite near the State line, and cut off communication between Bowling Green and Columbus, and perhaps run directly into Nashville." He elaborated in early January when Lincoln called for action, stating, "it will be of the first importance to break the railroad communications, and, if possible, that should be done by columns moving rapidly to the bridges over the Cumberland and Tennessee." The officials in Washington seemed to be leaning in that direction as well; McClellan asked for the depths of the Cumberland River to Nashville and the Tennessee River in early December. Lew Wallace summed it up best by saying, "most likely the conception was simultaneous with many minds."[30]

In reality, only one mind mattered and that was Henry Halleck's. Fortunately for the Union cause, he too was beginning to think in the same terms. William T. Sherman described how he, George W. Cullum, and Halleck plotted strategy one night in December 1861. Halleck asked the engineer Cullum to draw the Confederate line in his department, which he did from Columbus to Forts Henry and Donelson and on to Bowling Green. Then Halleck asked, "where is the proper place to break it?" The response was, "*Naturally* the center." Halleck took a blue pencil and drew a line perpendicular to the Confederate line at the center. Sherman marveled at how "it coincided nearly with the general course of the Tennessee River." Halleck informed his men, "that's the true line of operations."[31]

Problems nevertheless emerged even as the pros and cons were being sorted out and the realization came of a monumental opportunity being offered to the Federal high command. One problem was that any operations on the rivers, whether it be the Mississippi, Tennessee, or Cumberland, would have to be done with the cooperation of the navy, and its boats were not yet ready. Another problem was that any advance on the line of the Tennessee would necessarily need a similar effort on the Cumberland, and the troops making the effort would need vast support from nearby commands to provide covering forces, to make sure the enemy did not take troops from their front to reinforce the threatened area, and to send emergency relief if a setback occurred.

That fact brought Buell back into the picture. Unfortunately, the Tennessee and Cumberland region was somewhat of a gray area between Halleck's and Buell's commands, with inconsistency existing where they joined. Each commander was hesitant to operate on his extreme flank, fearing a lack of support from the other, who would not be under any obligation to send troops for help if asked. Unless a combined command in the west came about or the general in chief ordered something done jointly, little could be expected.[32]

Perhaps the biggest problem with an attack on the Tennessee or Cumberland rivers, or both, was the lack of knowledge about the enemy defenses and capabilities. There had been no operations as yet in the area, and the small timberclad gunboats had just barely even gotten sight of the enemy works, much less been able to develop their strength or find out how extensive the defenses were. Intelligence was thus desperately needed as thoughts began to turn toward a twin-river operation. It is not surprising that Ulysses S. Grant was the man who provided it.

Although the Confederate forts defending the crucial twin rivers were incomplete and pitifully garrisoned, the Federal commanders did not yet know exactly how undefended they were. Had they known, Halleck might have launched an attack immediately. Without any commanding naval presence like that which was about to come on line in the form of Eads's ironclads, however, Halleck could gain little intelligence without risking the priceless timberclads that were about all he had to work with. They could not be risked until the ironclads were nearly ready to enter service.[33]

As January proceeded, the boats were nearing completion, although if they entered service any time soon it would be with untrained crews and novice commanders. In the meantime, knowledge of the Confederate situation became a little clearer. C. F. Smith continually sent a gunboat up the Tennessee River to what he called "Fort Henry." Undefended by armor as the boat was, however, it could not approach too close. In addition, Smith had long felt grave worries when that gunboat left Paducah, terming the flotilla a "misnomer" in that it was only one gunboat and two coal barges lashed together into a floating battery: "I think it advisable to have another gunboat here as an additional security," he wrote Halleck. The navy was alerted as well, Phelps writing, "General Smith does not deem it prudent to leave this place without a gunboat."[34]

Given the lack of naval support in mid-January, it is not surprising that the army did the major intelligence-gathering, mostly as a result of peremptory orders from Lincoln for Halleck to do something. Lincoln's spurring of the commanders with such statements as "please do not lose time in this manner" seemingly also awakened the sick McClellan. On January 3, he wired Halleck that Buell should be supported at all cost, at the least by holding the Confederate garrisons in place in western Tennessee and Kentucky so they could not reinforce Bowling Green. Buell's department was obviously foremost on Washington's mind, probably because of the political, economic, and strategic importance placed on east Tennessee by the president. It was Buell who was to make that attempt, so the thought of Buell sending aid to Halleck was never considered. It did not help that intelligence from C. F. Smith at Paducah indicated that Confederate troops were indeed moving eastward toward Bowling Green. A force under John S. Bowen, replaced by the motley band of Mississippi militia, had in fact left Camp Beauregard in the area between Columbus and the twin rivers and was moving eastward toward Bowling Green.[35]

McClellan reacted strongly, ordering Halleck to send several expeditions south in order to keep the Confederates from dispatching any more troops eastward. McClellan stipulated that the available timberclads should be used as well, and that "not a moment's time should be lost in preparing these expeditions." After ordering Halleck to support Buell, Washington now turned its attention to the latter. "Please name as early a day as you safely can on or before which you can be ready to move southward in concert with Major-General Halleck," Lincoln wrote on January 7, adding, "delay is ruining us, and it is indispensable for me to have something definite."[36]

Obviously, Grant, as commander of the district that contained all these points of reconnaissance, was the man to do the work of pinning Confederate forces down in west Tennessee. Grant was more than happy to oblige. The aggressive general had been biding his time, desiring to be turned loose on the enemy line. He even asked for permission to travel to St. Louis to talk over a plan of attack he had in mind. Until he was allowed to do so, however, he tried to find out as much as possible about Confederate strength. He continually had spies or travelers report to him the condition of the defenses at Columbus and the surrounding area, and the picture they told was of a much weaker Confederate line than expected—"less than I have understood heretofore they had." Another spy indicated that the Confederates were badly supplied, Grant noting that "if salt can be kept out . . . they will have some difficulty in saving their bacon."[37]

In the meantime, McClellan ordered Halleck on January 3 to send out the reconnaissance. A nervous Halleck obeyed orders, but continually warned of danger if more troops were pulled from Missouri. He was also still nervous about beginning operations so close to Buell's department because of the lack of knowledge of the Confederate defenses. Yet he had no choice and issued his orders to Grant on January 6, also sending reinforcements to Cairo in the form of unarmed regiments as well as one from the interior of Missouri.[38]

Halleck ordered his aggressive commander Grant to send out two columns of troops to tie down the Confederates in west Tennessee and Kentucky and to conduct reconnaissance. One major column, under Smith and supported by Phelps's two timberclads, the *Lexington* and *Conestoga*, and the steamer *Wilson* on the Tennessee River, was to go forward toward Mayfield and Murray, Kentucky, near Camp Beauregard. Smith was to convince the Confederates that he was heading for Dover: "make a great fuss about moving all your forces towards Nashville, and let it be so reported by the newspapers." He was also to put word out that reinforcements from Missouri were arriving and that his troops were only the "advanced guards." In actuality, Smith was to try to keep the Confederates from reinforcing Bowling Green and was ordered to "by all means avoid a serious engagement." Such secrecy was maintained that the men and even staff officers were to be uninformed of the reasoning for the march. "Having accomplished this," Halleck ordered, "you will slowly retire to your former positions, but, if possible, keep up the idea of a general advance." Halleck cautioned once more against fighting a battle—"we are not ready for that." He did, however, allow Grant to "give your men a little experience in skirmishing."[39]

A second column under McClernand from Cairo was to move toward Columbus, which would of course keep that garrison busy as well as indicate how large and forceful it was, and how aggressive Polk would be. Grant had learned Polk would react swiftly on the opposite side of the river in November. Now, he would test the Confederate reflexes on this eastern side. McClernand would be supported by the only other gunboats now in service, the *Essex*, *St. Louis*, and *Tyler*.[40]

Grant quickly responded to Halleck's orders despite terrible weather, and he and Foote soon put in motion the infantry and gunboats. Trusting Smith more than McClernand, Grant decided to move with McClernand's force toward Columbus, leaving Smith to conduct his own operations to the east. Grant nevertheless informed Halleck, "the continuous rains for the last week or more have rendered the roads extremely bad, and will necessarily make our movement slow. This, however, will operate worse upon the enemy, if he should come out to meet us, than upon us."[41]

The operations were indeed delayed, even before the poor roads could affect travel. Grant reported how problems elsewhere affected his plans: a "steamer has got aground about 20 miles above here, where the channel is very narrow, and swung around so as to entirely cut off navigation from here during the present low stage of water or until removed." Fog at Cairo also delayed Grant's departure a day, causing him to notify Smith to likewise delay his movement. Then Halleck notified Grant to delay even longer until he sent more reinforcements. Grant had already sent McClernand's troops southward to Fort Jefferson, so he left them there instead of recalling them, worried about their morale.[42]

McClernand's movement finally began on January 14, and it made good headway despite the terrible roads and sleet. This force, with E. A. Paine's troops in the rear to guard Fort Jefferson and other routes to Cairo, marched toward Columbus, the cavalry getting closer than the infantry but all making a loud demonstration. Passing through such small towns as Milburn and Blandville, the cavalry made a 140-mile ride while the infantry marched seventy-five miles on what McClernand termed "icy or miry roads during a most inclement season." Once the demonstration was completed, the navy embarked the infantry and transported them northward to Cairo. Conversely, Grant with the gunboats *Essex*, *St. Louis*, and *Tyler* explored the river approaches to Columbus.[43]

The other column under Smith similarly moved forward from Paducah along the Tennessee River. He made some forty-six miles in three days despite what one Federal described as "marching all night through mud and water nearly knee deep. The rain pouring down in torrents all the time—in fact I never saw it rain harder in all my life—it took us three long hours to get two cannon and five wagons up one hill." Lew Wallace described the scene even more graphically: "the country had become an ocean of mud, and there was rain and melting snow, and from the beginning to end no dry place to set a foot could be discovered." He labeled the march "memorable to every man who participated in it." By January 20, when Smith moved through Murray, Kentucky, he was beginning to run out of provisions. He sent a courier back to Paducah, ordering a steamer to bring food to a point on the river. The steamer, food, and gunboat *Lexington* soon arrived.[44]

Perhaps the highlight of the operation came when Smith, while the supplies were being distributed, boarded the *Lexington* and proceeded upriver "to have a look at Fort Henry." The gunboat unfortunately hit a rock in the river, which caused an hour's delay and an inch and a quarter of water per hour to enter the boat. Lieutenant James Shirk grew angry at the pilot, "who represented himself as a Tennessee River pilot," and had him "confined in double irons." He thought better of it later, however, when the man appeared "to be so downhearted and distressed at the accident." In any case, Shirk was able to take Smith within two and a half miles of the fort, finding out that a rumored "masked" battery did not in fact exist. The *Lexington* fired four shots at the fort, receiving only one in return, and it fell well short. Despite a defender at Fort Henry writing home that "we were only bombarded by gunboats to no effect whatever," Smith was able to get a good look at the surrounding area and concluded that it was very similar to the maps back at his headquarters at Paducah. He reasoned, "I think two iron-clad gunboats would make short work of Fort Henry." Smith's reconnaissance thus proved invaluable in determining ranges of the Confederate guns as well as conditions in the river; it also gave some indication of the garrison. Smith returned to Paducah with much information, Grant crowing, "the expedition, if it had no other effect, served as a fine reconnaissance."[45]

Not everyone was so enthusiastic. The rank and file in the miserable Union columns complained bitterly that there was no real object for all their suffering. "The boys were very angry" when ordered back to Paducah, remembered one 12th Illinois soldier, adding that they "talked of rebelling. They wanted to push on to Fort Henry at all hazards." With the letdown of no fighting, the trek home was truly miserable, the men "feeling no ambition to march." In fact, many "fell out & had to be carried." Even so, they returned with much plunder, one soldier describing being "loaded down with plunder Such as geese turkeys chickens & everything else that is good to eat."[46]

Despite Grant's declaration that "we were out more than a week splashing through the mud, snow and rain, the men suffering very much," the operation provided large dividends. The people of the region were frightened, one Mississippian writing that "the people are much excited on account of the enemy having thrown a few shells into Fort Henry two or three days ago." Lew Wallace, who accompanied Phelps on one of his voyages, later wrote,

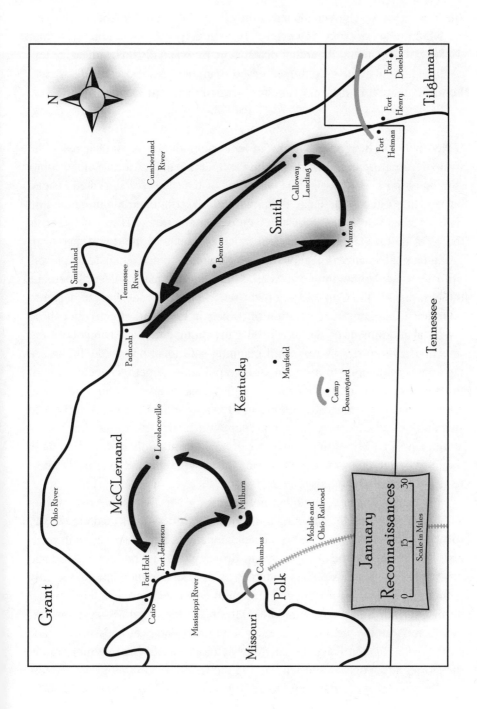

Grant

N

Ohio River

Smithland

Cumberland River

Tennessee River

Paducah

Calloway Landing

Smith

Benton

Murray

Fort Heiman

Fort Henry

Fort Donelson

Tilghman

Cairo

Fort Holt

Fort Jefferson

McClernand

Lovelaceville

Milburn

Kentucky

Mayfield

Camp Beauregard

Mississippi River

Columbus

Polk

Missouri

Mobile and Ohio Railroad

Tennessee

January Reconnaissances

0   15   30
Scale in Miles

"the gun-boatmen enjoyed the terror they inspired." The Confederate defenders were not so worried, however. A Fort Donelson Confederate wrote that we "are expecting a fight at that place [Fort Henry] daily." He added, "I feel confident that we can whip three times our number here [Fort Donelson], and I understand that Fort Henry is better fortified than Fort Donaldson."[47]

The stirring of the Federal armies in January produced major changes in the strategic situation in the west. On the Confederate side, Albert Sidney Johnston had long been ignoring the weakness of the twin rivers, fixated instead on Bowling Green's defense. Meanwhile, Polk continued his tunnel vision on Columbus's defenses. Johnston would continue to tout Bowling Green as the chief defensive area throughout much of January: "no doubt the strongest attack the enemy is capable of making will be made against this place." Still, he was also beginning to realize that his defensive line was perhaps the best chance the Confederacy had to gain its independence. He began to recommend a major concentration of forces on his front, effectively calling for an abandonment of the territorial garrisoning Jefferson Davis believed in. Thousands of troops were still manning safe locations while Tennessee lay almost wide open to invasion. "The rapid and energetic concentration of the power of the country to meet the mighty exigencies of the present movement," Johnston warned Richmond in January, "must be brought to bear to sustain our cause, which every one feels will justify every sacrifice for its attainment." To Mississippi Governor John J. Pettus, Johnston wrote, "here the most dangerous attack can be made on Mississippi, and here the stoutest resistance should be opposed to it."[48]

Few troops resulted, the most notable being Mississippi's Army of Ten Thousand. This motley force of militia or state troops had made their way forward in late 1861, and one brigade encamped at Camp Beauregard in western Kentucky while the other moved to Bowling Green. Their lot was sad and miserable. The Mississippians endured the disease common among recently gathered large bodies of men, and they endured such misery in a much colder climate far north of their normal deep South weather. One Mississippian remembered that the weather "exceeded anything I had ever known." Brigade commander Reuben Davis noted, "day by day the cold became more bitter, the storms grew darker and wilder, and the roads became more desperately bad." He added, "our men bore their sufferings heroically, but it was a fearful time." The combination of the disease and harsh weather in Kentucky doomed their ability to defend anything, and the "army" was soon dispatched back southward to recover. They had provided no effective service to the Confederacy.[49]

The major change in Johnston's thinking came with Grant's reconnaissances in mid-January. McClernand's movement toward Columbus and Smith's toward Murray seemed to frighten the Confederate commanders, with Polk at Columbus believing there were as many as fifty thousand Federal troops bearing down on him. He began to write anyone who would listen, including Johnston and even Jefferson Davis, reminding them that Columbus was the "key to the whole Mississippi Valley." Five days later, during Grant's maneuvers, Polk notified Bowling Green in what sounded like the last message of a frantic general that, as he had stores for twenty-five thousand men for a hundred and twenty days, "I have resolved, therefore, to stand a siege, and to look to the general for such aid as the War Department and the country may afford him for relief. We will, in maintaining our position, of course hope that the support required will be furnished as early as practicable." With news such as this, one observer noted that Johnston "suddenly awoke." Others also had a change in heart as rumors swirled throughout the South that Fort Henry had fallen to Smith's advance. Even Tennessee Senator Gustavas A. Henry became vocal: "I need not apologize for my urgency, for I cannot and ought not, in the position I occupy, to stand still in such a moment as this."[50]

The effect was widespread. Major fortifications and the establishment of heavy guns soon occurred at Clarksville, upriver from Fort Donelson. Local commanders under Tilghman began to seriously work on the twin-river defenses as well: Adolphus Heiman in command at Fort Henry and John M. Head at Fort Donelson until he was outranked by the arrival of Brigadier General Bushrod Johnson. Workers strengthened not only the river batteries but the landward approaches as well. In fact, the Donelson garrison could hear the gunboat firing at Henry, and the response was pandemonium. Head informed Tilghman at Fort Henry, "I have had the whole command turned out and put to cutting timber and preparing rifle pits, so as to protect the approaches." He also sent the sick away in preparation for action. Tilghman, in control of both forts, ordered more ammunition and two additional Tennessee regiments, although unarmed, northward from Henderson. Some of the Fort Donelson garrison also moved to Fort Henry amid the perceived crisis, particularly the 49th and 50th Tennessee. They did not have to fight the enemy but were, as one soldier reported, merely armed, before they were sent back, with "side arms—*spades and shovels*, and are now drilling in that manual."[51]

In the biggest change resulting from the Federal reconnaissances, Johnston finally awoke to the reality that no matter how strong Columbus and Bowling Green were, their defense rested on the twin-river forts. However, it was not until January 19 that he viewed the potential of Federal action on the Tennessee and Cumberland rivers as a serious threat. He had hardly mentioned the twin-river forts before; now, Johnston wrote Benjamin in Richmond twice on that day that the Federals tested Fort Henry on January 17 and indicated that it seemed probable that the enemy intended "to turn General Polk's right by the Memphis and Ohio Railroad." He admitted, "I desire the Government, if it be possible, to send a strong force to Nashville and another to Memphis," and he ordered additional guns to Fort Henry, Nashville, and Clarksville. Johnston now certainly saw the possibility of losing it all and needed garrisoned places he could fall back upon. But until reinforcements could come, Johnston had to act with what he had, and he dispatched some eight thousand men from his Bowling Green army under John B. Floyd westward to Russellville, nearer to the Cumberland River. There, they joined a small brigade under Mississippi general Charles Clark that had been holding Russellville as an outpost.[52]

The situation only grew worse for Johnston as January passed. Right in the middle of his quick change in strategic thinking, he received word that his right flank had been shattered in the debacle at Mill Springs and that his political general Zollicoffer was dead while his other commander Crittenden was drunk. Johnston confided to Samuel Cooper in Richmond, "to suppose with the facilities of movement by water which the well-filled rivers of the Ohio, Cumberland, and Tennessee give for active operations, that they will suspend them in Tennessee and Kentucky during the winter months is a delusion." As if to illustrate further his anxiety, he again counseled: "all the resources of the Confederacy are now needed for the defense of Tennessee."[53]

Then amazingly amid all such chaos, the crisis suddenly lessened as Grant's reconnaissance forces returned to Cairo and Paducah. Polk himself, so ready to go under siege, admitted when it was all over that "what the particular object of it was has not clearly transpired." Still, the operations may have been a blessing in disguise for Johnston and his subordinates. While it netted the Federals much intelligence, they gained no territory and the Confederate high command, especially Johnston, seemingly awakened. Johnston became thoroughly convinced of the twin rivers' importance, but time would tell if it was too late. Nevertheless, had Grant's troops not tipped their hand to future operations, they may have caught Johnston even more flatfooted than he was now.[54]

A similar change came over the Federal high command. With such glowing reports of possibilities, Halleck began to seriously consider action. Having already been thinking of a movement along the twin rivers instead of along the Mississippi, and being prodded by Grant and Foote at the same time, Halleck began to think seriously of an operation into Tennessee. It would be a bold stroke to be sure: his numbers were few and he would have to strip virtually all of his department to funnel troops to the area. Likewise, the naval assets were not ready yet, and much of the river system in the department would likewise have to be stripped of naval cover. Then there was the problem of command. Halleck had never really become comfortable with Grant and was even scheming behind the scenes to get the retired Ethan Allen Hitchcock restored to command to take over the operations. On the other hand, Smith and Grant were all the while informing Halleck of the possibilities that lay in a quick and bold movement. A now convinced Halleck grew warmer to the idea, but he still kept Grant in the dark despite allowing him to visit St. Louis, as Grant had been requesting. "The leave was granted," Grant later wrote, "but not graciously." Halleck's arrogance only grew worse once Grant got to St. Louis: "I was received with so little cordiality that I perhaps stated the object of my visit with less clearness than I might have done, and I had not uttered many sentences before I was cut short as if my plan was preposterous. I returned to Cairo very much crestfallen." Unbeknown to Grant, the sick (with measles) but recovering Halleck was thinking along the same lines anyway; as historian John F. Marszalek has described it, "Halleck was, in fact, reacting not to Grant's plan, but to Grant himself."[55]

The possibilities that could come from success were overwhelming. If the railroad bridge just south of Fort Henry on the Tennessee was severed, it would divide the Confederate line, virtually outflanking both Columbus and Bowling Green. Both of those garrisons might very well retreat. Even better, nothing apparently stood between Fort Henry and the deep cotton states, where the central nervous system of the Confederate railroad network could be put in grave danger. More ominously, word was out that P. G. T. Beauregard was coming west with fifteen regiments, which turned out to be false concerning the regiments at least, although the Union high command soon verified that an entire Virginia and Mississippi brigade under John B. Floyd had been sent west to Johnston. Obviously, the quicker Halleck moved, the better he would be able to take the weak forts.[56]

Halleck consequently began to prepare for such a move, asking Smith for detailed descriptions of the road and river network around the Tennessee and Cumberland rivers. Halleck asked Smith to report in "as much detail as your means of information will allow." He said that he was particularly interested in "the character of the country between these roads and rivers, and whether it is such that troops can sustain or be sustained by the gunboats." Grant and Foote had been conversing about such action as well, Grant wishing to move up the Cumberland first but Foote talking him out of it. Foote informed Halleck on January 28, "Grant and myself are of opinion that Fort Henry, on the Tennessee River, can be carried with four ironclad gunboats and troops to permanently occupy." He later added that based on additional reconnaissance by Lieutenant Phelps, "we have come to the conclusion that, as the Tennessee will soon fall, the movement up that river is desirable early next week (Monday), or, in fact, as soon as possible." In a follow-up note, Foote almost demanded: "have we your authority to move for that purpose when ready?"[57]

By this time, Grant was also increasingly calling on Halleck for such a move. He sent a short message on January 28: "with permission, I will take Fort Henry, on the Tennessee, and establish and hold a large camp there." He sent more details the next day, arguing for haste and reminding Halleck, "it will, besides, have a moral effect upon our troops to advance them toward the rebel States." He added, "if this is not done soon there is but little doubt but that the defenses of both the Tennessee and Cumberland Rivers will be materially strengthened." He also added, perhaps somewhat to goad the intellectual Halleck, "the advantages of this move are as perceptible to the general commanding as to myself, therefore further statements are unnecessary."[58]

Halleck thus agreed to the move, although historian T. Harry Williams has wondered if Halleck was acting egotistically. All the same, much planning would have to be done before the movement could be made. One of the key decisions was whether to go up the Tennessee or Cumberland river first. Many had their opinions, the common feeling being that Fort Henry was the stronger of the two Confederate forts as well as the most important: "Fort Henry has a garrison of about 6,000, and it is pretty strongly fortified," Halleck wrote Washington in late January. C. F. Smith agreed, writing, "the more important is Fort Henry, 71 miles up the Tennessee, just at the State line. It is a strong earthwork on the water front, but not nearly so strong on the land side." Conversely, Grant preferred moving up the Cumberland first, perhaps thinking Fort Donelson was weaker, but Foote talked him out of it. Foote later noted, "the General preferred the Cumberland and Fort Donaldson, as the more appropriate points of attack, but yielded to my views if General Halleck's assent could be obtained." He also added, "I made the proposition to move on Fort Henry first to General Grant." Perhaps trusting Foote more than Grant, Halleck consequently decided on the Tennessee River as the main line of attack. It offered a straighter and longer shot at the fort for the gunboats, access to the critical railroad just a few miles upriver, and the chance to move into the cotton states at some point in the future. Halleck therefore wrote Washington on January 30: "General Grant and Commodore Foote will be ordered to immediately advance, and to reduce and hold Fort Henry, on the Tennessee River, and also to cut the railroad between Dover and Paris." To Grant he wrote on January 30, "make your preparations to take and hold Fort Henry. I will send you written instructions by mail."[59]

Historian Kenneth P. Williams has called it "one of the most important dispatches of the war."[60]

4

"WE SOON UNDERSTOOD THAT THE GREAT WESTERN MOVE WAS TO BEGIN"

The Confederate Western Department was in crisis. Having been shaken from his lethargy concerning the twin rivers, Albert Sidney Johnston sent his chief engineer, Jeremy F. Gilmer, on an inspection trip to the forts, the engineer moving from Nashville on January 30 and arriving at Fort Henry the next day. There, he met Lloyd Tilghman and began to inspect all three forts on the two rivers. What he saw was not encouraging. One observant Mississippian at Fort Henry described the tense sentiment: "this is the place to test men, some stand the test and some do not. A mans character presents itself in its true colors, every trait is developed, you can almost read their very thoughts it seems."[1]

Gilmer himself was much of the problem. Having been tasked by Johnston to oversee the river forts' security, he had no heart for the work. He was homesick and uninterested, wishing he was with his wife in Georgia. The work on the forts thus lagged with Gilmer's lethargy. Even so, Gilmer first inspected Fort Henry, where he talked with engineer Joseph Dixon. Gilmer described the fort as "a strong field work of fine bastion front," while a Cairo newspaper later elaborated on its earthen defenses, describing walls "four to six feet high, and eight to ten feet wide on top, supported on the inner side by hickory twigs woven together, so as to prevent the crumbling away of the earth, with a ditch about twelve feet wide around it on the outside." The fort mounted a total of seventeen guns, the most powerful of which were a rifled 24-pounder, a 10-inch columbiad, and two 42-pounders. Smaller weaponry consisted of eight 32-pounders. Eleven of the guns fronted the river, poking through "embrasures formed by raising the parapet between the guns with sand bags carefully laid." Gilmer also inspected the outlying "extensive lines of infantry cover," which had been built "with a view to hold commanding ground that would be dangerous to the fort if possessed by the enemy." He concluded that the outer defenses were "capable of offering a strong resistance against a land attack coming from the eastward," but the river battery was a different story. One of the main guns, the 10-inch columbiad, had a defect that threatened to dismount the gun on every discharge, but a system of "ingenious mechanic clamps" was put in place, which all hoped would work. At the same time, Gilmer reported difficulty in finding "competent artillerists to man them." Lethargy among the troops did not help either, one Mississippian writing on February 2, "we have become so accustomed to the gunboats being two or three miles down the river, that we hardly go out to look at it. Everything has got quiet again."[2]

A more troubling area loomed on the west bank, where Gilmer described "a number of hills within cannon range that commanded the river batteries on the right bank." Gilmer had recognized the problem last November and ordered Dixon to build fortifications that would become known as Fort Heiman. Dixon had been promised "a large force of slaves, with troops to protect them, from Alabama," a result of those citizens' worry over the defense of the Tennessee River. However, these slaves were not forthcoming, and work at Heiman crawled slowly along. Gilmer complained, "the Negroes were not sent until after the 1st of January." Tilghman did the best he could in the mean time, and tried his best to fashion the works into formidable shape, working "night and day." By early February, Gilmer reported the work progressing well, and needing "only a few days' additional labor to put them in a state of defense." A Mississippian working on Fort Heiman was more optimistic, writing that if given another week or so to develop the earthworks, "we can whip 50,000 men under any circumstances."[3]

Meanwhile, Tilghman waited for the attack he thought was coming any day. Where and when grated on everyone's nerves. Gilmer wrote that "the attack of the enemy . . . was threatened at an early day either at Fort Henry or Fort Donelson, or possibly on both at the same time." One Mississippian had had enough and quit worrying. He wrote home, "I don't care if the Yanks do come now, as we have all the breast works finished and every thing ready to receive them according to the rules laid down in etiquette." Tilghman, on the other hand, had his doubts, especially about Fort Henry's ability to defend against the Union ironclads. He even confided to Gilmer "his fears that it

might cause disaster if the place were vigorously attacked by the enemy gunboats." A solemn Gilmer added, "this he thought his greatest danger." And
it was. As early as February 4, Captain Jesse Taylor wrote that as "far as the
eye could see, the course of the river could be traced by the dense volumes of
smoke issuing from the flotilla—indicating that the long-threatened attempt
to break our lines was to be made in earnest."[4]

The contest for Fort Henry was on.

A flurry of activity developed as word went out that Grant's command was
preparing a major thrust into the Confederacy along the Tennessee River.
When Halleck's permission message arrived, Grant's staff celebrated, knocking over chairs and throwing hats in the air. Grant jokingly told them to quiet
down so Leonidas Polk in Columbus would not hear their celebration. Planning began immediately. Grant ordered quartermaster Lewis B. Parsons to
find every available steamboat for the army's use. High-level officers tried
their best to keep as quiet as they could, but the unmistakable movement
of large bodies of troops and the corresponding movement of gunboats and
transports were too obvious. "We soon understood that the great western
move was to begin," D. C. Smith wrote home, "but not down the Mississippi
as we anticipated, up the Tennessee River by boat for Fort Henry." Others
guessed that was the place too, one soldier later recalling, "for we had hardly
heard of Donaldson." Given the deplorable weather, however, it was a question as to whether anyone could move at all. One staff officer noted how Fort
Holt near Cairo had been submerged and the roads were pitiful: "I fear Mr.
'Mud' says '*You cannot go*.'"[5]

The nervousness was even greater about what the expedition might find.
Foote's vessels continued exploring around the almost unknown river forts in
an attempt to get more information. In fact, while he and the navy had a pretty
good idea of Fort Henry, Smith at Paducah did not even know what to call
Fort Donelson: "Fort Gavock, or Fort MacGavock, or something else, usually
called Fort Gavock." There were also reported batteries on the opposite side
of the river just downstream from Fort Donelson. Phelps made another run up
to Fort Henry with the *Conestoga* and *Lexington* on January 30 and 31, and
returned with information that "torpedoes," or mines, had been emplaced and
that it would be necessary to remove them first. He also "enquired about the
roads along the ridge between the two rivers," learning that at that point they

were dry but the terrain was very hilly; any rain would cause major problems on the inland byways just as it did for the January operations.[6]

Despite the hurdles, Grant's army began mobilizing for action. In somewhat of a surprising development, the hedging Halleck stayed in St. Louis and allowed his subordinate Grant to command the expedition. That was strange because Halleck had never treated Grant as competent and even cast about to find a different commander for the expedition. He had approached Ethan Allen Hitchcock, who ultimately refused. He and McClellan even discussed Smith: "would not C. F. Smith be a good man to command that part of the expedition?" Yet it all came about so quickly and timing was such that Halleck determined to allow Grant to command. The decision would change Grant's life and career, and that of Halleck as well.[7]

Halleck certainly had his hands full with command of his department, but he continually ferried new regiments southward from the relative comfort of St. Louis. He also had to stay aware of Buell, who was shocked when he heard news of Halleck's offensive. Buell informed McClellan that Halleck had just recently told him, "I can do nothing; name a day for a demonstration." Now, Halleck informed him, "I have ordered an advance on Fort Henry and Dover. It will be made immediately." Buell wrote, "I protest against such prompt proceedings, as though I had nothing to do but command 'Commence firing' when he starts off." Buell nevertheless sent Charles Cruft's brigade to within supporting distance of Grant but added, "I fear very much that even that will be compelled to fall back for supplies, such is the condition of the roads over which they have to be hauled." Buell also offered his encouragement: "I think it is quite plain that the center of the enemy's line—that part which you are now moving against—is the decisive point of his whole front, as it is also the most vulnerable." In fact, he said that it was "well worth the risk of losing more than one or two gunboats." Then he got down to assets: "do you consider active co-operation essential to your success, because in that case it would be necessary for each to know what the other has to do?" Halleck surprisingly replied, "co-operation at present not essential." That shocked Buell even more. Halleck would soon get cold feet, however, and begin to ask for additional help, especially after it was rumored that Johnston had sent reinforcements from Bowling Green to the twin rivers. "Can't you make a diversion in our favor by threatening Bowling Green," Halleck asked Buell on February 5. Buell haughtily replied, "my position does not admit of diversion. My moves must be real ones." He told Halleck that it would be some time before he could help, but agreed to send one brigade by river to reinforce Grant. Halleck also began to ask Washington for more men: "can't you send me some infantry regiments from Ohio? Answer." McClellan could only tell Buell to "communicate with Halleck and assist him if possible," but Buell did little except engage Albert Sidney Johnston in correspondence about prisoner exchanges.[8]

In fact, Halleck gave Grant almost supreme control of the campaign. Perhaps he was giving Grant enough leeway that if the operation was not successful, Grant would bear the blame. He told his subordinate to "organize your command into brigades and divisions, or columns, precisely as you deem best for the public service." Perhaps because in Halleck's eyes McClernand was an even bigger novice than Grant, he added that this should be done "without the slightest regard to political influences or to the orders and instructions you may have heretofore received. In this manner the good of the service, and not the wishes of politico-military officers, is to be consulted." To make sure his point was taken, Halleck added, "such applications and arrangements are sheer nonsense and will not be regarded." Still, in giving Grant the leadership choices, Halleck could not help but suggest various approaches. A couple of days later he reminded Grant that few wagons and other transportation would be needed because of the waterborne movement: "don't cumber up the expedition with too large a train." He also suggested sending a cavalry force from Smithland down the neck of land between the two rivers while the main movement was on the Tennessee River itself.[9]

More specifically, Halleck told Grant to take his troops up the Tennessee in steamers, taking care to cover both sides of the river and to establish if necessary "a battery on the opposite side of the river." The obvious plan was to land the troops so they could cut off any retreat to Fort Donelson while the navy attacked on the riverfront. To aid in the effort, Halleck also sent Grant one of his engineers, Lieutenant Colonel James B. McPherson. After Grant carried the fort, moreover, Halleck desired him to cut the Confederate railroad to the south, perhaps even with cavalry sent out from the landed force. He cautioned haste, but he also desired that the "bridges should be rendered impassable, but not destroyed." Obviously, Halleck was thinking of using the rail line to his advantage in future operations. He also ordered a telegraph line strung to Fort Henry once it was taken.[10]

Grant took the opportunity and organized his command for the effort "without as yet having created a suspicion even that a movement is to be made," he wrote on January 31. He planned to have two divisions, one under Smith from the Paducah area and the other under McClernand brought over from the Cairo area. Grant informed Smith that he wanted a brigade from Paducah and the entire command at Smithland to take part except the 52nd Illinois and smaller units, which would guard the mouth of the Cumberland River. He then changed his mind and told Smith to take the entire command. As expected, keeping such a move secret was nearly impossible. When word went out in the partially flooded camps for the cooks to begin preparing rations in the middle of the night, one Iowan noted, "some of the boys happened to hear it and such a whooping and hollering they made. There was no more sleep that night." Grant cautioned Smith: "if possible, the troops and community should be kept from knowing anything of the design," but then added somewhat sheepishly that "I am well aware, however, that this caution is entirely unnecessary to you." Grant was not only learning to make bold offensives, but also learning how to command a man he deeply respected and one who had been his senior for many years.[11]

Grant had no such worries about telling McClernand what to do. He told him to bring two brigades under Richard J. Oglesby and W. H. L. Wallace to Paducah to prepare for the effort, leaving two other brigades, "and the sick of the entire command," under E. A. Paine and James D. Morgan at Cairo. General Paine was to command at Cairo during Grant's and McClernand's absence. McClernand moved his division toward Paducah on February 3 and went on ahead to prepare for their arrival. However, unfortunate incidents pervaded some of the ranks. While at anchor at Cairo, W. H. L. Wallace's brother Matthew fell from his transport and drowned, he being unable to stay afloat until help arrived due to his heavy clothing and weapons. Wallace's staff officer, I. P. Rumsey, wrote of the mourning brigade commander: "we saw the tenderness of his heart . . . but still the man and the soldier went bravely on with present duty." Then, one of the steamboats containing a portion of the 11th Illinois "about three O'Clock [AM] . . . struck a snag giving barely time to reach the shore before she went to the bottom," wrote Frank Whipple. "No lives were lost I believe although it created a great panic some jumped overboard and swam ashore." Whipple and a few of his comrades made it to an island and remained there for nearly three days, "with scarcely anything to eat," Whipple added. They were then picked up and taken on board a passing steamboat.[12]

It was not exactly the start Grant was hoping for.

Major action drew closer with new intelligence coming in, official permission to begin, and the naval forces ready. On the naval front, Foote first had to make the hard decisions of what he could take into battle and what he could not. Several of the ironclads were still not totally serviceable, including the *Benton*, and few if any had a full complement of sailors. Grant turned to equipping the vessels with infantry, although few were forthcoming because of opposition from "their captains and colonels." Some cavalrymen became available, mainly due to officers forcing unwanted members into the gunboat service. One 4th Illinois Cavalry trooper wrote, "the Captain took it upon himself to detail such men that he would rather spare and told them they had to go, and they went. They were mostly Norwegians and Germans that could hardly speak English. . . . Charley Walsh who was under arrest for drunkenness and attempting to kill Lieutenant Hapeman, was given the privilege to take service on a gun-boat or stand a court martial. He chose the former." Foote vehemently complained about the lack of men to Washington: "it is peculiarly unfortunate that we have not been able to obtain men for the flotilla, as they only are wanting to enable me to have at this moment eleven fully-manned, instead of seven partially manned, gunboats, ready for efficient operations at any point." He finally decided that he could take crews off of four city-class boats and the *Benton* and place them on three of the others along with the *Essex* and make four semicoherent crews. That, along with the three timberclads, would make a flotilla of seven gunboats, four of them ironclads. Foote obviously chose the already serviceable *St. Louis* and *Essex*, both of which had already seen some action. Along with those two, Foote also carried along the *Carondelet* and *Cincinnati*. Although he made the trip from Cairo to Paducah aboard the *Tyler*, he raised his flag on the *Cincinnati* at Paducah, thus making it the flotilla's flagship.[13]

Foote left the *Louisville*, *Cairo*, *Mound City*, and *Pittsburg* at Cairo, "very much to the annoyance of all our officers and those men left behind," one *Mound City* sailor wrote. Since the *Louisville* was "nearer completion than either of the others," he ordered her to be put into fighting trim and held ready for infantry soldiers to man in case of an attack on Cairo. He also took what he could from the other four gunboats to add to the crew. The *Louisville* accordingly took on almost the entire skeleton crews on board the others and proceeded to Fort Holt for defense of that important place. Also left behind was the fleet of mortar boats that no one except Lincoln seemed to want. Halleck wrote Washington openly that the mortar boats "cannot be used in

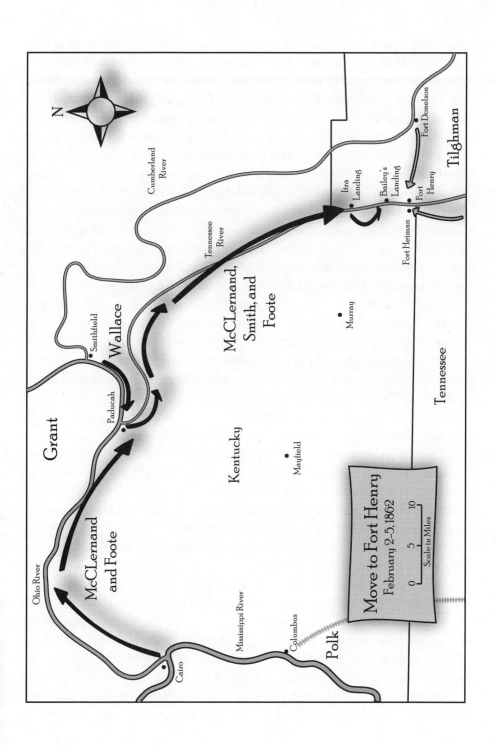

N

Ohio River

Grant

McClernand
and Foote

Cairo

Mississippi River

Columbus

Polk

Smithfield

Paducah

Wallace

Cumberland
River

Tennessee
River

McClernand,
Smith, and
Foote

Kentucky

Mayfield

Murray

Itra
Landing

Bailey's
Landing

Fort
Henry

Fort Heiman

Fort Donelson

Tilghman

Tennessee

Move to Fort Henry
February 2–5, 1862

0   5   10
Scale in Miles

the Tennessee or Cumberland, and I doubt if they will ever be of much use in the Mississippi. Neither navy nor army officers have much faith in them."[14]

Foote began his operations by moving the flotilla from Cairo to Paducah on February 2, and on February 3 sent the *Essex*, *Carondelet*, and *St. Louis* on up the Tennessee to Pine Bluff, nearly seventy miles up the river. At Paducah, he issued numerous orders preparing for the upcoming fight, including the governing principles in the engagement itself. He indicated which code of signals would be used, for instance, and reminded his captains how they should respond to those visual pennants. He also meddled in minutiae, reminding his officers to make sure to remove the hatch covers over the guns before the fight or "otherwise great injury will result from the concussion of the guns in firing." Once firing, the fiercely economical Foote dictated that the gunners not waste ammunition on bracketing targets: "there is no excuse for a second wild fire, as the first will indicate the inaccuracy of the aim of the gun." He added, "let it be reiterated that random firing is not only a mere waste of ammunition, but, what is far worse, it encourages the enemy when he sees shot and shell falling harmlessly about and beyond him."[15]

Amid all the minutiae, Foote also laid out the basic plan of attack. The four ironclads, termed the "main division," would proceed up the Tennessee River first in parallel formation, each only showing its bow to the enemy: "they will be much less exposed to the enemy's range than if not in a parallel line." Foote dictated that all vessels in this front line would follow "the motions of the flagship" and would not open fire until the *Cincinnati* did. The second line of boats under Phelps would be the three timberclads placed in the rear, "if practicable, inshore on the right of the main division" in order to protect them and provide long-range fire while the ironclads advanced and bore down on Fort Henry. Foote also cautioned that the entire flotilla should take special care to not fire on their own infantry, who would be in the area, "lest our own troops are mistaken for the enemy."[16]

Foote was certain of success, writing Welles that he had "every confidence, under God, that we shall be able to silence the guns at Fort Henry and its surroundings." He was so confident, in fact, that he issued orders about what should be done after the victory was won: "Lieutenant–Commanding Phelps will, as soon as the fort shall have surrendered and upon signal from the flagship, proceed with the *Conestoga*, *Tyler*, and *Lexington* up the river to where the railroad bridge crosses, and, if the army shall not already have got possession, he will destroy so much of the track as will entirely prevent its use by the rebels." Obviously, the larger aspects of the campaign were most important, that of eliminating the fortification and breaking the vital Confederate railroad that ran in the rear of Johnston's line. Such success would divide the Confederate defenses and, it was hoped, force both wings to withdraw. Foote wrote Welles as much, saying on February 3 that he planned to move southward "for the purpose of conjointly attacking and occupying Fort Henry and the railroad bridge connecting Bowling Green with Columbus." Thereafter, Foote told Phelps to "proceed as far up the river as the stage of water will admit and capture the enemy's gunboats and other vessels which might prove available to the enemy."[17]

With orders so issued, the navy gathered on February 4 and waited within just a few miles of Fort Henry, just beyond Panther Island. It was ironic that they were now waiting on the army.

The trip from Cairo, one 11th Indiana Federal noted in his diary, saw "everything in a bustle." Many suffered from being outside on the decks of the boats whipped with wind. Some were more fortunate; one member of the 20th Illinois remembered that brigade commander Richard Oglesby declared that only officers could be in the cabin of his boat, but the Illinoisan remembered, "we pressed on 'Dick' and his guards from all quarters, and some vowed they would throw him overboard if he did not submit." He did, the soldier noting, "this was our first victory." Others made the best of other circumstances. George Carrington of the 11th Illinois described his abode on the *A D January*, noting that most of the regiment slept warmly in the hold. "The boys have candles stuck along the sides of the hull to light up the dark place," he wrote, but his own company fared even better by being housed in the cabin. All were warm nonetheless, in direct opposition to the cold outside and the chunks of floating ice in the Ohio River.[18]

At Paducah, the boats took on other equipment, including cannon, which were lashed down at the bow. All the commotion obviously indicated something was happening. Those troops already at Paducah, just emerging from their garrison mindset, knew something was happening when McClernand's regiments arrived: "there is quite a strong force congregating here," one Iowan wrote, "but I am entirely in the dark as to our future movements."[19]

The details emerged quickly enough. Grant at Paducah sent his first wave of troops southward on February 3. McClernand himself arrived midafternoon that day, amid "a hurricane of cheers long continued," Lew Wallace remembered, "and the rivalry of bands playing, flags streaming." McClernand went immediately to see Grant. There, Grant told him to continue his movement just as soon as his transports arrived, making a column of steamers preceded by two gunboats. McClernand's transports soon reached Paducah and continued on toward Fort Henry since they were already loaded, there being insufficient shipping in the area to transport the entire army up the Tennessee River at the same time. Grant had twenty-three regiments in all, plus cavalry and artillery, and all could not move at once. Grant thus had to improvise, and there was no need to disembark McClernand's troops just to load Smith's. He simply informed Halleck that "not having sufficient transportation for all the troops, the larger portion of the steamers have to return to Paducah for the remainder of the command, under General Smith."[20]

The trip southward for McClernand's men was mostly uneventful, stopping only for fuel, although occasional shots from the bank greeted the Federals. Taylor's Illinois battery deployed two guns on the bow of their steamboat for protection if needed. Several of the 30th Illinois's soldiers had their legs hanging over the top deck when they were suddenly fired on from the bank. "All went over backwards, with their feet in the air, and scampered for the other side of the boat," one observer noted. The shift "caused a big creel or dip of the boat in that direction, and was more dangerous than the fire of the bushwackers." The captain and mate cursed the soldiers and made them return to their original side.[21]

Despite the occasional potshots, McClernand's transports and the gunboats *Cincinnati* and *Conestoga* proceeded up the river on the afternoon of February 3 and arrived in the vicinity of Fort Henry around 4:30 AM on February 4, ready for a fight despite multiple reports of drowning men and even mules during the river-borne operations. Tension developed as they neared the Confederate stronghold. One staff officer, I. P. Rumsey, described Fort Henry as "a rebel camp which we calculate to whip out or get beautifully whipped in a few days." To be perfectly careful in Confederate territory, McClernand stopped when within eight miles of the fort, at Itra Landing on the east bank, where he ordered his troops off the boats. He wanted to get his men on solid ground and a perimeter formed for defense, but the need of the transports to return to Paducah and ferry Smith's three brigades also factored into the decision. He sent Oglesby and Wallace inland, ordering them to quickly form a "line of battle before the encampment and fronting the enemy." He also reminded his troops, "the utmost discipline and most perfect subordination are required and expected," and told the officers to quickly "punish all depredators upon the persons or property of peaceful citizens."[22]

Just as McClernand was sending staff officers to lay out camp lines and to reconnoiter the enemy, Grant rode up and ordered the division reembarked. Grant had taken the opportunity to board the *Essex* and plod against the current up to within a mile of the fort. The *Essex*, accompanied by two other ironclads, fired several shells into the fort. "This drew the enemy's fire," Grant noted, "all of which fell far short, except from one rifled gun, which threw a ball through the cabin of the *Essex* and several near it." Grant had seen all he needed, especially with another boat drifting too near the bank and slamming into a tree limb. "We immediately turned back," he later wrote. A sailor on board the *Essex* simply noted, "found out range of their guns."[23]

Despite such scares, Grant had learned that McClernand was positioned much too far northward; there was no need for the division to have to march eight miles to Fort Henry when they could be disembarked much closer to the fort. He went back to Itra Landing and found McClernand, ordering him to reboard the transports and resume the advance southward. McClernand immediately moved up the river to Bailey's Landing, only three or four miles from Fort Henry. McClernand began landing his troops a second time around 10:00 AM and was finished by midafternoon. All was done under the watchful eye of Confederate scouts, however, Will Wallace writing his wife that "we can see the rebel flag for the first time floating over their forces." McClernand quickly ordered his men in line to move inland, which, he reported, "served both as a reconnaissance in force and as an occupation of the neighboring hills."[24]

In fact, there were Confederates closer than at Fort Henry. The 8th Illinois with Oglesby himself was on the first transport behind the gunboat, and one Illinoisan remembered seeing "two mounted officers [who] came galloping down from the fort [Heiman], halted on the low bank a half a mile above, and surveyed us with their field glasses." The leading gunboat fired its small deck howitzer at them "and they decamped with a suddenness that might have been taken for fright if they had been common soldiers." More ominously, a local civilian approached McClernand on the east bank and told him the Confederates had "mounted pickets . . . posted hard by." McClernand could also see Confederate scouts on the west bank of the river watching intently, until small-arms fire and especially "a shell from one of the gunboats . . .

dispersed them and another party of the enemy in sight farther up the river."
He also sent cavalry to the front to find the enemy, which they did, driving
them back a short distance.[25]

Meanwhile, the crisis feeling that accompanied the sight of the Confederates ebbed as the infantry and artillery trudged up the ridge overlooking the
river and went into bivouac, "prepared to meet any emergency," McClernand
noted. The trek was hard on the men who had been up since before daylight,
had landed, reboarded, and landed again, only to have to scale the heights,
dragging their artillery and wagons up "by hand and the aid of prolonged
ropes." Safety was the chief concern, however, and to be doubly safe, Mc-
Clernand ordered an artillery battery and two regiments southward to Panther
Creek, where these units took a defensive position. McClernand named his
armed bivouac site "Camp Halleck," and there one brigade of Smith's division under Colonel John Cook also joined him later.[26]

Despite the nearness to the enemy, the bands tuned up with the "Star Spangled Banner," "Hail Columbia," and "Yankee Doodle." They even played "St.
Patrick's Day in the Morning," which the listening Confederates of the Irish
10th Tennessee at Fort Henry declared was for them. Will Wallace wrote his
wife, "my quarters to-night are in a negro cabin, with my brigade bivouacked
on the hills about me." Having had no campfires since leaving Cairo on February 2, the troops were given permission to light fires and cook meals. The
hungry soldiers ate heartily, having already used up their two days' rations.
McClernand was even able to wax poetic about the scene: "our camp, marked
distinctly by its numerous fires, ranging along the crest and down the slopes
of lofty hills and in the valley toward the river, together with the many transports and gunboats which had come up and formed the foreground, exhibited
a most grand and imposing spectacle." McClernand also wrote that the scene,
"having been witnessed by the enemy's scouts on the opposite side of the
river, multiplied in their imaginations our numbers."[27]

Not all could revel in the idealistic scene. The men of the 41st Illinois were
none too happy about being connected to the regiment of Birge's Sharpshooters. One Illinois officer described them as "an unpleasant outfit" who "got on
board ahead of us and took all the cots so half the Officers had to sleep on the
floor." Once on land, the Illinoisans had picked out a fine campsite only to
find the sharpshooters had "worked General McClernand for an order moving
us into a muddy cornfield so they could get our campsite." The sharpshooters also maneuvered so that the Illinoisans "even had to haul the rest of their

stuff up the river bank for them." The Illinoisans were finally able to get the campsite order rescinded by McClernand, one officer writing, "I hope that we have had our last to do with them." The 41st Illinois was not the only antagonist of the sharpshooters, however; Henry Halleck wrote Grant: "look out for Birge's sharpshooters, they have been committing numerous robberies. I have the Col. locked up in the Military prison."[28]

Also busy were the transports preparing to ferry Smith's division southward. After disgorging McClernand's troops the second time, they, along with the *Lexington* and *Tyler*, returned downriver with Grant himself to Paducah to take on Smith's command. Smith's troops were soon levied out of their comfortable camps at Paudcah, James C. Parrott of the 7th Iowa writing his wife as late as February 3, "you are not the only one who is enjoying the good things of life." Parrott reported that the transports were late: "how soon they will come I know not, but we are looking for them hourly." They soon came, and the division boarded, leaving only the 40th and 55th Illinois and an assortment of cavalry and artillery under David Stuart to garrison Paducah, the 52nd Illinois and attending cavalry and artillery being similarly left at Smithland. The troops loaded onto their steamers with an immense amount of baggage, one 7th Iowa soldier tasked with helping load the gear writing, "after a great deal of swearing by some officer about our quantity of luggage, and after throwing lot of it overboard we got off at 9 A.M." The troops then made a much less hectic trip all the way to the forward-landing area, not stopping at Itra as McClernand had been forced to do. Smith's troops arrived on February 5, landing some of the regiments on the west side of the river but others remaining aboard the transports for the night, particularly Lew Wallace's brigade containing the 8th Missouri, 28th Illinois, and 11th and 23rd Indiana, which was, one Missourian noted, "about the last of the fleet." Other troops also arrived, including the 4th Illinois Cavalry, which had been plodding down the neck of land between the two rivers from Patterson's Ferry. McClernand noted that these troops had endured "a laborious march," but they along with infantry sent out from Paducah had accomplished Halleck's desire to place troops between the rivers. The 13th Missouri had also marched from Paducah inland and returned after three nights "in the open air, and having thoroughly explored the country between the Tennessee and Cumberland rivers."[29]

With all on the move, the Federal high command was confident. As Smith's brigades floated from the landing at Paducah and moved southward,

Grant was finally free of concern that Halleck might cancel the expedition. When he left Paducah for the last time he told Rawlins: "now we seem to be safe, beyond recall." He also wrote to his wife, "I do not want to boast but I have a confidant feeling of success." Farther south, McClernand was also feeling good, taking the daylight hours of February 5 to solidify his position and reconnoiter more ground toward Fort Henry. He certainly could not go ahead and attack the fort, because he needed Smith's men to help on the other side of the river. McClernand accordingly probed forward cautiously, sending Oglesby and a "strong detachment of infantry and cavalry" forward to "reconnoiter the country between Camp Halleck and Fort Henry, the approaches and accessibility of the latter, and its position and various external relations." Oglesby did so, leading the troops himself in conjunction with Grant's chief of staff, J. D. Webster, as well as McClernand's chief of staff and division engineer.[30]

This scouting effort on February 5 afforded McClernand great knowledge of the ground, and it also not surprisingly found the enemy. A few staff officers ahead of the main body located Confederate pickets, who fled but soon returned with larger numbers. Oglesby sent his infantry forward but the Confederates suddenly appeared "in the rear both of our infantry and cavalry." Oglesby's mounted cavalry drove them away in a ten-minute fight that produced one dead and several wounded. This skirmish had a marked effect on the green members of the 8th Illinois, one of whom remembered, "we ran bump against their cavalry pickets who fired into us quite unexpectedly. . . . For a wonder they didn't happen to hit any of us, but we got a large burly butternut with a shot in the forehead." Oglesby's skirmishing provided some intelligence, but not being able to get any closer to the fort, Grant still did not have a concrete idea of the Confederate numbers he faced. He amazingly wrote his wife late on February 5, "what the strength of Fort Henry is I do not know accurately."[31]

But he would soon find out. Now that Smith's command was up and positioned as well, Grant could attack the next day, February 6. Orders went out, Grant telling McPherson to guide McClernand's two brigades and one of Smith's east of the river at 11:00 AM on February 6 to "take a position on the roads from Fort Henry to Fort Donelson and Dover." These troops held the "special duty" to prevent escape from or reinforcement of Fort Henry, but also "to be held in readiness to charge and take Fort Henry by storm promptly on the receipt of orders." At the same time, Smith was to leave his position on the west bank and "take and occupy the heights commanding Fort Henry." If not all troops were needed west of the river, Smith was to send the extra units back to McClernand on the east side to aid in the assault. Grant was careful to remind Smith that "the west bank of the Tennessee River not having been reconnoitered, the commanding officer intrusted with taking possession of the enemy's works there will proceed with great caution, and obtain such information as can be gathered and such guides as can be found in the time intervening."[32]

There were, however, additional problems that erupted before those plans could be put into operation. The touchy McClernand objected to the words that he should move "under the guidance" of McPherson, and sent Grant a note explaining that the lieutenant colonel would not have any command authority over him. Grant had obviously meant that McPherson would act as a guide, so he no doubt rolled his eyes at the prickly politician's note.[33]

More ominously, a terrible storm system moved through the area during the night, causing the exposed Federals many more problems than the well-housed Confederates. "It commenced thunder and lightening as if the Heavens and earth was coming together," wrote one Illinoisan, "and the rain & Hail came down in torrents which made us like so many drowned rats in the morning." Another wrote of how he and his mates had made nice beds of cornstalks but were soon swamped in their tents; "I could hear the water rushing around our tent," he wrote, "and kept feeling down through the stalks with my fingers to see if the water was getting under us." The already insufficient roads quickly muddied, obviously affecting the next day's efforts. George Carrington of the 11th Illinois described the misery well: "as night came on a cold pelting rain set in and kept it up nearly all night." With abundant wood and rails nearby for a fire, he laid a "platform of rails in the mud to sleep on," alternating the soaked sides toward the fire. He could only remember his dry accommodations on the steamboat: "coming right out of warm cozy quarters, this night of weather horrors gave many a stout young man his death warrant." He added significantly, "but we kept our ammunition dry."[34]

The storm's effect was also felt on the river. Foote had been aboard his vessels running his crews "through the evolutions," cautioning them again not to waste ammunition that cost the government eight dollars per shot. Yet there was greater trouble brewing. The navy endured the rising river on the foggy February 5. Henry Walke on the *Carondelet* described how "the swift current brought down an immense quantity of heavy drift-wood, lumber, fences, and large trees, and it required all the steam power of the *Carondelet*, with both anchors down, and the most strenuous exertions of the officers and crew, working day and night, to prevent the boat from being dragged downstream." Perhaps more ominous were the Confederate torpedoes being washed along. These were white objects that Walke said "through the fog looked like polar bears." The crews were extremely glad of the high water then, rather facing the torpedoes unloosed than in their original positions. That they appeared at daylight was even better because the boats could more easily dodge them. The crews, Walke noted, took the good fortune "as a presage of victory." Nevertheless, a scare resulted as a now arrived Grant, Foote, and others examined a torpedo on board the *Cincinnati*. It let out a long hiss, which sent Foote up the ladder and Grant right behind him. The danger over, Foote turned and asked Grant, "why this haste?," to which Grant jokingly responded, "that the navy may not get ahead of us."[35]

Despite the nervous joking, there was a certain foreboding as all knew what was coming the next day. Those left behind at Paducah prepared, one Federal wrote, "quarters of 1000 wounded." On the expedition itself, F. C. Cromwell of the 12th Iowa wrote that, once their transports left Paducah and moved up the Tennessee River, "then for the first time we realized that we were really going to war." As good officers do, some calmed their own and others' frayed nerves; Lieutenant David B. Henderson of the famed 12th Iowa's "University Recruits," a company made up of students from Upper Iowa University in Fayette, went the extra mile: he described gathering his "Glee Club and telling the boys 'Let's sing and be merry for no one knows how many of us will be alive tomorrow night.'"[36]

The approach of Federal army and naval forces was certainly no surprise, but it still sent shock waves throughout the Confederate high command. Tasked with defending the twin-rivers sector, Lloyd Tilghman had a huge job and few resources. Word of the sudden appearance of Federals moving southward on the Tennessee River no doubt caused his heart to skip a beat. One Mississippian wrote that "we have been fortifying until we have rendered the place—I think—impregnable; and I defy the power of Lincolndom to take us." Tilghman knew better.[37]

The Confederate commander normally kept his headquarters at Fort Donelson, but in the days before the Federal advance he had ridden over to the Tennessee River to examine those defenses along with Johnston's chief engineer, Gilmer, who had arrived on his inspection tour. Both were busy inspecting the Henry and Heiman fortifications on the morning of February 3 and felt a reasonable safety, so much so that Tilghman deemed it acceptable to go back with Gilmer to inspect the Fort Donelson defenses as well. He made a quick check to make sure the scouts out to the north on both sides of the Tennessee River verified that nothing untoward was happening and thus departed for Dover. He left Colonel Adolphus Heiman of the 10th Tennessee in command on the Tennessee River.[38]

As fate would have it, Grant's armada appeared while Tilghman was away, leaving Heiman to decide what to do. His scouts first reported the approach of three gunboats by firing signal rockets from their position, which were answered from the fort itself. Heiman immediately called his cannoneers to their posts, and the guns were loaded and prepared for action as the steamboats at the fort fled upriver. Although the gunboats did not attack, Heiman received word that Federal transports were also arriving. He later noted, "smoke from several gunboats now became visible over the island." He quickly sent various portions of his command to cover the numerous roads and landings on both sides of the river, especially the roads in and out of the fort and running toward Dover. Heiman also had his men set out torpedoes in one of the channels of the river at the island, and likewise sent a courier to Tilghman informing him of the developments.[39]

To make matters worse, Heiman also had additional problems. At that very time the river was rising, causing major concern for the fort. The colonel noted that engineers had "a large force at work on the epaulements and [were] trying to keep the water out of the fort." He later described the problems: "the lower magazine had already 2 feet of water in it, and the ammunition had been removed to a temporary magazine above ground, which had but very little protection, but we had been at work day and night for the last week to cover it with sand bags and to protect it by a traverse."[40]

At that exact moment, the Union gunboats began to steam toward the fort. They had previously shelled the Bailey's Ferry area on the morning of February 4, in preparation for McClernand's landing, but now they steamed toward the fort itself around noon. Heiman ordered all troops except the cannoneers out of the fort and told the gunners to hold their fire until the enemy vessels came within range. When the gunboats opened up, easily reaching the fort, Heiman responded with fire from a rifle and columbiad. A defect on the 10-inch gun's carriage caused it to be shut down after one of the clamps broke and caused worry that another discharge would likely "upset the gun." The rifle performed admirably, however, Heiman reporting that it "was fired in quick succession and with good effect," one of the shells hitting the *Essex*. Eventually, the gunboats came nearer, and Heiman opened up with the smaller 32-pounders as well.[41]

Fortunately for Heiman, the gunboats backed off, leaving the fort alone after a duel of thirty minutes. Heiman was shaken anyway, and he continually sent couriers to Tilghman "requesting his orders, or, what I desired more, his presence." Heiman alerted Tilghman not to come without a guard, however, and not to use the Dover road as it was probably blocked. As night approached, Heiman was happy that he had held out, but was extremely nervous about the next day. He strengthened his pickets on the various roads and in the outward rifle pits and cast eager glances toward Fort Donelson for Tilghman.[42]

Tilghman had been busy inspecting the Cumberland River fortifications on the morning of February 4, working with Gilmer to solidify "the field work which had been constructed for the immediate defense landward." Gilmer also ordered better protection for the river batteries "by raising the parapet with sand bags between the guns to give greater protection to the gunners." As they inspected Fort Donelson, however, the calm was shattered. The sound of heavy firing came from the direction of Fort Henry around noon. Then, a courier from Heiman arrived in the afternoon with news that Federal gunboats had been up to the fort earlier in the day and that Union troops were landing at Bailey's Ferry on the east side of the river a mere three miles downstream. Tilghman quickly made arrangements to solidify the defense at Fort Donelson and headed back west to Fort Henry. He took Gilmer along once more, Gilmer writing that Tilghman "expressed with some anxiety a wish that I would accompany him." Tilghman also ordered three companies of Tennessee cavalry under Lieutenant Colonel George Gantt to escort him. After the long ride, he finally arrived at Fort Henry just before midnight on February 4 and quickly realized the dire situation he was in. "I soon became satisfied," Tilghman wrote, "that the enemy were really in strong force at Bailey's Ferry, with every indication of re-enforcements arriving constantly."[43]

Tilghman took control of the situation as best he could. He found out from Heiman that he had sent scouts out on both sides of the river to "within a very short distance of the enemy's lines." Heiman had also sent a section of artillery and a contingent of the 4th Mississippi out toward the outer works of the complex to cover the Dover road. Knowing there would probably be fighting, perhaps even the next day (he did not know Grant was waiting for Smith's division to arrive), Tilghman organized the Fort Henry garrison into two brigades and a heavy artillery contingent during the night. Only two of his regiments had much experience at all, Heiman's 10th Tennessee and Joseph Drake's 4th Mississippi, so he used each one as the core of a brigade. Heiman was given the 10th and 48th Tennessee, the 27th Alabama, and Culbertson's battery as well as Gantt's battalion from Fort Donelson, making a small brigade of around fifteen hundred men. Colonel Drake of the 4th Mississippi was given the other brigade, containing his own regiment, the 15th Arkansas, and the 51st Tennessee, along with Crain's battery and an assortment of individual cavalry commands. This brigade numbered a little over twelve hundred men, although there is question whether all of the 51st Tennessee ever actually joined the brigade. The heavy artillery contingent contained some seventy-five men under Captain Jesse Taylor, who would soon be superseded by Tennessee artillerist Lieutenant Colonel Milton A. Haynes. The Tennessean left Donelson during the night of February 5, "attended only by my servant," he noted, and arrived at the fort during the darkness and opted to wait until the next morning to cross the rising backwaters to the fort. Even with Haynes, however, Tilghman had less than three thousand men at his disposal to defend perhaps the most important piece of territory then in the Confederacy.[44]

As the long night passed, Tilghman realized his situation was even worse than he thought; all the infantry units that were needed to defend the fort were not even on site. The 27th Alabama and 15th Arkansas were currently across the river at Fort Heiman, and Tilghman judged that they could do little there and could certainly be used to greater effect on the east side of the river. Heiman had thought the same thing but "did not like to take the responsibility" because Tilghman had earlier "stated positively that these heights must be held." Now on site, Tilghman agreed with Heiman and calculated that "the extremely bad roads leading to that point would prevent the movement of heavy guns by the enemy, by which I might be annoyed." Tilghman effectively gambled that he could lose Fort Heiman in saving Fort Henry because the Federals could not emplace guns big enough to do any damage at Fort Henry. He accordingly ordered the two regiments across before dawn, leaving only small cavalry commands on the west side of the river.[45]

One member of the 27th Alabama, who wrote that the green regiment had already learned that midnight long rolls were mostly calculated for training, was in for a surprise. This time there came "soft tones from the officers, who opened the flaps of tents and commanded, 'boys, get up quick, leave everything except guns and cartridge boxes. Fall in without a bit of noise.'" The troops shuttled across the river, where they spent the rest of the night "propped up against trees, roosting on logs, and making all sorts of shifts to keep out of the mud." As morning dawned, staff officers hurried back and forth but yielded little information except that the woods to the north were "'swarming' with Yankees." One Alabaman wrote, "we felt that the time was at hand when we would have an opportunity of testing our double barreled guns and bowie-knives," but there was a problem: "an inspection showed that we had left our knives on the other side of the river; not half a dozen could be found in the regiment, some were left sticking in trees where we had practiced throwing them, others on stumps where the last beef had been carved, but the larger part probably scattered about camps and in tents." The Alabamians would have to rely solely on their shotguns.[46]

Tilghman also concentrated other troops at Fort Henry. He ordered Colonel John W. Head to have two regiments and a section of artillery ready and if no enemy forces arrived at Fort Donelson by the next morning to move to a position at Peytona Furnace, roughly halfway between the two forts. There, he would be able to move in either direction and was to "act as circumstances might dictate." Similarly, while two of the newer regiments were camped near the railroad bridge far to the south at Danville, Tilghman ordered them to the fort as well. The 48th and some of the 51st Tennessee made the trip northward and arrived during the night. Tilghman consequently had his full complement of regiments on site by daylight on February 5.[47]

Yet those units were inexperienced, and only the single core regiment of each brigade had any skill whatsoever. Heiman, in fact, noted that all the rest were "new troops, who had just entered the service. They were not drilled, were badly equipped, and very indifferently armed with shot-guns and Tennessee rifles." Perhaps even worse, the entire cavalry force consisted of a motley group of independent companies. "None of the cavalry had either sabers or pistols, and were only partly armed with double-barreled shot-guns," Heiman reported. On top of that, much of the command was sick. Heiman estimated that out of the nearly three thousand troops present, only twenty-six hundred were effective.[48]

Because of his plight of inexperienced troops and too few of them, Tilghman spent part of his preparation time begging for additional reinforcements. He realized that his best chance to get more troops was from Polk at Columbus, and he corresponded frequently with the bishop. Tilghman let it be known that he needed infantry instead of the paltry cavalry Polk had sent, and he wanted only good regiments. "I don't want raw troops who are just organized," he wrote Polk on February 5, "they are in my way." He also put another thought in Polk's mind: "I will await your orders, or, what I would more desire, your presence." Whether Tilghman was really desirous of instruction or someone in a higher position to take the blame for what was evidently turning into a cauldron for defeat is not known, but Tilghman was on his own. Polk would not leave Columbus, and he would be of little help to the twin-river forts over the next few days.[49]

Tilghman felt a little better because of the small number of reinforcements he had received, but dawn on February 5 also brought additional fears. He later reported that with daylight, "the enemy were plainly to be seen at Bailey's Ferry, 3 miles below." He also received frequent reports from his scouts, indicating "that the enemy was there in force even at that time, and the arrival every hour of additional boats showed conclusively that I should be engaged with a heavy force by land." He added that the numerous gunboats "indicated plainly that a joint attack was contemplated by land and water." Tilghman was especially concerned about his floating vessels, and made plans to have the five steamboats at Fort Henry moved southward in the event of an attack. These included the steamers *Dunbar*, *Lynn Boyd*, and *Appleton Belle*, which he had used to bring the Tennesseans from Danville to Fort Henry and also to ferry troops back and forth across the river. More worrisome was the possible fate of the steamers *Samuel Orr* and *Patton*, used as stationary hospital boats at Fort Henry.[50]

With daylight, Tilghman quickly went about deploying his meager force as best as he could. Because he had left his staff at Donelson, the general had to appoint new staff officers to assist him at Fort Henry. As the sun rose higher and higher on what he thought would be the day of decision, Tilghman quickly decided that he did not have enough troops to defend the outer works of the fort. He decided to concentrate his defense around the entrenched camps of the 4th Mississippi and 10th Tennessee closer to the river. "The wretched military position of Fort Henry and the small force at my disposal," Tilghman remembered, "did not permit me to avail myself of the advantages to be derived from the system of outwork built with the hope of being re-enforced in time." Moreover, troops in this position would be distant from the fort and the bombardment by gunboats if and when that occurred. Tilghman thus gave detailed orders and the "entire command was paraded and placed in the rifle pits." He and Gilmer soon had Heiman's and Drake's brigades placed and Tilghman concluded that "everything was arranged to make a formidable resistance against anything like fair odds." Gilmer remembered that the only personnel allowed inside the fort itself were "the men who had received some instructions in the use of heavy guns and such additional force as could be useful in bringing up full supplies of ammunition."[51]

Once the long night ended, the daylight hours passed quickly and Tilghman began to wonder if the Federals were indeed coming that day. Even as he taught the cannoneers "with as much care as possible his duty in anticipation of the threatened attack," by 10:00 AM Tilghman decided to send out a patrol of his own to find out what the enemy was doing, guessing they were trying to cut Fort Henry off from Fort Donelson. He already knew that the Federals had been operating on the Fort Donelson road the day before, and so sent out cavalry to investigate. The cavalry soon met Oglesby's reconnaissance less than a mile and a half out, whereupon they fell back. Tilghman decided to personally lead a larger effort and took with him half of the 10th Tennessee and half of the 4th Mississippi. He crossed the outer works, which were still defended by two companies of the 4th Mississippi—to which he added two more. By that time the Confederate cavalry had already gotten behind Oglesby's command, and the Federals had fallen back to Camp Halleck. Tilghman returned to Fort Henry around 5:00 PM, leaving the Mississippi companies still in the outer works.[52]

As the sun slowly sank to the west on this shorter winter date, Tilghman realized he had staved off defeat one more day. Gilmer remarked of "it being quite apparent that the enemy would not attack until next day." Consequently, Tilghman allowed his troops to be "relieved to seek food and rest." News nevertheless continued to filter in that more and more Federals were arriving; scouts continued to report additional landings on the east side of the river, but reports during the night also indicated a heavy landing on the west bank as well. The enemy in fact was already approaching within a mile or two of the Confederate lines on that west bank. Tilghman ordered Captain David Hubbard to try to surprise the enemy, but during the night "the rain having commenced to fall in torrents," Tilghman wrote, little else could be accomplished and both sides settled in for a miserable night that would no doubt bring action the next day.[53]

Indeed, one Illinoisan amid the mud and cries of "no bottom" was especially observant about the next day's activities. He noted, "there may be poetry in war, but there is no poetry in Camp Halleck." Even more observant, he simply remarked in his diary, "everything this evening looks warlike." Lew Wallace certainly thought so, writing his wife on February 5: "for the first time in my life I write you 'on the eve of battle.'" He was not surprisingly poetic in what he wrote, telling her,

> I linger over the good bye. I never said it under such circumstances. I have no apprehension as to the result personally—no superstitious dread. I only pray that I may do my duty tomorrow, so that if I come back to you, as I hope, and believe I will, it will be in honor and with another claim to the love which you have always nobly and faithfully given me in return for that which I again send you.[54]

5

"ALTERNATELY MUD AND WATER ALL THE WAY UP"

"[Day] dawned darkly after a thunderstorm," Lew Wallace wrote of that dreary daylight on February 6, 1862, yet it would be a red-letter day in American history. Numerous factors involved in the offensive effort would culminate this day, not the least of which was pressure from the highest levels of government to do something. George McClellan had sent a pronouncement out west just a few days before urging that action be taken in accordance with Lincoln's proclamation that all forces move by late February: "it is very desirable to move all along the line by the 22d February, if possible," McClellan wrote. None of the other commanders were willing to do so, but then Grant and Foote were not just any other commanders.[1]

The navy was obviously needed in this operation, and that caused more than a few officers and politicians to become nervous about the outcome. Lincoln himself took a special interest in the mortar boats, although few others saw any path toward victory riding these unpowered gun platforms. Henry A. Wise, in fact, wrote Foote, "Uncle Abe, as you already know, has gone into that business with a will." Foote was not impressed. The most veteran commander on the twin rivers, Ledyard Phelps, likewise wrote that these boats might help but "are probably not absolutely required at either fort." More to the point, Foote had no crews to man them, having to scrape enough sailors just to outfit four of his gunboats. Yet even those gunboats were questionable, all wondering how they would perform in this, their maiden battle. Another problem was the river current, which would force the gunboats to breast the tide during battle, slowing them in the approach and effectively making them easier targets. The good news, however, was that if one of the gunboats was disabled it would harmlessly float downstream out of danger rather than bob toward the enemy, raising the risk of sinking or capture. Halleck summed it all up when he wrote Buell on February 2: "it remains to be determined whether the gunboats are worth half the money spent on them."[2]

The lay of the land at Fort Henry made the gunboats vitally necessary, however. The fort sat on the bank of the Tennessee River, and the intricacies of the layout and its approach also caused concern among Federal commanders. They had not been able to get anywhere near the fort earlier as Confederate cannon fire had disrupted all attempts to gain information or intelligence. The Federal commanders would be learning as they went.[3]

The Federals did know that there were two main river approaches to the fort. The mile-long, wooded Panther Island sat in the middle of the river just north of Fort Henry, dividing it into a main channel on the east and a "narrow and crooked" chute on the west. While the main channel was susceptible to fire for a greater length, the chute provided some protection for the gunboats. Even that was slight, however, as the fort itself sat on a slight extension into the river where it made a slim jog to the west, allowing the guns of the fort to fire directly down the long expanse of the relatively straight river. It was also well known that the Confederates had placed "torpedoes," or mines, in the chute, but to what extent they would prove a barrier was questionable in the high water. If the torpedoes were tethered to keep a certain depth, then they would now be well below the surface of the water and below all the vessel's hulls. A few had broken from their lines and were bobbing on the river, and the *Essex* rounded them up. One sailor on board described these weapons as "ether bottle[s] filled with about 40 lbs. of powder."[4]

Just getting to the fort was thus problematic, but its defenses were also formidable. The major impediments included a layered defense consisting of three areas. The major bastion was the fort itself, a five-sided earthen stronghold somewhat in the form of a pentagon. The sides were not equal, creating a more pointed angle to the northeast. Although made of earth, the walls contained many nooks and crannies, making interlocking fields of fire possible and a landward defense available from many angles. The one road into the fort on the southwestern face contained a drawbridge, which could be raised and lowered, allowing or denying access to the fort. Sandbags placed around the guns created embrasures and protected the gunners.[5]

Inside the fort were seventeen pieces of heavy ordnance, which Tilghman hoped would stop any Union advance up the river. The most common pieces

in the fort were the ten 32-pounders mounted on barbettes. Three faced the
river to the northwest, with one in each angle of the five-sided fort and four
more on the northern facade fronting up the river (not counting the one in
the angle on the northwestern face). Three more faced the landward side on
the eastern face. While these ten 32-pounders packed a punch, they were far
too light to be able to stop the gunboats, having relatively small projectiles
and limited range. For better firepower, the engineers had also placed the
two 42-pounders and the 10-inch columbiad on the northern face looking up
the river. Scattered about were various smaller cannon as well, including a
24-pound rifle on the northwestern side fronting the river, a 24-pound siege
gun on the southeastern face fronting the landside, and two small 12-pound
siege guns, one of which also guarded the land approaches. Also inside the
fort were two magazines, one in the northeastern and one in the northwestern
angles, although river water was beginning to cause trouble for those. Likewise, a flagpole stood in the middle of the fort, as did three sets of garrison
quarters, two sets being made of logs and one of frame huts.[6]

The size of the fort was large, causing Phelps to remark that it was "of
considerable extent and peculiar construction, and apparently ill calculated
for defense against bombshells." He went on to explain: "the area in proportion to the guns mounted is extraordinary, and gives a better field than usual."
Yet given the lack of experience with ironclads and the perceived strength of
Fort Henry, no one really knew what to expect once an attack began.[7]

A second tier of defenses lay outside the fort proper and defended both
the approaches to the fort and the log huts housing the infantry garrisons.
A stockade ran from the fort to the river on the northern side, apparently
intended to keep landing Federal infantrymen from approaching. A swampy
slough ran along the eastern side; in high water this slough filled with water
and made entrance and exit difficult, the road leading away from the fort
crossing it south of the bastion itself. Along the road on the dry ground adjacent to the fort sat one group of infantry winter quarters in the form of huts,
with earthen defenses dug in a shielding manner facing the slough to the east
as well as blocking the road into the fort. Just across the slough was another
isolated area of higher dry ground surrounded by another swampy area. The
defending infantry had taken this bit of high ground and created a second area
of winter huts, likewise defended by a series of earthen works facing east.
As a result, the second layer of defenses were rifle pits covering the infantry

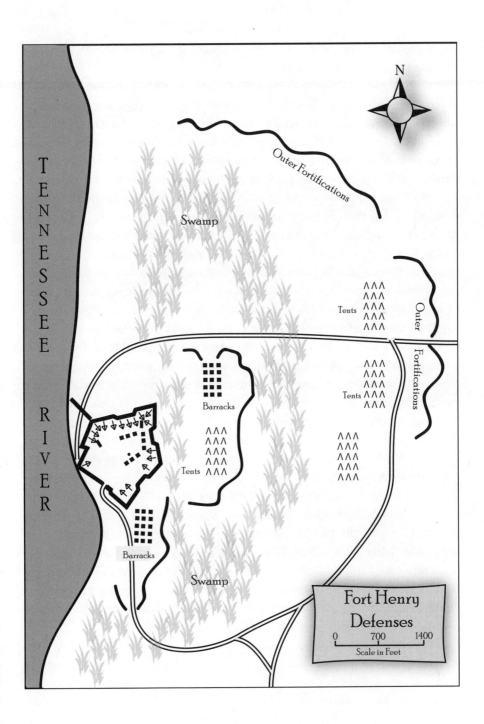

N

TENNESSEE RIVER

Outer Fortifications

Swamp

Tents ∧∧∧
∧∧∧
∧∧∧
∧∧∧
∧∧∧

Outer Fortifications

Barracks

Tents ∧∧∧
∧∧∧
∧∧∧
∧∧∧
∧∧∧

∧∧∧
∧∧∧
∧∧∧
∧∧∧
∧∧∧

Tents ∧∧∧
∧∧∧
∧∧∧
∧∧∧
∧∧∧

Barracks

Swamp

Fort Henry
Defenses

0   700   1400
Scale in Feet

encampment, where most of the soldiers had log huts but where other just-arriving troops also set up their tents.[8]

The last layer of defense consisted of outlying rifle pits on the higher and dryer ground east of the fort, out of the way of the rising waters or swampy sloughs. There, engineers placed earthen ramparts to defend the roads that entered the complex as well as the northern approaches to the fort. As additional troops entered the defense garrison, they found that the room in the fortified middle tier was gone, so they pitched their tents just inside these outer works.[9]

Out of this defensive complex ran two roads. One was the northernmost road, which ran straight to Dover and Fort Donelson. To the south ran an additional thoroughfare, which connected with more roads that also provided access to Dover. As a result, the defenders had choices concerning movement, but this meant the Federals also had choices on how to make their approach. Additional roads crisscrossed the area to the north, providing a maze of neighborhood paths on which the Federals could advance. On the other hand, all these roads meant that the Federals needed to close all of them if they hoped to seal off Fort Henry and capture its garrison and defenders.[10]

As the sun rose, all those questions had to be set aside, although not all the pessimists in the Federal high command could put their concerns behind them. McClellan in Washington was second-guessing the choice of commanding officer even on February 6, writing Buell that if he were reinforcing Halleck, "ought you not to go in person?" McClellan also added to Halleck, "I will push Hitchcock's case." Buell in Louisville also wrote on February 6 that "this whole move, right in its strategical bearing, but commenced by General Halleck without appreciation—preparative or concert—has now become of vast magnitude . . . and it is hazardous." Similarly in St. Louis, a worried Henry Halleck could not help but get more nervous since the expedition was out of his hands. He continued the pattern of hedging bets so that the claim of victory could still be his but blame for failure could be laid elsewhere. On February 6 itself, ironically after the fate of Fort Henry had already been decided, Halleck wrote McClellan, "I was not ready to move, but deemed best to anticipate the arrival of Beauregard's forces."[11]

He need not have worried.

If Beauregard's looming arrival made any difference in the Union high command's decisions, his presence made no impression whatsoever on the actual events. Beauregard had indeed arrived at Bowling Green, on February 4, for a meeting with Johnston. Significantly, he came alone, not with his fifteen regiments. Accordingly, one of the chief reasons why Halleck approved the attack was not even reality. For all the hype about Beauregard, Lloyd Tilghman awoke on February 6 with no help whatsoever coming from the Creole, or from anyone else for that matter.[12]

Tilghman spent the night of February 5 along with engineer Gilmer up the river on the steamboat *Dunbar*. He received word early the next morning from cavalryman Padgett of more Federal transports and an even larger buildup on the western side. Evidence also indicated further buildup on the eastern bank as well. Even worse, the navy showed every indication that it was preparing for action, causing Tilghman and Gilmer to quickly move to Fort Henry and cease all other traffic across the river. Colonel Heiman described the effect adequately: "early on the morning of the 6th heavy volumes of black smoke rose over the island, manifesting that the fleet was not to remain idle long."[13]

At some point in the morning, probably while getting reports of huge numbers of enemy infantry on both banks and seeing the billowing smoke of the gunboats on the river, Tilghman finally realized the unenvious position he was in. He later wrote of Fort Henry's inexcusable position, saying, "the entire fort, together with the intrenched camp spoken of, is enfiladed from three or four points on the opposite shore, while three points on the eastern bank completely command them both, all at easy cannon range." He added, "the history of military engineering records no parallel to this case," complaining that "an enemy had but to use their most common sense in obtaining the advantages of high water, as was the case, to have complete and entire control of the position." Although admitting "the work itself was well built," Tilghman concluded that he was fighting a losing battle.[14]

Even worse, Tilghman's garrison was not that dependable either. In addition to troubles among the regiments at Fort Donelson, causing some colonels to resign in protest to Tilghman, the Fort Henry commands were also in chaos. Captain Jesse Taylor described the 10th Tennessee as the "best-equipped regiment of his command," armed as it was with flintlock "Tower of London" muskets that had been used in the War of 1812. The only other seemingly dependable regiment was the 4th Mississippi, but it also had problems. The Mississippians were not used to such inclement weather, which was hard on their bodies; one member of the 4th Mississippi wrote in January, "the weather here is colder . . . than I ever saw in Miss." The leadership in the regiment was likewise questionable, John T. Megee describing their older Colonel Joseph Drake as "the old crazy fool." He went on to describe how "he is now being cussed throughout the whole regt as being the greatest old grannie in the world." Worse, Drake had placed several men under arrest for minor infractions but when he released them, they denied release and requested a court martial, intending "that the world should know what kind of an old fool he is." One of the arrested soldiers reveled in the fact that "we have the old fool scared half to death he thinks he has seen his last as Col of the 4th Regt."[15]

Tilghman became so despondent at his situation and his lack of resources that he later claimed that he determined upon his strategy even that morning. He claimed that the evidence he saw that morning "gave me no room to change my previously conceived opinions as to what, under such circumstances, should be my course." Tilghman concluded that with Grant and Foote bearing down on him and the water rising around him, Fort Henry was untenable and doomed. He consequently planned to withdraw the garrison to Fort Donelson for the major showdown, leaving only a token force to delay the enemy. Tilghman believed that "Fort Donelson might possibly be held, if properly reinforced, even though Fort Henry should fall; but the reverse of this proposition was not true." Making his argument more sound, Tilghman related that Fort Henry's fall would be disastrous and open up the Tennessee River into the cotton states, but Donelson's fall would jeopardize the army at Bowling Green as Nashville would probably fall before Johnston could retreat south of the Cumberland River. Tilghman stated as much: "the fate of our right wing at Bowling Green depended upon a concentration of my entire division on Fort Donelson and the holding of that place as long as possible."[16]

Tilghman was not the only Confederate officer despondent about Fort Henry's ability to withstand the Union assault everyone could see was on its way. Lieutenant Colonel Milton A. Haynes, chief of the Tennessee Corps of Artillery, had made his way during the night to Fort Henry but could not get in due to the submerged road. He opted to await daylight, but when he finally entered the fort he was aghast. Haynes immediately recognized that two major problems confronted Tilghman: the small number of defenders and the rising water in the fort, which was, he described, "on the point of being submerged." Either was bad enough, but both made evacuation immediately necessary. Moreover, he was not opposed to vocally espousing his opinion: "upon hastily examining the works with Captain Hayden, of the Engineers, I gave it as my opinion that Fort Henry was untenable, and ought to be forthwith abandoned." Hayden gave the same opinion to Tilghman when he arrived from his steamboat that morning, but Tilghman had little time for the engineer and quickly set about defending the fort, "without consultation with me," Haynes noted.[17]

Amid all the problems, Tilghman asked Taylor if he could hold out for one hour. During that time, he would get the garrison out of range of the gunboats and on the road toward Donelson. He realized the infantry could do little inside the outer works as they would still be well within range of the gunboats, so he put all except Taylor's artillery garrison in a position to get away quickly while Taylor's gunners readied for their sacrificial task. Consequently, orders flew out of headquarters; one started the process of "throw[ing] up earth to keep the water out of the magazine." Another mandate started work on a "temporary bridge across the backwater." Other officers were active as well, Haynes inspecting the guns in what he viewed as the doomed fort. All the while, reports from Tilghman's forward scouts alerted him that "General Grant [was] approaching rapidly and within half a mile of the advance work." He also received reports that Smith west of the river was quickly moving on Fort Heiman as well. Tilghman gambled that Grant (McClernand on the east bank) would not venture too near the outworks and engage his troops because of fear of being hit by gunboat fire. Such was actually the case as Grant had ordered McClernand to stop at the junction of the roads just north of Panther Creek. Tilghman quickly sent his infantry out the lower Ridge Road, or what he called the Stewart Road, but he decided himself to stay and defend Fort Henry until the last moment and then make his own getaway to Dover.[18]

Unknown, and perhaps unexpected to the worried Halleck, Grant and Foote had everything under control on the Tennessee River. While Foote was offering prayers on his gunboats, the crews were getting used to working together. One *Essex* sailor noted the melding of that gunboat's crew by force when necessary, writing, the "new part of crew has turned out to be good men when they found out that it was as Capt. Porter told the officer in charge of receiving ship that he had 40 that could hold them down." It was the same with Grant, who had issued orders the night before for his two divisions to begin their marches at 11:00 AM the next morning to operate in concert with the navy against Fort Henry. That was an exceptionally late hour to begin, but Grant later explained to Halleck that "my forces were not up at 11 o'clock at night when my order was written, therefore I did not deem practicable to set an earlier hour than 11 o'clock to-day to commence the investment." Indeed, some units of John McArthur's brigade of Smith's division did not leave Paducah until 10:00 PM on the night of February 5, arriving at the debarkation point around 9:00 AM on February 6. Grant of course did not want to delay the attack another day, adding, "owing to dispatches received . . . I thought it imperatively necessary that the fort should be carried to-day." Thus, the plan was relatively simple; as the gunboats engaged the fort, McClernand on the east bank was to cut off the Confederate retreat if there was one, or else storm the earthworks in a direct charge and take the site. On the opposite bank, Smith was to assault and capture Fort Heiman and then turn its guns on Fort Henry from across the river. If all worked according to plan, Grant and Foote would have sole possession of Fort Henry by nightfall.[19]

Preparations began at an early hour even though the march was set for late morning. Charles Kroff of the 11th Indiana noted, "at dawn of day we were all in a bustle preparing 2 d's rations." Kroff and the Indianans had managed to remain on their transport all night in the storm, but others were not so fortunate. Those who had already landed also rose from what slumber they had managed to get during the night. One Illinoisan reported that the men "twisted and wrung out their blankets getting most of the water out of both overcoats and clothing." More ominously, the flagstaff on the 11th Indiana's boat broke as it landed and fell on the nearby 8th Missouri's boat, killing one of the Missourians.[20]

While there would certainly be these kinds of hiccups to the plan, the Federal soldiers began their trek on time into what one Illinoisan described as "this outlandish portion of seceshdom." An Iowan was more impressed, writing in his diary, "tread on the Tennessee shore this morning for the first time." There was some anxiety as each waited their turn to move out; one Federal remembered waiting in line in the 20th Illinois: "Colonel [Carroll] Marsh lit a fresh cigar as he sat laxily on his horse, and asked if we could charge bayonets." The plan nevertheless began well on the western side of the river where Smith was to take Fort Heiman. Smith had two brigades under his command, led by Lew Wallace and John McArthur, with his third across the river operating with McClernand's division. Obviously, Fort Henry was expected to be much tougher than Fort Heiman, so the elevated troops levels were on that side. Still, there were daunting tasks on the west side as well, not the least of which was overcoming the effects of the massive storm during the

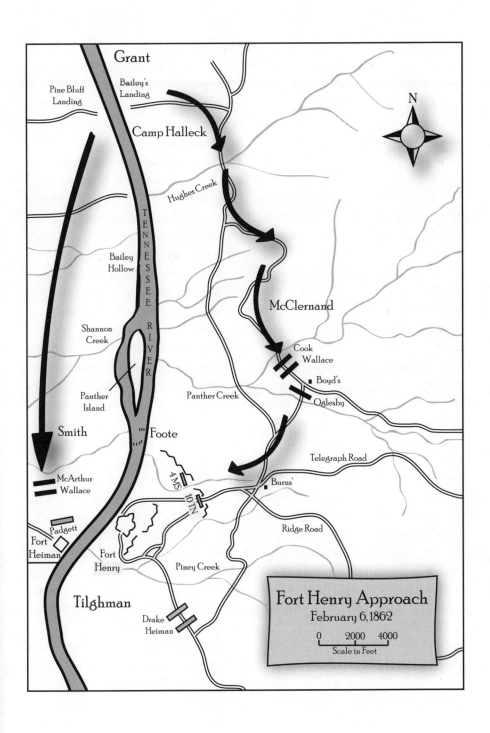

Grant

Pine Bluff
Landing

Bailey's
Landing

Camp Halleck

Hughes Creek

Bailey
Hollow

Shannon
Creek

T
E
N
N
E
S
S
E
E

R
I
V
E
R

Panther
Island

Smith

McArthur
Wallace

Padgett

Fort
Heiman

Fort
Henry

Foote

4 MS

10 TN

Panther Creek

McClernand

Cook
Wallace

Boyd's

Oglesby

Telegraph Road

Burns'

Ridge Road

Piney Creek

Tilghman

Drake
Heiman

N

Fort Henry Approach
February 6, 1862

0   2000   4000
Scale in Feet

night of February 5. As Smith gave Wallace his orders the evening before, he "looked then at the sky and at the coffee-colored water creeping over the low places of the land, and added, grimly, 'It will be a hard road—but we'll get there.'"[21]

It was a hard road. In fact, one of the major problems on the western side of the Tennessee River was a lack of a major road system. Some studies have conjured that Smith's division marched cross-country through the woods, but Wallace and Smith both left evidence that they took a single road. Wallace insisted that "there was but one" and Smith described it as "shockingly bad." Others confirmed as much, one 7th Iowa soldier writing, "the roads are in terrible condition, and men, as they march along cry 'no bottom.'" More troubling, the route so near to the river was inundated with major creeks the division had to cross, and being that near the rising river meant that they were large and formidable, if not impassable, by backwater from the river itself. Illinoisan Ira Merchant described how "we started in mud half knee deep. . . . We had to make a wide detour to avoid back water from the river and then did not altogether." At one point the column came to a slough that they could not move around so "the men plunged in cheering and yelling like tigers. They had to hold their cartridge boxes up to keep the powder dry The water was 200 yards in width And when we had passed out a halt was commanded to let the men empty their boots. After this we had alternately mud and water all the way up." On top of this misery, no one knew what kind of resistance the division would encounter as it advanced closer to Fort Heiman.[22]

Smith led the column forward anyway, preceded by cavalry and often accompanied by a gunboat, which threw a shell into the area in front of the marching troops, "whereat the toilers in the column cheered," Wallace wrote. As time passed, the brigades slogged ahead through the tough and muddy terrain, crossing Bailey Hollow and then Shannon Creek. "We had to wade through water several times waist deep," reported Charles Cochran of the 28th Illinois of Wallace's brigade, "but when we heard them fighting we did not mind being wet for we were anxious for a fight and thought we was going to get it." A Missourian in Wallace's brigade noted, "we marched about 21/2 miles wading streams 2 & 3 ft. deep of water & mud." The march was so agonizingly slow, however, that the navy passed the marching soldiers on the way down to Fort Henry. They began the action quickly, and the sound of the naval guns caused immense excitement among the infantry; Colonel Isaac

Pugh of the 41st Illinois wrote his wife, "you ought to have seen the boys and heard them send up the shouts of exultation at the prospect of the fight[.] they thought the fight was coming of in a few minutes." Wallace reported that although he could not see the river, he could tell the navy was ahead of the infantry by sound, and also by the residual effect of the fighting that occurred once the navy engaged the fort. "Presently they were between us and the fort," Wallace continued, "that we knew because the shells of the latter, over-elevated, sailed roaring and screaming into the tree tops, darkening the air with fragments of limbs." Ironically, the same thing was occurring to the Confederate forces arrayed south of Fort Henry. At any rate, Wallace noted that the "effect was to energize everybody in the march."[23]

Time and terrain took their toll as the increasingly weary Federals slogged on west of the river. Another major watershed flowed into the river between Panther Island and the fort, necessitating a harrowing passage. "We came to a swollen stream," remembered one 28th Illinois soldier, "and stripping to the waist and packing our accouterments on the muzzles of our guns, waded through." Wallace noted the tenacity of the command, writing, "did a sheet of backwater spread itself across a road, or a bog intrude, or a tree, no matter— there was a cheer, and a rush, and the obstacle lay behind." Wallace particularly marveled at his attached Battery A, Chicago Light Artillery "halloo[ing] their guns through a swamp without the loss of an inch of interval." At other places, the command successfully constructed bridges to get across.[24]

There were also messages from Grant that affected the column west of the river. Watching aboard the steamboat *Brown*, Grant took stock of all incoming information and disseminated it to the proper places. During the day, he wrote to Smith: "a prisoner just in states that all the Troops from, the West bank of the river have been withdrawn to Fort Henry. It would be well to send Cavalry forward as rapidly as possible to ascertain, if such is the fact, and to save as much march as possible of such of your troops as may be required to cross to the east bank of the river. The tents of an Alabama Regt. are said to be left standing, but . . . are not occupied by troops."[25]

Even as the gunboat battle was taking place, the infantry column continually made its way southward and eventually emerged in front of Fort Heiman. There, they saw the formidable-looking Confederate fort on the highest hill in sight, the trees all around it cut down to provide a good field of fire for the defenders. Smith rode with Wallace at the head of the column, with only cavalry to the front. He often stopped to listen to the quieting cannonading on the river, making him wonder if it was because the navy had reduced the fort or the fort had driven away the navy. Wallace recommended sending a regiment toward Fort Heiman, but Smith refused and led the entire column southward once more. After another stop, a mounted Federal approached Smith and reported the fort evacuated. Smith retorted, "how do you know?" The cavalryman blurted, "I have been in." A chagrined Smith quickly turned to Wallace and quipped, "it is just as well. Move on and take possession." One disappointed Missourian noted there "was not but one volley of muskets fired," and another Federal noted that they only "caught a glimpse of the rebel cavalry retreating as we came in sight."[26]

Isaac Pugh of the 41st Illinois was relieved, afraid as he was that the Federals would run into harsh resistance. The earthworks he found told him it could have been so: "they had no guns in the fort but had long Trenches made to protect the men from our attack but we approached on them from the side that was not protected and they run and left everything they had." Lew Wallace corroborated this account, writing his wife, "by purest accident I directed the head of my column by a road which turned the enemy's works." Wallace related that the enemy had fled only a few minutes prior to his arrival, and Pugh noted the disappointment among the troops; many of the men were chagrined "a little that the Boats done all the work at the fort & the enemy run away on this side." He added, "I expect they will have their curiosity satisfied before this thing is settled."[27]

The Confederates had indeed left, Heiman having taken his command east of the river a day or so earlier and the few remaining cavalry evacuating upon the arrival of Smith's forward troopers. Therefore, the heaviest firing west of the river came, as one 7th Iowa soldier described it, when "a flock of sheep came near our bivouac, and our men commenced firing as though it was a battle." He added, "our Col. stops it, though but few sheep were killed." Most of the Federals were indeed disappointed at the lack of Confederate targets. Charles Cochran wrote his mother, "we was put in line of battle three times but had no fight as they give up and run before we got up here." A Missourian in Wallace's brigade similarly wrote, "instead of resistance, which we expected, what was our surprise to find it entirely deserted." He went on to say, "their cowardly legs got the better of them," and

we did not get a shot at them. They were cooking dinner when the cannonading began and ran away leaving it on the fire. It was very nicely cooked when we got here and if it was Secesh, tasted well. We found many of their letters, some only half finished when the panic seized them. If they had whipped the Yankees the way they told their friends they intended doing, we would have fared badly, but they didn't.[28]

The surprised Federals west of the river, now totally safe, began to fan out and explore, finding all sorts of interesting items. Many soldiers swarmed over the earthworks, some declaring that the installation was very stout and that it would have been defensible had the Confederates chosen to defend it. Illinoisan James Drish described Fort Heiman as "a splendid fortification on the opposite side of the river on a high bluff a natural fortification that I would consider almost impregnable." Others found more of what the Confederates had left; Ira Merchant wrote home that "appearances indicated that they left in haste dinners were on the fire cooking, clothing hung out to dry, beeves half dressed in the slaughter house and everything lying around in admirable disorder." He was especially enthralled by the many long Bowie knives "with which the doughty heroes of C.S.A. had calculated to disembowel the d-d abolitionists." Another noted they found enough lances at Fort Heiman "to arm a regiment."[29]

The generals soon arrived and explored the camp and fort as well, Wallace riding over the parapet and noting that although the fort was not completed, "a stiff fight could have been made from it." Wallace immediately went to a large tent in the center that he soon learned had been Heiman's headquarters. He found a number of papers on a table, indicating a hasty withdrawal, and a prepared but uneaten feast confirmed as much. Wallace found a "block of fresh pork 'done to a turn,'" as well as freshly baked cornbread, hot coffee, and other delicacies just waiting to be eaten. He notified Smith, who "upon invitation, came and shared my good-fortune." The two generals had a lively time, but remembered their benefactor in all the celebration: "the absence of Colonel Heiman was never more sincerely regretted," Wallace wrote, but "out of a small contribution foraged from General Smith's right pistol-holster we drank the excellent German's health."[30]

Matters did not go quite so swimmingly for the Union infantry on the other side of the river. Obviously, Fort Henry was the major prize, Heiman being only a secondary and supporting bastion, and that brought the attention of the

navy mainly to the eastern side of the river. Thus, competition soon developed between the branches as to who would actually capture the fort. Given
the major storm systems that had moved through the area the night before, the
abundance of water only aided one of those branches. While the additional
water may have added to the already growing torrent that was the Tennessee
River, that in and of itself did not hinder the navy's efforts, and may in fact
have aided it. Conversely, the major rains played havoc with McClernand's
infantry as they slogged their way southward toward Fort Henry. One Confederate colonel declared, "I suppose the heavy rains which fell last night will
embarrass their operations," but not if McClernand could help it . . . and if
there was glory to be had.[31]

McClernand put his troops in motion in accordance with Grant's instruction at 11:00 AM. Realizing that the way would be dreary and slow, it is hard
to imagine McClernand not pushing for an earlier departure, with glory, after
all, on the line. Later, McClernand used every excuse he could to explain the
slow march, in this case legitimate, especially with the artillery of Schwartz's,
Dresser's, McAllister's, and Taylor's batteries in the column. "Notwithstanding the heavy rains throughout the previous night, which found my division
without tents and ill prepared for exposure," McClernand reported, he sent
his men forward "so as to enable the different brigades and arms of my command to afford mutual support in case of an attack." Halts were frequent,
however, especially when the large guns from the ironclads opened up. One
Illinoisan noted, "we halted for a short time and then moved on as fast as possible and that was not very fast for we had to guard the artillery and the roads
being very muddy and the artillery very heavy and teams rather light." An
Illinoisan remarked observantly, "it is evident the way the artillery is miring
down, that it will only be a naval battle." Indeed, one Illinoisan in Taylor's
battery reported "mud to the hubs of our carriages."[32]

The advance nevertheless moved determinably southward on the main
road to the fort. Once having moved eastward to the main road from Itra
Landing, McClernand's division took a right turn and moved southward across
the cultivated bottom of Hughes Creek, causing one Iowan to complain, "we
took a circuitous route so that we had to go ten or twelve miles to get five,
and such a road—mud, mud, mud, mud creek almost up to our knees." David
Reed of the 12th Iowa described how they were "hurried rapidly forward
over ground very soft and difficult, much of the way entirely without road,
crossing rapid streams on single foot logs, in this way stringing the regiment

out and then double quicking to close up until all were perfectly exhausted." On the high ground on the south side of Hughes Creek, from which the Federals could at times "see the fort through the smoke," the road split into two parallel routes, one running closer to the river across several small branches and the other running through dense woods on higher ground to the east. The two crossed Panther Creek separately and rejoined south of that watershed, but another road branched off the eastern route just north of Panther Creek at farmer Boyd's place and ran toward Dover. Grant had ordered McClernand to halt his column at the junction of those roads just north of Panther Creek, obviously to secure the junction as well as to provide a defensible area overlooking the creek bottom to the south.[33]

Unfortunately, McClernand's troops found these roads far too wet and muddy to allow any rapid movement at all toward the important crossroad. "The little streams through this mountainous country were swollen to rivers nearly," staff officer Rumsey wrote, "making them hard to ford. The land is also very springy, so that after 2 or 3 pieces had passed over the horses would sink clear to their bellies." McClernand estimated the circuitous route to the fort from his landing site at Bailey's to be roughly eight miles, and the division and John Cook's attached brigade of Smith's unit had made only four miles by 1:00 PM. "The march [was] extremely difficult," recalled brigade commander Cook, "the troops suffering intensely from fording the numerous creeks, often wading so deep as almost to submerge their cartridge-boxes." The infantry also frequently had to halt and help the artillery out of the "innumerable mud-holes," whereupon Grant eventually gave the order to proceed without the guns. One Iowan noted, "we started off in rear of the light artillery, but we soon passed the most of this and left it sticking in the mud." Then other problems emerged. Cook reported that "the guide led us off the road about a mile, which had to be countermarched." By that time there was additional trouble for the infantry, in the form of the loud noises they heard to the west. The gunboats had reached the height of their bombardment, which one Illinoisan recalled was "splendid music to march by," but the infantry was nowhere near the fort as yet. They still had some four miles to go, and were already meeting resistance. McClernand noted that the sound of the navy's bombardment, "being distinctly heard by my men, was hailed by loud shouts, and they pushed on with increased eagerness, hoping to reach the fort in time to cut off the retreat and secure the surrender of the enemy."[34]

As the afternoon wore on and the sounds of the gunboats waned, however,

McClernand could tell something was up. "Suddenly all was still," remembered one Illinoisan, "and the question ran along the lines, 'What does it mean? Is Foote beaten?'" Another related, "we did not know what was the cause of them stopping or what the result of the firing had been," but added, "during most of the time that our gunboats were firing we were standing in line in a meadow some of our artillery having got swamped on a hill and we had to wait on it." Either the fort had deflected Foote's gunboat attack or the navy had been able to bombard it into submission. Either way, McClernand came to believe that an eager push by his infantry to surround the fort would be needed, despite Grant's earlier order to halt the column at the junction of the road from Bailey's and the road to Dover. Obviously, Grant was worried about a flank attack from the Fort Donelson garrison, but McClernand seemed to have realized that the poor road conditions made that possibility remote. Plus, he had scouts on that road, who reported nothing of the sort. Then, when a rumor emerged that Tilghman was evacuating the fort, McClernand pushed forward his cavalry, reporting to Grant that "although the letter of your order required the halting of my column near the junction of the Dover and Bailey's Ferry roads, some two miles from the fort, in view of the information already referred to [rumors of evacuation] I did not deem it within its spirit to do so, and accordingly pressed on." McClernand sent his cavalry "to make a rapid pursuit if upon investigation it were found to be true." McClernand's forward brigade commander, Richard Oglesby, had already done the same thing, sending cavalry to the front and following with his infantry as best he could.[35]

Still, the heavy rains had made an enormous bog out of the roads, and the march across the large Panther Creek bottom resumed only slowly. McClernand later described the paths as "the worst possible roads, cutting a portion of them through woods and bridging several streams made too deep for fording by recent rains." Certainly, the major creeks were formidable, especially the two large watersheds of Hughes and Panther creeks. Each of those also had smaller tributaries, which the various roads crossed, as well as smaller branches that fed into the river itself. As Will Wallace phrased it, "the roads were terrible—but notwithstanding this they marched & took the heavy trains of artillery over the worst roads I ever saw."[36]

What McClernand would actually find at Fort Henry once he arrived was anybody's guess, but indications were that something momentous was happening. Even the Confederates were realizing a culmination of events was taking place. One 4th Mississippi soldier manning the Confederate rifle pits described what was going on: "this was our first sniff of gun powder, although we had not fired a musket, yet the powder smoke was so thick that in many places the smoke hung like a cloud over the river and near the shore."[37]

What was happening within that cloud was the real story.

6

"A Good Day's Work"

February 6, 1862, was destined to be an important day in the annals of the Civil War, but it also portended a major change in larger American and even world history. Troops marching against fortifications on land was nothing new; that occurrence had played out numerous times over many centuries on several continents. Naval forces approaching fixed-land fortifications was likewise not unusual, it also having been carried out previously many times. Even combined arms, with the naval and land forces coordinating their attacks, were not new. But what was about to occur at Fort Henry was indeed original. This time, the combined naval-land arm contained a new weapon, one never before seen in combat in the western Hemisphere. Iron-plated gunboats were a novel addition to warfare. Commanders hoped the plating would protect the otherwise normal wooden ships from incoming fire while seeking to defeat a garrison by steaming close aboard. One newspaper artist, Alexander Simplot, described the ironclads by saying, "they are certainly a novel sight in these waters and appear well adapted for fighting purposes." Whether they would actually work or not was anybody's guess; this was the first time they had been tried in battle. Perhaps because of this fact, Flag Officer Foote spent much of the morning on February 6 asking for God's help, writing his wife later that day, "I earnestly & almost agonized in prayer for victory this morning."[1]

Even as he completed his prayers, Foote took no chances concerning the duties of the various officers under his command. Commander Roger N. Stembel of the *Cincinnati* wrote that "my vessel had the honor of bearing the flag and person of then Flag Officer subsequently Admiral Foote." Foote called all his gunboat commanders together on this flagship that morning to go over the orders once more. It was even more dramatic when the big gunboats began to move. The sight was one of grandeur as the low, black city-class gunboats and the *Essex* one by one moved with careful precision through the chute on the west side of the river between the Kentucky shore and Panther Island. The Eads boats looked so similar that even Federal commanders could only distinguish between them by colored bands around the tops of the smokestacks. The *St. Louis* with its yellow bands worked its way through first, followed by the *Carondelet* with its red stripes. The flagship *Cincinnati* emerged as well with blue bands on its stacks, although the *Essex* was such a different animal that it did not have to carry any colored bands. Nor did the timberclads need differentiation, as each was originally unique before modernization and armament, and these boats retained their differences even after fitting out for service. Items that easily distinguished them were the placement of the stacks and paddle wheels, although the *Tyler* and *Conestoga* were strikingly similar.[2]

Whether they knew the historical significance of these developments or not, the watching Confederates were concerned about their current troubles more than their place in history. McClernand and Smith were getting uncomfortably close, but the main worries were the gunboats on the river itself. Billowing black smoke had been seen all morning, indicating an increase in activity, and by 11:30 AM the gunners inside the fort could see the first black monster poke its bow around the end of Panther Island. One by one, each emerged from the chute on the west side; engineer Jeremy Gilmer described how "one of the gunboats had reached the head of the island, about 1 1/3 miles below our batteries; another soon followed, then a third and a fourth, all coming as nearly abreast as the width of the river would permit."[3]

It was an awesome sight, one never seen before in North America.

It did not take long for history to be made. The action began once the ironclads established their parallel formation, around 12:30 PM. "Not a sound could be heard nor a moving object seen in the dense woods which overhung the dark and swollen river," Henry Walke remembered on the *Carondelet*. In such atmosphere the gunboats began to move southward. The *St. Louis* held its position along the eastern bank, Lieutenant Commander Leonard Paulding barking orders and keeping the gunboat in line with the rest of the squadron. Next to the west came the *Carondelet*, with Commander Walke governing his actions by the flagship as well. The *Cincinnati*, with Foote himself onboard, ran in line next to the west, Stembel keeping it in line against the current. Finally, Commander William D. Porter's *Essex* held the western end of the line near the Kentucky shore. All faced southward toward Fort Henry, their bow guns ready for action.[4]

It was quite a bit of firepower, eleven heavy guns encased in armor bearing on the fort. As the second wave of gunboats, Foote also positioned the timberclad squadron under Phelps immediately to the rear, "astern and inshore of the armed boats." Phelps's own *Conestoga* held the center of the formation, while Lieutenant Commander William Gwin and his *Tyler* ran nearer the western bank and Lieutenant Commander James W. Shirk's *Lexington* was in line nearer the eastern bank. These three boats—although the most veteran vessels on the river with the most veteran commanders and crews, Phelps especially—were simply too vulnerable to be in the first line. They were also capable of firing arched shot over the ironclads and into the fort, which made their rearward position a logical place.[5]

"The fire was opened at 1,700 yards' distance from the flagship," Foote noted, "which was followed by the other gunboats." Actually, although the *Essex* opened almost immediately after the flagship did, some of the boats waited to see the effect of the *Cincinnati*'s first shots from its three bow guns, all of which fell far short. One watching gunner on the *Essex* thought of Foote's admonition not to waste ammunition and concluded, "there was twenty-four dollars' worth of ammunition expended." The flag officer had ordered his other commanders to await his own ship's initial salvo before opening up themselves, but once the *Cincinnati* began to fire, the others did likewise and sailors on the *Essex* claimed to have put the first shot inside Fort Henry. Inside the tight quarters of the casemates, the gun crews worked their pieces furiously as the huge guns forced the naval carriages back with each recoil. Each gun would then be loaded by the bore, run forward out the hatches, aimed, and fired at the Confederate fort. The sound inside the metal and wood casemates, the smoke, the sweat even in February, and the screams of commands and eventually wounded all combined for a horrible experience here on the Tennessee River. All the while, the various commanders kept in line with the flagship *Cincinnati*, which steamed slowly southward toward Fort Henry. "We approached the fort under slow steaming till we reached within 600 yards of the rebel batteries," Foote noted. Captain Jesse Taylor inside Fort Henry described the effect as "one broad and leaping sheet of flame."[6]

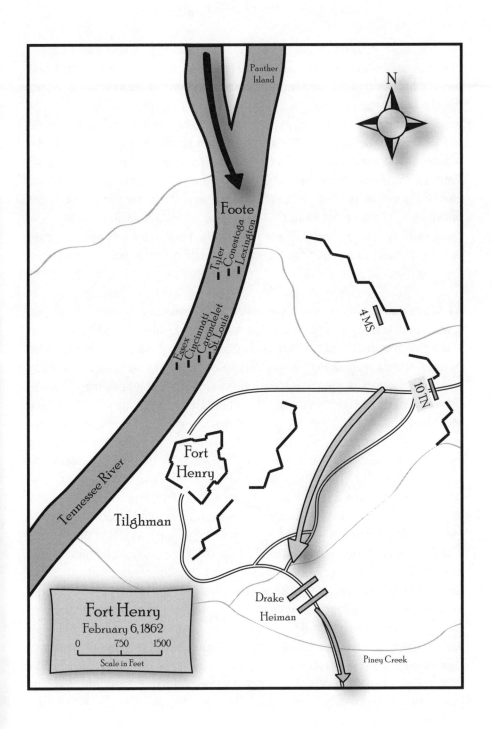

N

Panther
Island

Foote

Tyler
Conestoga
Lexington

4 MS

Essex
Cincinnati
Carondelet
St. Louis

10 TN

Fort
Henry

Tennessee River

Tilghman

Drake
Heiman

Piney Creek

Fort Henry
February 6, 1862
0   750   1500
Scale in Feet

That sheet of flame coming from the ironclads grew worse the closer the Federal gunboats moved toward Fort Henry. As the minutes passed, Foote pressed his flotilla forward according to the customs of naval warfare, pressing the attacks home. One gunner on the *Essex* described the result and the need for adaptation: "our shells, which were fused at fifteen seconds, were reduced to ten, and then to five seconds. The elevation of the guns was depressed from seven degrees to six, five, and four, and then to three degrees." Fortunately, unlike in the case of a group of newspaper correspondents who climbed trees on the riverbank but reported that "there was little to be seen but smoke," the slight wind carried the smoke far enough away from the ironclads to allow the gunners to view their shots. Foote was also able to gauge the ebb and tide of battle. What he saw was history in the making.[7]

By the time the Union navy approached, the Confederate gunners inside the fort, "eager for the contest" according to Jeremy Gilmer, opened up as well and Foote reported that "the fire both from the gunboats and fort increased in rapidity and accuracy of range." Walke declared that the "wild whistle of their rifle-shells was heard on every side of us." Taylor had assigned one vessel to each gun, and the return fire from Fort Henry was only slightly behind the initial Union fire, Tilghman writing that the enemy opened first but that he waited "a few moments until the effects of the first shots of the enemy were fully appreciated." It is questionable whether the gunners valued the delay and resulting one-sided bombardment, but Tilghman soon gave the order to return fire, which the "brave little band," as Tilghman called them, did. Taylor noted that it was "as pretty and as simultaneous a 'broadside' . . . as I ever saw flash from the sides of a frigate." Tilghman noted that the Federal gunboats nevertheless moved steadily forward, "firing very wild until within 1,200 yards." Then, the bombardment began to take increased effect. More and more Confederate guns opened up as the gunboats came closer, particularly the seven smaller 32-pounders that could fire down the river. Some of the fort's fire also went wild, as attested to by Union brigade commander Lew Wallace, who reported shots landing among the Federal troops marching southward toward Fort Heiman on the west bank.[8]

The massive bombardment in both directions soon began to take a toll, and the carnage increased as Foote's gunboats steadily bore down on Fort Henry and Phelps's timberclads poured in what one Confederate described as "cur-

veted shot, many of which fell within the work, but to the rear of our guns."
The earthen fort with its protective sandbags obviously took the harder hits,
with each landed shot causing damage. "Shot after shot was exchanged with
admirable rapidity and precision," one Confederate officer recounted, "and
the enemy's shell struck and exploded in every direction." Even the Federals
took notice; Walke on the *Carondelet* remembered how "we could occasionally see the earth thrown in great heaps over the enemy's guns."[9]

Problems quickly began to develop within the fort itself. One of the most
disconcerting for the defenders came around 12:35 PM, when the 24-pound
rifle mounted on the northwestern face of the fort, fronting the river but able
to shoot northward as well, burst as it was being fired. The explosion killed
or wounded every man at the piece as well as others on different guns nearby,
and took the cannon out of action. Perhaps the psychological effects of such
an accident were the greatest results. Engineer Gilmer watched and described
how "the effect of this explosion was very serious upon our artillerists; first,
because it made them doubt the strength of these large guns to resist the shock
of full charges, and, secondly, because much was expected from the long
range or rifled cannon against the gunboats."[10]

A similar misfortune occurred at the huge 10-inch columbiad. A priming
wire stuck in the vent while the crew worked the gun, perhaps too swiftly.
Tilghman himself went to the gun when he noticed it was silent and reported
the catastrophe: "we sustained another loss, still greater, in the closing up of
the vent of the 10-inch columbiad, rendering that gun perfectly useless and
defying all efforts to reopen it." Even a blacksmith could not pull it out. Even
so, Gilmer noted that the worker "labored with great coolness for a long time
exposed to the warmest fire of the enemy."[11]

With the demise of the rifled piece and the columbiad, the fort was down
to the two 42-pounders and the seven weak 32-pounders. Over time, even
these additional guns began to go out of service. A "premature discharge"
at one of the 42-pound rifles caused an explosion that killed three men and
injured many more, including the chief of the piece. Likewise, a Union shell
exploded when it hit the muzzle of one of the 32-pounders, killing two men
at the piece and wounding several others. With so many guns going down, the
artillerists began to doubt their success, and Gilmer even reported that many
of the crews on the small 32-pounders "ceased to work . . . under the belief
that such shot were too light to produce any effect upon the iron-clad sides of
the enemy's boats."[12]

So many guns were disabled, in fact, that by the time Foote's gunboats reached the six-hundred-yard range, Tilghman had only seven of his eleven guns able to bear on the river remaining in service. By a few minutes later, only four guns were serviceable. Making the situation worse, the cannoneers were beginning to slow down due to exhaustion after more than an hour of constant work at the guns. It was difficult work ramming down charges and positioning the huge guns, and even the hearty members of the guns crews were exhausted after such a long and uninterrupted period of service. The future was not looking too bright for Fort Henry.[13]

The only hope the Confederates were able to maintain was that there was also confusion in the Federal navy, some of it damage from the Confederate guns. It all began on the *Carondelet*, which tried to keep its station but unfortunately became tangled with the *St. Louis* because of the close quarters dictated by the relative narrowness of the river. Henry Walke on the *Carondelet* reported that his gunboat was "interlocked with the *St. Louis* a considerable portion of the time." Another problem developed when the pilot rang up the wrong orders and an impatient Walke continually yelled in "repeated orders" for the gunboat to move forward. The pilot, Daniel Weaver, later explained that "the bell lines of our boat had been reversed by the carpenter a few hours before we went into action, and when I ordered to go backed the boat about the half length of herself instead of going ahead as directed." Weaver also complained about the *St. Louis* "flanking against us on our port side, we being too near the flagship on our starboard side to keep away from her."[14]

Much more damage came from the Confederate guns. Catching the gunboats in their sights was problematic enough, as each gun had to be depressed and reaimed after each shot. Still, the gunners in the fort were able to hit the gunboats frequently as they came closer, and while many shots glanced off the sloping iron sides of the gunboats, many others registered and did damage. The worst case developed on the *Essex*. The Confederates recognized their success because they could see the gunboat drop out of line and float out of action downstream. Tilghman, in fact, reported, "this great loss [of the 24-pounder] was to us in a degree made up by our disabling entirely the *Essex* gunboat, which immediately floated downstream." Tilghman later reported that "a second one of the gunboats retired, but I believe was brought into action again." Foote and his officers made no record of another disabled vessel, even for a short time, so Tilghman could have misinterpreted a repositioning of vessels or even the *Carondelet*'s slight backward movement as a retreat.[15]

While the situation perhaps looked fairly calm from the Confederate vantage point, the *Essex* itself was a scene of horror. At first, the methodical deliberation of working the guns had been no different there than on any of the other boats. One fourteen-year-old gunner carefully counted shots on his gun with a rusty nail, marking on the whitewashed bulkhead. Then everything changed. One shot went through the *Essex*'s "No. 2 port hole breaking the handle of sponge between Jack Rogers hands and cutting the top of head off young Britton, Capt. Porters secretary and Masters mate." Then the shell went through a bulkhead and hit the worst place that a steamboat could be hit: the boilers. The boilers were extremely vital and dangerous, especially on warships. While not all of the exterior of city-class boats was protected by armor, the vulnerable engine and boiler section amidships was covered to cut down on the danger. Unfortunately, the *Essex* was different, and Foote sadly described how she "received a shot in her boilers." The steam that had been under pressure immediately erupted, and ultimately scalded twenty-nine crewmembers and officers, included the gunboat's commanding officer, William Porter. He was badly scalded on the face and hands even as he commanded in battle near the two pilots on board, James McBride and M. H. Ford, both of whom were scalded to death. There was also a contingent of infantry troops onboard, nine of whom were also scalded and four of whom later died. Without steam power from her boilers, the *Essex* was powerless and "necessarily dropped out of line astern, entirely disabled, and unable to continue the fight," Foote reported.[16]

The suffering on the *Essex* was horrible. Many gunners were scalded, and fate was a cruel factor. The gun crews had just swapped positions so that the tiring sailors on the bow guns could rest. Those who took their place from the stern guns were as a result killed after only one shot in their new positions. One crewman described his initial reaction at the rear of the gunboat when he met "a crowd of men rushing aft." Those to the front did not have that same luxury and actually had only one option for escape and that was out the portholes; many went directly into the river while a few managed to cling to the outside. Porter himself had been near the boilers when the scalding steam hit him and his first instinct was to dive out a porthole. A sailor clinging outside saw him and fortunately grabbed Porter around the waste, keeping him from going into the river. The sailor managed to get him to a ledge and then to the rear of the boat, where Porter turned over command with the orders to "man the battery again." They did so, and once crew members could get to the scene of the now steamless boilers, they found a horrid sight. One saw men "writhing in their last agony." At another point, he found a dead gunner "on his knees, in the act of taking a shell from the box to be passed to the loader." At the wheel, he found the dead pilot "standing erect, his left hand holding the spoke and his right hand grasping the signal-bell rope." Several who jumped in the river to get away from the steam drowned.[17]

Without power, the *Essex* began to drift northward with the current. A tug was soon on station to rescue the damaged gunboat that was still under heavy fire from the Confederate batteries. "The tug took hold of us and towed us out of range of the enemies guns," remembered one grateful sailor, and the small tug brought the gunboat down to the anchorage it had just left that morning. There, a larger river tug, the *Alps*, began preparations to tow the powerless ironclad back northward for repairs.[18]

Despite the carnage on the *Essex*, the *St. Louis*, *Cincinnati*, and *Carondelet* continued the fight, pressing ever forward toward Fort Henry. These gunboats took a pounding as well and casualties grew, the *Cincinnati* alone taking thirty-one shots, which killed one seaman and wounded nine. Foote later described the wounded "lying on deck groaning horribly." Walke told of seeing the *Cincinnati* hit: "it had the effect, apparently, of a thunder-bolt, ripping her side-timbers and scattering the splinters over the vessel." Perhaps that was why Foote said that the "rifle shots hissed like snakes." One of the shots came dangerously close to wounding Foote himself, who was encased in the pilothouse constantly signaling to the other boats to keep up in precise formation. "I had the breath, for several seconds, knocked out of me," he wrote his wife later that day, "as a shot struck opposite my chest in the iron clad pilot house on deck."[19]

The other boats fared somewhat better. The *St. Louis* took seven shots and the *Carondelet* was hit "nine or ten times," five bouncing off the iron on the bow casemate. Walke described how "their heavy shot broke and scattered our iron-plating as if it had been putty, and often passed completely through the casemates." Other shots took away some of the rigging and plank work. Another hit the starboard bow under water, which could have been a disaster had the shot penetrated the hull. Despite the hits, no one was killed or wounded on either vessel. Foote noted that the gunboats "resisted effectually the shot of the enemy when striking the casemate," and he was careful to present only the bows of each boat to the enemy, thereby "avoid[ing] exposure of the vulnerable parts of their vessels." Two cannon were disabled anyway, and one carriage damaged on the *Cincinnati*.[20]

The *Carondelet* seemed to do the most fighting, as several sources gave to it the lion's share of the credit for bombarding Fort Henry. Walke reported that the "aim was correct, their shot striking with terrible effect on Fort Henry." One of the Confederate gunners inside the fort agreed, later stating that "the center boat, or the boat with the red stripes around the top of her smoke-stacks, was the boat which caused the greatest execution." He was convinced that it was one of the *Carondelet*'s shells that exploded on the muzzle of the 32-pounder, adding that the gunboat "at each shot committed more damage than any other boat." In fact, he declared, "she was the object of our hatred, and many a gun from the fort was leveled at her alone. To her I give more credit than any other boat."[21]

All the while, the three timberclads continued their arching shot from the rear, taking a position on the eastern side of the river and firing southward. Each timberclad fired numerous shots, careful as Phelps reported to Foote to do so "without firing over your flagship or over the other iron-plated boats in close contest with the fort." Most exploding shells were set with ten- or fifteen-second fuses, and many landed within the fort itself, setting fire to the structures inside. While the Confederate gunners seemed to concentrate on the big ironclads up front, Phelps reported, "we were at times exposed to the ricochet of the close fire upon your vessel, as well as to the direct fire of a 32-pounder rifled piece till it burst."[22]

Despite the damage done to the *Essex*, Tilghman was growing increasingly worried as the bombardment continued. "He exposed himself during the whole fight without an idea of regard for his personal safety," one of his staff wrote home, "by walking from gun to gun, across embrasures &c &c and he worked one of the guns himself for a time when his small force were worn out." Yet such personal leadership could only go so far; his guns were being disabled one by one, his crews were beginning to drop from exhaustion, and the fort itself was riddled. "Many shot and shell were lodged in the parapet," Gilmer noted, "making deep penetrations, but in no case passing through, unless they struck the cheek of an embrasure." Milton Haynes added, "their heavy shot tore away the cheeks of several of our embrasures, throwing the sand bags upon the banquette, and exposing our gunners to the direct shot of the enemy." The Federal shells also set fire to the log and frame quarters in the center of the fort, and Tilghman's men had no way to extinguish them. Then another problem emerged. Colonel Heiman had taken the infantry and field guns out of the fort to a safe position along the southernmost road, but there they stopped to await Tilghman's orders. Although Tilghman had plenty of other worries, Heiman rode back to the fort to obtain directions. Tilghman later admitted: "at this time a question presented itself to me with no inconsiderable degree of embarrassment. The moment had arrived when I should join the main body of troops retiring toward Fort Donelson, the safety of which depended upon a protracted defense of the fort [Henry]." Tilghman was torn: "it was equally plain that the gallant men working the batteries, for the first time under fire, with all their heroism, needed my presence."[23]

It was crisis time for Tilghman, who recognized that "the effect of my absence at such a critical moment would have been disastrous." If he stayed, Tilghman could also see disastrous consequences personally, including potential captivity or death. But the overall desire was to buy time for the garrison to reach Fort Donelson and hold out there, and Tilghman determined that he would be most useful if he carried on the fight at Fort Henry as long as he could. His presence would inspire the weakening gunners to continue on, he believed. That many of his officers and men inside the fort were begging him to stay solidified his opinion. Tilghman consequently ordered Heiman to send additional men to work the guns while he stayed behind. He decided that he "should fight the guns as long as one man was left, and sacrifice myself to save the main body of my troops."[24]

Heiman quickly rode away and Tilghman returned to his work. "No sooner was this decision made known than new energy was infused," he remembered. Yet by that time only four guns were still firing and he readily admitted, "I could not well have worked a greater number." When one gun's chief became exhausted, Tilghman even leaped atop the carriage and worked it himself. "The general threw off his coat, sprang on the chassis of the nearest gun, stating that he would work it himself," one Confederate remembered. Tilghman reported that he gave the *Cincinnati* "two shots, which had the effect to check a movement intended to enfilade the only guns now left me." Haynes reported that by the time the gunboats were within several hundred yards, even the 32-pounders "pierced their sides, tearing holes plainly visible to the naked eye." Unfortunately for them, that success, if it was truly as

Tilghman and Haynes interpreted it, was only short lived, and as the range between the fort and gunboats continued to close, the Federal navy's shots became even more devastating. Tilghman reported, "the enemy were breaching the fort directly in front of our guns." More notably, Tilghman also reported, "I could not much longer sustain their fire without an unjustifiable exposure of the valuable lives of the men who had so nobly seconded me in this unequal struggle." Time was beginning to run out for Fort Henry.[25]

Tilghman was not the only one thinking of surrender, however. Major Gilmer was one who talked to Tilghman about "the propriety of taking the subject of surrender into consideration." He had earlier tried to get Colonel Heiman to do so, but Heiman retorted, "I would not like to make any suggestions to the general." Gilmer went himself, but Tilghman upbraided him, yelling, "I shall not give up the work," knowing that "every moment . . . was of vast importance to those retreating on Fort Donelson." Instead, he hoped to restart the fight and find new men to man the guns, as most were too exhausted after nearly an hour and a half fighting to continue. None could be procured from the retreating army, however. "My next effort was to try the experiment of a flag of truce," Tilghman reported. He hopped atop the gutted embrasures and waved a flag a little before 2:00 PM. The Federal gunners never saw it, Tilghman admitting that was because of "the dense smoke that enveloped it." He jumped back into the fort to save himself and continued the fight a few more minutes, but even he soon came to the realization that his time was up.[26]

About 2 o'clock, Tilghman ordered the flag lowered. He had requested Captain Taylor hold one hour, but it was now nearly two hours after the attack had begun. But not all had gotten out, and Heiman was even back in the fort once more. He had not been able to get fresh men to aid the gunners but had returned to state his reasons, to which Tilghman responded that the colonel had not been in the fort when the flag was lowered so he was immune from the surrender. He sent him to Fort Donelson, and Heiman rode swiftly to the east. Others were not ready to give up either. Haynes heard the command to cease firing, which he countermanded. Then one of his gunners showed him the white flag. Haynes was sure such an order should have been "given through me as chief of artillery," and ordered it lowered and "to shoot the man who ordered it." Not knowing Tilghman had actually given the order, Haynes was surprised when the soldier returned and said Tilghman himself was the cause. Haynes immediately went to Tilghman and confronted him, to which

Tilghman responded, "yes, we cannot hold out five minutes longer; our men are disabled, and we have not enough to man two guns." Haynes replied, "then, sir, I will not surrender, and you have no right to include me in the capitulation as an officer of this garrison, I being here only for consultation with you." Tilghman merely shook Haynes's hand and the latter departed, finding "a horse without a saddle or bridle, and, mounting him, I rode by the fort and passed up the bank of the river, and swam the sheet of backwater a mile above the fort." Haynes soon found Heiman's retreating infantry and joined them in their march to Fort Donelson.[27]

Ironically, the Confederate crisis played out as the Federal leaders experienced similar feelings. Although not known at the time, it was crisis time for Foote as well. He wrote his wife, "at a moment when it seemed as if we must be killed or sunk the big secession flag was hauled down and victory was ours." A cheer streamed from the watching Union gunners on the *Cincinnati*, "a yell in fact" Foote wrote, prompting three cheers from the other gunboat crews. The crews were so jubilant that Foote wrote, "I had to run among the men and knock them on the head to restore order." He told one officer who was especially jubilant that "he ought to be ashamed of himself," but he responded that having expected to be killed it was a "cheer he could not help voicing with all his might."[28]

As Foote steamed toward the fort to take possession, he encountered more problems. The boats seemed to be racing to get the glory, Foote yelling and signaling to halt so that the flagship could take the lead. The order for all engines to stop went out, which somehow occurred on the *Cincinnati* as well. About the same time, the *Carondelet* ran aground near the fort and was stuck fast. At the same time, Foote's own flagship, now without engines running, began to drift downstream, giving the flag officer the momentary sensation that Walke and the *Carondelet* were moving ahead of him, something similar to sitting on a train beside another on a different track and being unable at first to tell which was moving. Walke wrote that an agitated Foote gave "a few sharp technicalities to keep his station." When Walke did not seem to stop, Foote "in the midst of the excitement came forward in haste, trumpet in hand, and called out again and again to stop the '*Carondelet*' (unaware of the fact that his own vessel was all the time drifting down the river)." Foote had a younger officer continue the harangue and, Walke wrote, "the pantomime transformed itself into a comedy; but a satisfactory explanation was finally afforded by the action of the gunboat, sliding off the bank into deep water."

Cooler heads no doubt prevailed soon thereafter as officers on the *Cincinnati* shook Foote's hand, and later the commanders of the other gunboats boarded to offer their congratulations as well.[29]

After the flag came down, Tilghman sent his adjutant general and engineer out in a small launch to the gunboats. The two officers informed the sailors that Tilghman wanted to speak to the flag officer in command, and Foote sent Stembel of the *Cincinnati* and Phelps of the *Conestoga* into the fort to raise the American flag; their cutter sailed right into the sally port of the flooded fort, and Stembel called the act of raising the flag an "honor and unmistakable pleasure." They told Tilghman that Foote would receive him on his flagship. Soon thereafter, Tilghman took a launch to the *Cincinnati*, where he and Foote conferred on the surrender. Foote was evidently impressed with Tilghman, whom he described as fighting "with the most determined gallantry," but added that it was "worthy of a better cause." The two commanders agreed to a surrender of the fort, the general, his staff, and nearly a hundred prisoners (in addition to several killed and sixteen wounded in the fighting), as well as the sick on a hospital boat. Foote allowed the Confederate officers to keep their sidearms, and, knowing that his men, and he himself, would soon be prisoners of war, Tilghman also extracted a pledge that the prisoners would be "treated with the highest consideration."[30]

In surrendering the fort, Tilghman opened himself up to a great deal of criticism. Some came to his defense, such as John Burch, who wrote to Governor Harris three days later that "everyone compliments the conduct of Tilghman & all the officers and men during the engagement." He added that "the blame attached to Tilghman is for surrendering instead of leaving the flag flying & running with his men." Others were not so forgiving. One Confederate wrote from Fort Donelson four days after the surrender: "it is the impression of most every person here that Gen Tillman who was taken prisoner proved traitor to the south. It is said that when Tillman walked on board the Gun Boat to give himself up Col. Human [Heiman] of this place shot at him twice. I don't know whether to give it any credit or not as we can't hear the truth five steps here. But I will tell you what is the truth it was a perfect Bull Run on our side."[31]

Others gained disrespect as well. At one point when an officer railed on Jesse Taylor for burning all important documents at Fort Henry to keep them out of Federal hands, a now arrived Grant himself happened by and corralled the officer: "I would be very much surprised and mortified if one of my subordinate officers should allow information which he could destroy to fall into the hands of the enemy." Most associations were much more mild, including the renewal of friendships. Captain Taylor, the old navy man, saw many friends, among them Gwin and Shirk, commanders of the timberclads. Even C. F. Smith wrote his wife that he visited with "my old friend Genl Tilghman." Tilghman was very careful, however, to keep the fact silent that one of his staff, Lieutenant William Jones, was the son of a former US senator from Iowa, George W. Jones, who himself had been arrested for disloyalty.[32]

It was certainly odd, this trying to kill one another and then renewing friendships as if nothing had happened. And there was a lot of both, one Confederate calculating that there were 1,014 shots fired on both sides. Such was the essence of a gentleman's Civil War, especially this early in the conflict.[33]

Just because the navy made quick work of the fort and its garrison did not mean that major operations had ended. In fact, there was still much to do. On the *Essex*, for example, the wounded were in horrible shape but rejoiced at the news of the surrender. Porter himself "immediately rallied, and, raising himself on his elbow, called for three cheers, and gave two himself, falling exhausted on the mattress in his effort to give a third." A similarly scalded crewman was so enthused with the news that he jumped up and exclaimed, "Surrender! I must see that with my own eyes before I die." He bolted up the ladder to the upper deck and shouted, "Glory to God" before falling back down; he died later that night.[34]

The land forces on both sides, one to get away and the other to trap what they could inside the fort and the narrow swamps leading from it, were also still on the move after the surrender. The shocked Confederate garrison quickly began to realize the gravity of the situation. All during the fight they had watched and listened. Richard L. McClung of the 15th Arkansas noted, "here I saw my first bombshell and heard the first cannon that I heard in the war." Another admitted, "our appetites were completely 'knocked out in the first round,' empty stomachs no longer realized the vacancy caused by the absence of both breakfast and dinner." Then tension grew as it appeared the Federal land forces would also be coming. "When we were ordered to pile overcoats, load and cap our guns, with suppressed excitement we awaited the approach of the enemy; but nothing more dangerous looking than trees and lagoons appeared in the direction from which we expected them to come." Then came the cessation of the gunboat fire "as suddenly as it had begun," an Alabaman recalled, and the order sounded to march to the south, which he deemed "a little strange, as the enemy were supposed to be in the opposite direction." The garrison marched southward along the river until

it soon dawned on us that the fort had surrendered, and we were retreating—
running from the Yankees! We who had so recently left home with visions of glory
to be achieved on the field of battle—of hundreds of Yankees to be slain with our
'buck-and-ball,' and our long-bladed knives steeped in Yankee gore, actually running before we had fired a gun, or even caught a glimpse of a blue-coat.[35]

The reality of the situation similarly dawned on the Federals. McClernand realized that he had been beaten by the navy, but there was still glory to be had. Certainly, Tilghman had surrendered the fort to the navy and was even then in their custody, but McClernand could still make sure his division was the first of the Union army forces in the fort. While McClernand had a contingent of Smith's division with him in the form of Cook's brigade, there was no chance they would lead the way. McClernand would make sure his division was triumphantly first into the fort, and thus pushed on rapidly. "We came the last two miles at a double quick," remembered one 30th Illinois soldier.[36]

Adding to the haste, there was possibly more to be had than just the surrendered fort. McClernand's cavalry in the vanguard made contact with the enemy even as they were departing. A small contingent led by McClernand's staff officer, Warren Stewart, first attacked the rear guard of the enemy, McClernand writing that they "boldly charged his rear while he was in the act of clearing the outer line of his defenses." A larger, more substantial body of cavalry under Lieutenant Colonel William McCullough of the 4th Illinois Cavalry then took up the chase and soon had the Confederate garrison traumatized even more. One Alabaman remembered, "when it became known that we were retreating the impulse to go faster and faster seemed to strike all of us at the same time, while the dashing past of small squads of frightened cavalrymen and an occasional shot in the rear served to accelerate our speed until short-legged fellows like myself had to go in a lively trot to keep up with the procession."[37]

Heiman's Confederate command marched away southward toward Standing Rock Creek, crossing it five times at "five deep and rapid fords," Haynes reported. An Arkansan remembered: "we waded creeks—plunged mudholes ascended mountains and crossed ravines." Another Confederate with the measles noted he had to choose between the raging creek "running like a mill-race" and the Yankees, and he chose the "cold bath." With the water raging so fast, several men aided one another: "locking together, tall and short, by fours, we plunged in." McCullough kept up the chase until nightfall, garnering a large lot of arms and equipment, "in short, everything calculated to impede his flight," McClernand noted. He also captured thirty-eight prisoners, along with killing one soldier. The same Arkansan described one small fight with the Federal cavalry; he and his comrades "gathered together on the apex of a hill to sell our lives as dear as possible choosing rather to die with a steady aim and face to the foe than a surrender." The cavalry turned around, likely no more interested in dying than the Confederates. Heiman's men then continued on their way to Donelson.[38]

The march soon became mass chaos. Gilmer, who had escaped Fort Henry on foot, wrote in understatement, "as soon as this movement was commenced confusion among the retiring troops followed." The major prize left behind in the chaos was an entire Confederate field battery of six guns, Culbertson's Tennessee battery, captured when the miry roads and need for haste caused the artillerymen to abandon the cannon. Those six guns, added to the seventeen captured in the fort itself, netted a total of twenty-three pieces of Confederate artillery captured in the fighting that day. There was some good news, however, in the form of a two-regiment relief party under Colonel John Head sent out from Fort Donelson toward "Camp Tilghman," but Head was probably not that enthused about helping Tilghman, with whom he had recently had bitter struggles, which had led him to contemplate resigning. Nevertheless, the small brigade met the retreating garrison near Peytona Furnace and turned back as well, the retreat growing more and more chaotic. One Tennessean under Head noted that most of the Fort Henry garrison arrived at Dover the next day "nearly all wet to their armpits. . . . Scattering men from all the regiments outstripped all and went in without any order, some two on a horse." One of the unfortunate participants agreed, writing that they got into Fort Donelson "hungry, cold and mad." The following Federals noted as much, one writing, "from appearance it was rather a stampede than a retreat for in their flight they threw away their knapsacks and some of their arms and left their things all along the road for several miles." Another simply noted, "as soon as the secesh saw our forces coming they took to there Heels and rund in all directions."[39]

Even as the Federal cavalry harassed the Confederate retreat that afternoon,

McClernand and company rushed onward, hoping still to catch at least part of the Confederate garrison. One of the leading officers wrote how "I ordered a double quick and rushed with a shout to cut off the retreat but when I arrived at the Fort they had fled." Many dove headlong into water waist deep trying to catch the enemy, all to no avail, one writing that "although we marched very fast through the mud & water, we were too late however to catch many of the rebels." The troops strode triumphantly into the fort anyway, determined not to let a little navy luck beat them out of the glory of taking official possession of the fort. While Walke was in charge by Foote's orders, McClernand arrived and took official possession. Led by the gigantic Colonel Michael K. Lawler of the 18th Illinois, McClernand's first brigade streamed into the fort around 3:30 PM, followed later by Will Wallace's brigade, which had been stalled due to having with them "a battery of heavy siege guns and the aggravated condition of the roads." Cook's brigade of Smith's division, with no chance at glory or plunder, trailed to the rear.[40]

When they arrived, the Federal infantry found a thoroughly shot-up fort. Will Wallace described it vividly to his wife: "the effect of the fire on the fortifications here was terrible — guns dismounted — earthworks torn up and the evidences of carnage meet the eye on every hand." Lew Wallace later described the same: "the devastation astonished me all the more when I recalled the short time in which it had been accomplished." A staff officer wrote his father about seeing "a man's tongue and an eye lying around loose, and any quantity of blood and brains," and another confided that some Confederates were "blown to atoms" and that "it would be horrible at any other time except in time of battle which time it does not seem to affect a man."[41]

If there was any consolation, it was in what the Federals found around the fort, including what one described as "about twenty of the heaviest and best looking guns . . . that ever I saw, besides this we got 10 or 12 pieces of brass cannon." The Northerners were particularly impressed with the big 128-pounder, one Iowan calling it "a whopper." Another noted, "they have thrown up breastworks enough to make five miles of railroad." Individual items were much more in demand as the soldiers took possession of the tents and log huts that had been inhabited by the Tennesseans and Mississippians the night before and had survived the bombardment. Other Federals were more sinister in their occupation; one Illinoisan described how "we stacked arms and after breaking ranks the boys broke for the barracks to see what we could find." Another wrote of how "we had a good time searching and pilfering their camp," one Iowan describing reading Confederate letters. An Illinois staff officer noted, "there was everything that can be thought of taken by the first ones in; — gold watches, splendid uniforms, blankets, a large number of tents as well as barracks. Some I hear got 50 to 300 dollars in money out of officers' trunks; one got 100 half-dollars." Brigade commander Jacob Lauman, who was battling a bad cold, noted that the Confederates left so hurriedly that some of the men found "bread baking in the ovens and meat cooking." One grateful Indianan across the river at Fort Heiman noted, "we have taken up our quarters this evening where the rebels were this morning, living on their 'grub.'"[42]

Numerous Federals also commented on the dead inside the fort, the first that many had even seen. While few in number, they were still badly mangled because of the bursting of the gun inside the fort. David Poak wrote his sister of the grisly details: "I saw 4 rebels that were killed in the fort[.] One of them had his head and both arms blown off, and his body burned black, another had his head blown all to pieces, another his neck was cut about two thirds off and the other his head was split right in to." Some of the sailors also got a look inside, and the site caused these new warriors to take stock of what it meant. "On every side lay the lifeless bodies of the victims, in reckless confusion, intermingled with shattered implements of war," one sailor wrote. "Our eyes then met each other's gaze with a sadness, full of meaning, that forbade any attempt to speak, and, in the quietness like that of a graveyard, we walked slowly over the desolate scene."[43]

Grant himself arrived within an hour of the time that Foote took Tilghman's surrender. He then took command, going aboard Walke's *Carondelet* to offer his congratulations to the crew. He later went aboard his own steamboat, where some of the Confederate officers were brought. One observer noted the Confederate proclivity for show by writing that "the captured Rebel officers, in a profusion of gold lace, were taken to Grant's headquarters." Grant had numerous duties to attend to, but he took a moment to write a quick note to Julia: "Fort Henry is taken and I am not hurt. This is news enough for to-night." His confidence, despite not knowing the strength of the defenses, was well placed.[44]

Even though Grant was in command, McClernand took the limelight. He placed Captain Stewart of his staff in command of the fort but surprisingly renamed it Fort Foote, in honor of the naval commander. One Illinoisan noted that it was renamed after "the commander of the gun-boats which shot it to pieces." That McClernand would give anyone else glory, besides himself, was remarkable, but he took the opportunity to write that his division "was the first of the land forces to enter the fort, and I may truly say for them it is their greatest regret that circumstances beyond their control prevented them from accomplishing their greatest desire, which was to cut off the enemy's retreat and force him to fight or surrender." McClernand also sent out a flurry of letters to important politicians, such as Illinois Governor Richard Yates and even President Lincoln, emphasizing his own part in the battle. He even joked with Foote about naming the fort after him: "please pardon the liberty I have taken without first securing your concurrence, as I am hardly disposed to do, considering the liberty which you took in capturing the fort yesterday without my cooperation." Still, McClernand had to give credit where credit was due. He wrote, "their hasty surrender without a more protracted struggle can only be accounted for by the terrible cannonade from our gunboats." He could not help but add: "and their apprehension of being cut off from retreat by the rapid advance of our land forces." Foote perhaps summed it up best when he described February 6 as "a good day's work."[45]

Grant calmly let McClernand swagger, but he took firm control. He was also compassionate. Will Wallace came down with a massive headache after the march and fighting, "the worst I ever had," he told his wife Ann, "induced doubtless by long continuous exposure & loss of sleep & irregularity in my meals." Grant took pity on his brigade commander; as Wallace wrote to his wife: "Genl. Grant invited me to take a state room on his boat & perhaps I will for tonight."[46]

The demise of Fort Henry came so swiftly that it took almost everyone by surprise. Grant even had second thoughts, writing Halleck, "had I not felt it an imperative necessity to attack Fort Henry to-day I should have made the investment complete and delayed until tomorrow, so as to have secured the garrison." He added, "I do not now believe, however, that the result would have been any more satisfactory."[47]

Foote thought so too and reveled in the victory, careful to give the glory to God. "Bless the Lord who has given me the victory after a horrible fight of an hour and fifteen minutes," he wrote his wife later that day. Others sent word up the chains of command, and communications about the event quickly spread across the nation. Grant himself crowed to headquarters: "Fort Henry is ours." Similarly, Halleck sent word on to both Buell and Washington when he received it on February 7: "Fort Henry is ours. The flag of the Union is re-established on the soil of Tennessee. It will never be removed." Lower-level soldiers also wrote home, one Illinoisan writing that Fort Henry was "very strongly fortified for miles around" and that "the rebels have been at work here for 8 or 9 months, but [we] took it in one hour and 10 minutes."[48]

Grant even allowed Lloyd Tilghman to send a report to his superiors on February 7. "Through the courtesy of Brig. Gen. U. S. Grant, commanding Federal forces, I am permitted to communicate with you," Tilghman wrote Richmond. He told of the disaster and noted, "I communicate this result with deep regret, but feel that I performed my whole duty in the defense of my post." Many took up for Tilghman, Milton Haynes writing that "the fault was in its [Fort Henry's] location, not in its defenders." He also added, "we lost . . . everything but honor." Nevertheless, Tilghman was now a prisoner, and his Federal captors sent him and his men northward. At the same time, with the Fort Henry garrison marching away that afternoon without securing any of its equipment, the Federals soon took all they could. One Arkansan in Drake's brigade described how "my regt. left all of our blankets and clothes save the clothes we wore. As we expected on leaving camps, to return again after a few hours fighting. Yet we went to Donelson."[49]

In all the flurry of correspondence that looked back at the news with either pride or disgust, one simple message got the most attention at Halleck's head-quarters in St. Louis. Fort Henry was by no means going to be the climax of the campaign. In writing to Halleck on February 6, Grant nonchalantly added, "I shall take and destroy Fort Donelson on the 8th and return to Fort Henry."[50]

It was the mark of Ulysses S. Grant and his bulldog mentality. The campaign was far from over.

7

"THE ENTERING WEDGE TO ALL OUR SUBSEQUENT SUCCESSES"

Congressman Charles B. Sedgwick, chairman of the House Naval Affairs Committee, took the floor of the US House of Representatives on the afternoon of February 7, 1862. He wanted to share the urgent news he had just received from the Navy Department, and the clerk quickly read Flag Officer Foote's initial report of the capture of Fort Henry, including Confederate commander Lloyd Tilghman. Members in the chamber erupted, the official *Congressional Globe* describing "great applause upon the floor and in the galleries." About the same time, Tennessee Senator Andrew Johnson rose to the floor of the US Senate and had the same message read. "I merely wished to have that dispatch read by way of refreshing the Senate, that we might see that the Union is going along," Johnson noted. Washington was abuzz over the victory.[1]

Foote later learned just what a stir his short note had caused; Assistant Secretary of the Navy Gustavus V. Fox wrote on February 8: "your telegram came at noon and we sent it immediately to Congress, where it gave intense satisfaction." Gideon Welles himself notified Foote that his note was "read in both houses of Congress in open session." Another Navy Department officer, Henry A. Wise, added, "we all went wild over your success, not unmixed with envy, when the news came of the reduction of Fort Henry. Uncle Abe was joyful, and said everything of the navy boys and spoke of you—in his plain, sensible appreciation of merit and skill." Even more celebration occurred later when Foote sent two flags to Welles, one of which had been "displayed during the action at the flagstaff in the center of the fort until hauled down as the signal of surrender to the squadron."[2]

The nationwide response was just as joyous, although some Federals at Fort Heiman complained as late as February 11 that "we on this side of the river, although only about a mile from Fort Henry, could obtain but little information until we received the Chicago and Cincinnati papers of the 8th inst last night." George Templeton Strong wrote in his diary: "excellent tidings from Tennessee; Fort Henry, a rebel earthwork on the Tennessee River, bombarded and taken." Some steamboat companies even planned excursions to Fort Henry. In all the celebration, Foote received most of the accolades. Fox, for example, wrote, "you are being rewarded for the trials and sublime patience of the labors you have given to your work, now crowned with victory. Of yourself we all knew that the hour of trial for you was the hour of success." Secretary Welles agreed: "the labor you have performed and the services you have rendered in creating the armed flotilla of gunboats on the Western waters, and in bringing together for effective operation the force which has already earned such renown, can never be overestimated." Humbly, Foote gave his men credit, especially considering how undermanned and chaotic the preparations had been amid the transfers from one boat to another. He notified his men that their "brilliant services and gallant conduct [has been] formally noticed by the commanding general of the Western Army and by the Secretary of the Navy, conveying the assurance that the President of the United States, the Congress, and the entire country appreciate their gallant deeds."[3]

The navy's new gunboats also came in for acclaim. Many had wondered on the eve of battle whether the gunboats would stand up to the heavy ordnance about to be unleashed on them, particularly with some vulnerable areas not covered with iron and with their patchwork crews. All worry was dispelled with the victory at Fort Henry, however. Foote wrote, "all the officers and men gallantly performed their duty, and, considering the little experience they have had under fire, far more than realized my expectations." Grant likewise noted, "the gunboats have proved themselves well able to resist a severe cannonading." Even lower-level Federal infantry praised the ironclads, one doubting Illinoisan writing, "our gunboats proved an entire success," with another adding: "our gunboats have achieved something of which they may justly be proud and which I think will effectually silence the growlings about useless expense in constructing them, which have from time to time been urged."[4]

Not everyone was so enthused about the navy's victory, however. One 4th

Illinois cavalryman complained, "the papers don't say anything about any-thing but the gun boats." While the navy accrued most of the acclaim, Halleck was not about to let the army miss any glory. He sent a flurry of reports and congratulations to Washington on February 7 when news reached St. Louis. It had obviously taken a while for the news to reach Cairo, the nearest telegraph line, but when it did, it spread quickly. Halleck wrote, "Fort Henry was taken yesterday, with seventeen heavy guns, General Lloyd Tilghman and staff, and 60 men, after a bombardment of one hour and a quarter by gunboats." He also included word of the forty-four Union wounded, including "Cap-tain Porter [who] is badly but not dangerously scalded." Halleck also sent Foote his warmest congratulations but sent no praise to his army commander Grant; few others did either. Only Grant's native Ohio legislature sent their congratulations to both Foote and Grant. Still, all gloated in the victory, one Illinoisan writing, "they can say nothing more about Bull Run." Lew Wallace noted, "altogether this is the best thing of the war."[5]

Just the opposite feelings emerged in the Confederacy. Lunsford Yandell in Memphis wrote on February 7 of the news of the fall of Fort Henry: "this is a heavy blow upon us. . . . God be on our side & help us." War Depart-ment clerk John B. Jones simply noted, "Fort Henry has fallen. Would that were all!" The news hit Albert Sidney Johnston especially hard: "no reli-able particulars of the loss of Fort Henry have yet reached me," he wrote to Richmond, but he was encouraged that the troops had escaped. The enormity of the disaster was evident, however: "the capture of that fort by the enemy gives them the control of the navigation of the Tennessee River, and their gunboats are now ascending the river."[6]

Others were just as distraught. Tennessee Governor Isham G. Harris noti-fied Confederate Secretary of War Judah Benjamin of the disaster on February 7, writing, "a large increase of force to defend this [State] from Cumberland Gap to Columbus is an absolute and imperative necessity. If not successfully defended the injury is irreparable." Even Lloyd Tilghman was upset at more than his surrender. He asked Foote to correct his report that Fort Henry had seventeen mortars. Foote responded that he got several other things wrong in his official report, but he had not stated that the fort had any mortars. The "mistake, no doubt, arose at the printer's office," Foote explained. For his part, Foote wanted to give Tilghman the benefit of the doubt, writing that he fought gallantly and "I see nothing in him but admirable points of char-acter, except his perverted notions about his duties to the Union." Others

thought similarly, one 8th Wisconsin soldier writing about their duty guarding the Fort Henry prisoners: "Genl. Tilghman is a very intelligent man and I
was surprised to think, that so smart a man, should ever think of secession."
One 12th Illinois soldier in Paducah wrote that Tilghman and the staff were
guarded in a fine house on Broadway Street, and the people of his native city
bowed to him. An Ohioan noted that some prisoners were kept on a boat in
the river "guarded by a gun boat," but others were in a house in town. "We
can see them from our boat," he marveled, "looking out at the windows."[7]

Even worse, almost all in the Confederacy could sense the next disaster
waiting to happen: Fort Donelson. "Operations against Fort Donelson, on
the Cumberland, are about to be commenced, and that work will soon be
attacked," Johnston wrote Benjamin on February 8. Given the lackluster defense offered at Fort Henry, little could be expected of Fort Donelson. Johnston and indeed the entire Confederacy were at a crisis point.[8]

Johnston was absolutely correct in his assessment that Fort Donelson was
next, because the Federal commander was already thinking ahead. Instead of
casting about for his own glory, instead of positioning himself for the greatest
limelight, instead of making his own contributions obvious to all who would
see, Ulysses S. Grant simply kept planning and moving, desiring to keep up
the pressure and continue the victories. So came his notification that he would
simply march over to Dover and capture Fort Donelson in a couple of days.[9]

Grant later sent a more detailed explanation to Halleck, stating, "owing to
the intolerable state of the roads," few wagons and "but little artillery" would
be taken. Halleck was still scheming to replace him with what he deemed a
more competent and experienced leader, but there was little Halleck could
do now. Grant's note did not arrive until February 7, and the chances of a
Halleck order getting back to Grant before he left for Fort Donelson were
slim if Grant moved on February 8. Halleck could only inform Washington,
"General Grant's infantry and artillery have gone to attack Fort Donelson at
Dover, on the Cumberland."[10]

That was the essence of Grant. Not caught up in the glories of victory, he
continued forward, confident in his own ability. He obviously had to be cognizant of Halleck's concerns, but in a classic episode of asking forgiveness
rather than permission, Grant wrote, "hoping that what has been done will
meet the approval of the major general commanding the department." With
that, Grant planned to be off for Fort Donelson and the next round of fighting
in what was already a significant strategic campaign.[11]

Grant's casual mention of moving on and taking Fort Donelson on February 8 shocked the highest Federal commanders, but Henry Halleck in St. Louis knew there was little he could do to stop Grant if he had already marched eastward. "I can do no more for Grant at present," he wrote McClellan, but showed his nervousness: "it is the crisis of the war in the West. . . . We are certainly in peril." Halleck wrote Buell as much on February 7, stating, "I suppose the mud there, as it is here, is too deep for movements outside of railroads and rivers. The enemy has the railroads, and we must use the rivers—at least for the present." Then he added significantly, "unfortunately our gunboats are badly disabled." In his worry, Halleck could only shuttle new troops southward, hoping Grant would not get into more than he could handle. To McClellan, Halleck nervously wrote, "I am sending everything I can rake and scrape together from Missouri." He also asked for any help he could get from Buell.[12]

McClellan was no more enthused about Grant's latest foray than was Halleck. While congratulating Halleck, as if that general did anything other than allow the Fort Henry advance to take place even while distancing himself from it, McClellan toasted Halleck "upon the result of your operations. They have caused the utmost satisfaction here." Even so, the new operations worried him, and McClellan and Halleck continued to scheme to find what they considered a competent commander to lead the advance along the twin rivers; they obviously still distrusted Grant. At the outset, McClellan informed Halleck, "either Buell or yourself should soon go to the scene of operations." Halleck countered that William T. Sherman outranked Buell and should have the command before him ("his health is greatly improved," Halleck wrote). He also had another idea—one large western department with him in command and smaller departments commanded by Buell and others. At the same time, Halleck continued to try to give Hitchcock the command. He wrote the secretary of war that since Grant, Sherman, McClernand, and a host of other generals all ranked from the same date "and each [was] unwilling to serve under the other," he needed Hitchcock as soon as possible. Of course, the underlying issue was his mistrust of Grant for such a massive operation. "If it can be done there should be no delay," Halleck added, "as an experienced officer of high rank is wanted immediately on the Tennessee line." In the meantime, Halleck himself planned to make his way to Fort Henry early the next week.[13]

Despite his concerns, Halleck continued to shift all the troops he could to

Grant to solidify his hold on Fort Henry and allow for a greater chance of success on the hasty offensive. Halleck had sent his chief of staff, George W. Cullum, to Cairo, he told Grant, "to give any necessary orders in his name to facilitate your very important operations." As early as February 7, Halleck also sent the 49th Illinois and 25th Indiana to Fort Henry from Cairo and forwarded the soon-expected 57th Illinois as well. Several other regiments were also in the pipeline, including the 48th Indiana, 32nd Illinois, 1st Nebraska, and 2nd Iowa. Halleck also sent engineering tools for entrenching. All the while, Halleck cautioned Grant to face Fort Henry's guns to the landside and hold the fort "at all hazards."[14]

An additional reason for concern was the matter of the navy's role in any upcoming operations. Although under army command, Foote was still a force within himself, especially after his glorious victory at Fort Henry. Unfortunately, the lines of authority were not always clear military lines of command in the mixed-up situation. The army officers had the authority but were loath to use it often, Halleck and Grant mostly "suggesting" what they would like done. Foote mostly accommodated, but a more contentious naval commander could have created great difficulty for the combined arms operations along the western rivers.[15]

In truth, logistics played a greater role in naval cooperation than did squabbles over command. Foote's strength was severely limited in the two or three days after Fort Henry, which included Grant's target date of February 8 for capturing Fort Donelson. Foote had already sent Phelps and the three timberclads up the river to the railroad bridge and beyond on the evening of February 6; when he would return was anybody's guess, but he certainly would not be able to get back in time to make his way out of the Tennessee River and up the Cumberland by February 8 to support Grant. Likewise, two of Foote's ironclads had been damaged and the flag officer himself left Fort Henry that same evening bound for Cairo and repairs. Foote had remained at the fort for only three hours or so, never even entering the works, and left the same afternoon with the damaged *Cincinnati* and *Essex*; the *St. Louis* eventually made its way back to Cairo as well. Then too, Foote was already showing peskiness. The *Essex* was so badly hit that it needed towing, so Commander Porter sent a note to Grant asking permission for the *Alps* to tow her. Foote responded that the request should go through him, but allowed the towing anyway, only asking that they all go down to Cairo together: "as I am going down to-night, I wish you to remain till this vessel reaches you, as we are so

badly cut up I do not like to go down alone." Foote and company accordingly
left that evening, dropping critically wounded and scalded sailors off at both
Paducah and Mound City. The flotilla arrived at Cairo on February 7, the
gunboats, one sailor writing, "came down with the rebel colors flying under
the American flag." It was no doubt quite a sight, but the gunboats themselves
stole the show; one amazed 2nd Iowa soldier viewed the ironclads and wrote
that "they are riddled considerable." They certainly were, and Foote notified
the Navy Department that repairs on the two gunboats would require ten days
(actually, the *Essex* would have to return all the way to St. Louis for repairs).
That left only the *Carondelet* and *St. Louis* operable, and one was needed to
guard Fort Henry. As a result, only one active gunboat was able to make its
way to Fort Donelson, unless more were sent from Cairo. However, none
could be on station in the Cumberland by February 8. If Grant was hoping
for naval support for his quick advance, he certainly would not get it by his
desired date. Something had to give.[16]

A major reason that naval support for an operation against Fort Donelson
was not available on February 8 was because a large portion of Foote's flotilla, the entire timberclad division under Seth Ledyard Phelps, was gone.
Federal efforts in the hours and days after the capture of Fort Henry were
more than reorganizational. There occurred one major Union offensive that
proved to have long-lasting implications, carrying the war into places little
dreamed of just days before.[17]

Flag Officer Foote had issued instructions to his most veteran naval commander even prior to the attack on Fort Henry to continue up the Tennessee
River once the victory was won. Phelps was just the man for the job, having
been up and down each of the rivers from Columbus to the twin forts numerous times throughout the previous fall and winter. Although of lower rank
than others, Phelps had a solid division of the three timberclads. In fact, Foote
had slotted Phelps to take over the ironclad *Cairo* until the arrival of Lieutenant Nathaniel C. Bryant, who outranked Phelps, hindered the promotion and
Phelps had to stay abroad the *Conestoga*. It was a good thing for Foote, as
Phelps would now make a raid that would cause the Confederacy to tremble.[18]

When Fort Henry fell, all Federal eyes were initially on the major prize
of the railroad bridge across the Tennessee River just a few miles south of
the fort. In fact, the bastion itself was of little strategic consequence except

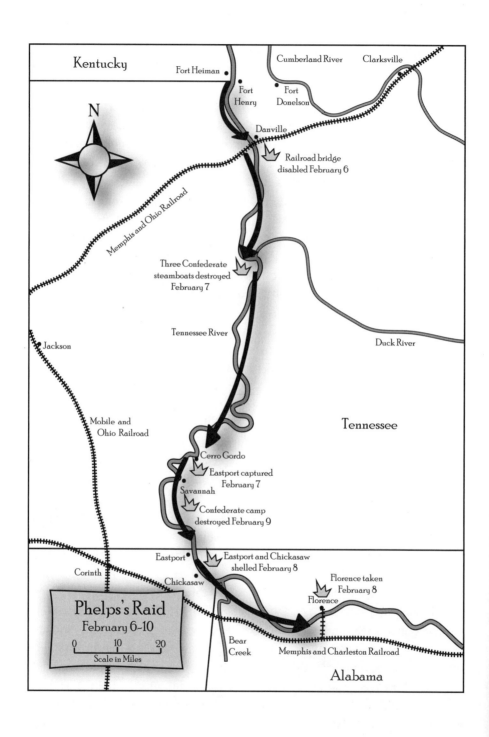

Kentucky

Fort Heiman

Cumberland River   Clarksville

Fort Henry

Fort Donelson

Danville

Railroad bridge disabled February 6

N

Memphis and Ohio Railroad

Three Confederate steamboats destroyed February 7

Tennessee River

Duck River

Jackson

Mobile and Ohio Railroad

Tennessee

Cerro Gordo

Eastport captured February 7

Savannah

Confederate camp destroyed February 9

Eastport

Eastport and Chickasaw shelled February 8

Corinth

Chickasaw

Florence taken February 8

Florence

Phelps's Raid
February 6–10

0   10   20
Scale in Miles

Bear Creek

Memphis and Charleston Railroad

Alabama

that it was the door to the larger prize. This bridge was on everyone's mind, even in the midst of victory. Word even arrived from Halleck to remember the bridge. Foote responded that in accordance with prior instructions he had sent Phelps "to remove the rails, and so far render the bridge incapable of railroad transportation and communication between Bowling Green and Columbus, and afterwards to pursue the rebel gunboats and secure their capture, if possible."[19]

As a result, while Fort Henry itself was important, it was by no means the total goal of the initial action. Rather, Halleck, Grant, and Foote wanted to cut the transportation line between the Confederates at Bowling Green and Columbus: the Memphis, Clarksville, and Louisville Railroad. It was that primary route that allowed the Confederates to utilize interior lines of communication along at least part of the western defensive line. If the rail line was severed, the two major wings of the Confederate defensive line would then be out of rapid contact with each other, with two broad rivers between them. The next series of rail lines that could connect the two were the cotton state lines in Alabama and Mississippi. Consequently, as important as Fort Henry was, it was really the opening to additional opportunities, and Phelps was just the man to take advantage.[20]

There was also more than just the railroad bridge at stake. It was well known that there was Confederate shipping on the Tennessee River south of the fort, with reports of the enemy even building an ironclad along its banks. That shipping, with nothing to stop Phelps, was now wide open for destruction. Moreover, with nothing to stop him, Phelps could also range at will along the river into the cotton states of Alabama and Mississippi, gathering vital intelligence, supplies, and perhaps even recruits. Most notably, a naval flotilla ranging along the river into Mississippi and Alabama, far behind the tottering Confederate defensive line in Kentucky, would be a tremendous strategic advantage for Union operations.[21]

Phelps accordingly led his three timberclads, the *Tyler*, *Lexington*, and *Conestoga*, southward immediately after the fighting at Fort Henry ended. Foote was taking a chance sending the three unarmored boats alone, but there was nothing south of Fort Henry to disrupt the Union naval advance, so the ironclads would not be needed for a major fight. Likewise, the ironclads, some of them heavily damaged in the fighting, were too big and slow to proceed at the rapid pace that Phelps would keep. Also, Phelps had worked with all three boats and knew their capabilities and limitations. The flotilla was a finely tuned unit, and Phelps could utilize its effectiveness much more quickly than if he was saddled with the larger ironclads that were actually not needed. Phelps thus set out quickly, his first goal to reach and render unusable the bridge over the river just to the south.[22]

Phelps steamed hard, occasionally stopping to destroy "a small amount of camp equipage abandoned by the fleeing rebels." Because of his late hour of departure, he did not reach the bridge until after dark on February 6. There he encountered another delay. The railroad bridge swung on a central pivot, which had to be opened to allow traffic on the river through. Phelps found that the Confederates of the 51st Tennessee under Colonel John Chester had closed the bridge and disabled the machinery before they fled; it could not be opened. All the while, Phelps watched as "about 1½ miles above were several rebel transport steamers escaping upstream." Phelps had reached his main objective point, but he wanted so much more.[23]

Thinking quickly, Phelps sent a party of machinists to get the bridge working. "In one hour," Phelps noted, "I had the satisfaction to see the draw open." Phelps was now torn between the bridge and his desire to catch the enemy boats, now with an hour's head start. He quickly decided to leave the slowest of his three gunboats, the *Tyler* under Lieutenant Gwin, at the bridge while he and Lieutenant Shirk and the faster *Lexington* and *Conestoga* pursued the Confederate boats. While Phelps sped away, Lieutenant Gwin and his crew spread out along the railroad and destroyed some of the trestlework leading to the bridge but not damaging the structure itself. It would, after all, become a major asset to the Federal war machine when the Union armies pushed on southward along the river. The *Tyler*'s crew also destroyed Confederate camp equipage and found a set of papers belonging to Confederate naval officer Isaac N. Brown. Later, it was determined that these papers faulted Tilghman for surrendering Fort Henry too early. Indeed, cries of "Treason, Treachery, and Avoidance" were increasingly being hurled at Tilghman, but one of his staff officers chalked it all up to "a spirit of bad feeling on the part of Tennesseans towards Kentuckians." Phelps knew Brown, writing he was "formerly a lieutenant in the Navy, now signing himself 'Lieutenant, C. S. N.,'" so he was happy to report that Brown "had fled with such precipitation as to leave his papers behind." He eventually sent the documents to Foote, where they provided "an official history of the rebel floating preparations on the Mississippi, Cumberland, and Tennessee."[24]

All the while, Phelps raced southward trying to catch the fleeing Confederate steamers. Over the course of the next five dark hours, Phelps and the *Conestoga* outran the *Lexington* and managed to close the gap with the Confederate vessels, eventually forcing all three to a halt. The first Confederate boat, the *Samuel Orr*, Phelps reported, "had on board a quantity of submarine batteries, which very soon exploded." The other two, the *Appleton Belle* and *Lynn Boyd*, huddled near the bank at the mouth of the Duck River and were destroyed by the Confederates themselves. One of them turned out to be laden with "powder, cannon shot, grape, balls, &c." and provided quite a firework show deep in the night. The massive explosion caused major damage, especially to a local residence on the bank of the river. Phelps believed it was "the house of a reported Union man," Judge Creavatt, and he suspected that "there was design in landing the rebels in front of the doomed house," which was, in Phelps's words, "blown to pieces."[25]

So too would have been Phelps, had he not realized what was happening and halted short of the two enemy steamers. Even at a distance of a thousand yards, Phelps's gunboat sustained damage from the falling debris of the two steamboats. "Even there our skylights were shattered by the concussion," he noted, "the light upper deck was raised bodily, doors were forced open, and locks and fastenings everywhere broken." He added, "the whole river for half a mile around about was completely 'beaten up' by the falling fragments and the shower of shot, grape, balls, &c." Having caught the enemy steamers and survived to tell the tale, Phelps wisely stopped his advance to await daylight and the arrival of the *Tyler* and the *Lexington*. The latter had no pilot on board, so was especially vulnerable in the dark. Fortunately, both timberclads soon arrived safely, and Phelps's flotilla was again intact.[26]

Apparently the destruction of only the trestlework leading to the bridge was not enough for Grant. Still at Fort Henry, he received word that the bridge was still standing, and guarded by Confederates. Obviously, the enemy reappeared after the *Tyler* had continued on upriver. Grant asked Commander Walke of the *Carondelet* to move upriver and finish the job, which he did despite leaking magazines and shell rooms. Grant's chief of staff, Joseph D. Webster, Rawlins, and McPherson accompanied him as well. Walke was back at Fort Henry by February 8, the bridge damaged even more. Meanwhile, Phelps was far to the south. There was an apparent miscommunication among the Federal officials; Grant and Foote had not discussed the extent of bridge destruction, and Phelps and Walke certainly had not either. Amazingly, the miscommunication damaged a significant portion of the bridge so that it inhibited river traffic even while three Union gunboats were on the other side of the obstruction.[27]

Phelps knew nothing of the problems to his rear but set out the next morning to inhibit more shipping on the river and to see how far he could go into Mississippi and Alabama. While the deeper draft ironclads could not have made it over some of the lower points, most likely Phelps with the lighter boats would be able to go at least to Florence near the Muscle Shoals, Alabama, the location where only the lightest launches could pass. That would be far enough to instill panic in the Confederate commanders and citizenry.[28]

Phelps moved southward all day on February 7. By dark, the flotilla had reached Hardin County, Tennessee, where they found another prize. At the landing at Cerro Gordo, Phelps discovered the fabled Confederate ironclad *Eastport* under construction. The Confederate workers had fled at Phelps's advance, although a few innocuous rifle shots greeted the Federals. One sailor onboard the *Tyler* remembered, "when we fired two 24 pounder shots at her the crew left it to us." Phelps wisely sent men to check for "means of destruction that might have been devised." Sure enough, the Confederate workers had scuttled the boat, allowing water in through broken suction pipes. Phelps's naval personnel were able to quickly stop the leaks, and the Federal navy now had yet another ironclad. Phelps noted the *Eastport* was "in excellent condition, and already half finished." Around the yard also lay large quantities of lumber and iron plating as well as sundry other items intended for use on the gunboat. Phelps had made a major catch.[29]

Capture of this prize meant Phelps had to make another decision. He had always intended to move on up the river as far as he could go, but he certainly could not leave the *Eastport* alone, even with a small guard. Such security would easily be overrun, and the boat sunk for good. Phelps decided once more to split his force, again leaving the slower *Tyler* at Cerro Gordo to guard the *Eastport* while he and Shirk continued up the river. In the meantime, the *Tyler*'s crew was to load all the valuable supplies and materials for transport back northward; some of the *Tyler*'s crew later tried to claim monetary compensation for a captured prize.[30]

Phelps and Shirk continued southward on February 8, passing Eastport, Mississippi, quietly but capturing two Confederate steamers at Chickasaw, a little farther up the river. The *Sallie Wood* was laid up and not worth much, but the *Muscle* was laden with iron for the Confederate government. Both were taken. Phelps then continued on into Alabama, where he approached

Florence, "at the foot of the Muscle Shoals," he reported. He also described three Confederate steamers that had been driven ahead of him, the *Sam Kirkman*, *Julius*, and *Time*, all three of which were torched by the Confederates to keep them out of Federal hands. Despite some limited fire from the banks, Phelps quickly sent men aboard to save anything they could, and did manage to save some supplies marked "Fort Henry." Numerous other supplies, including more iron plating for the *Eastport*, were on the bank. Phelps had his men load all they could and destroyed the rest.[31]

While his crew was in the midst of destruction, "a deputation of citizens of Florence" came to see Phelps. The locals had gathered some old relics, including a cannon on a carriage but missing its wheels, to defend their homes, but then thought better of it, opting to ask for mercy instead. Thinking the Federals were marauding vandals, they first asked "that they might be made able to quiet the fears of their wives and daughters with assurances from me that they should not be molested." Phelps told them in no uncertain terms "that we were neither ruffians nor savages, and that we were there to protect them from violence and to enforce the law." Relieved, the citizens then turned to their economic concern, their prized railroad bridge over the river. While it aided Florence economically, the bridge was not on a main line, but rather connected the town with the trunk line Memphis and Charleston Railroad south of the river. Phelps again responded compassionately, stating that he could not proceed upriver even if the bridge was not there and "that it could possess, so far as I saw, no military importance." He left the bridge intact.[32]

Having gone as far as he could, the shoals blocking further transit, Phelps turned around and began his voyage back down the river. It had been an extremely profitable invasion, however. Phelps had captured three boats including the *Eastport* and had forced the Confederates to destroy six more that he knew of; Southern reports indicated others were scuttled or burned out of the enemy's view. Only two other large boats were known to be on the river, "and are doubtless hidden in some of the creeks," Phelps noted, "where we shall be able to find them when there is time for the search." Indeed, the *Robb* and *Dunbar*, which had evacuated Fort Henry on February 6 and brought word to the upper-river areas of the pending Federal navy's arrival, had made their escape up Cypress Creek, though Confederate newspapers claimed the *Dunbar* later sank in the creek. Despite all such success, Phelps had nevertheless left a couple of major bridges intact. One was the Florence bridge, which if it did not carry any real military importance would have certainly been destroyed if this raid had occurred later in the war. More troubling was Phelps's passage of Bear Creek, just south of the state line. His two gunboats passed the creek twice (a second time on his way home), little knowing that the Confederates' worst fear was that he would ascend the creek to the vital Memphis and Charleston bridge across the large watershed. While the Florence bridge would have done little damage to the Confederate rail network, destruction of the Bear Creek bridge on a major Confederate trunk line that Leroy Pope Walker described as the "vertebrae of the Confederacy" would have been disastrous. Leonidas Polk, in fact, had sent troops to guard it, portions of James Chalmers's 9th Mississippi and Robert Looney's 38th Tennessee. The people of the region were likewise frightened at the prospect of a Federal attack; one Alabamian correctly notified Judah Benjamin in Richmond, "since the fall of Fort Henry there is nothing to prevent the enemy during high water from ascending the Tennessee with their gunboats and invading North Alabama and North Mississippi."[33]

Phelps missed the opportunity, however, and turned his two gunboats and two captured steamboats northward on the evening of February 8. They reached Cerro Gordo during the night, meeting up once again with Gwin and the *Tyler*. That gunboat's crew had been busy for the last twelve or more hours, loading the lumber on board and preparing to set sail. The crew of the *Lexington* and *Conestoga* joined in the work when they arrived. Phelps reported that he "brought away probably 250,000 feet of the best quality of ship and building timber, and the iron machinery, spikes, plating, nails, &c., belonging to the rebel gunboat." Not wanting the local mill to provide any more lumber, Phelps had it destroyed.[34]

Hoping to be quickly on his way, Phelps then learned of another possibility that he could not resist. During his absence, Gwin had dealt with local citizens, about twenty-five of whom actually joined the Union naval service. They told of a regimental encampment at Savannah just upriver. Phelps had passed the town twice that day but had noticed nothing out of the ordinary. Now, he wanted to return and destroy the camp and break up the regiment. He discussed the plan with Gwin and Shirk, who were of the same opinion. Phelps this time left the *Lexington* to guard the *Eastport* and took the *Tyler*, whose crew had missed some of the more exciting aspects of the raid twice, and the *Conestoga* to Savannah. There, he landed Gwin and several troops as well as a howitzer in the wee hours of the morning on February 9. They found the camp but "had the mortification to find the encampment deserted."

That did not stop them from taking equipment and nearby rifles, as well as mail. They burned what they could not remove, including log huts used as quarters.[35]

The raid on the Confederate camp was made to exploit the obvious Unionism of the area. Gwin reported that much of the regiment at Savannah was "'pressed' men," and the flotilla had seen enormous evidence of Unionism during its voyage. Phelps himself wrote, "we have met with the most gratifying proofs of loyalty everywhere across Tennessee, and in the portions of Mississippi and Alabama we visited most affecting instances greeted us almost hourly." As examples, Phelps reported, "men, women, and children several times gathered in crowds of hundreds, shouted their welcome, and hailed their national flag with an enthusiasm there was no mistaking. It was genuine and heartfelt." The officers talked to some of these people, who indicated that the Confederates had treated them badly. "Tears flowed freely down the cheeks of men as well as of women, and there were those who had fought under the Stars and Stripes at Monter[r]ey who in this manner testified to their joy."[36]

Phelps admitted that the Unionism in Tennessee "astonished us not a little," and even in Mississippi and Alabama the feeling was the same although "what was said was guarded." There, the people told him, "we know there are many Unionists among us, but a reign of terror makes us afraid of our shadows." He also told of "whole communities who on our approach fled to the woods," but he blamed that on the Confederate steamers who had spread the word of "our coming with fire-brands, burning, destroying, ravishing, and plundering." That said, Phelps brought back with him the twenty-five recruits who had joined the Union military, and said that he could have raised a regiment had he stayed a week. "The people of the South are heartily sick and tired of this Rebel government," noted one Kentuckian, "they say it promised much and performed nothing."[37]

Once reunited with the *Lexington* at Cerro Gordo, Phelps set sail later on February 9 with the three gunboats as well as the *Eastport*, *Sallie Wood*, and *Muscle* all in tow. Some trouble emerged as the *Muscle* began leaking too badly to continue. Phelps reported that "all efforts failing to prevent her sinking, we were forced to abandon her, and with her a considerable quantity of fine lumber." More trouble developed when the flotilla reached the railroad bridge, which Walke and the *Carondelet* had damaged further while Phelps was south of it. Phelps reported, "we are having trouble in getting through the draw of the bridge here"; the main trouble was getting the large *Eastport* through. Delayed several hours, Phelps in the meantime wrote a report for Foote. The little flotilla reached Fort Henry later on February 10, and Foote was obviously overjoyed at the news. He wrote Gideon Welles, "his work has been thorough and merits the highest praise." He later wrote that Phelps "has, with consummate skill, courage, and judgment, performed a highly beneficial service to the Government, which no doubt will be appreciated."[38]

Taken all together, this "cruise up the Tennessee River," as Foote described it, blazed a trail that the Federal armies would ultimately follow. It refocused attention on the mess the Confederate defensive line was in out west, and just how vulnerable the Confederacy was. Taking all the information in at his headquarters at Bowling Green, Albert Sidney Johnston had some difficult decisions to make—mainly courtesy of Ledyard Phelps and his three little gunboats that pierced the Confederacy to its heart.[39]

The South reacted with panic at the events of early February 1862. A Confederate soldier in Columbus, Kentucky, wrote his wife, "I hear the Yankee gunboats are at Florence, Alabama!!!" Newspapers reported, "the Lincoln gunboats seem to have had quite a frolic up the Tennessee." Not only were the details of the loss of Fort Henry given but also the effects. Fort Henry was literally the key that unlocked the lower South, and newspapers in places like Memphis, Nashville, and New Orleans nervously reported the continuing movements of the Federal navy's thrust southward along the Tennessee River. "Private and general dispatches sustain the report that reconnoitering gunboats had gone up the Tennessee River as high as Florence," read one New Orleans paper. The Lynchburg *Virginian* reported, "the Federal gunboats reached Florence about 4 o'clock PM yesterday."[40]

The Confederate high command was similarly shaken. In Richmond, Jefferson Davis informed Alabama officials that he was sending troops to Tuscumbia. "I hope you may also capture the gunboats," he added naively. The government also sent a new general, former Secretary of War Leroy Pope Walker, to take command in north Alabama. The shock also hit army headquarters in Bowling Green. Hardee wrote, "the loss of the Tennessee River and the probable loss of the Cumberland renders our position here not so formidable." Johnston was likewise distraught. He began issuing a multitude of orders to contain some of the damage, for example, moving all boats as far up the Tennessee River as they could go. Evidently concerned that the enemy could use the railroad to get in the rear of Columbus, he issued orders to destroy the railroad bridges from the Tennessee River to Humbolt. Johnston also cautioned Polk to send telegraph messages via Montgomery, Alabama, rather than Florence, because he was concerned that the enemy had captured the telegraph station and had the capability to listen in. The telegraph operator at Tuscumbia reported that the enemy had indeed taken the Florence office and "found out nearly everything that was passing over the line before he was informed of their having landed." The quick-thinking operator disconnected the Florence line "and cut them off." Even so, one newspaper claimed the perpetrators sent "some wondrous message to Richmond."[41]

To determine exactly what could and should be done, Johnston's inner circle in Bowling Green quickly met to plot strategy. By this time that circle also included a sick Beauregard, who had been transferred from Virginia and had come to talk with Johnston at his headquarters in Kentucky. One Tennessean described him as "a small man—gray hair, dark complection, would weigh about 130 or 35—large mouth, black eyes . . . restless looking man." Johnston, Beauregard, and Hardee met on February 7 in Beauregard's quarters at the Covington House, and despite the need for positive morale-building rhetoric, all agreed that these dire times required significant actions. In effect, they all agreed it was imperative that "preparations should at once be made for the removal of this army to Nashville, in rear of the Cumberland River."[42]

To be sure, any retreat was bound to cause morale and political problems. Johnston had been hailed as the savior of the west, and a retreat would entail giving up large swaths of Kentucky and Tennessee. Indeed, a retreat could not stop even at Nashville, because a defeat at Fort Donelson would put the Cumberland River in Union hands and allow the Federal gunboats to travel at will up and down its navigable stretches as well. Johnston accordingly had to get his army south of the Cumberland River soon if he intended to avoid interference from the gunboats. To really be safe he would have to get out of the bowl of the Tennessee River as well, which meant retreating all the way into Alabama. There seemed no other choice, as Fort Donelson evidently could be depended on no more than Fort Henry had been against the vaunted ironclads. Johnston so wrote Secretary Benjamin in Richmond the next day: "the slight resistance at Fort Henry indicates that the best open earthworks are not reliable to meet successfully a vigorous attack of iron-clad gunboats, and, although now supported by a considerable force, I think the gunboats of the enemy will probably take Fort Donelson without the necessity of employing their land force in co-operation, as seems to have been done at Fort Henry."[43]

All the information Johnston could gather from his generals nearer the scene confirmed his concerns. John B. Floyd, recently transferred from Virginia with his brigade of four Virginia regiments and one from Mississippi, agreed. He wrote, "if the best information I can gather about these iron-clad boats be true they are nearly invulnerable, and therefore they can probably go wherever sufficient fuel and depth of water can be found, unless met by opposing gunboats." Even Beauregard, whom Johnston ordered to go to the now separated Columbus, added that "it also becomes evident that by the possession of that river [Tennessee] the enemy can concentrate rapidly, by means of his innumerable transports, all his disposable forces on any point along its banks, either to attack Nashville in rear or cut off the communications of Columbus."[44]

Johnston added it all up in a letter to Richmond on February 8: "the occurrence of the misfortune of losing the fort [Donelson] will cut off the communication of the force here, under General Hardee, from the south bank of the Cumberland," he wrote. "To avoid the disastrous consequences of such an event I ordered General Hardee yesterday to make (as promptly as it could be done) preparations to fall back to Nashville and cross the river." Johnston added that it would have come to that anyway: "the movements of the enemy on my right flank would have made a retrograde in that direction to confront the enemy indispensable in a short time. But the probability of having the passage of this army corps across the Cumberland intercepted by the gunboats of the enemy admits of no delay in making the movement." For political cover, he added, "Generals Beauregard and Hardee are equally with myself impressed with the necessity of withdrawing our force from this line at once."[45]

Consequently, Johnston's central Kentucky army, followed by numerous civilians, was in full retreat by mid-February, having been flanked out of position without a single shot being fired in Kentucky. Those fateful shots at Fort Henry had done all the damage. Moreover, the Bowling Green enclave was not the only bastion affected. While Grant, Foote, and Phelps in dramatic fashion turned Nashville and made it untenable, the same movement also made the Columbus defenses unsustainable. For all the work Polk had put into making the area one of the most heavily defended Gibraltars in the Confederacy, the simple turning movement at Fort Henry had made it all for naught. "It was also determined," Beauregard wrote that same February 7, "that the possession of the Tennessee River by the enemy, resulting from the fall of Fort Henry, separates this army at Bowling Green from the one at Columbus, Ky., which must henceforth act independently of each other until they can again be brought together." As a result, the generals decided, "the main body of that [Columbus] army should fall back" to Humbolt or perhaps Grand Junction, Tennessee, Beauregard even suggesting Grenada or Jackson, Mississippi. Because of the layout of the rivers, Columbus was not quite the emergency that Nashville was due to being able to withdraw along the Mississippi River instead of across it, but Beauregard especially was convinced that it too was useless. He talked of leaving a small force to delay the Federals at Columbus while taking the material and weaponry to Island No. Ten and Fort Pillow for similar delaying actions. He saw the next real defensive point as Memphis, however, "where another bold stand will be made." In fact, Beauregard, who was soon on the way to command that force, talked of Columbus being "abandoned altogether, its armament and garrison being transferred." He went so far as to say that trying to maintain Columbus would "be to jeopardize not only the safety of that army, but necessarily of the whole Mississippi Valley."[46]

It is ironic that such minor bloodshed at Fort Henry, less than fifty casualties on each side, could result in such large strategic changes, but that was the essence of working with rivers and railroads. The mere capture of the main impediment on the Tennessee River had allowed the Federals to break the key Confederate railroad joining the two halves of the Confederate western defensive line. The further incursion of Federal gunboats along the entirety of the southward leg of the river forced a rethinking of all Confederate strategy. Certainly no garrison was safe with the Federals possessing the ability to land troops hundreds of miles to the rear of each wing. Additionally, the performance of the gunboats at Fort Henry caused the Confederate high command to place little confidence in Fort Donelson. It therefore quickly became the crisis point in that blocking the Cumberland River for at least a time would allow Johnston to get his entire right wing south of that river and out of immediate danger. For all its having been overshadowed in the postwar history of the Civil War, the capture of Fort Henry certainly paid tremendous dividends to the Federals, and it caused miserable hours of contemplation for the Confederate high command.[47]

If the fall of Fort Henry had a major effect on the Confederate line at Bowl-ing Green and Columbus, it also had an even greater effect on the rest of the Confederacy. Leonidas Polk argued correctly on February 8 that "active preparations on the part of the Government for the defense of this frontier seem now indispensable." He was not the only one thinking that way, and all across the Confederacy troops were marshaled for movement to Tennessee. In fact, the highest levels of the Confederate government suddenly awakened to the Fort Henry crisis, and order after order began to flow from Richmond to solidify the northern border. Whether it would be in time or not was any-body's guess.[48]

Secretary of War Judah P. Benjamin was the main cog in ordering troops to Tennessee. He sent numerous units from all over the Confederacy in addi-tion to the earlier movement of John B. Floyd's five regiments from Virginia. He wrote Governor Harris on February 11, "I have also sent a fine regiment to Decatur from Pensacola, and have ordered three Tennessee regiments and one Georgia regiment from Virginia to Knoxville."[49]

By far, however, the major reinforcement came from the Gulf coast, where Jefferson Davis's political policy of assuring everyone a defense had caused huge problems in the actual defense of the Confederacy. Thousands and thousands of Confederate troops were frittering away their time guarding the coastal regions of Louisiana, Mississippi, Alabama, and Florida while the Federals were overrunning the northern defensive line. Davis now began to wake up to the problems, which were already snowballing out of control.[50]

Benjamin called on two main commands to send reinforcements to Ten-nessee. One was the New Orleans defense under Major General Mansfield Lovell. On February 8, Benjamin wrote Lovell: "the President desires that as soon as possible on receipt of this letter you dispatch 5,000 men to Colum-bus to re-enforce that point, sorely threatened by largely superior forces." He went on to state the rationale, that "the menacing aspect of affairs in Kentucky has induced the withdrawal from points, not in immediate danger, of every man that can be spared to prevent the enemy from penetrating into Tennessee or passing Columbus." Benjamin also added, "we hope to stem the tide till the new levies called out from the State shall be in condition to take the field." Knowing Lovell would not be in favor of reducing his command, Benjamin lectured, "New Orleans is to be defended from above by defeating the enemy at Columbus; the forces now withdrawn from you are for the defense of your own command, and the exigencies of the public defense allow us no alternative."[51]

As expected, Lovell was none too happy about losing troops, and especially his best ones (Lovell was to send "five or six regiments of his best troops at New Orleans"), but he could not argue with direct orders. He could, however, negotiate where they were sent. A few days after Fort Henry fell, Johnston and his commanders had decided Columbus was untenable anyway and asked Lovell to send the troops to lower-tier areas along the Memphis and Charleston Railroad. Johnston, in fact, wanted four regiments to go to Memphis and one to Iuka, but Lovell countered that Corinth, Mississippi, would be the most logical place. "Corinth is, in my judgment, an important strategical point," Lovell argued. Of course, Corinth was also a good place from which he could also recall his troops quickly if he needed them.[52]

In the end, Lovell wound up sending one of his best brigades under Brigadier General Daniel Ruggles. He first sent the 13th Louisiana and then followed it with four more regiments and Ruggles himself. In all, the 13th, 16th, 17th, 18th, and 19th Louisiana regiments all made their way northward in mid-February, some as early as February 14. They went to various spots such as Corinth and its nearby river landings, hoping to stop some of the Federal navy's incursions into the area.[53]

Braxton Bragg's enclave at Pensacola and Mobile was also asked to send troops to Tennessee. "The President desires that you will as soon as possible send to Knoxville all the troops you can spare from your command without immediate danger," Benjamin wrote Bragg on February 8, "and he hopes that the number will be at least four regiments." As with Lovell, Benjamin explained the administration's thinking: "the condition of affairs in Kentucky and Tennessee demands from us the most vigorous effort for defense, and General A. S. Johnston is so heavily outnumbered, that it is scarcely possible for him to maintain his whole line without large additional reinforcements." The secretary then went on to explain that "by thus subtracting something from other points, where the pressure is not so great, we hope to enable him to defend his lines until the new levies ordered from all the States shall be in condition to take the field."[54]

Bragg responded two days later. "I send a regiment to-day to Decatur, Ala., to save our railroad bridge," he wrote, but with a Union naval column approaching the gulf under David Farragut and Benjamin Butler, he did not feel safe to send any more. "If Farragut and Butler are destined for this point my force is too weak to spare more," Bragg wrote. He continued his equivocal posturing two days later when he informed one of his commanders, "I am not yet decided to send them," arguing that the affairs in Tennessee were not so bad and that "our disaster at Roanoke Island is much more serious." Bragg quickly came to realize just how wrong he was. On February 15 he sent the War Department a lecture on his views of what should happen. "Our means and resources are too much scattered," he wrote, adding that everything of less importance should be abandoned and the forces "concentrated for a heavy blow upon the enemy where we can best assail him. Kentucky is now that point."[55]

Bragg first sent the 9th Mississippi, and a few days later he also dispatched the 5th Georgia and 20th and 23rd Alabama to Knoxville. Many more troops soon followed, especially after the ensuing events at Fort Donelson, and Bragg eventually brought several more brigades as well as coming northward himself in late February. By that time, Lovell at New Orleans was also sending additional troops, a motley combination of state troops and militia. In any case, the first efforts to reinforce Johnston in Tennessee were begun not as public memory believes after Fort Donelson, but after Fort Henry. As such, Fort Henry serves as the key stroke of breaking the Confederate defensive line *and* starting what would ultimately become the concentration at Corinth that would result in Shiloh.[56]

"This is a great victory and a *big* thing," wrote Union staff officer I. P. Rumsey after Fort Henry's fall. Indeed it was, as Foote described it, a good day's work. Contrary to what many historians depict, the major crisis for the Confederacy emerged because of the fall of Fort Henry. Although many buffs and not a few historians maintain that the events of mid-February were the real awakening of the Confederate high command, it was clearly early February and Fort Henry that actually first sent the South reeling. Most significantly, Fort Henry allowed the Union forces access by naval as well as land forces all the way into the interior of the South, into the lower cotton states of Alabama and Mississippi. While it would be some time before they took advantage of this opportunity, the Federals nevertheless opened the gate at Fort Henry that would never again be shut. The citizens of the Tennessee Valley certainly realized the ramifications, one writing that with the fall of Fort Henry there was "nothing now to stop them." Commander Stembel of the *Cincinnati* said it best when he argued, "suffice it to say it was the entering wedge to all our subsequent successes in the South West; and the first step toward the opening of the Mississippi River."[57]

And Fort Henry was not out of the limelight even after its capture. Certainly, it was in constant danger of being attacked in an effort on the Confederates' part to retake it and once again close the river to Union use. Halleck was afraid of such a development and ordered Grant to fortify the place. At the same time, however, Fort Donelson was also growing in importance. The fact that the Confederates were already transferring and concentrating troops there just a couple of days after Fort Henry's fall made such a situation extremely bothersome for the Federals at Fort Henry. Consequently, the importance of capturing Fort Donelson was partly an effort to make Fort Henry totally safe.[58]

The other logic to attacking Fort Donelson was its position on the Cumberland River, which opened the way to Nashville. If the Confederates could be driven from Fort Donelson, Federal gunboats could, much as they did on the Tennessee River, range far and wide along the waterway and capture Clarksville and Nashville, the latter being an extremely important supply, political, and psychological center for Tennessee and the Confederacy. Thus the primary importance of Nashville and Fort Donelson to the Confederacy was to hold them long enough for Johnston's army at Bowling Green to withdraw (because of Fort Henry's fall) out of the shallow bowl of the Cumberland River's path. If Fort Donelson was untenable, as Confederate commanders thought immediately after Fort Henry's fall, then a temporary holding of the fort would at least allow Johnston's wing of the army to escape. As a result, Fort Donelson, to both Union and Confederate commanders, became a temporary strategic goal while the really important prizes were the Tennessee River, the railroad bridge at Danville, and the gateway, Fort Henry.[59]

Such a Fort Henry/Tennessee River–centric mindset is seen in the correspondence of the day. Grant himself wrote in his early missives to Halleck after Fort Henry that he would take Fort Donelson on February 8 "and return to Fort Henry with the forces employed, unless it looks feasible to occupy that place [Fort Donelson] with a small force that could retreat easily to the main body. I shall regard it more in the light of an advance grand guard than as a permanent post." Clearly, the Tennessee River, running parallel with the Mississippi River down the entirety of the State of Tennessee, was the true line

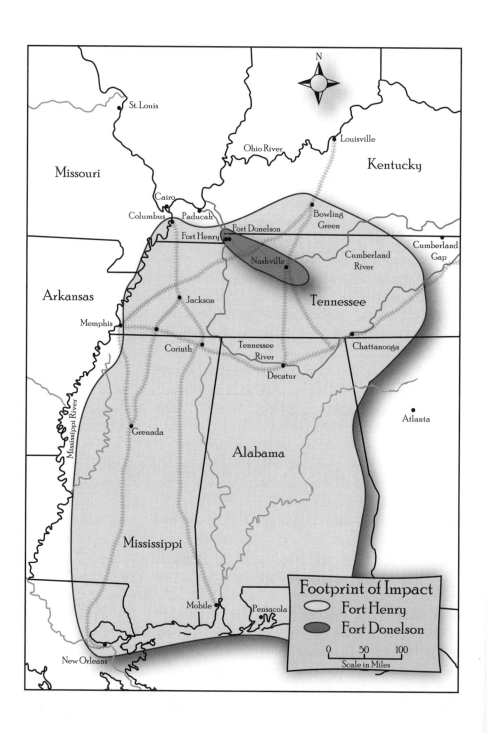

of operations to Grant. Others had a Mississippi/Tennessee Valley context firmly in mind as well; George B. McClellan in Washington wrote on February 7, "a combined movement on Memphis will be next in order." Lower-level officers exhibited the same attitude, Navy Department officer Henry A. Wise writing Foote: "then, if you don't get down first, the blue jackets will paddle up and down the great [Mississippi] valley, and make a name to ring in all time to come."[60]

The Tennessee River thus continued to be the focus of current and future operations for the strategic Union advance and Confederate defense via concentration, which was already occurring in the wake of Fort Henry's fall. On the other hand, it would be dangerous to discount altogether the coming operations on the Cumberland River because they would play an extremely, and in fact undreamed-of, role in the war in the west. Both the Union safety of Fort Henry and future Federal movements along the Tennessee River depended on what happened next. Major interests were therefore at stake, so all attention quickly turned to the Confederate bastion on the Cumberland River. Still, one Confederate soldier's wife from East Tennessee was completely accurate in predicting four days before: "if the Federals ever take Fort Henry we are ruined."[61]

8

"I Think We Can Take It; at All Events, We Can Try"

Ulysses S. Grant kept a firm eye on his next objective. If the capture of Fort Henry was the key that opened the Confederate heartland, Fort Donelson now took on the next critical role. Action picked up quickly as a result. While Phelps faced little confrontation with the enemy, it was not so with the other major activity going on at the time. While the Confederates did not, and could not, combat Phelps, they threw much of their western defense capability into holding Fort Donelson.[1]

Even if Fort Donelson was a level below that of Fort Henry's large strategic significance, its importance was still clear. Grant and Foote could not consolidate their victories and continue operations while a nearby Confederate fort held out. Protection of their Fort Henry gains, therefore, was paramount in their minds. Then, too, capture of Fort Donelson would open crucial strategic areas such as middle Tennessee and Nashville, which, although not as vast or important as the areas unlocked by Fort Henry's demise, were still extremely important. Any damage done in the process to the enemy armies, whether those at the Confederate garrison at Donelson or Johnston's retreating army if Donelson fell, would be an added benefit. In fact, if the army at Donelson could be captured or the passage of Johnston's troops over the Cumberland River blocked, either might result in the elimination of a large portion of the enemy's troops.[2]

The opposite was true for the Confederates. They had to hold Fort Donelson to retake Fort Henry and close the floodgates into the Confederate heartland. If that was not possible, they had at least to hold long enough for Johnston to withdraw south of the Cumberland River before giving up the defense and getting the Fort Donelson army out safely. Albert Sidney Johnston later famously declared, "I determined to fight for Nashville at Donelson," but the record is clear that Nashville was already doomed. In fact, in the same statement Johnston noted that the evacuation of Bowling Green and the move south of the Cumberland River were "ordered before and executed while the battle was being fought at Donelson."[3]

Either way, all attention now turned to Fort Donelson. Despite its more limited strategic and operational possibilities as compared to Fort Henry, it was nevertheless center stage for the coming operations and would in large part determine just how extensive Fort Henry's consequences would be.[4]

Fort Donelson presented significantly different military circumstances than had Fort Henry. "Fort Donelson is not a mud fort, like Fort Henry," declared one Confederate newspaper, "and we have properly based confidence in its strength." It was impressive, especially to those new to the war-making business. One Tennessean wrote that it was "the first fort I ever saw," and then described it in detail: it was "formed by a deep ditch about 8 feet deep and 10 feet wide and an embankment about 10 feet wide and about every 50 yards or one hundred yards a big cannon planted in the imbankment." He marveled at the big guns, especially the river batteries, when they were fired for practice. He wrote that if "any one had have told me that I could have sean the ball I would have told them it was not so but I could see the ball as plane as you can see a bird a flying."[5]

As with Fort Henry, everyone expected the Federal naval arm to be the all-determining factor at Fort Donelson. After his escape from the Tennessee River, engineer Jeremy Gilmer warned, "the attack expected here is a combined one; gunboats by water and a land force in the rear." He then stated what everyone was thinking: "the greatest danger, in my opinion, is from the gunboats, which appear to be well protected from our shot." He went on to blame Fort Henry's fall on "the want of skill in the men who served the guns, and not to the invulnerability of the boats themselves," but he clearly saw that Fort Donelson's gunners, just as green and inexperienced as Fort Henry's had been, would be overmatched by the now comparatively veteran gunboat crews. The newly minted veteran Confederate gun crews would not be a factor as they were even now on the way north to Union prison camps. Most of the lower-level Confederates did not believe that the gunboats were susceptible, either; Jacob Culbertson, manning the batteries, agreed with Gilmer, writing that the disaster at Fort Henry served "to inspire distrust of our own guns and a belief in the invulnerability of the gunboats." Ironically, while all concern seemed to center on the enemy navy, Gilmer was much less concerned about Grant's infantry. "With the preparations that are now being made here I feel much confidence that we can make a successful resistance against a land attack," the engineer said. "We are making Herculean efforts to strengthen our parapets—making narrow embrasures with sand bags, and if we can have ten days we hope to make bomb-proofs over the guns." While the covers would never be built, the sides of the embrasures were lined with "rawhides" and tarpaulins were placed over the guns when not in use.[6]

Other Confederate officers were more upbeat about the chances of holding Fort Donelson at least for a time, especially if the Confederacy had a few breaks. One officer reported that the river was falling "and often falls from 5 to 6 feet in twenty-four hours." Obviously thinking mainly in terms of the chief threat that had so confounded Fort Henry, the Federal navy, he recognized the possibilities: "if it runs down rapidly as I hope it will from the cold weather, we will not be attacked this rise; before another rise I will have the works safe."[7]

The chief concern was obviously the water approach, but a few hoped they could even defeat the Union navy. Unlike the Tennessee River, which split around Panther Island north of Fort Henry and was wide enough to accommodate all the gunboats Foote had side by side, the Cumberland River was much narrower. Even in the wider Tennessee the gunboats had found it difficult to keep apace, but the significantly smaller Cumberland would no doubt hem in the Federal navy to a localized area. Moreover, the chute that led to Fort Donelson was long and straight, allowing the Confederate gunners a wide-open field of fire. The guns of Fort Donelson also sat much higher on the bank than those at Fort Henry, and this too was a major plus, allowing plunging fire on the unarmored decks of the ironclads. One Confederate summed it up well: the "great advantage it has is in the narrowness of the stream and the necessity of the boats approaching our works by straight and narrow channel for 1½ miles. . . . This makes the field of fire required for the guns so very narrow, that it admits of the construction of very narrow embrasures, which we are now constructing."[8]

Largely because of the terrain features and the hope for some luck, many Confederates managed to be upbeat even amid the crisis engulfing the western

Confederacy. One surprisingly wrote home, "we have able and experienced generals here, and as fine a body of troops as can be found anywhere nearly all of them are well armed." He was optimistic about keeping Fort Donelson, but Ulysses S. Grant would have something to say about that.[9]

For all Grant's impulsiveness, aggressiveness, and willpower, he simply could not will matters to move as quickly as he wanted. He had intended to move as early as February 8, even sending out detailed instructions for the movement pending reconnaissance and supply. He did the same thing almost every day thereafter, but he was sorely mistaken in the army's abilities and the weather's cooperation. In fact, on that very day Jacob Lauman wrote that he held his command in readiness to march according to orders, but "there could not well be a worse day for marching." The weather turned cold and disagreeable with light snow, and Grant just could not move. Federal reinforcements (as well as officers' wives) consequently began to stack up at Fort Henry, one Illinoisan writing in his diary, "a fine sight opened to my view this morning the river was high and the shore was lined with steamboats and the ground was covered with tents and soldiers." Another described the area around Fort Henry: "to look at the river has the appearance of St. Louis from the number of steamers tied up." Another described a nighttime view as the boats were lit up with "red and blue lights" while "along the bluffs thousands of fires were blazing." Still, these handsome accommodations were not as fine as what many were used to at Fort Holt and Paducah. One soldier wrote that without their stoves they built "a big fire of logs and set on our coffee pot & camp kettle & do our cooking and stand round in the smoke till our eyes are nearly out and we don't sleep as warm on the ground as we did in our houses."[10]

The delay certainly did not keep Grant from planning. One newspaper correspondent reported telling the general goodbye, whereupon Grant alerted him that he was about to attack and he had better remain to get the scoop. The correspondent asked what he knew about Fort Donelson, and Grant admitted he did not know how strong it was. "But," he added, "I think we can take it; at all events, we can try." To help plan, Grant did something he rarely if ever did: he held a council of war on February 10 in his quarters in the rear cabins on the *New Uncle Sam*. Smith and McClernand were there, of course, and Lew Wallace was also invited. He responded almost like a boy going to town for the first time: "how often had I read of such affairs in books of war! Now I was to see one and have a voice in it." Unfortunately, Wallace only saw a theatrical show by John A. McClernand. The quiet Grant simply stated, "the question for consideration, gentlemen, is whether we shall march against Fort Donelson or wait for reinforcements. I should like to have your views." He polled Smith first, being senior, and Smith indicated they should advance "without the loss of a day." Grant next turned to McClernand, but the politician would not give such a simple answer. In fact, he took out a proposition paper and read for what must have seemed like hours. "The proceeding smacked of a political caucus," Wallace remembered, "and I thought both Grant and Smith grew restive before the paper was finished." Wallace studied Grant as "he smoked, but never said a word. In all probability he was framing the orders of march which were issued that night." Once McClernand was done, Grant turned to Wallace, who was smart enough to simply answer, "Let us go, by all means; the sooner the better." Grant responded, "Very well, gentlemen, we will set out immediately. Orders will be sent you. Get your commands ready."[11]

Even with the consensus, Grant still could not move on such a fast timetable as other problems surfaced as well. Although he explored eastward with his staff to within a few miles of Fort Donelson on February 7, he later wrote that on February 8, the very day he had wanted to take Fort Donelson, "at present we are perfectly locked in by high water and bad roads, and prevented from acting offensively, as I should like to do. The banks are higher at the water's edge than farther back, leaving a wide margin of low land to bridge over before anything can be done inland. . . . I contemplated taking Fort Donelson to-day with infantry and cavalry alone, but all my troops may be kept busily engaged in saving what we now have from the rapidly-rising waters."[12]

Grant also had to incorporate the vast influx of new troops arriving at Fort Henry, including the regiments Halleck was shuttling down to Cairo as well as the ten regiments Buell sent, four in Charles Cruft's brigade already sent to the Green River and six green regiments just organized, four from Ohio and two from Indiana. Those were delayed in coming, but enough arrived by February 10 that Grant organized a new brigade of three or four regiments for both McClernand's and Smith's divisions. He also sent out an order that "all regimental officers will immediately take up quarters with commands and not board on steamers, as the general commanding regrets to see has been done." Grant likewise had to curb the "pilfering and marauding disposition shown by some of the men of this command." He ordered that all offenses "be traced back to their officers for punishment," and warned: "in an enemy's country, where so much more could be done by a manly and humane policy to advance the cause which we all have so deeply at heart, it is astonishing that men can be found so wanton as to destroy, pillage, and burn indiscriminately, without injury." The men thus endured a tight rein, one Illinoisan writing home that they "get as much Crackers and Bacon as we want but not a drop of whiskey I have seen offered 5 dollars for a quart of Rat gut."[13]

Another reason for the delay was the absence of the navy. Halleck informed Washington that "Commodore Foote, with disabled gunboats, has returned to Cairo—gunboats for repairs; will soon return to the field." That could not happen soon enough for Halleck. Very desirous of naval support, especially with an army commander he did not fully trust, Halleck began to put pressure on Foote to send what he could to the Cumberland. He even had Cullum at Cairo to act as his eyes and ears. Halleck wrote on February 9, "if three gunboats can be spared from Cairo and made efficient, I wish them sent up the Cumberland to Dover and Clarksville." The next day he wrote Cullum again, "persuade Flag Officer Foote, if possible, to send gunboats up the Cumberland. Two will answer if he can send no more. They must precede the transports. . . . All we want is gunboats to precede the transports." Assistant Secretary of War Thomas A. Scott, also in Cairo, was similarly pushing for naval support.[14]

Halleck and Cullum found Foote stubborn. Indeed, the flag officer had written his wife after Fort Henry, "I never again will go out to a fight half prepared." Cullum informed Halleck of Foote's resistance to new operations on February 9, writing, "I have already consulted with Foote, anticipating your orders. He can't send gunboats up Cumberland. Will see him again." Grant got into the politicking as well, writing Foote, "I do not feel justified in going without some of your gunboats to co-operate." Halleck even appealed to Foote's vanity, writing, "you have gained great distinction by your capture of Fort Henry. Everybody recognizes your services. Make your name famous in history by the capture of Fort Donelson and Clarksville." He then added, "the taking of these places is a military necessity. Delays add strength to them more than to us. Act quickly, even though only half ready."[15]

Foote had far too many things on his mind to be hurried. He still had to prepare the boats for action, the largest issue again being crews. Then, the devout Foote took time for church as well, attending services that Sunday, February 9, in Cairo. When informed that the minister was sick that day, Foote himself took the pulpit and gave a sermon on John 14, reading the verse in which Jesus stated, "Let not your heart be troubled: ye believe in God, believe also in me." Although one *Mound City* sailor reported it was "a real good plain common sense sermon, with which everyone seemed pleased," Foote expected to be reviled for his words but decided to do so anyway, stating, "we are dependent upon God as individuals and as a nation, and that without his blessing we must ignominiously fail in the great work before us." While expecting to be criticized, he did not anticipate it from one particular quarter. His small six- or seven-year-old niece retorted that the flag officer had said it wrong in the sermon; he should have said, "Let not your heart be troubled: ye believe in God, believe also in *the gun-boats*."[16]

The army officers finally wore Foote down despite his promise never again to sail half prepared. On February 11 he wrote the Navy Department, "I am off again to-night with other gunboats and have to transfer the men again, which causes the greatest dissatisfaction among them and 30 have run from one steamer to avoid transfer. We suffer for want of men." Continuing, he wrote, "I regret that the want of men will render this expedition less efficient than it should be, considering its object." Foote wrote Secretary Welles himself on February 11: "I leave again to-night with the *Louisville*, *Pittsburg*, and *St. Louis*. . . . I go reluctantly, as we are very short of men, and transferring men from vessel to vessel, as we have to do, is having a very demoralizing effect upon them; 28 ran off to-day, hearing that they were again to be sent out of their vessels." He added significantly, "I shall do all in my power to render the gunboats effective in the fight, although they are not properly manned, but I must go, as General Halleck wishes it. If we could wait ten days, and I had men, I would go with eight mortar boats and six armored boats and conquer."[17]

Complicating matters even more was army meddling. Grant at Fort Henry issued orders that the *Carondelet*, which had been left in the Tennessee River at Fort Henry, be sent to the Cumberland as well as Phelps's timberclads upon their return from their voyage up the Tennessee River. As a result, Commander Walke, commanding the *Carondelet*, was in a quandary. He was torn between Foote's desires to defend Fort Henry and Grant's orders to move to Fort Donelson. He decided he must follow Grant's instructions but wrote Foote about his concerns: "I am (or the *Carondelet* is) very slow, and General Grant desires that I should be at Fort Donelson as soon as I can get there."

Foote once more acquiesced, sending Phelps orders to join the expedition as well.[18]

The naval contingent moved forward from Cairo on the evening of February 11, Foote bringing the returned *St. Louis* (now his flagship) as well as the undamaged and uninvolved *Louisville* and *Pittsburg*, the latter with thirty-four men transferred from the damaged *Essex*; the *Louisville* carried thirty-three of the *Cincinnati*'s sailors. The flotilla moved through Paducah despite a problem with a boiler on the *Pittsburg* and a fire that broke out on the gunboat; Lieutenant Egbert Thompson reported, "prompt action in extinguishing the fire saved us, perhaps, from a fearful calamity." The *Pittsburg* was able to be repaired en route and kept up with the formation, which picked up two of the three timberclads on the way. At various places, the flotilla also took on pilots familiar with the Cumberland River and began steaming up the Cumberland against the current, hoping to be in position near Fort Donelson in time to aid the army or, better yet, to reduce Fort Donelson just as they had Fort Henry.[19]

But the navy would have to hurry to beat Grant. He was already probing eastward, sending cavalry "to within a mile of Fort Donelson" as early as February 7. Numerous scouting patrols went forward in the ensuing days, prompting Colonel T. Lyle Dickey of the 4th Illinois Cavalry to argue, one relieved trooper wrote home, "that his men was tired and the horses was not fit to go until they got some rest." Engineer James B. McPherson scouted toward the fort as well, creating some slight skirmishing. Grant was champing at the bit more and more as the days passed, eager to be off and see what this fabled Fort Donelson was like. Confidence was thus rampant in the Federal high command. Assistant Secretary of War Thomas A. Scott, in fact, crowed on February 11, "victory seems to crown all our efforts."[20]

Unknown to Grant, Fort Donelson was growing stronger and stronger by the hour. In just a few days, the garrison had come a long way from the timid fear of February 7 when word of a Union attack forced the entire complement of troops to the lines, "hourly expecting an attack by an overwhelming force by land and water," one Tennessean remembered. It was obviously a false alarm, but it illustrated the fort's weakness at that point. Now, Fort Donelson was growing stronger each day, one Confederate staff officer noting that additional troops "are arriving by every boat that can be found to bring them down from Clarksville." Unknown to them, those troops were enjoying their last bit of good times. One 18th Tennessee soldier wrote in his diary, "went gliding down the beautiful stream of Cumberland River favored with cabin passage."[21]

Albert Sidney Johnston had awoken from his malaise and was acting not only on the strategic front (in coordination with Richmond), by withdrawing from Bowling Green, beginning the process of withdrawing from Columbus, and reinforcing Tennessee from the Gulf Coast, but also on the more limited operational level. The center of that level of attention was Fort Donelson, which he saw correctly as the key to getting his army south of the Cumberland. The Confederates realized Fort Donelson would be in jeopardy soon; Jeremy Gilmer wrote succinctly, "the capture of Fort Henry was for the enemy a great success, which it was felt would embolden him to make an early attack upon Fort Donelson." While the actual attack would not come as early as February 8 as Grant had desired, it would come soon enough. Yet, delay could only aid Johnston, and his Confederates grew more confident by the day. One soldier wrote his wife on February 8 that the enemy had taken Fort Henry but "we will pay them for it when we get hold of them."[22]

Johnston's immediate reaction to the crisis was to send more troops, and in particular their generals, to Fort Donelson. With word that Tilghman had surrendered and was on the way to a Northern prison camp, the twin-rivers command was left without a general officer. Colonel Heiman, marching in from Fort Henry after his self-described "very tedious march," was the senior officer, although Colonel John Head was in nominal command at Fort Donelson while Tilghman was at Fort Henry. Heiman did not make an issue of command: "expecting the arrival of General B. R. Johnson and other general officers in a few days I did not assume command, which would have been my duty, being next in command to General Tilghman." Others heard that Gideon Pillow would soon arrive as well, some said "in a few hours."[23]

In the earliest stages of the crisis of command, Johnston did indeed have a general officer nearby, and he sent the newly appointed brigadier general Bushrod Johnson from Nashville to take "instant command." Johnson had actually been at Fort Donelson in January while Tilghman concentrated his efforts at Fort Henry during Grant's reconnaissances, although no reason was given why he later moved back to Nashville. Perhaps there was such animosity toward Johnson that he was sent back; Milton Haynes, manning the river batteries at Fort Donelson at the time, wrote Tilghman, "I am informed that there is much dissatisfaction in regard to the assignment of Gen. B. R. Johnson to command here, and that several officers will send in their resignations." Haynes notified Tilghman that he recommended they not do so, saying, "I have as much & better reason to object to him than any of them." Instead, he counseled: "this is not the time to do anything to weaken ourselves, and that redress ought to be sought in a way which would not embarrass our army." Whether the officers followed Haynes's recommendation is not known, but Johnson was soon sent back to Nashville; perhaps it is telling that Johnson was not immediately sent to Donelson when another crisis emerged and Tilghman once again moved to Fort Henry.[24]

Now that the evolving crisis was growing more problematic, however, Johnson was once more the most available general officer. The order went out the night of February 6 itself, and Johnson sped down the Cumberland River along with the 2nd Kentucky on the first boat he could get out of Nashville. He passed Clarksville but continued on, arriving early on the night of February 7. What he found was not positive. In addition to the refugees from Fort Henry under Colonel Heiman, Johnson found only four Tennessee regiments and a battalion of infantry and one field battery, all under Colonel Head. Two companies of infantry were acting as gunners on the big guns on the river. Johnson began his work despite the lack of resources, toiling to store the mammoth amount of supplies pouring into the fort, mostly at Dover, and removing wounded to rearward areas. Indeed, one Confederate remarked, "the little town of Dover at once became full of bustle and confusion." Johnson also began to organize a defense, but that was almost an impossibility, Johnson noting that he had to position troops "without definite knowledge of the strength of the re-enforcements destined for the place." Fortunately for him, those reinforcements continually poured in, the first of them arriving as early as the night of February 7: two Virginia regiments of Floyd's command brigaded under Colonel Gabriel C. Wharton of the 51st Virginia. Others arrived the next day. The Virginians were disappointed because they had just finished building permanent chimneys for their tents at Russellville, Kentucky, but the ensuing steamboat ride to Donelson made up for it. One Virginian wrote, "I set down to a steam boat Breakfast this Morning. I had the pleasure of setting down in a Chair and eating off of a *Table with* a *knife* and *Fork*."[25]

Johnston soon had second thoughts about entrusting Donelson to Bushrod Johnson, however, and on February 9 he ordered Gideon Pillow at Clarksville to the fort. Pillow arrived the next day and took command, making his head-quarters in the Rice House (one of his staff officer's residences), a block up from the Dover Hotel. This time, troops again accompanied an arriving general. When taking command, Pillow placed Johnson in command of the left section of the Confederate line and the momentarily expected Simon Bolivar Buckner in command of troops on the right.[26]

Reveling in the independent command, Pillow went to work with gusto, and the weather helped. One Confederate wrote in his diary that February 9 was "clear as a bell but very cold," although even the chill warmed up in the next few days, allowing Pillow and his Confederates ample time and conditions to get Fort Donelson in order for the attack all knew was looming. Gilmer noted that Pillow "took active measures to inform himself as to the character of the defenses and had the additional works pressed forward with the greatest activity." He also began to implement additional measures to defend the fort and by extension Nashville and Johnston's army. Finding, as he said, "the work on the river battery unfinished and wholly too weak to resist the force of heavy artillery," he mounted more guns, including a rifled 32-pounder and a 10-inch columbiad. Additional plans were made to mount more big guns, but time was the determining factor. Pillow had his gunners practice firing along the river in the meantime, fixing range indicators along the riverbanks. Pillow reported he "tried them and the other guns in battery. The trial was most satisfactory."[27]

Pillow also saw to other defensive efforts even as skirmishing with Federal cavalry began to increase. One of his labors was establishing "a line of vedettes on the east bank of the Cumberland to within 8 miles of Smithland, so that I will be posted as to the movements and advance of the enemy." Pillow was therefore extremely busy and even asked John B. Floyd, now at Clarksville, to send on reports to Johnston at Bowling Green—"my engagements and duties press me so much that I cannot address you both and, knowing his anxiety, I am anxious to place before him the intelligence contained in this letter." Pillow's lack of protocol could seemingly be forgiven because of all his effort, and it was hoped he was producing an upbeat boost of morale in the midst of crisis. And that was certainly needed. Pillow noted that when he arrived, "deep gloom was hanging over the command, and the troops were greatly depressed and demoralized by the circumstances attending the surrender of Fort Henry and the manner of retiring from that place."[28]

Making morale much better, Pillow also benefited from more reinforcements. Johnston sent additional troops to the area, including Simon Bolivar Buckner's division from Russellville, Kentucky, although Buckner initially moved his troops to Clarksville. "Hope to get all my troops to Clarksville by daylight," he wrote from Russellville on February 8. Over the course of the next couple of days Buckner went personally to Fort Donelson along with his "jaded and worn out" division. Buckner's arrival caused more tension, however, because he and Pillow were old political enemies, mainly stemming from a nasty 1857 senate race. If that were not enough, militarily and politically, yet another general was also at Clarksville by this time, the politician John B. Floyd. He had received his orders from Johnston the night of February 6 as well, and had his brigade in Clarksville by daylight on February 8, although he complained that the town was undefended: "the defenses here amount to about nothing," he wrote. "I think they have mistaken the location of the work upon the river hill about 200 yards, whilst the one in the bottom is nearly submerged."[29]

Unfortunately for Johnston, all these newly arrived strong-willed generals did not communicate well. Floyd was senior, but he was at Clarksville; Pillow was senior at Donelson itself. And a difference of opinion soon surfaced. Floyd had no trust in Fort Donelson's defense, desiring to defend the Cumberland River at Cumberland City while the independent Pillow was busily making Fort Donelson his own little fiefdom: "upon one thing you may rest assured," he wrote Floyd, "viz, that I will never surrender the position, and with God's help I mean to maintain it." Floyd had other ideas, including concentrating all available troops at Cumberland City just upriver from Fort Donelson and using the army as a mobile striking force rather than a defensive garrison. Buckner alluded to Floyd "operating from some point on the railway west of that position in the direction of Fort Donelson or Fort Henry, thus maintaining his communications with Nashville by the way of Charlotte." Floyd even sent Buckner to Fort Donelson on the night of February 11 to order Pillow to evacuate the fort and join him at Cumberland City.[30]

Open rebellion ensued as Pillow was challenged in his authority at Donelson. In fact, when the abhorred Buckner relayed Floyd's order, Pillow refused to obey "until he should have a personal interview with General Floyd"; he quickly prepared to travel to Cumberland City to confront the Virginian. Pillow consequently left Buckner in command at Donelson on the morning of February 12, Buckner making his headquarters in the Dover Hotel. Pillow told Buckner "in no event to bring on an engagement should the enemy approach in force." Buckner also said that "General Pillow left me under the impression that he did not expect an immediate advance of the enemy, and regarded their approach from the direction of Fort Henry as impracticable." Pillow then took a steamboat to meet Floyd at Cumberland City.[31]

This was not the first time that Pillow had been corralled, and not the first time he had anguished in perceived humiliation. He was in his own view one of the heroes of the Mexican War, having been a division commander under Winfield Scott. When Polk had taken over from Pillow at Columbus in 1861, Pillow admitted: "that I should have felt deeply humiliated at being thus deprived of my command, reduced in rank, and placed under the orders of a priest, who had devoted his life to religious pursuits and had no experience in the field as a military man, ought not to excite surprise." Pillow later complained of "the promotion of my juniors in rank, who, when promoted had fought no battle, had no experience in high command and little of any sort." The Tennessean obviously had a thin skin when it came to his honor and command, and now he did not like a Virginian, and a political general at that, being placed over his carefully constructed lair at Fort Donelson.[32]

Pillow chose this moment to take a stand. Although he missed Floyd, who had gone to Clarksville, he returned to Fort Donelson about noon, telling Buckner that he and Floyd, mostly Pillow as it turned out, had decided that Fort Donelson would be maintained and that all troops at Cumberland City and Clarksville would be sent there as reinforcements. He had successfully lobbied Albert Sidney Johnston, saying he could hold Fort Donelson with Buckner's troops, but he could not do so without them. Pillow thus kept his command and placed Buckner's division in a defensive line on the right despite their tents and baggage being left behind and the men "suffering very much." Lower-level accounts bore this out. Colonel Joseph B. Palmer of the 18th Tennessee wrote that his men "encamped mainly without tents or other protection from the weather, and with scarcely any cooking utensils." A compassionate Buckner soon rode his lines, telling his men to cook what they could and keep three day's rations prepared. Johnson's troops of course manned the left.[33]

By February 12, Gideon Pillow had his fort in the best-conceivable shape he could, and had proven unshakable in the need to continue its defense. Ominous signs were nevertheless appearing, on both land and water. A recently arrived (February 10) Nathan Bedford Forrest and his 3rd Tennessee Cavalry soon reported Federal troops approaching on land, and Pillow's vedettes down the river reported steamboats moving toward the fort on February 12. Pillow also reported, "I have heard ten heavy discharges of artillery." Still, he was in his element, in total charge, and counseled his command to have as optimistic an outlook as he did. He challenged the troops to "drive back the ruthless invader from our soil and again raise the Confederate flag over Fort Henry." The battle cry, he said: "Liberty or death."[34]

Not everyone was so enthralled. The troops were miserable, receiving few rations and living on flour dough "knead[ed] . . . on stumps some on bark and some on a log and wind it round our musket rammers and bake and eat it without grease or salt." The high command was not happy either; John B. Floyd, just up the river at Cumberland City, wrote Johnston in those intervening days: "I wish, if possible, you would come down here, if it were only for a single day." Likely, Gideon Pillow thought he needed no such help from Johnston or anyone else, but he was about to unexpectedly get a new superior on site, changing his entire attitude.[35]

Had Grant been able to keep to his original timetable of marching on Fort Donelson on February 8, he could probably have swept in and captured it with much less resistance than he later faced. Then again, he might not have come away with all he did later in the delayed operations. At any rate, Grant was unable to keep to his timetable and slowed down his effort, all the while receiving reinforcements and preparing for the advance. James B. McPherson summed it up: "the time was chiefly occupied in making reconnaissances up the Tennessee River to a short distance above Danville and of the roads leading to Fort Donelson, getting our forces in condition to march against the latter place and awaiting the co-operation of the gunboats." He might also have included waiting until the roads dried out sufficiently for overland movement. A perturbed Grant chafed at the delay, almost daily writing his division commanders that he intended to move the next day.[36]

Even though Grant's military units did not march eastward from Fort Henry on February 8, he still had cavalry and his engineers probing toward Dover in an effort to find out as much as they could before the actual march began. The major player in finding out the best route to Fort Donelson was engineer McPherson, who actually found there were two good routes. The main road out of Fort Henry split into the northern branch and the southern branch, while the Confederate forces under Heiman took an even lower road in their roundabout march to Fort Donelson. Roundabout as it was, it was not feasible for the Federal approach. Fortunately for the Federals, the northernmost road split into the two different paths just northeast of the fort, in fact between the fort and Panther Creek. The northernmost branch, or the Telegraph Road, wound its way south of Panther Creek and across several of its feeder branches. Farther on, past the miniature "continental divide" between the two rivers, the road also negotiated the upper reaches of Bear Creek and many of its tributaries. This path was as a result one of ups and downs and numerous creeks. The southernmost route was termed the Ridge Road for good reason; it filed along the high ground largely between the tributaries of Panther Creek to the north and Lost Creek to the south. It passed Peytona Furnace midway to Dover and then climbed the high Tennessee and Pumpkin ridges before becoming mired in the valley and tributaries of Hickman Creek closer to Fort Donelson. Neither road was free of hindrances, but both were good routes that were definitely usable for Grant's advance.[37]

McPherson kept cavalry patrols out along these roads throughout the days after Fort Henry's fall. He reported that "the roads had not been obstructed in any manner by the rebels, from the fact that after the fall of Fort Henry our cavalry scoured the country so continually and effectively that they did not venture to send out men for the purpose." As the days passed, however, these cavalry patrols began more and more to meet their Confederate counterparts in the form of Nathan Bedford Forrest's Tennessee cavalry regiment, which had arrived at Fort Donelson from Kentucky on February 10. Forrest made a reconnaissance out the Telegraph Road on the afternoon of February 11 and fought some of the exploring Union cavalry.[38]

The short interval of several days gave Grant time not only to organize his efforts a little better but also to have his son Fred down for a few days, although he was sent home before the actual movement toward Fort Donelson began. It also gave Grant time to build up his forces even more. Grant had two divisions under McClernand and Smith, and they were continually being fed newer regiments that were formed into new brigades. By the time the divisions marched off toward Fort Donelson, McClernand commanded three brigades under colonels Richard J. Oglesby, W. H. L. Wallace, and William R. Morrison, the entire division of infantry, artillery, and cavalry all being Illinois troops except for two small companies of US regular cavalry. Smith's division by this time had grown to four brigades under Colonels John McArthur, John Cook, and Jacob Lauman, and Brigadier General Lew Wallace.

This division contained an assortment of troops, many of them from Illinois but some also hailing from Missouri, Indiana, and Iowa.[39]

Some changes in command occurred as Grant further organized his troops, leaving the sick of McClernand's division at Fort Henry along with the 23rd and 28th Illinois and one of Smith's brigades and the 5th Iowa Cavalry at Fort Heiman, all under the command of Lew Wallace. The Indianan was livid about being left behind. The decision had been Smith's, and Wallace seethed with anger toward what he described as his jealous division commander. He wrote his wife, "through old Smith, I am left behind in command of the Fort and Ft. Henry. 'French Statement.' I have been sick from rage since yesterday." Wallace told her his patience with Smith was "played out" and he would begin to assert himself more amid the breach that was growing between the two generals from the disobedience of orders by Wallace at Paducah that had landed Smith in a lot of trouble. Wallace evidently complained elsewhere as well, but Grant's aide Hillyer counseled patience: "you will [soon] have a position that will suit you *in every particular—having no intermediate commander.*"[40]

All the while, other troops continually arrived, Grant telling Halleck: "send all troops to arrive to Fort Henry." He was still nervous that "that point is in danger" and wanted as many troops as possible to cover it while he was gone to Fort Donelson. Grant displayed more of his nervousness when he admitted, "Johnston, Buckner, Floyd, and Pillow are all said to be here," although he seemed less concerned about Pillow, about whom he wrote his sister that he intended "to give him a tug before you receive this." In the end, Grant need not have worried, because the Confederates were extremely disorganized at this point and were in no way pondering any attack on Fort Henry. He obviously did not know that, however. Fortunately, he continued to receive troops shuttled up the Tennessee, including eventually by a new commander at Paducah, William T. Sherman.[41]

With so many troops gathering and the weather clearing, the operation began moving forward in earnest. Grant gave orders on February 10 to move two days later, "at as early an hour as practicable," and delineated what the troops should take with them: "neither tents nor baggage will be taken, except such as the troops can carry." The latter included forty rounds of ammunition per man and two days' rations in haversacks. Behind the column, clearly behind the marching troops, would come wagons with three days' rations, but Grant was careful to remind his officers these should "not impede the progress of the main column." Some soldiers wrote quick notes home; "marching orders have just come to camp to be ready in an hour," wrote one Illinoisan, "and I take a few moments to write goodbye."[42]

More detailed orders were issued the next day. Grant stipulated that one of McClernand's brigades was to move on the Telegraph Road, eventually stopping two miles from Fort Donelson. McClernand's other brigades were to move by the lower Ridge Road, stopping at the same distance "and throw[ing] out troops so as to form a continuous line between the two wings." Smith's brigades were to follow on the Ridge Road, one of them, Grant wrote somewhat naively, moving into Dover "to cut off all retreat by the river, if found practicable to do so." Lew Wallace of course would remain in command at Forts Henry and Heiman, setting up a defense as well as services such as a post office. In addition, Cruft's brigade from Buell's army as well as additional regiments under John Thayer that had also arrived on transports at Fort Henry were ordered to turn around and move by water to Fort Donelson, keeping for protection the *Carondelet*, which was also by this time moving into the Cumberland. One Kentuckian could only surmise that with so many troops at Fort Henry, "they had no use for us." Along with the four Indiana and Kentucky regiments under Cruft, Grant sent the 57th Illinois, 1st Nebraska, and 2nd Iowa under Thayer by water as well, one Iowan reveling in the trip, writing, "spent the evening on deck as it is a beautiful one, and the scenery along the River fine." He added that the boys were entertaining themselves in various ways, one preaching "a hard shell sermon to the great amusement of his hearers while others of a more serious mood were thinking of the morrow." Thayer was more concerned about his orders to stop additional transports moving to Fort Henry, and he turned around eight more boats as he moved northward toward Paducah. There, the transports stopped and waited for the naval contingent from Cairo before moving on.[43]

Meanwhile, much of the army, particularly McClernand's division, actually moved forward on the evening of February 11 to get on high, dry ground that would allow them to begin the march at an early hour the next day. From there, Grant hoped to reach and engulf Fort Donelson the same day. Indeed, the backwater from the rising river had almost inundated Fort Henry and was creeping toward the outer earthworks, causing many problems for the Federals camped around the fort. One staff officer even noted, "there have been several men drowned by getting in and miring." McClernand's division thus utilized both of the main roads according to Grant's orders, W. H. L. Wallace's brigade on the upper Telegraph Road while Oglesby in the lead and Morrison in rear marched on the Ridge Road on February 11. McClernand interestingly wrote that "in compliance with your order for marching upon Fort Donelson on the morning of the 12th, I directed in the afternoon of the 11th instant the transfer [of the brigades] . . . to a night bivouac . . . about 5 miles in advance." Such compliance took the division nearly half way to Fort Donelson, but McPherson offered some context and noted that "the heaviest part of the whole route was from the Tennessee River at Fort Henry back 2 miles to the high ground. To overcome this and have the forces in good condition to march against Fort Donelson the artillery and a great portion of the infantry were moved back to the high ground on the 11th instant."[44]

Will Wallace's brigade, with his prized former regiment the 11th Illinois in the lead, marched out the Telegraph Road to the accompaniment of the drum corps around 4:00 PM, moving to a point where the high ground began as the road rose out of the bottoms of Panther Creek. The Illinoisans camped in line of battle in a field that moonlit night, using nearby rails for fires. Just a little to the south on the parallel Ridge Road, Oglesby left about the same time and camped around 8:00 PM where the road ran on the high ground between the watersheds of Panther and Lost creeks. Charles Tompkins of the 17th Illinois wrote of the fine day: "the pleasantest march I ever made. We encamped in a fine forest. The boys soon had bright fires of dry pitch blazing & as we lay on the dry leaves looking up at the reflection of the fires from the green pine above us it was decidedly beautiful and romantic." Unfortunately the bliss ended when the wagons arrived later in the night and the spooked mules got loose. They went "over us two or three times," Tompkins wrote, the first time "we were asleep & hearing them coming awakened us so suddenly we sprang about ten feet from our bed of leaves the first jump."[45]

Despite the chaos, the day itself had been beautiful, and so was the next. One Federal described February 12 as "pleasant" while another noted that after the cold snap "the weather is spring-like and we are in the best of health and spirits." One Illinoisan went so far as to write his father, "it is clear and warm so warm that the frogs is a hallowing lik birds." Charles Kroff noted in his diary, "this is a delightful day, it is much like spring, birds are singing sweetly." In high spirits indeed, most of the Federals were extremely confident in their future success. James Drish, for example, wrote home, "I think

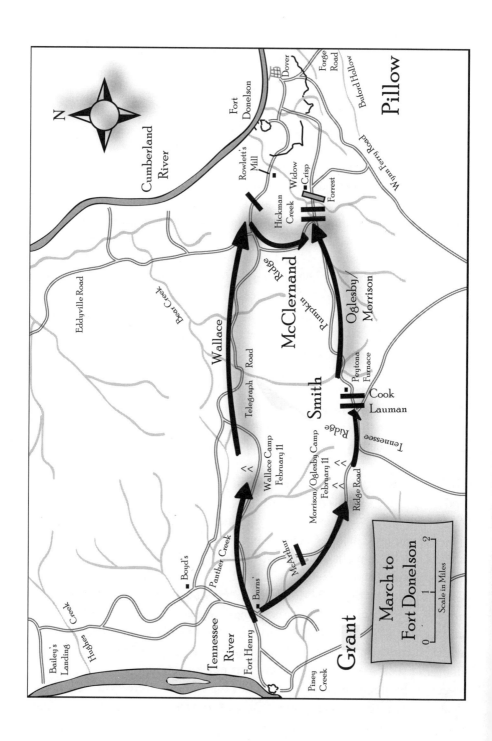

N

Cumberland
River

Fort
Donelson

Rowlett's Mill

Hickman Creek

Widow
Crisp

Forrest

Dover

Forge Road

Buford Hollow

Pillow

Wynn Ferry Road

Eddyville Road

Bear Creek

Wallace

Telegraph Road

Pumpkin Ridge

McClernand

Oglesby/ Morrison

Peytona Furnace

Smith

Cook

Lauman

Tennessee Ridge

Bailey's Landing

Hughes Creek

Tennessee River

Fort Henry

Piney Creek

Panther Creek

Boyd's

Burns'

McArthur

Wallace Camp February 11

Morrison/Oglesby Camp February 11

Ridge Road

Grant

March to
Fort Donelson

0   1   2
Scale in Miles

we will bag a fine lot of them this time if we don't get thrashed ourselves which is not very likely." One Illinois cavalryman was definitely caught up in the excitement, writing, "looking back over the long column in full view there was an army with banners marching to battle. . . . The burnished arms glistened in the morning sunlight which seemed to make ruddy the faces, and rugged the forms, of the men in column. All were in the best of spirits."[46]

The actual march began early on February 12, McClernand noting that "at 8 o'clock on the morning of the 12th my whole command was in motion." One Illinoisan wrote that the men ate breakfast and "filled our Canteens with nice pure watter that run in a little streem at the foot of the hill on which we were camped." Wallace, with his father-in-law's 4th Illinois Cavalry leading the way, marched alone on the Telegraph Road while Oglesby and Morrison continued past Peytona Furnace on the lower Ridge Road. Cavalry led the way on the lower road as well, Colonel Silas Noble of the 2nd Illinois Cavalry leading Oglesby with skirmishers and flankers. Wallace also noted that he was careful in "keeping frequent communication with Colonel Oglesby's First Brigade." The two roads actually joined each other inside the Confederate defenses, but fortunately for McClernand several crossover roads connected the two outside the Confederate earthworks. As he neared the Confederate garrison, Wallace thus joined the remainder of the division on the Ridge Road after sending his cavalry forward to Rowlett's Mill and finding the crossing of Hickman Creek underwater and impassable. Indeed, the Confederates were counting on the backwater from the river to shield that right flank of the fortifications. Wallace's troops simply took the connecting road southward to the Ridge Road, where Oglesby's regiments were already forming in response to meeting a stiffer Confederate defense. One teamster simply reckoned in his diary, "the ball opened this evening."[47]

It is remarkable that Grant's forces were able to march right up to the defenses of Fort Donelson on February 12, but then the state of the Confederate command explained this fact. Grant of course famously declared that he knew both Pillow and Floyd and knew he could get away with such boldness. Obviously, Floyd and Pillow were away at Cumberland City and Clarksville at the time. Buckner, who was chafing to get out of Fort Donelson with his troops, did not offer any resistance, and was actually under orders not to bring on an engagement. As a result, Grant was able to march right up to Fort Donelson and the Confederates missed what some historians have declared was a golden opportunity to strike Grant's forces while they were on separate roads and the gunboats would not be of any help. A terribly fractured Confederate command system precluded such offensive action, however, and the Federals easily moved all the way to the Confederate defenses.[48]

That said, resistance stiffened the closer the Federals came to Fort Donelson. Leading the Federal advance, Major John J. Mudd was out front with a scouting party and located what McClernand described as "a detachment of the enemy's cavalry strongly supported, indicating the determination to resist our farther progress." Oglesby formed an advance guard of his brigade under Major George A. Bacon and the 30th Illinois while the remainder of his brigade deployed in the rear. Wallace and Morrison did likewise. It was a good thing, because their harassment came from Forrest's Tennessee cavalry as well as a company of the 18th Tennessee of Buckner's division. McClernand described the Confederate horsemen making "a vigorous and determined attack upon our grand guard" and then trying to flank the advance guard and "cut it off from its support." Forrest had far too few men to do much damage to three deployed brigades and artillery, George C. Gumbart's Illinois battery even getting off one shot, but he at least let McClernand know the Confederates were apprised of the situation and there would be no more ground gained freely. Indeed, the small action with Forrest cost Bacon's advance guard one killed and four wounded, but the Confederates were the ones truly surprised. Colonel Palmer of the 18th Tennessee reported that his company on skirmish duty "suddenly . . . discovered several thousand Federal troops advancing towards our encampment." Captain W. R. Butler immediately conducted a "prudent and skillful retreat," Palmer noted. Forrest likewise fell back up the Indian Creek Road with his wounded. One Federal put it more succinctly: "they only fired one voly and run."[49]

By this time, a light-traveling Grant (carrying only a toothbrush and extra shirt) himself was on the field, arriving around 2:00 PM. He had left Fort Henry earlier, making the entire twelve-mile trip that morning and early afternoon. He was apparently in a good mood, joking with Surgeon John Brinton, who rode a spirited horse who kept nudging ahead of the others: "Doctor, I believe I command this army, and I think I'll go first." Making his headquarters at a farmhouse owned by a widow named Crisp, Grant soon took firm control of the situation, apprising McClernand that Smith was immediately behind and that he would take the left and McClernand should move his three brigades and assume the right of the line. Grant thus described how "the fortifications of the enemy were from this point gradually approached and surrounded, with occasional skirmishing on the line." At places, in fact, the Federals could well see their goal, Fort Donelson. One Illinoisan remembered a "rattle snake ensign upon the heights of Donaldson."[50]

Smith was indeed right behind, although he had to continually endure many problems. The newspapers were still calling him disloyal, or as Smith described to his wife the Chicago *Tribune* "keeps up its fire on me." Perhaps for that reason Smith had declined to allow reporters access to his head-quarters with a "very prompt negative," adding that he regarded reporters as "little better than a nuisance." Then, too, some of Smith's command also had a much longer march to make. One of his brigades, McArthur's, had started the morning at Fort Heiman and had to be ferried across the river before they could begin their march. Once on the way, however, these troops moved quickly, brigade commander Cook noting, "the road being excellent and all transportation having been left at Fort Henry." The 52nd Indiana in his brigade even found time on one break to enjoy honey some of the members found in a nearby beehive. The division wound its way on the Ridge Road, Cook in front, Lauman next, and the delayed McArthur in the rear, to a point behind McClernand's deployed division. Smith then moved them to the left, placing Lauman's brigade on the far left near Hickman Creek and Cook's brigade on his right, connecting with McClernand's division. Smith held McArthur's troops in reserve behind this line, although there was a good bit of moving and redeploying during the night. The artillery also deployed, but with difficulty. One Federal described the process of placing the guns: "the officer had to find a vantage-ground first; then with axes a road to it was hewn out; after which, in many instances, the men, with the prolongs over their shoulders, helped the horses along."[51]

All the while, McClernand's brigades were filing off to the right, Oglesby in the lead taking the extreme right position with Wallace on his left. Mor-rison's small brigade took the left of the division along the Ridge Road, con-necting with Cook's brigade of Smith's division. McClernand described that he ordered the brigades "to ascend the range of steep hills which overlook the center and right of the enemy's works, and to form in order of battle." To move to the right, the troops eventually had to cross the wide valley of Indian Creek in the face of Confederate fire, and each regiment in turn responded the same way: "on the double quick his [McClernand's] men passed through it; and when, in the wood beyond, they resumed the route-step and saw that nobody was hurt, they fell to laughing at themselves." All the while, Oglesby maneuvered the most on the right, continually pushing down the Wynns Ferry Road, causing rearward personnel such as surgeons to repeatedly have to relocate their regiments after moving their hospitals.[52]

McClernand's artillery was likewise "brought to the crest of the hills," Wallace commenting on "dragging the artillery up the steep, wooded hills." Oglesby brought up artillery once the infantry reached the point of being "in full view of the enemy's tents on the opposite hill." He brought up one howitzer of Gumbart's battery but found it could not reach the required distance. He then ordered forward one of the three James rifles of Jasper Dresser's Illinois battery, which fired twenty-one times and caused obvious concern in the Confederate lines: "the result," Dresser noted, "was to disperse a body of infantry which was drawn up in line of battle and to compel the enemy to strike their tents in that camp." George Durfee of the 8th Illinois agreed, writing that the guns felled "some of their tents and [made] them advance rapidly to the rear under the hill, and out of range." A Confederate confirmed it, writing how the shells "came whirling through the air, now striking a house, now going beyond the town and plunging in the angry waters of the river."[53]

Under cover of the rifle, Oglesby's brigade made a farther movement forward to a better location, and once more sidestepped to the east a half-mile to better encircle the enemy works. Colonel Michael K. Lawler's 18th Illinois led the way "over a high ridge," one Illinoisan reported, followed at sunset by the remainder of the brigade despite an unfortunate friendly fire incident in the growing darkness causing several casualties in the 29th Illinois. One soldier in the 8th Illinois wrote that "one of our regiments come up behind us and not knowing but what we were there enemy fired into the rear of our regiment, the bullets whistling about us in every direction." The rear of the 8th Illinois returned fire, killing three and wounding three in the 29th Illinois. Wallace's and Morrison's brigades meanwhile followed the eastward movement, keeping the line fully formed despite, Colonel Morrison recalled, moving "over underbrush, fences, ravines, and brooks in the best possible order, [the men] casting away their knapsacks, overcoats, and every inconvenience to their most speedy advance." Another officer described the dense thickets "making it impossible for even colonels to see their regiments from flank to flank." The confusion ranged all the way up to the brigade level; Will Wallace's staff officer I. P. Rumsey described "the crooks and maneuverings in the woods, trying to find the enemy."[54]

It was all very confusing to the watching Confederates, one Tennessean writing of their surprise when the enemy neared: "a hatless horseman came rushing by crying, 'Yankees! Yankees!' Old man Arbegast blew the assembly call on the bugle and 3rd [Tennessee] fell in line." A wagon train of volunteers on the way to Dover to gather supplies was immediately left: "in less than one minute every mule was unhitched and mounted," wrote the commander, the boys wanting to get back to their regiment to fight. The continual encirclement also kept the watching Confederates busy, one of whom reported, "we saw a regiment of bluecoats march up in line of battle but has scarcely become visible before they formed fours and marched directly to the left." Some wanted to fire on the enemy several hundred yards away, but the officers managed to keep them calm, knowing that muskets and shotguns would not reach that distance. "The excitement among us as is usually among fresh troops was intense," remembered one Confederate, but they were confident. "Our army had whipped at Manassas and other places and we would whip here too."[55]

The solid line of Union regiments also confused one of Grant's staff officers, who was then subjected to a little ribbing. Surgeon Brinton had ridden out to look at matters and inadvertently got in front of the line of battle. When he tried to return, the regiment on his front realized the situation and "it seemed to afford the men great pleasure," Brinton remembered, "to close up so as to keep me from getting through. I, and a solitary scared dog, were in front. After a while, when the men had had their joke at my expense, I passed through."[56]

Despite the humor, the continual Union envelopment also brought with it more ominous activity; numerous Federal batteries began to unlimber and take the Confederate defenses under fire. "Suddenly the silence was broken by the boom of a cannon," one Tennessean remembered, "a light puff of smoke appeared high in the air in front of our line, then the busting of the shell was heard, and the smoke ascended in the form of a delicate ring up into the heavens out of sight." He thought, "many a time have I seen it ascend from the bowl of a pipe in a quiet room in exactly the same manner." But this was no such peaceful place. In fact, more rounds began to fall, and the area resembled anything but a quiet room. It was now a battlefield.[57]

As fate would have it, the final phase of Grant's concentration also came about on February 12. The army general was wary about carrying on his campaign without naval support and the troops the navy was ferrying around the rivers as reinforcements. A worried Grant had little information on the gunboats' whereabouts, those under Foote having left Cairo several days ago. Closer in contact was the *Carondelet* at Fort Henry, which was sent around by Grant with instructions to let him know when the gunboat appeared off Fort Donelson. It was a harrying trip for the large, leaking gunboat, towed as it was by the steamer *Alps*. Commander Henry Walke nevertheless got his boat up the Cumberland River and approached Fort Donelson by midday on February 12. "Seeing or hearing nothing of our army," Walke reported, "I threw a few shell into Fort Donelson to announce my arrival to General Grant, as he had previously desired." He marveled at the "echo from the hills." He also marveled that the place looked even more ominous than it sounded. Walke described the Confederate fort with its batteries dug into the side of the hill in eerie terms: "the black rows of heavy guns, pointing down on us, reminded me of the dismal-looking sepulchers cut into the rocky cliffs near Jerusalem, but far more repulsive."[58]

The Confederates in Fort Donelson interpreted Walke's shelling as a full-fledged attack. When the large, black ironclad poked its bow around the bend a couple of miles down the river from the fort, complete with rockets fired above obviously indicating to those ashore its position, the gunners manned their pieces for the showdown that all expected. "The smoke exactly marked the progress of the boat and we knew when to expect her appearance," Reuben Ross related, "a low black nose soon glided beyond the point shaped exactly like that of a R.R. Engine, having two steamboat pipes at the upper part of the nose." Some of the newly minted artillerymen were still training on their pieces when an officer "suddenly informed me that the gunboats were coming," one artilleryman remembered, "and we set to work to prepare for them." Despite the extreme range, the Confederate gunners opened on the *Carondelet* with the heaviest gun in the fort, the large rifle, and, one Confederate crowed, "by using great pains succeeded in striking much more frequently than we expected." The gunboat and fort traded a dozen or so shots before Walke eased the *Carondelet* back around the bend, his purpose fulfilled. The Confederates were amazed that they had survived their baptism of fire, one writing that they received "no damage to us at all, though all her shot reached us easily. This was considered remarkable, as we had no covering overhead and moderately high epaulements."[59]

While Walke was content to just throw a few shells forward, the Confeder-

ates, perhaps awash in "driving away" the enemy gunboat or gunboats, celebrated what seemed to them to be a great victory. Although Walke reported
no hits, one of the officers commanding the Confederate gunners noted, "our
balls could be heard to strike with tolerable distinctness." Likewise, they soon
received word from a civilian who had been at the bend during the exchange:
"a respectable citizen, from in view of the boat below the bend, sent us up
word that this boat was taken off in a sinking condition between two other
boats, but that she could not be kept up and that he saw her sink finally."
One officer noted, "we could not know and hesitated to believe in such good
news." Such deliberation was wise, because Walke and the *Carondelet* were
fine around the bend in the river. The commander had dropped anchor a few
miles to the north and waited for word to come from Grant or Foote, or both.[60]

With the army approaching the Confederate works on land and at least a
portion of the navy on station, the operation was now beginning in earnest.
Yet little else could be done this day, while large components, army and navy,
were still filing in and taking position. By the time Grant had his two divisions deployed and moved forward to the last ridge in front of the Confederate works, night had set in. The gunboats and reinforcements sent around by
river had not arrived either, so major action would have to wait until the next
day. Grant in fact wrote that a halt took place "owing to the non-arrival of
the gunboats and re-enforcements sent by water, . . . but the investment was
extended on the flanks of the enemy and drawn closer to his works, with skirmishing all day." Despite the delay, the Federals went into bivouac confident
but watchful. The 12th Iowa's Colonel Joseph Woods remembered, "slept on
their arms ready for action." Brigade commander Cook in Smith's division
noted: "in fine spirits, with full assurance of success, the troops passed the
night, prepared for an attack should a sally be made from the fort." The artillery remained in constant readiness as well; Jasper Dresser reported, "we lay
in the woods with our teams hitched up and the men with their equipments
on." Unfortunately for the troops, they were so close to the enemy that fires
were not allowed, Captain S. B. Marks of the 18th Illinois noting that his
regiment "remained on arms during the night without fires." Others had left
tents and blankets in the rear at Fort Henry. Fortunately for the Federals, the
supreme confidence of what would occur on the morrow negated most of the
discomfort on this comparatively mild night.[61]

One Federal particularly exhibited such confidence. An Indianan was captured and taken to a Confederate camp, whereupon an officer interrogated him, asking who commanded the Union army. "General U. S. Grant" came the reply, to which the Confederates asked "where he came from, as we had never heard of him before." The Indianan quietly responded, "you will [soon] know him well enough."[62]

Major General Henry W. Halleck was the attentive if nervous commander of the Department of the Missouri, under which Grant's offensive fell. He did not fully trust Grant to lead the campaign but wasted no time in claiming the spoils of victory. Courtesy Library of Congress.

Brigadier General Don Carlos Buell commanded the Department of the Ohio and was a thorn in Halleck's side, being hesitant to support Halleck's operations and only grudgingly sending reinforcements once Halleck acted on his own. Courtesy Library of Congress.

Brigadier General Ulysses S. Grant commanded the District of Cairo, which included the twin rivers. His insistence on attacking the enemy gave the Union its first major victories and made Grant a national hero in the process. Courtesy Library of Congress.

Brigadier General John A. McClernand commanded Grant's First Division. He was a politician general that caused Grant many headaches, but he fought well. McClernand's division bore the brunt of the fighting at Fort Donelson. Courtesy Library of Congress.

Brigadier General Charles F. Smith commanded Grant's Second Division. He was an old army officer who suffered under rumors of disloyalty early in 1862. Perhaps for that reason, he bravely led his division in the thickest of the fighting at Fort Donelson, contributing largely to the victory. Courtesy Library of Congress.

Brigadier General Lew Wallace commanded Grant's newly created Third Division at Fort Donelson. His opportune stand stalled the Confederate advance, and his counterattack retook much of the lost ground on February 15. Courtesy Library of Congress.

Colonel W. H. L. Wallace commanded a brigade under McClernand. His bold stand bought time on February 15, but his brigade suffered heavy casualties. Courtesy Library of Congress.

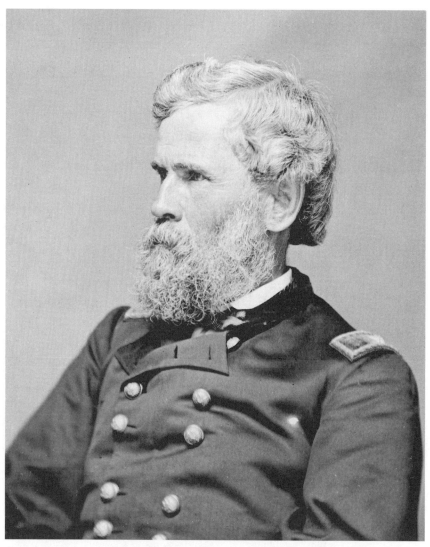

Colonel Joseph D. Webster served as Grant's chief of staff. He was a seasoned advisor to the young general but was not above carrying orders during the battle. Courtesy Library of Congress.

Flag Officer Andrew H. Foote commanded the naval contingent on the twin rivers. His bold attack at Fort Henry won the victory and made him a hero, but the same tactics failed miserably at Fort Donelson, where he was also wounded. Courtesy Library of Congress.

Lieutenant Commander Seth L. Phelps commanded the timberclad division of gunboats, with which he patrolled the rivers and gained much intelligence for the Union land efforts. His raid into Mississippi and Alabama after Fort Henry created shock throughout the Confederacy. Courtesy Library of Congress.

Commander Henry Walke commanded the USS *Carondelet*, which saw action at both Forts Henry and Donelson. The ironclad was heavily damaged in the campaign. Courtesy Library of Congress.

General Albert Sidney Johnston commanded the vast Confederate Department Number 2. His concentration on the Bowling Green, Kentucky, defenses allowed the enemy to break his defensive line in an unexpected area—at the twin rivers. Courtesy Library of Congress.

General P. G. T. Beauregard arrived in the west as Johnston's second in command in February 1862. The rumor of his arrival, with reinforcements, was one of the reasons the Federals decided to hurry up operations on the twin rivers. Courtesy National Archives.

Major General Leonidas Polk commanded the Confederate Gibraltar at Columbus, Kentucky. Although the twin rivers were technically in his command area, he was consumed with Columbus's defense and gave little thought to the area. Courtesy Library of Congress.

Brigadier General Lloyd Tilghman commanded the twin-river forts after November 1861. He pleaded for men, material, and help, but Johnston and Polk were obsessed with their own defenses elsewhere, and the twin rivers were as a result woefully undermanned. Courtesy Miller's *Photographic History*.

Brigadier General John B. Floyd was a political general who found himself in command at Fort Donelson. His passiveness and ability to be controlled were much of the problem in the Confederate high command. His cowardly escape did not endear him to Confederates either. Courtesy Library of Congress.

Brigadier General Gideon J. Pillow saw himself as the hero of the twin rivers, but his usurpation of authority from Floyd only caused trouble. His questionable decisions in battle and in retreat left him a vilified man. Courtesy National Archives.

Brigadier General Simon B. Buckner commanded one division in the Fort Donelson army. He was left with the overall command when Floyd and Pillow chose to escape the surrender, but he endeared himself to his soldiers by staying and suffering the same fate as they. Courtesy Library of Congress.

Brigadier General Bushrod R. Johnson was often left out of the Confederate high command's decisions. He ostensibly commanded a division, but the overbearing Pillow often took it over in battle. Courtesy Library of Congress.

Tennessee governor Isham G. Harris was appalled at the fall of Forts Henry and Donelson, although many of the underlying reasons were his fault. The fall of his capital at Nashville caused Harris and the state government to become a government on the run, remaining so for the rest of the war. Courtesy Library of Congress.

The USS *Essex* was the first Union ironclad in service. A Confederate round hit a boiler at Fort Henry and put the vessel out of action. The shot killed and wounded, mostly by scalding, many of the crew. Courtesy Library of Congress.

The USS *Louisville* was one of the city-class ironclads that made its maiden entrance into battle at Forts Henry and Donelson. The *Louisville* was not in action at Fort Henry but was part of the flotilla that unsuccessfully attacked Fort Donelson. Courtesy Miller's *Photographic History*.

The USS *Lexington* was one of the stout timberclads that roamed the western rivers under Ledyard Phelps. The *Lexington*'s reconnaissances and raids up the Tennessee River provided much intelligence and instilled fear into many Confederates. Because of damage, the *Lexington* was not engaged at Fort Donelson. Courtesy Miller's *Photographic History*.

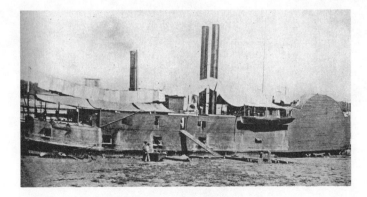

The USS *Tyler* was one of the workhorses of the US Navy in the twin-rivers campaign. The vessel took part in both the Fort Henry and Fort Donelson action, as well as Phelps's raid up the Tennessee River. Courtesy Miller's *Photographic History*.

The USS *Pittsburg* was another city-class ironclad that saw action at Fort Donelson. The *Pittsburg* had among its crew many of the surviving *Essex* sailors. Courtesy Miller's *Photographic History*.

Fort Henry was a star-shaped fort on the Tennessee River, and its outline can still be seen in this 1937 aerial view. Sadly, in just a few years the fort would be submerged in the depths of Kentucky Lake as the Tennessee Valley Authority dammed up the river. Courtesy Fort Donelson National Battlefield.

This postwar view shows the battlefield of Fort Donelson looking east. The photo illustrates the undulating nature of the terrain. Courtesy Fort Donelson National Battlefield.

The postwar view of the Forge Road shows the nature of the battlefield. The Forge Road was the anticipated avenue of Confederate escape, but the attempt was never made. Courtesy Fort Donelson National Battlefield.

This 1884 view looking southward across the Cumberland River toward Fort Donelson illustrates the size of the river as well as how the terrain looked prior to the damming of the Cumberland River. Courtesy Fort Donelson National Battlefield.

This postwar view of the Dover Hotel shows the structure as seen from the river landing below. The Dover Hotel became the scene of much drama, including Simon Bolivar Buckner's surrender of Fort Donelson to Ulysses S. Grant. Courtesy Fort Donelson National Battlefield.

9

"PRETTY WELL TESTED THE STRENGTH OF OUR DEFENSIVE LINE"

The signs were unmistakable. All through the day on February 12, Grant had encircled almost all of the Southern lines, the exception being the extreme Confederate left near Lick Creek. Likewise, the Union navy appeared on the river and while not offering much of a fight, it still showed itself, as much to the Union army ashore as to the Confederates. The defenders inside Fort Donelson knew exactly what it all meant. "The smoke of his gunboats was seen in the distance," Confederate engineer Jeremy Gilmer wrote, "warning us that a combined attack was to be expected."[1]

This day, February 13, would certainly see the beginning of major hostilities around Fort Donelson, both on land and on water, but it would also see additional fighting as far back as Fort Henry. Lieutenant Colonel J. H. Miller of the 1st Mississippi Cavalry led his troopers on raids against Fort Heiman, hoping to disrupt some of Lew Wallace's foraging parties who were, Miller said, "committing terrible depredations on the citizens." Miller had with him many of the units from Fort Heiman that had not escaped across the river, including Padgett's, Hubbard's, and Houston's companies of cavalry.[2]

By far, the biggest decision of this day came in once and for all committing the Fort Donelson garrison to live or die with the result of the defense there. Pillow and Floyd had made the decision the morning before, and regiment after regiment began to flow into the fort. Some, such as Colonel William E. Baldwin's brigade from Cumberland City, including the 26th Mississippi and 26th Tennessee, arrived in the early hours of February 13 and were immediately sent to the works. Others arrived after daylight, when the significant artillery and sharpshooter fire picked up once more; "every time a head appears above the earthworks," one Federal wrote, "a ball goes through it." The 42nd Tennessee marched off their transport at Dover "under a heavy fire," the adjutant remembered. They had two or three men wounded as they marched through the town toward the lines. The Virginia battery under John H. Guy had two shells hit their steamboat as they approached the landing around noon. Others had a safer time, including Floyd's last two Virginia regiments under Colonel John McCausland of the 36th Virginia as well as the attached 20th Mississippi.[3]

Perhaps the most important arrival was that of one man. Not satisfied with his current crop of generals at the fort, Albert Sidney Johnston sent one last general officer into the growing confusion of Fort Donelson, and this decision would play out significantly over the course of the next few days. Johnston telegraphed on the evening of February 12 for John B. Floyd, currently at Clarksville and Cumberland City, to move to the fort; he also gave him complete command: "I give you full authority to make all the dispositions of your troops for the defenses of Fort Donelson, Clarksville and the Cumberland you may think proper." Such was a huge task for a politician-soldier, but Johnston continually refused to move to the crisis point himself and take command. Consequently, Floyd would be the decision maker. He took a steamer immediately and reached Fort Donelson the morning of February 13, even before the sun rose. Floyd immediately rode the lines to see for himself what kind of defense could be made and then made his headquarters at a house just two blocks up from the Dover Hotel.[4]

Floyd's arrival was significant, but not so much because another general was needed; in fact, there were more generals of perceived high rank than positions. All except for Johnson, who with his civilian cap and cloak caused one Mississippian to state that he "resembled more a little Jewish merchant than a Confederate general," perceived themselves as higher-level commanders despite their actual rank as brigadier generals. Buckner had commanded a division in Johnston's army at Bowling Green, and even Johnson had claim to commanding a division here at Fort Donelson. Pillow had certainly commanded larger organizations and was in command of the fort as a whole prior to Floyd's arrival. Floyd technically outranked them all by date of appointment. So, while all the brigades in the Confederate army were commanded by ranking colonels, none of the brigadier generals was willing to command a lowly brigade, while several actually desired command of the fort itself.[5]

The major problem was between Pillow and Floyd. Buckner and Johnson were seemingly content to command their divisions, but Floyd's arrival put the Confederate command system in jeopardy. Pillow had been extremely active and efficient in his command of the fort. His messages while in command rang with optimism, almost daring the enemy to come and attack him and his fort. When Floyd arrived and took command, Pillow seemed to slink back into the masses but remained unable or unwilling to let this slight pass. In fact, Pillow seemed determined to maintain at least some of his independence and power, now writing Governor Harris much more frequently than he did Johnston or anyone else. It seemed Pillow was grasping at anyone who would listen and reverted back to his old power base within Tennessee's politics and militia.[6]

On the other hand, an extremely hesitant Floyd took command from the passionate Pillow. The two had already sparred over whether to reinforce or evacuate Fort Donelson. The result was that Floyd changed his mind despite the fact that Pillow was his junior. Floyd had a tendency to waffle, especially when confronted by a forceful personality such as Pillow's. Pillow now had little to do except exert his forceful personality against the man whom he viewed as an interloper. A volatile mixture thus emerged. Albert Sidney Johnston would have been much better off had he placed one or the other in command. Retaining both when only one was actually needed was a formula for disaster.[7]

Such command chaos is evident in the account of Virginia battery commander John H. Guy. His unit arrived around noon on February 13, and Bushrod Johnson immediately ordered him to move to the line. Guy wrote that although Johnson seemed nice enough, "I saw no manifestation of generalship." When on the way, the battery ran into Pillow, who asked who they were and where they were going. When told Johnson had ordered them to the line, Pillow "exhibited some indignation" and countermanded the orders. Then the Virginians met Floyd, whom they knew well. Guy wrote that "Genl. Floyd was present, but seemed not to be exercising Command, Genl. P. was giving orders, & would occasionally mention one of them to Genl. F & explain it to him. Whence I inferred that Genl. P was in Command."[8]

On top of such a hesitant character, Floyd was also not well liked even in his Virginia brigades. One Virginian told of an episode when the generals came riding by their lines. Floyd never acknowledged the Virginians, and Buckner and Johnson merely "touched their caps to our flag." Pillow, on the other hand, reined up his horse and addressed the troops: "I trust to old Virginia my safety and my honor." A watching soldier remembered, "the effect was electrical, and inspired the Virginians with renewed hopes and courage." A Mississippian in Floyd's command similarly wrote home, lamenting, "we are still under General Floyd," also noting that it was "unanimously agreed to petition to be transferred from Floyd." Of course, Pillow had his detractors too, perhaps more from political than military associations. Former Nashville mayor Randal McGavock of the 10th Tennessee said, for example, "I regret very much that Gen. Pillow has been placed in command, as I have no faith or confidence in him as an officer."[9]

Such was a formula for Confederate disaster, already brewing at Fort Donelson.

Although he knew little of the chaotic command situation in the Confederate lines, Grant was not about to let up. He had deployed his divisions and the navy had tested the river batteries the day before, and everyone expected this would be the deciding day. As expected, the fighting recommenced at daylight on February 13, Floyd writing that the firing "announced the opening of the conflict" and that the Federals "opened a general and active fire from all arms upon our trenches." The Confederates were not fully ready, however, so they had to depend on what defenses they had created so far.[10]

There were four parts to the Confederates' defenses. One, the most important because of the emphasis on the Federal navy and its victory at Fort Henry, was the river batteries. The entire fort's armament included eight 32-pounders, which had proved too light at Fort Henry, and a larger 10-inch columbiad and 32-pound rifle, both of which were more effective. There were also three smaller guns, including an 8-inch howitzer and "two nondescript 9-pounders." Cannoneers had trained on these guns since January, marking ranges on the riverbank at a thousand, fifteen hundred, and two thousand yards and practicing with their pieces. Another company of artillerymen, Captain R. R. Ross's men of the Maury Artillery, gave their field pieces to the other batteries and manned the rifle and two naval guns in what Haynes described as the "half-moon battery." This group sat farther up the riverbank across a small depression and was most often referred to as the "upper battery," because it was located farther up the river. Captain Joseph Dixon commanded all the guns, ably assisted by Captain Jacob Culbertson, who was without a battery

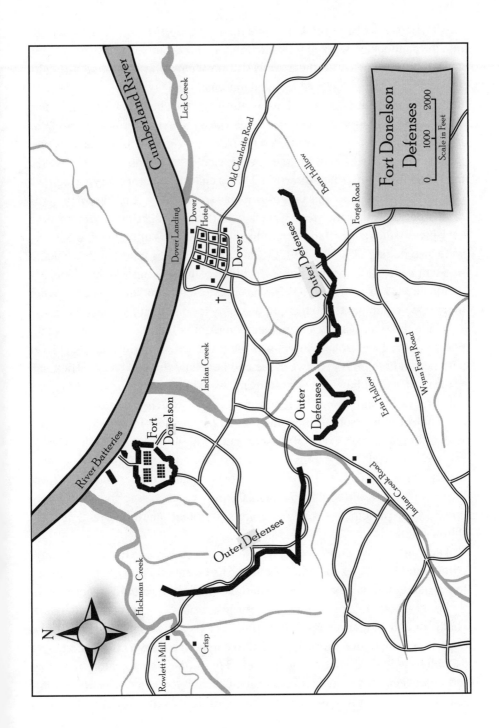

now that his guns had been left on the road from Fort Henry. While not drilling, the cannoneers worked on the defenses, embrasures, and magazines.[11]

Despite the firepower, there were still problems. Similar to the difficulty at Fort Henry, the columbiad recoiled too much; in Haynes words, "its recoil threw the gun back against the hurters, throwing the chassis off the pintle, and seriously damaging the iron barbette carriage." Haynes termed it "useless" in such condition and soon replaced the traverse wheels with larger versions, thereby raising the level of incline to work against the recoil. Haynes reported that "with these new wheels it worked like a charm," but not everyone agreed. One officer wrote that "this depression was so great that it produced a valley or bed out of which the front wheels could not be rolled, thus diminishing very greatly the range of the gun right or left." At the same time, the gunners were also having difficulty with the large rifle. Haynes reported that when it was sent to the fort, "neither pintle nor pintle plate (without which it could not be mounted) was sent with it." Haynes had to send another officer to gather the needed equipment, and the gun was only mounted on February 11.[12]

While the river batteries were the main focal points, a second major component of the Donelson defenses was the fort itself sitting just atop the river batteries on high ground between the two large and flooded creeks, Hickman to the north and Indian to the south. Inside were hundreds of small cabins, one soldier describing them as "log houses . . . all of which are of uniform size, and built in regular order, they are about 12 by 15 feet inside and provided with a fireplace each." The 30th, 49th, and 50th Tennessee of John Head's brigade occupied these cabins and manned the fort itself. A third major area of concern was the town of Dover a mile or so up the Cumberland River from the river batteries and fort. It contained the only good landing and accordingly housed "our principal supplies of commissary and quartermaster's stores," Pillow wrote.[13]

The fourth area consisted of the landward defenses. Engineer Jeremy Gilmer laid out "lines of infantry cover," as he called them, "on commanding grounds around the place and fatigue parties were daily employed in their construction." Initially these were just around the fort itself, between Hickman and Indian creeks, but as more troops and supplies arrived in the days after Fort Henry, Gilmer decided to extend the lines to surround Dover as well, reaching almost to Lick Creek. These lines ran for more than two miles between Hickman Creek and Lick Creek, but dangerously crossed Indian Creek in the process, one observer writing that the creeks and ravines were "almost wide and deep enough to be called valleys." Unfortunately for the defenders, the trenches were not formidable as yet. One Texan described them as "small saplings, with which that country abounds, thrown lengthwise along the outside margin of ditches, dug some 5 feet wide and 2 feet deep, the dirt having been thrown upon the saplings, and giving us protection of about 5 feet."[14]

Confederate soldiers toiled night and day on these works and abatis, one Mississippian writing in his diary, "made Breast Works of brush and through up a ditch on the inside which took us all night to do." Without much opposition, the Confederates were initially not that enthused with the task: "we were at first much more careless than afterward," another Mississippian reported. As more and more Federals appeared, however, the entrenchment effort increased, especially when a sudden burst of musketry "was heard in front of us and simultaneously a shower of balls were whizzing along our works." Soldiers digging outside the trenches dropped their tools and scampered inside while those atop them "rolled or jumped to the same place."[15]

Even as they grew stronger, the outer defenses were a source of concern for the Confederate high command. Buckner characterized them as "in a very imperfect condition," and wrote that they "consisted of a few logs rolled together and but slightly covered with earth, forming an insufficient protection even against field artillery." He also complained that the defenses had been located "near the crests of a series of ridges, which sloped backward to the river, and were again commanded in several places by other ridges at a still greater distance from the river." He also noted that the Confederate line was periodically broken by "deep valleys and ravines, which materially interfered with communications between different parts of the line." Pillow complained as well: the entire area "was commanded by the heights above and below on the river and by a continuous range of hills all around the works to the rear." Once Floyd arrived, he seconded Pillow's grim assessment, writing that they were "in many places . . . injudiciously constructed, because of the distance they were placed from the brow of the hill, subjecting the men to a heavy fire from the enemy's sharpshooters." Yet these outer works were all that the defending Confederates had, and they were manned continually from February 12 onward, although most commanders opted to keep only a portion of their troops on the front line at the same time. Nathaniel Cheairs of the 3rd Tennessee, for example, remembered "occasionally alternating" his companies. The officers also tried to instill some faith in the works, Bushrod Johnson himself walking along the line of Thomas Davidson's brigade "and direct[ing] us how to manage for the best in our fortifying land[.] reminded of the invaluable benefit we might derive from them."[16]

There was precious little time given to prepare further. The Federal artillery and sharpshooters opened up at daylight on February 13, harassing the Confederate lines. The firing even reached the officers' slave cooks behind the lines, who found "there were more Negroes than holes so they piled up three or four deep in a hole." One Tennessee soldier told the story that "Old Ike Suttle was at the bottom and Ned Brown was on the top in one hole when old Ike yelled out 'git offen me — you is mashing the life outen me.'" A shell burst at that exact time, and Ned Brown obliged: "Unker Ike, if youse tired down dar, you git up here and let me git down dar awhile."[17]

Perhaps because of such flimsy defenses, the Confederates inside Fort Donelson put their trust in God. Captain Dabney Carr Harrison of the 56th Virginia was not only a company captain but also a Presbyterian minister, and he gathered his company in the works as dawn crept forward that morning. He read to them from Psalm 27: "The Lord is my light and my salvation: whom shall I fear; the Lord is the strength of my life; of whom shall I be afraid? When the wicked, even mine enemies and my foes, come upon me to eat up my flesh, they stumbled and fell. Though a host should encamp against me, my heart shall not fear; though war should rise against me, in this will I be confident." An onlooker remembered, "all the men around him listened with heads uncovered and bowed on that solemn and still, cold winter morning. Some repeated after him."[18]

If the Confederate garrison at Fort Donelson was not completely ready for action as dawn came on February 13, neither were the Federals. Most were more interested in getting breakfast that morning than fighting because most had nothing to eat for hours now. One Federal in the 17th Illinois wrote of having "hard crackers & raw ham for breakfast," adding in his letter to his wife, "by the way it tasted *mighty good* too." As a result, the onslaught from land and water that the Confederates expected did not come about. The ironclads and land reinforcements moving by river had not all appeared yet, and Grant chose to take his time and continue to solidify his position, tightening the noose around the Confederates inside Fort Donelson. Consequently, February 13 did not develop into a critical day at Fort Donelson but rather morphed into a series of isolated attacks that produced little effect except indicating to the Confederates the trouble they were in.[19]

One of the isolated attacks came on the Cumberland River, "very high and angry from recent rains," as one Confederate described it. The ironclad *Carondelet* once again tested the Confederate river batteries alone because Foote's flotilla from Cairo would not arrive until after dark. Accordingly, despite its reported sinking the day before, the *Carondelet* soon produced a ruckus, what Pillow described as "quite a lively cannonade."[20]

Commander Walke weighed anchor early that morning, moving slowly up the river toward Fort Donelson. Fortunately for him, he received a dispatch from Grant indicating that his army had encircled the Confederate works and that "most of our batteries . . . are [now] established, and the remainder soon will be." Grant added, "if you will advance with your gunboats at 10 o'clock a. m., we will be ready to take advantage of every diversion in our favor." Grant obviously did not know that only Walke and the *Carondelet* were present, but the navy man set out to accommodate the army general.[21]

The *Carondelet* rounded the bend in the river more than two miles from the fort and immediately began to pepper the river batteries with shot and shell. Walke utilized his three bow guns and reported that he fired "some 139 15-second and 10-second shell into the fort, receiving on return the enemy's fire from all their batteries." Milton Haynes reported, "the gunboats opened a spirited cannonade of shot and shells from heavy rifled and smooth-bore guns upon the batteries and fort." Captain Ross on the big rifle reported, "during this hour and forty minutes' cannonade 14 of her balls were collected in the battery within the narrow radius of as many yards."[22]

Some of the gunners were still training on the guns when the gunboat appeared, so the Confederates quickly returned fire. Soon the river batteries were ablaze with fire down the valley. All guns opened up, Haynes noting that it was done "though at too long a range." Culbertson, commanding at the 32-pounders, wrote that he opened with the smaller pieces "at our maximum elevation; but our shot all fell short." Captain Bidwell similarly noted that he "opened with my guns at the highest possible elevation. I soon found, however, that I could do no good, as they were beyond my range, and, the boat falling below the point, I ceased firing." The 10-inch columbiad and the rifle did good work, on the other hand, Captain Ross reporting that "we returned her fire with great vigor from the rifle, firing as often as the heat of the gun would allow."[23]

The Confederate guns only hit the *Carondelet* twice, one of which was not serious. The other proved a cause for Union concern. One of the rifle's 128-pound solid shot "passed through our port casemate forward, glancing over our barricade at the boilers, and again over the steam drum, it struck and, bursting our steam heater, fell into the engine room without striking any person." Walke was amazed that no one had been hit or killed by the large cannonball bouncing around inside his gunboat. One of his crew described the feeling that the ball "seemed to bound after the men . . . like a wild beast pursuing its prey." Miraculously, only a few sailors received minor splinter wounds when the ball went through the wood portions of the vessel. Flying splinters wounded six of the crew, but that was remarkable compared to the damage that could have been caused had the ball hit a truly important part of the gunboat such as the engines or the boilers. Despite only the steam heater having been knocked out, Walke decided he had provided enough of a disturbance for Grant and, as he reported, "I then dropped down to this anchorage," firing as he retired.[24]

The Confederate gunners were elated that they had hit and perhaps fatally damaged yet another ironclad. Not knowing that this was the same *Carondelet* from the evening before, one Confederate officer noted that the effect was "driving the boats back under the shelter of a bend in the river, from which they continued to throw shells." Captain Ross went so far as to declare, "it was seldom that the rifle missed now, we supposed, as we could tell by the spray to the right or left when we did not strike."[25]

Unfortunately for the Confederate gunners, the next-to-last shell fired by the *Carondelet* caused most of the killing inflicted by the gunboat that day. The shell tore through an embrasure and hit one of Bidwell's 32-pounders on the cheek, dismounting it in the process. Captain Dixon, in command of the river batteries, was just then passing from Bidwell's first gun to the second when it was hit. Freakishly, the captain was stooping because of the incoming shells "when a screw-tap struck him in the left temple, killing him instantly." Ross noted that it hit him in the head, "smashing in his whole forehead." In addition to Dixon, a few other gunners were killed and wounded, and Captain J. P. Shuster was temporarily disabled, Bidwell reported, "by negligently standing too near the muzzle of one of my guns." Others atop the hill were also hit when shells went among the infantry or the cabins, one hitting a mule.[26]

Floyd immediately ordered the gun remounted, and Gideon Pillow told one of Bidwell's boys that he would give "one hundred dollars in gold" if he could remount it. Unfortunately, the man had no tools, and Haynes had to send a dozen artificers and carpenters to do the work. Ross ordered his men to collect the unexploded Parrott shells in the vicinity, and they lined fourteen of them "in a row in our little fort intending when the victory was gained to place them in the capitol at Nashville." More problematic was the loss of Dixon, whose death caused a crisis in command at the batteries. An injured Haynes was having to rely on crutches to get around and could only walk in "great pain"; he obviously could not be the mobile commander he needed to be but nevertheless took a position amid the batteries to offer what leadership he could. Instead, Haynes placed Captain Culbertson in charge of the batteries, although Captain Ross ranked him. Ross did not make an issue of it and "found no necessity nor had any desire to take any authority over so accomplished an officer as Major Culbertson, as we called him, and [we] continued virtually as before."[27]

Walke had clearly provided Grant some cover for any landward attacks, and as the afternoon approached, he could continually hear the "sound of distant firing." Wondering whether he could make any more difference, Walke again set out to engage the Confederate river batteries and threw around forty-five shells into the works during the afternoon's bombardment. Although the Confederate gunners hit the *Carondelet* once more, Walke reported he received "but little damage" and soon departed back downstream where he hoped to meet Foote and the rest of the flotilla. When he got there, another note from Grant was waiting for him indicating that Foote would be on station "on the following morning." Grant also wrote that the landward operations were going fine: "we are doing well on the land side. How are you?," he wrote. No doubt the isolated Walke breathed a sigh of relief.[28]

Despite its limited duration, the small naval fight that afternoon had major repercussions. It had not inflicted much damage, but the Confederates misinterpreted the events once again. One artilleryman noted that "it really appeared as if the boat was diabolically inspired, and knew the most opportune times to annoy us." Captain Ross declared that it was a different gunboat from the morning's action and was seen to "be in distress and finally dropped down." Haynes wrote that the gunboat "returned to the contest, keeping up a continued discharge of shells and solid shot upon our batteries, without, however, doing us any material damage." He also reported, "our fire was for some time carefully withheld in order to draw the boats nearer to us." Haynes again reported that the 10-inch columbiad and the rifle drove the gunboat away, adding, "one of the boats being so seriously injured that she (as we afterwards learned) was with difficulty kept from sinking." If Walke's crew had trouble keeping his vessel afloat, he certainly knew nothing about it. Still, the Confederate gunners were joyous, as were Pillow and Floyd, who came down to the batteries and offered their personal commendation for the stellar work. Thrice now they had "driven" away an enemy gunboat. Morale was inching upward in the beleaguered Fort Donelson garrison.[29]

Thanks to the *Carondelet*'s shelling, Grant had what he wanted: a diversion that he could use to help his actions on the land side. Historians have long argued whether or not Grant intended to fight on February 13, and several statements made in official reports do not add up. For instance, Grant told Walke that he was interested in any navy diversion that he might be able to use for an advantage on land. On the other hand, McClernand noted in his report that he was ordered to "avoid everything calculated to bring on a general engagement until otherwise directed." Grant himself made no comment on the February 13 land attacks until his memoirs appeared decades later. In those memoirs, he castigated one division commander while not complaining of the other, both of whom launched attacks. It could be that Grant had issued orders not to bring on an engagement and then changed those orders. A tantalizing February 13 note to McClernand, in fact, appears in Grant's papers: "men on the left have charged up to the Abattis but found it impossible to get through." Whether the note came to McClernand before his assault and thus influenced him to conduct his own attack is not known, but Grant used the word "charged," which could only have indicated to McClernand that Grant was sanctioning an assault.[30]

Whatever the cause, there were at least two major assaults on the Confederate works that day. The smaller of the two occurred on the extreme Confederate right or Union left, where a portion of one of C. F. Smith's brigades attacked Buckner's division. Unfortunately for the attacking Federals, the assault came through some of the most difficult terrain on the lines, where the Confederates had a distinct tactical advantage. In the area overlooking Hickman Creek on the far Confederate right, the ridges were mostly parallel, with the Confederate position located on the highest point around. Buckner could afford to man this section with fewer troops, concentrating larger numbers and the artillery batteries on the more approachable areas farther to the east. Buckner essentially had two brigades inside Fort Donelson, one Tennessee unit of three regiments under Colonel John C. Brown of the 3rd Tennessee, which had a fine brass band attached, and the other a mixed brigade under Colonel William E. Baldwin of the 14th Mississippi, although Baldwin and the 26th Mississippi and 26th Tennessee manned the line farther to the east. Baldwin complained that his brigade had been split up, but reported, "neither representations nor solicitations on my part could avail in inducing such change as would reunite these regiments." Buckner placed one of Baldwin's regiments, the elite 2nd Kentucky under Colonel Roger W. Hanson, on the extreme right, bounding the Hickman Creek bottom farther west, and filled in the remainder of the line to the east toward Porter's Tennessee battery with the 18th Tennessee of Brown's brigade. Buckner kept another of Baldwin's regiments, the 14th Mississippi, in reserve behind Porter's salient, and continued the line eastward with the rest of Brown's regiments, the 3rd and 32nd Tennessee extending to the left from Porter's position. Filling in the line from Brown's left to Graves's battery, also in a salient on high ground covering the Indian Creek bottom, was another of Baldwin's units, the 41st Tennessee. As a result, the majority of the line was studded by Brown's Tennessee brigade, with the three present regiments of Baldwin's brigade, temporarily assigned to Brown, sparsed out on the right and left and in reserve. In front, the timber had been cut, one of Graves's artillerymen declaring "to the bottom of the hill & in some cases up to the top of the opposite hill."[31]

Smith's Federal division began to confront this Confederate line even on the afternoon of February 12 and continually made its way forward that day and the next, placing batteries to duel with Porter's and Graves's guns. In the 18th Tennessee, William McKay wrote, "it was amusing (but serious) to see our actions when the Yankee battery opened on our line. We had never heard bomb shells whistle by and had heard but few minie balls. At first we looked surprised and uneasy[.] about the second round every fellow fell to his knees and at the third fell flat on the ground." Sharpshooters also raked the Confederate line, one hitting Mississippi Secession Convention delegate, former US Federal judge, and future Confederate general Samuel J. Gholson (now a captain in the 14th Mississippi) in the chest. He was soon removed to Nashville with the other wounded. In response to the sharpshooters, brigade commander Brown ordered his men to put head logs atop their breastworks, leaving "port holes" to shoot through. Then, of course, the Federal

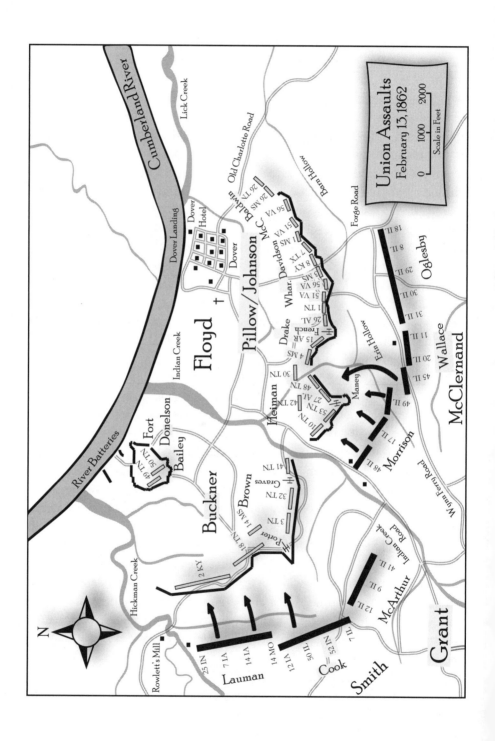

Union Assaults
February 13, 1862

0   1000   2000
Scale in Feet

Cumberland River

Lick Creek

Old Charlotte Road

Barn Hollow

Forge Road

Dover Landing

Dover Hotel

Dover

Floyd

Pillow/Johnson

McC.
Baldwin
26 TN
56 VA
51 VA
3 MS
8 KY
7 TX
Davidson
Whar.
56 VA
51 VA
1 TN
26 AL
French
13 AR
4 MS
Drake
30 TN
Maney
42 TN
48 TN
53 TN
27 AL
Heiman
10 TN
17 IL
48 IL

Erin Hollow

Wallace

Oglesby
18 IL
8 IL
29 IL
30 IL
31 IL
11 IL
20 IL
45 IL
49 IL

Morrison

McClernand

W. Jun Ferry Road

Indian Creek

River Batteries

Fort Donelson
Bailey
49 TN
50 TN

Buckner

Indian Creek

Brown
41 TN
Graves
32 TN
3 TN
Porter
14 MS
18 TN
2 KY

Smith

McArthur
41 IL
6 IL
12 IL
7 IL

Cook
50 IL
52 IN
121 IN
14 MO
14 IA
7 IA
25 IN

Lauman

Indian Creek Road

Hickman Creek

Rowlett's Mill

Grant

N

sharpshooters began firing through the holes. Meanwhile, the artillerymen of Graves's and Porter's batteries were not anxious to respond, one cannoneer writing, "we did not intend they should find us out until they were within good range & were visible."[32]

The aggressive Smith was not content with mere artillery and small-arms fire, however; he was looking for an opportunity to assault and perhaps break the enemy line and so earn a victory. Numerous exploratory parties accordingly went forward to locate soft defenses. At one point, Confederates in Graves's battery and Brown's brigade saw "an engineer mounted upon a white horse [who] rode coolly down the valley to within six hundred yds of our line & surveyed us with his field glass." He went on to describe the result: "a sharpshooter having obtained permission, crept down the hillside to within three or four hundred yards of him & tried several shots at him without effect; he bowed gracefully, wheeled his horse & rejoined his escort."[33]

With some information in hand, Smith pushed his three brigades forward on the morning of February 13 with the same deployment as the day before. Jacob Lauman's mixed Iowa and Indiana brigade held the far left near Hickman Creek, and John Cook's Illinois, Indiana, Iowa, and Missouri brigade manned the right. All the while, Smith kept John McArthur's all-Illinois brigade in reserve behind the two frontline units. Looking for an opening, Smith pushed his brigades forward but noted, "the ground covered by the division was thickly wooded and exceedingly hilly and broken," and added, "the enemy's works were on the highest ground in the vicinity." He described those works as "an infantry breast-work in front of his main line (vaguely called rifle pits), crested with logs, from under which they fired." Only portions of the works could even be seen, as Colonel James C. Veatch of the 25th Indiana reported: "the timber was so thick that we could only see here and there a part of the rebel works, but could form no idea of their range or extent." By far, the most troubling aspect of the defenses was that the entire Confederate line was "strengthened by a wide abatis from felled timber of large size." Smith admitted that without much information on the terrain and the Confederate defenses, he had to move forward slowly and "feel our way cautiously." The brigade commanders therefore strengthened the skirmishers and moved on, with orders from Smith to "press forward as steadily and rapidly as the ground would admit, and, if the opportunity offered, to assault with the bayonet."[34]

Smith was on the ground and active in prodding for an opening. He pushed the brigades onward, covered by the Missouri artillery batteries on a ridge to the rear; there Stone's, Welker's, and Richardson's Missouri batteries, collectively known as Cavender's artillery battalion, fired into the Confederate works and dueled with Porter's battery farther to their left. Porter's cannoneers did good work, several of the Missouri gunners having to change their position because of hot incoming artillery fire. Yet even as the artillery exchanged shots, Smith determined that an infantry assault was indeed needed and chose to send a portion of Lauman's brigade forward.[35]

Smith ordered Lauman to send the left of his brigade, that farthest toward Hickman Creek, forward against the Confederate line. The left consisted of the 25th Indiana on the left and the 14th Iowa on the right, the 7th Iowa remaining behind for the time being in reserve. Lauman led the troops forward over intervening ridges and ravines; Colonel James C. Veatch of the 25th Indiana reported that just as he topped "the hill which was between us and the enemy's breastworks," about 10:00 AM, Lauman ordered him to "fix bayonets and charge the rebels, and, if possible, drive them from their works." Lauman wrote, "the advance was made steadily and in as good order as the nature of the ground would admit of until we reached the ravine at the base of the hill on which were the enemy's fortifications."[36]

The lines were necessarily deformed while moving into the valley, and Lauman called a halt to re-form before sending the troops up the steep incline toward the waiting 2nd Kentucky. Throughout, the Confederates poured a heavy fire into the Indianans and Iowans, Veatch writing that "at the foot of the hill the enemy poured on us a terrible fire of musketry, grape, and canister, with a few shells." It only became worse once starting up the long hill, and the Indianans and Iowans soon met three terrible problems. One was the blistering fire of the 2nd Kentucky, which by this time had been reinforced by two companies of Colonel Joseph B. Palmer's 18th Tennessee. Lauman reported that the regiments "moved steadily up the hill and toward the entrenchments under a most galling fire of musketry and grape." His report then alluded to a second major problem, which was the flanking fire sent into the brigade from Porter's battery farther down the line to the east. One Federal wrote how he hit the ground "as the grape shot as large as walnuts whistled over a few inches above my head, [and] I rooted down till I buried my face in the sand to get my head lower. I do not think mother earth ever received a closer or more affectionate embrace. It was also the first time I was ever compelled to 'root hog or die.'" By far, the third and most problematic issue was the abatis. Veatch wrote, "the heavy timber on the hillside had been felled, forming a dense mass of brush and logs. Through and over these obstacles our men advanced against the enemy's fire with perfect coolness and steadiness." Yet Lauman not surprisingly reported, "their onward progress was obstructed by the fallen timber and brushwood."[37]

Caught as they were in the interlocking branches of the felled trees, the Indianans on the left were stymied, but that did not stop them from trying again. "After a halt of a few minutes," Veatch reported, "they again advanced within a short distance of the enemy's breastworks." Artillery fire from Porter's battery swept the hillside, however, and Veatch wrote that "it became necessary to halt and direct the men to lie down to save us from very heavy losses." Casualties resulted anyway, including Captain Samuel Laird of Company K, who despite being hit in the leg refused to leave until compelled to do so; even then, "he cheered his men when he retired." Even worse, the Federals could see that the Confederate lines extended far beyond their own left, and Veatch sent a few flanking companies toward the west to keep Confederates manning those works occupied, thus "preventing a fire on our flank from the enemy's rifle pits." Veatch also reported small artillery fire from that direction. All the while, the infantry remained in their position, trading fire with the Kentuckians on the hill in an unequal contest. Casualties of course began to mount as the Indianans lay stationary for two long hours, waiting to see if any success could be had elsewhere.[38]

There was none. The 14th Iowa to the right was having no better success, running into "a heavy fire of musketry," which they could only see by the smoke. Some found the going easier by using a small hill on their right as cover for the right wing, although the left wing remained exposed. One member of the regiment described the sprint to get behind the cover on the right, and several men were lost in the process, although one Espy McKune was hit right in the cartridge-box buckle and spared. Others had near misses as well, one Iowan writing, "a miss of an inch is as good as a mile." Even behind the hill, the fire of Porter's battery was still heavy, although Colonel William T. Shaw reported that it "did but little damage, as the range was too high." There, he re-formed the companies, "the line being much broken, owing to the unevenness of the ground and the thick fallen timber." In fact, Shaw wrote that it was "impossible to advance in line of battle." From their stopping point, the Iowans poured their fire into the works above them but were shielded somewhat better than were the Indianans, experiencing far fewer casualties. "We carried on the fight in Bushwhacking style for several hours as we could neither advance nor retreat," wrote one Iowan. "It was rather an uncomfortable predicament we had got into."[39]

Fearing that his regiments were fatally separated, Lauman sent one of his reserve units, the 7th Iowa, into the breach between the Indianans on the left and the Iowans on the right. Their numbers could not materially change the dynamics of the fight, however, and Confederate fire and the thick abatis stopped the advance. Lauman then settled for sending a regiment of sharp-shooters farther to the right and a portion as skirmishers in the front to harass the Confederate defenders, most notably the gunners of Porter's battery to the east that were making life so difficult on the slope of the ridge.[40]

The battery was indeed a problem for the Federals. Colonel Hanson wrote that Porter's gunners "always fired at the right time and to the right place," allowing Hanson to have an easy time of his defense. With only his Kentuck-ians and two companies of the neighboring 18th Tennessee sent over for help, he held the ridge easily against what he declared were three different attacks. Certainly the 25th Indiana advanced twice, and he might have construed the advance of the 14th Iowa as a separate attack, or the arrival and advance of the 7th Iowa as such. No matter how many attacks came, Hanson easily held his own.[41]

After a couple of hours of useless sacrifice, Veatch and Shaw had seen enough. "With no opportunity to return the fire to advantage, the enemy be-ing almost entirely hid, and seeing no movement indicating a further advance from any part of the line," Veatch wrote, " I asked your permission to with-draw my regiment, to save it from heavy loss where we could do no good." Shaw also began a withdrawal "after waiting about an hour, and seeing no movement on my left." He first withdrew his more exposed left but then took the entire regiment to the rear. Lauman certainly agreed about the need to fall back, and Smith did as well: "the reports of the different commanders," he wrote, "partially confirmed by my personal observations, satisfied me that an assault on almost any part of the entire front covered by us was not practi-cable without enormous sacrifice of life." He consequently ordered Lauman to withdraw to the bottom of the hill and take cover until nightfall, when the troops were withdrawn even farther over the tall ridge in their rear, back to the jumping-off point of that morning. Some withdrew a different way; one Iowan noted, "we saw the way it was going and retreated round the hill about dark without losing any more men." He concluded, "we blundered ahead a lit-tle too far but we got out pretty safe considering the place we had got into."[42]

It was the first major land attack on Fort Donelson, and if this was any indication, the Confederate bastion was not going to easily fall. In the assault,
the 25th Indiana had lost fourteen killed and sixty-one wounded while the
other regiments had fewer casualties. It had been worth a try, but now Smith
knew that it was going to take much more effort than one isolated assault.[43]

Smith's attack on the far Union left came at about the same time that the
Carondelet advanced against the water batteries. The major attack of the day,
however, came a couple of hours later and in the center of the Confederate
line. Working off the same orders as Smith, McClernand came to the same
conclusion and advanced against a Confederate salient in the line, hopeful of
breaking through and winning a victory.[44]

McClernand might also have been influenced by additional insights from
Grant. The division commander has been roundly criticized for attacking
against Grant's orders, historians citing his own words "to avoid everything
calculated to bring on a general engagement until otherwise directed." Grant
added fuel to the fire in his memoirs decades later, criticizing McClernand for
attacking "without orders or authority." Historians have followed this thinking ever since, despite the fact that Grant made no objection at the time and
despite the fact that Smith was not later criticized for doing the same thing
McClernand did. There might possibly be more than we know, however,
Grant's note about the "charge" on the left potentially fueling McClernand's
determination. McClernand also wrote Grant that day asking for clarification: "I would be pleased to be advised of any plans of operations and attack
which you may have designed and decided upon." For whatever the reason,
McClernand was soon obeying what he called "the spirit of your order." He
opened with his artillery and later contemplated attacking with Oglesby's
brigade. He countermanded that order but then did indeed advance another
of his brigades with additional support, writing, "I deemed the opportunity
favorable for storming redan No. 2."[45]

The attack came in the center, against one of the strongest sections of Confederate earthworks manned by infantry and a battery of four guns. The line
was under the command of Colonel Adolphus Heiman. The Tennessean noted
his position "was a hill somewhat in the shape of a V, with the apex at the angle." Essentially, Heiman held the isolated position between Indian Creek on
his right, where Buckner's command in the form of Graves's battery ended,

and its tributary, Erin (also called Aaron) Hollow, which branched off to the southeast and flowed in a large curve back to the southwest. The two creeks joined in rear of the Confederate line, and the high ground between the two south of the confluence was manned not only by Heiman's infantry but also by Maney's Tennessee Battery. Heiman was first under Bushrod Johnson and then Pillow's command, so the Indian Creek watershed was the junction of the two divisions and Erin Hollow was the junction of Heiman's and Drake's brigades. Consequently, Heiman stuck out from the line, detached from the rest by two creeks and large hollows that joined in his rear. He was virtually alone inside his own hilltop bastion.[46]

Fortunately for him, Heiman had ample power in his little cul-de-sac. His line ran from the valley of Indian Creek, where it joined Buckner's division, westward up the summit of the extremely high hill and then down the equally sloping eastern side to Erin Hollow. Fearing for the larger Indian Creek watershed, Heiman placed the capable 10th Tennessee on the right sloping down into the hollow, with the 53rd Tennessee manning the line as it climbed to the apex, where Maney's four guns held the salient itself. The 27th Alabama and 48th Tennessee manned the southeast face of the V, the Alabamians supporting Maney's guns and the Tennesseans holding the line down into Erin Hollow. Heiman also had additional firepower sent to him later on, including the 42nd Tennessee that was held in reserve, although several of its companies entered the earthworks during the fighting. Colonel Head's 30th Tennessee was also detached from the actual fort's garrison and sent to the outer lines. Head took a position in Erin Hollow itself, between Heiman's and Drake's brigades, although no one informed Heiman of the addition: "I was afterwards informed that this regiment was also placed under my command," Heiman wrote, "but, the colonel not having reported to me, I did not know it."[47]

As a result, McClernand faced a powerful line, and for some reason chose his least powerful brigade to make the assault. Oglesby and Will Wallace had already shifted to the right down the Wynn Ferry Road, leaving Morrison's recently created brigade in the general area of Maney's defensive salient. Desiring to attack there, McClernand used this small two-regiment brigade (a third regiment having been left at Fort Henry), although he added additional regiments as needed to the assault force. In particular, McClernand ordered the detached 48th Illinois, a part of Wallace's brigade that had been left behind in the eastward movement to support McAllister's battery west of Indian Creek, to join in on the left of the assault. McAllister was in a heavy fight himself and needed the support, although he was smart in pulling his pieces back behind the ridge to load and only then running the guns up to fire over the heights. "The recoil would throw the guns back out of sight, and thus we continued the fight," McAllister reported. Still, a Confederate shot cut a wheel in two on one of his three guns. Despite the fire, Colonel Isham N. Haynie moved his 48th Illinois eastward from the high ground west of Indian Creek about five hundred yards to a position on Morrison's left, which placed the regiment just across Indian Creek and on the western slopes of the ridge running toward Maney's position. The 17th Illinois of Morrison's brigade was next in line, the left of the regiment across the ridge and taking fire from Graves's battery, which had by this time opened up. The right of the 17th Illinois and the 49th Illinois were on the far right down the eastern slope of the ridge and in the valley of the upper reaches of Erin Hollow.[48]

Morrison's February 13 attack is misunderstood in many ways. The attack has almost always been presented as occurring northwestward across the valley of Erin Hollow toward the apex and left face of Maney's battery salient. Part of the reason is probably the fact that Morrison said that he formed the regiments southeast of Maney's position, but he was evidently off on his directions, as was very common. Another indication could be that the War Department placed a tablet for Morrison southeast of the salient in the 1920s or 1930s, when the Fort Donelson National Battlefield was first established. A series of National Park Service maps that have been the basis for almost all maps since the 1950s shows the attack occurring from southeast to northwest, and historians since then have almost always taken that as the true angle of attack, particularly in map presentations.[49]

In actuality, the attack moved from the southwest to the northeast mainly against the apex and southwestern face of the salient rather than the southeastern front. Multiple pieces of evidence bear this out, including Heiman's report that the enemy deployed "in the woods in front of my right and center." The terrain at the battlefield also indicates that since Graves's Confederate gunners clearly fired into the attackers, that could only have happened if the attack occurred west of the ridge and not through Erin Hollow. Moreover, the southwestern face of the salient provided much better ground over which to attack; the southeastern face fronted the curving sweep of Erin Hollow and provided much the same type of almost impossible terrain that Smith faced on the far left. There was also a large clearing in that direction, which was easily swept by Maney's guns; Confederates of Drake's brigade down the line could see all the way to Maney's position and watched the show, one Arkansan excitedly noting, "I saw it all. . . . the sun was shining their bayonets." Much better ground for the attack thus existed on the southwestern face, including a sliver of high ground that constituted the ridge on which Maney's battery sat. In fact, the tongue of high ground ran from the confluence of Indian Creek and Erin Hollow southwestward into the Union lines, providing much better terrain over which to launch the attack. While the position of Maney's battery and the apex of the line were higher than the narrow ridge leading to it, the main portion of the column was able to utilize much better ground on the gently sloping ridge rather than crossing the steep and precipitous valley of Erin Hollow.[50]

Despite the fairly favorable terrain, much more so than Smith had faced on the left, Union miscues threatened to derail the attack even before it began. One was a potential argument over command. Once in position, Morrison learned from McClernand that he would "make the first assault upon the enemy's works, with an order to move against the enemy's redoubts to my right." He also learned that Haynie's regiment would be added as well, and Haynie soon arrived where Morrison and McClernand's staff officer Warren Stewart were conferring. Morrison wrote that "he believed he ranked me." Morrison added, "knowing that this was not time to dispute about a question of rank, I observed to Colonel Haynie that I would conduct the brigade to the point from which the attack was to be made, when he could take command, if he desired to do so." Morrison did so, but later complained that Haynie "neither declining nor assuming the command, said, 'Colonel, let us take it' (meaning the enemy's redoubt) 'together.'" Morrison took that to mean that he would retain command of the brigade. Unfortunately, Haynie did not mean it the way Morrison took it, writing that he ordered the commander "to communicate with me at or about the center of the brigade . . . and to control their movements upon the right and left wings by the center."[51]

Despite the confusion, the Union regiments swept up the length of the high ridge from the southwest toward Maney's battery. Haynie's 48th Illinois moved along the western slope of the ridge, parallel with Indian Creek. For his part, thinking he was independent, Morrison moved with his own 49th Illinois, leaving the 17th Illinois in the capable hands of Major Francis M. Smith. Morrison later admitted that he had "more confidence in the Seventeenth . . . not in their superior courage, but in their power for efficiency in an assault, acquired by length of service and consequent skill in the use of arms, as well as in evolutions and movements in the field, and having entire confidence in the ability and courage of Major Smith." Indeed, the 49th Illinois had been organized only a few weeks before and had received their arms only five days ago.[52]

Preceded by skirmishers, the three Illinois regiments moved forward astride the ridge leading to Maney's battery. "The troops moved forward with much spirit and eagerness," Morrison wrote, noting that only on the right, where he was, were the troops "sweeping down the hill some 200 yards through the thick brush in perfect order, at once commencing the ascent of the opposite ridge or mound upon the top of which the redoubt was situated." The regiments made good progress at first, the 49th Illinois on the right making better speed than the others due to more open ground. Once they reached within fifty or so paces of the Confederate line, however, "we encountered an almost impassable abatis, made by felling small trees crosswise of each other, the tops always meeting us, the difficulty increasing the nearer we approached the breastworks, where brush had been piled upon brush, with the sharpened ends confronting us." Major Smith, commanding the 17th Illinois, did not mention traversing any declivity as his regiment moved astride the ridge itself, but he did report that "the ground was difficult to get over, being composed of thick underbrush . . . [and] fallen timber."[53]

Miraculously, most of this advance was made without any return fire, but then Morrison realized what was happening. "We had advanced to within less than fifty paces of the enemy's works without his offering any opposition," he wrote, "and were making our way slowly but surely." Then the Confederate line opened up: they were "undoubtedly waiting for us," Morrison concluded. He ordered his Illinoisans over on the right to hold their fire until they reached the breastworks, hoping "I could create such confusion with one volley as would enable us to get over before the enemy recovered from the shock." That was not to be. The Illinoisans could not wait and began to fire at will, Morrison noting, "they fired without orders, though with fair precision and some effect." The same was occurring on the western side of the ridge with the 48th Illinois, Haynie writing, "from their rifle pits and earthen breastworks, which greatly protected them, the enemy opened a brisk and galling fire."[54]

Indeed, Heiman's Confederates opened a heavy fire on the Illinoisans, mostly the 10th and 53rd Tennessee on the southwestern face of the salient but also including the 27th Alabama and 48th Tennessee on the left face. Maney's guns also tore great swaths in the Union ranks. The result of the heavy abatis and the even heavier fire was that the Federal lines stalled before reaching the Confederate trenches. Morrison over on the right noted that he had to stop the 49th Illinois and take cover, waiting on the 48th Illinois on the left to make an attack, which he said never came. Obviously, Haynie disputed that, but that regiment was also stalled after trudging as far as it could go. Morrison was nevertheless bitter, perhaps more so toward Haynie than the regiment itself, but he later reported that the Illinoisans "failed to support me."[55]

Not only were the isolated units of Heiman's brigade giving the Federals plenty of fire, but others down the line were also doing so. Of even more help were the Confederate forces of Buckner's division on the high ground west of Indian Creek. Heiman had cooperated with Colonel Brown, commanding Buckner's left brigade, during the previous night to cover the Indian Creek valley, and these troops were still in the front as the Federals began to advance. Of particular aid was Graves's battery, sitting atop the apex of the high ground on the west side of Indian Creek and sweeping that lowland; "we opened an enfilading fire with shell and shrapnel," one of the cannoneers wrote, describing how "they wavered, rallied & were again repulsed falling back in disorder. A portion of the time the combatants were not forty yards apart." Although part of Buckner's division, they could plainly see the advancing Union column west of the ridge and sent a steady stream of fire into the Union flank, similar to Porter's effect on Smith's earlier attack on the 2nd Kentucky. Heiman reported that Graves "with excellent judgment opened his battery upon them across the valley." Brigade commander Brown, across Indian Creek, wrote that "before the column came within range of Colonel Heiman, and, indeed, before it could be seen from Colonel Heiman's position, I directed Captain Graves to open fire from all his guns, which he did with such spirit and fatal precision that in less than fifteen minutes the whole column staggered and took shelter in confusion and disorder . . . when Colonel Heiman opened fire upon it." The effect was not lost on Haynie and the Illinoisans trudging toward the Confederate line; he wrote, "the enemy's batteries, situated so as to be concealed from us and not before known to bear upon us, were opened and a well directed fire of shell and canister poured upon our ranks."[56]

Despite the heavy fire, the Confederate defenders suffered as well. The infantry units all sustained casualties, but Maney's battery was hit particularly hard. Several reasons existed for this carnage, including the fact that there had been insufficient time to build a worthy parapet in front of the guns. Heiman reported that the cannon were "entirely exposed" because "no time could yet have been spared to protect his guns by a parapet; besides, we were ill-provided with tools for that purpose." Likewise, the positioning of the guns was not ideal, the cannon being deployed on the geographic crest of the hill rather than on the military crest. Consequently, the Federals had some cover as they surged up the gentle incline along the narrow ridge leading to the guns. As a result, Morrison's Federals killed several officers in the battery. Bushrod Johnson described how Maney "was unable afterwards to man but two guns of the four which composed his battery," but Heiman reported, "the gallant Maney, with the balance of his men, stood by their guns like true heroes, and kept firing into their lines, which steadily advanced within 40 yards of our rifle pits, determined to force my right wing and center." Indeed, Heiman later reported that although his total casualties did not reach over forty killed and wounded, most came in Maney's battery and the 53rd Tennessee on its right.[57]

Still, Maney and the supporting infantry caused many more casualties than they sustained. McClernand was so worried that he decided to send in another regiment on the right of Morrison's brigade, the 45th Illinois detached from Wallace's unit. Like the others, the Illinoisans were no better able to reach the guns, and Haynie himself took some exception, writing, "I had not received notice until I found them on the right in this action." Even so, the brigade commander Wallace reported how the far right of the attacking column "advanced in beautiful order down the slope, across the valley, and up the opposite steep." Yet even the arrival of the 45th Illinois could not sustain the attack, and something had to give after an hour or more under heavy fire. Colonel John E. Smith wrote that "balls whistled around me (for I was exposed on horseback and the men under cover of logs) and I believe I dodged once when a shell whistled so close that I thought I felt the wind." The breaking point came when Colonel Morrison went down with a painful bullet in the hip; all order broke loose, especially on the eastern slopes of the ridge. "I was struck in the right hip with a musket ball," Morrison noted, "knocked out of the saddle, and compelled in consequence to relinquish my command."[58]

With Morrison's departure, what was left of the attack fell apart and the troops began to wind their way back down the ridge. Haynie reported, "seeing that the redoubt could not be taken without great destruction and loss of life, I at length reluctantly gave the order to retire down the hill." The colonel reported it was done "in good order and without confusion," and Haynie was further relieved when he met McClernand himself: the retreat was "greatly to my gratification, sanctioned by yourself [McClernand] when reported by me to you."[59]

Heiman noted that the enemy made as many as three attacks, probably counting the late arrival of the 45th Illinois as a separate one, but the overall assault had been costly. Morrison's two regiments lost 128 casualties, about equally divided among the two. Haynie's 48th Illinois lost only one killed and eight wounded, indicating it went to the ground amid Graves's first shots from across Indian Creek and did little thereafter. The wounded suffered the most, although surgeons aided those they could reach. This included the surgeon of the 32nd Illinois, "whose regiment was not in the engagement, and generously volunteered his professional services in the absence of my surgeon," Morrison wrote. Unfortunately, the surgeons could not get to all, and they could only do so much. One Confederate later told of "one poor wretch [who] had strength enough left to crawl up to the breastworks on our left this (Friday) morning & was helped over the logs & laid on a blanket by a fire but death soon relieved him." A similarly sad episode emerged as the cannon fire lit leaves afire in front of the Confederate salient. "The dry leaves took fire from the heavy firing and many of the wounded burned to death," Illinoisan George Smith later wrote. One Confederate described how "the groans and screams of the poor helpless men suffering this double torture were agonizing, but no help was sent and death finally put an end to their misery." A few still lingered, and their cries prompted some to offer help if the opposing skirmishers would promise not to fire, but neither side could agree and the suffering continued. Ultimately, several Confederates chanced death to go outside their lines to save those they could, but it was still a morbid scene.[60]

Besides the three major attacks, continuous fighting also raged on other parts of the lines as Grant tightened his grip on the Confederate defenders. One Confederate, in fact, wrote, "from my position I could see heavy masses of troops passing around to their right, they were evidently determined to surround us." Preceded by cavalry, McClernand did indeed continue to shift to the right on the Wynn Ferry Road during the day, Oglesby and Wallace (without the 48th Illinois, which joined him later) following. Taylor's, Schwartz's, and Dresser's batteries deployed at multiple points on the high ridge as well throughout the day, Wallace noting that "the open space afforded a fine opportunity for artillery practice at long range" and that the firing from both sides "presented a rare example of the use of that arm of the service." This was so much the case that Dresser's battery, with longer-range rifles, ran out of ammunition and was only resupplied the next day. Ezra Taylor was more fortunate in that he had brought from Cairo extra ammunition, which was then at Fort Henry. He dispatched "two six mule teams with two large baggage wagons" to fetch it, and the battery was thus resupplied by dawn the next day despite one of the wagons breaking when hitting a stump and being delayed. Other minor tactical changes also occurred, including temporarily attaching the wounded Morrison's regiments to Wallace's brigade and Smith bringing McArthur's brigade up from reserve to man the line between Cook, his right brigade, and Wallace's brigade of McClernand's division across Indian Creek.[61]

A few casualties resulted during minor skirmishing throughout the afternoon, prompting some of the batteries to erect small earthworks over the course of the next couple of days. Taylor's battery moved to one of its numerous positions during the day and became caught in a "gauling" fire as the cannoneers attempted to deploy the guns in the heavy brush. The battery lost a few men as a result but soon opened up on the Confederate artillery across the way, which responded in kind. One of the section commanders, Samuel Barrett, described "one cannon ball, passing over my horses ears, and striking a tree just behind me." He concluded, "they had a perfect range on us." Similarly, as McAllister's battery west of Indian Creek fought Graves's Confederates on the opposing hill, Graves utilized "his favorite rifle piece" to hit one of the wheels of a cannon, cutting it in two. McAllister had no additional wheels and had to replace it with one from a limber. In one of the most unexpected events of the day, Dresser's rifled guns were employed in an "experimental" fire up Erin Hollow and into Fort Donelson itself, McClernand writing that it could be seen "dispersing a considerable body of men observed lining the parapet facing its river front" and also damaging the barracks inside the fort. Certainly, all the firing took a toll, but Confederate Colonel William E. Baldwin noted, "this fire, kept up with but little intermission throughout the entire day, produced but little effect upon the left until late in the evening, when, the enemy having reduced his charges, several of the shells, which had previously passed too high, fell in our midst." All the same, the men seemed to take it in stride: one noted being "in the ditches," while a Virginian related that "the men and officers behaved well under the circumstances, and soon became accustomed to the firing."[62]

Little therefore changed tactically throughout the day and the Union artillery eventually pulled back behind the ridges to shield themselves from the sharpshooters. Buckner summed up the day's exchanges, writing, "the fire of the enemy's artillery and riflemen was incessant throughout the day, but was responded to by a well-directed fire from the entrenchments, which inflicted upon the assailants considerable loss and almost silenced his fire late in the afternoon." Jeremy Gilmer wrote more ominously: "the enemy had gained no footing on our works nor produced any important impression upon them. But our forces were much fatigued, having been under arms all day, and this after three or four days' hard labor upon the intrenchments."[63]

What did change drastically, however, was the weather, one Confederate remembering how "dark clouds came rolling up from the northwest." John A. McClernand eloquently described the wet cold front that moved through: "during the afternoon of the 13th the weather turned intensely cold, a driving north wind bringing a storm of snow and sleet upon the unprotected men of my division. The night set in gloomily, and the mingled rain and snow congealed as they fell, thus painfully adding to the discomfort of a destitution of tents and camp equipage, all of which had been left behind." A lesser-rank soldier put it more succinctly: "about that time our boys thought Tenn was rather a rough climate for soldiering." Low rations and no fires only added to the misery, one Federal noting, "being in point-blank range of the enemy's batteries and sharpshooters, camp fires, inviting shot and shell, were not lighted." One Iowan disagreed, writing, "in my opinion it would be less destruction in health and life than the cold will prove." Perhaps worst of all, the wounded from the two isolated attacks suffered horribly. One Mississippian noted the irony of the wounded in front of Maney's battery: "some of the wounded scratched around to save their lives from the burning woods . . . and remained there to perish in the snow." Sadly, Grant noted that "the thermometer indicated 20° below freezing," or twelve degrees at its coldest. The wind chill was even lower.[64]

The accounts of the operations around Fort Donelson are replete with the misery of that night, one Iowan noting to his wife, "in the morning we had a pretty good Iowa winter!" Making it even worse was the drastic change from the preceding days, one Illinoisan writing home, "it looked about as mutch like winter as it had looked like summer two or three days before." In the Union lines, numerous officers and men reported on their dreary circumstances, although a few brigade and regimental commanders had tents;

James Parrott reported that he and Lauman shared a tent "and spent the night as comfortable as the circumstances of the case would permit." Meanwhile, the troops had nothing for cover. C. F. Smith recalled his skirmishers after the attack and noted, "the troops [were] ordered to remain in position, but from necessity without fires, as the night was very inclement—rainy, snow, sleet, and cold—and the discomfort of the men was very great." The 18th Illinois, its commander moaned, "remained with arms in their hands during the night; the extreme cold and snow forbade their lying down." Samuel Barrett of Taylor's battery wrote home, "the only way I could keep from freezing was, by walking up and down all night." An Iowan admitted, "I shaked like I had the ague, if not worse." Lew Wallace indicated that "even the horses, after their manner, betrayed the suffering they were enduring."[65]

Despite one of the most prevalent myths of the Civil War, the men did have blankets and many had overcoats. Some accounts later told of throwing away blankets and overcoats on the warm trek from Fort Henry, but those descriptions date from decades after the war. Not a single contemporary February 1862 account of throwing away items on the march has been found. What did happen was that the Federals either left much of their equipment back at Fort Henry or deposited it as regiments before going into line on February 13. Many reported bringing their equipment but "we had lost our blankets during the day in the field." Another noted, "we left our knapsacks so as not to have any trouble with them in battle." Brigade commander Cook mentioned "everything but arms and ammunition having been cast aside on approaching the fort." Still, most Federals had blankets. David Reed of the 12th Iowa remarked that their orders were to go in "light marching order" and thus all left their overcoats at Fort Henry but took a blanket each. Even so, the effects were obviously disastrous, including frostbite.[66]

Making the night even worse for the Federals was the constant firing and fear of a Confederate attack. Colonel Carroll Marsh of the 20th Illinois noted that his men were kept in line of battle, the skirmishing "leading me to fear an attack at any moment." Many took the suffering in stride, one 17th Illinois officer writing, "my regiment was in line of battle nearly all night, suffering from cold and hunger, yet no one complained, and all were even cheerful." Oglesby wrote that the blizzard was "one of the most persecuting snow-storms ever known in this country" and found by passing along the lines of his brigade that "there was one universal wish to meet the enemy, to carry the fort, and to end the sufferings of the men." At least one colonel,

James M. Smith of the 52nd Indiana, decided he would take his chances with fires, saying he "would rather be shot and have his men shot by Rebs than all of us freeze to death."[67]

George Carrington of the 11th Illinois related in his diary that he was sleeping warmly under a "burr oak bush" that still had its leaves and with dry leaves underneath. Then word came to fall in, and he was astonished that so much snow had fallen. Fires built far behind the ridges warmed men who were fortunate enough to be allowed off the front; the men left their muskets in line sticking in the ground bayonet first for immediate use. "We are something like 'Napoleon's shivering Battalions in that blinding snow storm at Eylau,'" Carrington thought. Another miserable Federal could only hear the men "coughing and shivering with cold." One Iowan noted that his fellow soldiers circled a fire all night, governed by orders: "by company, in a circle, double quick, march!" He later noted that was something "entirely new to Casey's tactics." An Illinoisan told a similar tale, writing that he circled a fire in the snow and "invited" his comrades to join him by shouting, "fall in." To his surprise, the words filtered up and down the line until many regiments went into formation. He later surmised, "I think I was the only fellow there who could identify the ass that started the false alarm."[68]

Adding insult to injury was the fact that the Federals had to man their lines, leaving many of their possessions behind in camp where these were frequently stolen. Colonel John E. Smith of the 45th Illinois reported to his wife that he had no blankets as "mine were stolen." He also added, "my pocket Book was stolen out of my over coat pocket while we we[re] out fighting so that I am cleaned out entirely."[69]

The Confederates also suffered greatly during the cold night and similarly left vivid descriptions. Colonel Edward C. Cook of the 32nd Tennessee reported, "the weather was extremely cold, and being kept continually at labor and on duty, we suffered much from exposure." Colonel Hanson on the far right reported that during the night they had to dig a parapet for Captain Thomas E. Jackson's four Virginia guns: "although the night was cold and inclement, and the men much exhausted from the day's fighting and several days of hard work, we succeeded in getting these pieces in good position and well protected." The same was occurring at Maney's position. Heiman reported that Pillow sent him another section under Captain A. H. Parker, which required work: "the night was unusually cold and disagreeable. Snow and sleet fell during the whole night; nevertheless we constructed a formidable parapet in front of the battery." Heiman described the work as "this hard and most unpleasant labor," and admitted, "the troops suffered dreadfully, being without blankets." Even those not in the fought-over areas suffered. The 20th Mississippi replaced the 7th Texas on the front line and Major William N. Brown, in command because of an ankle injury to Colonel Daniel R. Russell, reported, "the breastworks were thought insufficient, . . . so the remainder of the night was occupied in strengthening them and cleaning out the trenches, now partially filled with water and snow." One of his soldiers insisted that the snow was a foot deep, but he may have been exaggerating because the Mississippian may not have seen twelve inches of snow in his entire life. Another simply wrote in his diary, "cold, cold, cold." Others indicated that there were ice and water in their trenches, and officers had to make sure that their men did not stay in their "place of pretended repose" too long, because without movement, frostbite would set in.[70]

Added to the suffering was the similar Confederate fear of a Union night attack, one Mississippian writing, "we would often imagine that the whole line of the enemy was approaching by stealth and aimed to catch us asleep." Jeremy Gilmer noted, "inclement as was the weather, it was necessary (to guard against surprise) that the troops should be all night in position along the lines of infantry cover." Similarly, Captain Ross reported that "rain and snow and a final freeze of the same rendered this a dangerous night for the gunboats passing [the batteries] in obscurity. We therefore masked for the night firing." He even periodically fired a shell, which he described "sound[ing] almost double as loud as in the daytime" and which produced a staff officer from Floyd inquiring why he was firing at night. Fortunately for the gunners, the garrison of the fort aided these cannoneers during the long night. Ross reported, "remaining much of their time with us at night, thus encouraging us to persevere; also that they cooked our rations for us and sent us spirits, all from their regiments."[71]

The fear of night fighting was not without reality for both sides. Samuel Barrett wrote that "we expected a charge, every minute from a large force." As a result, artillery and sharpshooters from both sides fired throughout the night, Floyd writing that the artillery "deprived our men of any opportunity to sleep." He added, "we confidently expected at the dawn of day a more vigorous attack than ever." One Mississippian similarly described how his regiment fired at phantom Yankees, "lighting up our works with our discharges." Moreover, the concern came from both land and water, Pillow reporting that they could see "the smoke of a large number of gunboats and steamboats a short distance below."[72]

Despite the turn of events, Pillow believed that "the result of the day's work pretty well tested the strength of our defensive line, and established beyond question the gallantry of the entire command, all of which fought gallantly their portion of the line." It was quite a day, but unfortunately it was only going to get worse.[73]

10

"You Are Not at Fort Henry"

If fighting a war was hard work, the armies arrayed around Fort Donelson saw that difficulty compounded exponentially as dawn broke over the Cumberland River valley on February 14. A combination of factors had come together to make the previous night one of the most miserable certainly during the war and perhaps in the lives of almost all involved. The major culprit was the weather, one Federal declaring that snow fell "full 3 inches deep." Snow itself was not such a desperate concern because many of the soldiers, especially those from Northern states such as Iowa and Illinois, had seen plenty of it in their lives and even the Southern soldiers had at least experienced it. What made this night so particularly bad was the cold and the fact that because of the continuing military operations, the troops could not take shelter or build fires. Neither army could get inside a cabin or tent, and the Federals had even left knapsacks, blankets, and other personal items in the rear. The Confederates likewise could not leave their lines for fear of a breakthrough. The lack of food added to the misery, one Federal writing that he had "nothing but hard crackers to eat and few of them." Other resulting issues also caused problems. One Illinoisan declared that "our clothes were frozen as stiff as a board."[1]

Despite the continued cold and icy conditions, the armies began to shake off the snow and resume their proper roles as dawn neared. In the Union lines, John McClernand wrote how "the morning of Friday, the 14th, dawned cold and cheerless upon men already severely tired by hunger, exposure, and long-continued watching and labor." Yet he described them "rising promptly to the duties of the day." Brigade commander John Cook wrote that his men "shook the thick covering of snow from their overcoats, partook of a meager breakfast, and cheerfully resumed their old position under the intrenchments." Oglesby noted his men were "nearly torpid from the intense cold of the night," but some fortunate units received a break of sorts because fires could be lit in the daylight. They also chugged down coffee, that being all that was available because the wagon trains were still a day away from arriving. Lieutenant Colonel Frank L. Rhoads of 8th Illinois took his regiment to the rear for an hour's respite, he reported, "but only coffee could be obtained."[2]

That morning the Confederate army similarly uncovered itself from the snowstorm. Captain Bidwell at the river batteries declared, "I spent another very disagreeable night, sleepless and severely cold." He added that "the suffering from severe cold was intense. I had to carry several of the men to the quarters next morning so nearly frozen that they were unable to walk." Perhaps the cold added to already short tempers within the Confederate garrison, because even some of the slaves serving as body servants to the officers became embroiled in conflict. One of John C. Brown's slaves, Ned, got into a heated argument with Major Pointer, the servant of a captain. The officers decided to mock the two slaves and teach them a lesson. They brokered a duel with, unbeknown to the slaves, unloaded pistols. The white officers acted as seconds. The officers counted one but when they got to two both slaves ran away. They were quickly brought back but fled once again before the full count was reached. Having enough, Ned finally screamed, "Gen. Brown, you knows I love Major better 'an anybody 'cepin tis you." One amused observer noted, "this broke up the duel but Ned and Major were ever afterwards good friends and quit quarreling."[3]

Despite such theatrics, every soldier knew that daylight meant more fighting, and officers quickly positioned their units. They found the enemy once more in the changed surroundings that the large snow had made to the terrain. Changes in enemy positioning did not help the reorientation process either. Captain Ezra Taylor of the Chicago Light Artillery, for example, noted, "during the night the enemy changed the position of all his guns which bore on my position, as, with the experience of the day, I had secured a perfect range on all his batteries which I had been able to discover." The captain thus had to locate the enemy guns again and find their ranges all over.[4]

All that preparation was done in the expectation of major fighting that day. No doubt all had wondered when the long cold night would end, hoping that daylight would bring some relief even if it also brought renewed fighting. Some no doubt thought the chance of death in battle was better than the misery of freezing to death.

"Early on Friday morning, the 14th," wrote Captain Reuben Ross at the Confederate river batteries, "we looked for a renewal of the attack, but for some reason we did not yet understand there was no sign of an advance." Others wrote of the same expectation, and the resulting sound of relative silence was odd. Roger Hanson, who had driven back Smith's attack the day before and fully expected worse today, wrote, "we remained under arms and in ranks all day Friday, expecting the attack to be renewed." Only sharpshooting took place, however, with both small arms and artillery. Nevertheless, he wrote that this went far in "disturbing and almost destroying the repose of my command." Will Wallace's staff officer I. P. Rumsey was likewise disturbed; he wrote his father that he was in the act of "getting the snow and ice off my saddle, [when] there came a cannon ball above my head, and soon there came another, so low as to strike Col's oilcloth that hung in a tree, it being right by our headquarters." Although heavy, the firing never reached large proportions, however; even a surprised John Floyd wrote that "the day advanced and no preparations seemed to be making for a general onset."[5]

Floyd soon realized why; the Federals were retooling, expanding their reach, and adding reinforcements. In fact, huge columns of smoke just around the river bend to the west indicated transports were discharging troops, and soon those troops could be seen marching toward the battlefield. Commanding the big rifle in the river batteries, Ross wanted to shell the transports, but Colonel Bailey, commanding the fort, would not agree until he talked to Floyd. The general agreed to let him shell a column of troops that could be seen marching inland, but Ross noted that by the time word got back to him they had gone out of sight. He later admitted, "I did not resist the temptation to fire on their immense fleet of transports." He opened with the rifle and the columbiad at extreme elevation and after only two or three shots from each gun saw the transports moving away. Later reports indicated "the water [was] covered with . . . wrecks, intermingled with arms, legs, and fragments of every form." Understandably, Ross was hesitant to believe it: "this is what he stated, but I am satisfied he much overstated these things."[6]

Others wanted to make sure that the Confederate lines were as tight as possible for the assault all expected at any moment. On the isolated spit of a ridge between Indian Creek and Erin Hollow, Heiman was most concerned about his right and moved two guns down the hill to the valley of Indian Creek. Back on the far right, Hanson was concerned about another attack and more companies of the 18th Tennessee reinforced him. The expected assault never came, though, although the growing skirmishing and artillery fire were just about as bad. Floyd wrote that "an extremely annoying fire was kept up from the enemy's sharpshooters throughout the whole length of the intrench-ments. . . . While this mode of attack was not attended with any considerable loss, it nevertheless confined the men to their trenches and prevented their taking their usual rest." One soldier in the 20th Illinois agreed, writing that Union fire "made them hunt their holes double quick." Some just had to grin and bear it. Colonel Roger Hanson scolded his Kentuckians for dodging bul-lets until a minie ball zinged close by his head and he himself ducked. As his men laughed, Hanson retorted, "Boys, you may dodge a little if they come too close."[7]

The Confederates on the western trenches had a particularly tough time with C. F. Smith's sharpshooters, Birge's regiment. They found they could not reach the Federals with their shotguns and smoothbores. One Confeder-ate managed to obtain three "Minnie muskets" from the 49th Tennessee and when put to use "in less than three minutes . . . brought a Yankee out of the forks of a tree. He fell full fifty feet to the ground." Down the line and in the opposite ranks in the 17th Illinois of McClernand's division, A. F. Gilbert similarly wrote of this type of fighting. "Directly opposite my position was a ten-inch oak behind which was a gray," he wrote, adding, "he emerged at intervals to fire at me." Gilbert continued, "I had also fired twice at him, but while reloading for a third shot he got me in the left shoulder, spinning me around like a top . . . I fell, but scrambled up as well as I could and hustled to the rear." On Davidson's front, his Mississippians were being pestered by a sharpshooter they could not reach, but one 8th Kentucky soldier with a "long-ranged gun" shot the man, one observer noted, "and he fell from the tree a lifeless corpse." The 50th Illinois dubbed one particular Confederate sharpshooter behind a stump as "old red shirt," which they finally shot. At times, even higher officers were involved. A sharpshooter fired at Colonel Oglesby while he watched the fighting, hitting him in the stirrup. One of his men shouted, "are you wounded, general?" He merely replied, "I don't know; haven't had time to see."[8]

Although there was heavy skirmishing, the reason no major attack came on this day was because Ulysses S. Grant had other means to reduce the fort and capture the enemy. Foote and the five gunboats from Cairo and twelve transports had finally arrived at Bear Creek Landing after a lengthy voyage, which was slowed to the pace of the sluggish gunboats. They arrived a little after 10:00 PM the night before during the heavy snowstorm. The flotilla anchored next to the *Carondelet*, Henry Walke no doubt happy to have more firepower to aid his lone vessel. Also arriving were the Federal reinforcements, particularly the many regiments Grant had sent around from Fort Henry. These were certainly ready for battle, one Ohio chaplain writing that the troops were "inspired with delight." Grant was just as pleased to have more land forces, but he was most eager for the arrival of Foote and the navy. They had worked wonders at Fort Henry, and Grant wanted them now at Fort Donelson to perhaps do the same thing. With all the new troops and gunboats, and with the Confederates seemingly bottled up inside Fort Donelson, Grant had options and time was on his side. Hence, he did not rush into a costly resort of storming Fort Donelson's defenses.[9]

The reinforcements actually came in two ways. One of course was by water, but the other was by land from Fort Henry. Realizing this was going to be a longer operation than Fort Henry, Grant ordered Lew Wallace on the evening of February 13 to gather the troops he could and march to Fort Donelson. The troops left behind had heard the cannon fire, with some of the dead and wounded already being brought back there; they were, therefore, itching to get into the fight. The official order came around 2:00 AM and one Federal remembered, "the drums were beat rousing up the men." Three day's rations went out and some of the troops at Fort Heiman soon ferried the river and began their march. Wallace took with him two regiments, his old brigade consisting of the 8th Missouri and 11th Indiana, his old regiment. Grant ordered him to leave a guard at Forts Henry and Heiman and so he left the 23rd Indiana with the 23rd and 28th Illinois of McClernand's division and the 5th Iowa Cavalry, much to the chagrin of the men: "the stay order was received with a tremendous howl," Wallace remembered, "which I pretended not to hear."[10]

Wallace had been forewarned as early as February 12, but when the call came it was still thrilling. He described the joy: "very seldom in life have there been instances in which my signature has been given more willingly than to the receipt for that bit of paper." He quickly set off on the Telegraph Road with his 11th Indiana and 8th Missouri, along with Wood's Chicago Light Artillery and a company of the 32nd Illinois; he later added a patrolling cavalry force. Throughout the morning the brigade came nearer and nearer to the fighting as judged by the sounds and sights; newspaper artist Alexander Simplot, who accompanied Wallace, noted, "soon the continuous booming with the smoke rising over the hills and tree tops marked the battleground." The brigade marched on until they reached Grant's headquarters at the Widow Crisp's house around noon on February 14. Wallace went inside while the troops remained in column, and there he received more orders. Wallace lost his old brigade, which was placed under the command of the senior colonel, Morgan L. Smith. Wallace lamented losing his prized regiments, but Grant had larger ideas for the Indianan. Needing to organize a new division of all the arriving troops, Grant created the Third Division and assigned Wallace as its commander.[11]

Most of the troops for this division arrived by the other means of transportation, by steamboat. Some of the units such as Cruft's brigade of Kentuckians and Indianans had arrived at Fort Henry earlier, but Grant had sent them around by water to Fort Donelson, they being on the steamboats for a total of five days without going ashore. Others came as well, one Illinoisan writing his wife, "we had a splendid voyage up the Ohio and Cumberland Rivers & I wished that you could have been along to enjoy it." It was nevertheless slow due to the high water, a strong current, and the slow gunboats. Arriving at the landing west of the operations, Cruft marched inland and became one of Wallace's new brigades, quickly coming under fire and causing at least one Kentuckian to wish "that I was a home guard." Other arriving troops sent from Cairo and St. Louis were formed into another brigade under John Thayer, colonel of the 1st Nebraska. Still other unattached regiments such as the 46th, 57th, and 58th Illinois were considered for a new brigade, but in the confusion they were simply attached to Thayer's unit for the time being. A few of the arriving regiments were assigned elsewhere, such as the 2nd Iowa. Upon landing, their knapsacks being hurriedly thrown on the bank by the boat's crew under fire from the Confederate guns, the Iowans marched to Smith's headquarters, where he assigned them to Lauman's brigade and they quickly took their position on the front line. A few were late in arriving, such as the 57th Illinois, which marched off its transports after breakfast on February 14. According to one soldier, it "started for the fort in the forenoon, but got on the wrong road, and returned to the boats and got our dinner, and started out again in the afternoon."[12]

Grant ordered Wallace and his new division to take a position between Smith and McClernand. "My orders, received from General Grant, were to hold my position and prevent the enemy from escaping in that direction; in other words, to remain there and repel any sally from the fort." Wallace also noted, and Grant must have impressed it upon his new division commander, that "under the orders I had no authority to take the offensive." The brigades thus went into line between Indian Creek and Smith's division, Thayer on the left and Cruft on the right, his flank within supporting distance of Will Wallace's expanded brigade on the Wynn Ferry Road. There, the newly arrived troops faced the brutal cold as well, Wallace describing how "we walked about and beat our bodies to keep up circulation, our teeth chattering meanwhile like castanets." Fortunately, he had thought to bring Heiman's large tent captured at Fort Heiman, and this provided some cover. Less than a mile away, Heiman himself would have been chagrined had he known his massive tent was now providing headquarters for a Union division commander.[13]

Throughout the day, these three divisions continued the skirmishing, but they did not attack. McClernand continued to extend his lines eastward after he and several staff officers, along with cavalry and infantry, probed toward the right and found that without help the division could not reach the river. McClernand decided instead to rest his flank on Lick Creek, which was mostly impassable and would hem in the Confederate garrison just as well, although they could not interdict as planned the river traffic from that position. The division consequently shifted throughout the day, mostly taking cover along the reverse slope of the ridge on which the Wynn Ferry Road ran. McClernand ordered his brigade commanders to form their lines well, telling Oglesby to "take the strongest *defensive* position whether it be purely defensive or aggressive in its character." In the ensuing hours, the men also erected more earthworks for batteries, McClernand remarking, "a want of additional implements prevented me from carrying into effect my design to intrench the right of my line." Meanwhile, the sharpshooting continued; Carroll Marsh reported his men "picking off the rebels as they exposed themselves above the breastworks."[14]

Smith's division likewise skirmished, although troubles with problematic colonels caused some gaps in the line. Brigade commander John Cook noted that the often rouge Crafts J. Wright of the 13th Missouri had pulled his men out of line without orders during the day so they could refresh in the rear. A furious Cook wrote that he "proceeded on foot, and in person ordered his return." Smith himself reconnoitered to the left of his division toward Hickman Creek and "satisfied myself that the only apparent practicable point of assault was in that quarter." Still, only skirmishing, sometimes heavy, continued throughout the day.[15]

Much of the skirmishing was done by the artillery, which had a difficult time in the wet and icy slop. Edward McAllister reported that the fire on his front became so hot that he had "to move our horses far down the slope in rear of the Forty-fifth Regiment." He also related that in some of the sparring, one of his guns "broke its trail short off by its own recoil on the frozen ground and was completely disabled thereby." On the other hand, Taylor's battery took advantage of a lull to move "back to a ravine to water and feed my horses."[16]

In short, Grant had the situation well in hand, even joking with some of his soldiers at times. He asked two injured Federals if they had been wounded "hunting bear." They responded that they had the bear treed and went on to describe how even while wounded they kept fighting, silencing an enemy battery. A jovial Grant responded, "you didn't hurt anyone, did you?," to which one soldier responded, "why, General, I dunno—I reckon I just scared 'em and they fainted." Yet while Grant was continually being strengthened, he refused to attack with those greater numbers. One Mississippian recognized the irony, later writing, "while we were rejoicing over our victories they were being greatly reinforced." Grant certainly could have attacked, but he knew he had the upper hand and saw no need to create hundreds if not thousands of casualties when Fort Donelson could be reduced in other ways. The false account of Grant being a butcher was certainly not true at Fort Donelson. Instead, Grant opted to primarily use his other major reinforcement on February 13, the US navy.[17]

While the armies skirmished on the landward side of Fort Donelson and almost all began to conclude that the day would pass with no real fighting, suddenly what many thought would be the climactic attack occurred later on the afternoon of February 14. Everyone by this point knew of the navy's startling success at Fort Henry just a few days earlier, and many expected a repeat at Fort Donelson. The Federals, Grant included, were particularly desirous of a naval attack, especially one that would provide the kind of success seen at Fort Henry. The Confederates were likewise mindful of the looming gunboat threat, many outwardly admitting that the land defense concerned them much less than a naval attack. Perhaps only Andrew H. Foote was not so sure. He later wrote that he joined the expedition and attacked "at the urgent request of Major-General Halleck and General Grant, who regarded the movement as a military necessity, although not in my opinion properly prepared." He brought his gunboats south anyway, their vulnerable areas now covered with anything such as chains, lumber, and coal that might deflect a shell. The fleet slowly moved toward the final bend before reaching Fort Donelson and then toward what many thought would be the operation's final action. Ulysses S. Grant even took a position on the bank of the river to watch the victorious show.[18]

All seemed to think this would be Fort Henry all over. Even as the gunboats rounded the bend, Captain Ross, commanding the Confederate rifle himself as he "trusted no one else to point it," noted that "it must be confessed we felt unequally matched with this fleet, armed with ten times or more our number of their best artillery. We had resolved to defend the fort, however, and would not allow ourselves time to be alarmed." This time he made sure there was none of the frivolity of the two prior days when his men had "chattered like so many wild geese, each one having a great deal to tell others to do, but not seeming disposed to do much himself." Now, he ordered no talking and complete concentration. There was also a change in morale from the previous days. If the Federals intended the earlier days' shelling to disrupt Confederate morale, the opposite had happened. Because of Walke's demonstrations, Ross had been able to get his men calmed down before the big fight on February 14. In that sense, the earlier days' semiattacks had been favorable for the Confederates. A conscientious Ross also prepared even more than previously. He set fires to be able to light the guns in case "the Friction Primers should fail."[19]

As a result, Foote led his flotilla, actually smaller than his fleet at Fort Henry, against the much stronger and confident Fort Donelson around 3:00 PM on the afternoon of February 14. Watching from the fort, the Confederates could see the huge columns of black smoke and knew something was afoot. B. G. Bidwell remembered how "four boats came around the point, arranged themselves in line of battle, and advanced slowly, but steadily, up the river." Foote once more aligned his ironclads bow first across the river, with the *St. Louis* and *Carondelet*, veterans of Fort Henry, and the two new gunboats, *Louisville* and *Pittsburg*, the replacements for the damaged *Essex* and *Cincinnati*. The four ironclads formed across the river, the *St. Louis*, *Louisville*, *Pittsburg*, and *Carondelet* west to east. Behind the ironclads came two of the timberclads, the *Tyler* and *Conestoga*, again under Phelps. The *Lexington* had been damaged on the Tennessee River run and was sent back to Cairo. Foote had the *St. Louis* as his flagship.[20]

The gunboats moved forward slowly, Foote signaling to *Louisville* and *Pittsburg* to "steam up" when they fell slightly behind. The *St. Louis* opened fire about 2:40 PM a mile or so from the fort, followed by the rest of the iron-clads. Walke in the *Carondelet* later wrote the flag officer that despite a signal from Foote "not to fire so fast," they eventually produced "a deliberate and well-directed firing from the instant your vessel commenced." In accordance with what had worked so well at Fort Henry, Foote steadily drove forward and the gunboats closed the range until after an hour they were within four hundred yards. All the while, the gunners cut the fuses shorter and shorter, from fifteen eventually down to five seconds.[21]

Meanwhile, the Confederate defenders were having problems, making it indeed seem like Fort Henry all over. Even though the rifle opened as soon as the first gunboat nudged its bow around the bend, each of the guns had a different set of problems. For one, because of the increased wheel size on the columbiad, "the gun could only fire when their boats passed the field of its range, and probably on the right boat all the time." That right boat was the *Carondelet*, and it would definitely be hit hard throughout the afternoon. Even worse, the rifle had multiple issues. A shot jammed halfway down the bore early in the fight, but the gunners "hunted up a long log just fitting the bore, all mounted the parapet, in the height of the bombardment, and drove the ball home." More fatally, a priming wire later jammed in the rifle's vent, the result of a charge being rammed after a gunner forgot to remove the wire. It bent and could not be extracted. Culbertson blamed "the want of skill of the cannoneers in loading. They had had but two days' experience." More ominously, Pillow was on site and ordered Culbertson to respond at first only with the rifle and the columbiad, saving the smaller 32-pounders for closer work. "This was opposed to my judgment," Culbertson wrote, "as it showed the enemy the positions of our two heavy guns, which I regarded as constitut-ing our only hope." Captain Bidwell, commanding four of the 32-pounders, similarly remembered, "we remained perfectly silent, while they came over about 1 ½ miles, pouring a heavy fire of shot and shell upon us all the time." Pillow added, "it was a severe restraint to their patriotic impulses," but they obeyed. A relieved Culbertson went on to say, "they took no advantage of it, however, but fired almost at random."[22]

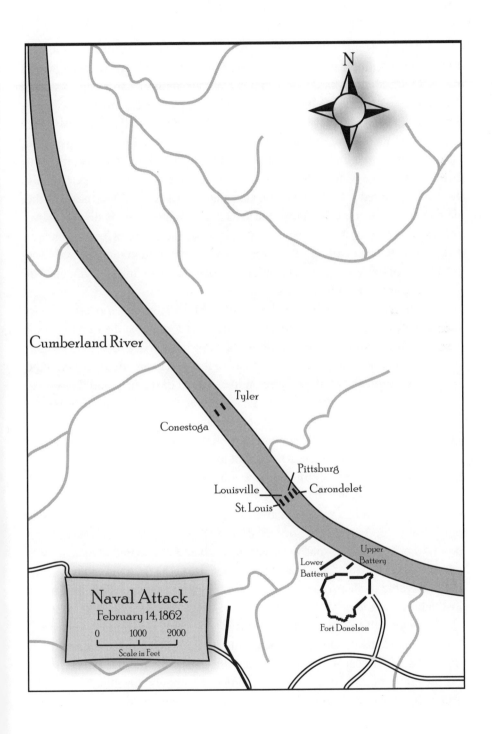

N

Cumberland River

Tyler

Conestoga

Pittsburg

Louisville

Carondelet

St. Louis

Upper
Battery

Lower
Battery

Naval Attack
February 14, 1862

0   1000   2000
Scale in Feet

Fort Donelson

All soon got in on the action, however. When the front line of the flotilla reached within four hundred yards of the fort, the Confederates gunners opened with all they had. One watching infantryman was in awe: "A dence cloud of smoke arose from the battery while peal after peal are clear as a bugler blast they sending terror and confusion on the enimys fleet at evry shot." The 32-pounders were able to do damage as well as the howitzers, several of the guns utilizing ricochet shot. And it told. The closer the Federal gunboats came to the water batteries, the more significant hits they took. Captain Bedwell declared, "I am confident that the 32-pounders did almost all the damage to the boats, although I have seen it stated otherwise by distinguished officers." Whoever did the damage, one by one, each of the Union ironclads began to receive crippling hits, with Pillow relaying, "I could distinctly see the effects of our shot upon his iron-cased boats" and that the shots made "her metal ring and her timbers crack."[23]

The two right gunboats succumbed first. Foote's own St. Louis was perhaps the most resilient if the most battered. He reported that the ironclad took upward of fifty-nine shots, including "4 between wind and water," which was a naval term meaning in the hull where the water sometimes covered the hull and sometimes not, depending on the rocking of the boat and the waves. Needless to say, these were dangerous hits because water often flowed in. In perhaps one of the most significant shots of the war, one cannon ball also hit the pilothouse and mortally wounded the pilot and wounded others. Foote wrote, "the wheel of this vessel, by a shot through her pilot house, was carried away." The St. Louis therefore became unmanageable.[24]

The same thing was happening on the Louisville. Its "tiller ropes" that controlled the rudders were shot away in the fighting, meaning that it too was uncontrollable. At what one officer described as "the height of the fighting point," Foote reported that the steering problems "rendered the two boats wholly unmanageable" and that "they drifted down the river, relieving tackles not being able to steer or control them in the rapid current." The flotilla had lost half of its punch.[25]

The other half was doing even worse, one Confederate gunner describing "the two flank boats closing in behind them and protecting them from our fire in retreat." Because they remained a little while longer, the Pittsburg and Carondelet took the brunt of the Confederate gunners' fire, the Carondelet especially taking a beating from the columbiad that could not turn widely. Foote reported that the other two gunboats were also "greatly damaged between wind and water and soon followed us, as the enemy rapidly renewed the fire as we drifted helplessly down the river."[26]

The *Pittsburg* indeed took a severe pounding. Likely hearing of the scalding on board the *Essex* at Fort Henry, the *Pittsburg*'s commander Lieutenant Egbert Thompson "had 100 bread bags filled with coal and stowed around the boilers as likely to afford some protection to the latter against shot." Later, the crew added their hammocks as additional protection. Covering the boilers could not help the outlying parts of the gunboat, however, and the *Pittsburg* took "at least 30 shots," according to her commander. The most damaging were two large shells in the bow (one on each side) right at the waterline, "between wind and water." Another shot from the rifle (then still in action) went through the pilothouse at the same spot where an earlier round had "weakened the joints of the iron plates in that particular locality." Thompson even marveled that "another shot entered the middle bow port, and passed out at the stern, through the cabin, first cutting its way through a stack of hammocks and coal bags, escape pipe, wheelhouse, etc., not touching a man." Still other shots tore away the flagstaffs and other items on the decks.[27]

Miraculously, no one was killed on the boat and only two were wounded. One of the wounded was Seaman George Smith, "whom it was difficult to draw from his gun after receiving his wounds, he insisting that he could still go on fighting." The other was similarly brave. Thomas Merwin "had his skull fractured; he also wished to join in the fight again after being for a few moments in the hands of the surgeon." While the crew was in good shape, the boat was in dire trouble. Thompson reported that he decided to get away while he could, "discovering that the flagship had fallen astern and all the other boats but one were drifting out of range." That was easier said than done, and he soon found the ironclad filling with water so rapidly from the bow hits that he had to take drastic countermeasures. Realizing "we could not float much longer from the way the boat was making water," Thompson wrote, "I fell downstream and only kept afloat long enough to get out of the range of the enemy's guns by running my guns aft, thus lightening her at the bow." Back atop the river batteries, Captain Ross wrote that his target "left the line and ran in to the shore—we reverently hoped to sink."[28]

As bad as the *Pittsburg* was, the *Carondelet* suffered the most on the far side of the river, or the left of the formation. That was probably because of the narrow range of the Confederate columbiad stuck in its wheel ruts. Yet, some of the trouble was not even from Confederate fire; the gunboat lost a bow gun during the action when one of the rifles burst. One of the crew remembered, "for about two minutes I was stunned, and at least five minutes elapsed before I could tell what was the matter. When I found out that I was more scared than hurt, although suffering from the gunpowder which I had inhaled, I looked forward and saw our gun lying on the deck, split in three pieces." The stunned crews nearby quickly recovered, Walke reporting that his gunners served "the remaining two guns faithfully as long as the enemy were within reach." Still, the ironclad suffered more the closer it came to the Confederate guns, with one shot "striking our wheelhouse and jamming the wheel," Walke reported. He also described the shells "taking flag-staffs and smoke-stacks, and tearing off the side armor as lightening tears the bark from a tree." A couple of shells that tore through the boat killed four men, one observer describing "three with their heads off. The sight almost sickened me, and I turned my head away." Walke reported, "before the decks were well sanded, there was so much blood on them that our men could not work the guns without slipping." To make matters worse, an eight-inch shell from the *Tyler* farther to the rear exploded astern the vessel, "the fragments of which penetrated our casemate." To add insult to injury as the gunboat floated helplessly away, the *Pittsburg* attempted to turn around in the river and struck the *Carondelet* "on our starboard quarter and broke off our starboard rudder iron." One perceptive Confederate described how the vessel "floated around against the bank of the river, but turned her bow straight across the river, ran to the middle, fired several shots, and retired." In all, the *Carondelet* was hit thirty-five times by the Confederate guns, losing four killed and thirty-two wounded, including the pilot. Walke described how "we leak[ed] badly forward and aft, and require[d] extensive repairs above and below watermark, and in almost every department." Yet out of the chaos did emerge one good outcome; Matthew Arther won the Congressional Medal of Honor for his actions on this day and on February 6 at Fort Henry.[29]

All the while, the timberclads to the rear also added their firepower, although they had to do so over the gunboats to the front. One Confederate recognized the difference: "they threw shells, while the boats threw shot, shell, and grape." Gilmer described them as "curveted shot, which passed over our works, exploding in the air just above." One Federal infantryman watching the show similarly described the timberclads' actions as different from the bow firing of the ironclads. The two smaller boats opened with their bow guns at first but then began "swinging and giving the broadside, and turning fired the other broadside. This being steadily repeated was a grand sight."[30]

The Confederate gunners began to realize their success as the Federal gunboats one by one began to fall to the rear. They could tell when a shot hit water, Ross describing the interesting effect when "instantly the spray is in a perpendicular column, 30 to 50 feet high, where it appears to remain stationary for a distinct interval of time before it falls. It is almost perfectly white in appearance." Some artillerymen became especially excited at the sights, gunner John G. Frequa telling his crew, "now, boys, see me take a chimney." He did, and then threw his cap in the air and shouted at the enemy: "Come on, you cowardly scoundrels; you are not at Fort Henry." On another occasion, Pillow described George S. Martin, who, when "the wadding of his gun having given out, pulled off his coat and rammed it down his gun as wadding, and thus kept up the fire." Even so, the Federal bombardment took a toll, especially on the fortifications themselves, which were, one Confederate described, "damaged considerably."[31]

As bad as all the damage was, one special wounding did even more harm. The shot that hit the St. Louis's pilothouse and killed the pilot also wounded flag officer Foote, coincidentally in the foot. He had already been hit by splinters while overseeing a gun crew, but his wounding by the piece of shrapnel seemed to take away from the flotilla much of the impetus to continue the fight. To be sure, Foote had not been especially interested in tangling with the Confederate batteries in the first place. Yet, he later claimed (erroneously) that the Confederates were fleeing their guns at the moment when the St. Louis's steerage was hit. "We have every reason to suppose [that the fighting] would, in fifteen minutes more, could the action have been continued, have resulted in the capture of the two forts bearing on us, as the enemy's fire materially slackened and he was running from his batteries when the two gunboats helplessly drifted down the river." Obviously, he mistook movement within the batteries as a retreat.[32]

Foote actually told more of the truth when he described the hornet's nest he had awakened. Almost shell-shocked, he related how "the enemy must have brought over twenty heavy guns to bear upon our boats from the water batteries and the main fort on the side of the hill, while we could only return the fire with twelve bow guns from the four boats." He also reported, "I am informed that the rebel batteries were served with the best gunners from

Columbus." Foote was obviously convinced that he had failed, as were the
Federal infantry soldiers ringing Fort Donelson; McClernand reported that
they could easily hear "the shouts of the enemy that [confirmed] the gunboats
had been disabled in their attack upon the fort and had fallen back."[33]

In all, fifty-four sailors were killed and wounded on all boats in Foote's
flotilla, including the commander, who had to use crutches to get around. That
was a staggering number considering the number engaged, and especially so
when put alongside Foote's dearth of sailors in the first place. But as harsh as
it sounds, men were replaceable while the gunboats were not. Perhaps in the
worst case, the *Pittsburg* was having trouble even staying afloat. "The pumps
on board were not sufficient to keep the boat afloat," Thompson wrote, "nor
had we material of which to construct others." Without them, the boat could
not be made ready to fight and Thompson had to run the *Pittsburg* aground to
keep her from sinking: "we made the boat fast to the shore," he wrote, "had
leaks stopped by working steadily through the night as well as the work could
be done under the circumstances." Henry Walke similarly reported his dilapidated state on the *Carondelet*, adding, "we are in want of coal, provisions, and
ammunition."[34]

The Confederate reaction was understandably different. One Tennessean described the feeling in the midst of the fighting, stating, "it seemed to
shake the hills of Donelson and the earth itself seemed to tremble beneath the
mighty thundering of the big guns." Another eloquent if not perfect speller
wrote, "tha prest up the river stidly firing upon us and our Battreys while the
Bum shells were bursting in the air with loud and wild confusion threatening
them with sudden distrucktion. Stil tha came onn." Ross admitted that up
until the navy's retreat, he and his men "had gone so far as to conclude how
we would resist them when they landed and stormed our batteries." Now with
the prevailing silence that seemed that much more dominant, cheers from the
watching infantry and the gunners "yet panting from their exertion" accompanied the retreat as it suddenly dawned on the Confederates that this was
no retake of Fort Henry. A chorus of shouts emerged from the soldiers, one
Texan describing how it "commenc[ed] on the right wing and soon caught up
and became universal along the entire line." Even citizens of Dover who had
gathered on the bank of the river farther upstream were "testifying the joy by
tossing their hats in the air." Watching and fearing that the end had come, Nathan Bedford Forrest was suddenly euphoric: "never were men more jubilant
than when the victory crowned the steady bravery of our little fort; old men

wept; shout after shout went up." The Federals obviously heard these cheers, one describing that they "sounded like small boys, school boys, yelling." A Confederate was convinced, writing, "we could here the shouts of triumph reverberate through the hills and vallies which doubt less went to the ears of the enemy for they seemed infuriated and soon we hear the keen crack of there cannon and the whirling of shot and shell around us."[35]

Many tried to make sense of what had just happened. Having lost no casualties, Ross declared, "I am unable to account for so remarkable a circumstance, except that our always prompt and vigorous firing at long ranges had intimidated them and destroyed their capacity to take aim." Colonel J. E. Bailey, commanding the two regiments inside the fort, lost one man wounded in the melee, but noted, "the boats were repulsed and evidently seriously damaged." Rumors of at least one gunboat later sinking swirled around the fort, but Pillow related, "this information may or may not be true." Nevertheless, although the 32-pounders fired only around fifty shots per piece and the others less, the Confederates soon realized they had bested the gunboats. Captain Bidwell remarked, "I am confident the efficiency of the gunboat is in the gun it carries rather than in the boat itself." He went on to crow: "we can whip them always if our men will only stand to their guns." Bidwell also learned about the misperception of range amid all the ordnance coming at him, writing "they must have fired near 2,000 shot and shell at us." He noted, however, that "their fire was more destructive to our works at 2 miles that at 200 yards. They overfired us from that distance." Indeed, some shells fell among the land armies to the rear, prompting Bushrod Johnson to take cover and several of his men from the Goochland Virginia battery to "deem . . . ourselves justified in following so illustrious an example."[36]

With no other resort, an unhappy Foote next contemplated sending a gunboat past the river batteries to break up Confederate transportation east of Fort Donelson. Then he decided to slow down and do it right. In no mood to be told what to do any longer, the wounded Foote decided "my services here, until we can repair damages, by bringing up a competent force from Cairo to attack the fort, are much less required than they are at Cairo." He accordingly decided to move back to his base early Saturday afternoon with one of the damaged gunboats, the *Pittsburg*, leaving the *Louisville, Carondelet,* and *St. Louis* at Fort Donelson to guard the river and the transports and provide interservice cooperation. The *St. Louis* was operable and had to bear much of that burden; the *Carondelet*, on the other hand, was not even able to be moved. Fearing reinforcement from Columbus, Foote also sent the *Tyler* up the Tennessee once more to damage the railroad bridge even more, leaving only the timberclad *Conestoga* for Grant's use.[37]

Foote has been castigated for using the blunt tactic of steaming straight at the enemy fortifications. Had he held back and methodically shelled the fort, he could have been more successful with much less damage, as most of the Confederate guns could not reach long distances. That, of course, was not the tactical doctrine of the navy at the time, or what had succeeded at Fort Henry, so he steamed close. He learned his lesson well. Foote soon wrote his wife, "you need have no fears about us now, as we will keep off a good distance from rebel forts in future engagements." He later wrote, "I won't run into fire again, as a burnt child dreads it."[38]

Disappointment was understandably rampant among the Federal ranks. One Kentuckian began counting the shots, only stopping his count at 667. Lew Wallace later wrote, "I recollect well—indeed, I shall always remember—the disappointment of the army at Donelson when Commodore Foote's attack upon the water battery failed." He later wrote, "we looked at one another like sick men." A lower-level Federal similarly wrote his wife, "we all expected great things of the gun boats but they did nothing at all & our boys were much disheartened." Grant was also evidently shaken, writing, "I retired this night not knowing but that I would have to intrench my position, and bring up tents for the men or build huts under the cover of the hills." With the flotilla all but shattered, attention therefore turned back to the landside of the operations. If Grant was to become the victor at Fort Donelson, it would be without the navy's help, and he began to think in terms of a long siege, even writing Julia that he might be tied up a while and telling her where to go, what money to obtain, and what to do with his personal effects and horse. It seemed Grant was getting ready for a long stay at Dover, even writing of a "protracted siege."[39]

That had been the furthest thing from his mind earlier in the day when the gunboats were still the most feared portion of the Federal force.

In addition to the repulse of the gunboats, the afternoon of February 14 proved to be important in other ways. The fact that the Confederate earthen fortifications had defeated the vaunted Union ironclads upset all the expectations on both sides. The Confederate high command had always been more concerned about the naval attack than the landward threats, but that seemed to literally float away with the swirling, bobbing gunboats that drifted helplessly down the river that afternoon. Had Foote not attacked upriver, the four ironclads would certainly have been shot up even more than they were or, even worse, captured.[40]

That increase in respect for the Confederate river defense was but one of the major changes that developed that afternoon, particularly on the Federal side. For two days, Grant had kept the initiative, slowly but surely easing his land forces entirely around the Confederate lines. Meanwhile, the Confederates kept on the defensive. Now, other decisions were made this day that would alter the nature of the Confederate high command's outlook. Because ammunition was at a premium, Floyd and Pillow worked to get more brought in from Clarksville. Second, the threat of the Federals extending their lines so far eastward that they came to the river east of Dover portended major trouble. The erection of artillery there would end all river transportation and communication, supply, and even retreat options for the garrison. "Such appeared to be their design," engineer Gilmer wrote, adding that Grant evidently "resolved to invest us, and, when prepared, to attack us in overwhelming numbers or press us to capitulation by cutting off supplies and reenforcements." Third, the large numbers of Union reinforcements that could be seen marching from transports on the river signaled to Floyd and Pillow that the already surrounded garrison could not endure much longer, especially with so many fresh Federal troops fronting the thin Confederate lines. While the earlier attacks had failed, it would not be a major problem for Grant to mass much larger numbers and punch a hole in the garrison's lines, dooming all involved. It was thus ironic that the very land defense that had caused so little worry in the face of the victorious Fort Henry gunboats now seemed to be the real danger, and much greater than previously thought. "A child could see how the drama would end," recalled one Mississippian.[41]

At the same time, Grant was slowly losing the offensive mindset that had brought him to Fort Donelson in the first place. Indeed, he took little initiative throughout February 14 to move closer and attack the Confederate lines. Grant's division commanders attested to this, Smith writing, "the same system of annoyance was kept up, but, under the orders of the commanding general, to a more limited extent." McClernand similarly related that he received orders from Grant "that all aggressive operations on our part must be avoided," and Grant, in fact, later admitted that with the repulse of the gunboats, "I concluded to make the investment of Fort Donelson as perfect as possible, and partially fortify and await repairs to the gunboats."[42]

As the cold and white day of February 14 wore on, however, the Confederate high command increasingly realized that they would not be able to withstand either an attack by Grant's obviously swelling numbers or a siege. Nathan Bedford Forrest later wrote that "the army was in the best possible spirits [after the naval victory], feeling that, relieved of their greatest terror, they could whip any land force that could be brought against them." That was unfortunately not the feeling among the Confederate high command, which seemed to be fading into a growing melancholy despite the victory over the gunboats. Floyd correctly remarked, "I had no doubt whatever that their whole available force on the Western waters could and would be concentrated here if it was deemed necessary to reduce our position." It is ironic that even as the Confederate water batteries won a signal victory over the gunboats, the morose feeling of being trapped was growing greater, prompting the Confederate high command to act to do something. As a result, Floyd and Pillow, evidently mostly Pillow, began to think of taking the initiative even that afternoon, actually even before the victory over the gunboats, and forcing a way out of Fort Donelson. Floyd noted, "but one course was left by which a rational hope could be entertained of saving the garrison or a part of it—that was to dislodge the enemy from his position, on our left, and thus to pass our people into the open country lying southward toward Nashville."[43]

It would take a heavy blow to open a way out of the fort, but it could be done, if done quietly. As of the afternoon of February 14, the Federal line did not reach all the way eastward to Lick Creek, which was the obvious direction of escape. Grant's emphasis was on the western side of Fort Donelson, where he communicated with the navy and received his reinforcements. Moreover, a Confederate escape eastward, toward Nashville, would take the army, or the portion that survived a breakout attempt, toward Johnston's command rather than away from it. The meandering rivers also played a critical role; an attempt to break out and escape to the west would only mean the Confederates would face the daunting Tennessee River, and there was no way to quickly cross it. The army would no doubt be tracked down and destroyed by Grant's larger force or the naval gunboats, or both. A withdrawal to the east toward Johnston and Nashville could be done, however, because the Cumberland River made a huge turn in its bowl shape, which meant that the Confederates could march all the way to Nashville if need be on the western or southern side of the river, never having to cross it. And, it was hoped, Johnston's army coming to the rescue could aid any units that escaped from the trap that Fort Donelson was becoming.[44]

The Confederate high command held a conference around midday on February 14, with Pillow pushing an idea to use a portion of his division to pry open an avenue on the extreme Federal right. Buckner and Floyd evidently agreed with the idea and Pillow went to work forming his troops, although most stayed in the trenches and soon became enamored with the gunboat attack. One commander reported that his troops could hear the "terrific cannonading between the gunboats and the fort" and that "some of the shells from the boats [were] exploding in and near our lines, but doing no injury." Brigade commander Colonel John McCausland of the 36th Virginia wrote of "the shells passing over and taking the line of works in reverse, and many passing over and through this brigade." His curious men picked up some of the huge unexploded cannonballs, some they estimated to be as large as sixty-four pounders.[45]

All the while, several Confederate brigades made their way to the east, including eventually McCausland's Virginia brigade, Davidson's Mississippi, Kentucky, and Texas troops, and William E. Baldwin's 26th Tennessee, 26th Mississippi, and attached 20th Mississippi. "About noon General Pillow directed the left wing to be formed in the open ground to the left and rear of our position in the lines, for the purpose apparently of attacking the enemy's right," Baldwin reported. He and others such as the Virginia Goochland battery formed in the road that led across Lick Creek "in column by platoon," ready to march forward to the right until contact with the enemy occurred. Nathan Bedford Forrest's cavalry was also included in the redeployment, holding the left of Baldwin's brigade and making a wider sweep to the right as they advanced out of the works.[46]

Baldwin and Forrest began to move that afternoon, but other events quickly derailed the planned attack. Pillow soon called off the entire advance, perhaps becoming more interested in the gunboat action that was taking place around the same time; he soon rode to the scene for a firsthand look. Perhaps Pillow thought that if the vaunted gunboats would end the fighting immediately, there was no need to launch an infantry attack. Other issues were working on Pillow as well. A staff officer later described how he, at the head of the column, was caught off guard when a soldier went down from a Union sharpshooter almost immediately upon starting out: "Captain, our movement is discovered," Pillow barked, "it will not do to move out of our trenches under the circumstances." For whatever reason, Buckner wrote that "the [attack] order was countermanded by General Floyd, at the instance, as I afterwards learned, of General Pillow, who, after drawing out his troops for the attack, thought it too late for the attempt." Baldwin similarly wrote, "General Pillow ordered a countermarch, saying it was too late in the day to accomplish anything; and we returned to our former position in the lines." Only Forrest's troops became engaged in "maneuvering a short time and some sharp shooting between the cavalry and the enemy," while Baldwin reported he advanced "not more than one-fourth of a mile."[47]

Floyd was surprised at Pillow's single-handed usurpation of power over the attack, but he should not have been, and it would not be the last time Pillow would assume such authority. "Tell General Pillow," Floyd snapped, "he has lost the opportunity not by being discovered, but by the delay in sending the message and the consequent delay in getting a message back to him at this late hour." It was a definite letdown, but even the muted attempt illustrated that the initiative was changing hands.[48]

Although the contemplated Confederate attack on the afternoon of February 14 was recalled, it was somewhat of a blessing in that such a hurried and minor attack could potentially have done nothing more than alert Grant to Confederate thinking. Fortunately for Floyd and Pillow, no Federals reported the fairly large movement as anything more than skirmishing. Now, the Confederate high command had an entire night to plan, reposition, and launch a much larger morning attack that could involve nearly the entire army and that would have more potential for success. Even as the generals planned, however, the troops of both sides endured another long harrowing night of cold, snow, and misery.[49]

There were two different meetings held that night, one right before and one right after midnight. The high command of Floyd, Pillow, and Buckner, with Gilmer invited, met first and came up with a larger version of Pillow's plan from the afternoon before. Pillow wrote, "it was determined unanimously to give the enemy battle next day at daylight, so as to cut open a route of exit for our troops to the interior of the country, and thus save our army." It would be a tricky thing to accomplish, to be sure, as almost the entire army would have to be redeployed on the left and left center, leaving the right extremely vulnerable. Then the attack would have to go off flawlessly for the pathway of escape to be open. Finally, all remaining elements of the Confederate defense and garrison would have to be evacuated out of the opening, which would be held ajar by Buckner's division as a rear guard. It would take perfect timing for the entire army to escape, but after some minor debate, all agreed to proceed.[50]

With the decision made, another council of war took place right after midnight, to which the brigade commanders were added. Others such as Forrest and engineer Gilmer were also there, and the plan was laid out and explained so there would be no misunderstanding. Floyd later wrote, "this plan was laid before them, approved, and adopted, and at which it was determined to move from the trenches at an early hour on the next morning and attack the enemy in his position." Bushrod Johnson added, "to provide for every contingency, even that of failure, a rallying point, far beyond the enemy's lines, was designated, and all the plans were skillfully and minutely adjusted." There was unfortunately even then some doubt, such as when Adolphus Heiman, who was to maintain his salient position, noted that he and the others that would remain in garrison were afraid they could not hold against an attack. "I stated my fears to General Floyd," Heiman reported, "who replied, if I was pressed to fall back on the fort or act as circumstances would dictate." Such a vague answer evidently did not help Heiman's concern.[51]

The plan was nevertheless solidified during the night. Pillow was to mass his units on the far Confederate left and lead the assault, "assisted by Brigadier-General Johnson," who had basically been in the way since Pillow took command of his division upon Floyd's arrival. Buckner was to move from the right and man the center, where he would also take up the attack once Pillow rolled the Union line back westward. "In other words," Pillow wrote, "my success would roll the enemy's force in retreat over upon General Buckner, when by his attack in flank and rear we could cut up the enemy and put him completely to rout." Once the door was swung open, Buckner was to cover the retreat and the Confederate army would slip away in safety before the Federals could react.[52]

The Confederate brigades began to move in the early hours of the morning of February 15, and most were in position by the set time of 4:00 AM. Staff officers frequently arrived and nudged brigade commanders "to marshal their forces with the utmost dispatch" or to "hurry the formation of the brigade." Most of the brigade commanders did their job perfectly, John McCausland, for instance, writing, "about midnight I received orders to concentrate my brigade near the left wing, which was done promptly." Baldwin related they were to form at 4:00 AM "on the same ground and in the same order as on the previous evening." Once again, Forrest's cavalry was on the far left and would make the largest swing to the right or west, while five other Confederate brigades eventually massed on the far left, including those under Baldwin, Davidson, McCausland, Wharton, and Drake.[53]

As would be expected, the predawn darkness and icy conditions threatened to disrupt the carefully laid plans. Colonel Davidson's brigade was late in taking its assigned position, so Pillow sent Bushrod Johnson to his headquarters and he found that the colonel was "severely indisposed, and had only given orders that his command should be held in readiness to move." Pillow then remembered that Davidson "was complaining of being unwell" at the earlier council. Johnson quickly got the brigade moving and placed Colonel John M. Simonton of the 1st Mississippi in command, the third commander the brigade had received in just a few days; a dissatisfied Charles Clark had given over to Davidson at Clarksville on February 9, and now Simonton was in command. Auspiciously, this change was not fatal and Simonton soon positioned his four regiments in rear of Baldwin's troops "in column under the crest of the hill."[54]

More troubling was the delay on the right wing. Buckner was to move his division eastward and man most of Pillow's trenches, moving his regiments across Heiman's rear and into line east of Erin Hollow. Because of the already thin line especially on the far right, he was ordered not to move until the position was manned by the reserve forces from the fort's garrison. Floyd ordered Colonel Bailey to remain in the fort with his own regiment but to send a part of Colonel Head's 30th Tennessee to man Buckner's stretch of the line. Only then was Buckner to shift to the left. Unfortunately, there was a mix-up in communication and Head was nowhere to be seen when it came time for Buckner to march. One of the Confederates later blamed the delay on the fact that "Lieut.-Col. Murphy was sick and Col. Head unwell." For his part, Head reported that upon receiving his orders, "this I did without delay." If true, the foul-up came higher up the command chain.[55]

Buckner and his commanders chafed as the minutes passed and Head was nowhere to be seen. Hanson waited for Head but reported, "the failure of this regiment to arrive as soon as contemplated delayed me in reaching the point assigned me." Brown's brigade left only a token force and went anyway, not waiting. It was probably a good thing; once Brown arrived on Pillow's lines, he found the entrenchments unmanned, inviting a night attack by the enemy. Buckner had the same experience, reporting that he found the works empty: "even a battery was left in position without a cannoneer." Buckner deployed his lead regiment, the 3rd Tennessee, to hold all the trenches while the rest of his division marched in.[56]

Other factors also delayed the shift to the left. Buckner reported that his men were plagued "by the slippery condition of the icy road, which forbade a rapid march." Major W. L. Doss of the 14th Mississippi similarly stated, "it was with great difficulty that we progressed, owing to the country, which was hilly or mountainous, and covered with snow and ice." One of Graves's cannoneers wrote how "the hills [were] slippery with ice, requiring all the strength of the cannoneers at the wheels & all the sharp points of the drivers spears to get the Battery up one hill in an hour." Even so, Buckner's men soon slogged their way to their assigned positions, filling the potentially hazardous void in the Fort Donelson outer works. They warmed up in the process: "we was very cold at first," one Tennessean remembered, "but having to move double-quick for a time, we soon became quite warm." The crisis on the far right eased as well when Head's Tennesseans eventually arrived and manned the line formerly held by Buckner's division. It remained thin, however; only three companies stood in place of the entire 2nd Kentucky on the far right, while others held Brown's former trenches all the way to Indian Creek.[57]

No one in the Confederate army knew it at the time, but other potentially fatal problems were also developing. Although the Federal right flank had been wide open and resting on nothing all day, McClernand had finally garnered reinforcements and placed them exactly where the Confederates planned to assault the next morning. John McArthur's reserve brigade of Smith's division was finally detached and sent to McClernand, who put it on the right of Oglesby's troops, closer to Lick Creek. Although the brigade still lacked several hundred yards reaching the actual valley, it did provide more firepower in the exact area the Confederates targeted. McArthur's troops were not happy, however, having been shelled by the Confederates on the march along the Wynn Ferry Road. Worse, they did not arrive until after dark and consequently had little time to form much of a line. McArthur himself was upset that his men "encamped for the night without instructions, and, as I regret to add, without adequate knowledge of the nature of the ground in front and on our right." His colonels were just as upset, Issac Pugh of the 41st Illinois writing that "after some instructions from Colonel McArthur, commanding brigade, I hastily examined the ground, but it was too late to form any correct idea of the ground." Even so, the brigade took a position just under the brow of Dudley's Hill, and McClernand sent cavalry to McArthur's right to help plug the gap even more.[58]

While the Confederate high command knew nothing of McArthur's chance arrival and could not have done anything about it if they had known, miscommunication within their own ranks also plagued their efficiency. Despite Bushrod Johnson's insistence that all contingencies had been worked out and minute plans prepared, one glaring misunderstanding threatened to tear apart the Confederate escape timetable. Buckner understood his directions to include having his men march with knapsacks and equipment, or basically whatever they desired to carry with them out of the fort. The understanding on his part was that his men, once they made the breakout attack, would not return to the trenches or fort to retrieve their personal possessions and food. Unfortunately, Pillow understood differently, although one of his brigade commanders, Baldwin, sided with Buckner, stating that the men were "directed to take knapsacks, blankets, and all the rations that could be immediately provided." Tellingly, despite having operated under Pillow for the past couple of days, Baldwin was technically under Buckner, who apparently still issued orders to him. Buckner's other brigade commander, John Brown, had his men sufficiently prepared as well, while none of Pillow's brigades moved to their positions carrying their equipment, blankets, or knapsacks. He apparently planned to return once the door was open and retrieve those items. It was a grave misunderstanding and a formula for disaster.[59]

In fact, the whole plan was a potential disaster. It was certainly a gamble to mass everything on the far left for one colossal escape attempt. Fortunately, because of Grant's growing lethargy, but perhaps even more so because of the gunboat defeat that day, the Federals had not taken advantage of any of the vulnerable holes in the Confederate lines. In fact, they had not even detected the large mass movement to the east. Lew Wallace later wrote,

> it seems incomprehensible that columns mixed of all arms, infantry, cavalry, and artillery, could have engaged in simultaneous movement, and not have been heard by some listener outside. One would think the jolting and rumble of the heavy gun-carriages would have told the story. But the character of the night

must be remembered. The pickets of the Federals were struggling for life against the blast, and probably did not keep good watch.

Indeed, most Federals were simply trying to stay warm on this second in-clement night. Yet the danger of detection significantly increased with the dawn. If the timing went wrong in any way, or if Grant realized what was occurring and counterattacked on the weaker fronts on the Confederate right, the entire timetable and escape plan would be disrupted.[60]

And as that dawn approached, the ability of the Confederate commanders to stay on that timetable was severely tested.

11

"NOT GENERALLY HAVING AN IDEA THAT A BIG FIGHT WAS ON HAND"

"The morning of the 15th dawned clear and hopeful," John A. McClernand wrote later that month, "and both officers and men, unshaken by another night of intense suffering, stood to their arms, ready for the work of an eventful day." McClernand may have been unshaken in his comparatively comfortable headquarters, but Illinoisan George Carrington wrote that the men "threw off our snow covered blankets while the chill wintry air penetrated our very bones." And while the skies may have remained clear, hope for the end of the misery soon faded into grave concern for the general and many other Federals as the dawn indeed brought an eventful day, starting as always with the artillery and sharpshooters. One Iowan noted, "when a Rebel showed his head above them [fortifications], he was shot at by a dozen rifles at once." It was not just small arms either. One Kentuckian wrote, "this morning I was aroused from my sweet slumbers by the bursting of those damned bomb shells."[1]

Yet little did the Federals know that as day approached they were about to fight the battle for Fort Donelson. Because of the inclement conditions, most, like Grant, figured the Confederates would simply await the next Federal move. He had no qualms about delaying the proceedings to allow the men some respite and to await the return of a more powerful naval flotilla. That would take time, and in the mean time, the Union commanders had learned from the previous night, when they had kept nearly the entire army in the ranks throughout the darkness. With so little happening this night, numerous officers allowed their commands to retire behind the safety of the ridges and build fires during the night. That had helped to alleviate some of the bone-chilling misery, but nothing could remedy all the concerns except daylight, to which the Federals longingly looked. They obviously did not know what that dawn would bring.[2]

Indeed, the previous night had been miserable for all involved. Colonel Joseph J. Woods of the 12th Iowa, like other commanders, allowed most of his regiment to retire behind the ridges, keeping only a couple of companies on the actual line. Despite the fires, Woods still noted that the men "passed an unpleasant night." Colonel Crafts J. Wright of the 13th Missouri noted, "the clothes of the men were drenched and frozen upon them. I sat upon a log wrapped in my blanket until 3 o'clock, when permission was given to go back half a mile and build fires to dry the men." Lew Wallace also described his troops making fires behind the ridges but that "they laid down as best they could on beds of ice and snow, a strong, cold wind making the condition still more disagreeable." Even his horse, John, was miserable; the general had not had any water for John and thus staked him on a rope to let him get all the snow he could reach in a large circle. John met him the next morning and Wallace saw he had "lapped up all the snow in the circle of his tether, and that, not to speak of the appeal in his eyes, told me how he suffered for water." Others had to perform outright military duties despite their misery; Lieutenant Colonel T. E. G. Ransom of the 11th Illinois called his men into line in the night "when the firing became heavy." They remained two hours before being allowed to go back to a safe area, but again and again they were called out, with only coffee distributed in the ranks to warm them. Others built small earthworks to shield the artillery batteries on McClernand's front.[3]

The Confederates across the lines were not as fortunate as their Federal opponents. Those who remained stationary had to man their lines, including those in the river batteries who, Captain Culbertson wrote, had to "sleep by their guns ready for an attack." Those on the move since around midnight, the five Confederate brigades that congregated on the left, were not able to build fires, nor were the replacements of Buckner's division and the fort's garrison allowed to gain any comfort. They were hungry as well, having had little to eat since Thursday. One noted that while there was plenty of food in camp and a means was even worked out to get food and water to the front lines, they "did not get much of either."[4]

While the Federals had no idea that a major attack was coming at dawn and settled into the long, bleak night, wishing for daylight and higher temperatures, the Confederates had a boost of adrenaline and activity that made up for some of the chill. The Confederate troops stayed busy during the night, causing their exertion to remedy some of the cold that would have been even worse standing idle. Then too, the Confederates experienced an adrenaline rush realizing they were about to attack the enemy. One Mississippian described the feeling perfectly: L. J. Bailey of the 20th Mississippi wrote of how his regiment was called out of the trenches during the night and allowed to warm at a bonfire and prepare three days' rations. Then they moved forward, but he noted,

> we started back toward the ditches, not where we had left them, but more to the
> left, and went on over and into the timber, then out into an old field, where we
> were formed in line, and I noticed other lines just in our front. I could see men
> on horses riding down the lines and talking to the soldiers. Presently, our Major
> Brown came riding down our line, talking in a low tone to the boys, for we were
> near the enemy. I soon understood what was up.[5]

Thus as the first gray streaks of dawn began to emerge over the Confederate brigades waiting in column on the road leading out of the defenses, they hoped by the end of the day to be rid of the trap that Fort Donelson had become. If all proved successful, they would break out and be free of the coiling Union constrictor that was continually wrapping itself around Fort Donelson and its garrison.

Ulysses S. Grant was up before the break of day as well. With headquarters at the comparatively warmer Crisp House on the Federal left, he had been mulling over his options in the wake of the gunboat defeat the afternoon before. He informed George Cullum at Cairo, "I fear the result of an attempt to carry the place by storm with raw troops." Little else seemed possible than to hold what he had, wait for additional reinforcements, keep the Confederates hemmed in, and endure until the gunboats could be repaired and return. He was seconded in this thinking by Cullum in Cairo, who told him, "you can afford to have a little patience." All the same, he had his staff out—particularly his trusted chief Joseph D. Webster—looking for areas to the right where he could extend his lines to the river and block Confederate waterborne movement. For himself, he planned to ride as early as possible to the river landing and confer with Foote, who could not make it inland because of his wounds.[6]

In all his planning, however, it never entered Grant's mind that anyone else could dictate the tempo of operations. Grant later admitted as much: "when I left the National line to visit Flag-officer Foote I had no idea that there would be any engagement on land unless I brought it on myself." While historians and certainly later Americans tend to view Grant as the warrior at his peak at Vicksburg or in Virginia in 1863 or 1864, this was the Grant of February 1862, less than a year away from his father's dry goods store in Galena. Certainly Grant grew as a commander over time, and one of the most important ways he matured was in quelling the overconfidence that he displayed often in the early stages of the war. While his bulldog mentality and refusal to be turned away likely were inbred in his personality, so apparently was his great confidence, so much so that it caused him to blindly view operations as of his own making, rarely factoring in early in the war that the enemy could act independently from what he wanted them to do or what he thought they would do.[7]

Clear examples abound indicating that Grant, early on, had a real problem with overconfidence. When he routed the Confederates at Belmont, he seemed to disregard any chance of a counterattack, which occurred, and it almost cost him the battle and his life. Obviously, the prime example came a couple of months later when he just could not fathom that the Confederate army at Corinth would march out of their entrenchments and attack him on open ground at his campground around Shiloh Church and Pittsburg Landing. He certainly found out then that the enemy could do unexpected things, but in each case his dogged determination not to give up saved the day. Fortunately for him, he learned as he went.[8]

A large part of that growth process occurred at Fort Donelson on February 15. Grant had convinced himself that the Confederates would not or even could not act offensively, or perhaps it just never even crossed his mind that they would or could. In his mind, the fighting would only restart when he decided it would, and until then both sides would simply watch each other and wait. How wrong he was; he was caught in a most compromising position when the Confederates did act.[9]

Grant was indeed up early that morning, even sending Halleck a message that everything was going well despite the gunboat setback. He also received a message from Foote about 2:00 AM asking that he come to the gunboats and meet with him because of his foot wound. Seeing no chance of fighting he did not bring on himself, Grant set out for the landing four or five miles to the north, even as the Confederate brigades were massing on the other end of the Union line. Significantly, Grant issued orders for his division commanders to stay where they were until he returned, not bringing on an engagement. The fact that he issued only orders to quell an offensive move is telling about his mindset. And that he met regiments such as the 20th Ohio moving to the field from the landing could only have confirmed his feeling of security.[10]

Grant found the path toward the river very difficult; the frozen roads "made travel on horseback even slower than through the mud," he later wrote. The meager roads had been churned into quagmires by the reinforcements trudging to the battle lines, and the frigid night had frozen those ruts and holes into almost nonnegotiable terrain for his horse. He nonetheless made his way as best he could to the river, where a small boat waited to carry him out to the gunboat and Foote. The two officers conferred, Foote telling Grant he would need ten days for repairs and to get a more powerful flotilla back to attack Fort Donelson. He also told Grant he was departing for Cairo that morning, leaving Commander Benjamin M. Dove in charge of the remaining flotilla at Fort Donelson. Grant's heart must have sunk at news of the long delay, but that was nothing compared to the news that awaited him as his small boat landed on the riverbank for his return trip about 9:00 AM. One of his staff officers, William S. Hillyer, was there, Grant remembered, "white with fear not for his personal safety, but for the safety of the National troops." The news was indeed frightening: the Confederates had attacked![11]

Gideon Pillow had indeed launched his attack, which was fairly simple on paper but very difficult to actually accomplish. One Texan in line labeled it "an indiscreet though a bold movement, as we did not know the force of the enemy or the number and locality of his batteries." Indeed, the chances of any operation going totally according to plan, much less this one in the dead of winter and its attending inclement weather, were miniscule, as illustrated by the old military adage that "no plan survives initial contact." In this case, the Confederate plan hardly even survived the march to get into position, much less contact. When that contact came, it certainly went off schedule, causing massive delay in the Confederate attempt to break out of Fort Donelson.[12]

The problems began even before dawn. Intended to be launched at daylight, the attack was delayed half an hour because of Davidson's brigade not being in line at the proper time. The problems in Davidson's brigade were quickly fixed, with Colonel John M. Simonton taking command, but the delay in arrival necessitated a delay in launching the attack. Consequently, the Confederate brigades did not advance until well after daylight, around 6:00 AM.[13]

Yet Pillow still amazingly had the element of surprise, because the Confederates had not given away their intention and were actually still within the Confederate defenses. When the brigades began to file by the right flank out the Old Charlotte Road to the east and then turn northward, forming columns at a right angle to the entrenchments, that element of surprise quickly faded, however. Federal cavalry commands were exactly where the Confederate brigades intended to form, and, even worse, an entire Union brigade was atop Dudley's Hill, the key terrain feature on the Union right. John McArthur had led his brigade of three Illinois regiments (detached from Smith's division) eastward the night before and had taken a position on the high ground around the hill. Unknown to him, of course, that was exactly the area in which the Confederate brigades planned to form and assault. Ironically, McArthur's presence was also unknown to the Confederates. It seems both sides received a shock when daylight finally appeared.[14]

Once daybreak literally shed light on the surroundings, all could get a glimpse of what kind of terrain they would be fighting on, the fresh snow adding to the ability to see almost every nook and cranny of the ground. Essentially, the Confederates would be ascending the gradual but narrow slope of Dudley's Hill, the ridge initiating the high ground on which the Wynn Ferry Road ran to the west. The Federals had deployed on this ridge, placing their artillery on the high ground and sheltering some of their infantry behind it. The ridge was narrow, falling off abruptly to either side in a series of valleys that fed the defining watersheds. Just to the north of the ridge and Dudley's Hill was Barn Hollow, which flowed from the high ground on which the Wynn Ferry and Forge roads met. The Confederate outer works ran directly on the north or opposite side of Barn Hollow. Directly to the south of the high ground, the steep slopes of Lick Creek first defined Dudley's Hill, and its tributary Bufford Hollow paralleled Barn Hollow, although at a longer length and leading all the way to the ridge that separated that watershed from Indian Creek. Thus, the narrow ridge between Lick and Bufford creeks on the south and the succession of Indian Creek, Erin Hollow, and Barn Hollow on the north created only a small space in which the Confederates could deploy and roll up the Union battle line. The plan was to march out the Old

Charlotte Road to the base of Dudley's Hill, where the long ridge fell into the bottomland at the confluence of Barn Hollow and Lick Creek, turn right on a "narrow and obstructed by-road," and ascend the hill, rolling up the Federal flank in the process.[15]

Colonel William E. Baldwin commanded the lead Confederate brigade, consisting of the 20th and 26th Mississippi and the 26th Tennessee. It was not the full brigade, as portions had been left back with Buckner, and indeed the 20th Mississippi was nominally a part of the Virginia contingent but was assigned to Baldwin this day. Baldwin was ready to go at the appointed time, writing that "precisely at 4.10 on the morning of Saturday, the 15th, General Pillow arrived on the ground, and found my three regiments, which were to constitute the advance, formed and ready to march." Yet it was 6:00 AM before Baldwin actually led the five brigades out of the Confederate defenses toward the rising ground of Dudley's Hill. Baldwin reported he marched "by the right flank in a narrow and obstructed by-road." The entire force moved in column on the road as best it could, preceded by one company of the 26th Mississippi as skirmishers.[16]

Because of the Federals' presence on Dudley's Hill, Baldwin could not ascend the slope before he met resistance, the initial shots coming from the Union cavalry in the area. The troopers soon fell back to a reserve position, where, according to McClernand, they "were posted in positions favorable for the pursuit of the enemy if the fate of the day should justify it." They took little part thereafter, one 4th Illinois trooper writing, "we once dismounted and ran up the hill to help them, but were too late." With the cavalry gone, McArthur's Illinoisans soon took up the fight, one Confederate writing that "by the time we had gained 300 yards we were under a brisk fire, which came from a hill in front covered with timber." One 41st Illinois soldier agreed, writing, "at daylight Saturday morning while some of the boys were yet asleep, firing commenced on top of the hill where our pickets were posted, and in less than a minute the engagement became general." He went on to say, "we briskly returned the fire of the enemy, who were advantageously posted behind the hill, while we were in the open field exposed to a heavy fire." The Illinoisans managed to offer such resistance that Baldwin was unable to make much headway with only one company as skirmishers and the rest of the Confederate attacking force piling up behind him. If McArthur was surprised, Baldwin was just as surprised finding a Union brigade on the hill; it had not been there the night before. Showing his surprise, Baldwin reported that his

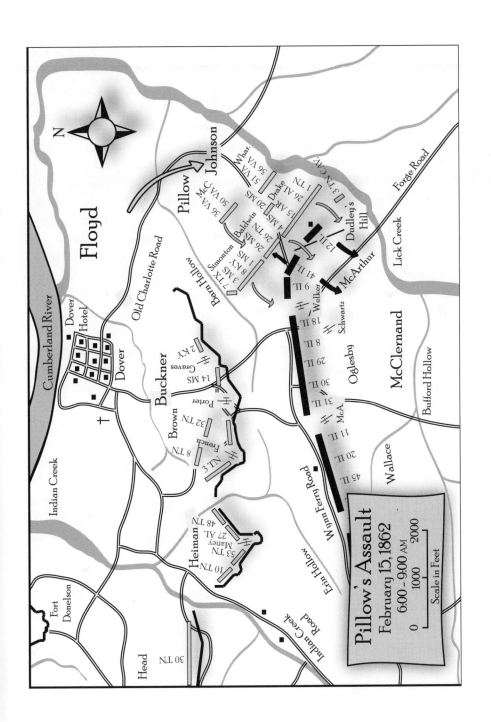

Pillow's Assault
February 15, 1862
6:00 – 9:00 AM

0   1000   2000
Scale in Feet

Mississippi company "was fired upon by what was supposed at first to be only the enemy's pickets." He quickly sent out another company of the 26th Mississippi to reinforce the skirmishers, "but," Baldwin noted, "both were soon driven back by a brisk and well-sustained fire, which indicated the presence of a considerable force."[17]

It was indeed a considerable force, McArthur's three Illinois regiments. But they were just as awed by the approaching spectacle as the Confederates were surprised that they were there. The shock was evident to R. H. McFadden, who wrote home: "about daylight, we were aroused by the firing, of our pickets, and in about five minutes we were formed in line, but received a galling fire as we were forming." With only three regiments, McArthur could not do much, but he placed the eight companies (the other two having been left in the rear for other work, one in Paducah in fact) of the 9th Illinois in line extending Oglesby's brigade, facing north, with the 41st Illinois farther to the right and facing northeastward just under the crest of the main hill. McArthur also shifted the 12th Illinois, which had been held in reserve the night before behind the brow of the hill, to the right to cover that flank behind the 41st Illinois. Colonel Augustus L. Chetlain of the 12th Illinois was concerned about his green troops, this being their "'maiden' flight," as he described it. What he saw when he arrived farther to the right did not help his concern; Confederates were even then swarming in that direction near an open field, so Chetlain sent several companies even farther to the right to guard against a flank attack. Companies A and B moved out, but Captain J. Tyler Hale of Company B fell dead while posting his line. Company C also went out to several buildings in the area, also losing their captain, Robert V. Chesley, in the process, while a portion of Company D manned a fence near the field. It was unfortunately a small plug for a big hole. McArthur later wrote that his men "were surrounded by the enemy, who opened on us a heavy fire of musketry, at the same time outflanking us by one regiment on our right."[18]

Even worse for the Federals, more Confederates were on their way. The presence of such a force and the heavy Federal fire emanating from the hill convinced Baldwin to deploy his entire brigade. He sent the 26th Mississippi into line on the right of the road, but regrettably ordered them to do so "by company," which meant that each would leave the road and form successively down the line to the right on the initial company at the road. "This method of forming line of battle was rendered advisable," Baldwin reported, "by the particular features of the ground, which sloped gently to the right, thickly covered with timber." A large field of several hundred acres to the left of the road also factored in, because if the regiment had deployed into line on its center company on the road, the left would have been exposed in the field to the heavy Union fire.[19]

Unfortunately for Baldwin, his deploying maneuver caused major confusion among the green Mississippians. Baldwin reported that the regiment "was three times thrown into confusion by the close and rapid fire of the enemy, taking the men in flank, and three times were they rallied, finishing the movement some 50 yards to the rear and a little to the right of the exact point where their line should have been placed." He decided, "any other than forward movements are extremely dangerous with volunteers." Despite the confusion, Baldwin then brought the next regiment into line, placing five companies of the 26th Tennessee between the Mississippians on the right and the field and fence on the left. The other five companies were held in reserve in the road, basically in the center at what Baldwin called the "center and pivot point of operations."[20]

As Baldwin slowly deployed, John McClernand, though lacking any military academy education, could see what was happening and that it was not good. As he later described it, there were "large masses of the enemy, rushing towards my right." As more and more Confederates deployed and entered the fighting, in fact, they began to take more than just McArthur's brigade in the flank. By around 7:00 AM, the 41st Illinois had shifted until it faced more east than north, which left portions of Oglesby's brigade uncovered. There, the 8th and 18th Illinois dispensed with their meager breakfasts and coffee and formed a line on Lieutenant Colonel Frank L. Rhoads's orders to "hold the height of the ridge, and not to yield an inch." One Illinoisan admitted that "as there had been as much of that [firing in the previous days] we were not disturbed," but the Illinoisans soon found out this was for real and quickly formed up on McArthur's left. An Illinoisan remembered his feelings that cold morning:

> I remember that when I first caught sight of the crowd, with their slouch hats
> and shaggy beards, coming over the ridge en masse, loading and firing, something
> like the advance of a skirmish-line, that my fingers were so numb and useless from
> cold, and that I was so chilled and nervous from cold and excitement together, that
> I thought I never would get a cap on my gun-tube, as every one I would take
> from my cap-box would slip through my fingers and drop in the deep snow.

While tempted to turn those regiments to the right and battle the oncoming enemy, McClernand and Oglesby had to be concerned about their front facing north as well. By this time numerous Confederate batteries had opened up on the Federals across Barn Hollow and infantry could be clearly seen, no doubt preparing to make an attack from that direction. With Confederates on their front and flank, the Union right was getting into a major predicament.[21]

By 7:00 AM, other Confederate commanders were also on the front, helping move forward the stacked-up brigades in the rear but in the process also confusing the chaotic situation even more. Primarily, Gideon Pillow rode forward in response to a message from Baldwin that "the enemy was before us in force," and he quickly took stock of the problems. Pillow later noted, "the enemy was prepared to receive me in advance of his encampment, and he did receive me before I had assumed a line of battle in which and while I was moving against him without any formation for the engagement." The usually vain Pillow admitted, "for the first half hour of the engagement I was much embarrassed in getting the command in position properly to engage the enemy."[22]

Once on the ground, Pillow went to work to rectify the situation. One of the first things he did was to send Baldwin's third regiment forward on the left. Evidently not knowing of the large field there, Pillow sent Major William N. Brown and his 20th Mississippi to form on the 26th Tennessee's left, which placed them squarely in the field. Brown recalled that the enemy "commenced firing upon us soon after the order to advance, and by the time we had gained 300 yards we were under a brisk fire, which came from a hill in front covered with timber." That is where the 41st Illinois was, one of its members writing, "we engaged them freely, pouring in such a fire that they retreated back over a field." That brisk fire continued as the Mississippians fell back across the field, and the problems were compounded when Pillow ordered the regiment to wheel to the right, which exposed their left flank farther out in the field. Brown noted that such a move "subjected us to a cross-fire, and very much exposed us to the enemy on both sides, under cover of the woods." Brown sent a messenger to Pillow to have the order revoked, which he did, but not before numerous Mississippians in the left wing of the regiment went down. In fact, the recall order was not heard on the left, where the companies were in heated combat with the Illinoisans, and their withdrawal was thus delayed. Even some of the injured refused to budge, a wounded Lieutenant O. R. Eastland barking at his men, "never mind me, boys; fight on! fight on!" Many did, one member of the regiment relating later, "here I kill[ed] my first Yankee."[23]

The Mississippians eventually retired into the woods east of the field, but Pillow soon brought more of his brigades forward to create a heavier line of battle. The two small Virginia brigades under Colonel Gabriel C. Wharton and Colonel John McCausland moved forward, Wharton's 51st and 56th Virginia taking a position in the field to the left of Baldwin's brigade. The 20th Mississippi had just been in that fire-swept field and had retired. Now, the Virginians had the same experience. Baldwin noted that the Virginians "twice endeavored to gain ground forward to a point where their fire could be effective, but were unable to stand the destructive effect of the Minie balls." The 20th Mississippi apparently used the Virginia diversion to their own good and reentered the field farther down the line to the south to face the 12th Illinois, taking a position "slightly covered by an irregularity of the ground," Baldwin noted. Next in line came the two regiments of McCausland's brigade, the 36th and 50th Virginia, which were held in reserve on the road behind Baldwin's troops.[24]

The 56th Virginia's Presbyterian minister, Dabney Carr Harrison, fell in the midst of the fighting. He had read to his men from the Psalms just a day or two before, and one Confederate now described the events as "a strange dispensation of the Almighty." In the thick of the fighting, Harrison took three balls through his cap and another hit his temple but did not stop him. He continued on, leading his men, when a shot through the lung felled him for good.[25]

With more troops funneling into the field on the left of the road, Pillow also sent more troops to Baldwin's right. The next brigade in line was Simonton's, and after "filing around the base of the hill upon which the enemy were drawn up," as well as experiencing confusion in the 3rd Mississippi as to how to deploy, Simonton positioned the 3rd Mississippi to Baldwin's right, followed by the 8th Kentucky, the 1st Mississippi, and the sick-decimated 7th Texas. The latter included future Confederate generals John Gregg and Hiram Granbury and sloped down the hill to the right toward the bottom of Barn Hollow. Bushrod Johnson noted this was "about half way up the hill occupied by the enemy," and the brigade soon began to feel the effects of the Federal fire. In fact, the right regiment of Texans was actually "thrown back perpendicular to our line, to prevent the enemy's taking advantage of the cover afforded by the slope of the ground to turn our right." They remained there just across the small hollow from Graves's battery in its new position. The other flank of the brigade was similarly a mess, with a portion of the 3rd Mississippi cut off and winding up on the far left, south of Baldwin's troops, where they took a position along the fence at the large field. One Mississippian distinctly remembered the "ball[s] cutting the fence rails and wounding some of our men." While under heavy fire, especially during the confusion among the Mississippians that caused the Kentuckians to endure a grueling volley, most of the other regiments sustained little loss due to "the balls passing over us," Simonton related.[26]

The final brigade in line, Joseph Drake's, moved out to the far left Confederate flank under the careful eye of Bushrod Johnson. The four regiments had the farthest to travel, Johnson elaborating on some of the concern: "in passing from the left towards the right of our trenches, as did our line of battle, our left had to traverse a much larger circle than our right, and as our right moved near the trenches our left was the only wing liable to be outflanked. I therefore found ample occupation in pressing forward the left wing, keeping a regular, well-directed line, and in guarding the left flank." To this brigade was joined at least a portion of the 3rd Mississippi cut off from Simonton's brigade, and Johnson simply pushed them forward as well, ordering them to fix bayonets and advance. Even though on the extreme left, the brigade took some fire. Timothy McNamara of the 4th Mississippi described how they were "greatly annoyed by a fire from some old houses," which came from the companies Colonel Chetlain of the 12th Illinois had sent to the buildings. Fortunately, also on the left flank was Forrest's cavalry, he noting "the first gun from the enemy killing a horse in my regiment." Forrest kept his cavalry on the far left but found "the undergrowth was so thick that I could scarcely press my horses through it." Later, Forrest admitted that he attempted to attack the enemy flank using the open field "but found the ground a marsh and we were unable to pass it." He did provide good work, however, in parading in front of the enemy and keeping them pinned down and hence unable to turn Pillow's left.[27]

Despite the chaos in the Confederate ranks, the weight of their numbers soon told and McArthur's line began to bend. The Mississippians of both Drake's brigade and the 3rd Mississippi felt a major sense of accomplishment at taking the small two-story house occupied by some of the 12th Illinois. The troops quickly entered, seeking to stop any more resistance from it but finding only a wounded Illinoisan. One Mississippian noted that he had "his back mangled or broken" and was soon carried to the rear, where unfortunately he was "openly abused by Southern civilization." The Mississippians also searched the upper story but again found no one there. They did scare one more Federal from a thicket, and when he tried to run back to his own lines, "two quick shots brought him to the ground."[28]

Despite taking the buildings, the Confederates made little forward headway. Their concern for both flanks was obvious, even to the point of refusing the line on the right, and that was not altogether inappropriate. One Kentuckian of Simonton's brigade was not ashamed to tout his state's ability on one of those flanks, writing, "dispair seemed to be knit upon every brow to such a degree that any other people except Kentuckians and Texans would have given away before the enormous number which they had to contend with." And despite Confederate artillery opening up from the trenches to the north, there was a distinct possibility that the enemy could try to counterattack, and in fact that actually happened. Numerous reports bore this out, with Bushrod Johnson writing that Simonton was "being heavily pressed by the enemy." McCausland reported the enemy "advancing just in front of the Thirty-Sixth Virginia Regiment." Others stated that the enemy advanced as well. Indeed, the 41st Illinois's colonel Isaac C. Pugh had ordered an assault.[29]

The 41st Illinois had taken its position near the Forge Road, just under the brow of Dudley's Hill and facing the open field. It was in this position that they caused much of the damage in the Mississippi ranks. One Illinoisan remembered, "not succeeding in drawing the enemy up on top of the hill, we were ordered to advance up the hill and formed in line, exposed to a heavy fire from the centre, and also from the right where the rebels [were] concealed in the timber." The regiment steadily advanced up the hill toward the Confederate line, hitting it roughly at the junction of Baldwin's and Simonton's brigades. Seeing his men beginning to waver from the vicious assault, Simonton sent an aide to fetch reinforcements, and Pillow moved a regiment from McCausland's brigade, then in reserve behind Baldwin. Colonel McCausland with the 36th Virginia "at once moved up to his support," with Simonton's aide, Lieutenant R. B. Ryan, leading the Virginians along the crest of Dudley's Hill back to his brigade at the junction of its left and Baldwin's right. There, Ryan "suggested to the major to form and bring his men into action so as to take the enemy, that was pressing us so hard, in the flank."

Although Pugh later claimed that his assault drove the enemy clear back into the trenches half a mile away, it was not that successful and he soon realized "this movement (the charge) had not been general on the part of our troops." Now, his regiment was alone forward of the line. Worse, Pugh related that "the enemy returned with renewed force and recommenced the conflict." It was the Virginians, who hit Pugh's Illinoisans in the right flank. Even in the midst of being taken in the flank, however, Pugh was somehow able to steady the line while the Illinoisans fell back down the hill, one noting that the enemy "fired into us, in front, on the right and left."[30]

All the while, the 9th and 12th Illinois were battling on their own fronts. Chetlain of the 12th Illinois described how the enemy "in large numbers was trying to force in the right of our line." In the process, they lost the houses. Colonel August Mersy of the 9th Illinois had his own problems, his right being engaged the most. Making the situation worse, after some two and a half hours Mersy's men were beginning to run out of ammunition, although some of it was apparently wasted; Confederates reported their firing as "generally overshooting, while ours were constantly warned to aim low."[31]

And as fate would have it, Pillow restarted his advance at that critical moment. After repelling the foray by the 41st Illinois, Pillow and his commanders once again began to move forward themselves. He admitted, "we fought him for nearly two hours before I made any decided advance upon him. He contested the field most stubbornly." Baldwin echoed those thoughts, writing, "our line advanced some 50 or 100 yards up the slope and remained stationary for more than an hour, the position of the enemy being so well chosen and covered that it seemed impossible to gain an inch of ground." Brigade commander Simonton agreed: "for one long hour this point was hotly contested by the enemy." He added mistakenly that the brigade nevertheless "marched up the hill, loading and firing as they moved, gaining inch by inch on an enemy at least four times their number." Casualties were mounting too, Lieutenant R. B. Ryan of Simonton's staff relating, "in some places it seemed as if a whole rank fell at a time." Officers also went down, including the colonel of the 26th Tennessee, John M. Lillard, as well as the 7th Texas's lieutenant colonel, J. M. Clough. Clough had had an earlier near miss two days before when a shell "sung through his whiskers," one Texan remembered. Now he was not so fortunate. Others were individually easy targets, such as Captain D. H. Spence on Baldwin's staff, who "was severely wounded in the head while gallantly exposing himself on the top of a fence and urging Tennesseans onward."[32]

Despite such casualties and more than two hours of chaos on the northern slopes of Dudley's Hill, Pillow and Baldwin ultimately succeeded. Baldwin reported that he spied "a regiment or more" farther to the left, in actuality Drake's brigade, and sent word for help. The brigade was in an area where the small declivity his men were using as protection ran into Lick Creek. Baldwin asked Drake to "throw forward his left and advance up the hollow in a direction nearly parallel to our line of battle, and attack the enemy's right flank." Drake did so, hitting the right companies of the 12th Illinois and driving them back. At the same time, Baldwin and Pillow ordered a surge by the remaining brigades, all "throwing forward their left wings, [and] we succeeded in executing a change of front to the right, turning the right of the enemy and driving him at once from his opposition." Augustus Chetlain in the 12th Illinois agreed: "the fire of the enemy at my right became heavy and very destructive." He reported that "at the end of twenty to twenty-six minutes," his forward companies were routed and the 41st Illinois next in line to the left had retreated from their counterattack, their right passing directly through the 12th Illinois. Chetlain thus ordered his prone men to fall back as well. With the break of the 41st Illinois and 12th Illinois farther to the right, McArthur had little hope left for this line. One 12th Illinois soldier wrote of the brigade commander's disgust at the 41st Illinois, whose Colonel Pugh was already in trouble, having had numerous charges of neglect brought on him at Paducah: "Col. McArthur was very mad. Very angry. He said it was because of their cowardly officers." Even so, the Illinoisans fell back all across the board. McArthur insisted, "I deemed it my duty to give the order to retire." The Virginia regiments of McCausland's brigade, Bushrod Johnson noted, then "planted its colors on the top of the hill."[33]

Also lost near the top of Dudley's Hill were the two Union guns of Welker's Missouri battery, McClernand describing "two 10-pounder Parrott guns, on the extreme right." Apparently they never entered action, McClernand writing that McArthur's infantry was "unsupported by their artillery, which had not been brought into action for want of opportunity." The Confederates described capturing the two guns, Baldwin relating that they were pointing toward the Confederate trenches and were "seized before they could be turned upon us or taken from the field." Bushrod Johnson gave the credit for capturing the two pieces to the decimated 8th Kentucky of Simonton's brigade.[34]

As a result of the Confederate surge and flanking movements, McArthur's Illinoisans were by 9:00 AM in full retreat to the west. In the midst of the retiring Illinoisans of McArthur's brigade was John Kerr of the 41st Illinois.

He had been upset at missing the march toward Fort Heiman on February 6 because he was with the baggage. He wrote his wife, "I have resolved that after this . . . I will not serve on detached duty for the Regt any more." Now that he and his regiment were bearing the brunt of Pillow's attack, he changed his tune, next writing his wife, "I wish and pray God that I may never [again] have the painfull nesisity of witnessing such a hard fought battle." Another admitted, "possibly some of us wondered why we had been so anxious to leave home and mother."[35]

Despite the personal feelings, it was in the larger context a notable Confederate success, Baldwin himself writing that "up to this time our condition was one of extreme peril." There was, he declared, even a chance of "being thrown back in confusion into our trenches." Jeremy Gilmer similarly wrote, "for some time the result of the day appeared doubtful and but little advantage was gained." Nevertheless, the Southern regiments, despite already running low on ammunition, swarmed up and over Dudley's Hill, Simonton writing that "the enemy's lines gave way, and the rattle of musketry was drowned by the shouts of victory that rose along the lines of men conscious of superiority and right."[36]

Gideon Pillow could indeed claim initial success, despite it taking five brigades three hours to dislodge three Union regiments. Obviously, terrain played a key role in the Federal defense, but Pillow was not yet able to declare full victory. He had indeed driven away the right of the Federal army, and perhaps more importantly he had affected a lodgment on the high ridge on which the Wynn Ferry Road ran to the west, Dudley's Hill being the highest point on the ridge. Even so, Pillow was still well short of his goal, that of acquiring the Forge Road. It still lay to the west, crossing the Wynn Ferry Road on Oglesby's front. The Confederate brigades would have to take that key thoroughfare if they were to have any chance of escape. Unfortunately for Pillow, several more Union brigades waited on the Forge Road ridge.[37]

The Confederate line consequently surged onward toward this new enemy position, one Mississippian near the left writing, "we formed a good line as we advanced." The heavy forest caused a vast reduction in sight lines, "but we knew the enemy was close." He went on to describe: "we found the enemy had taken their [next] stand but a few hundred yds from where they first were. They had thrown their extreme right wing farther south which caused us to change our front slightly. We moved up a hollow and a heavy engagement soon commenced, whereas that before was only heavy skirmishing."[38]

Of the nine principles of war touted as keys to winning battles, campaigns, or wars, surprise is perhaps the most obvious. It can also be one of the most complicated. As with many other battles, there is room for debate about the level of surprise achieved by the Confederates at Fort Donelson and how effective it really was.[39]

Fort Donelson does not stand out as a primary example of surprise during the Civil War. Normally, Shiloh and Chancellorsville gain that distinction. One historian has even proclaimed Shiloh as "the Pearl Harbor of the Civil War." Unlike Pearl Harbor in 1941, however, the Civil War battles did not rise to that level of surprise, when bombs started dropping with no indication that a major enemy force was even remotely close. In all three cases in the Civil War, Fort Donelson included, both sides were already in contact and knew the enemy was at least within striking distance. At Chancellorsville, for example, Joseph Hooker's Army of the Potomac had been battling Robert E. Lee's Army of Northern Virginia but was not expecting Stonewall Jackson's flank march, which ultimately surprised the Union right. Similarly at Shiloh, Federal forces under Grant had been in contact with lead elements of the Confederate army, but they were not expecting a vicious, all-out attack. At Fort Donelson, certainly the armies had previously been engaged, but Federal officers believed they alone held the initiative (another principle of war) and could dictate when and where the fighting occurred. As a result, they were surprised when the Confederates took the initiative and attacked the open right flank.[40]

It is in the levels of surprise that Civil War battles differ. At Chancellorsville, the Confederate attack came so suddenly that there was no time for the initial attacked regiments to form lines of battle or prepare for action. At Shiloh, on the other hand, the Confederate attack began far out in front of the Union camps, allowing the entire Union army to form their lines and meet the enemy prepared, most of the time firing the first volleys. Tactical factors obviously made a difference, with a well-timed patrol causing the forward fighting at Shiloh that alerted the rest of the Union army. In fact, even at Chancellorsville, the fighting on the far Union right alerted units farther down the line to the east that the battle was raging, allowing them time to prepare for action.[41]

So it was at Fort Donelson. The initial Confederate attack fell on a small, almost detached Union brigade that held its position for nearly three hours, thus allowing the rest of the Union army time to realize what was happening and to respond. Report after report indicates that the Federals were able to form their lines in response to the fighting farther to the east, and even McArthur's regiments had ample time to form their lines because of the skirmishers giving fair warning, which was exactly what they were intended to do. So, while definitely a surprise in the sense that the Federals did not expect the Confederates to assault that day, the actual surprise fell only on a minuscule portion of the Federal army, and these regiments held long enough to allow the rest of the brigades to react. It may well be noted, too, that the Confederates were also surprised that morning when they discovered McArthur's Union brigade in the exact spot where they planned to deploy and launch their attack.[42]

Accordingly, both sides faced a surprise that morning, although more so the Federals than the Confederates. Still, McArthur's troops recovered well and held for a time. In fact, McArthur's little band of three Illinois regiments held the critical Union right flank for nearly three hours. The Confederate attempt to break out of Fort Donelson was far from reality.

12

"THE WHOLE LINE JUST SEEMED TO MELT AWAY AND SCATTER"

John A. McClernand could tell something was amiss by the sounds and then sights of Confederates to his right. "At early dawn this morning," the general wrote, "he [the enemy] was discovered rapidly moving in large masses to my extreme right." Even worse, McArthur was falling "back before the pressure of overpowering numbers." Logic told the Illinoisan that he was next, but he was going to put everything he had into a defense of the important Forge Road.[1]

Indeed, with McArthur withdrawing in disorder, McClernand's Illinois regiments were now the extreme right of the Union army. He had always acted the part, because even though McArthur was technically from Smith's division, he had been detached and put in McClernand's sector and under his command. With McArthur's retreat, McClernand's original units now had to defend against Confederates to the front and flank. Thus, the Illinoisans in the division set to work. Because there were so many Illinois regiments in both McArthur's brigade and McClernand's division, one Ohioan actually dubbed the fighting as "largely an Illinois affair."[2]

A new phase in the February 15 action accordingly began, one that would see the fighting expand from just an attack on the Union right to one involving most of both armies. For the Federals that meant bringing up reinforcements from the next division in line to the west, Lew Wallace's. For the Confederates, it meant Buckner's brigades still situated in the trenches north of McClernand's lines would also become engaged. The fighting therefore expanded to include much larger numbers, which unfortunately meant producing much higher casualties.

It would take time to get those other divisions involved, however. Gideon Pillow later wrote, "while my command was slowly advancing and driving back the enemy, I was anxiously expecting to hear General Buckner's command open fire in his rear, which, not taking place, I was apprehensive of some misapprehension of orders." While Pillow was perhaps too hard on Buckner, he nevertheless felt the need to leave his command and ride back into the trenches with engineer Gilmer to find Buckner and see what was delaying him. As Pillow described it, he "came from the field of battle within the work to ascertain what was the matter." Pillow and Buckner talked and soon Buckner's Confederates were in the fight.[3]

A similar delay occurred on the Union side. Realizing around 8:00 AM that he was in deep trouble, McClernand sent off a staff officer, Major Mason Brayman, to Lew Wallace for support. Such a request caught Wallace in a predicament, because he had just received Grant's earlier order not to act offensively while he was gone. Wallace could hear "the sound of battle raging on the extreme right, supposed at first to be General McClernand attacking." Wallace thus sent an orderly to Grant's headquarters for clarification and to state "the absolute necessity of prompt and efficient succor." Of course Grant was not there, having gone to meet with Foote on the gunboat. Wallace later added that "the suspense became torturous," and Brayman came rushing back a second time, indicating that "the enemy had turned his flanks, and were endangering his whole command." Wallace decided that reinforcing McClernand was not offensive but was required to save the army. He therefore sent his right brigade under Charles Cruft eastward at about 8:30 AM to reinforce McClernand. Like Pillow, McClernand was later harsh on Wallace, writing even that Cruft took the responsibility for moving while Wallace was away, but Cruft made it plain that Wallace gave the order to reinforce the right. Moreover, Wallace was not the only one who hesitated. McClernand also sent Captain G. P. Edgar to C. F. Smith for support, but he also returned with the same response that Smith had been ordered not to go on the offensive. "Genl. S was under orders not to move," McClernand wrote amid the battle in his memorandum book, "So Genl. W."[4]

It was a good thing that Wallace ultimately recanted his initial hesitation, because the Confederates were even then bearing down on McClernand's right flank. Richard Oglesby's brigade was in the crosshairs of the massive Confederate attack that was snowballing even as the minutes ticked by.

Richard J. Oglesby had a bright future ahead of him, including the governorship of Illinois, but first he would have to endure some terrifying days as a brigade commander under Ulysses S. Grant. One of the most harrowing days would come months later in the war when he would be dreadfully wounded and given up for dead. Another would be this day, February 15. With McArthur's departure to his right, there was nothing between his brigade, straddling the all-important Forge Road, and the Confederate attack. He had to move fast to meet it as best as he could, but he had the confidence of his men. James Butterfield wrote home, "a braver and cooler man never went upon a battlefield." Oglesby would indeed need to be calm and collected if he was going to defend the desired avenue of Confederate escape.[5]

Like everyone else, Oglesby had been taken aback when he heard the ruckus to his right earlier that morning. "The enemy dared to pass out of his trenches for the first time in a desperate effort to turn our right and escape into the country," he wrote. One of his captains added, "we were aroused about daybreak by a rapid and heavy firing on our right and front." The same sentiments continued on down the line; Dietrich Smith of the 8th Illinois wrote home that the fighting "commenced early in the morning before we had anything to drink or eat." In response, Oglesby immediately put the brigade in line facing north on the south side of the ridge that faced the Confederate trenches, allowing his men to use it for cover. He also sent a few skirmishers across the crest of the ridge to watch for the enemy but then rode eventually over to McArthur's position, where he saw the extent of the trouble. "From the large force of infantry and cavalry moving in front of their line," he later wrote, "it was obvious the contest was to be upon our right." Asking whose troops he was with, Oglesby learned that it was the 12th Illinois. "Excuse me, Colonel," Oglesby added, "I believe I am out of my brigade." He quickly rode back to his own troops and prepared as best he could for the worst.[6]

By that time, the Confederate attack was already engaging the rightmost units of his own brigade. Colonel Simonton had briefly halted his Confederates after the fighting on the north slope of Dudley's Hill: "the line of my brigade, in the charge over the hills and in passing through the enemy's camp, having become somewhat broken, I ordered the commandant to halt and rectify their alignments, which was quickly done." Then Simonton renewed his advance and the regiments, especially on the right where the 7th Texas and 1st Mississippi trudged forward through the slopes leading to Barn Hollow, curled around McArthur's position and engaged the right of Oglesby's line at a distance. Artillery fire from the Confederate trenches across Barn Hollow was also falling thick and fast: "the enemy did not spare their grape and canister," Oglesby wrote. The fighting quickly became more general as Confederates of Simonton's brigade continually moved toward the leftmost regiments of Oglesby's brigade. Colonel John Gregg of the Texas regiment reported how "just before reaching the crest of the hill, their line, drawn up behind it, delivered fire, and a most galling one it was." The 8th and 18th Illinois indeed opened up, too green to know to lie down, as did a section of Schwartz's battery under Lieutenant Gumbart, who was soon wounded and taken away to a hospital. Eventually, the fighting surged down Oglesby's line as far as the 29th Illinois as well, one Illinoisan describing the enemy in waves, "adopting a mode similar to that of street fighting, firing and falling back."[7]

Problems quickly emerged in the Federal brigade. Gaps developed in the Union line because of the undulating ground. There had been gaps in McArthur's troops to the right, but even in Oglesby's brigade, one Illinoisan reported, the men of the 8th Illinois could not see their next flank regiment to the left. Another problem was a growing lack of ammunition. Daniel Brush of the 18th Illinois described how the regiment had left Fort Henry with forty rounds per man but they had used a good deal of that in skirmishing during the last two days. Brush and other officers paced the lines: "I ordered them to be very careful about wasting what they had, and to withhold their fire until sure of doing execution." The Illinoisans did so, eventually lying down while loading and firing, which obviously prevented casualties.[8]

The fundamental problem quickly became clear, however. While Oglesby's line faced northward, the attack came from the right, or east. Captain Samuel B. Marks of the 18th Illinois next to McArthur's men described how "they approached us diagonally, their line forming an angle of about 20 degrees with ours." Even worse, he described how "the enemy, so far as we were able to distinguish through the brush, appeared to approach in columns of six or eight files deep. . . . So rapid was their firing, it was almost impossible to distinguish an interval."[9]

Moving six or eight deep was of course the earlier staggered approach of the Confederates in column of regiments, and some of its effect was still felt even as the center of the Confederate line hit Oglesby's right. Baldwin pushed his 26th Mississippi and 26th Tennessee forward in the center, and other units followed in the rear, including the 50th Virginia of McCausland's brigade and even the 36th Virginia, which had been sent to Baldwin's right earlier at the approach of the 41st Illinois. The 20th Mississippi also went in and out of the line, being eventually detached from Baldwin. Farther to the left, Drake and his attached Mississippians likewise moved through the heavy growth, firing blindly to the front, "with very little direct aim," remembered one Mississippian.[10]

With McArthur gone and so many layers of Confederates approaching, Oglesby had to do something about his right flank. He sent a staff officer to find McClernand, telling him that "unless promptly supported the First Brigade must give way." McClernand sent the messages off to Grant and Wallace pleading about the "absolute necessity of prompt and complete succor," but those returning from Grant's headquarters merely assured that "my appeal would be communicated upon [his] . . . return." Back in the thick of the fighting, Oglesby quickly decided he was on his own and turned his left-flank regiment, the 18th Illinois, to the right, refusing the line, and sending it farther in that direction. Oglesby filled the space between the 18th Illinois and the 8th Illinois by bringing up the 30th Illinois from its reserve position. The main line of the brigade then faced north on the ridge, with the line turning back southward (facing east) at the junction of the 8th and 30th Illinois. From there, the refused 30th and 18th Illinois held the critical right flank.[11]

Unfortunately for Oglesby, his careful plans were quickly shattered, mostly by a high attrition rate in the 18th Illinois, which was bearing the brunt of the Confederate fire. Officers gave commands to fire at the Confederate flag-bearers, and Daniel Brush commented, "it was but a short time until the dirty rags disappeared from our view." The Confederates came on anyway. The fact that the regiment was running out of ammunition did not help, and leadership was becoming critical as well. Colonel Michael K. Lawler was soon wounded in the left forearm and removed from the field. That left a captain in command, Daniel Brush, whom a bleeding Lawler told to "do the best I could with the regt." Brush did, meeting Oglesby, who ordered him to move the men to the right "for the purpose of extending our lines in that direction." Brush was then wounded in the shift, a bullet going completely through his shoulder without hitting a bone. Captain Samuel B. Marks took over although Brush remained for some time, after which he "came to what I considered a reasonable conclusion . . . I was not dead." However, while Brush was testing "my limbs to see if I was disabled—found I could move my hands & feet," disaster was befalling the regiment as a whole. The final straw came as only

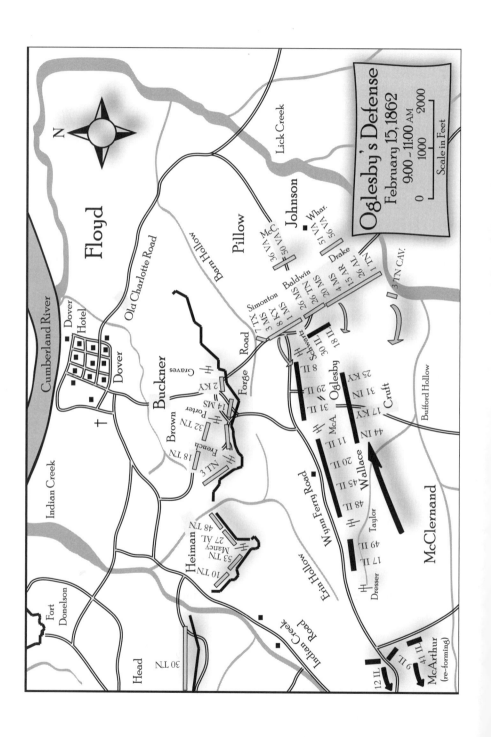

Oglesby's Defense
February 15, 1862
9:00–11:00 AM

0   1000   2000
Scale in Feet

a portion of the regiment repositioned to the right. Brush had given the order on the right of the regiment, but the left had not heard them and did not move with the others. Marks reported, "the enemy poured in in such overwhelming numbers and with such rapidity, that both wings were speedily flanked by them and almost surrounded." Marks later reported that "further resistance seemed useless," adding in understatement, "it was deemed prudent to retire."[12]

Other units were having problems as well even as Simonton's Confederate brigade steadily approached the angle of the Union line while Baldwin and the Virginians moved toward the refused right. Schwartz's battery was firing as fast as it could, losing at one point a gun because its trail was shot away. More ominously, the 30th Illinois was just coming into line when it met the massed Confederate attack as best it could. At the angle, the 8th Illinois was taking heavy casualties as well as running out of ammunition, gathering what they could from the dead and wounded. A Confederate battery also continually fired into the flank, Lieutenant Colonel Frank L. Rhoads reporting that the enemy guns "never ceased to pour grape and canister into our ranks for three hours." While being ordered to "hold the height of the ridge, and not to yield an inch," Rhoads wondered how he would do that as his men were running out of ammunition. He sent word to Oglesby, who told him to hold until he could bring reinforcements to the front.[13]

Somewhat miraculously the 30th Illinois was able to stem the tide for a few minutes. "It was here that the hardest fighting that I ever saw was done," wrote David Poak, "the rebels were not more than 60 yards from us pouring in a very deadly fire." But how long they could last against the repeated Confederate surges was anybody's guess, and Oglesby was already thinking ahead about what to do next if help did not arrive soon. "I was tempted to use the bayonet," he later wrote, "but the risk of breaking my lines in an effort to go through the thick brush, when the result under the most favorable circumstances could only be to drive them into their lines and expose my command to a raking fire of artillery and musketry upon emerging in broken files from the thick woods, determined me to hold my line to the last." How long he could do that was questionable; Oglesby needed help, and he needed it now.[14]

Fortunately for him, he soon saw fresh troops moving up the road. It was Cruft's brigade of Wallace's division, led by the 25th Kentucky "with flags flying," one grateful Illinoisan noted. Help had arrived.[15]

$\mathbf{R}$einforcements are almost never a bad thing, unless they appear in the midst of a disaster. That is exactly what happened as Cruft's brigade moved toward the already shaky Union right flank around 10:00 AM. Cruft commanded four regiments, two Indiana and two Kentucky, one time a part of Buell's army until he transferred them to Grant in the midst of all the confusion surrounding the twin-rivers invasion. They had arrived by boat and were one of the two brigades of Lew Wallace's brand new division. Despite enduring the discomfort of the cold, one Kentuckian writing that "I was as hungry as a wolf and we all suffered terribly with cold during the night," the regiments marched quickly, the 25th Kentucky in the lead. The brigade marched eastward past Will Wallace's brigade now deployed in line. They also passed McClernand's headquarters, where they saw the general and his staff, who admonished them to hurry at the double quick. Obviously, they were entering a crisis.[16]

More confusion developed as the brigade neared the fighting. Cruft reported that his orders to deploy behind Oglesby's line were not heeded because the 8th Illinois's commander, Rhoads, quickly sent word for the lead regiment to replace his ammunitionless men. As a result, the brigade continued on farther than intended, right into the chaos, one Indianan writing that the lead 25th Kentucky was "run almost into the enemy's ranks." Even worse, Cruft explained that "the guide sent with the head of the column here shamefully abandoned it, not, however, until he had given Colonel Shackelford an improper instruction." Colonel J. M. Shackelford of the 25th Kentucky reported that he was "in utter ignorance of the point at which I was needed and the position of the enemy." Accordingly, the column, in Cruft's words, "became suddenly engaged with a superior force of the enemy in front and to the right." Cruft worked hard under the "continued volleys of the enemy's musketry" to form the 25th Kentucky and the next regiment in line, the 31st Indiana.[17]

Unfortunately, Cruft's arrival only made matters worse, even as the Confederate surge neared the all-important Forge Road. As Oglesby was showing Colonel Shackelford of the 25th Kentucky where he wanted him and was instructing the 8th Illinois commander, Rhoads, to swap places with the Kentuckians, the left wing of the 25th Kentucky "from some unaccountable cause," Oglesby wrote, opened fire, hitting those in front. In particular, the volley hit portions of the 8th and 29th Illinois as well as some of Schwartz's cannoneers, and the effect was immediate. Both the 8th and the 29th Illinois broke as a result of the confusion, George Durfee of the 8th Illinois describing how the men "were then ordered to fall back, and got confused and retreated in disorder." Another Illinoisan gave more detail, writing that the reinforcements "that came upon our rear mistook us for the enemy, gave us a volley and run. We were then utterly, completely and eternally disgusted and quit." The nearby 30th Illinois also fell back in the confusion, and since most of the Illinoisans rushed through the ranks of the 25th Kentucky, that regiment also broke in two and fled to the rear. The 31st Indiana, next in line, sustained similar problems, especially when the elderly Lieutenant Colonel John Osborn's horse became unmanageable and he had to go afoot. One of the Indianans later wrote, "for a while I thought another Bull Run was to be inaugurated." Fortunately, companies K, D, and B did good service in holding while the others reorganized and headed off to the right to secure that flank. Still, the bullets came fast, one Kentuckian noting, "I am certain that the missiles of death came through our columns thicker and faster than ever the raindrops descended from Heaven." Perhaps most important in the grand scheme of things, the retreat left the Forge Road completely in Confederate hands.[18]

With such chaos brewing in his brigade, Oglesby had only one regiment still in line, Colonel John A. Logan's 31st Illinois on the far left next to Wallace's brigade. It was nevertheless a force within itself; Logan's "eyes flashed like fire," one Illinoisan remembered, and the colonel continually called to his men, "Give it to 'em." In the midst of disaster, Oglesby quickly ordered Logan to refuse his right wing, "so as to form a crochet," he reported, thus forming a ninety-degree angle with his left wing, thereby hoping to provide some stability on which the others could re-form. Logan did so with "highly expressive and forcible language" and despite receiving terrible wounds himself, one in the left shoulder, splinters from a bullet hitting his pistol, and a flesh wound in the thigh. All these injuries began inaccurate rumors back home that he had been killed, but his lieutenant colonel, John H. White, was indeed killed in the fighting. One of the famous "fighting McCooks" (a captain) was also wounded, and another brother, Latimer A. McCook, who was the regimental surgeon, took command. Fortunately for Oglesby's ammunition-low soldiers, by this time "the fire of the enemy had materially slackened," as he described it, although they could never really be sure when another attack might come. He noted that the enemy "sought refuge in the oak leaves, between which and their uniforms there was so strong a resemblance, our men were continually deceived by them." All the same, any break was welcomed, and Oglesby turned his attention to forming the rest of Cruft's regiments on Logan's right, facing the same direction as his refused right wing, eastward. McClernand later described the effect: "my line was swung around like a gate on a pivot."[19]

Cruft managed to place the remainder of his brigade in line beside the 31st Illinois, particularly the 17th Kentucky and the 31st Indiana farther to the right. The 44th Indiana held a position a little to the left rear, behind the Illinoisans who were on the slope of the hill to the front. Facing east, the Indianans endured a heavy flanking artillery fire from the Confederate works to the north. They also then faced a new Confederate advance. As soon as the regiments took their new positions, the Confederates again bounded down on them from both front and flank. Particularly concerning was Drake's Confederate brigade that continually moved around the Union right flank, firing into the new line from the south and even getting in the rear of the Union regiments. A portion of the 31st Indiana, particularly Company K, was sent across a small valley to protect that flank, but to no avail. Drake's much larger brigade was easily able to swamp the small company and its parent regiment. Major William N. Brown of the 20th Mississippi, by now attached to Drake's command, could not always tell what the larger plan was, but he could make out some of the results: "our movements . . . seemed to take the enemy by their flank and rear." Major Fred Arn of the 31st Indiana on the extreme right agreed, woefully noting, "their line extended a considerable distance beyond our right." The Indianans shifted once more to the right and threw out several companies even farther to the south, but Drake's Confederates continually outflanked them, Bushrod Johnson marveling at their "regular, well-connected line." It was all they could stand and Cruft soon pulled the 31st Indiana and 17th Kentucky back to a line with the 44th Indiana behind Logan's position. At one point, Cruft even claimed to have made a short counterattack to stall the enemy advance, but the general movement was a chaotic retrograde. One Kentuckian admitted that "it came near being a general stampede throughout our Brigade, but was prevented, to a great extent, by the skill and experience of our officers."[20]

The major rupture came when more friendly fire from the left of the brigade caused Logan's nearly ammunitionless 31st Illinois to break. Although word had been sent back that the Illinoisans were in front supporting Schwartz's guns, the Indianans found it very difficult to believe they were not confronting the enemy. In a momentary lull, Colonel Hugh B. Reed even sent his colors a few paces forward of the line but failed to elicit a response. Captain William B. Bingham of Company H then took them several more

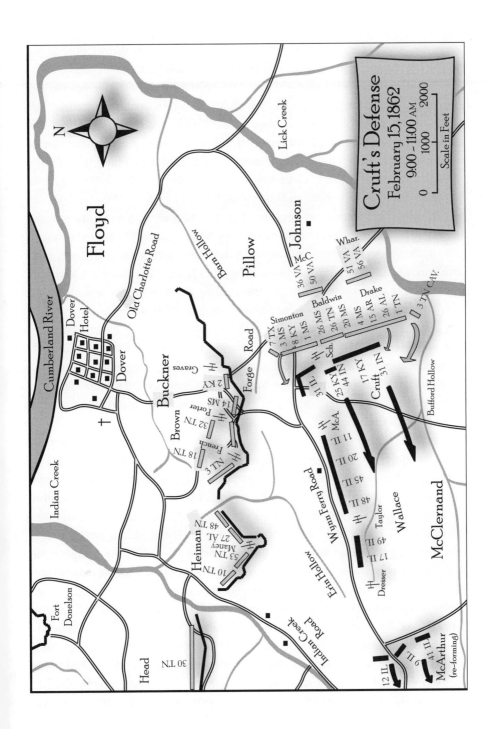

Cruft's Defense
February 15, 1862
9:00 – 11:00 AM

0   1000   2000
Scale in Feet

paces to the front and "waved our colors in the air." This drew Confederate fire, upon which the Indianans opened up. In actuality, they still fired mostly into the Illinoisans who were on the slope of the hill between them and the enemy. Not surprisingly, Logan's men broke and fled through the ranks of the 44th Indiana and what had re-formed of the 25th Kentucky. Those regiments again broke, and the others to the right had a hard time keeping the line as well, especially with Drake's Confederates on their flank. As a result, Cruft's entire brigade had to fall back in confusion, leaving the line at differing times but nonetheless falling back in full retreat.[21]

Officers tried to re-form the line, but it was useless. One Illinoisan remembered topping a hill and seeing John Logan himself "in a furious rage" gathering men to re-form a line, although he could only get about fifty men to join him. On another part of the field, Captain Herman Lieb of the 8th Illinois decided he was going back into the fray, telling his men that he was returning if he retrieved just one man. One Illinoisan admitted that

> none of us were anxious to go back just then and he took his sword—which was made of tin or pewter but silver plated, and put his foot on it to break it, he was so [mad]. He beat it nearly double, and as it had no spring in it, it remained in a shape like this. He then waved it over his head and used language which is not proper to put on paper.[22]

Meanwhile, the Confederate brigade commanders took full advantage of this self-imposed chaos in the Union lines. Baldwin pressed on straight down the ridge, approaching Schwartz's battery with his 26th Mississippi and 26th Tennessee. On his right Simonton's Mississippians, Kentuckians, and Texans curved their way around the Union angle, while Drake's brigade continually pressured the refused Union line, at times reaching well beyond their flank and into the rear of the Union troops. Schwartz's guns were particularly inviting, Schwartz noting, "the Kentucky Regt fired in my battery, killing horses, & men." Indeed, dead and wounded littered the ground. Richard McClung of the 15th Arkansas of Drake's brigade described "a stream of blood that had run for 20 steps down a hillside, here were friends and foes lying together." Still, some isolated pockets of Union resistance hampered the Confederates. Colonel Gabriel Wharton remarked that the enemy "were either rallied or re-enforced." Their own lack of ammunition was also becoming a factor;

the Confederate soldiers rifled through the cartridge boxes of the dead and wounded for all they could find.[23]

Perhaps the biggest loss in the chaos was Schwartz's battery itself. Sitting atop the ridge of high ground west of Dudley's Hill, the battery fought long and hard but sustained severe casualties, including Gumbart earlier in the action. Much of the attrition occurred among the horses that pulled the guns, and that loss doomed the battery to capture once the infantry surrounding it fell back. Baldwin reported that the guns were still pointed northward to counter the Confederate artillery in the trenches and "were rushed upon in flanks and seized before they could be turned upon us or be taken from the field." Apparently, the four guns were fighting in detached sections; the 26th Tennessee took one section of guns, the 26th Mississippi the other. With Schwartz on staff duty under McClernand and Gumbart down, only Lieutenant George L. Nispel was left to get the men out. Schwartz wrote that he "was the last to retire, when the Bayonets of enemy were nearly thrust in his breast." In addition to the guns, a wounded Colonel John M. Lillard of the Tennessee regiment reported capturing "two flags, the instruments of a band, and several prisoners."[24]

By 10:00 AM, then, the Confederate assault had plowed forward over three Union brigades, McArthur's, Oglesby's, and Cruft's, as well as Schwartz's battery and the section of Missouri guns atop Dudley's Hill. Even better, the Confederate surge had now completely taken the Forge Road, the planned escape route. But while the road was entirely in Confederate hands, the Union lines were still far too close to allow unfettered access for an escape, especially with any wheeled vehicles. Consequently, the attack would have to continue, driving, it was hoped, the next Union brigade away and gaining more room to utilize the all-important escape route.

That next brigade was Will Wallace's, and it now became the focus of the Confederate onslaught: "the enemy's undivided attention was turned upon us," wrote one of his Illinoisans. Even worse, it came from multiple directions.[25]

W̲ill Wallace was a quick study and certainly knew what all the ruckus to his right meant. He sent staff officer I. P. Rumsey to McClernand, telling him: "Rumsey, you go to McClernand, tell him McArthur has broken, Oglesby is breaking and it is necessary to withdraw and change our front, and form a new line to the left and rear." The staff officer rode away and soon returned with word from McClernand to hold, but he added: "tell General [Colonel] Wallace if it is absolutely necessary, to withdraw and form the new line." Wallace soon found it very necessary.[26]

Wallace's Illinoisans had easily heard the early morning fighting on Dudley's Hill slowly creep toward them. Each regimental commander had his men up and formed into line, sending out skirmishers to the front. Colonel Carroll Marsh of the 20th Illinois, for example, reported, "repeated volleys of musketry on the right caused me to form in line of battle." Wallace's regiments remained for the early hours in their line on the reverse slope of the Wynn Ferry Road ridge, using it to shield themselves while keeping skirmishers over the top so they could advise of any attack. Still, the effects of the fighting to their right and the attending movements, including the retreating Federals, Cruft's reinforcing brigade, and then Cruft's retreating brigade, played on their morale. But what came from the front caused them even more concern.[27]

If the brigades trying to hold the extreme right of the Federal line were having major trouble, they only had to contend with Confederate attacks from the right flank and at times the rear. While that was difficult enough to handle, the men of Wallace's brigade faced perhaps an even larger issue in that while they received attacks from both the right flank and rear, the entire brigade still faced northward along the Wynn Ferry Road and they also received direct frontal assaults from the Erin Hollow area.

The first enemy presence on their front came in the form of artillery. William H. Tibbets of the 45th Illinois gave a vivid description of the enemy fire as he returned from fetching water from a creek in the rear. "They then commenced pouring grape an canister and bom shell at us to a rapid rate[.] they ranged from about 5 feet to 20 above us and stripped the saplings clean and killed and wounded some by the fall of the limes[.] after a while they got our range a little better and then pored it write in among us for about 2 rounds an then they got too low and struck the hill side below us." Fortunately for the Illinoisans, their own artillery, Taylor's, McAllister's, and Dresser's batteries, took up the fight and returned fire.[28]

The artillery was not the only Confederate force arrayed to Wallace's north. Also fronting him was the division under Simon Buckner, with Floyd himself watching from behind. Buckner had deployed his division behind the trenches, keeping most of it in reserve to protect the men from the Union artillery on the Wynn Ferry Road ridge. Buckner explained that while Pillow was attacking, his own troops were under heavy artillery fire from the Federals: "in view of the heavy duty which I expected my division to undergo in covering the retreat of the army," he wrote, "I thought it unadvisable to attempt an assault at this time in my front until the enemy's batteries were to some extent crippled and their supports shaken by the fire of my artillery." Brigade commander John C. Brown added, "we were awaiting the proper moment of co-operation." Accordingly, Buckner only opened with Graves's battery, particularly the one 10-pound Parrott rifle among the other smoothbores.[29]

Throughout the morning, Buckner and the others watched and listened to what was happening to their front, one cannoneer in Graves's battery declaring they were "the pivot on which the line was moving." At times, Buckner's troops could only tell what was happening by sound: "the fighting had been steady all along the line all morning. Sometimes the musketry would be steady, continuous & severe, telling of the stubborn stand the enemy were making, & then the scattering discharges told of their falling back." It was in this covered state, with only the 3rd Tennessee actually manning the works, that Pillow found the division when he returned to the trenches to get Buckner moving.[30]

Pillow soon had Buckner under arms, and the two decided to send out a small force to relieve some of the pressure from the Union artillery. Buckner ordered to the front one of his "best regiments," as he termed it, the 14th Mississippi detached from Baldwin's brigade. Brown likewise sent the 3rd and 18th Tennessee ahead of the lines to support the Mississippians if they found much trouble. Most knew they would, as Brown noted, because "the enemy [was] occupying a hill in considerable force not far distant." Buckner himself was amid the danger as well, one Tennessean describing him on "the crest of the hill 15 or 20 steps in front of our line and walked back and forth with his hands behind him while the shells—solid shot and musket ball—was cutting the dirt both before and behind him."[31]

This first small attack on Wallace, although it had a stuttered start, developed around 9:00 AM. The Mississippians had to negotiate their own abatis and then move across open ground. Buckner's staff officer gave the command to move forward, to which Major W. L. Doss, commanding the regiment, responded, "where to?" The staffer ordered the regiment forward once more, Doss again replying, "where to?" Finally, the staffer yelled, "over the ditches," and the satisfied Doss led the Mississippians forward, the call of "charge Mississippians" passing down the line. One of them remembered that "over the earthworks goes our flag & over goes the regt after it—over the fallen timbers." If the abatis was not enough, they then met the Union skirmishers of Wallace's brigade, who fell back. The Mississippians deemed this a signal victory, thinking they were driving the main Union line rearward. They then surged across the higher ground connecting the Wynn Ferry Road ridge with the high ground on which the Confederate trenches stood, essentially the divide separating Barn Hollow and a small feeder branch of Erin Hollow. Unfortunately, the trajectory led them across the fire of Graves's battery, forcing the cannoneers to shift to support Pillow's attacking columns. The Mississippians moved on anyway, forcing the Union skirmishers back but not without casualties, including Captain Francis Marion Rogers, lately a delegate to the Mississippi Secession Convention. Indeed, the fire was so heavy that one hospital steward caring for the wounded noted he "could have held up my hat and caught it full."[32]

Artillery fire was also heavy from the Union batteries on the opposite ridge, particularly McAllister's and Schwartz's guns before they fell to the flanking Confederates. Graves's and Porter's batteries had taken their new positions with Buckner's command, but were soon located and shelled by the Union artillery. One of Graves's gunners noted, "their rifled shot & shells tore up the ground around us & cut off saplings & limbs around & above us, killing some of our horses & knocking the end of a caisson off." One shell landed among the guns and wounded five, one mortally.[33]

Being a small force despite Wallace declaring it to be "a heavy force of the enemy's infantry," the Mississippians moved on nonetheless. Wallace described how he used the shield of the ridge to aid his men's defense: "they charged up the hill and gained the road in front of my position, but the moment the rebel flag appeared above the crest of the hill a storm of shot from the Eleventh and Twentieth drove them back in confusion." John C. Brown echoed those sentiments from the other side, writing that the Mississippians made good progress until they topped the hill on which the road ran: "especially upon reaching the summit of the hill, they were met by a murderous fire." Calls to cease firing because of friendly fire rang out, causing even more chaos in the Mississippi regiment. Colonel Marsh of the 20th Illinois took the defense one step farther, writing that just as "the rebels appeared, coming over the brow of the hill," he ordered an attack. The regiment made one slight change to the east while doing so, one member writing, "our regt. made a right half whirl and drove two regts. back inside their breastworks." The small attack had hit only the two regiments making up Wallace's right, and because of the timidity and smallness of the force, the Illinoisans easily handled it, although more was surely to come. In fact, several officers were already leading in re-forming the Mississippians, including a small lad of fifteen, who one Tennessean declared "was calling on his regt . . . to reform and charge the Yankees again[.] the tears were rolling down his face and I think he would have gone alone if an officer had not taken him to the rear." With such exemplary courage in view, Doss re-formed the Mississippians for another try, but Buckner's staff officer Major Alexander Casseday, who had been sent along for guidance, ordered Doss back to the trenches. The Mississippians quickly fell back, Brown noting "further pursuit being impracticable in that direction."[34]

Buckner met the Mississippians, riding among them to stabilize the regiment for another assault. He tried to shame them as well, yelling, "Mississippians, look at those Virginians driving the enemy from our soil. Is it possible that you are going to leave them to do the fighting? No, never; your general will lead you."[35]

Consequently, Wallace had to confront another frontal advance on his brigade. One 45th Illinois soldier wrote, "they rallied again and came ten times as strong as they were before." By this time, Pillow was back in the trenches and ordered Brown's regiments forward again, but this next advance came a little to the west of the earlier attack. Brown chose to utilize the more covered expanses closer to the valley of Erin Hollow this time. Under cover of Porter's, Graves's, and Maney's batteries, Brown soon led his brigade forward, the 3rd, 18th, and 32nd Tennessee (left to right) now included, negotiating once more the abatis and the open ground east of Maney's battery that the 49th Illinois had encountered two days before in their attack. One member of the 3rd Tennessee wrote how he "heard someone behind us and on turning around saw Col. J. C. Brown who was commanding the brigade jump from his horse, wave his sword over his head and cry, 'Men of the 3rd Tenn., come out of the pits.'" Pillow was also on the ground, shouting to the 32nd Tennessee, "Boys I want you to take that battery." The ground was difficult, however, Colonel Joseph B. Palmer of the 18th Tennessee reporting that "we found some, I may say much, embarrassment in having insufficient information in regard to the enemy's location, as we could only judge in reference to that by the smoke and reports of pieces lately heard and seen in that direction." Brown added: "we found also very considerable difficulty in marching in the requisite order, owing to the timber and denseness of the undergrowth, on which the snow was thickly depositing and melting somewhat rapidly." Colonel Edward C. Cook of the 32nd Tennessee agreed, writing, "we moved forward through woods with thick undergrowth; the bushes were covered with snow, which was melting slowly, and it was very difficult to move forward." The Tennesseans pushed on nonetheless, Brown ordering a quick time advance.[36]

With so many obstacles, however, the Confederate advance soon slowed as officers called a halt within a few hundred yards of the ridge so they could learn more about the enemy line. The skirmishers quickly returned and formed on the regiments but were unable to tell the commanders any more than they already knew. Colonel Cook of the 32nd Tennessee and Palmer of the 18th Tennessee even went ahead of the lines themselves to ascertain any information they could glean; they soon found the enemy "just over the point of a hill in our front." The colonels returned to their commands and deployed the regiments from their columns to battle lines and then moved forward again.[37]

Behind the ridge, Wallace feared that the enemy would sneak up on his brigade; plus, the 20th Illinois had already advanced somewhat, counterattacking the Mississippians. He therefore moved the other three regiments, but not the attached 17th and most of the 49th Illinois (formerly of Morrison's brigade), up to the top of the hill in the road. Wallace noted they "advanced boldly and in fine order to the brow of the hill," but there they were taken under fire not only from the attacking Tennesseans but also from the Confederate batteries still in the trenches; Graves's battery, in fact, advanced some distance with the brigade, Brown noting that "Graves came in full speed to our assistance." Wallace also had artillery, of course, in the form of McAllister's and Taylor's batteries, and these opened up as well despite one of McAllister's guns being disabled. The infantry fired too, Colonel Palmer reporting that "the enemy opened a terrific fire upon us about the time or before we had fairly executed the deployment." The forward 20th Illinois was caught in its exposed position but was able to meet the attack head on. The 45th Illinois likewise advanced to aid their forward sister regiment as well as to bolster McAllister's battery. Wallace remembered that "for some time the conflict was strong and fierce," and Ransom of the 11th Illinois reported that the enemy "brought their colors up in front of ours and not over 100 yards distant, when the fight again commenced with renewed energy." One of his soldiers agreed, writing, "we waited until they were about 30 yards away from us and then let them have it."[38]

Meeting such heavy fire, the Tennesseans were forced to halt but they opened up on Wallace's regiments, Ransom describing the fighting as "an exceedingly firm and bloody one." Major casualties resulted, including Lieutenant Colonel Thomas H. Smith of the 48th Illinois, killed while leading his men to the top of the hill, Lieutenant Colonel William Erwin of the 20th Illinois, killed when hit in the chest by a cannonball, as well as Lieutenant Colonel Jasper A. Maltby of the 45th Illinois wounded. On the opposing side, Lieutenant Colonel W. P. Moore of the 32nd Tennessee was also mortally wounded.[39]

Even worse for Wallace, further infusions of Buckner's troops came just as the fighting ebbed on his left. Colonel Baldwin rode across Barn Hollow in the midst of the fighting against Cruft's brigade and then the 31st Illinois, looking for anyone he could find to aid his attack on what was evidently a fresh Union brigade studded by artillery. He first ran into Colonel Hanson and his 2nd Kentucky, which was holding the Forge Road area of Buckner's line. Baldwin told Hanson that his men were running out of bullets and that "unless he could get ammunition and re-enforcements there was a great danger of losing the ground which had been won." Hanson had already sent two companies in that direction, on the command of a staff officer, "supposing it to be the order of Generals Pillow or Buckner." Now, Hanson sent a quartermaster and another officer to provide the ammunition, but he was wary about moving his entire regiment across Barn Hollow without firm orders from Buckner. Colonel McCausland then appeared and agreed with Baldwin, adding that the enemy was bringing up reinforcements. Hanson surveyed the scene and realized that he was on the Forge Road, the escape route, and that he had to do more to maintain it. "I concluded to take the responsibility and make the effort," he reported. He marched the Kentuckians across the abatis and joined in the Confederate advance, losing around fifty men but adding weight to the Confederate surge. Also on hand was Forrest's cavalry, having shifted to the right from the defiles of Lick Creek, attempting to use the valley of Barn Hollow to outflank the enemy. Joining Hanson's movement, Graves's battery also moved forward across Barn Hollow, adding even more firepower.[40]

Wallace was able to hold against all these piecemeal advances by Buckner's troops, but that was not the major problem spot. "There were indications,"

Wallace later wrote with understatement, "that the enemy were gaining some advantages on the right of the whole line." He could easily hear the sounds of battle growing closer and closer, but the telltale sign was when "the enemy's shot . . . began to rake my line from the rear of my right." Wallace held, but he quickly surmised the situation and sent McClernand a courier and warned that he would not be able to hold his position unless reinforcements "should be speedily sent to that quarter." McClernand replied that he had none to send at the moment and loosened Wallace's orders to act upon his own discretion "if I found my position untenable." Wallace was nearing that point, being assailed as he was from the front, flank, and rear. Worse, his regiments were reporting that they were out of ammunition. The situation was growing desperate for the Federal line.[41]

By this time, the rout on the Union right was nearly complete as the 31st Illinois of Oglesby's brigade had fallen back from its isolated position. The Federal line had continually shifted farther to the west and south in response to the Confederate flank attacks, but Logan had been unable to hold, especially because of friendly fire from the rear. His retreat uncovered the right regiment of Wallace's brigade, Thomas Ransom and his 11th Illinois, and Ransom initially bent the regiment's right back to connect with Logan's troops before their retreat while keeping several companies on the left facing the Confederate trenches to the north. The 11th Illinois thus anchored Wallace's right and remained there to help fend off a renewed Confederate advance while the 31st Illinois retreated, taking much of Cruft's brigade with it. That left only the 11th Illinois to stem the tide, and when Logan's Illinoisans retreated, Ransom shifted his regiment even farther to the right. Wallace described them as "changing front to the rear under a most galling fire with all the coolness and precision of veterans." One of Wallace's staff officers described the event in even more detail: "'right flank, file left,' a move which is laid down in tactics as almost impossible to be made in the face of the enemy, but it was done." The 11th Illinois consequently took the place of the 31st Illinois in the trampled-down snow "stained with the crimson life blood of so many of our brave boys," one observer noted. As a result, the Illinoisans created something of a rear guard while Wallace figured out what to do. Will Wallace had written his wife of the disappointment of missing the fighting at Fort Henry earlier in the month, "but hope for better luck next time." Isolated as his unit

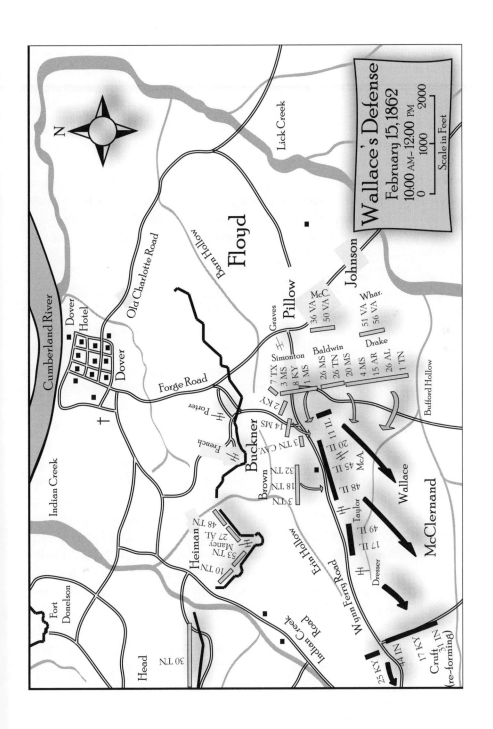

Wallace's Defense
February 15, 1862
10:00 AM–12:00 PM

Scale in Feet
0   1000   2000

was fronting multiple Confederate brigades, the Illinoisan probably wished for no more such luck.[42]

While his old regiment blocked the Confederate advance temporarily from the east, Wallace acted on his discretionary orders from McClernand and ordered his brigade "to the rear up the road." With the remainder of the brigade as well as Oglesby's and Cruft's shattered regiments fleeing to their rear, distractedly leaving the skirmishers to the front and in danger of being cut off, the detached 11th Illinois unfortunately did not get the order and continued to hold out. Their stand resulted in a gift for the rest of the brigade, which managed, with little pressure from Buckner, to file away westward along the Wynn Ferry Road. Colonel Marsh of the 20th Illinois reported that he "remained here without further molestation from the enemy till ordered to march to the left"; he did note, however, that the 11th Illinois was "still fighting bravely." Similarly, John E. Smith of the 45th Illinois reported he had only "continual though irregular skirmish with the rebels" before he filed away. Colonel Haynie of the 48th Illinois noted that he received the order to "retire by the left flank," adding, "this was done by my regiment in the best possible order and without any appearance of fear or panic." Because of the 11th Illinois's stand, the rest of the infantry was able to march away in order.[43]

Yet the brave stand certainly cost the Illinoisans. By this time, the regiment had lost all but one of its color guard, only Corporal William S. Armstrong of Company H remaining to carry the flag. He too was wounded, but he managed to survive with the colors. The flag itself was "riddled with shot & the staff was struck twice with bullets, breaking off the spear at the top," Wallace informed his wife. The Illinoisans stayed anyway, George Carrington writing, "we did not know enough of war to run away, so we hung on."[44]

Others suffered as well. The infantry could quickly file to the left and retire, but it took much longer for the artillery to limber up and get away. Taylor's battery had been firing constantly, one cannoneer writing, "it was load and fire and drop, flat as a pancake. We watched the smoke of the enemy's guns and down we went, except when we were loading, where there was nothing to do but to grin and bear it." That battery was farther to the left and had time to limber up and retire according to the retreat order, but McAllister's guns farther to the east could not. McAllister had fought hard against the Confederate advances and was taken aback by the suddenness of the order to retreat. As fate would have it, the enemy arrived at the right gun "before I could throw my saddle on my horse." With one gun already taken, McAllister concentrated on getting the left gun out and hitched up. He reported that "it was so heavy we could not haul it through the brush, and abandoned it, bringing off the limber." The guns therefore fell under the combined weight of Buckner's renewed advance, pressure from Pillow's brigades on the right, and even Forrest's cavalry advancing in the rear. One perplexed Union soldier in the 11th Illinois later wrote, "my attention was first drawn to this by the fact that our men were being shot in the back, and on looking to the rear saw the cavalry." Forrest's troopers had been all over the field during the morning but because of the lowland moved to the right near Barn Hollow. Seeing an opportunity, Forrest advanced behind the Illinois guns and aided in their capture, claiming also to capture another piece down a ravine. A Mississippian described the cavalry tactics, telling of how the Tennesseans moved "up by platoons and divisions alternately that those who had just emptied their arms could reload and every succession bringing them nearer the batteries."[45]

A young Thomas Duncan described the cavalry charge:

> I lost control of my horse, and he carried me beyond the battery into the infantry support of the enemy. I made a circuit, and on my return a Federal soldier fired at me when I was not more than twenty paces from him. I was mounted on a spirited animal, and it was running and jumping so unevenly that I happily made a very evasive target, and the soldier missed his aim, just grazing my right shoulder, taking the width of the ball out of my coat and cutting a crease in the flesh. The shot was fired as I was approaching the man; and as I passed within a few feet of him, I shot at him twice with my six-shooter, but could not tell whether or not my shots struck him. I was a good marksman, and under ordinary circumstances I would have been sure of my aim; but it behooves me to tell you that I was far more bent on getting out of this dangerous situation than on killing an enemy.[46]

Others were escaping as well. Wallace himself got out, although he later declared he did not know how. "Darling Angel wife, God has indeed heard your prayer & that of our little innocent," he wrote his wife Ann. "I little expected when amid the fierce storm of lead & iron that beat around me for hours, striking down my men by hundreds, that I should come off unscathed—but I never thought of the surrounding dangers without a mental prayer for mercy for myself & for you, darling." Even if Wallace somehow survived, around him was still mass confusion as the Illinois regiments jock-

eyed for position and an escape route. At one point, the 45th Illinois ran up on
the 12th Illinois, fresh from its retreat on the far right. Colonel Smith simply
noted, "we saw Chetlain conducting his Regt through Ravines in order to take
the position I was ordered. I had to go through his lines. The Col rode up to
me with his face very much elongated. [']My dear Col how glad I am to see
you. My rgt is very badly cut up,[']" Chetlain confessed.[47]

As a result, only one lone regiment remained out of four Union brigades,
sixteen regiments with artillery, to stem the tide of the Confederate advance.
The 11th Illinois was the sole unit east of Indian Creek that was still formed
and resisting the enemy onslaught, and the Illinoisans paid dearly for it, losing 329 casualties in total, the largest of any regiment in the Union army at
Fort Donelson. One of those casualties was Ransom himself, who was hit in
the shoulder and had to have his wound treated, but he soon returned to take
command again from Major Garrett Nevins. In uncommon praise, Colonel
Marsh of the 20th Illinois noted, "at the time of my being ordered off the field
[the 11th Illinois] were still fighting bravely. Had I received a fresh supply of
ammunition I would gladly have gone to their assistance."[48]

Not surprisingly, the Illinoisans could not hold forever, being assailed as
they were on three sides. The crucial moment came when Forrest's cavalrymen were also able to get in the 11th Illinois's rear as well, despite Ransom
continually moving the regiment to the right. Having suffered mostly head
wounds because of their shielded position behind the ridge for much of the
fighting, the breaking point came when the cavalrymen appeared in the rear,
and one Illinoisan described how "the whole line just seemed to melt away
and scatter. There was a blind rush to get away." The regiment fled down the
hill they were holding and up the next, the men slipping in the snow that was
now beginning to melt with the sun's warmth. It all seemed so surreal; George
Carrington described losing his musket when the bayonet became caught in a
fallen tree. He described a corporal who was hit multiple times losing his cap
and getting it back on only to lose it again: "the second time it fell off he let it
go." Upon reaching the other side of the valley Carrington turned and looked
back to see a Confederate battle line, "and it seemed to me every man was in
the act of firing." Bullets clipped the bushes around him and one nipped his
hip but "it did not interfere with my running."[49]

The wounded Ransom saw it all from his higher level. He reported, "the
movement [Wallace's retreat order] was executed, but too late to prevent the
cavalry from getting in rear of most of my command, who bravely cut their

way through with terrible loss." The Illinoisans were also hit in the front, the 2nd Kentucky joining in Baldwin's and Simonton's advances. Colonel Roger Hanson noted that his attack "was not, strictly speaking, a 'charge bayonets,' but it would have been one if the enemy had not fled." Ransom later wrote that he "found what was left of the Eleventh a few hundred yards in the rear." He marched them across Indian Creek to safety, but he was immensely proud of the stand they had made.[50]

By 11:00 AM, therefore, the Confederate surge had driven back four Federal brigades, all of which were streaming in confusion toward the valley of Indian Creek. Yet this advance had taken a toll on the Confederate brigades as well, and a lull developed on the field. Colonel Baldwin remarked, "uncertain as to the movements of our right wing, I paused to obtain the information necessary to render our future movements effective and to restore order from the confusion incident to a continuous combat of nearly six hours in the woods." There was much gained in those nearly six hours, though. The way was now open and secure for the Confederate army to escape on the Forge Road, with no resistance being organized at this point to stop them. Gaining even more ground, the Confederate brigades were now following slowly toward the west, and met little resistance for nearly half a mile. The ultimate time of escape had come. "The day is ours," rang out from the officers in the Confederate lines.[51]

Unfortunately for the Confederate army defending Fort Donelson and trying to break out, that would not be so easy. The success of such a move hinged on two generals, one on each side. Acting differently, these two would come to define the successes and failures at Fort Donelson and onward. Certainly, the differences between Gideon Pillow and Ulysses S. Grant were stark, and those differences emerged crystal clear on the afternoon of February 15.

13

"Up to This Period the Success Was Complete"

Abraham Lincoln was a troubled man, his fifty-third birthday three days before causing him less concern comparatively than his two very sick boys. He was also keeping track of the developments around Fort Donelson as best he could. He received delayed reports from Grant's expedition, because after Grant sent messages they traveled to Cairo, then to St. Louis, and thence to Washington. Obviously interested, Lincoln offered advice in the midst of the campaign, telling Halleck, "you have Fort Donelson safe, unless Grant shall be overwhelmed from outside." To keep that from happening, especially by railroad from Johnston's army between Nashville and Bowling Green, the president suggested, "in the midst of a bombardment at Fort Donelson, why could not a gunboat run up and destroy the bridge at Clarksville?" Lectures aside, Lincoln came to the main point at the end, writing "our success or failure at Fort Donelson is vastly important, and I beg you to put your soul in the effort."[1]

Had Lincoln been on site at noon that afternoon of February 15, he most likely would not have been encouraged. Neither would Jefferson Davis for that matter, because neither army leader actually commanded his forces at the time. Grant was of course off to see Foote, making his long way back over miserable roads and then taking stock of what was happening. Floyd was not operating as his army's commander either, being one-upped by Pillow, who was riding his and Buckner's lines, giving orders about what needed to be done. As a result, neither army had an effective head coordinating all movements during the morning and even into the early afternoon. It consequently fell to the division commanders, who did not always agree and who could not be expected to provide a coherent plan, to fight the battle. At any rate, the emerging pattern was clear; the steady tide of Confederate attack drove the Union line rearward continually, one Mississippian describing the effort as "find the enemy, then charge, rout him, re-form line and move forward again."[2]

Clear victory and defeat would nevertheless emerge this afternoon, largely because one of those army commanders chose to assert his command authority and take control of the situation. The other, sadly for his cause, continued to dawdle, letting slip by a golden opportunity to change the course of events. The ramifications would be great for these men; one would become a hero while the other would be the butt of criticism and be dead within two years.

The stakes were high on that afternoon of February 15. It was clearly one of the first truly consequential days of the now yearlong civil war.

Prior to Grant's arrival back at the scene of battle, it was up to the Federal division commanders to solidify another line of defense on the right. For his part, C. F. Smith was still operating under strict orders to hold his ground and not to go on the offensive. A major attack had occurred on the right, but there was no certainty that an attack would not come on his front as well. Smith stayed put, even while one of his brigades under John McArthur was caught up in the fighting taking place on the Union right. Consequently, it fell to McClernand and Wallace to handle the situation.[3]

The view Wallace had of what was happening was not good. Effectively, five Union brigades, McArthur's, Cruft's, and John McClernand's entire division of three brigades, were even then chaotically withdrawing westward along the Wynn Ferry Road and the woodlands to its south. Lew Wallace could hear the fighting, noting that "the woods rang with a monstrous clangor of musketry, as if a million men were beating empty barrels with iron hammers." Fortunately, Confederate pursuit had slowed down, but everyone realized a new line had to be formed quickly.[4]

Lew Wallace first saw the signs of crisis when retreating Federal soldiers began to appear behind his line, which at this point was facing north. More and more beaten soldiers came, "bringing the unmistakable signs of disaster," Wallace wrote. At one point, even a "mounted officer" galloped past shouting, "we are cut to pieces." Wallace was, at the time, talking to John Rawlins of Grant's staff, so with some verification of what he had seen he felt safe in sending his other brigade to help. Plus, he did not want the panic to spread to his stationary men; troops on the move with adrenaline are much more hardy than troops left to stand idle. Wallace therefore ordered John Thayer late in the morning to move his brigade to the right and intercept the Union retreat and the expected Confederate pursuit.[5]

Wallace rode on ahead of Thayer's marching troops to see for himself the extent of the damage; he later remarked on the eerie sight of the dead and wounded "reddening the snow with their blood." He found some regiments totally disorganized, but most, especially Will Wallace's, were still in a good state of organization. All they wanted was ammunition, "want of which was the cause of their misfortune," Lew Wallace concluded. Soon, he met the other Wallace, whose "coolness under the circumstances was astonishing," the division commander noted, later saying he merely "looked like a farmer from a hard day's plowing." The two quickly realized they were the two Wallaces, at one time colonels of the 11th Illinois and Indiana, prompting Will Wallace to reflect that they "have been the cause of great profanity in the post-office." Lew Wallace asked if the Federals were being pursued and how rapidly. Will Wallace "calculated," according to Lew, and, spying the head of Thayer's brigade emerging up the road from the west, coolly responded, "you will have about time to form line of battle right here." Both Wallaces bade each other farewell with "Good-day," and Will worked to re-form his brigade while Lew sent word for Thayer to take the position to stem the tide. "The crisis had come," Lew Wallace wrote, "my Third Brigade had to be thrust between our retiring forces and the advancing foe." Fortunately, Thayer quickly deployed, Wallace positioning him "at a right angle with the old one" on the Wynn Ferry Road, on the military crest of a small ridge that ran almost perpendicular to the road. Wallace also sent for Peter Wood's Chicago Light Artillery; turning to an aide he yelled, "ride and tell Pete Wood to come. Tell him he has the right of way, and to stop at nothing." Wallace also sent word to Smith for additional help.[6]

The regiments marched quickly to their positions, taking stock of the evidence of battle. One Illinoisan in the 46th Illinois related, "every few Rods we would pass some poor fellow with an arm shot off or his head bound up & blood running down over his clothes. Oh Nellie! You can have no idea of the Horror of War so far away from all the sights & sounds of it." He added, "when we passed our Boys with our Colors flying & Band playing more than one poor fellow would turn to take a last look at the Glorious Flag he had fought for & given his life to support." Colonel John Davis described that band, writing that they entered the action "with banners flying in sight and the band and field music playing Yankee Doodle."[7]

Thayer's line took shape on the high ground east of Indian Creek, led into place by Captain Warren Stewart of McClernand's staff. The Chicago artillery became the main defense in the road itself. Wallace was amazed how quickly the artillery moved: "it drove forward full speed, the horses running low, the riders standing in their stirrups plying their whips, guns and caissons bouncing over root and rut like playthings, the men clinging to their seats like monkeys." Wood's guns, later joined by a section of Taylor's battery, shelled the woods as the lead elements of Confederate pursuers appeared, the Chicago gunners averaging about two rounds a minute for fifteen minutes. The infantry also took their positions, the 1st Nebraska to the right of the road and the green 58th Illinois farther to the right; one of the newly minted Illinois soldiers marveled: "it was to bad leaving camp on Tuesday receiving arms on Wednesday and going to battle on Friday." The 58th Ohio held the area to the left of the road, their line re-fused a bit to cover the front. In the rear, a second line consisted of the 76th Ohio and the 46th and 57th Illinois, with the 68th Ohio farther to the left on the road in the valley of Indian Creek and the 20th Ohio even farther back. Despite forming the line, the Federals were miserable, one Illinoisan remembering, "the weather was raw and disagreeable, a cold wind blowing in our faces." Another Ohioan noted, "we discovered as we moved on, the air was full of objects that flew like birds, and seemed to whisper softly as they went. When once or twice we heard these flying objects hit trees with a sharp crack, it occurred to us that they were bullets from rebel guns." One marching Ohioan declared that a cannon ball "passed the whole length of our line"; he noted, "it made us open our eyes." Even worse, Confederate fire was increasing. The Federals first heard "commands in the thick woods a short distance in front and to the left," but those commands soon turned into small-arms fire and eventually artillery. One Illinoisan wrote home, "I tell you the way the grape & canister did fly also musket balls & buckshot. The shot ploughed up the ground about us also cutting off large limbs of trees as large as my body." An Ohioan already in awe with their march through the "mountains" was even more impressed when "we had just time to form and turn round when the balls came like hail." Another Ohioan sent out with his company as the skirmish line was even more intimidated: "our Co. was right between our men and the enemy each side fired mostly over our heads. We lay flat on the ground. Canon ball and bullets flue around us like hail."[8]

In addition to Thayer's line, Wallace had other troops at his disposal. McClernand soon sent out some of the 2nd Illinois Cavalry to his right and they located the following enemy. It so happened that Cruft's brigade, as it withdrew from a couple of successive positions, formed a line directly in that area, on the right of Thayer's position but not connected to it as yet. It took some time for communication to be opened with Wallace, but the general soon arrived and approved the position, telling Cruft to "hold it at all hazards." "Riding down its front," Wallace marveled, "I found the regiments in perfect order, having done their duty nobly but with severe loss, and eager for another engagement."[9]

Adding to the strength of Wallace's line, C. F. Smith had also relented and sent troops to the east. Eventually Morgan L. Smith's small brigade of two regiments from Smith's division, the 8th Missouri and 11th Indiana, also filed into line between Cruft and Thayer, but not without seeing horrible sights on the way as well. Charles Kroff noted in his diary, "we met hundreds of soldiers who had been in the conflict—many were wounded—some were in ambulances, others being carried on stretchers—some hobbling along, &c. All seemed to tell the same tale, that their Reg't was 'cut to pieces.'" He added, "this was indeed discouraging, but we marched swiftly on." Wallace was not immune to fear either, writing his wife later, "I confess when I saw McClernand's thousands come driving back, I thought of Bull's run. . . . Altogether that moment tested my nerve more than ever before." It unfortunately got no better once Smith's small brigade arrived and formed in line. One Missourian noted that "the Rebels, who were in a dense thicket, unexpectedly to us, opened a deadly fire." But, he added, "we were soon in line and returned it as warmly as they gave it." To locate the enemy accurately, Smith sent forward a company of Missourians to "draw their fire, and ascertain their position." This was a difficult chore because the hill before them was "covered at intervals with forest and dense underbrush."[10]

A crisis within the larger crisis faced the Federals, but Lew Wallace had managed to place a strong line of battle containing three brigades in the Confederate path of advance. Whether it would be enough was unknown, as the Confederate assault had rolled over several other brigades already and the fighting here was now beginning to grow once more. One Indianan wrote, "I don't think I ever heard hail fall faster than the balls flew over us. But we were

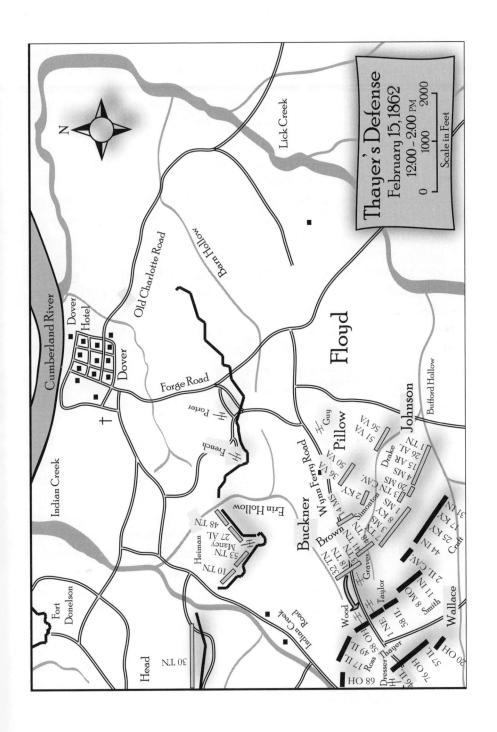

Thayer's Defense
February 15, 1862
12:00 – 2:00 PM

0   1000   2000
Scale in Feet

N

Cumberland River

Dover Hotel

Dover

Indian Creek

Fort Donelson

Head

N.L. 30 T.N.

Old Charlotte Road

Barn Hollow

Lick Creek

Forge Road

Porter

French

Erin Hollow

48 T.N.

Heiman
53 T.N.
Maney
27 AL.

10 T.N.

Indian Creek Road

Floyd

Johnson

Bufford Hollow

Pillow

Guy

56 VA.

51 VA.

50 VA.

36 VA.

2 KY

14 MS.

Buckner

Wynn Ferry Road

Drake
4 MS
20 MS
15 AR.
26 AL.
TV
1 T.N.
3 T.N. CAV.
1 MS.
8 KY
3 MS.
1 T.N.
7 T.N.

Brown

18 T.N.

32 T.N.

Graves

Wood

Taylor

Simonton

Ross
58 OH
49 OH

17 IL.

1 NE.

58 IL.

Dresser Thayer
46 IL.

HO 89

Smith

Wallace

2 LL CAV.

44 IN
11 IN.
8 MO

25 KY
17 KY
31 IN.

Craft

57 OH
76 OH
20 OH

lying down so that they principally shot over us but if we had been standing up we would have nearly all been killed." He added, "and there it is that the ZOUAVE saves himself and gets pay for his extra drilling."[11]

Within the line, soldiers left accounts of what they were feeling in this, their first taste of combat. D. P. Grier of the 8th Missouri wrote home,

> sometimes when a cannon ball or a bomb shell would pass over my head, the peculiar whizzing noise would cause me to dodge down my head. This is impossible for any man to avoid for it is perfectly natural for any one to do so. At first I commenced dodging the musket balls, but I soon gave this up for they came so thick and fast that one had no chance to move his head in any direction.

Another Missourian noted, "all the way that we could do anything with them was to lie down and load on our backs." He went on: "they thought they had killed all our men on the first fire but when their guns was empty we was up and a firing and they could see us lying on our backs striking as though we were in great agony and all the time we was loading." To reassure all the green soldiers, officers continually roamed the lines. Colonel James M. Shackelford of the 25th Kentucky lost his horse after dismounting, but one Kentuckian remembered him "poping up and down the lines on foot through the woods."[12]

Cruft's line was especially important in that it deployed near the Union hospital east of Indian Creek, where Surgeon Thomas W. Fry and others were working on the wounded who were already crowding the medical facilities. Fry described how "the slightly wounded, the mangled, the dying, and the dead presented a scene which baffles description." Some were beyond hope while others were raised to a frenzy. George Carrington described one member of his 11th Illinois who was holding his bleeding hand "going around swearing at the rebels, the doctors, the government, and everything else." Others were more calm, such as when Colonel Logan was brought in with his many wounds. Laid beside Colonel Morrison, who had been wounded two days before, the two old politicians talked it up: "Bill, did you get a bad lick?" Logan asked, and Morrison quipped, "Yes, John. I think I got enough to go home and beat Phil Fouke for Congress," which he later did. Worse, quite a few well Federal soldiers also crowded into the hospital area, sick with fright. The mass of well soldiers was soon cleared, however, when the Confederates arrived close enough to actually fire a volley into the hospital. Such instances of rearward fire were not uncommon; Joseph Skipworth had a cannonball go through the cover of his wagon behind the lines. Yet a hospital was different. Surgeon Fry and the others quickly evacuated what wounded they could and moved to a new hospital at Grant's headquarters at the Crisp house. In fairness to the Confederates, Fry reported that later some Southerners told him "the fire on the hospital was accidental and ceased the moment the flag was seen." The same thing occurred on the Confederate side as well, one Southern hospital steward noting that several artillery rounds landed among their tents and "we went to work to raise the flags higher." The fire soon stopped.[13]

Eventually, McClernand's re-formed troops also added force to Wallace's new line. Will Wallace had stopped his brigade's withdrawal on the ridges overlooking the valley of Indian Creek. Watching the other Wallace, Lew Wallace and others described him as cool under pressure. "I have always thought the Colonel was a cool man," wrote the chaplain of the 11th Illinois, "but could you have seen him that morning, on his black steed, moving from one point to another, directing the conflict as composedly as if on dress-parade, watching every movement, you would have said that prayer from some pure heart had been answered on his behalf." The cool Wallace soon placed his Illinois regiments in line "at right angles with their first lines," and McClernand reorganized Oglesby's brigade in a similar fashion behind Wallace's troops. There, both brigades were issued ammunition and food, which the tired and dazed soldiers definitely needed. "In two hours the whole brigade was reformed, and having received a new supply of ammunition, awaited orders to march onto the field again," Oglesby reported. Artillery was also placed in the line, Schwartz putting a section of Taylor's battery under Samuel Barrett on the Wynn Ferry Road near Wood's position and setting the other guns in the rear "to guard against a flank approach either from the right or left." On the road itself, Wood's Chicago Light Artillery shared with the weary cannoneers of Taylor's battery some of their stock of ammunition, one Chicagoan writing that Taylor's battery "was just about to spike their guns."[14]

McClernand's other units also took positions in the newly re-formed line. Jasper Dresser's rifled artillery deployed on the left so they could cover the Indian Creek valley; they dueled with Confederate artillery to the west of the creek. Also on site was brigade commander Leonard F. Ross, colonel of the 17th Illinois. He had previously led the small brigade that Colonel Morrison had assaulted with two days before, but as Morrison was wounded in the attack, the two regiments had been attached to Wallace's brigade. Now, Ross returned to command the brigade once more, placing the 17th and the 49th Illinois on the left of the division. In addition, McClernand also had the re-formed regiments of McArthur's brigade, who, although not engaging again and later moving back to Smith's division on the far left, were nevertheless temporarily available if needed. McArthur reported that he ordered his rolls called and supplied his men with food, something they had not had in thirty-six hours. No doubt these veterans of McClernand's earlier defense agreed with one of the Nebraskans then holding the line in Thayer's brigade: "it was no child play."[15]

The Confederate advance, including surgeons seeing to the wounded of both sides, proved just as uncoordinated as the Federal defense. Where the Union commanders managed to meld together a solid line, however, the Confeder-ates essentially divided into two uncoordinated efforts: Buckner's along the Wynn Ferry Road and Bushrod Johnson's farther south. Neither had seen each other throughout the morning, as the heavy woods precluded sight even though the forces were relatively close. Now, both had within their force units from each other's divisions. In fact, Pillow noted that "General Buckner's forces became united with mine." But Pillow was still inside the trenches, so Buckner took it upon himself to pursue as best he could along the Wynn Ferry Road while Johnson pushed forward the other troops to the south.[16]

Buckner first moved out with one gun of Graves's battery, ordering the 14th Mississippi to follow in support. Major Doss of the Mississippi regi-ment wrote that "we marched down the Wynn's Ferry road about 1 mile, and were halted on the top of the hill by General Buckner, when the enemy's bat-tery opened a galling fire of shot and shell upon us." One of Doss's soldiers illustrated the surprise, writing, "on the declivity beyond a monstrous fire of grape, canister & shell suddenly opened on us from an unseen battery in front." Another described how the Federals formed "beautifully, in the shape of an open V the point toward us." The Chicago artillerymen indeed opened up, Samuel Barrett writing that "we had not been in position more than ten minutes, when the rebel force hove in sight, not a stones throw from us in a turn of the road." Buckner knew he needed much more firepower, but he had little to work with at this point; Major Doss, in fact, concluded, "it was soon ascertained that Captain Graves's battery could do but little good there, and was ordered back." Lew Wallace confirmed as much on the other side of

Graves's guns: "the Confederate artillery, having to fire up-hill, was of no service. Their shot and shells flew over the trees." Consequently, Buckner sent couriers to John C. Brown to bring up his brigade, to Colonel Hanson to rejoin him, and to assorted other commands to buttress the line along the road.[17]

Additional Confederate units soon began to arrive, including more artillery. Cannoneers of Captain John Guy's battery had been holding their position in line east of Maney's battery when Pillow rode up and asked them where they were from. They answered that they were Virginians, and Pillow asked, "Will you follow me?" The men responded that they "were not afraid to follow him anywhere," and Pillow led them across the hollow to one of the abandoned Federal guns of McAllister's battery. The Virginians began to work the gun, firing in support of Buckner's push down the Wynn Ferry Road. Captain Guy was thrilled with his newly acquired weaponry: "I got its caissons and equipments & six very fine horses with harness & equipment complete." Yet in the confusion of advancing in heavily wooded terrain, the artillery could only fire by sound: "we had to follow the Progress of the Fight more with the Ear than the Eye & several times ceased firing for a while, from the difficulty of distinguishing friends from foes."[18]

Obviously, one more gun would make little real difference, but larger units soon arrived as well. When Brown's brigade approached along the Wynn Ferry Road, Buckner sent it forward despite what he perceived as "a strong [enemy] position on the road." Riding his "noble white steed," Brown quickly deployed his three Tennessee regiments across the road, the 3rd Tennessee on the south side and the 18th and 32nd Tennessee on the north, along with the 41st Tennessee and six companies of the 48th Tennessee, which had also crossed the rifle pits. Buckner also repositioned Graves's one gun in the road. Then, with the shout of "Forward! Storm the battery!," Brown led his Tennesseans into the teeth of Thayer's waiting regiments. He managed to drive back some skirmishers but was unable to dislodge Thayer's strong line, writing, "when within 100 yards of the enemy, who was upon higher ground, we were met by a fire of grape and musketry that was terrific, but fortunately passing above our heads." Colonel Palmer ordered his men to fire while kneeling, so that "the main body of the enemy's fire would and did pass over us." Calvin Clack of the 3rd Tennessee remarked they "received a volley from a battery and about 2000 men." J. T. Williamson provided a more individual picture, writing, "the Yankee bullets were knocking up the snow all around me and buzzing by like bees." Unfortunately, some of the Tennesseans were kept idle in line under fire, prompting one to write, "this is the time to try men. While they are firing themselves they have something to occupy the mind, but compel them to stand under a heavy fire with nothing to do, they will grow weak in the knees."[19]

The brunt of Brown's advance fell on Wood's and Taylor's Chicago Light Artillery and the adjacent 1st Nebraska. As Brown's Tennesseans swooped into the low spot and tried to ascend the slight rise, the cannoneers began firing with the Nebraskans doing likewise, mostly from the left of the regiment. "We opened perfect lanes through the underbrush," artilleryman Barrett remembered during the fifteen-minute fuselage. A Nebraskan remembered the same: "we opened fire on them and had about ten or fifteen minutes hard work." Some of the Nebraskans had a better field of fire than others, one noting, "some of us were down in a hollow and had bushes between them and the enemy so that they could not see them. I could see the smoke from their pieces through the brush when they first commenced firing on us and always blazed away in that particular direction as near as I could. The men on the left of our company saw them plainly."[20]

Such heavy fire was certainly hard on Brown's Confederates. One Tennessean declared that the enemy fire cut "the bushes over our heads and plow[ed] up the snow at our feet." Even so, Graves's Confederate guns responded and the infantry surged ahead but was soon turned back by the massed vollies of the Nebraskans; they continued their "almost incessant discharge of musketry for three-quarters of an hour, the battery continuing its firing at the same time," Thayer wrote. Meanwhile, he added, "the enemy poured volley after volley upon us, but, fortunately, aimed too high to do much execution." Thayer later claimed that Brown had tried three times to take his position, but he probably mistook various aspects of the same attack as individual assaults. No matter how many advances there were, none succeeded, and a wounded Lieutenant Colonel Thomas M. Gordon of the 3rd Tennessee soon panicked and ordered his regiment to retreat. Brown re-formed it after only a hundred yards or so, but the damage was done; the other regiments also fell back in response. By this time other problems also surfaced, such as a lack of ammunition as well as flintlocks "coming in contact with the melting snow, [having] become too inefficient for use until they could be dried and put in proper order." Brown's Tennesseans accordingly fled rearward, and Thayer thought momentarily of chasing after them: "nothing but the thick underbrush prevented a charge with the bayonet." He decided against it because of the ground cover, which actually had played into the Confederate force's hands all day. Brigade commander Baldwin noted that in this type of terrain where they could close rapidly with the enemy, their smoothbore muskets with buck and ball and "our rapid loading and firing proves immensely destructive and the long-range arms of the enemy lose their superiority." A Tennessean agreed, writing that "our buck & ball cartridges could kill one and wound three and as is well known one wounded man takes three out of action as it takes two men to help him off the field." At least one Mississippian was convinced in that "the enemy's fire ranged by the marks of the shot upon the trees and bushes from breast height to eight feet. Our fire ranged from half leg to above the head in height. We suppose they generally over shot our men with their long range guns."[21]

Pillow soon learned of the halt, writing that his and Buckner's troops "engaged the enemy in a hot contest of nearly an hour," but added significantly, "with large forces of fresh troops that had now met us." Those troops were of course Thayer's and Smith's brigades from the Union left, and they were indeed fresh. Nevertheless, the Confederates managed to re-form a line and traded shots with the enemy, many having taken to the ground for protection. One Tennessean remembered firing while "falling upon our knees loading in the greatest possible haste others would load lying flat upon the snow." Unfortunately, their flintlocks soon fouled to the point that they stopped working altogether, forcing many to pull their rounds and clean the pans before they could be used again. Even so, the Federals were impressed, one of Morgan Smith's Indianans writing, "they stood their ground well for a short time pouring volley after volley over our heads."[22]

At the same time, other Confederate brigades also tested the new Federal line, primarily farther south. Colonel Simonton led his four regiments forward to Buckner's left, although this brigade never really confronted the enemy but did move across scores of wounded and the Federal campsites complete with knapsacks and blankets. Simonton wrote, "the enemy had disappeared behind the crests of a range of hills about half a mile in our front and in the direction of their transports." He added tellingly, "at this point I was ordered to halt my command and await further orders." Other Confederate commanders said the same thing, Colonel Baldwin, who had his horse shot from under him during the fighting, writing that he could get no orders from Pillow "except to do the best I could." Simonton took advantage of the lull to resupply his troops with ammunition, "chiefly gathered from the slain of the enemy," he noted, and re-formed his line. Yet all around lay destruction; Colonel John Gregg of the 7th Texas noted, "for more than the distance of a mile through the woods the earth was strewn with the killed and wounded of the enemy." Prisoners also abounded. One private in the Texas regiment, George Blain, captured Major John P. Post of the 8th Illinois.[23]

Farther to the left, Drake's brigade likewise moved up and confronted the right of the Union line, mainly Cruft's brigade as well as the Union hospital set up near the Indian Creek road. There, more of a fight occurred, something along the lines of Buckner's and Brown's advance on the Wynn Ferry Road. One Mississippian remembered, "we had just crossed this hollow and begun to ascend the projecting point of the hill in front when we were greeted with a shower of Minnie balls so sudden that it almost threw our line into confusion." The Confederates soon calmed down, and "rapid musketry began now on both sides." Cruft, who was especially concerned about the wounded and the surgeons, gave much of his attention to defending the hospital from any attack. But it was especially difficult to even see the enemy, Cruft wrote: "the deadened leaves of the oak shrubs were almost identical in color with the brown jean uniforms of the enemy, and rendered it almost impossible to distinguish their line until a fire revealed its locality." He further noted that such a problem caused "a feeling of uncertainty among the men." Although he managed to learn that some of the troops he faced were Roger Hanson's 2nd Kentucky and a portion of Forrest's cavalry to the right, Cruft was never able to be sure. The rest were Drake's brigade farther to the left with the attached 20th Mississippi on their right. Even with all the firepower, though, much less fighting occurred on this Confederate left than along the Wynn Ferry Road. There was even a Confederate foray across Bufford Hollow to the south, although a small detachment of the 17th Kentucky stopped the Confederate exploration, but at the expense of the men's baggage. Colonel John H. McHenry noted, "this engagement was at the place where the regiment had encamped the night previous, and resulted most disastrously to our knapsacks and blankets, which had been left hanging upon the trees."[24]

Numerous other odd experiences occurred as a lull began to settle over the battlefield. A singularly strange thing happened in the 48th Tennessee, where Andrew Campbell expressed amazement at the enemy fire. He wrote in his diary, "we engaged the enemy for some time while iron and hail was falling all around from the belching cannon and deadly musket. Our battery, in the meantime, was firing over our heads at the enemy." Amazingly, Campbell spied an old friend even during this cannonade. "Here I met up with my old friend Lieut. Joe Love (of Culleoka, Tenn.) and shook hands with him amidst a shower of bullets, this being the first time that I had seen him since we parted at Camp Maury." Similarly, farther to the south, the men of the 3rd Mississippi watched as a small bird "about the size of a tame pigeon" meandered in the snow in front of the line. "It would fly a few steps and then alight and as we approached it would fly again a few steps and then alight again on the ground as before, repeating the same movement a number of times."[25]

Others were taking in the horrid sites behind the lines. Many thirsty Confederates found Federal canteens full of ice and water. Others took in the morbid sights. While his guns were not in action, Captain John Guy of the Virginia battery went exploring. "I next went farther to the left & followed the main line along which the Battle had raged from one end to the other," Guy wrote a few weeks later.

Our own men had there removed most of the Enemy's wounded, that they had not carried off with them as they fell back. But the dead were still lying there in Numbers that astonished me, for the duration of the Conflict had not been such as to prepare me for such slaughter. It was terrible. The dead lay in every conceivable position & were shot in every part of the body. Whenever a face was turned up to view as many were, its ghastly pallor was rendered more horrid by contrast with blood & gaping wounds. The ground was all along strewn with blankets, canteens, Haversacks, Knapsacks, guns, cartridge boxes & every kind of equipment. The trees and saplings were all sacrificed and torn & many of the latter cut down, by balls. In one place, where the Battle raged with greatest fierceness, where in fact our forces having first driven the Enemy back, were themselves forced to retreat a little way & there again drove the Enemy back, I could but stop & note the marks of the storm that had passed & repassed over it. . . . The growth was mostly small & it was cut down by the balls, so that it looked something like I have seen a thick growth of corn, that had been swept over, & cut down & shattered by a severe hail storm. . . . The dead were mostly slain by the balls of the infantry, those slain by the Artillery were of course more mangled & torn, but were not I thought so horrid to look on as those who [were] killed by smaller arms, retained most or all of their features & limbs & thus seemed to force on the mind a stronger realization of the scene around him.[26]

A Mississippian similarly described Federals with their heads blown off, one "leaving only a little of his chin and the skin under it." In another case, he wrote of a head wound: "his hair and skull lay mangled on the ground with his brains scattered over them. The blood had flowed so freely as to make its way fifteen or twenty steps down the tracks their artillery had made."[27]

Perhaps in part because of such harshness during the fighting, but more so because of the new Federal line that lay in front, Buckner and the rest of the Confederate commanders called a halt. "In this position I awaited the arrival of my artillery and reserves," Buckner later wrote, "either to continue the pursuit of the enemy or to defend the position I now held, in order that the army might pass out on the Forge road, which was now completely covered by the position occupied by my division." He waited in vain. As it turned out, Pillow had countermanded orders to some of Buckner's infantry and artillery, not allowing them to support him, Pillow admitting, "I called off the further pursuit, after seven and a half hours of continuous and bloody conflict." The Confederate high-water mark had as a result been achieved in terms of the attempt to open the way for escape. Jeremy Gilmer correctly noted, "our success against the right wing was complete."[28]

Unfortunately for the Confederate effort at Fort Donelson, Pillow was not content with just stopping the pursuit. What happened next almost took Buckner's breath away. In a case of incompetence that Buckner could not believe, Pillow ordered Buckner himself and his troops back into the entrenchments. "After the troops were called off from the pursuit," Pillow wrote, "orders were immediately given to the different commands to form and retire to their original position in the intrenchments." The reason for Pillow's order would be debated for decades, but suffice it to say that because John Floyd had ridden to the far right to check on Colonel Head's defense, Gideon Pillow made the fateful decision of the day. Most significantly, Pillow doomed all chance of the Confederate army's escape. Pillow seemed not to understand that whoever went on the offensive would have a morale advantage and, even worse, called for a retreat, thus giving up everything so hard won during the day. Significantly, part of what was ultimately given up was the Forge Road, the all-important Confederate avenue of escape. A retreat to the entrenchments was the death knell for the Confederate army.[29]

Buckner quickly rode rearward to find out what was going on. In doing so, he met Floyd and told him what was happening. Floyd "seemed surprised at the order," Buckner related, and asked Buckner what he thought. The Kentuckian told him in no uncertain terms that he still believed the army should escape: "I replied that nothing had occurred to change my views of the necessity of the evacuation of the post, that the road was open, that the first part of our purpose was fully accomplished, and I thought we should at once avail ourselves of the existing opportunity to regain our communications." Floyd immediately told Buckner to stop any withdrawal while he went and talked to Pillow, who was inside the trenches. Buckner was soon astonished once more when word arrived from Floyd to withdraw inside the earthworks.[30]

What happened in the intervening moments as Floyd and Pillow met clearly indicated that Floyd had not taken control of the situation. The commander had ridden to the right just after giving orders to Buckner to hold the roads opened by the Confederate attack. His idea was to make sure the right was firm and then to march out the left side of the garrison while Buckner held the Federals back on the Wynn Ferry Road. Floyd was returning when he met Buckner and heard the devastating news. He angrily confronted Pillow: "General Pillow, what have we been fighting all day for? Certainly not to show our powers, but solely to secure the Wynn's Ferry Road [Forge Road], and now after securing it, you order it to be given up." Floyd could of course protest all he wanted, but the withdrawal was already happening and the precious ground gained so bloodily during the morning was already being given up. "This movement was nearly executed before I was aware of it," Floyd wrote despondently, adding that because of the timing involved, nothing was left but to resume the defense of the trenches. A distraught Colonel Hanson realized the gravity of the movement: "up to this period the success was complete."[31]

Bushrod Johnson later gave an explanation from his vantage point. He had pushed the Confederate left (Drake's brigade, the 20th Mississippi, as well as Forrest's cavalry) up toward the final Union line, confronting Cruft's brigade. He deliberated about what to do next but saw no real chance of making much progress without additional troops. "Observing the enemy in force in front and no troops supporting us on our right," Johnson sent an aide to ask for reinforcements. The courier returned with orders for Johnson to "report in person to the commanding general within our defensive works." A stunned Johnson rode to Floyd inside the trenches and there offered his views that the enemy should once more be attacked. He was stunned to hear that Pillow and Floyd were thinking of retreat. "After slight discussion," Johnson remembered, Floyd ordered him to keep Drake's brigade as a rear guard, or in Johnson's words "displayed before the enemy," while the rest of the troops returned to the trenches. A shocked Johnson could only ride back to the brigade and follow orders.[32]

Almost everyone who heard the order was dumfounded. The 3rd Tennessee's Major Cheairs balked at Pillow's order, arguing to Pillow himself that Buckner had told him to hold out. An incensed Pillow "rose in his stirrups & said 'I am Genl in command of the forces of Donalson. Obey my order.'" The regiment fell back but broke apart in the confusion; Cheairs remembered that even he and Brown "could not arrest [the retreat] until they fell back some two or three hundred yards." For his part, Forrest was incredulous, writing that they had "opened three different roads by which we might have retired if the generals had, as was deemed best in the council the night before, ordered the retreat of the army." Colonel Joseph B. Palmer of the 18th Tennessee similarly remembered that when news of the retreat came, "I was every moment expecting to receive orders to march my regiment, together with the balance of our troops, in the direction of Nashville." Colonel Edward C. Cook of the 32nd Tennessee related the same feelings: "at this moment we felt satisfied that the Wynn's Ferry road [Forge Road] was clear and the way back to Nashville open; that fortune had smiled upon us, and that we ought to prove to her we were worthy of her favors." Instead, orders came to man the trenches once more.[33]

Most of the brigades reentered the Confederate works that afternoon, leaving only Drake's brigade and the 20th Mississippi as a rear guard. The troops brought with them many of the wounded. One Tennessean remembered ambulances bringing numerous wounded Confederates inside the works during the lull provided by the lack of a Union attack. "As it passed through the gap in the breastwork where the ground was very rough," noted the soldier, "the careless driver urged his horses forward. The vehicle passed over with a severe jolt and the cries and groans of the poor, mangled sufferers were heart-rending."[34]

It was only adding insult to injury, much like what was happening with the Confederate army as a whole.

Gideon Pillow later tried to cover over his glaring blunder, writing, "we had accomplished our object, but it occupied the whole day, and before we could prepare to leave, after taking in the wounded and dead, the enemy had thrown around us again in the night an immense force of fresh troops and reoccupied his original position in the line of investment, thus again cutting off our retreat." In truth, the Confederate army could very well have marched out that afternoon. Many men and much material would have been lost, but the chance was there even if the Confederate high command had not taken advantage of it. One Confederate succinctly summed up the situation when he wrote, "our Generals were so elated over our victory that they lost their heads." His story was corroborated by a staff officer who reported Pillow "riding about Donelson exclaiming: 'Another Manassas defeat! Another Manassas defeat!'" Confederate artillery captain John Guy similarly noted in his journal, "the general opinion among the Colonels seemed to be that Genl. Pillow was so elated with the success of the attack, that he abandoned the idea of retreating." Another was less generous, although he tempered his words somewhat, writing, "his head was turned with the victory just gained, & he was too short sighted a fool to see that it was entirely thrown away unless we used it to escape."[35]

A major debate took place later over what had actually been said in the council the night before, and whether Pillow was at fault for not having his men loaded and prepared to march, as Buckner had clearly understood was supposed to be the case. Later, Pillow said that "General Buckner seems to have understood it differently." But he insisted, "I solemnly aver before God that I never understood it to be the purpose, object, or determination of the general officers, or of any of them, to march in retreat from the battlefield if we won it." Pillow even had several officers later make statements on his behalf, including Nathan Bedford Forrest. The cavalryman wrote in contradiction to his other statements, "nothing was said about our retreating from the field. No order was given to that effect and no preparation was made for that purpose; no suggestion was made of that character and no such determination arrived at." Bushrod Johnson likewise came to Pillow's defense, writing,

the plans and preparations necessary to commence the retreat, after the way was opened, or the circumstances which should determine exactly when it should commence, were not settled more definitely than indicated in general terms. . . . How and when the retreat should begin was not determined in conference, and these were clearly things to be determined at a subsequent period. There was no proposition made in the conference to retreat from the battle-field and no determination made to do so.

Jeremy Gilmer also backed Pillow, writing that none of the issues of numbers of rations prepared, taking blankets and knapsacks, order of march on the retreat, or those manning the advance and rear was discussed. Even so, Pillow's biographers concede that the blame for the confusion should rest on his shoulders as he was "the briefing officer" at the council the night before.[36]

While Pillow made a terrible decision, he admittedly had been caught with no good choices. He could not go forward and he could not hold his lines outside the trenches, especially as he and others could see additional Union reserves moving toward them. Gilmer correctly noted that "it was a choice of evils," but Pillow certainly chose badly. One Confederate gave him the benefit of the doubt by writing, "Gen. Pillow was overconfident or incompetent, either of which was fatal to us." Yet if there was a time for the Confederates to make an escape attempt, it was late in the afternoon on February 15. Lew Wallace, no stranger to controversy himself, concluded, "it must be evident that he should have made the effort." And although not known to the Confederates, Grant was away until after noon and no Union pursuit would have been likely anyway.[37]

Pillow cannot shoulder all the blame, however. Also at fault was John Floyd, who as commander at Fort Donelson should have been in a position to make sure the chief objective of the operation was being carried out. Not being in control allowed his prickly and humiliated subordinate to take command, as had been happening all along. This time, Pillow's decision meant life or death to the Confederate garrison. At the least, there should never have been any confusion about what was to happen. It was Floyd's duty to make sure that all of the generals had specific instructions regarding the plan, which Buckner and Pillow most certainly did not. As a result it falls to Floyd's systemic lack of leadership as well as Pillow's terrible decision to explain the Confederate failure.[38]

One Confederate succinctly summed up the command situation years later, writing:

> the Senior General arrived at the eleventh hour, and seems to have been lacking in disposition, or in power to hold his second in due subjection. The latter had been on the ground for about a week; he was full of energy and physical activity, and possessed rare executive ability. He was restless under restraint, probably prone to insubordination, and it was almost impossible for him to yield his scepter to a new comer. He gave orders affecting the whole army without any known rebuke or remonstrance from his chief.[39]

Ulysses S. Grant also described the Confederate chaos. In his memoirs, he later claimed that he took the actions he did because he was able to read both Pillow and Floyd. He had known Pillow in Mexico and "judged that with any force, no matter how small, I could march up to within gunshot of any intrenchments he was given to hold." That had certainly been the case on February 12, although Pillow had been at Cumberland City during those critical hours. Grant also commented on Floyd, writing, "I knew Floyd was in command, but he was no soldier, and I judged that he would yield to Pillow's pretensions." Whether Grant wrote from hindsight or actually knew those personalities at the time is somewhat debatable, but in those detailed depictions Grant described both Floyd and Pillow perfectly.[40]

As a result, all those lives were lost and the wounded mangled in vain because of the theatrics of two of the Confederacy's most incompetent generals. Putting Floyd and Pillow together at Fort Donelson was a recipe for disaster, and in that sense Albert Sidney Johnston must also bear some blame for the Confederate fiasco at Fort Donelson.

14

"THE ONE WHO ATTACKS FIRST NOW WILL BE VICTORIOUS"

Into the mass of Federal brigades that were in the process of repelling an equally disfigured mass of Confederate brigades strode perhaps the most important arrival on the Federal right, Ulysses S. Grant. While his presence was not that inspiring, one beaten Federal writing that "he is a savage looking oll cuss," his determination made up for any other shortcoming. He rode onto the battlefield complete with one of Foote's cigars, which would portend a later fatal switch from a pipe. He was encouraged that his division commanders had a new line formed and were ready and seemingly eager to fight once more. Still, a defensive attitude hung over the army and it showed no inclination to attack. It was even evident in his division commanders. Grant rode up to Lew Wallace and McClernand, who had just had a laugh together over a shell that flew over their heads "not more than a yard above us." As soon as they saw Grant, both "gave him instant attention." He "seemed irritated and bothered" to Wallace, and McClernand did not help matters by observing, "this army wants a head." To this, the perturbed but restrained Grant replied, "it seems so." Others thought so as well, one Illinoisan writing that for most of the battle the army was like "a decapitated snake, we were all tail and no head." Fortunately, Grant could look past the egotistical comments to what really mattered. He later described how the men complained of being without ammunition, yet there "was an abundance of ammunition near by lying on the ground in boxes." He described how "I saw the men standing in knots talking in the most excited manner." Obviously, the men wanted to be led.[1]

Grant had to hurriedly decide what to do. He told the division commanders that Foote was withdrawing and they would have to form a new line and even "throw up works" while they waited, obviously in conformity with his decision the day before to slow down and lay formal siege to Fort Donelson. The first step in that process was to form a defensive line around the enemy, from which later approaches could be built. Then Grant received information that changed his thought process, and it was here that he made his most tangible impact on the battle: Grant realized that if the Federal brigades were this fought out, so also must be the Confederates. He wrote as early as February 16 that after realizing the enemy was not taking advantage of his victory, "that equal confusion and possibly greater demoralization existed with him [the enemy]." He intended to take full advantage of it.[2]

Then further information spurred him to an altogether greater realization. When Wallace and McClernand informed Grant that the Confederate escape route was open and that some of the enemy had their knapsacks and blankets with them, Grant changed his thinking entirely. Wallace noted that his "face, already congested with cold, reddened perceptibly, and his lower jaw set upon the other." Grant's determination was coming out. Wallace later wrote, "in every great man's career there is a crisis exactly similar to that which now overtook General Grant, and it cannot be better described than as a crucial test of his nature." Viewing the situation, Grant began to put two and two together—that the Confederates were trying to force back the Union right wing to escape. More reports of Confederates carrying their knapsacks, blankets, and haversacks with them confirmed such a notion, and Grant realized he was not dealing with a set-piece battle fighting for the upper hand. He was dealing with a Confederate escape attempt.[3]

Realizing the gravity of the situation, as well as its possibilities, the decisive Grant ordered an offensive across the board. Flushed with concern and crumbling papers in his hand, he immediately ordered McClernand and Wallace: "gentlemen, the position on the right must be retaken," adding that he would go and order Smith to attack as well. Turning to Webster, he told him, "the one who attacks first now will be victorious and the enemy will have to be in a hurry if he gets ahead of me." It was the perfect decision. On the Union right, at worst he could stall the Confederate advance permanently, but he hoped he could also retake the lost ground and slam shut the open door, if, that is, the Confederates had not already marched out of the trap. He also realized that if such a mass attack had occurred on the Federal right, Floyd must have weakened the rest of his defenses to create it, so the rest of the lines must be correspondingly weaker. While that was not true everywhere, especially on

Heiman's front, where the same contingent of troops still defended the area unsuccessfully assaulted on February 13, it certainly was the case farther to the Union left, where Buckner had turned over the defense to a small force. If Grant could attack and gain entrance to Fort Donelson, a victory might still be won quickly. If he could do that while closing the door on the right and keeping the Confederate army trapped inside, it might mean a truly momentous triumph.[4]

Grant accordingly ordered offensive operations all along the lines, "to press upon enemy at all point[s]," McClernand staff officer Mason Brayman wrote in his memorandum book. Grant himself rode along the lines and told Webster to call out to the men that the Confederates were trying to escape and not to let them. "This acted like a charm," Grant later wrote, adding: "the men only wanted some one to give them a command." When he reached Smith's position, he similarly told his former commandant, "General Smith all has failed on our right—You must take Fort Donelson." One aide noted that "Smith sprung to his feet and brushing his moustache with his right hand said 'I will do it.'" It was a significant moment; for the first time that day there was a cohesive command of Union operations, coordinating efforts all across the board. Others realized the importance, McClernand writing, "your arrival gave promise that the general wish to advance would soon be gratified."[5]

Not forgetting the asset he had in the US navy, Grant also sent word to Foote that

> if all the gunboats that can will immediately make their appearance to the enemy
> it may secure us a victory. Otherwise all may be defeated. A terrible conflict
> ensued in my absence, which has demoralized a portion of my command, and I
> think the enemy is much more so. . . . I do not expect the gunboats to go into ac-
> tion, but to make appearance and throw a few shells at long range.

Grant's curious note to Foote that afternoon perhaps betrayed Grant's uneasiness. After all, he would have been extremely embarrassed had the Confederates been able to break out since he had told Halleck over and over that he had the enemy hemmed in. Whether Grant really believed the potential was there to be defeated is unclear, but he indicated his thinking by also telling the navy, "I must order a charge to save appearances." Obviously, Grant was worried to some degree.[6]

Although Foote had already departed, Commander Benjamin Dove was now in charge of the flotilla and Grant's message changed his plans. The naval contingent had heard the fighting but was not involved, rather burying their dead in a field north of the river. Walke read "the Episcopal service on board the *Carondelet*, under our flag at half-mast" before the sailors moved the bodies to land for burial. As they were doing so, "a Roman Catholic priest appeared, and his services being accepted, he read the prayers for the dead." All the while, the battle seemed to be raging more and more furiously, and closer, throughout the day. Grant's note only confirmed the fact. "It seemed of so much importance for us to keep up a show of force," Dove wrote, that he canceled one gunboat's departure and went aboard the heavily damaged *Carondelet* to check on its availability. Finding that it "could not well be moved," Dove utilized the *St. Louis* and the *Louisville*, with the former shelling the Confederate water batteries.[7]

The naval bombardment certainly aided the land effort. Lew Wallace later admitted, "I recollect yet the positive pleasure the sounds gave me . . . how well timed his attack was, if, as I made no doubt, it was made to assist General Smith and myself." Even more significantly, it was the first coordinated effort all across the board for the Union forces at Fort Donelson.[8]

The goal of the attack by the Union right was to slam the door on any Confederate escape. By retaking the lost ground and closing once again on Dudley's Hill and Lick Creek, McClernand and Wallace could prevent further Confederate movement. Once Grant had the enemy hemmed in, he could again slow down and implement siege operations if need be, this time obviously more wary of a Confederate breakout attempt and thus entrenching fully. Having accomplished this, Grant could then await the gunboats, as he had planned earlier. But for all that to happen, the escape route had to be solidly shut once more, and until the Federals on the right moved forward, no one knew if that was possible. For all the Federals knew, the Confederates could even then be marching out the Forge Road with the majority of their troops.[9]

Fortunately for Grant, he had the bulk of the Union army on this eastern half of the battlefield. A full seven of the army's nine brigades were east of Indian Creek, although McArthur's re-formed units would be sent later in the afternoon back to the west side to rejoin Smith's division. In fact, Grant had so many brigades on this east side that he did not utilize them all in the counterattack to retake the lost ground. He could pick and choose which brigades to send, or let his division commanders do so, and they had fully enough troops to do the job even though the bulk of the Confederate army was on that flank as well.[10]

Grant soon issued the necessary formal orders to get the troops moving on the eastern side. While indications of a similar movement could be heard to the west toward Smith's division, McClernand reported that "Colonel Webster . . . brought your order to press upon the enemy at all points." Lew Wallace remembered, "General Grant rode up the hill and ordered an advance and attack on the enemy's left, while General Smith attacked their right."[11]

Given the thrashing McClernand's brigades had taken during the morning, McClernand asked Wallace to take the lead. Wallace remembered McClernand telling him, "the road ought to be recovered — Grant is right about that. But, Wallace, you know I am not ready to undertake it." Wallace gladly obliged. McClernand therefore kept Oglesby's brigade in the vicinity of the Wynn Ferry Road while sending Will Wallace's to the left to cover the Indian Creek valley. McArthur's three regiments marched back to Smith's division west of the creek, so the only force under McClernand's command that made an advance was Ross's newly reinstituted brigade consisting of the 17th and 49th Illinois. McClernand reported that Lew Wallace "requested" that he send troops to support his forces, and McClernand sent this small brigade as well as the 46th and 58th Illinois of Thayer's brigade. The rest of Thayer's brigade likewise remained in place on the Wynn Ferry Road, although a couple of Oglesby's regiments, the 8th and 18th Illinois, moved forward to the high ground facing Heiman's position between Indian Creek and Erin Hollow.[12]

Ross was accordingly the main element of McClernand's division to move forward, and he met very little resistance as Buckner's Confederates had already withdrawn by that time. The Illinoisans nevertheless retook the westernmost portions of the Wynn Ferry Road ridge, as far as the earlier position of Taylor's and McAllister's batteries (Brown's Tennesseans had already removed the two guns). The only resistance prior to reaching the Confederate defenses on Ross's front consisted of "straggling parties of the enemy." Once the Confederate trenches were reached, however, skirmishers sent forward over the hill "drew from them a heavy discharge of grape, canister, and shrapnel." For protection, Ross wisely ordered his regiments to hold a position "about twenty paces behind the summit."[13]

More fighting occurred to the Union right. Actually leading the way on Lew Wallace's front was Morgan Smith's brigade of C. F. Smith's division.

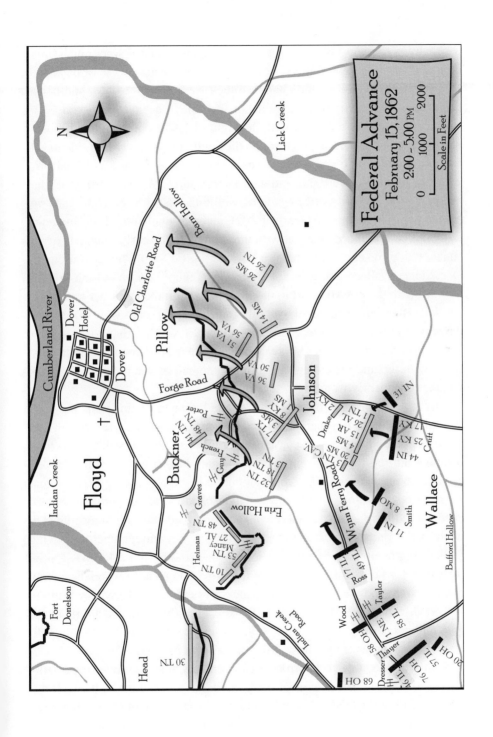

Federal Advance
February 15, 1862
2:00 – 5:00 PM

0   1000   2000
Scale in Feet

N

Cumberland River

Lick Creek

Barn Hollow

Old Charlotte Road

Dover Hotel

Dover

Pillow

Forge Road

26 TN

14 MS

56 VA

51 VA

50 VA

36 VA

1 MS

Johnson

31 IN

8 KY

3 MS

7 TX

1 MS

Drake

N I 1

26 AL

15 AR

1 TN

25 KY

17 KY

Cruft

44 IN

Buckner

41 TN

48 TN

Porter

French

Gwynn

32 TN

18 TN

3 TN

Graves

4 MS

20 MS

30 TN CAV.

Wynn Ferry Road

8 MO

11 IN

Smith

Wallace

Bufford Hollow

Floyd

Indian Creek

Heiman

10 TN

53 TN

Maney

27 AL

Erin Hollow

Wood

49 IL

17 IL

Ross

Taylor

1 NI

58 OH

58 IL

Thayer

Dresser

46 IL

76 OH

57 IL

HO 89

HO 76

HO 20

Head

30 TN

Indian Creek Road

Fort Donelson

Normally, a wayward brigade of another division would not get much lime-light, but this was Lew Wallace's old brigade until just a couple of days ago, with his old regiment of Indianans, so they were special to him and hence garnered a major part of the action. In fact, they cheered him loudly, and Wallace was just as enthused with the sight of his old brigade and officers, writing of Colonel Smith: "all through the conflict I could see him ride to and fro, and could hear his voice, clear as a bugle's, and as long as I heard it I knew the regiments were safe and their victory sure." Wallace also wrote that he knew their Zouave tactics would be well fitted to the terrain and that "my confidence in Smith and in George F. McGinnis, colonel of the 11th [Indiana], was implicit." Wallace even sat with the brigade in the early moments of the attack, ready to send them forward but waiting on Smith "to light a cigar." Once done, Wallace bellowed, "Forward it is, then!" Smith led the brigade forward with the 8th Missouri in the lead, the 11th Indiana farther to the rear and left. Bickering had developed within the brigade as to who would lead the way, and Smith reported that "the gallant Eleventh Indiana would have gladly been in the lead, but kindly yielded to their brothers, the Eighth Mis-souri, with the understanding that it opens the ball on the next occasion, for which it is patiently waiting."[14]

The attack promptly moved forward, one Indianan writing that "our Regt and 8th Mo. Fixed bayonets and took at them in warlike style." Smith met more resistance than Ross because Simonton's brigade was still near its final position, but retiring to the entrenchments and, farther to the south, Drake's brigade, along with the 20th Mississippi and Forrest's cavalry, was the rear guard to cover Pillow's withdrawal. Other Confederate brigades were also encountered during the advance, but they provided little resistance as they were in the process of marching back toward the entrenchments, leaving Drake's regiments to fend for themselves. One soldier in the 4th Mississippi related that his regiment "stood there for more than an hour when the enemy came in sight and we were in great danger of being cut off." Major William N. Brown of the 20th Mississippi on Drake's far right explained a little more: "the regiments on my right very soon commenced retiring to the intrench-ments; I did not learn by whose order or for what purpose."[15]

Smith reported that he "stormed the hill on which the enemy were posted," but failed to mention that most of the Confederates were gone by then. He en-countered only skirmishers from Simonton's brigade, although some resisted the advance and provided a few close calls for the Missourians. Smith himself had his cigar shot near his lips, whereupon he took out another and called for a light. A soldier ran and lit it, and Smith responded, "Thank you. Take your place now. We are almost up." Smith also explained the novel situation when at times his own skirmishers and those of the enemy were "occupying each side of the same tree for cover." A few losses occurred, including Captain George B. Swarthout of the 8th Missouri, Smith relating: "in his efforts to keep his men under cover he forgot himself, and received two rifle bullets, either of which would have killed him instantly." Smith's Indianans and Missourians took a few prisoners as they moved diagonally toward the Wynn Ferry Road, enough for Smith to place the 1st and 3rd Mississippi, the 8th Kentucky, and a regiment of Texans he misnamed. They also took three flags from Mississippi, Texas, and Tennessee regiments. Sadly, as they were being moved to the rear, some of the prisoners were killed by Confederate artillery fire. Obviously, Simonton's brigade faced his advance, although the bulk of the troops fell back to the entrenchments without becoming engaged. It was a good thing, as much of Smith's path was cleared, the only defining features being "outcropping ledges of rock" and underbrush. He noted that his losses were small, "owing to the admirable manner in which all orders were executed and the perfect confidence that existed between the officers and men, the officers all vying with each other in accomplishing their object with the least possible loss of their brave men."[16]

Although Wallace gave the choice assignment to his old brigade, even spinning that it led the advance and Cruft supported it, the advancing brigade of his own division did the hardest fighting. Cruft's brigade stood to Smith's right and advanced at nearly the same time, all its Indiana and Kentucky regiments in a line despite Wallace's order to form by columns of regiments, as Smith had done. Wallace rode among his troops as they surged ahead, telling them of the danger and being answered with "cries of 'Forward!' 'Forward!'" A portion of Dickey's 4th Illinois Cavalry followed behind at Cruft's insistence, but despite encountering Drake's line, they were not needed.[17]

While Smith's brigade moved across open rocky terrain, Cruft's advanced up a wooded area with thick underbrush against the enemy line of battle "distinctly visible on the hill-side," according to Wallace. The Confederate fire from Drake's brigade alerted Wallace to their position and strength, and he later marveled at the musketry on Cruft's front: "the woods through which he was moving seemed actually to crackle with musketry." Cruft's regiments nevertheless moved forward along a road leading into the Wynn Ferry Road, the 44th Indiana behind the Missourians of Smith's brigade. The rest of the brigade fanned out to the right, the extreme right turning and flanking Drake's Confederates, as Cruft described it, "in a line at a right angle to the main advance." In a singularly poignant moment, at one point the 17th Kentucky of Cruft's brigade confronted Colonel Roger Hanson's detached 2nd Kentucky of the Confederate army. One Kentuckian in Cruft's line noted that the regiment made "three desperate charges with the bayonet, the third one being successful." He later termed it a "hard, hard fight."[18]

Drake's Confederate brigade, acting as the rear guard, was obviously not big enough to cover enough ground to keep from being flanked, and Bushrod Johnson recognized as much very quickly. He had already learned that the far Confederate right near Hickman Creek was under attack and requesting reinforcements, so he correctly predicted that no support would be sent to aid his defense even if called for. The only sizable force he had to send to Drake's aid was Forrest's cavalry, which he did. But even Forrest was wary of this fight, and soon reported to Johnson that he had advised Drake to retreat.[19]

There would be quite a firefight before he did so, however. Drake was soon swamped by the advancing regiments of Cruft's brigade, even as Morgan Smith's troops to the left followed up Simonton's withdrawal and turned that flank as well. The initial meeting on Drake's front was extremely loud, from both musketry and yelling soldiers, particularly the 44th Indiana. Cruft described it as "a sharp and desperate fight of a few minutes' duration [and] the hill was carried by storm, and the enemy, with tremendous cheers, driven up to and within his breastworks." It was not quite that simple in reality, and it took some Herculean efforts by the officers to lead the men up the steep hill. Colonel Hugh B. Reed dismounted and took a position in front of the regiment, a pistol in each hand. He led them forward through the bullets with the simple command, "Come on." Major Fred Arn of the 31st Indiana similarly described "the storm of iron which raked the bushes and plowed the ground around them." Consequently, Drake did not go quietly and easily but maneuvered for a bit until Major Brown of the 20th Mississippi reported Federals turning their right and getting in their rear. Drake shifted to the right and rear to counter this threat, but he could do little and continually fell back. By late afternoon, many of Drake's companies were out of ammunition, and the rear guard itself quit and marched back to the trenches.[20]

A wounded Federal, First Lieutenant James Churchill of the 11th Illinois, described the overall effect well. Although terribly wounded in the leg and hip and unable to move, he had conversed with several Confederate surgeons who told him, "to tell you the truth, we haven't the facilities to get our own men off. We are taking as prisoners now only those of you we think will live. If I can return and take you, I will." Churchill had just finished conversing with a Confederate about weaponry, the Southerner even giving him his gun for examination, when he "heard heavy musket firing in the rear." He went on to describe: "it drew nearer me by degrees when suddenly I saw a large number of Confederate infantry passing by, many directly over me. I held up my hand and none stepped on me. They were immediately followed by the 'blue coats.'" Almost miraculously, Churchill recognized an officer and asked him who they were, to which the officer responded, "the 8th Missouri and 11th Indiana." The Federals did not remain long as the Confederates "passed down the ravine below me, and over the rise on the opposite side." Some of Smith's troops, topping the hill and realizing they now confronted the Confederate entrenchments, fell back under cover of the ridge. Churchill was caught in the middle but somehow survived.[21]

The bulk of the Federal brigades followed Drake's retreat almost blindly, Wallace later writing "that we were moving in the direction of the fort I knew rather as a surmise than a fact." Then Wallace described how "the situation revealed itself" as the division pressed on; topping the ridge on which the Wynn Ferry Road ran, Cruft and Smith met a massive force of artillery fire from the Confederate outer works. Like the others to the left, Cruft met "a terrible fire of grape, shrapnel, and shells," reported Major Fred Arn of the 31st Indiana. One of Smith's Indianan's related how "we followed them up till we came within 75 yds of their rifle pits when they opened fire on us with . . . artillery, and we fell back about 50 yards, behind a rise to get out of range of their artillery." A Missourian admitted, "the way the shell, grape and canister flew around us was far from pleasant, I assure you."[22]

Even so, the Union troops basked in the fact that they once again fronted the Confederate outer defenses, one Illinoisan declaring that the enemy was "sent back to their intrenchments howling." A Missourian who had not felt a tinge of panic in the fighting now admitted, "I commenced feeling a little excited and considerable nervous and I must confess a little scared for I then had time to realize what I had come through and how wonderfully my life had been preserved." The momentous results likewise began to dawn on all involved. It was certainly worth all the suffering inflicted as the Union line on the right had been restored. Of course, just the opposite reality dawned on the Confederate side, where John Floyd dejectedly sighed: "we had to submit to the mortification of seeing the ground which we had won by such a severe conflict in the morning reoccupied by the enemy before midnight."[23]

If Grant's offensive on the Union right brought magnificent results in shutting the trap once more on the Confederates, the attack on the left similarly brought major dividends. Grant used the majority of his army against the Confederate escape route, but he also held back a significant portion on the west side of Indian Creek to assault there as well. Recognizing that an attack by the Confederate left had to weaken other portions of the line, particularly the Confederate right, Grant anxiously sent Smith's division forward at the same time Wallace and McClernand moved out. The results would be just as significant on the Union left.[24]

The soldiers of Smith's division spent the morning of February 15 quietly, recovering from another long night of cold. Brigade commander John Cook remembered that the regiments had "been permitted to fall back by companies out of range of the enemy's guns to cook their breakfast and thaw their frozen clothes." Jacob Lauman received two letters from his wife while awaiting action, written days ago of course, in which she congratulated him on his comfortable quarters in Smithland. "I had to laugh," he wrote back, "when for two nights I had been camped under a tree, and it raining and snowing on me, without a tent." Despite the misery, the men listened intently to what was occurring to the east, James Parrott commanding the 7th Iowa writing his wife, "we were for some time held in suspense on our wing." Although snow had a tendency to shroud the sound, Smith's Union troops could tell that the fighting was growing closer to them throughout the morning and early afternoon. Yet Smith himself wrote that "under the orders of the commanding general the division remained quiet, . . . except to keep up the annoyance by skirmishers and slow artillery fire."[25]

That all changed around 2:00 PM, roughly the same time that Grant sent Wallace forward on the right. Smith recalled that around that time, "I received the general's personal order to assault the enemy's right, a half mile or more from my habitual position." Smith eagerly went to work planning, Grant writing that he did so "in an incredibly short time." Smith ordered Cook's and Lauman's brigades to move forward with heavy lines of skirmishers proceeding them. The artillery was also ordered "to open heavily." More than that,

Smith planned the actual assault in minute detail, unlike the bold thrust on the right. Smith desired Lauman's brigade to make the advance in column of regiments, led by the 2nd Iowa, "on the left of the position attacked by us on the previous Thursday," Lauman noted. Smith had to do much of the preparatory work himself because he had only a few staff officers, and he did not fully trust them, saying he had "little fancy for constantly playing dry nurse to the staff officers." He even noted, "I am my own staff officer." Smith consequently rode up to the 2nd Iowa and shouted, "I want this Regt. to carry that fort, yonder, at the point of the bayonet and without firing a gun until you get inside of their works. You will be well supported, a whole brigade will follow at your heels." The Iowans were excited, one having noted, "the 2d Iowa has performed nearly all kinds of military service except fighting." Now they had their chance, and Colonel James Tuttle shouted, "now, my bully boys, give them cold steel. Do not fire a gun until you have got on the inside, then give them h—l!" The rest of the regiments were indeed to support the Iowans, and Cook's brigade was likewise to advance, all being ordered to "rely on the bayonet and not to fire a shot until the enemy's ranks were broken." Still, it was clear that the Iowans were to be the point of the assault, Smith even dividing the regiment into left and right wings, the left in front and the right in rear, he himself accompanying the right section. One Iowan noted that the regiment attacked "by battalions because there was no room for reg to go in so they had to go by battalion."[26]

While Grant had a hunch that the Confederate defenses in this area would be weak, he had no idea just how indefensible they really were. A total of three companies of the 30th Tennessee under Major James J. Turner manned that section of works, which until that morning had been defended by the 2nd Kentucky, while the rest of the regiment under Colonel Head defended the line toward Porter's and Graves's former positions, where John C. Brown's entire brigade had recently manned the line. Major Turner soon heard the ruckus of the forming attack and "rode to a point overlooking our works, and could see the enemy in two lines, and numbering several thousand, moving rapidly upon us." The Tennesseans quickly opened fire and had some effect as the Iowans began to advance. "They held their position with great gallantry," Colonel Head noted of his few Tennesseans, "pouring a destructive fire into the ranks of the enemy."[27]

They were obviously no match for the Federals. "Right gallantly was the duty performed," Smith later remembered, comparing the charge to "any of

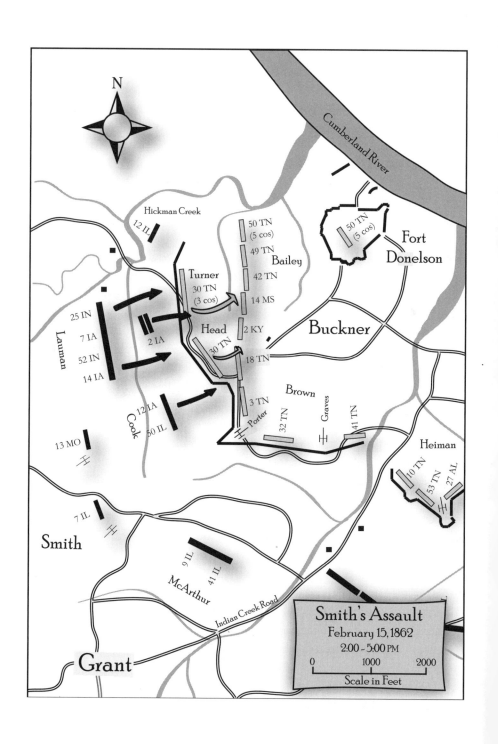

N

Cumberland River

Hickman Creek

12 IL

50 TN
(5 cos)

49 TN

42 TN   Bailey

50 TN
(5 cos)

Fort
Donelson

Turner
30 TN
(3 cos)

14 MS

2 KY   Buckner

25 IN

7 IA

Lauman

52 IN

14 IA

2 IA

Head

30 TN

18 TN

Cook

12 IA

50 IL

3 TN   Brown

Porter

32 TN   Graves   41 TN

13 MO

Heiman

10 TN

53 TN

27 AL

7 IL

Smith

9 IL   41 IL

McArthur

Indian Creek Road

Grant

Smith's Assault
February 15, 1862
2:00 – 5:00 PM

0   1000   2000

Scale in Feet

the charges of Napoleon's 'Old Guard.'" He was particularly fascinated with the Iowan's conduct but berated them until he was hoarse in old-military style: "Damn you gentlemen, I see skulkers, I'll have none here. Come on, you volunteers, come on. This is your chance. You volunteered to be killed for love of country, and now you can be. You are only damned volunteers. I'm only a soldier, and don't want to be killed, but you came to be killed and now you can be." The line thus moved forward over the scene of the attack two days before, prompting one Iowan, Peter Wilson, to note, "we came up over the same ground and the sight of so many dead and wounded was shocking. The smell of powder was strong and seemed to have the effect of making me [men] feel as though they did not care." Some cared perhaps too much. That same Iowan noted that in their first attack two days before, they did not know enough to be scared, but admitted, "the second time I was somewhat excited before we got into the battle but when we got among the balls my nerves were as calm as they are at present." Indeed, battle had a way of determining who was brave. Wilson wrote, "it is disgraceful to see some of our greatest fist-cuff rowdies running away into the timber and not coming back until the battle is over, then hold up their heads and try to make a joke of it."[28]

This was no joke, of course. Colonel James Tuttle led the left wing of companies B, C, G, K, and F, Smith describing them as moving "steadily over the open space, down the ravine, and up the rough ground, covered with heavy timber, in unbroken line, regardless of the fire poured into it." The Iowans faced a rail fence at the bottom of the ravine, a short span of open timber, and then the band of felled trees. Turner's Confederate defenders fired into the column as they reached the bottom of the hill, but Iowan William Holden noted the regiment "answered it with a *deafening shout*" and contin- ued forward without firing. The abatis caused more confusion, one Federal remarking, "it looked too thick for a rabbit to get through." Future presiden- tial candidate James B. Weaver noted that because of the abatis, which he said "the enemy had felled in wild confusion," only half the regiment was sent in the first wave: "it was enough to sacrifice." Lauman similarly described how Tuttle led the Iowans "without firing a gun, up to and charged into the rebels' works, driving the enemy before him and planting the colors on their forti- fications." Slightly behind, the right wing under Lieutenant Colonel James Baker was just as brave, although Baker had a ball pass through his cap, exiting near his temple. Smith reported that these companies moved just as gallantly and soon joined the right wing near the top of the ridge on which the

Confederate line sat. Not surprisingly, there were casualties, including Tuttle "taking a ball through his glove and cuff." Major Norton P. Chipman fell in the advance but "refused to be carried from the field, but waved his sword and exhorted the men to press forward." He shouted to them, "forward my brave boys. We will gain the fort yet." A couple of captains also went down, Charles C. Cloutman killed instantly, but Captain Jonathan S. Slaymaker, after being mortally wounded, kept waving his sword and "shouting to his men to go forward and consummate the work." Smith was obviously impressed; "the movement of this regiment was a very handsome exhibition of soldierly conduct," he wrote approvingly.[29]

Particularly impressive was the regiment's color guard in the heavy fire that Weaver described so well: "all around us and amongst us flew the missiles of death and all around and on every side of us men were falling in the agonies of death." All in the color guard were hit. First was the color sergeant, Henry B. Doolittle, who was hit four times and terribly wounded. Corporal Garfield S. Page grabbed the colors but was immediately killed, whereupon Corporal James H. Churcher fell at the trenches with a broken arm. Corporal Voltaire Twombly took the colors but was immediately hit by a spent ball, which knocked him down. He simply got up and bore the flag the rest of the day, the only member of the color guard still active. He later won a medal of honor for his actions.[30]

Others showed similar bravery, but with a mixture of fear. One nearby Iowan noted, "we took it as cool as a cucumber and wasn't scart until the thing was all over." Another 2nd Iowa soldier was frightened throughout, writing that "in the midst of the conflict I poured out my heart to God in prayer, that he would preserve my life through the battle or fit and prepare me for the last great change." Once he arrived safely at the top, he "returned thanks to God for my miraculous preservation," writing, "Glory be to God who giveth us the victory."[31]

Taking the Confederate trenches did not end the advance, however. A mounted Smith (most officers were afoot) and staff officer Thomas J. Newsham with the right wing of Iowans pushed the attackers onward, Smith inspiring numerous Federals with his actions. Lauman described the general as "brave as a lion," and another Federal took special inspiration from Smith, who beckoned, "No flinching now, my lads?—Here—this is the way! Come on!" One soldier remembered, "I was nearly scared to death, but I saw the old man's white mustache over his shoulder, and went on." Others took courage as well, James Butterfield writing of Smith: "he sat upon his horse as stern as a man could look, and he one of the finest looking men I ever saw. His head is as white as snow, and as he advanced in front of his men. . . . It was a fine picture for a poets pen or an artists pencil." And it was successful, despite the casualties that included Smith himself. He later wrote in his journal that he had exposed himself to "keep in position the Vols," and "my horse and self both hit." He took a spent ball in the stomach that he did not discover until bathing later. He also wrote his wife soon thereafter in response to reports of his actions: "my blood runs cold when I read such stuff as that I put my cap on my sword etc. I did no such ridiculous thing. I certainly did use my sword in waving people on etc, & would like to have used it extensively on those who went back; but not the cap business." He was candid enough to admit, however, "I was ridiculous enough to curse and damn those most heartily who seemed to feel a reluctance to move on and expose their precious persons as I thought ought to have been."[32]

Fortunately, Smith's wound was not major and he was able to spur his men onward. "On reaching the works," Tuttle noted, "we found the enemy fleeing before us, except a few, who were promptly put to the bayonet." Tuttle ordered the Iowans to fire at the retreating Tennesseans, an Iowan noting, "as soon as the boys got near enough to use the bayonet the Secesh broke and ran and many a greycoat got a bullet in his back in the race." Not to be outdone, Smith continually motioned the Iowans onward. They soon crossed a deep ravine and began to mount another hill. This time, however, they would not be as successful.[33]

Matters quickly deteriorated for Tuttle, over and above the slight wound he received. First of all, the Confederate defenders were steadily receiving reinforcements, which the three small companies defending the entire Confederate right flank sorely needed. They had a long way to come, mainly Buckner's troops that had lately been in action against Wallace's advance east of Indian Creek. Buckner reported that as he was withdrawing and barely back within his trenches, Floyd ordered him to "repair as rapidly as possible to my former position on the extreme right, which was in danger of attack." Buckner obeyed, although he reported, "my troops were already much exhausted, but returned as rapidly as possible, a distance of 2 miles, to their positions." Buckner led the way with Brown's troops, whom Floyd and Pillow both also ordered westward, followed by the remaining portion of Baldwin's brigade. Only Hanson's 2nd Kentucky and 41st Tennessee were left behind to cover the lines east of Indian Creek to see if the enemy planned to follow. Fortunately for Buckner they did not, and he called the Kentuckians to join him as well. Later, additional regiments and artillery also moved to the right, including part of Simonton's brigade fresh from engaging Wallace's counterattack. One Mississippian noted how the firing on the right and the call to move westward created chaos in their lines, writing "all was now hurry and confusion." All were weary as well, one Tennessean writing, "cold and benumbed as were the troops, they double-quicked for 1½ miles through the mud, slush, ice, and snow."[34]

Some in the Federal army realized what was happening with the Confederate shift back to the west. A watching soldier of the 46th Illinois near the Indian Creek valley bemoaned the fact that he and other Federals had watched with loaded muskets "for nearly four hours, before we so much as even saw any of them." The Illinoisans soon moved forward to the high hill west of Indian Creek to support a battery and "in a few minutes a Reg of Secesh cam along on the run." The battery opened on them, but it was hit so hard by Graves's artillery, now also back in its original position, that it limbered up and moved away. The Illinoisan noted, "the next fire from the Fort came almost exactly where they had been." The Illinoisans lay down close to the ground and endured the barrage, which largely passed over their heads. Meanwhile, under cover of Graves's guns, Buckner continued to move his troops westward.[35]

Threatened with disaster, Major Turner galloped to the arriving regiments and told them of the crisis, whereupon Brown ordered the double quick. The Tennesseans were able to man their original lines from Graves's position to Porter's, but the west side of Porter's position was the trouble spot where Lauman's Federals were already breaking through. A trailing Hanson and his 2nd Kentucky arrived just as the Federals broke the line, and they did not have time to put all the companies into the trenches. As a result, the Kentuckians became part of the general chaotic withdrawal as well, even though Buckner considered them "as good a regiment as there was in the service." Buckner, in fact, had to "take at least twenty men by their shoulders and pull them into line as a nucleus for formation." It worked, but not before the Kentuckians fell back across a ravine to another bold ridge in front of Fort Donelson itself. At the same time, Turner and his three companies were losing the entrenchments on Lauman's front, although Colonel Head ordered more companies of his 30th Tennessee to the right to aid Turner.[36]

A new Confederate line soon formed on the next ridge, primarily when the 3rd and 18th Tennessee of Brown's brigade helped stabilize the position amid the heavy firing. Major Cheairs of the 3rd Tennessee, in fact, called this last engagement "the hardest fight and heaviest rattle of musketry that was had during the entire day." Buckner rode among his weary and cold troops to instill one last bit of morale among them, but actually the arrival of sections of Graves's and Porter's batteries, the latter having to be brought into action by hand after the horses had been shot down, as well as additional infantry regiments such as the 14th Mississippi and 42nd Tennessee, helped instill confidence more than anything else. Fire from a couple of the guns inside Fort Donelson that bore on the area of Smith's attack also helped. Captain Ross wrote that he "took charge of a small siege gun on the infantry fortifications of the fort, and played on the enemy's land forces over the heads of our troops." Another officer worked a howitzer "from another salient at the same time." Colonel Head, commanding the brigade at the fort itself, also ordered out the 49th and half of the 50th Tennessee (the other half remaining in the fort) to help sustain Buckner's forces on the new line. Unfortunately, in the double quick movement and subsequent fighting, Lieutenant Colonel Alfred Robb of the 49th Tennessee was mortally wounded with a shot through both lungs and Captain Porter "fell dangerously wounded by a Minie ball through his thigh while working one of his guns, his gunners being nearly all of them disabled or killed." Brigade commander Brown reported that command of the battery then went to Lieutenant John W. Morton, "a beardless youth, who stepped forward like an old veteran, and nobly did he emulate the example of his brave captain." As Porter was being carried away, he called to Morton, "don't let them have the guns, Morton." The young lieutenant responded, "no, Captain; not while I have one man left."[37]

The climax of the crisis was therefore emerging. A 14th Mississippi soldier described his fright when "I ran over the hill and Lo! The whole hill was moving with blue coats." That fright was also in the Union ranks, causing some to act before they thought. An Iowan noted several soldiers seeking any shelter they could find and getting behind Confederate canvas tents for cover and shooting from behind them. "It being natural for soldiers in battle always to get behind some tree or stump for protection," he wrote, "but to get behind their thin canvas tents to fire from, was too much."[38]

Amid the fright, another problem for Tuttle surfaced from the rear. By this time, the rest of Lauman's brigade had topped the hill, including the 52nd

Indiana of Cook's brigade but attached to Lauman for this action, as well as the 25th Indiana, 7th Iowa, and 14th Iowa. All of these regiments took casualties, Sergeant Major S. H. Smith of the 14th Iowa being "shot dead" next to Colonel William T. Shaw. Even so, they succeeded in driving away what was left of the Confederate line, James Parrott writing that they "drove the enemy like chaff before the wind." In a bit of confusion, however, the "cowardly," according to one 2nd Iowa soldier, 52nd Indiana was supposed to move to the left of the 2nd Iowa but came up in rear of the regiment and once atop the hill let out a volley. The Iowans were ahead testing Buckner's new line and received the brunt of the fire. C. F. Smith was still chagrined a couple of months later, writing that the Indianans did not do "as I had intended," but "from some unexplained cause, fired a number of fatal shots into their friends in front." The 2nd Iowa understandably could not stand fire in their rear as well as in their front from the re-forming Confederate line, and thus broke in some confusion, a wounded Tuttle writing a few days later, "I am not able to name the regiment which fired upon our rear, but I do know that the greater part of the casualties we received at that point was from that source, for I myself saw some of my men fall who I know were shot from the hill behind us." Fortunately, the trailing 25th Indiana soon appeared and helped stabilize the line, advancing to the left and into the ravine north of the Confederate trenches. The 2nd Iowa soon re-formed as well, behind the line of Confederate trenches on the first ridge, where they awaited ammunition. To stabilize the situation even more, Smith sent a staff officer to the rear to bring up artillery. He soon found engineer McPherson, who related, "General Smith's aide came galloping down in great haste, stating that the general wanted some more pieces of artillery." McPherson ordered forward a section of Stone's Missouri battery, and Lieutenant Thomas Haynes placed one gun in action at the trenches despite heavy artillery fire and was soon joined by the other. Stone's section of guns very much aided in holding the Confederate trenches, and the arrival of Cook's brigade on the right likewise helped stabilize the chaos.[39]

In fact, Cook's regiments had moved up the hill in the wake of Lauman's advance, although because of detachments the brigade was essentially down to two regiments. The 52nd Indiana was with Lauman and the 13th Missouri and 7th Illinois had earlier been sent to the right to cover different batteries left alone by McArthur's transfer the evening before. That left Cook with only the 50th Illinois and 12th Iowa, but he moved out with them behind and to the right of Lauman's assault, arriving at the top of the ridge with the Confederate breastworks under a heavy artillery fire. He received word that "the Stars and Stripes were flying over the main battery of the enemy," but he later determined that they "were raised by the rebels that we might be drawn within their reach." The brigade remained under heavy fire, but their numbers were soon augmented by the return of the 7th Illinois. Colonel Cook reported, "the discharges caused but little damage, overshooting us just enough to tear into shreds the colors of the Seventh Illinois." The two guns the Illinoisans had previously been defending also soon arrived in the Confederate trenches, and they took the Confederate line under fire as well, easing some of the tension among Cook's troops.[40]

In the 12th Iowa was Lieutenant David B. Henderson, a native of Scotland but destined to become an Iowa representative in Washington and speaker of the house. He was dreadfully wounded, a ball clipping his shoulder and "passing under his chin and cutting his throat nearly to the windpipe." Henderson survived and went on to become one of the most powerful men in the country; he used that power to preserve many of these Civil War battlefields as national parks. But for now, he was one of the many casualties lying in the bloodied snow at Fort Donelson.[41]

By the time Lauman and Cook stabilized their lines at the Confederate trenches, nightfall was not far away and Smith decided to forgo any further advances. The enemy was forming a new line on the next ridge, the 2nd Kentucky digging new rifle pits, and Parrott reported "they again made a stand and gave us all some warm work!" Smith paused: "as it was getting late I deemed it better to dispose of the troops for the night and be in readiness for a renewed assault on the morrow." He quickly prepared the men for the attack early the next morning, shouting to them, "we will advance and drive them from the next tier of works or loose every man in my division." To stabilize the line until then, Smith brought up more artillery, three pieces of Welker's battery to the cheers of the infantry, and placed Lauman's regiments in the Confederate trenches while holding Cook's in reserve down the ridge in the rear. McArthur's Illinois regiments had also arrived by this time, and Smith rode the lines of the 9th Illinois with head uncovered in a show of respect for what they had done earlier in the day; the Illinoisans responded with loud cheers. Smith then sent the 12th Illinois to the left "around the base of the hill toward the enemy's main work" while holding the rest of McArthur's brigade in reserve. In this position, Smith's brigades awaited more action, although the cold night that had to come first was very much dreaded. Smith fortunately noted, "the night was very cold, but without the cruel storm."[42]

So ended the fighting on the left, where Smith had actually advanced farther than Wallace and McClernand had on the right. Granted, it had been necessary for the two divisions on the right to stop the determined Confederate advance and then counterattack over nearly a two-mile distance just to get back to the outer works of the Confederate line. Smith had only faced three small companies on his front, but the fact remained that Smith had managed to break through the outer defenses of Fort Donelson. Floyd and Pillow rode over to the extreme right to survey the situation, and Pillow plainly saw the trouble that lay ahead:

> the position thus gained by the enemy was a most important and commanding one, being immediately in rear of our river batteries and field work for its protection. From it he could readily turn the intrenched work occupied by General Buckner and attack him in reverse, or he could advance, under cover of an intervening ridge, directly upon our battery and field work. While the enemy held the position it was manifest we could not hold the main work or battery.[43]

Nightfall may have saved the weary Confederates for a few more hours, but time was obviously ticking away.

By nightfall, it was very much a relief for McClernand and Wallace when they realized they had indeed shut the door on the Confederate escape attempt, with the Confederates still inside, and even more that Smith had broken the outer Confederate defenses. The fighting died down with darkness, however, McClernand noting that the dwindling fire indicated "the termination of a battle which had continued the greater portion of ten hours." He also reveled in the fact that the lost ground had been retaken "and the intrenched position of the enemy again invested, cutting off his hope of escape." Oddly enough, some of the troops that had shut the door were ordered to fall back during the night, Cruft's brigade receiving such orders while in the act of "deliberating upon an attack upon their fortifications," remembered Colonel Hugh B. Reed of the 44th Indiana. They were told to withdraw to the hill they had carried earlier. Ross's two regiments likewise fell back. The trap was closed, but the Federal advance had not made it watertight.[44]

Other odd thoughts also ran through the minds of the Union high command as darkness shrouded the field, thoughts that if put into action were capable of reversing all the hard fighting. Both McClernand and Wallace reported that Grant had some type of scheme in mind to move both divisions west of Indian Creek, perhaps for safety or perhaps for a greater assault the next morning. A somewhat more astute McClernand responded that "night had set in before compliance by my division with this order," but Wallace admitted: "satisfied that the general did not know of our success when he issued the direction, I assumed the responsibility of disobeying it, and held the battleground that night." In fact, Webster had personally delivered Grant's order and, when Wallace balked, simply stated, "I give you the order as he gave it to me." Wallace quipped, "very well, give him my compliments, and say that I have received the order." Webster smiled and returned to headquarters. Perhaps McClernand's political astuteness had saved him in the short term, but neither he nor Wallace would develop into Grant prodigies. In any case, it was fortunate that neither obeyed this questionable order.[45]

Grant never mentioned the plan anywhere again, and indeed there is very little commentary on exactly what he had in mind. Pulling the divisions west of Indian Creek would have been ludicrous and ran opposite to his earlier orders. Grant realized the larger importance of the situation when it was confirmed that the Confederate army had indeed withdrawn back inside the works instead of making an escape attempt. Now that he had the Confederate army bottled up, it was preposterous to throw that advantage away. It is possible that Grant's orders were misinterpreted in some way, or that Grant merely meant to fall back to a protected position and there restart what he had intended doing all along: to implement siege operations by first establishing a secure line around the enemy's position. If misunderstanding was the case, who to blame is not evident. However, the fact that all had been in action most of the day with nerves frayed could have played into Grant being less articulate than he should have been or the division commanders being more judgmental than was warranted.[46]

Whether Grant was on top of this particular situation or not, he had unquestionably been the key ingredient in the counterattacks in the afternoon and the surging Union fortunes at the end of the day. He had seemed to be everywhere, urging his men on personally amid the horrifying conditions. A humorous example even occurred in Grant's interaction with the problematic colonel of the 13th Missouri, Crafts J. Wright. Although the colonel had been assigned to support a battery, Grant found the regiment in line with knapsacks and blankets fully on. Wright noted, "to be better prepared, our men threw off their knapsacks and blankets at the suggestion of General Grant." Grant's thoughts can only be imagined, but it is known that he similarly instilled preparation and confidence in other regiments that day.[47]

In doing so, he set his forces up for the greatest victory of the war to date.

15

"We Got the Place"

The rainy and cold night of February 15 was anything but calm and peaceful. Like previous nights, brigades were on the move, decisions were being made, and fates were determined as the events at Fort Donelson drove toward a climax. And as usual in this dreary mid-February, it was all done in the worst of cold snaps. The fact that it was uncommon in Tennessee was as difficult to take as the conditions themselves, soldiers wondering why they had to endure not only the terrible war conditions but also one of the coldest periods of the war thus far. It was pure misery, made worse by the weariness brought on by days of constant effort.[1]

The cold was relentless. "The night was one of the coldest of the season," noted Colonel George F. McGinnis of the 11th Indiana, "but being within 800 yards of the enemy's guns, we were not, of course, permitted to build fires, although greatly needed." Others echoed his sentiments. One Mississippian described how "a keg of good (so called) whiskey" was acquired and divided into buckets set all along the line." Some "of the Washingtonian creed . . . [were] disappointed when they mistook it for water."[2]

Making matters even worse, February 15, unlike the previous days, had been one of long and almost continuous fighting, Pillow describing it by arguing that "such carnage and conflict has perhaps never before occurred on this continent." As a result, hundreds if not thousands of dead and wounded had been produced, and it fell mainly to the Federals who held the battleground to care for the casualties. While some Confederates had managed to gather their wounded and take them back inside the trenches for care, Forrest's cavalry in particular scouring the battlefield most of the afternoon, many wounded still lay on the Wynn Ferry Road ridge and on Smith's front. Basic humanity dictated that they be taken care of as quickly as possible even in the bitter cold weather conditions.[3]

The already exhausted Federals worked through the night to care for the wounded. Morgan L. Smith noted that the troops of his brigade carried "the wounded from the battle ground of the morning to the rear nearly all night." Most of these were wounded from the 8th, 11th, and 20th Illinois. Lew Wallace also described the Federal humanitarian efforts. "All night and far into the morning," he later wrote, "my soldiers, generous as they were gallant, were engaged in ministering to and removing their own wounded and the wounded of the First Division, not forgetting those of the enemy." While the wounded were certainly the top priority, many Union soldiers also sought to bury the dead even that night, although the task was difficult due to the frozen ground.[4]

Most of their horrible work was done with an eye toward ultimate victory on the Union side. Grant himself wrote the next day, "the troops encamped for the night, feeling that a complete victory would crown their labors at an early hour in the morning." Many reflected that they expected to assault the Confederate works at daylight, and they fully believed that they would be totally successful. This was especially the case on Smith's front, where he had already broken through the outer Confederate defenses and was nearing the actual fort itself. Smith gave brigade commander Cook simple directions during the night while discussing the Confederate position: "Take it, sir!" To strengthen his men as much as possible, Smith allowed them to withdraw somewhat from the lines to build fires, "which enabled them to rest more comfortably," he added.[5]

While optimism was prominent in the Federal ranks, no such feeling resided among the bone-weary Confederates. Pillow described them well when he wrote, "the command had been in the trenches night and day for five days, exposed to the snow, sleet, mud, and ice-water, without shelter and without adequate covering and without sleep." Not all of Grant's army had been engaged at all times, allowing them rest at differing periods. Conversely, all the Confederates except Heiman's command had moved and shifted several times throughout the last few days, consequently gaining little rest. While they were worse for the wear, they also were in a less defensive state, especially on the far right. Having lost their trenches and fallen back to a new defensive line, which Colonel Hanson actually argued "was a stronger one than the one lost," it still displayed the problems that were growing in his command: "every effort was made that night to construct defenses; but the men were so exhausted from labor and loss of sleep that it was utterly impossible." Illustrating that fact was Colonel Robert Farquharson of the 41st Tennessee, who admitted that after less than five minutes of sleep in four days, he "went to sleep standing up . . . in the trenches at the head of my regiment." He also described how his men "tumbled over where they stood." Another Tennessean wrote, "men were so exhausted that they actually slept in their position while shells were exploding around them and the deadly missile of the sharpshooters flying around their heads." He also noted, "during these four or five days I never had time to get water to wash my face and hands, being glad to get enough to drink. Having no canteens we were compelled to bring water in our cooking-pans." Perhaps one Mississippian summed it up best by writing that his unit "had been employed three days up to Friday night without rest, sleeping in the trenches by night, fighting by day, in the snow & sleet, poorly clad & poorly fed."[6]

Problems continually compounded inside Fort Donelson on the night of February 15, but no one knew they were only about to get worse, mainly due to the swirling incompetence of the Confederate high command.

While the Federal troops calmly awaited the renewal of fighting the next morning, there was indeed pure chaos inside the Confederate lines. A definite melancholy pervaded the Confederate troops concerning all the fighting to open the escape route and then simply throwing it away, but there was nevertheless a desire to do it all again and finally escape this trap that was growing more fatal by the hour. To discuss options, Floyd again called his division and brigade commanders into conference after dark, where they discussed the next day and what should be done. Oddly enough, not all were there; the often-ignored Bushrod Johnson was not included. Those present were testy; Pillow, never a fan of Buckner, mumbled, "if Buckner had have been up in time according to his promise, the enemy would have been routed." Tension precipitously increased when Buckner himself arrived and the two men were in the same room.[7]

According to Buckner, the prevailing thought was that "if the enemy had not reoccupied in strength the position in front of General Pillow the army should effect its retreat." This thought developed into a plan to attempt the same movement they had tried the day before—to shove open an escape route and move toward Nashville and safety. Orders accordingly went out around 1:00 AM for the brigades to mass once more on the extreme left flank "as noiselessly and cautiously as cats," one Confederate remembered. The tired Confederate soldiers therefore began the same process all over again, finding themselves in the same old field they had gathered in the night before and the afternoon before that. John C. Brown related that his orders were to gather on the left but to leave his artillery behind and spike it. Others noted that the wounded were to be brought along as well. The orders also called for "three days' cooked rations prepared, and, with knapsacks packed, to be ready to march." Even Adolphus Heiman went this time as well, under orders to march "without the least noise," and Bushrod Johnson reported that "the left wing was duly paraded in column of regiments outside of the left of our intrenchments by 3 a. m." The troops themselves were restless, however, one Texan describing how "we immediately took to our line of march, and had advanced some distance to an open field, when a halt was ordered. At this order the men became much dissatisfied. It was exceedingly cold and uncomfortable." A Mississippian described how they were "marched out in the same direction that we took yesterday. When we got outside our pits we were halted and stood there about 2 hours when we were about faced and marched back into our pits." Obviously, the uncertainty in the high command had not yet been resolved.[8]

Causing the change was word that the Federals had indeed followed up the Confederate withdrawal into the trenches the evening before. With that news, optimism for a Confederate offensive began to wane. Back at his headquarters, with staff officers coming and going, Pillow remembered, "we received intelligence from the troops in the trenches that they heard dogs barking around on the outside of our lines and they thought the enemy were reinvesting our position." Some soldiers also wondered if escape had not been achieved during the unarguable success of February 15, why it would work on February 16. The Confederate soldiers were also now even more tired than they had been twenty-four hours earlier, and there were major concerns about whether the army could fight another battle or march to safety in their depleted condition. The officers decided to send Forrest out to check to see exactly how tight the Union cordon was on the left.[9]

Forrest returned to his command and sent two men out on the far left. They returned, reporting that Federal troops were in their old positions and that fires could be seen. Other scouts sent along the Old Charlotte Road beside the river stated at the same time that the backwater was too deep for infantry to escape. The generals even called in a local citizen, Dr. James W. Smith, who expressed no optimism for an escape along the backwater route, saying the mud was "half-leg deep" and the water "saddle-skirt deep to the horses." Forrest reported that he believed that the fires seen by his scouts were only old campfires that "the wind, being very high, had fanned . . . into a blaze." The cavalryman reported this information to the generals, but they ignored it.[10]

With such news arriving at Pillow's headquarters at the Rice House, Floyd turned to Pillow and Buckner and asked, "well, gentlemen, what is best now to be done?" Neither answered, whereupon Floyd repeated the same question individually to Pillow and Buckner. The generals discussed the breakout attempt, for which the brigades were already on the move. Certainly, it would result in the destruction of the Confederate supplies. Worse, "it would result in the slaughter of nearly all who did not succeed in effecting their escape." "The question then arose," Floyd noted, "whether, in point of humanity and a sound military policy, a course should be adopted from which the probabilities were that the larger proportion of the command would be cut to pieces in an unavailing fight against overwhelming numbers." Apparently Buckner had the firmest grasp on reality (some argue despair) and by this time "regarded the position of the army as desperate, and that an attempt to extricate it by another battle, in the suffering and exhausted condition of the troops, was almost hopeless." He ran through his thinking: the troops were "worn down with watching, with labor, with fighting"; they were "frosted by the intensity of the cold"; they had no rations issued to them for days; they were out of ammunition; they were completely "invested"; the gunboats would maul the troops that remained; and all would be "assailed on their front, rear, and right flank at the same instant." The Kentuckian further argued that it would cost three-quarters of the troops to get one-quarter out, and "it was wrong to sacrifice three-fourths of a command to save one-fourth, and that no officer had a right to cause such a sacrifice." Buckner effectively argued that "the result would have been a virtual massacre of the troops, more disheartening in its effects than a surrender."[11]

The discussion soon turned to holding out within Fort Donelson, but Buckner said he could not do so. "Why can't you?" Pillow asked Buckner, adding, "I think you can hold your position; I think you can, sir." Pillow then suggested holding out one more day so that much of the army could be removed across the river by steamer. Buckner replied, "I know my position," and related that daylight would end the game either way: "I replied that my right was already turned, a portion of my intrenchments in the enemy's possession—they were in position successfully to assail my position and the water batteries—and that, with my weakened and exhausted force, I could not successfully resist the assault which would be made at daylight by a vastly superior force." Buckner did, however, concede that if it was correct that the entire need to hold at Fort Donelson was to give Albert Sidney Johnston time to cross the Cumberland River at Nashville, then it might be worth trying to hold, "as the delay even of a few hours" might benefit Johnston. When Floyd said (erroneously) that Johnston had crossed the river, Buckner was adamant: "it would be wrong to subject the army to a virtual massacre when no good could result from the sacrifice, and that the general officers owed it to their men, when further resistance was useless, to obtain the best terms of capitulation possible for them." Floyd later admitted, "I was myself strongly influenced by this opinion of General Buckner."[12]

With surrender virtually agreed upon, self-centeredness emerged. Floyd suddenly announced that he was wanted in the United States (actually under indictment for traitorous actions as secretary of war immediately prior to the conflict) and would not surrender with the command: "you know my position with the Federals; it wouldn't do; it wouldn't do." In fact, Grant later commented that indeed Floyd would, if captured, probably have been "tried for misappropriating public property, if not for treason." Instead, Floyd proposed taking his Virginia and Mississippi brigade and leaving on two steamers that were scheduled to arrive at the Dover landing about daylight. Pillow quickly jumped on the bandwagon and selfishly announced, "there were no two persons in the Confederacy whom the Yankees would prefer to capture than himself and General Floyd." He added, "I will never surrender the command nor will I ever surrender myself a prisoner. I will die first." Buckner countered that those were personal opinions and "personal considerations should never influence official action," to which Floyd agreed that it was personal but that he would not change his mind. Pillow asked Floyd about the propriety of escaping with him, Floyd responding that it was a question "for every man to decide for himself." Pillow asked Buckner the same thing, and Buckner replied as Floyd had, but added that he "regarded it as my duty to remain with my men and share their fate, whatever it might be." Buckner's lecture notwithstanding, Pillow announced his intention to escape as well.[13]

If it were not for the seriousness of the situation and the lives at stake, it would have been almost comical. (Charles F. Smith's son described the scene "as rich in humor as a capital comedy," adding that it was "a scene irresistibly ludicrous.") Buckner agreed that he would surrender if he had the command, so Floyd immediately turned over control to Pillow, who was next in line of authority, Floyd noting that he was taking his brigade with him. Pillow described the next action: "thereupon the command was turned over to me, I passing it instantly to General Buckner, saying I would neither surrender the command nor myself." A flabbergasted Buckner took the responsibility, asking for a pen, ink, and paper, as well as a bugler. In the meantime, he could not refrain from lecturing the two cowering generals before him, stating that "a capitulation would be as bitter to me as it could be to any one, but I regarded it as a necessity of our position, and I could not reconcile it with my sense of duty to separate my fortune from those of my command."[14]

Despite the lecture, Pillow left to devise a way out, but later returned, perhaps feeling guilty but more probably out of concern for his reputation. Some of his command asked him if the rumors of surrender were correct. Colonel W. A. Quarles of the 42nd Tennessee wondered if there was not a way to fight it out. Pillow replied, "no; I have fought against the surrender in the council, but my senior and junior in command overrule me. I can do nothing; I am powerless; the surrender had been positively determined on; had I my way I would fight the troops; I believe I could get them out." Pillow apparently had this conversation on his mind when he returned, and told Floyd and Buckner that "he wished it understood that he had thought it would have been better to have held the fort another day, in order to await the arrival of steamers to transport the troops across the river." He sat between Buckner and Floyd and made sure that they understood him. They replied, "we understand you, general, and you understand us," but Buckner again related the reasons why escape could not occur. He also reminded his fellow generals that if they did not decide the outcome by morning, Grant would decide it for them—in much bloodier fashion.[15]

After the fateful decisions had been made, the two top Confederate generals began to execute their escape even as their worn-out troops were trudging to implement a plan that the high command was no longer using. Fortunately, word soon went out to the troops to cease their deployment to the left and return to the trenches, for some another march of a mile or more. By this time, the Confederate soldiers were far too exhausted for much of anything else, however, especially a defense if Grant attacked at daylight. Plus, their artillery was already spiked. Brigade commander Brown noted that his troops were "wholly unable to meet any spirited attack from the enemy on Sunday morning."[16]

While the rank and file suffered, the generals planned their getaway. Pillow notified Gilmer around 3:00 AM that he was leaving and "invited me to join himself and staff, as they were not included in the proposed surrender." Gilmer may have had qualms about doing so and did not agree with surrender either, writing his wife a few days later about the breakout attempt: "*which was possible.*" Whether he said so in the deliberations is unknown, but he recognized that as a member of Johnston's staff and only on detail at the fort he was not part of the garrison. "This I accepted," he noted. Pillow and company also had to act fast as Buckner would soon recommend a six-hour "armistice" under a flag of truce. "Before this flag and communication were delivered," Pillow noted, "I retired from the garrison," although it was not easy. He and his staff paddled across the river on a "small hand flat, about 4 feet wide by 12 long" that one of his aides who lived in Dover somehow procured. Pillow, Gilmer, and staff quietly made their way across the river and fled to safety on the north side. The horses were later more easily taken away by one of the steamboats, while some of Pillow's slaves and his trunk were carried on the boats to Clarksville.[17]

Floyd's departure was more complicated. He first ordered Forrest to get him through the lines but then determined to leave by the two steamboats that arrived at the Dover landing before daylight, ironically loaded with men, corn, and ammunition. Consumed with taking his brigade with him, primarily his beloved Virginia regiments, he sent word for them to desist from their deployment on the far left and march to the landing, where they would board the boats. Floyd also sent word to Major William N. Brown of the 20th Mississippi to join him, as they were officially part of his brigade, having come from Virginia with Floyd's other regiments. Bushrod Johnson was surprised when the Mississippians turned for the landing but acquiesced when he learned it was on Floyd's orders.[18]

With the *General Anderson* and *John A. Fisher* now returned to Dover, Floyd told his commanders that they would embark in order of rank, which put the 20th Mississippi under Major Brown last. It thus fell to them to form what Brown called "a strong guard around the steamboat landing to prohibit stragglers from going aboard." Meanwhile, Wharton and McCausland led their regiments to the boats when they arrived, although rumors of the surrender caused many Confederate soldiers to "flock to the river, almost panic-stricken and frantic, to make good their escape by getting on board." Brown reported that his Mississippians "stood like a stone wall" in a semicircle around the landing, all the while expecting to board after the boats ferried the Virginia troops to the opposite bank. That was not to be. As daylight neared and Floyd became more anxious, one of the boats left upriver for Nashville. The other was still loading, but Buckner sent word that out of respect for the terms of capitulation and honor, he would surrender whatever was still at the landing at daylight and would even throw a "bomb-shell" into the boat if it was still present. The captain not surprisingly slipped away, Floyd yelling, "come on, my brave Virginia boys" but leaving the outraged Mississippians standing at the landing. The last boat actually pulled away with scarcely anyone on board, leaving some Virginians behind as well.[19]

Lower-level officers similarly fled without their men. Colonel John W. Head of the 30th Tennessee immediately began to scheme to get away when he realized surrender was coming. He later reported that his surgeon warned him that, suffering as he was from "exposure and threatened with pneumonia," imprisonment "might cost me my life." He went to Buckner and asked about his views of escape, to which Buckner, by this time likely tired of the flight of officers, responded that it was a decision Head had to make for himself. Head decided that he "could be of no service to my command or to the country by a surrender" and quickly made his way up the river to safety.[20]

Nathan Bedford Forrest escaped more forthrightly. Once he had returned from his reconnaissance and the generals had decided to surrender, Forrest flatly stated, "I neither could nor would surrender my command." The commanders gave him permission to cut his way out and for a time both Pillow and Floyd planned to go with him. Once the cavalryman had everything in order and was ready to move, he went to headquarters to get the generals, but Floyd told him Pillow had already left and that he was going by boat. Forrest then led his regiment and an assorted group of attached Confederates to the east, crossing the backwater of the river in Lick Creek, which was indeed "saddle-skirt deep," Forrest related. The cavalryman chose to cross at the little-used Smith Ford near Dr. Smith's house, the main crossing at Hay's Ford being deeper. With Forrest went the members of his Tennessee cavalry as well as some infantry. Not all the cavalry escaped, however, Forrest denigrating George Gantt in his report: he "failed to fight on Saturday, and refused to bring his men out with my regiment on Sunday morning when ordered to do so." Two Kentucky cavalry companies likewise refused to leave. Once across the creek, Forrest left a company as a rear guard, but no Federals followed. In fact, Forrest noted, "not a gun had been fired at us. Not an enemy had been seen or heard."[21]

Many others also escaped in much smaller groups or even individually as the minutes ticked on toward dawn. Forrest related that the road remained open as late as 8:00 AM that morning, and he firmly believed that the vast majority of the army could have gotten out. More interestingly, Dr. Smith's ten-year-old girl and a slave girl ferried soldiers across the backwater in a small boat. Many others crossed the river on anything that would float, such as rafts or skiffs. Captain Jack Davis of the 7th Texas managed to cross the river on a "flat-boat," while Henry Williford of the 20th Mississippi jumped into the river after the steamboat left and "clambered over the guards of the boat." Lieutenant Colonel T. N. Adair of the 4th Mississippi and his brother escaped across the river in a dugout canoe, while a couple of 15th Arkansas soldiers paid five cents apiece for a ferry across the backwater of Lick Creek. Bushrod Johnson later reflected that "many of [the] men and officers commenced to leave Fort Donelson as soon as they were aware of the proposed surrender, and hundreds of them no doubt have made their way to their home and to the Army. I have not learned that a single one who attempted to escape met with any obstacle." Johnson himself admitted that he too had thoughts of fleeing. "Almost immediately upon discovering that steps had been taken towards surrendering our forces, the question occurred to me whether the example of our commanding general [Floyd] was an appropriate one." Like Buckner, he "concluded to stay with the men, promote their comfort as far as possible, and share their fate."[22]

Such a noble sentiment was obviously not shared by the entire Confederate high command, or even by an unknown number of soldiers of all rank.

The surrender process was already starting as the Confederate generals and soldiers were making their way out of Fort Donelson. Once in command, Buckner took firm control, first ordering the troops that had massed on the far left back to their entrenchments. Bushrod Johnson, still full of fight, had earlier sent word that he was ready to move out in the attack; in response, he received notice from Buckner of the command change and to await orders from him. He then learned that Buckner was searching for him and went himself to Buckner's headquarters, where he learned they were to be surrendered. Buckner asked Johnson to "communicate with the enemy's pickets and to request that our forces should not be fired upon." Buckner also ordered a white flag flown over Fort Donelson. Having no such flag, "nobody expecting to need one," wrote a miffed soldier of the 50th Tennessee, the garrison ran up a white sheet. Buckner then sent a note by courier to Grant recommending an armistice so that terms could be discussed. He wanted the cease fire to last until noon, during which time "commissioners . . . [could] agree upon terms of capitulation."[23]

"In the morning, as day dawned," Jacob Lauman wrote, "we were attracted to the inner fortifications by the sound of a bugle, and saw the rebels displaying a white flag." One Iowan deduced, "I guess they were as much afraid we would attack them in the second breastwork as we were that they would attack us in the first." Lauman sent his 7th Iowa lieutenant colonel, James Parrott, to investigate, and Parrott met the Confederate, Major Nathaniel Cheairs of the 3rd Tennessee, who offered terms of the armistice. Lauman quickly sent the news up the chain of command to Smith. The division commander also met with Cheairs, telling him, "I make no terms with rebels with arms in their hands—my terms are unconditional and immediate surrender." The major protested that it would take him forty-five minutes to get permission from Buckner, but Smith cut him off: "I will give you one half hour to be back here with your answer—if not here in that time I will move on your works. Go." While the Confederate was gone, Smith sent a staff officer to Grant, who replied, "tell Smith that I approve all that he has done."[24]

In the meantime, Smith himself took the news to Grant's headquarters, but Grant's response was not what Buckner had expected, or what he desired. The oft-told story of Grant and Buckner having known each other before the war and Buckner even bailing Grant out by covering his debts during one of the latter's lowest points obviously did not enter into Grant's thinking. Nor did the more memorable moments such as their three years together at West Point or their service in Mexico, during which both, with others, went to climb Mount Popocatepetl, Buckner making it to the top while Grant turned back with many others. Now, Grant was in no mood to be merciful, and even if he had been, Smith was pushing him to be firm. When Grant read Buckner's note, the crusty old division commander Smith blurted firmly, "No terms with traitors." Grant laughed and sat down to write his response, showing it to Smith with a frank, "General, I guess this will do." Smith responded, "it could not be better." Grant thus sent one of his most famous communications, writing Buckner: "no terms except unconditional and immediate surrender can be accepted," adding somewhat strongly: "I propose to move immediately upon your works." Consequently, without commissioners or even a cease fire, Buckner was out of options as daylight neared. His men were not yet back in their trenches, including the water batteries, and some of the guns had been spiked when left for the breakout attempt. Buckner described "a degree of confusion, amounting almost to a state of disorganization" attending everything. Further resistance was obviously out of the question.[25]

Buckner quickly decided he had no other choice but to "accept the terms demanded by our ungenerous enemy." He told Grant as much, writing that the situation "compel[s] me, notwithstanding the brilliant success of the Confederate arms yesterday, to accept the ungenerous and unchivalrous terms which you propose." Even if the terms were really as ungenerous as Buckner claimed, the world would not see it that way. Grant's immediate and unconditional surrender stance soon made him a Union hero.[26]

The official surrender was accordingly done, as one Texan phrased it, "between daylight and sunup." Orders went out for the Confederate troops to raise the white flag; John C. Brown, who one of his regimental commanders described as "mad as a hornet," indicated that his orders were to "display flags of truce from the front of our works." Clearly, he did not agree. The individual units were surprised as well, indicating that they perhaps had more fight in them than Buckner had thought. Colonel Palmer of the 18th Tennessee wrote that he had moved all the way to Dover and even met "Generals Floyd, Pillow, and Buckner, all of whom were still there, and who ordered me to halt and await further directions." He reported, "it was . . . well understood among all parties that the object of the march was to evacuate our entire position." Then he received orders to go back to his trenches, another mile and a half back, where Brown told him they were surrendering. "This was the first notice of that fact," Palmer wrote, "and was thus received on Sunday morning at 5.30 o'clock." Another member of the brigade described "the white flag floating where the 'Bonnie Blue' had waved. . . . Then our hearts sank within us." One Texan added, "when the intelligence of our surrender was communicated to the troops there was a general feeling of indignation, mingled with surprise, among all. The men were frantic to be permitted to fight their way out." Timothy McNamara of the 4th Mississippi agreed. The news "fell like a thunderbolt among the men. We had whipped them for three days and on the day before drove them like sheep before us." Perhaps most surprised was Colonel Robert Farquharson of the 41st Tennessee, who after little sleep in four nights finally gained some rest this night; he noted he "awoke to find myself a prisoner." A few, particularly the younger soldiers, feared they "would be massacred, for we had never considered the matter of surrendering."[27]

One by one, the shocked Confederate regiments stacked arms; "oh, it was hard to see the enemy take possession of the guns we had handled so well," one Tennessean wrote, "and the beautiful banner presented by the ladies of Giles and Maury." A momentary resurgence of enthusiasm hit Simonton's brigade when it received orders to move forward, but the excitement quickly left when it was found that the move was to man the works in order to surrender. Perhaps most bitter were the men of the 20th Mississippi, who despite "the orders and promises of General Floyd" had been left to surrender while the Virginians got away. Major Brown illustrated the rage: "we realized the sad fate that we had been surrendered, and the regiment stacked arms in perfect order, without the least intimidation, but full of regret." Others in the regiment simply refused to hand over their arms and equipment: "rather than surrender their flag which was so much loved it was buried on the bank of the Cumberland River and their guns thrown into the river." Federal brigade commander Jacob Lauman corroborated the occurrence, writing his brother several days later, "they either destroyed or secreted their flags, as none could be found." Others damaged their weapons: "some broke their guns others threw them in the river & many raved & cursed[.] I gave vent to a small oath for which 'I hope' the recording angel dropped a tear upon it as he wrote it down & blotted it out forever against me." Colonel Joseph Drake, commanding a brigade, broke his sword and threw it into the river rather than have it captured. A Federal later described many muskets "with broken stock and bent barrels, evidently having been struck against trees to prevent their further use." Another described how some of the Federals "fished out several revolvers & guns." In one of the saddest episodes, one unfortunate Confederate did not destroy his sword but lost it anyway. Federal Harley Wayne described telling a Confederate officer to give up his sword, to which he protested, saying his father had carried it with him at the Battle of New Orleans. Wayne told him bluntly that "he had forfeited his right to the relic by his treason," and having no recourse, the Confederate turned it over. Wayne inwardly felt bad:

"I heard his deep down sigh as he unbuckled it from his waist and handed it over and could but pity the man."[28]

The Federals were just as surprised as the Confederates at the appearance of the white flags. James B. Weaver of the 2nd Iowa had just gone out looking for his company's wounded: "found Job Dunn J. Z. Neidy, Jas. Duckworth, A. J. Patterson Wm. Drake, and Joseph Rhodes laying upon the field dead, Phillip Stoner, our orderly with his arm broken so as to Compel amputation. Pirtle and John Jones wounded severely in the groin, Fouts with a leg shot all to peaces since amputated. Wert Stevens Gabriel Johnson, Sloan, Kinnick, Collier severely wounded and many others shot though not so severely." In the midst of the carnage, a bugle suddenly erupted and white flags appeared, Weaver thinking "it was Sabbath morning and we supposed they wanted to bury their dead." Colonel John Davis of the 46th Illinois gave his men a speech early that morning, informing "us that we were assigned to a column for assault on the fortifications and he trusted no man would falter but bravely do his duty and win glory for the regiment." They then began marching toward their assault point when word arrived of the surrender. At first they did not believe the news, although all were soon relieved that it was true. One Iowan noted, "my heart leaped with joy for the times indicated a verry bloody time that day if they had not surrendered."[29]

On the far right, Lew Wallace was also preparing to attack "about breakfast time," having moved Cruft's brigade up from its rearward position as well as placing Thayer's larger brigade on Cruft's right near Dudley's Hill. Then a Confederate courier with a white flag appeared, Major W. E. Rogers of the 3rd Mississippi. Wallace sent a staff officer with Rogers to Grant to inform him of the surrender and ordered the rest of his division forward to take possession of the works. This he did compassionately: "I want the business done as delicately as possible. Not a word of taunt—no cheering." His division then took possession of the Confederate trenches on the right, but Wallace had by this time taken it upon himself to ride into the Confederate lines. He rode on into Dover by himself, past what one Federal described as "regiment after regiment of rebels, standing in line, with the white flag waving at the center of each regiment." The obviously outnumbered Wallace began to have second thoughts. "They eyed me sullenly," he later wrote, "and several times it crossed my mind that I was doing an imprudent thing." He nevertheless went on, and eventually met Buckner at the Dover Hotel.[30]

Wallace and Buckner, like Grant, had known each other prior to the war, the Indianan knowing the rest of Buckner's military family as well. Buckner and his staff were at breakfast, and when Wallace arrived, Buckner stated, "General Wallace, it is not necessary to introduce you to these gentlemen; you are acquainted with them all." Buckner then nonchalantly asked Wallace to join them "while waiting for General Grant." Wallace remembered how they all then "engaged, eating and talking the battles over." Humorously, in the midst of the wait Commander Benjamin Dove, commanding the ironclad *Louisville*, also arrived at the landing and was ushered in as well. He talked with Wallace a bit but then left to return to his gunboats. Wallace remarked to an aide, "the navy seemed to be abroad very early; they were looking for swords, perhaps."[31]

In the meantime, other Federals also began to march in and take possession of the Confederate fort, one Illinoisan marveling at "the long lines of infantry marching in from every direction." Wallace's brigades moved into the fortifications on the right, and Charles Kroff of the 11th Indiana wrote how, contrary to Wallace's orders, "our troops gave cheer after cheer, threw their hats in the air, while the rebels looked grim and sullen." Another noted that even "Colonels threw their hats in the air." Much of the ill will soon departed, however, and the same Indianan then noted how "Union and rebel soldiers met and talked over, in a friendly manner the last 3 day's fighting." Others were not so enthused, one 3rd Mississippi soldier describing how the Federals immediately broke the surrender terms regarding private property, including the regiment's brass band. The Federals took most of the pieces, arguing that "you captured one of ours yesterday," meaning the 11th Illinois's instruments. The enraged Mississippians were in little position to argue, one Indianan writing of the reaction when he took a piece of meat: "you should have seen the look on the Mississippians face that he gave me when I took it!"[32]

In the center, McClernand noted that he was likewise preparing to attack when the "welcome intelligence" came of the surrender, mostly through white flags made of torn tents hoisted above the Confederate works. Will Wallace rode ahead toward the Confederate trenches when the news arrived, his brigade following once formed. He met his regiments at the Confederate works, telling a staff officer, "Rumsey, it is true; their arms are stacked and they stand behind them." Rumsey was forever taken by the "look on his face [which] showed a feeling far deeper than words could express; seldom have I seen a more expressive face than his." Wallace moved into the Confederate lines with his brigade, even though a staff officer from Smith's command ordered him to stop. Wallace continued on, barking, "General Smith is not my commander." He turned to Rumsey and stated, "I am going, to the fort; I commenced this battle, and it is my right."[33]

McClernand led the rest of the division into Fort Donelson and down to the water batteries and the nearby small landing. He raised the US flag inside Fort Donelson and had a "national salute" of thirteen guns fired from Taylor's battery as the US flag went up. Lieutenant Colonel Frank L. Rhoads of the 8th Illinois displayed his pride when he reported that the regiment, hit so hard the day before, marched "full of pride" into Fort Donelson. A satisfied Will Wallace likewise took it all in, telling his staffer, "Rumsey, this is glorious." The staff officer agreed but mentioned how sad it was that some were no longer there "who, forty-eight hours ago, were with us." Wallace agreed: "Yes, but they died in a noble cause." Another Illinoisan stated it more bluntly: "many of our troops were killed, but we got the place."[34]

The Federals also began to probe forward on C. F. Smith's front, obviously wanting the honor of being first inside the fort. Smith sent the 2nd Iowa into the Confederate lines first at "the post of honor," they planting their colors on the Confederate trenches as the gunboats fired a salute. Future presidential candidate Weaver wrote home, "here I wept like a child." Jacob Lauman also led his brigade in amid "drums beating and colors flying." He noted the Confederate troops "drawn up in line, with their arms in great heaps, and looked quite woe-begone, I assure you, as the victors passed along." Not all were so enthused, however; one Federal described the march into the fort as "a lengthy and tiresome parade—as useless as it was irksome." Both Lauman and Colonel Cook nevertheless wrote of the cheering from the troops. The Confederates were nonappreciative, one Tennessean writing that they heard and then "beheld the head of a Yankee regiment with streaming banners making for the center of the town. We held our places and looked." Even then, the Confederate could not give the impressive scene its total due. The same Tennessean said about the cheers of the Federals: "the Yankees never during the entire War learned how to utter a decent yell. Their attempts at it were simply ridiculous, not to say hideous."[35]

The gunboats likewise reacted to the surprise. Commander Dove received a note from Grant, and he immediately prepared the *St. Louis* and *Louisville* for action, sending the wounded to transports. He was soon "steaming up toward the batteries at Fort Donelson, both vessels cleared for action." When he neared the fort, the Confederates displayed two white flags. Dove boarded a smaller tug and with a white flag hoisted on it ran in to the bank, where a Confederate officer met him and "offered me his sword, which I declined to receive, thinking it most proper to consult with General Grant." Dove took the officer on board and continued to the Dover landing, where he found Lew Wallace already at the hotel. Even the steamboats in the river joined in the celebration. One Illinoisan remembered that "some [were] playing 'Yankee Doodle' some 'Columbia' and others 'America.'" Others reported hearing the tune "Dixie Land."[36]

The Federal high command also soon arrived in Dover. Smith rode to the hotel and refused Buckner's outstretched hand, to which Buckner responded, "General Smith, I believe I am right." Smith retorted, "that is for God to decide, not me, for I know I am right." Grant himself arrived a few minutes later, no doubt chagrined that not only had a political general beat him to the site, but the navy had beaten him again as well. It had taken him a while to ride from the left of the Union lines to Dover, having had some interesting experiences along the way. Major Cheairs later claimed to have met Grant, who asked how many troops were in the Confederate army. Cheairs responded about seven or eight thousand, to which Grant, likely without thinking, blurted that it was a lie. Cheairs took exception and removed his coat, amazingly challenging Grant to a fistfight. Cheairs noted that he was a prisoner indeed, but his father "taught me to take the lie from no man, and if you will get off your horse and take off your shoulder strap (of rank), I will give you the worst beating a man ever had." Grant wisely withdrew his comment and that satisfied Cheairs's sense of honor. Even so, Grant had the last laugh, of course. Cheairs and the others were prisoners, soon headed to prison camps in the various Northern states.[37]

Grant then went on through the teeming Confederates, one account even describing how John C. Brown stopped a mounted lieutenant on horseback who intended to shoot Grant. Eventually, Grant, perturbed at Wallace's preempting him, met Buckner at the hotel in Dover. Apparently there was no formal surrender of swords or any of the show that Grant disdained (one Confederate erroneously described such a scene many years afterward). Another described the meeting as "formal, though after the style of Military men." By then all ill will seemed to be gone and the two talked like old friends. Grant asked where Floyd and Pillow were, Buckner responding that they had fled. Grant retorted, "I am very glad to hear that because if they are men of that type they will do me much more good in command of Confederate troops than as prisoners." Grant remembered Buckner saying, "if he had been in command I [Grant] would not have got up to Donelson as easily as I did." Grant retorted "that if he had been in command I should not have tried in the way I did."[38]

Grant was also kind in many other ways, despite one Confederate describing "a very grave military looking official [who] passed . . . [and] was pointed out as Gen. U. S. Grant." He noted Grant "looked as sour as a crabapple." Grant told Buckner that he remembered his kindness years previously when he was out of money in New York, and he offered to cover his expenses now. Buckner declined, saying he was well cared for, but he did have other concerns for his men. He asked Grant to detail a staff officer to see after them continually, but Grant responded that he had just set up his staff, it was very unorganized, and he could not spare anyone right now. Buckner told him his staff was very organized and asked if it could be put under his command, which Grant accepted: "I know you well enough to realize that you will not take advantage of this and will therefore give instructions that any orders which you issue on that subject will be obeyed by my troops as though I had issued them myself." Buckner's son, himself a military officer, later noted, "this presents the remarkable picture of a recently captured general issuing orders to the members of his captor's command."[39]

Grant's staff and troops were indeed busy. McClernand thought to send Dickey's Illinois cavalry back out to the perimeter to prevent any Confederates from wandering away. In the ensuing hours, they brought in numerous wayward Southerners. Others were also told to watch any escape, particularly Leonard Ross, who had moved his small brigade up near the river on the right; McClernand wanted no Confederates to escape the way Forrest had. Meanwhile, McArthur's brigade was tasked with guarding the nearly fourteen thousand Confederate prisoners and captured stores in Dover. Amazingly, the Federals quickly made sense of the situation even as they took stock of what they had done. One was astonished that they had been so successful, describing Fort Donelson: "as strong as the famous pass of Thermopaly. I don't see how in the world we ever took it."[40]

"This has been a day full of sad offices," Will Wallace wrote his wife, "collecting and caring for the wounded, burying the dead and doing all that could be done to allay the distresses of those who suffered in the terrible fight." Indeed, the work of repairing the damage done to armies, bodies, and numerous other items began immediately after the fighting ended and continued for several days. One of the worst was writing home to tell friends or family of the death of loved ones. Wallace continued his morbid letter, writing, "among the saddest duties is one just accomplished, of writing to Mrs. Erwin & Mrs. Capt. Shaw letters of condolence on the death of their husbands." He added, "thank God, Ann, no friend has been called to do this sad duty for me." Jacob Lauman cut a lock of Captain Slaymaker's hair for his family, fearing that the body would not be in any condition for viewing when it got home. Similarly, a 2nd Iowa captain wrote a father, "William fell inside the entrenchments while nobly and bravely fighting for the Union of the States. He died shouting aloud for the Union. His last words 'Hurrah for the Union' were heard distinctly by his comrades. He died with the name of his country trembling on his lips."[41]

In addition to the letters, the prisoners and wounded took first priority, the prisoners because of sheer numbers and the possibility of escape. The wounded were obviously a concern because of the weather and the good chance that they would die. "The wonder was to find any of them alive," Lew Wallace noted. The roaming Union soldiers did indeed find many alive, along with an assortment of other materials; one 11th Illinois musician found the regiment's cornets, "pounded over the logs and hammered flat." He concluded, "they evidently had no use for silver cornets." Surgeons, band members, and chaplains all cared for the wounded, something they had been doing for days now. Will Wallace wrote that his chaplains were "indefitatiguable in their attentions to the wounded and in collecting and burying the dead."[42]

The wounded were sheltered, one Illinoisan said, "in every house in Dover." Unfortunately, this early in the war the Federal surgeons were a mixed lot. Most were very conscientious, working for twenty-four hours or more at the height of the fighting. Others were less able, and Surgeon Charles Tompkins of the 17th Illinois wrote home, "our wounded I am sorry to say are only tolerably well cared for," concluding, "there is as much red tape connected with the Medical department as any other." Surgeon Thomas Fry complained that he received no medicine, food, or bandages to work with, and his surgeons had to use only what rudimentary tools they had in their mobile packs. Other surgeons had a different type of trouble: "Dr. Sexton, an efficient and skillful surgeon when sober, was so much under the influence of liquor for twenty-four hours as to be incapable of discharging the responsible duties of his office." Fortunately, aid soon arrived from the North in the form of the US Sanitary Commission as well as women nurses, but one surgeon worried, "what was to be done with those women for the night?"[43]

Many of the Confederate wounded had been sent by boat to Nashville before the surrender, one Virginian shot through the body remembering that "a soldier in the struggles of death fell across my body and died there. He lay on me a long time for there was no one to remove him and I was to weak from the loss of blood to do it." Another described, "the scene on the boat . . . was truly heart rendering, one would beg the doctor to dress his wound, another would call in his dying moments, for a Mother, a Sister, or brother, so beseechingly that when I think of it, I can't help but shed tears." The Federals faced the largest task, however. "As soon as I got possession of Fort Donelson I commenced sending the sick and wounded to Paducah," Grant wrote. "No distinction has been made between Federal and Confederate sick and wounded." Fry railed against moving the wounded too early, desiring rather to leave them in the local houses until they became stable enough to transport. Such postoperative care was unfortunately not instituted until later in the war, and many consequently suffered unnecessarily at Fort Donelson. Fry cited the example of sending the steamboat *Tuts* northward crowded with wounded but with no surgeons onboard to watch the cases. Fry called this "unwise and highly injudicious, endangering the lives of those who might otherwise recover." Nevertheless, the wounded were all sent northward as quickly as possible.[44]

The prisoners posed a far different problem, simply because of their numbers. There were fairly few Union prisoners at issue, and those were taken throughout the siege to Nashville and points farther south. Union prisoners taken to Nashville were given "Cahn-Pones," one noted, and "nothing ever tasted sweeter." Ladies of Nashville also brought "refreshments, both of whom and which were received with great gusto." Even Mrs. John Bell came and stated that "had my husband been elected this war would never have taken place." One Federal prisoner added, "for the first (and only) time, I most heartily wished he had been."[45]

More problematic was the sheer number of Confederate prisoners, some actually from the Dover area; Lieutenant Colonel H. C. Lockhart of the 50th Tennessee related that he had been taken prisoner "within one mile of my home." One Illinoisan wrote that they had "thirteen thousand live rebels," and another wrote his mother that he had "captured 4 horses and 6 revolvers 5 sabres and 1 colnel." Grant initially issued orders that all prisoners be corralled near Dover "under their respective company and regimental commanders." There, he offered two days' rations "preparatory to [them] embarking for Cairo." He also allowed the prisoners to keep their clothing, blankets, and private property that could be carried on their persons, while the officers were allowed their side arms. That said, Bushrod Johnson noted instances when "some officers at least were disarmed as they passed aboard the transports." A Tennessean also described the enemy coming around "buying what they could not steal." Even so, Grant was able to report that "generally the prisoners have been treated with great kindness, and I believe they appreciate it." It was indeed a trying time for these Confederates and kindness was certainly cherished. One Tennessean displayed the dejectedness: "I wrote a hasty note to my wife, gave it to a citizen who hoped to be allowed to return home, and resigned myself to my fate."[46]

One episode particularly showed Grant's conciliatory attitude. A probably drunk Union soldier paraded in front of a large group of Confederate prisoners in a woman's bonnet and cape. Although the Confederates laughed, Grant took exception and had the man, still in female attire, hung by his thumbs barely on his tiptoes onboard the headquarters boat. Another example of the kindnesses was the ability to write home. One Confederate, Horace Lurton of Kentucky (who went on to become a US Supreme Court justice), wrote his mother, "I am well and not wounded except a slight graze on my leg not at all painful. I will write when opportunity occurs. We will probably be sent to Illinois." Others had special favors done by the Federals. Although many Northerners were keeping Confederate horses (Colonel Valentine Bausenwain of the 58th Ohio reported that "our company officers walk no more; they are supplied with secesh saddles, horses, and mules, and happiness beams from their eyes and lips,") James B. Weaver of the 2nd Iowa obtained a fine horse from a Confederate captain in return for him sending the Confederate's sister another horse. Weaver agreed to do so and told his wife, "I call him after his owner, Capt. Graves."[47]

Even more conciliatory, Grant allowed Buckner to address many of the men before they left. Buckner told the 14th Mississippi:

I could have made escape but I preferred staying to make your lot easier if possible and friends I leave you, remember you still have a country. And bear your captivity with fortitude. Do nothing to sully your bright name and the day is not far distant I trust when I may again lead you to the charge as I did on Saturday — Gentlemen I know you will not forget your homes, and your country, I will do all in my power for you. Goodbye friends.

Buckner tipped his cap and the prisoners responded with loud yells, which prompted the Federals to stop the shouting.[48]

Still, there were escapes among so many prisoners. Buckner asked Grant to allow his men to bury their dead, and Grant later admitted that some Confederates just walked off while doing so. Oddly enough, some Southerners came to Grant himself and admitted that they were tired of war and wanted to go home and would never fight again. "I bade them go," he wrote. The rest remained in a pitiful state of boredom, waiting on the Federals to do something with them. One member of the 14th Mississippi related, "we had nothing to do but to stand around our fires and talk of our experiences and narrow escapes during the four days carnage."[49]

After long hours of waiting "in the mud . . . first on one foot and then on the other," the prisoners were "marched in long lines from their camps to the landing to be sent to Cairo." "They are a strange and motley crowd," Will Wallace wrote Ann, "but they shoot terribly sharply." More humiliation occurred at the landing, where one Illinoisan described how "the steep bank soon became very slippery while this trampsing was going on and raining in sheets, and the clumsy fellows commenced to negotiate down trip on their backs, knocking the feet from under others as they went, sometimes two or three deep at the bottom." Then, the trip northward proved agonizing, the men packed as they were on the boats like "freight," one chaplain noted. Another Confederate described how the steamboats "appeared to be rotten from bottom to top," adding, "we were in much more danger on the decks of these old boats than we were when we were facing the Yankee bullets." There was some presumed firing at the prisoners, such as when guards shot into the water after they thought a Confederate had jumped ship trying to escape; they later found out that a dog had jumped overboard. More conspiratorial, one Tennessean wrote later, "the capture of the boat was freely talked of an would have been done if it had been attempted, but the whole of the lowlands were covered with water and if we had captured the boat we could not have made our escape."[50]

As the notion to take over their steamboat indicated, there was fight left in the Confederates, over and above the "cocky" rooster Jake that served as the 3rd Tennessee's mascot (along with Frank, the dog mascot of the 2nd Kentucky). They still had a lot to be proud of, one Mississippian writing, "we felt that they had the whistle but had payed for it dearly." Many took heart at how well the Confederates had fought; Colonel Farquharson was amazed, noting that the soldiers fought "admirably for troops only a month or so from the plough." Federal Jacob Lauman wrote that "such a lot of humanity I never saw before—all butternut color; but they can shoot, as many of our boys can testify." Moreover, the Confederates were apparently still ready to fight, if prompted; at one point John C. Brown almost got into a fistfight with Major Wesley Boyd of the late-arriving 52nd Illinois. On another occasion an Illinoisan took three "colts revolvers" from Colonel Bailey, all while the colonel was "denying that he was armed." One Iowan was amazed that "after being so badly whipped here, [they] did not hesitate to say that one of their soldiers was good for half a dozen of ours. I think they will begin to lose conceit of themselves by and by." Still, open conflict was rare, and one Iowan even related, "they were sociable fellows and we were on good terms with them before they left."[51]

Grant eventually sent all but a few prisoners northward, the commissary at Cairo listing rations issued for 14,623 Confederates. Grant decided while sending the bulk of Confederate prisoners to Northern camps that he would "retain enough of the enemy to exchange for them." The prisoners accordingly moved by boat to St. Louis and Alton, citizens along the way at times throwing tobacco and fruit to the prisoners on the boats and schoolchildren giving the "Rebel Yell." Numerous other odd experiences also occurred, such as one day when "a genial sun for a few minutes caused so many of us to go to the sunny side of the boat." One Confederate noted, "the captain was alarmed." Once they disembarked from the boats, the prisoners moved by train to Chicago and other prison sites, but even the trips by rail were troublesome in blizzard conditions. The Confederates were certainly an odd-looking sight to Northerners who came to view them every chance they had, carrying as they did their "camp kettles, skillets, ovens, frying pans, coffee pots, tin pans, tin cups, and plates. We had them on our heads, on our backs, swinging to our sides and in our hands." Chicagoans, for example, turned out by the thousands to see the defiant prisoners who whistled Dixie as they marched from site to site, eventually to Camp Douglas; others went to Camp Chase in Columbus, Ohio, and Johnson's Island on Lake Erie. The prisoners sometimes cheered Jefferson Davis when Union citizens decried them. "Some would curse us and call us poor ignorant devils," remembered M. A. Ryan of the 14th Mississippi. "Some would curse Jeff Davis for getting us 'poor, ignorant creatures' into such a trap." The children who had obviously been told that Confederates were monsters were heard to ask, "where are their horns and tails? I don't see them."[52]

Back at Fort Donelson, the dead, while past help, had to be attended to as well, although the cold weather made this duty somewhat less time-critical than at summer battles. Still, the battlefield was by all accounts a terrible spectacle: "it was the most horrid sight I ever beheld & I hope I may never see such another one," Charles Tompkins wrote his wife. George Durfee noted, "the damned rebels stripped our dead of their boots those that had them on and turned their pockets inside out." Although officers were often sent home for burial, the rank and file were buried right on the field. George Carrington described the burial of the 11th Illinois's dead: "a trench six feet wide was dug and the dead laid in side by side. They were then covered with blankets. A few words by the chaplain. The trench is then filled with earth. 76 were buried in this one grave on the line where they fell." Members of the regiments cut headboards to identify the dead, and many poignant moments occurred during the doleful duty. Carrington noted a member of the 45th Illinois beholding the body of his brother: "I saw him stand and look at his Brother lying there dead, He said nothing and soon turned away and left him there." At the same time, details of Confederates buried their dead on the battlefield, and continued all the way until February 18. Luther Cowan noted that even several days later, "we find them piled up in the woods, old houses and thrown into holes." Perhaps most troubling, various newspapers in the North carried the story of the Federals finding several Union dead in the Dover jail without wounds. Most surmised they had been there for months and were either starved to death or poisoned.[53]

Grant also had to do something with all the captured stores at Dover, which one Confederate described as "presenting nothing but one consolidated scene of confusion and strife." Grant was amazed at the haul: "the amount of supplies captured here is very large," he wrote, "sufficient, probably, for twenty days for all my army. . . . Of rice I don't know that we will want any more during the war." The only item that was scarce seemed to be coffee. There were also plenty of weapons of all sorts piled up in great heaps, one Federal wrote, but they were so deficient that the government had no use for them.

Federals could walk by and get any they wanted. Occasionally, a soldier would examine a weapon and throw it back on the pile only to have it "go off sending a bullet singing off in most any direction." As in many cases during the war, Grant also had to issue explicit orders to keep his soldiers from looting captured stores or private items. He did so with humor: "pillaging and appropriating public property to private purposes is positively prohibited."[54]

It is amazing that anyone could retain a sense of humor amid so much suffering.

16

"THE TROPHIES OF WAR ARE IMMENSE"

The USS *Carondelet* arrived at Cairo in a heavy fog on February 17, one observer noting the ironclad actually "passed below the town unnoticed, and had great difficulty in finding the landing." While slowly moving back toward Cairo blowing her whistle, numerous people in the town thought it was a Confederate gunboat raiding from below. Once Commander Henry Walke landed, however, fright turned to joy as the gunboat brought news of the surrender of Fort Donelson, including the capture of fifteen thousand prisoners and two generals. But all who saw the gunboat knew it had been a tough victory; one *Cincinnati* sailor wrote that the *Carondelet* looked "very much the same as we did" but noted the small loss of life "shows that the boats can stand a great battering without much loss."[1]

News quickly spread from Cairo as Union commanders sent word up the chains of command. Cullum wrote Halleck, "the Union flag floats over Fort Donelson." Foote sent word to Gideon Welles in Washington: "the trophies of war are immense and the particulars will soon be given." The news spread elsewhere as well. The Iowa House of Representatives was in the middle of a roll call vote when, around 11:00 AM that morning, a local newspaper editor burst into the chamber "in a manner betokening intense excitement." He made his way hurriedly to the speaker's stand, at which point Speaker Rush Clark shouted, "Gen. Grant has captured Fort Donelson!" Pandemonium erupted, one eyewitness writing that "the members sprang to their feet with the wildest cheers and hurrahs that ever woke the echoes of the Old Capitol building. . . . the members went fairly wild, hugging each other, shaking hands, cheering, and in every possible manner giving way to expressions of extravagant delight." The commotion was so loud that the neighboring senate heard the uproar, and senators, "startled by the noise and confusion," began to enter the chamber wondering what was happening. When informed of the news, they also joined in the celebration. Iowans had played a major role in the victory and it was worth celebrating. Yet the victory came at a cost, and that news similarly soon arrived in Des Moines. An eyewitness grimly noted, "it was but a few hours until joy over the great victory gave place to sorrow for the fate of the gallant dead."[2]

The celebrations that occurred in Iowa were but one example of the process playing out all over the North, eventually as far as the west coast. News spread in every direction, correspondent Alexander Simplot noting that the report "flash[ed] over the north like a glorious gleam of sunshine following the gloom of the Bull Run disaster." Students at Oxford, Ohio's, Miami University were ecstatic: "we went around with 4 or 5 drums and tin pans and serenaded every person in town." In Chicago, where citizens quickly raised two thousand dollars to aid the wounded, one witness declared: "flags, bells, cannon, rockets, bonfires, illuminations, and shoutings vainly strove to give expression to our wild rejoicings." Similarly, Randall Cooke wrote his daughter from Wallingford, Connecticut, that flags were floating and bells ringing because of the news of Fort Donelson: "there is great rejoicing among the politicians who are looking for an early termination of the war." One Northern woman even wrote, "I believe that the general opinion is <u>now</u>, that the Donelson affair, is one of the greatest victories that we have gained <u>at all</u>." The same joy exploded in numerous Federal camps. One soldier wrote how "about dark yesterday, we received the news of the capture of Fort Donelson, the Camp was perfectly wild with excitement for about an hour. One fine Brass Band played Yankee Doodle, Hail Columbia, Dixie, & e, & e. while the 'boys' united in cheer after cheer for the success of our arms."[3]

George Templeton Strong commented in his diary, "*Laus Deo* again! We are victorious at Fort Donelson." He then reported the losses and capture of prisoners, including at first Albert Sidney Johnston, although he later corrected himself: "the captured General Johnston is not the genuine A. S. Johnston. He is a bogus Johnston, a 'Bushrod Johnston' [Johnson] that nobody ever heard of." He also erroneously reported Floyd captured but wondered what to do with him, finally recommending "commit[ing] him to Barnum's custody as a special deputy United States marshal *pro tem*. . . . He could be most profitably exhibited along with Commodore Nutt and the 'What-Is-It?'"[4]

The South reacted quite differently, not only over the loss of friends and family but also over the staggering defeat—a defeat that was hard to deny or explain away. No one could get enough information. The Clarksville *News Chronicle*, its readers within earshot of the fighting, knew it had to produce and editorialized: "we have kept our paper back some eighteen hours awaiting news." Families wondered what happened to their beloved—dead, wounded, captured. "This is all we now know of their fate," wrote one concerned loved one, "lists of killed and wounded have not been published."[5]

By early March, word even reached Europe, and Confederate commissioners there had a hard time explaining why European nations should support this new Confederacy. John Slidell wrote from Paris: "I need not say how unfavorable an influence these defeats, following in such quick succession, have produced on public sentiment." J. M. Mason similarly wrote from London, "the late reverses at Fort Henry and Fort Donelson have led an unfortunate effect upon the minds of our friends here." P. A. Post echoed their sentiments but reminded the Spanish foreign secretary that Spain itself was conquered and ruled by Napoleon but still, on its last leg, "rose in their might and drove the imperial legions beyond the Pyrenees."[6]

Such isolated events as Fort Henry and Fort Donelson had caused worldwide reverberations. Sadly, they were only the entering wedge in a war that would last several more years.

While the news spread like wildfire across the globe, the misery at Fort Donelson itself did not wane. For those who were involved in the campaign, especially in the terrible weather conditions, the aftermath only brought more misery. The weather remained cold and rainy after the surrender, prompting one Federal to write, "if this is 'good old Tennessee' I have had enough of it, maybe when I get to Nashville I will have a better opinion of Tenn." He added significantly, "I have got so I cannot bear to hear it rain." Everyone was tired and grumpy, one writing that the soldiers "cant keep from quarreling about everything. The rattle of a leaf startles us. Any rasping sound sets the shivers going. Sounds like the whistle of a bullet. I reckon we're nervous." A Kentuckian on the way back to Fort Henry simply noted that he was "sick and tired and hungry and mad." The misery, of course, did not confine itself to the lower ranks. Lew Wallace wrote his wife that he had "a terrible cold . . . my lungs and throat are very sore, tho' I am better today."[7]

The despair began to ease as the days moved on, the Federal soldiers finding other things to occupy their time. "Some of the boys have quite exciting times fishing guns from the River," wrote one soldier. The living quarters also improved, with many Federals moving into the Confederate cabins. "We are quartered in the Rebels shanties," one noted, but "the straw they left in the bunks was alive with gray backs, and in less than half hour we were salted with them completely." The continual appearance of reinforcements also helped take Federal minds off the misery, most of the new men arriving by steamboat at the Dover landing. Their trip had been interesting in itself, some reporting the various effects of the fighting. One Federal described seeing the gunboats heading back to Cairo, all shot to pieces. Another Illinoisan reported seeing prisoners early in his voyage: "we seen Gen. Tilghman and about 25 of his men, on board the steamer *Hannibal* as prisoners of war." Once in the Cumberland after Fort Donelson's surrender, he wrote, "we met five steamboats this morning, coming down the river laden with prisoners and soldiers." Once at the fort, he noted the bluffs "are still full of them."[8]

A decidedly different set of people also arrived, the tourists. One Federal described arriving steamboats containing excursionists who had come to see the battlefield, another numbering them as "hundreds of citizens." One described "visitors from Cincinnati to see battle ground, a great number of ladies." Many gathered bundles of sticks to take home to make canes: "I expect that there will not be a stick left soon," wrote one Federal, "the most of them were cut to pieces by the musket balls that were fired by both parties. O Kate, you have no idea how it looked." Of particular note were northern state governors, including Richard Yates of Illinois, Oliver P. Morton of Indiana, William Dennison of Ohio, and Samuel J. Kirkwood of Iowa. Governor Kirkwood "paid us a flying visit a few days ago," one Iowan remembered, "they remained one day, gathered some trophies, and left again for Iowa." The governor took with him the flag of the 2nd Iowa, it "having 17 bullet holes through it." Many soldiers sent home other trophies as well.[9]

What these visitors and soldiers alike saw after the battle filled them with horror. One Federal declared, "let a person visit the battle ground. And see the trees And bushes cut to pieces with Cannon balls And musket balls. they would think it impossible for a man to escape without being Shot some place." Others described the fort itself, one Federal writing, "this place is naturally a very strong place, and to this they have added all that labor, and expense would do, so that now it is rather a formidable place."[10]

Making the scene more horrendous, there were still wounded and dead on the field in the first few days after the surrender. Wounded survivors were still being found as late as February 22:

> some of our men while strolling about the entrenchments yesterday found a secessionist in a brush heap with both legs shattered by a cannon ball his hands both froze off. His face frozen until it was black. He was in his shirt sleeves and had been lying there ever since last Friday a week on the cold ground & was still able to faintly ask for a drink of water.

Those who could be moved were sent to hospitals all along the Ohio and Mississippi rivers, some as far as Cincinnati and St. Louis. Dead bodies were still being found as well for days after the fighting ended. As the days passed, many citizens from the North also arrived seeking bodies of loved ones.[11]

A major attraction, especially early on, was the Confederate prisoners, although many continually escaped through the porous net of Union guards. Bushrod Johnson, for example, had determined to stay with his men on February 16, but by February 18 he was still at the fort despite the fact that his men had already been transported northward. He had no thoughts of escape until he and another officer walked out toward Heiman's position between Indian Creek and Erin Hollow. "Finding no sentinel to obstruct me," he wrote, "I passed on and was soon beyond the Federal encampments." Understanding what Floyd and Pillow had done, he wanted it understood that he had remained as long as his men were there and that he had no honor to fulfill because he "had been given no parole, and had made no promises." In fact, he thought he had not even been recognized as a higher-level officer, although several communications among the Federal high command noted him as a captured Confederate general. In fact, like George Templeton Strong, other Federals initially confused Johnson with the overall Confederate commander, writing home that Albert Sidney Johnston had been captured at Fort Donelson. When the truth came out, this Johnson gained little sympathy, a hometown Ohio newspaper writing, "none of his relatives, so far as I know, have the slightest sympathy for his treason, which they regret far more than his capture."[12]

In the middle of all the chaos of reorganization and visitors, Grant kept his mind firmly on the future and began to consolidate his victory. First of all, he arrayed his forces for defense, Smith on the right with Lauman in command of the fort itself and McClernand on the left of the Confederate trenches. As further defense of his gains and as a precursor to more action along the Tennessee River, Grant sent Lew Wallace back to the soggy Fort Henry with two of his brigades and artillery: "I was as glad to get back to Fort Henry as I had been at being ordered to Fort Donelson," Wallace noted. Grant also organized another division at Fort Donelson to take over the rearward town areas and oversee the stores—the Fourth Division under newly arrived Brigadier General Stephen A. Hurlbut. To keep the soldiers in line, Grant issued orders that "prohibited [them] from entering the town of Dover or any houses therein situated without permission. . . . Any officer violating the above order will be at once arrested."[13]

There was some celebration too. On February 22, a thirty-four-gun salute occurred for George Washington's birthday. It was the deadline Lincoln had set for a general advance of the Union armies. Grant had certainly complied . . . and then some.[14]

"We heard all of the cannon at Fort Henry and Fort Donnelson it made all nature quake and jair and trimble." So wrote one of the many civilians in the twin-rivers area affected by the massive amount of military movement that was punctuated by short but intense and deadly combat. While the soldiers themselves and their families suffered the major effects of being killed or wounded, the stark reality was that the local population was very much affected as well. Even the shortest travel was curtailed; in the midst of the campaigning, one old man who lived near Fort Henry wanted the Federals to provide him with an escort to return to his home. He was nearly deaf and he "feared someone would call for him to halt and he would not hear them."[15]

After the fact, many Federals gave detailed observations of the local area and in doing so provided a glimpse of the suffering of the civilians, some even before the fighting had erupted. James B. McPherson, for example, described the area as "very rolling, thickly covered with timber, and sparsely populated; the soil, as a general thing, being poor." An Iowan agreed, writing, "the country between Fort Henry and Donaldson [Donelson] is as rough as Connecticut and the soil very poor. The timber is good both in quantity and quality. There are not many houses and the niggers have all been carried off." Many Federals took an extremely negative view of the locals, one asserting that only women remained, and most claimed to be widows. He continued

that the people were "the most ignorant and God forsaken set of human be-
ings that I ever saw. In traveling over two hundred miles we only passed two
school houses and they looked as though they had not been occupied for
some time. Most all live in log cabins with mud chimneys. We saw only six
frame buildings on the rout. The land is very poor. Tobacco is the principal
product."[16]

Many Federals described Dover in the same manner, especially after the
siege. One called it "an old dilapidated town," and most of the residents had
fled upon realizing that their little village would soon be a war zone. Correspondent Alexander Simplot noted, "the town being bare of its inhabitants,
gave a very deserted appearance to the entire locality." An Indianan similarly
wrote, "many dwellings are deserted. Farms are laying neglected, the owners having fled at the approach of the armies leaving most of their property
behind them which the soldiers confiscate when they find it and our teams
subsist principally on forage when in the neighborhood." An Illinoisan gave
a detailed view of Dover, writing home that it was "about the size of Millers-
burg, and has been laid out for the last 30 or 40 years." He went on to describe
a courthouse, jail, two taverns, and "3 or 4 stores and as many groceries
together with the shops and other resorts necessary to make a southern village. . . . The Furniture was nice and tasty which fell prey to the Soldiers and
was destroyed by them in great measure until prohibited by order of General
Grant." That same Illinoisan wrote,

> the citizens are returning to their homes now and they find their Houses in a very
> bad condition all of which had been used for to stow the sick and wounded and
> dead. . . . there is nothing here to support a town as I can see the farms are small
> and far between the Citizens have no enterprise and it looks like they have a hard
> road to travel at the best.[17]

It did not help that the Federals were not always on their best behavior,
even this early in the war, when Federal policy was to treat Southern civilians
with kid gloves. One Confederate described a trip toward Fort Donelson and
"when within about 12 miles of the point I met the citizens of the country
fleeing from their homes with terrible rumors of a Northern army marching
through the country." Grant specifically dealt with the issue of looting before
he sent the men out on their expeditions, outlawing "plundering and disturbing private property." He noted that terrorizing the civilians made "open

and armed enemies of many who, from opposite treatment, would become friends, or at most non-combatants."[18]

All the lectures and orders did not help much. Charles Cowell scribbled in his diary after the January marches, "the boys were very ha[r]d on the natives of the country." That said, there was a fine line between what was not allowed and what was accepted. McClernand, for instance, noted during the mid-January movements that he had to feed his men somehow and not taking large trains saved the government much money: "finding live stock, provisions, forage, &c., the owners of which had abandoned it and gone into the rebel army, I took and appropriated it to the uses of the United States without hesitation. In other cases I purchased from loyal citizens such supplies as were indispensable, and caused certificates to be issued, charging the Government for the fair value of the articles thus obtained."[19]

Telling the difference between legitimate gathering of materials and unnecessary foraging was very hard, and instances of abuse occurred. One 4th Illinois cavalryman, for example, wrote, "it is considerable fun to scout . . . through the country. . . . They are as scared as if they was a going to be killed and the people through the country when we get up to their houses they have them shut up as tight as if no one lived in them and when they do come out they are all wimen men are scarce." He added, "if their country is all like this it aint worth fighting for."[20]

Many others corroborated this account. "We went out scouting and killed 3 or 4 cattle & hogs sheep chickens and every[thing] that was fit to eat. The people had all left these farms and villages," wrote one Federal. Another told of how "in the afternoon a part of our men went out without leave & shot a lot of chickens, sheep &c. at an inhabited place & also brought in some sweet potatoes." An Iowan at Fort Henry wrote, "the country abounds with cattle, sheep, hogs, geese, ducks, chickens, &c. Our Reg. killed two good big fat oxen yesterday. A number of our boys go out daily and bring in all they can carry of the feathered tribe so we are having good times." One Federal summed it up succinctly: "we get lots of forage from the secesh farmers as we just take anything we want from them and don't ask them anything about it."[21]

A particular area of activity was to take slaves away from civilians. The Confederates certainly utilized slaves for the war effort, although Johnston, Tilghman, and company quickly found that the owners were not as willing as they had hoped to loan out their money-making assets. When the armies

came to the Dover region, for example, most owners opted to get out themselves and take their expensive property with them. One Illinois cavalryman
was thus surprised to find a slave in the vicinity, noting on February 14 that
while near Randolph Forge, two miles from Dover, "I got my supper tonight
from an old black woman." He added, "nearly all of the niggers have been
sent to Nashville." He further noted, "the country is owned by small farmers,
saw but few darkies along the road."[22]

Still, numerous slaves did remain in the area who were either left there or
had escaped. One poignant episode occurred as the navy patrolled the rivers.
In this instance, Phelps reported, "just before dark a negro ran down to the
river bank, near the boat, chased by blood hounds in full cry after him, and
begged to be taken on board." The slave said Confederate cavalry was chasing him: "he had run 18 miles," Phelps reported, and was to be taken when
captured to Fort Donelson to work on the fortifications. Phelps took the man
with him as he returned to the Ohio River. Those slaves still in the area or
able to escape to Union lines were quickly put to work for the Federal forces.
Somewhat surprisingly this early in the war when the Union slave policy
was still extremely conservative, Halleck issued orders to Grant to "impress
slaves of secessionists in vicinity to work on fortifications." He warned that
slaves "should be kept under guard and not allowed to communicate with
the enemy, nor must they be allowed to escape." Consequently, the Federal
camps quickly began to fill with contraband. One Iowan at Smithland wrote,
"there are lots of contrabands in town and they seem to welcome us by looks
if no other way. The white inhabitants mostly claim to be Union men but
some of them act strangely." One racist Illinoisan noted, "I should like to
live down here [but] you see plenty of darkies our camp is full much to our
annoyance."[23]

While some fought back, one woman complaining to C. F. Smith that
Federal soldiers confiscated the children of her contraband who had fled to
safety, many Confederate civilians sided with whichever army seemed to be
in control of their area at the time. Locals aided in the care of Confederate
cavalry at Fort Henry, but many soon became Unionists when the Federals
arrived. After Fort Donelson, Grant reported, "great numbers of Union people
have come in to see us, and express great hope for the future. They say secessionists are in great trepidation—some leaving the country, others expressing
anxiety to be assured that they will not be molested if they will come in and
take the oath." An Illinoisan gave a specific example: "stopped at the house

of a Mr. Winn. He owns 1400 acres of land for which he paid $8,000.00. It is the nicest place I have seen in Dixie. He has been in the Secesh army, but claims to be a Union man. He treated us very cordially, and invited us to stay for supper, which I declined."[24]

The generalities of the local civilian population's suffering are bad enough, but specific examples demonstrate the tough spot in which these Tennesseans found themselves. Southern newspapers carried the account of a disturbance between a citizen of Dover and a captain in the local 14th Tennessee in January 1862, resulting in the captain's death from "a wound inflicted from a pistol shot." One farmer near Fort Henry was so afraid when the Federal army landed that he immediately asked for a guard on his property, and one Illinoisan noted the disgust that he felt: "the idea of enlisting to fight for 'Old Glory' and save the Union, and the first thing he had to do was to guard a lot of dirty pigs that were not half as good as those in his father's farm yard, but 'orders is orders.'" The marching Federal army so frightened Flora Sykes that she could only resolve to hide behind a chest in her house as they passed. It was obviously worse when actual combat raged around those who could not get out. One Federal later wrote of a wretched scene right in the midst of the fighting at Fort Donelson: "I remember one day while moving thus to the right, we passed a small dwelling, around which was a mother and a lot of children, little girls and boys, wringing their hands and crying. The mother was frantic with fear and apprehension. Cannon-balls had already perforated her house in several places, and the air was blue with shell, balls, and bullets."[25]

Even so, some civilians took chances to provide services to one side or the other. Some remained in Dover and hid Confederate prisoners in their lofts or houses. Numerous Federals wrote of the kindness offered them even as they were on the march, perhaps something as simple as receiving a cup of coffee during a cold day's trek. Even war could not dampen the kindness of some who were themselves in their hardest hour.[26]

On the other hand, the suffering also brought out the worst in others. John A. McClernand described how Major John J. Mudd, "while performing an act of kindness at the request of one of two or three countrymen, one of the party dropped behind and shot him in the back, inflicting a severe, but I trust not mortal, wound."[27]

The Federals were quickly getting versed in dealing with occupation issues.

Albert Sidney Johnston received updates all through the fighting at Fort Donelson, even as he retreated to Nashville. One staff officer later remembered
the retreat, writing, "it was a sad journey, for all along the rout we received
telegrams of disaster." While Pillow kept Polk informed at Columbus, Floyd
primarily wrote Johnston of the fighting and offered little good news as early
as February 13: "we will endeavor to hold our position if we are capable of
doing so." This was of course before the feared gunboats attacked. At that
time, Johnston had replied, "if you lose the fort, bring your troops to Nashville if possible." Whether it was a statement that Floyd should not lose the
army in losing the fort or if it was a direction for where to retreat is not known,
but Johnston reacted by sending orders for railroad bridges to be burned and
hastened Hardee's march to Nashville. Then things changed as Floyd and
Pillow sent a glorious message of victory on February 14, Pillow calling
it "the fiercest fight on record." More glorious news came on February 15,
which Johnston sent on to Richmond, calling it a "brilliant victory." Then on
February 16, Johnston received the fatal news, unexpected especially after he
had received such good tidings just hours before. He notified Richmond on
February 17, telling Davis, "at midnight on the 15th I received the news of a
glorious victory; at dawn, of a defeat."[28]

The Confederate high command reeled at the news of the loss. Beauregard
had recently written, "the loss of Fort Donelson (God grant it may not fall)
would be followed by consequences too lamentable to be now alluded to."
Governor Harris was similarly distraught, realizing that Nashville now lay
defenseless. He had tirelessly asked for reinforcement of Donelson, telling
Johnston, "if there is anything that State authorities can do to aid this or any
other matter they are at your command." He later wrote, "Fort Donelson has
fallen and Nashville will fall into the hands of Federals. No stand can be made
there. . . . I will rally all the Tennesseans possible and go with them myself
to our army." Lower-level Confederates were upset as well; one Southerner
wrote, "the terrible news of our defeat at Donelson came this morning. I have
seldom felt so deep a pang of grief." A Virginian noted, "to your list of disas-
ters the greatest of all has now to be added—we have been defeated in a great
battle—Tennessee seems to be lost—with it Columbus—Memphis—the Valley of the Mississippi."[29]

The ramifications of this Confederate defeat were not lost on the now
defenseless people of Nashville. One Tennessean noted, "before ten o'clock
Sunday morning a vague rumor that Fort Donelson had surrendered and that

the entire Confederate force had been taken prisoners, had found its way into the streets and was spreading with a rapidity which only such rumors can spread." Then came confirmation: "the fall of Fort Donelson was announced by the ministers—from their pulpits—at 11 o'clock service—just after some had returned thanks for the victory." The effect was electric. "The people were possessed with the idea of getting out of the City and stood not on the order of going—Hacks went up to ten, twenty, dollars an hour." Governor Harris and the legislature, along with the state archives, left on a train that night, full as it was of citizens as well: "the Engine was taxed to carry its load of refugees."[30]

The arrival of Confederate survivors from Donelson did not help; they straggled into Nashville, providing a human face to the facts of the defeat. The wounded also began to pour in. "The wildest excitement prevailed in the city," one observer noted, "very many persons left the city in vehicles—many on the cars. The Gov. & Legislature decamped. Nashville was a panic stricken city. The Union men alone seem to have their wits about them." It was no better the next day, the same observer adding: "as a day of panic and terrified confusion this was equal to the preceding—Large bodies of the retreating army were hastening through, and getting supplies as they passed. Many citizens and their families left on the cars and in vehicles." The writer went on to indicate there was little hope: "what I saw of Johnston's army to day and yesterday fully equaled any description I have ever read of an army in hurried retreat before a superior force, whose fangs they must avoid. There was hurry, confusion, alarm, and on the part of many a sullen dissatisfaction at not being able to fight."[31]

The arrival of the Donelson commanders proved shocking too. When Floyd and Pillow arrived, they were already under a cloud. Rumors swirled, one Illinoisan even declaring that Pillow and Floyd "got away with womens clothes on." Cullum referred to the Virginian as "Floyd the traitor" and another Federal stated erroneously that Floyd had been captured: "they got the old fellow that robbed the treasury." An Indianan more correctly related, "our men were very much vexed at the escape of Floyd and Pillow. Every soldier wanted to see Floyd the thief." One Virginia Confederate was extremely upset: "I think to cashier them & dismiss them [Floyd and Pillow] from the service is necessary to show the world that the Southern heart appreciates their dastardly conduct & smarts under the disgrace of the Surrender at Ft. Donelson." A Kentuckian similarly noted, "no sort of engineering in the way of forts and rifle-pits could have saved that army from disaster, commanded, as it was, by officers who, from beginning to end, were guilty of a perfect medley of errors."[32]

Although Pillow and Floyd put the best-possible justification on their actions during speeches at Nashville, it fell to Forrest's cavalry to make some sense of the bedlam and get out what stores and supplies they could. He did so, but eventually fell back with Johnston's army, leaving the city defenseless. The people of the larger Confederacy also soon realized what the people of Nashville were witnessing, that the twin-rivers defeat had been an unmitigated disaster. Civilians all over the Confederacy strove to learn all they could, one writing that he "walked in to town this Evening as I was anxious to hear what was to be heard." It was only bad news, and getting worse by the day.[33]

In Richmond, Jefferson Davis had to boldly bluff at his inauguration just six days later, on February 22, although he privately told his brother, "I cannot believe that our army surrendered without an effort to cut the investing lines and retreat to the main body of the army." At any rate, the stark reality was that the Confederacy had endured a major defeat, and the Southern population responded to the news with sadness. But there was a glimmer of stubbornness as defeat tended to prompt additional resolve. One Confederate wrote, "as soon as I heard of the fall of Fort Henry and Donelson I knew that it would take every available man in the south to check the invaders." Perhaps in part because of the major defeats on the twin rivers, many Southerners joined the Confederate army in this second spring of the war.[34]

"We have been waiting here in the greatest anxiety for two or three days to hear the result of the battle at Fort Donelson." So wrote Lincoln's secretary John Nicolay, expressing even Lincoln's deep concern over what was happening. Just as all the South waited for news from Fort Donelson, so did the North wait in anxious expectation. While all waited, a nervous Halleck could only send more troops to Grant, writing Sherman at Paducah, "send to General Grant everything you can spare from Paducah and Smithland; also General Hurlbut."[35]

Then came the joyous news, provided by the *Carondelet* as it moored at the Cairo landing. Celebrations quickly emerged in Union camps. Bands played, cannon fired, and prayers of thanks went up all across the nation. Other forms

of information also spread the news, including a high number of personal letters sent home to let families know of the individual results. One staff officer
wrote his family, "Glory to God in the Highest. . . . The number killed on
both sides is awful, but your *two sons* are *here, safe* and *sound, unharmed*."[36]

The joy felt in the North was unequaled in the war, but there were many
who learned sad tidings that emanated from the battlefield as well. Those who
lost loved ones were stricken with grief, as were those who knew little of their
loved ones' fates, whether killed, wounded, or in prison. Newspapers such as
the Cairo *Gazette* published false rumors of many killed, including colonels
Lawler, Morrison, and John A. Logan. "The telegraph office was besieged
night and day, and the streets were filled with distressed men and women,
each looking with penetrating eagerness into the face of every person from
whom they could hope to receive the least tidings," wrote Logan's wife, who
had a special interest in those lists. Her husband had been wounded three
times and was at first listed as dead, but she, for one, soon received the happy
word that the news had been all in error. Other wives were just as distraught.
Will Wallace's wife, Ann, wrote on February 14 that she was invited to a
party at a judge's house, "but the thought of you before Fort Donelson is in
my mind every minute." Even Abraham Lincoln's joy was stifled amid the
celebrations. His son Willie died at the Executive Mansion in Washington on
February 20, just four days after the surrender. Not only did Lincoln have a
nation at war to run, but he also bore the incredible burden of losing a son and
staying strong for his grief-stricken wife and son Tad, who was just as sick.
While Tad would eventually recover, Lincoln knew not at the time whether
he would die too. February 1862, with all its victorious joy, certainly carried
with it much sadness for many in the North.[37]

Still, it was a huge success, and the glory was spread around far and wide.
State legislatures and towns passed resolutions of congratulations. Ottawa,
Illinois, for example, sent congratulations to its two favorite sons, brigade
commander Will Wallace and his father-in-law T. Lyle Dickey, colonel of
the 4th Illinois Cavalry. Many other Union commanders also came in for
their own praise, especially all of Grant's division commanders. Lew Wallace
gained some notoriety; Grant staff officer Hillyer wrote Wallace that he had
"save[d] the day on the right," and Wallace was not slow in telling his wife
that he had indeed done so. Charles F. Smith received the most acclaim of
Grant's division commanders. Smith, one of his officers noted, "is a perfect
gentleman, is perfect in military matters and brave as a lion." Even Halleck

went so far as to ask McClellan: "make him a major-general. You can't get a better one. Honor him for this victory and the whole country will applaud." Smith received the promotion, but perhaps more important was his vindication as a loyal Federal among his troops, who now supported him completely; perhaps he had so exposed himself in the fighting to show his loyalty. Specifically, Lorenzo Thomas wrote him that his actions "afford the most positive refutation of the charges which had been brought by individuals not of the military." McClernand also received praise, although most of it was from his own pen. It was no doubt McClernand that Smith referred to in speaking of how newspaper reporters shied away from him; Smith later remarked how "the other Generals (Grant excepted) feed them and make much of them for a purpose."[38]

By far, although there were still some detractors such as 45th Illinois colonel John E. Smith, who wrote, "Rowley has been appd one of that Drunken Cuss Genl Aids," Grant received the most glory, including promotion to major general. He wrote Julia after the surrender, "I am most happy to write you from this very strongly fortified place, now in my possession, after the greatest victory of the season." That is as far as he would go in touting himself, the humble general even pointing toward others in the process. To his new friend Sherman, he hoped that "should an opportunity occur, you will win for yourself the promotion which you are kind enough to say belongs to me. I care nothing for promotion so long as our arms are successful and no political appointments are made." Naval officer Phelps readily recognized this streak of humility, writing Grant that he noted and admired "your generosity toward others in the hour of your triumph."[39]

If Grant would not sound his own praise, many others did it for him. "General Grant has . . . won great laurels and I hope they will never be tarnished," wrote one Iowan under him. "General Grant has redeemed his Belmont Blunder and his stock is now at a premium," noted another. Details of what Grant had accomplished made more fame come his way; he had taken a fort to which, "though strongly fortified by nature, all the safeguards suggested by science were added." The haul also included the "greatest number of prisoners of war ever taken in one battle on this continent." Grant, not surprisingly, gave the credit to his soldiers, writing that "Fort Donelson will hereafter be marked in capitals on the maps of our united country, and the men who fought the battle will live in the memory of a grateful people." Perhaps the best-known adulation came when news of Grant calmly smoking a cigar flashed around the nation; so many people sent cigars that the pipe smoker switched on the spot.[40]

Many also took time to offer thanks and praise to God for the victory, and sermons appeared on the Sundays thereafter touting the victory and God's hand in it. Not the least among those offering praise to God was Flag Officer Foote: "Let us thank God from our heart, and say not unto us alone, but unto Thy name, O Lord, belongs the glory of the triumph of our arms." "Te Deum laudamus—Let the people praise Him," wrote Will Wallace. Many individual soldiers were also grateful to God for the victory and for sparing them. "I have been on the Tennessee River where Fort Henry is and also on the Cumberland where Fort Donnelson is," wrote one Federal. "It is the most mountainous place except Harpers Ferry I ever saw, how our troops could fight an enemy entrenched there unless an Almighty power helped them, I cannot tell. I believe God is on our side and that our cause is just." James Fogle of the 11th Indiana wrote of such a religious experience on the way back to Fort Henry:

> we passed through a pine grove several miles in extent. It is the most beautiful grove I have ever seen and it was so green and nice that it fully looked like summer and I thought that I would like to worship God in such a place as this for it made me feel like I wanted to fall on my knees and make offering my prayers to the most high God and then I thought of the many blessings God has bestowed on me since I have been in the army.

He added, "the birds are singing all nature is rejoicing as there is no thing disturbing the land." Nevertheless, his mind was obviously also fixated on the present war, writing, "but the cloud of war hangs darkly over rebellious Tennessee."[41]

Despite the praise heaped on the generals and the thanksgiving to God, the fighting produced some irritability among those who thought they deserved more praise than they had received. While fighting competently, McClernand lusted mightily for glory, but Grant had grown weary of the politician, writing that his report "is a little highly colored as to the conduct of the first division." McClernand had indeed written that his division bore "the brunt and burden of the battle." Grant also noted that he had not heard McClernand recommend an all-out advance on the afternoon of February 15, as he had claimed. Grant was not the only one. Lew Wallace also took issue and noted that McClernand had not mentioned his stand late on February 15, writing, "all he plausibly can he appropriates to himself." Even McClernand's brigade commander Richard Oglesby later wrote on the back of McClernand's congratulatory order, "we did the fighting. He did the writing."[42]

Others bickered over glory as well. Ezra Taylor complained that Peter Wood's Chicago battery unfairly received much more credit than his own Chicago unit; Taylor claimed he had driven the enemy back before Wood had arrived and "I have not the least idea that their shots hurt anybody as they fired at random not being able to see anybody from the fact of the enemy having retired." Taylor indicated he was not against the other battery getting any glory, but "I wish them to earn their reputation by gallant *deed*." Similarly, many took issue with the newspapers, Colonel John E. Smith referring to an account that said his 45th Illinois had run during the battle. "I would rather have been shot than have seen it," he noted. An Iowan was also miffed at his state's lack of glory: "I see the Chicago papers give all the praise to the Ill. Troops. They scarcely mention the Iowa Reg."[43]

The bickering also extended to the navy. One *Louisville* sailor on the *Carondelet* related that the *Carondelet* did not get the credit she deserved because "there is an animosity between the Commodore and our Captain, which accounts for us not receiving the credit that is due us." He went so far as to say that Foote "showed the white feather, for had all the boats of staid as long as us, the 14 of Feb would of decided it, instead of the 16th."[44]

Despite all such bickering, no larger controversy emerged than that between Grant and Halleck. Although McClellan wrote Halleck to "thank Gen. Grant, Flag Officer Foote and their commands for me," Halleck congratulated everyone, including Smith and Foote, *but* Grant. He even singled out David Hunter in Missouri for sending reinforcements and thus making the difference. In all his communications there was no praise for the man who deserved it most, Ulysses S. Grant.[45]

In fact, Halleck eventually turned on Grant, using a lack of communication (not Grant's fault) to remove him from command of future operations. Lincoln soon became involved and Halleck had to reinstate Grant, but the relationship was materially damaged. Worse, Halleck used Grant's victory for himself. He wrote McClellan, "make Buell, Grant, and Pope major-generals of volunteers, and give me command in the West. I ask this in return for Forts Henry and Donelson." Later, he wrote of the west: "give it to me, and I will split secession in twain in one month." Halleck was certainly seeking to benefit from the glorious victory earned by his subordinate Grant, and indeed received some of the glory, the citizens of St. Louis going so far as to offer their congratulations and a dinner on his behalf.[46]

All the same, the quiet man from Galena deserved the praise, and found much of it when Northerners began to label the meaning of his initials U. S. as Unconditional Surrender.

The strategic significance of the February 1862 Confederate defeats was enormous. Henry Halleck certainly realized as much, writing on February 15: "Fort Donelson is the turning point of the war, and we must take it at whatever sacrifice." While Forts Henry and Donelson were certainly front and center, other Confederate mishaps were likewise seen in combination with them as bad omens for the future. "We have all been disturbed by the defeats at Fort Donelson, Roanoke & other places," wrote one Southerner who understood the mammoth hole the Confederacy was digging for itself. Still, while those other defeats were large, they did not compare to the losses suffered in west Tennessee. With the Confederate strategic line in the west already severed at Fort Henry and Johnston's wings already falling back or preparing to begin the concentration that would result at Corinth, Mississippi, the humiliating defeat at Fort Donelson simply added insult to injury.[47]

Indeed, the ramifications of Fort Donelson were huge. Not only did it spur Union morale and conversely diminish Southern hopes for independence, but it also brought to the forefront a legitimate Union hero, Ulysses S. Grant. Perhaps more consequentially, the removal of around fifteen thousand Confederate troops from the war was devastating to Confederate defense of the west. The way these men were lost infuriated Southerners even more. Additionally, the tangible territorial loss forced by not only the Fort Henry defeat but also the Fort Donelson disaster loomed large. Johnston, with Hardee's force, was already retreating from Bowling Green as a result of Fort Henry's fall, but as long as Fort Donelson remained in service Nashville was at least partially protected. With that fort's loss, however, the road was open to Nashville. Therefore Johnston ordered Hardee to fall back fast so he would not be caught north of the Cumberland River if Fort Donelson fell and the Federals beat Johnston to Nashville. "General Johnston wishes the command to march day and night until the Cumberland is crossed," one of his aides wrote during the withdrawal. One soldier even linked Johnston's order for retreat to a lack of pay: "the retreat commenced and we have not stopped at any one place long enough to get it." With Donelson's fall, Johnston marched right through Nashville, knowing it was untenable.[48]

Grant did not let the pressure lessen on Johnston and Nashville but sent another of Buell's divisions under William "Bull" Nelson on up the river. This unit arrived after the surrender, and Grant sent it on to Clarksville aboard their transports. Despite his injured foot, which he described as "much inflamed," Foote was also back from Cairo with two ironclads, all the others being "badly cut up and require[ing] extensive repairs"; he ordered 150 carpenters to board the boats as quickly as possible. In addition to the ironclads was the *Conestoga*, as well as eight new mortar boats. Foote easily captured Clarksville on February 19 by taking possession of the three forts. The Federals received a cool reception from Clarksville's white citizens, one noting how "Lincoln gunboats arrived at Clarksville" on February 19 and "Lincoln troops arrived in Clarksville" on February 22. Such coolness was not the case with the slaves, however, one Illinoisan recording how "the negroes flocked to the shore." Foote then informed Grant that he could also take Nashville just as easily because of "great panic" in the Confederate army, but Halleck "frustrated" the plan by ordering the gunboats not to go beyond Clarksville. Grant prepared for the eventual movement nevertheless and sent Smith's division to Clarksville too.[49]

Despite Halleck's interference, a stymied Grant was not about to give up, and with the theme "Onward to Nashville," he opted to send Nelson on to Tennessee's capital. The city was in a different department under Buell, but Nelson hailed from Buell's army so Grant felt free to send those troops back to their own department, capturing Nashville in the process. Nelson beat Buell there, which caused a rift among the Federal high command. Also let loose was the navy, and the Federal ironclads soon made their appearance as well.[50]

The Federal soldiers were anxious to get to Tennessee's capital. One said, "hope we will get through in time to plant the Old flag on the dome of the Capitol of Tennessee, Think I would be willing to lose an arm for the privilege of doing it myself." The city did not disappoint: "the State House is the finest one in the Union. It is built of stone entirely, except the stair railings which are iron and the doors which are oak—it is decidedly the finest building I ever saw." Other factors at Nashville were not so great, despite the fact that the city surrendered "without firing a gun." One Federal noted that "the people here have made no demonstration of either welcome or hostility, and the Union sentiment here is either expressly latent or insignificant." Another commented on the continuing chaos: "arrived at and was disgusted with Nashville. Saw the citizens seizing bacon on the wharf. The town in a perfectly demoralizing panic." The Federals quickly brought the city under control, employing former slaves to turn it into one of the bastions of Federal strength for the rest of the war. Meanwhile, others marched on through, chasing the Confederate rear guard; one Federal wrote they were camped south of Nashville "on the ground said to have been occupied by Genl Jackson for an encampment in 1814."[51]

Meanwhile, the problems continued to compound for the Confederates. Because of Fort Henry's fall, other large swaths of the Confederacy were affected, including the concentration of troops in north Mississippi and west Tennessee from Florida, Louisiana, and eventually the trans-Mississippi. The events at Fort Donelson sped up that concentration. More tangibly, the turning of Columbus forced that Gibraltar's evacuation in early March, just days after the losses at Forts Henry and Donelson. Beauregard had clearly seen that its days were numbered and began urging evacuation as early as February 7. That reality eventually came to pass a few weeks later after Donelson fell, Beauregard prophesying that holding Columbus "could only result in an early fate like that of Fort Donelson and the loss of the Mississippi Valley as a necessary consequence."[52]

The loss of Nashville, Columbus, and a large swath of Tennessee and Kentucky certainly affected the Confederate high command. Albert Sidney Johnston was severely castigated; one probably overhyped Confederate wrote, "if Old Johnson had have acted as he should have done, we could not only [have] sustained ourselves, but captured and killed all of the enemy, and rid Tenn of the foul invader." Others in higher positions agreed. The Tennessee delegation in the Confederate Congress, with the exception of William G. Swan, asked Jefferson Davis to remove Johnston. "Confidence is no longer felt in the military skill of Gen. A. S. Johnston," the group wrote. They also called on Davis to come west and take command himself, or appoint someone else to defend the theater. Ever since, historians have similarly faulted Johnston for his indecisive actions. Most significantly, biographer Charles P. Roland faulted Johnston for declaring Fort Donelson "untenable" and then pouring reinforcements in: "There lay the rub; for this defense had to be all or nothing at all."[53]

Johnston himself was not immune to the same feelings. He wrote that "the blow [Fort Donelson] was most disastrous and almost without remedy." Even Davis wrote Johnston a private letter telling how he had made a defense for Johnston that "friendship prompted and many years' acquaintance justified." But now he needed facts. Johnston responded that he well understood, and that "the test of merit in my profession with the people is success. It is a hard rule, but I think it right." While Johnston would retain command, he was nonetheless startled by the vitriol, which allowed Beauregard to take a larger role than was probably necessary or desired. Beauregard ran with it, writing, "I am taking the helm when the ship is already in the breakers and with but few sailors to man it. How it is to be extricated from its present perilous condition Providence alone can determine, and unless with its aid I can accomplish but little." Beauregard would clearly wield increasingly more influence, which would severely come to hamper Confederate efforts in the future.[54]

All this occurred while the Federals continued to put pressure on the reeling Confederate western defense. Eventually, Halleck, Grant, and company turned their attention back to what Halleck called "the great strategic line of the Western campaign," the Tennessee River. Grant's army, although he was temporarily removed and then reinstated, mostly made their way back to Fort Henry and the Tennessee River for movement southward. There, some of the same naval forces that had surveyed the river before, namely the *Lexington* and *Tyler*, led them. They continued to patrol the river, shelling landings and any perceived Confederate defensive area along the waterway as the campaign shifted into this new phase along the upper stretches of the river in west Tennessee.[55]

And so it happened, in this southward moving process, that the two timberclads, the vanguard of the eventual larger Union thrust up the river, located and fought a small action on March 1 at one of the numerous but soon to be important stops along the river.[56]

The name of the landing: Pittsburg.

Epilogue

Forts Henry and Donelson were watershed events in the Civil War, especially at the specific moment they occurred. As the first meaningful Federal victories, they propelled the Union war effort deeper into the South and galvanized Northern morale. They were also defining moments for the soldiers involved. One Confederate wrote in early March, "I have actually seen the elephant." A Federal told his father, "I had my curiosity satisfied at Fort Donaldson." Colonel John E. Smith of the 45th Illinois noted that before Fort Donelson his troops "were more eager then than they ever will be again to get into a fight. The Boys were constantly wishing they could have a fight. You do not hear any such wishes now."[1]

Obviously, the staggering (for that point in the war) casualties had something to do with the change. Federal official reports placed their losses at 500 killed, 2,832 wounded, and 224 missing for a total of 2,832 out of some 27,000 engaged. Of those, McClernand's division, not surprisingly, sustained the lion's share of the casualties, with some regiments such as the 11th Illinois losing 329 men, more than all the losses of Lew Wallace's entire division. The 9th Illinois sustained 210 total casualties. The very much debated Confederate losses, as documented in Confederate reports, listed 273 killed, 949 wounded, 11,738 surrendered, and 2,286 missing or escaped out of around 18,000 engaged. The surrendered number is certainly low, the Federal commissary at Cairo listing rations given to 14,623 Confederates. Neither side ever really got over these first overwhelming numbers, especially in the South, where so many more prisoners were included in the figures. One Mississippi woman declared it "the beginning of our political troubles," and a member of the 4th Mississippi acknowledged that the events were "the greatest horror of the war to me." Another Mississippi woman two years later wrote, "many yet mourn the loss of fathers, husbands, brothers, and children who perished." Explaining the largest context of all, one contemporary writer noted the campaign was "the most bloody and desperate ever witnessed on the American continent, excepting, perhaps, the earlier conquest of Mexico by the Spaniards."[2]

The war would continue, but a sense of partial finality set in for all. One stunned Federal wrote about how "we deeply mourn & grieve over the loss of our comrades who only a day or two ago were yet in our midst setting around our camp fires with us full of life, spirit and patriotism." Fortunately, some relief came as the wounded returned home, but it took time for the huge numbers of injured to make it home. Only there did the full human results of the fighting become evident in stark reality; "a great many of our men were disabled so that they will never be fit for anything after they get out of the service," wrote Charles H. Floyd of Illinois. A particular case in point was William A. Nichols of the 31st Indiana, who "was struck by a musket ball in front, on the nose, which ball passed through his head below the brain, and came out on the back of the neck." He somehow survived, and his lieutenant had the marvelous insight to write him a letter later that year supporting medical aid. He wrote of the wound "rendering said private Nichols entirely unfit for *any* military duty."[3]

The arrival of some of the dead most certainly made the finality of war evident to many in the nation. One Kentuckian noted in his diary a particularly poignant scene:

> this was the first one of the young men who left this Portion of the county that
> has ever returned or been brought back and as I stood to day and looked upon
> that cold inanimate form sleeping calmly in death I could but hope he had gone
> to that land where wars can never come. I could but hope that though his body
> was in the hands of friends to be consigned to the Mother earth that his mortal
> spirit was in heaven. I could but feel sad at the fate of a Poor Prisoner away from
> home and friends surrounded by those who look upon him as an enemy to lie
> down and die in a Miserable hospital such is the fate of hundreds almost daily
> and if this war continues which God forbid this must increase on both sides.
> Oh how little did this young man think when a few months ago he bade me
> good by and told me he was off for Dixie that this would be his fate that he was
> never again to meet those friends he had left behind on earth or that he would be
> brought back to his native county a corpse.[4]

As time passed, however, some began to see a larger context for their actions. One Illinoisan wrote, "I have went through hardships enough in the last six days to have killed me if I had been at home." Another wrote his sister, "we have reason to praise the Lord." Many echoed Grant's claim that it was the largest battle on the continent to date, one soldier writing that it was "the greatest victory that was ever gained having taken the gratest amount of prisoners that was ever taken on the contenant." Another summed it up particularly succinctly: "I never before knew what hard times were." A few soldiers had had enough; a captain in the 46th Illinois resigned after the fighting and a member of his company testified: "we were glad of it as he showed the white feather plainly." Others petitioned for their officer's removal, the case of the 31st Indiana being curious to be sure: "notwithstanding our profound regard for you as a personal friend and Gentleman and our respect for your former service to your Country," Charles M. Smith wrote to Lieutenant Colonel John Osborn,

> we are nevertheless sorry to inform you that your conduct on the field at Ft. Donalson has caused us to lose that confidence in your efficiency as a Regt. Com. that we had formerly entertained and which is so indispensable to success. We are glad to believe that your inefficiency is wholly attributable to your advanced age and not to any want of courage and that, therefore, you can tender your resignation without dishonor which we as officers of the 31st Regt Ind Vol respectfully request you to do.[5]

Yet there was some good news amid the lingering suffering. Years later A. F. Gilbert reflected on Fort Donelson. He had been wounded and taken prisoner, but was reported killed at home. He soon arrived there and remembered, "I had the pleasure of reading my own obituary and of remarking, like Mark Twain, that 'the report of my death was some what premature and greatly exaggerated.'"[6]

For the next several months at least, the twin-rivers campaign had a definitive impact on the lives of those involved. For most of the Confederates, they could expect six to eight months of imprisonment. Fortunately for them, prison life at the many Northern camps such as Johnson's Island, Camp Chase, Camp Douglas, and others was far from the miserable existences of Andersonville or Elmira later in the war. One Confederate wrote, "I am treated a great deal better than I expected." Still, the lack of freedom was the common denominator in it all, but most Confederates managed to keep up their strength and commitment to the Confederacy. One Chicago resident told of just such spunk, writing of visiting the Southern soldiers at Camp Douglas: "a tall Massachusetts Yankee was walking around passing some cutting remarks about the prisoners when all at once a prisoner came forward and said to the Yankee, 'what remark is that you just made?' The Yankee answered 'If you'd a known what old Abe was made of you wouldn't a taken up arms agin the government but I don't blame you cause you warn't taught nothing better down there among the *poor* niggers.' He scarcely had the words out of his mouth when the Southerner gave him a shot (or a stroke) under the Ear that tumbled him at the Guard's feet."[7]

While life was fairly tolerable in the prison camps this early in the war and the prisoners were mostly fed well, there were certainly still problems ranging from the lack of freedom to write letters to the lack of personal effects. Many prisoners complained of not getting news from home. On some occasions, prisoners got crushing news from their families; Mississippian James Z. George received a letter from his mother while at Johnson's Island: "PS—Your boy Frank died last spring since you was a prisoner." On a few occasions, the captivity became so bad that some Confederate prisoners galvanized, or were released upon joining the Federal army. These were obviously not sent back to the Confederacy to fight but were instead sent out west.[8]

The Confederate field and general officers were treated better, although one Indianan wrote home of the intended treatment of Buckner: "we are going to skin him alive and have some shoes made out of his hide for the Union soldiers." Many noted the movements of well-known officers, Sherman, for example, writing of Buckner as he passed through Paducah: "he seemed self-sufficient, and thought their loss was not really so serious to their cause as we did." Most officers, including Buckner and Tilghman, were taken to Fort Warren near Boston, Massachusetts. Buckner referred to this fort as his "celebrated resort," although there was some solitary confinement for him as well as Tilghman. Others were allowed to roam the fort in Boston Harbor, watching the boats, which helped pass the time. Most lived comfortably and remained healthy; the only major officer to die in confinement was Colonel Thomas J. Davidson of the 3rd Mississippi, who had led a brigade during the fighting. He died at Fort Warren on April 29.[9]

Eventually, the Confederates were exchanged, most lower-level officers and enlisted men going to Vicksburg and the officers being taken to Virginia. Their joy was evident: "we laughed, and sang, and shed tears of joy at our release from prison," noted one Mississippian. Most reentered service and fought the rest of the war, some living through it and others not. Tilghman, of course, was killed a little over a year later at Champion Hill. Buckner, on the other hand, lived well into the next century.[10]

Contrary to the Confederate viewpoint of survival and thankfulness at being exchanged, the Federals gained different attitudes from the twin-rivers campaign. Most were convinced that the war was just about over. "I think we will see home about the first of July to spend the fourth of July with you," wrote one Federal. "It is my opinion they will soon get weary of these Foolish ways," added another. "If we continue to catch them at this rate we will soon have the whole of them," yet another posited.[11]

Those predictions were not just in Grant's army, either, but extended to other forces as well. Buell's army "received the news in camp of the surrender of the Rebels at Fort Donelson which caused great enthusiasm in camp. All are now hopeful that the end of the war is not far distant." One Iowan in Buell's army wrote: "I guess the transactions lately taken place at Fort Henry, Mill Springs, Roanoke Island, and Fort Donelson begin to make them think that we have a will as well as a way to teach traitors that the United States Still have a government and all the brave spirits she needs to maintain that Government. The news of the glorious victories above named was received with Shouts of joy by the boys here and soon the bands was out making the hills of Old Kentucky re-echo with the heart of Stirring and patriotic Strains of Hail Columbia, Yankee Doodle, The Star Spangled Banner &c."[12]

A few actually thought the war would be over that summer: "I think three months more will make them come under or sing out compromise." James Parrott noted that the "rebels in this state are about gone up." One especially observant Federal noted, "the opening of these two important Rivers, must show the Rebels, that they must go under."[13]

Of course, all woefully misjudged the situation. "How badly mistaken we were history proves," remembered an Illinoisan years later.[14]

Those involved in conducting the twin-rivers campaign were likewise affected as the weeks passed into months and years. The gunboats that were so heavily damaged were soon repaired and recrewed, and went on to provide stellar service on the western waters despite being immediate sensations, especially in their damaged state. One sailor aboard the *Essex* so frightfully damaged at Fort Henry commented on its return to St. Louis for repairs: "a great many visitors on board to see the damage." Unfortunately, the gunboats' commander would not share in their victory; despite later promotion to rear admiral, Foote died in the summer of 1863.[15]

Grant obviously rose to great heights, becoming commander of the Union armies by 1864 and president of the United States by 1869. Yet it was not easy, the miscommunication and opposition of Henry Halleck stunting his growth throughout 1862. He steadily gained promotion nevertheless, first to command the District of West Tennessee and then higher commands. At times Lincoln himself intervened on Grant's behalf, but he eventually produced massive results, confirming Lincoln's confidence in him.[16]

Grant's division commanders were not so fortunate. McClernand eventually rose to corps command, but not being a Grant insider he did not survive the Vicksburg campaign in command. Neither did Lew Wallace, who was another victim of miscommunication at Shiloh and remained under that cloud the rest of his life. Perhaps most unfortunate was Charles F. Smith. While in command of the early expedition farther up the Tennessee River from Fort Henry in March, prompting some confusion among the soldiers as to who was actually in command, Smith or Grant, Smith suffered a freak accident and died of infection just a little over two months after his heroics at Fort Donelson. Thirteen-gun salutes were ordered on many posts and vessels, and flags flew at half-staff in memory of the general.[17]

The Confederate commanders did little better. Albert Sidney Johnston lay dead on the plains of Shiloh a mere month and a half after the disaster at Fort Donelson, and Beauregard did not survive Jefferson Davis's wrath much longer. The seemingly forgotten Bushrod Johnson served solidly in the Army of Tennessee, as did Buckner, who had forever won the praises of his men for surrendering with them at Fort Donelson. Pillow and Floyd, on the other hand, were much different stories. While they held small commands later, neither ever really played any major role in the war again.[18]

The Davis administration found Pillow's and Floyd's reports "incomplete and unsatisfactory," setting off a political firestorm. A congressional inquiry resulted. Soon, Davis relieved both men of their commands and the congressional investigation asked each to explain why the army failed to escape, the turnover of command, and the escape of each general. Floyd tried unsuccessfully to explain away the fact that he gave up command and then escaped by saying that his goal by the morning of February 16 was to get as many troops as possible out of the trap. He further said that it just so happened that his Virginia troops were the nearest when it came time to board the boats. Obviously, such weak excuses did not sway many minds. Never able to make much headway against popular or political dissatisfaction, Floyd termed his treatment the "gravest injustice."[19]

Pillow also railed against the government, but Secretary of War George W. Randolph would not budge. Pillow chalked this up to Randolph being Nicholas Trist's brother-in-law. Trist was an important figure during Pillow's Mexican War dispute with Winfield Scott, and he even testified against Pillow; the Tennessean thus termed Randolph his "personal enemy." Pillow wanted his report published, thinking it would clear his name: "my report gives a truthful history of the incidents of the battles as I saw them." Nothing ever worked, however, and Pillow went down as one of the worst generals of the Civil War.[20]

Not only did the official government statements bother Floyd and Pillow but so also did the popular memory of the two generals. One Confederate remembered Pillow: "his insufficient conceit has probably not yet allowed him to comprehend that he is totally incompetent to command a brigade." As for Floyd, he perhaps endured the most vitriol, even having a mocking song written about him. Tellingly, few who had served under him were dismayed when he passed away a year later. "Floyd has at last gone up," wrote one Mississippian. "All of our old politicians are failures as generals." A Virginian noted, "I am sorry to say that we was badly out Generaled." Perhaps the best that could be said of him was by another Confederate who later took shots at both: "his fault was his weakness in yielding to Pillow & his being overruled & in not discovering Pillow's incompetence." Even the Northerners hated Floyd, one Union citizen writing, "I hope they will capture him yet, and make an example of him the traitor and thief. I think he ought to have it branded on his forehead."[21]

Although Floyd tried to make amends with his senior commanders, the leading Confederates at Fort Donelson complained bitterly about Floyd and Pillow while in prison. William Baldwin was irate and wrote that the Mississippians were "guarding the embarkation of troops while their chief was seeking safety." Later he wrote of the passage of command: "[when] seniors endeavor to escape responsibility by throwing the same upon the former, comment is unnecessary." Nathaniel Cheairs of the 3rd Tennessee described Pillow's and Floyd's "disgraceful flight," and Colonel Robert Farquharson of the 41st Tennessee, in prison at Fort Warren, labeled the affair a "criminal blunder." He also wrote that Buckner and the garrison were "victims of the *in competency* or *crime* of Pillow or Floyd or both."[22]

As more and more months passed, the twin-river forts fell out of the public eye as larger battles such as Shiloh took the spotlight. Fort Henry nevertheless continued to serve as a base for further operations, especially in the movement eventually to Corinth, Mississippi, which culminated the Tennessee River campaign that included Forts Henry and Donelson, Shiloh, and the fighting and siege around Corinth itself in May 1862. Still, Fort Henry was a place to see even later. Many noted passing the site while on transports destined for stations farther south. One Illinoisan viewed Fort Henry later in April, after Shiloh: "passed Fort Henry at 1¾ o'clock in the night moonlight and clear seen the fortifications. The riverbank is only about 5 feet from the fort." Another noted, "we came up to Ft Henry that great place there has been so much talk about lately. . . . I was surprised to find it such a small place." One Federal actually got to tour the site: "I went off and looked at the fortifications on the east bank."[23]

Fort Donelson also received more attention later in the war. The Federals continued to man the site even after the movement southward, and actually built a new fort just east of the original, across Indian Creek. It was there that Confederates attacked on several occasions, including August 1862 but most famously in February 1863, just a year after the defining events in February 1862. These later battles were Federal victories too.[24]

Later in the war and even afterward, the public as well as the Federal government remembered Fort Donelson. A "musical description" of the fighting appeared later in 1862 and the navy, in addition to naming a gunboat USS *Fort Henry*, renamed a captured blockade runner as USS *Fort Donelson*. The major memorialization began after the war when the Federal dead were reinterred in the Fort Donelson National Cemetery, situated at the site of the new Union fort. One worker described the process of digging up soldiers: "a large auger was used to drill into the graves on the battlefield and if they found something blue they were carried to the cemetery if it was gray they were left on the field." Most of the graves were found to be in the breakout area along the Wynn Ferry Road. Eventually, in the 1920s, Congress established what is now the Fort Donelson National Battlefield, today under the National Park Service. Unfortunately, Fort Henry is today under the waters of Kentucky Lake, a victim of the Tennessee Valley Authority dams built in the 1930s and 1940s.[25]

Just like the battlefields, the connections made at the twin rivers similarly remained. Some fifteen or so years later when Grant was president, he still respected his old division commander, C. F. Smith. When he learned one of Smith's daughters was in need, he wrote proffering help; Grant called Smith "one of our most gallant Generals in the rebellion," and added, "there is nothing that I would not do to aid the children of my once old chief and afterwards subordinate in their life struggles."[26]

Perhaps the most riveting Fort Donelson connection that was remembered decades later was between Grant and Buckner. The two old adversaries reconciled just like the sections they had once fought for. In fact, Buckner visited the dying Grant at his New York cottage. Because of his terminal throat cancer, Grant by then was only able to communicate by writing on a piece of paper. Just a few days later, Buckner served as one of Grant's pallbearers at the funeral.[27]

The old adversaries at Fort Donelson had been reunited in peace once more, much like their sections.

Appendix A

FORT HENRY ORDER OF BATTLE
FEBRUARY 6, 1862

Union Forces

ARMY OF THE TENNESSEE
Brig. Gen. U. S. Grant

FIRST DIVISION
Brig. Gen. John A. McClernand

First Brigade
Col. Richard J. Oglesby
8th Illinois
18th Illinois
29th Illinois
30th Illinois
31st Illinois
Stewart's, Dollins's, O'Harnett's, and Carmichael's cavalry companies
Schwartz's/Gumbart's Battery (E), 2nd Illinois Light Artillery
Dresser's Battery (D), 2nd Illinois Light Artillery

Second Brigade
Col. William H. L. Wallace
11th Illinois
20th Illinois
45th Illinois
48th Illinois
4th Illinois Cavalry
Taylor's Chicago Light Artillery (B), 1st Illinois Light Artillery
McAllister's Battery (D), 1st Illinois Light Artillery

SECOND DIVISION
Brig. Gen. Charles F. Smith

First Brigade
Col. John McArthur
9th Illinois
12th Illinois
41st Illinois
Battalion, 2nd Illinois Cavalry

Second Brigade
Brig. Gen. Lew Wallace
8th Missouri
11th Indiana
23rd Indiana
28th Illinois
Battalion, 2nd and 4th US Cavalry

Third Brigade
Col. John Cook
7th Illinois
50th Illinois
7th Iowa
13th Missouri
Wood's Chicago Light Artillery (A), 1st Illinois Artillery

Western Flotilla
Flag Officer Andrew H. Foote
USS *St. Louis*
USS *Carondelet*
USS *Essex*
USS *Cincinnati*

Timberclads
S. Ledyard Phelps
USS *Tyler*
USS *Conestoga*
USS *Lexington*

Confederate Forces

Brig. Gen. Lloyd Tilghman

First Brigade
    Col. Adolphus Heiman
        10th Tennessee
        48th Tennessee
        27th Alabama
        Culbertson's Battery
        9th (Gantt's) Battalion Tennessee Cavalry

Second Brigade
    Col. Joseph Drake
        4th Mississippi
        15th Arkansas
        51st Tennessee
        26th Alabama (2 cos.)
        Crain's Battery
        Hubbard's and Houston's Alabama Cavalry Battalions
        Milner's Cavalry Company
        Padgett's Cavalry Company
        Milton's Ranger Detachment

Fort Henry Gunners
    Captain Jesse Taylor
    Taylor's Tennessee Artillery Company

Appendix B

Fort Donelson Order of Battle
February 12–16, 1862

Union Forces

ARMY OF THE TENNESSEE
Brig. Gen. U. S. Grant

FIRST DIVISION
Brig. Gen. John A. McClernand

First Brigade
Col. Richard J. Oglesby
8th Illinois
18th Illinois
29th Illinois
30th Illinois
31st Illinois
Stewart's, Dollins's, O'Harnett's, and Carmichael's cavalry companies
Schwartz's/Gumbart's Battery (E), 2nd Illinois Light Artillery
Dresser's Battery (D), 2nd Illinois Light Artillery
Battalion, 2nd and 4th US Cavalry
Battalion, 2nd Illinois Cavalry

Second Brigade
Col. William H. L. Wallace
11th Illinois
20th Illinois
45th Illinois
48th Illinois
4th Illinois Cavalry

Taylor's Chicago Light Artillery (B), 1st Illinois Light Artillery
McAllister's Battery (D), 1st Illinois Light Artillery

Third Brigade
    Col. William R. Morrison (wd)
        17th Illinois
        49th Illinois

SECOND DIVISION
    Brig. Gen. Charles F. Smith

First Brigade
    Col. John McArthur
        9th Illinois
        12th Illinois
        41st Illinois

Third Brigade
    Col. John Cook
        7th Illinois
        50th Illinois
        52nd Indiana
        12th Iowa
        13th Missouri
        Maj. J. S. Cavender's Battalion Missouri Artillery
            Richardson's Battery (D), 1st Missouri Light Artillery
            Welker's Battery (H), 1st Missouri Light Artillery
            Stone's Battery (K), 1st Missouri Light Artillery

Fourth Brigade
    Col. Jacob G. Lauman
        25th Indiana
        2nd Iowa
        7th Iowa
        14th Iowa
        Birge's Sharpshooters (14th Missouri)

Fifth Brigade
    Colonel Morgan L. Smith
        8th Missouri
        11th Indiana

THIRD DIVISION
Brig. Gen. Lew Wallace

First Brigade
Col. Charles Cruft
31st Indiana
44th Indiana
17th Kentucky
25th Kentucky

Second Brigade
Attached to Thayer's Brigade
46th Illinois
57th Illinois
58th Illinois
20th Ohio

Third Brigade
Col. John M. Thayer
1st Nebraska
58th Ohio
68th Ohio
76th Ohio

Not Brigaded
Wood's Chicago Light Artillery (A), 1st Illinois Artillery
Company A, 32nd Illinois

Western Flotilla
Flag Officer Andrew H. Foote
USS *St. Louis*
USS *Carondelet*
USS *Pittsburg*
USS *Louisville*

Timberclads
S. Ledyard Phelps
USS *Tyler*
USS *Conestoga*

Confederate Forces

Brig. Gen. John B. Floyd

PILLOW'S DIVISION
  Brig. Gen. Gideon J. Pillow
  Brig. Gen. Bushrod R. Johnson (c)

Heiman's Brigade
  Col. Adolphus Heiman (c)
    10th Tennessee
    42nd Tennessee
    48th Tennessee
    53rd Tennessee
    27th Alabama
    Maney's Tennessee Battery

Drake's Brigade
  Col. Joseph Drake (c)
    4th Mississippi
    15th Arkansas
    1st Tennessee Battalion
    26th Alabama (2 cos.)

Davidson's Brigade
  Col. Thomas J. Davidson (s) (c)
  Col. John M. Simonton (c)
    1st Mississippi
    3rd (23rd) Mississippi
    7th Texas
    8th Kentucky

Baldwin's Brigade
  Col. William E. Baldwin (c)
    20th Mississippi
    26th Mississippi
    26th Tennessee

McCausland's Brigade
  Col. John McCausland
    36th Virginia
    50th Virginia

Wharton's Brigade
    Col. Gabriel C. Wharton
        51st Virginia
        56th Virginia

BUCKNER'S DIVISION
    Brig. Gen. Simon Bolivar Buckner (c)

Brown's Brigade
    Col. John C. Brown (c)
        3rd Tennessee
        18th Tennessee
        32nd Tennessee
        Graves's Kentucky Battery
        Porter's Tennessee Battery
        Jackson's Virginia Battery

Baldwin's Brigade
    Attached to Brown's
        2nd Kentucky
        14th Mississippi
        41st Tennessee

Fort Donelson Garrison
    Col. John W. Head
    Col. James E. Bailey (c)
        30th Tennessee
        49th Tennessee
        50th Tennessee

River Batteries
    Cpt. Joseph Dixon (k)
    Cpt. Jacob Culbertson (c)
        Maury Tennessee Battery
        Stankiewicz's Tennessee Battery
        Company A, 30th Tennessee
        Company A, 50th Tennessee

Cavalry
    Lt. Col. Nathan Bedford Forrest
        3rd Tennessee Cavalry
        9th Tennessee Cavalry Battalion
        1st Kentucky Cavalry Battalion

Artillery
    French's Virginia Battery
    Green's Kentucky Battery
    Guy's Virginia Battery
    Parker's Battery
    Adams's Virginia Battery

NOTES

Prologue

1. *The Goodspeed Histories*, 896–898, 901–902; Link, "An Inquiry into the Early County Court Records of Stewart County, Tennessee," 13.

2. *The Goodspeed Histories*, 901, 904, 913–917; "Union Inn," September 14, 1859, Dover *Weekly Intelligencer*, copy in Dover Weekly Intelligencer 1859 Newspaper Dover Hotel Info File, FDV; Wallace, "The Capture of Fort Donelson," 1:398.

3. Kennedy, *Agriculture of the United States in 1860*, 136–139; *The Goodspeed Histories*, 900; McClain, "A History of Stewart County, Tennessee," SCPL, 21.

4. *The Goodspeed Histories*, 894–895; Cooling, *Forts Henry and Donelson*, 45–46.

5. *Manufactures of the United States in 1860*, 573; McClain, "A History of Stewart County, Tennessee," SCPL, 22–23; *Stewart County Heritage, Dover, Tennessee*, 1:11–13.

6. Johnson, *Engineers of the Twin Rivers*, 61, copy in Western Rivers/Steamboats/Twin Rivers File, FDV.

7. Kennedy, *Population of the United States in 1860*, 459, 461, 463, 465, 467; *The Goodspeed Histories*, 900–901; McClain, "A History of Stewart County, Tennessee," SCPL, 36.

8. *The Goodspeed Histories*, 910–911; "For the Chronicle," May 10, 1861, Clarksville *Chronicle*; John Franklin Locke Diary, July 16, 1861, SCPL; *OR*, 1, 7:737.

Chapter 1. "The Keys of the Gate-Way into Her Own Territory"

1. Davis, *Jefferson Davis*, 336.

2. For an overview of the east, see Simpson, *The Civil War in the East*.

3. For the west, see Hess, *The Civil War in the West*; Woodworth, *Decision in the Heartland*.

4. Connelly, *Army of the Heartland*, 16–17.

5. Ibid., 3–22.

6. McPherson, *Battle Cry of Freedom*, 337.

7. For a detailed contemporary map of the Tennessee River, see "Tennessee River from Paducah, Ky. To Florence, Ala.," 1865, UMEM, copy in TSLA.

8. Longacre, *The Early Morning of War*; Piston and Hatcher, *Wilson's Creek*.

9. Hess, *The Civil War in the West*, 7–8.

10. Eubank, *In the Shadow of the Patriarch*.

11. McPherson, *Abraham Lincoln and the Second American Revolution*, 31.

12. Albert Sidney Johnston to Samuel Cooper, October 5, 1861, Correspondence of the Eastern Department and the Army of the Mississippi, 1861–1862, RG 109, E 103, NARA; Woodworth, *Decision in the Heartland*, 3.

13. McPherson, *Battle Cry of Freedom*, 293–295.

14. Connelly, *Army of the Heartland*, 25.

15. Elliott, *Isham G. Harris of Tennessee*, 86.

16. *OR*, 1, 7:684; Elliott, *Isham G. Harris of Tennessee*, 85–87.

17. Elliott, *Isham G. Harris of Tennessee*, 86–88.

18. *OR*, 1, 7:689.

19. "Southern News," March 27, 1862, Nashville *Evening Bulletin*.

20. Millett, Maslowski, and Feis, *For the Common Defense*, 110–111.

21. Jones, *Civil War Command and Strategy*, 51, 143; *OR*, 1, 7:749.

22. Ibid., 51, 143.

23. Connelly, *Army of the Heartland*, 16–17.

24. Hess, *The Civil War in the West*, 11–17.

25. Elliott, *Isham G. Harris of Tennessee*, 87–88.

26. Parks, *General Leonidas Polk*, 21–152.

27. McPherson, *Battle Cry of Freedom*, 296.

28. Parks, *General Leonidas Polk*, 180–187. See also Girardi, "Leonidas Polk and the Fate of Kentucky in 1861," 3:1–19; Gott, *Where the South Lost the War*, 55.

29. B. West to Lizzie, January 27, 1862, 12th Illinois File, FDR.

30. *OR*, 1, 7:788; Johnston, *The Life of Gen. Albert Sidney Johnston*, 496. See also Roland, "Albert Sidney Johnston and the Defense of the Confederate West," 1:12–23; Woodworth, "When Merit Was Not Enough," 9–27; and Engle, "Thank God, He Has Rescued His Character," 133–163.

31. *OR*, 1, 7:692, 746–747.

32. Roland, *Albert Sidney Johnston*, 270–277.

33. Jones, *Civil War Command and Strategy*, 48–49.

34. *OR*, 1, 7:684.

35. For Belmont, see Hughes, *The Battle of Belmont*.

36. Clarence L. Johnson, "The Story of Forts Henry and Donelson," undated, Kentucky Library and Museum Papers, WKU; "Fort Donelson," October 18, 1883, *National Tribune*; "Mouth of Sandy Tenn," June 11, 1861, Isham G. Harris Papers, TSLA, copy in FDC; Felix Zollicoffer and W. G. Harding to Adna Anderson, April 27, 1861, Confederate Military and Financial Board Papers, TSLA.

37. *OR*, 1, 7:689, 710–711; *ORN*, 1, 22: 797, 800; Taylor, "The Defense of Fort Henry," 1:368–369; Clarence L. Johnson, "The Story of Forts Henry and Donelson," undated, Kentucky Library and Museum Papers, WKU; J. P. Cannon, "History of the 27th Regiment Ala. Volunteer Infantry C.S.A.," undated, 27th Alabama File, ADAH, 2; "Recruits Wanted," December 20, 1861, Clarksville *Chronicle*.

38. "Anniversary of the Battle of Monterrey," Nashville *Union and American*, October 2, 1861, copy in Fort Henry Newspaper Accounts, FDV.

39. *OR*, 1, 7:734, 757; Cooling, *Forts Henry and Donelson*, 41–42.

40. W. W. Mackall to Felix Zollicoffer, October 3, 1861, Letters and Telegrams Sent, September 1861—April 1862, RG 109, chapter 2, volume 217, NARA.

41. For more on the Confederate railroad system, see Black, *The Railroads of the Confederacy*.

42. James Bailey to wife, December 22, 1861, 49th Tennessee File, FDR.

43. *OR*, 1, 7:144, 689, 710–711; Taylor, "The Defense of Fort Henry," 1:369.

44. H. L. Bedford Memoir, 1883, UT, 6; Wesley Smith Dorris Diary, December 24, 1861, UT; J. A. B. Rogers to Cornelius Bell, January 29, 1862, J. A. B. Rogers Letter, FDA; James Bailey to wife, February 2 and 6, 1862, 49th Tennessee File, FDR. For the 49th Tennessee, see Cross, *Cry Havoc*.

45. *OR*, 1, 7:711.

46. *OR*, 1, 7:698–700, 710; Connelly, *Army of the Heartland*, 83–85; Gott, *Where the South Lost the War*, 65; John Shorter to Green Strother, December 28, 1861, and Shorter Memo, January 6, 1862, Governor John G. Shorter Administrative Files, ADAH.

47. *OR*, 1, 7:698–699, 709; Brumbaugh, "A Letter to Fort Donelson," 31–35, copy in 50th Tennessee File, FDR; "Army Correspondence," December 31, 1861, Clarksville *Chronicle*; H. L. Bedford Memoir, 1883, UT, 2; John T. Hodges to family, November 21, 1861, 49th Tennessee File, FDR; F. E. Willey to friend, December 12, 1862, 49th Tennessee File, FDR.

48. *OR*, 1, 7:699, 723, 735; Eisterhold, "Fort Heiman."

49. Ibid., 709.

50. Roland, *Albert Sidney Johnston*, 266–267.

51. *OR*, 1, 7:684–685, 692–695, 719.

52. Ibid., 688, 694, 732–733, 739, 769, 771, 779, 788, 796.

53. Ibid., 707, 718, 728, 758, 788–790, 792–795; Gott, *Where the South Lost the War*, 72; Cooling, *Forts Henry and Donelson*, 44.

CHAPTER 2. "YOU HAVE NO IDEA HOW MUCH WORK IS REQUIRED
TO IMPROVISE"

1. Jones, *Civil War Command and Strategy*, 10.

2. For the complicated politics of Lincoln's presidency, see Paludan, *The Presidency of Abraham Lincoln*. For a good overview of Lincoln and the military, see Marszalek, *Lincoln and the Military*.

3. Symonds, *Lincoln and His Admirals*, 106.

4. Hess, *The Civil War in the West*, xii.

5. McPherson, *Battle Cry of Freedom*, 333.

6. Marszalek, *Lincoln and the Military*, 22–23, 26.

7. McPherson, *Battle Cry of Freedom*, 367.

8. For Fremont, see Chaffin, *Pathfinder*.

9. *ORN*, 1, 22:390.

10. *OR*, 1, 7:439; Winthrop B. Everett to Henry Halleck, February 12, 1862, Henry W. Halleck Papers, RG 94, E 159, NARA. For Halleck, see Marszalek, *Commander of All Lincoln's Armies*.

11. Daniel, *Days of Glory*, 3–14.

12. Marszalek, *Sherman*, 157–165.

13. *OR*, 1, 7:443–444, 447, 457. For Buell, see Engle, *Don Carlos Buell*.

14. For McClellan, see Sears, *George B. McClellan*.

15. McPherson, *Battle Cry of Freedom*, 290–292, 367; Daniel, *Days of Glory*, 33–56; Panhorst, "'The First of Our Hundred Battle Monuments,'" 31.

16. Cooling, *Forts Henry and Donelson*, 1–3.

17. Ibid., 3–10.

18. Jones, *Civil War Command and Strategy*, 8.

19. *ORN*, 1, 22:283–284, 286, 318–319, 495; *OR*, 1, 7:691; Joiner, *Mr. Lincoln's Brown Water Navy*, 23–24; Untitled Article, Clarksville *Weekly Chronicle*, October 18, 1861, copy in Newspaper Clippings on Fort Donelson and Dover Folder, FDV; John Rogers to Montgomery Meigs, July 12, 1861, George McClellan to John Rogers, June 26, 1861, and Survey of Steamboat *Lexington*, n.d., all in USS *Conestoga* File, RG 92, E 1403 Water Transportation, NARA; Daniel Collier to Montgomery Meigs, September 21, 1861, USS *Tyler* File, RG 92, E 1403 Water Transportation, NARA. For more on the timberclads, see Smith, *The Timberclads in the Civil War*.

20. *ORN*, 1, 22:283, 287, 292, 296, 304; Niven, *Gideon Welles*, 378. For more on Rogers, see Johnson, *Rear Admiral John Rogers*.

21. *OR*, 1, 7:691; *ORN*, 1, 22: 283–284, 286, 299, 318–319, 371–372, 375, 397, 430, 458, 461, 495; Joiner, *Mr. Lincoln's Brown Water Navy*, 23–24; untitled article, Clarksville *Weekly Chronicle*, October 18, 1861, copy in Newspaper Clippings on Fort Donelson and Dover Folder, FDV. For a list of the crew of the *Conestoga*, see "List, Officers and Crew," 1862, Seth Ledyard Phelps Papers, Christopher Newport University.

22. *ORN*, 1, 22:314, 495; Joiner, *Mr. Lincoln's Brown Water Navy*, 26–29; Bearss, *Hardluck Ironclad*, 190–191.

23. *ORN*, 1, 22:314, 358, 377, 438, 495, 505; Joiner, *Mr. Lincoln's Brown Water Navy*, 25–27.

24. *OR*, 1, 7:477; *ORN*, 1, 22:331, 365, 384, 387, 438.

25. *ORN*, 1, 22:462–463; Joiner, *Mr. Lincoln's Brown Water Navy*, 28–29; Bearss, *Hardluck Ironclad*, 27.

26. *ORN*, 1, 22:297, 320, 349–350.

27. *ORN*, 1, 22:297, 306–307, 313–314, 317–318, 321–322, 324, 465–467. For more on Foote, see Tucker, *Andrew Foote*.

28. *ORN*, 1, 22:390–392, 394–395, 42, 431, 435.

29. Ibid., 470–471, 473–474.

30. For Grant, see Simpson, *Ulysses S. Grant*.

31. *OR*, 1, 7:442; Simon Cameron to John Fremont, September 19, 1861, Ulysses S. Grant Papers, RG 94, E 159, NARA.

32. Grant, *Personal Memoirs*, 1:225; *OR*, 1, 7:515.

33. *OR*, 1, 7:442, 463.

34. Ibid., 442, 462–463, 515; *ORN*, 1, 22:317.

35. *OR*, 1, 7:442, 462–463, 515; *ORN*, 1, 22:317; James Parrott to wife, February 4, 1862, James C. Parrott Papers, SHSI; Milton Rood to father, January 29, 1862, Milton Rood Letters, SHSI.

36. John A. McClernand to John A. Logan, January 8, 1862, John A. Logan Papers, LC. For McClernand, see Kiper, *Major General John Alexander McClernand*.

37. General Orders No. 1, September 5, 1861, John A. McClernand Papers, RG 94, E 159, NARA.

38. Richardson, *A Personal History of Ulysses S. Grant*, 207; Wallace, "The Capture of Fort Donelson," 1:405; *OR*, 1, 7:929.

39. Simon and Marszalek, *The Papers of Ulysses S. Grant*, 4:188; Stephens, *Shadow of Shiloh*, 42–43, 48; Charles Smith to George Cullum, December 26, 1861, Charles F. Smith Papers, RG 94, E 159, NARA.

40. *OR*, 1, 3:267–268.

41. For Belmont, see Hughes, *The Battle of Belmont*.

42. Grant, *Personal Memoirs*, 1:280–281.

CHAPTER 3. "TOO MUCH HASTE WILL RUIN EVERYTHING"

1. Burns, *The Civil War*.

2. Smith, *Mississippi in the Civil War*, 96–97, 106.

3. Davis, *Jefferson Davis*, 396–397.

4. *OR*, 1, 7:533; Donald, *Lincoln*, 330.

5. Donald, *Lincoln*, 334–335.

6. *OR*, 1, 7:444, 517, 524, 526, 928; Abraham Lincoln to D. C. Buell, January 6, 1862, Don Carlos Buell Papers, FHS; Don Carlos Buell to Charles Smith, December 1, 1861, Charles F. Smith Papers, USMA.

7. *OR*, 1, 7:527, 532–533, 928.

8. Ibid., 563; James Bailey to wife, February 2, 1862, 49th Tennessee File, FDR. For Mill Springs, see Hafendorfer, *Mill Springs*.

9. *OR*, 1, 5:41.

10. R. H. Elam to mother, December 24, 1861, Elam Family Papers, TSLA; James Bailey to wife, December 22, 1861, 49th Tennessee File, FDR; W. C. Stewart to family, December 10 and 30, 1861, and January 8, 1862, W. C. Stewart Letters, FDA; *OR*, 1, 7:144–145, 396, 817; T. M. Sayars to cousin, January 19, 1862, Martha Farmer Anthony Papers, TSLA; "The Excursion" and "The Flag Presentation," January 10, 1862, Clarksville *Chronicle*; Samuel Smith to brother, January 9, 1862, Seamans Family Papers, LTU.

11. *OR*, 1, 7:144–145, 396, 817; Elliott, *Soldier of Tennessee*, 22; T. M. Sayars to cousin, January 19, 1862, Martha Farmer Anthony Papers, TSLA; Samuel R. Simpson Diary, November 10, 1861, TSLA; J. W. Wall to Jim and Sallie, January 30, 1862, 49th Tennessee File, FDR.

12. *OR*, 1, 7:144–145, 396, 817; T. M. Sayars to cousin, January 19, 1862, Martha

Farmer Anthony Papers, TSLA; Samuel R. Simpson Diary, November 10, 1861, TSLA; J. W. Wall to Jim and Sallie, January 30, 1862, 49th Tennessee File, FDR.

13. *OR*, 1, 7:532–533.

14. Hess, *The Civil War in the West*, 20.

15. Bearss, *Hardluck Ironclad*, 34–36.

16. *ORN*, 1, 22:481; Bearss, *Hardluck Ironclad*, 34; *OR*, 1, 7:455.

17. *ORN*, 1, 22:493, 496.

18. *OR*, 1, 7:534, 552, 565–566; *ORN*, 1, 22:489, 493–494.

19. *OR*, 1, 7:540; *ORN*, 1, 22:500, 502–504, 506, 516, 522.

20. *ORN*, 1, 22:485–486, 520–521.

21. *OR*, 1, 7:446.

22. Ibid., 530–531, 547.

23. McPherson, *Battle Cry of Freedom*, 333–335.

24. *OR*, 1, 8:509.

25. Ibid., 509; Connelly, *Army of the Heartland*, 79; Jones, *Civil War Command and Strategy*, 45.

26. *OR*, 1, 7:693; James Parrott to wife, February 3, 1862, James C. Parrott Papers, SHSI.

27. *OR*, 1, 8:509; Virginia Hanson to mother, January 21, 1862, Roger W. Hanson Papers, LC.

28. *OR*, 1, 7:440.

29. *ORN*, 1, 22:452, 458.

30. *OR*, 1, 7:451, 528–529, 925; Wallace, "The Capture of Fort Donelson," 1:399.

31. Sherman, *Memoirs*, 1:220.

32. McPherson, *Battle Cry of Freedom*, 394.

33. *ORN*, 1, 22:428.

34. *OR*, 1, 7:462–463; *ORN*, 1, 22:486.

35. *OR*, 1, 7:527, 926.

36. Ibid., 527–528, 535.

37. Ibid., 482, 507.

38. Ibid., 533–534, 539–540.

39. Ibid., 533–534; *ORN*, 1, 22:489–490, 507.

40. *OR*, 1, 7:533–534; *ORN*, 1, 22:489–490, 507.

41. *OR*, 1, 7:537–538.

42. Ibid., 540–541, 543, 545–546, 552; Force, *From Fort Henry to Corinth*, 27.

43. *OR*, 1, 7:68–71, 540–541, 543, 545–546, 552; Martin Wallace to Ann, January 17, 1862, Martin R. Wallace Papers, CHM; Thomas B. Hicks to Lowry Hinch, January 11, 1862, 7th Illinois Cavalry Papers, Lowry Hinch Collection, USAMHI.

44. *OR*, 1, 7:561–562, 565; *ORN*, 1, 22:507–509, 520–521; Frank Watters to sister, January 29, 1862, Walter Letters, FHS; Wallace, *An Autobiography*, 1:356; William Gilliam to S. E. Gilliam, January 26, 1862, Gilliam-Chason Family Letters, MDAH; Frank Smith to friend, February 2, 1862, Frank B. Smith Papers, USAMHI; Charles Smith to wife, January 21, 1862, Letter Extracts, Charles F. Smith Papers, USMA.

45. *OR*, 1, 7:561–562, 565; *ORN*, 1, 22:507–509, 520–521; Charles Smith to wife, January 22, 1862, Letter Extracts, Charles F. Smith Papers, USMA; Frank Watters to sister, January 29, 1862, Walter Letters, FHS; Wallace, *An Autobiography*, 1:356; William Gilliam to S. E. Gilliam, January 26, 1862, Gilliam-Chason Family Letters, MDAH; Frank Smith to friend, February 2, 1862, Frank B. Smith Papers, USAMHI.

46. B. West to Lizzie, January 27, 1862, 12th Illinois File, FDR.

47. *OR*, 1, 7:561–562, 565; Grant, *Personal Memoirs*, 1:234; John A. Neilson Diary, January 24, 1862, Irion-Neilson Family Papers, MDAH; Wallace, *An Autobiography*, 1:358; David Clark to cousin, January 18, 1862, 30th Tennessee File, FDR.

48. J. P. Hollowell to sister, January 3, 1862, J. P. Hollowell Letter, UT; *OR*, 1, 7:820, 823, 825; Hattaway and Jones, *How the North Won*, 69.

49. Davis, *Recollections*, 422, 425; "An Autobiography," undated, Mark P. Lowrey Papers, CWD, USAMHI.

50. *OR*, 1, 7:828–829, 831, 835–838, 841–844, 850–851; Wallace, "The Capture of Fort Donelson," 1:401.

51. *OR*, 1, 7:831, 835–836, 838, 841–844; A. Ricks to aunt, January 25, 1862, Eliza Barry Ricks Papers, MDAH; Wesley Smith Dorris Diary, January 17, 1862, UT; Lloyd Tilghman to W. W. Mackall, January 19, 1862, Lloyd Tilghman Papers, MOC; "From Fort Henry," January 25, 1862, Clarksville *Chronicle*.

52. *OR*, 1, 7:839–841, 849; *ORN*, 1, 22:801, 807, 816.

53. *OR*, 1, 7:844–845.

54. Ibid., 847.

55. "Fort Donelson," October 25, 1883, *National Tribune*; *OR*, 1, 7:561–562, 565, 930; Grant, *Personal Memoirs*, 1:234; John A. Neilson Diary, January 24, 1862, Irion-Neilson Family Papers, MDAH; Wallace, *An Autobiography*, 1:358; David Henderson to Mrs. Warner, January 19, 1862, Willaim W. Warner Papers, SHSI; Marszalek, *Commander of All Lincoln's Armies*, 116.

56. *OR*, 1, 7:571, 933 Grant, *Personal Memoirs*, 1:235; Woodworth, *Nothing but Victory*, 69.

57. *OR*, 1, 7:121, 930; *ORN*, 1, 22:524–525; Henry Halleck to Charles Smith, January 24, 1862, Charles F. Smith Papers, USMA.

58. *ORN*, 1, 22:525; *OR*, 1, 7:121.

59. Williams, *Lincoln and His Generals*, 59; *OR*, 1, 7:121, 571–572; *ORN*, 1, 22:314, 427–428, 524.

60. *OR*, 1, 7:121; Williams, *Grant Rises in the West*, 193.

CHAPTER 4. "WE SOON UNDERSTOOD THAT THE GREAT WESTERN MOVE WAS TO BEGIN"

1. *OR*, 1, 7:131; William Gilliam to S. E. Gilliam, February 2, 1862, Gilliam-Chason Family Letters, MDAH.

2. Connelly, *Army of the Heartland*, 80–81; *OR*, 1, 7:131–132; "The Work Progresses," January 13, 1862, Cairo City *Gazette*, copy in Fort Henry Newspaper Accounts, FDV; William Gilliam to S. E. Gilliam, February 2, 1862, Gilliam-Chason Family Letters, MDAH.

3. *OR*, 1, 7:132; John A. Neilson Diary, January 25, 1862, Irion-Neilson Family Papers, MDAH; John T. Megee to wife, January 20, 1862 (mislabeled 1861), John T. Megee Papers, MDAH.

4. *OR*, 1, 7:132–133; Taylor, "The Defense of Fort Henry," 1:369; William Gilliam to S. E. Gilliam, February 2, 1862, Gilliam-Chason Family Letters, MDAH.

5. Catton, *Grant Moves South*, 134; Gott, *Where the South Lost the War*, 77; I. P. Rumsey to mother, January 27, 1862, I. P. Rumsey Papers, NL; Dietrich Smith to Carrie, February 20, 1862, Dietrich C. Smith Papers, ALPL; James Butterfield to unknown, February 19, 1862, James A. B. Butterfield Correspondence, ALPL.

6. *ORN*, 1, 22:427–428, 528; *OR*, 1, 7:572. For the batteries on the north side of the Cumberland River, see the map in "Fort Donelson, Tennessee," undated, FHS.

7. *OR*, 1, 7:473; Croffut, *Fifty Years*, 434.

8. *OR*, 1, 7:573–574, 576, 583–585, 932–933, 936; Henry Halleck to Don Carlos Buell, February 1 and 5, 1862, and Buell to Albert Sidney Johnston, February 2, 1862, Don Carlos Buell Papers, RG 94, E 159, NARA; Albert Sidney Johnston to Don Carlos Buell, February 6, 1862, Letters and Telegrams Sent, September 1861–April 1862, RG 109, Chapter 2, Volume 217, NARA; Voltaire Twombly to cousin, January 12, 1862, Voltaire P. Twombly Papers, SHSI.

9. *OR*, 1, 7:572, 577, 579.

10. Ibid., 121–122.

11. Ibid., 575, 578; B. West to Lizzie, January 27, 1862, 12th Illinois File, FDR; Milton Rood to father, January 29, 1862, Milton Rood Letters, SHSI; Grant to J. C. Kelton, January 31, 1862, Lew Wallace Papers, RG 94, E 159, NARA.

12. *OR*, 1, 7:126, 578–579; Wallace, *Life and Letters*, 153; Kiper, *Major General John Alexander McClernand*, 68; Frank Whipple to mother, March 16, 1862, 11th Illinois File, FDR; Thomas K. Mitchell Diary, February 9, 1862, 4th Illinois Cavalry File, FDR.

13. *ORN*, 1, 22:528, 530–532, 534–535; Avery, *History of the Fourth Illinois Cavalry Regiment*, 51.

14. *ORN*, 1, 22:531, 533–535; *OR*, 1, 7:572; Milligan, *From the Fresh-Water Navy*, 23.

15. *ORN*, 1, 22:531, 534–536; Edward M. Galligan Diary, February 3, 1862, MTHS.

16. *ORN*, 1, 22:535–536.

17. Ibid., 534, 537.

18. Mattingly, *I Marched with Sherman*, 41; Charles Kroff Diary, February 4, 1862, Sheery Marie Cress Collection, UO; George D. Carrington Diary, February 3, 1862, CHM; James Parrott to wife, February 3, 1862, James C. Parrott Papers, SHSI.

19. Charles Kroff Diary, February 4, 1862, Sheery Marie Cress Collection, UO; James Parrott to wife, February 3, 1862, James C. Parrott Papers, SHSI.

20. *OR*, 1, 7:126, 581; Wallace, *An Autobiography*, 1:366; Douglas Hapeman Diary,

February 3, 1862, ALPL. For more on the transports used in the operation, see Gibson and Gibson, *Assault and Logistics*, 67.

21. Boring, "From Cairo to Donelson"; Crummer, *With Grant*, 14; Hackemer, *To Rescue My Native Land*, 142.

22. *OR*, 1, 7:126–127; I. P. Rumsey to father, undated, I. P. Rumsey Papers, NL; Adolph Engelmann to Mina, February 10, 1862, Engelmann-Kircher Family Papers, ALPL; Edward M. Galligan Diary, February 4, 1862, MTHS.

23. *OR*, 1, 7:581; Catton, *Grant Moves South*, 141; Grant, *Personal Memoirs*, 1:237; Edward M. Galligan Diary, February 4, 1862, MTHS.

24. *OR*, 1, 7:127; Wallace, *Life and Letters*, 154; Dan Young to Vance, February 12, 1862, John Vance Powers Papers, NJHS.

25. *OR*, 1, 7:127; David Cornwell Memoir, undated, CWD, USAMHI, 58.

26. *OR*, 1, 7:127–128; John Rawlins to Charles Smith, February 1, 1862, Charles F. Smith Papers, USMA.

27. *OR*, 1, 7:127; Wallace, *Life and Letters*, 154; Gower and Allen, *Pen and Sword*, 583.

28. Adolph Engelmann to Mina, February 10, 1862, Engelmann-Kircher Family Papers, ALPL; Woodworth, *Nothing but Victory*, 79.

29. *OR*, 1, 7:128; George C. Kindelsperyer Diary, February 5, 1862, FDR; Grant, *Personal Memoirs*, 1:237; James Parrott to wife, February 3 and 4, 1862, James C. Parrott Papers, SHSI; E. W. Herman Diary, February 5, 1862, 7th Iowa File, SNMP; Thomas K. Mitchell Diary, February 4, 1862, 4th Illinois Cavalry File, FDR; Channing Richards Diary, February 9, 1862, FHS; General Orders 16, February 3, 1862, Charles Smith Letterbook, Charles F. Smith Papers, USMA.

30. *OR*, 1, 7:128; Woodworth, *Nothing but Victory*, 73; Simon and Marszalek, *The Papers of Ulysses S. Grant*, 4:149.

31. *OR*, 1, 7:128; Oliver Bridgford to wife, February 5, 1862, 45th Illinois File, FDR; Simon and Marszalek, *The Papers of Ulysses S. Grant*, 4:153; David Cornwell Memoir, undated, CWD, USAMHI, 58.

32. *OR*, 1, 7:125, 585–586.

33. Kiper, *Major General John Alexander McClernand*, 70.

34. George D. Carrington Diary, February 5, 1862, CHM; Boring, "From Cairo to Donelson"; Stowell, "'We Will Fight for Our Flag,'" 213, originals in Thomas Barnett Papers, ALPL; James T. Mackey Diary, February 5, 1862, MOC.

35. Walke, *Naval Scenes*, 54–55, 61; Walke, "The Gun-Boats at Belmont and Fort Henry," 1:362; Henry H. Baltzell Memoir, 1916, ALPL, 8; Cunningham, *Shiloh and the Western Campaign of 1862*, 40–41.

36. John Roe to A. K. Stiles, February 6, 1862, John H. Roe Letter, Chicago Public Library; F. C. Cromwell Journal, February 6, 1862, 12th Iowa File, FDR.

37. William Gilliam to S. E. Gilliam, January 26, 1862, Gilliam-Chason Family Letters, MDAH.

38. *OR*, 1, 7:137, 131, 149.

39. Ibid., 149.

40. Ibid.

41. Ibid., 150.

42. Ibid.

43. Ibid., 133, 137, 149.

44. Ibid., 137, 145, 148; death notice, undated, G. W. Paris Papers, CHM; David Goodwin to Miss Bettie, March 2, 1862, David G. Godwin Letters, AHC.

45. *OR*, 1, 7:138, 150.

46. J. P. Cannon, "History of the 27th Regiment Ala. Volunteer Infantry C.S.A.," undated, 27th Alabama File, ADAH, 4–5.

47. *OR*, 1, 7:138, 150.

48. Ibid., 148–149.

49. Ibid., 858–859.

50. Ibid., 138, 149.

51. Ibid., 133, 138, 150.

52. Ibid., 133, 138–139.

53. Ibid., 133, 139.

54. Ambrose, *History of the Seventh Regiment Illinois Volunteer Infantry*, 25–26; Lew Wallace to wife, February 5, 1862, Lew Wallace Papers, IHS.

CHAPTER 5. "ALTERNATELY MUD AND WATER ALL THE WAY UP"

1. *OR*, 1, 7:931; Wallace, "The Capture of Fort Donelson," 1:401.

2. *ORN*, 1, 22:512–514, 523; *OR*, 1, 7:578; Foote, "Notes on the Life of Admiral Foote," 1:347.

3. Simon and Marszalek, *The Papers of Ulysses S. Grant*, 4:153.

4. *ORN*, 1, 22:512; Edward M. Galligan Diary, February 5, 1862, MTHS.

5. Davis, Perry, and Kirkley, *Atlas*, 11. For a good description, see Jesse Connelly Diary, February 18, 1862, IHS, copy also in ISL.

6. Davis, Perry, and Kirkley, *Atlas*, 11.

7. *ORN*, 1, 22:512.

8. Davis, Perry, and Kirkley, *Atlas*, 11.

9. Ibid.

10. *ORN*, 1, 22:512. For an overview of Fort Henry, see Bearss, "The Fall of Fort Henry," 85–107.

11. *OR*, 1, 7:587–588.

12. Williams, *P. G. T. Beauregard*, 115.

13. *OR*, 1, 7:139, 151; Gower and Allen, *Pen and Sword*, 584.

14. *OR*, 1, 7:139.

15. James Bailey to wife, February 2, 1862, 49th Tennessee File, FDR; Taylor, "The Defense of Fort Henry," 1:370; John T. Megee to wife, January 14, 1862 (mislabeled 1861), John T. Megee Papers, MDAH.

16. *OR*, 1, 7:139–140.

17. Ibid., 145.

18. Ibid., 140–141, 146; Taylor, "The Defense of Fort Henry," 370.

19. Edward M. Galligan Diary, February 5, 1862, MTHS; *OR*, 1, 7:124; Walke, "The Gun-Boats at Belmont and Fort Henry,"1:362; Isaac Pugh to wife, February 10, 1862, Issac C. Pugh Papers, UCR.

20. Charles Kroff Diary, February 5–6, 1862, Sheery Marie Cress Collection, UO; George D. Carrington Diary, February 6, 1862, CHM; James S. Fogle Diary, February 6, 1862, 11th Indiana File, SNMP.

21. *OR*, 1, 52, 1:11–12; Mattingly, *I Marched with Sherman*, 42; Wallace, *An Autobiography*, 1:368; Ira Merchant to Henry Yates, February 26, 1862, Ira Merchant Letter, ALPL; Garrett Schreurs Diary, February 6, 1862, SHSI.

22. Wallace, *An Autobiography*, 1:369; Ira Merchant to Henry Yates, February 26, 1862, Ira Merchant Letter, ALPL; E. W. Herman Diary, February 6, 1862, 7th Iowa File, SNMP; Charles Smith to wife, February 7, 1862, Letter Extracts, Charles F. Smith Papers, USMA.

23. George C. Kindelsperyer Diary, February 6, 1862, FDR; Wallace, *An Autobiography*, 1:369–370; Charles Cochran to mother, February 11, 1862, Mark A. Chapman Collection, UWY; "He Was at Fort Heiman," February 23, 1899, *National Tribune*; Isaac Pugh to wife, February 10, 1862, Issac C. Pugh Papers, UCR; J. P. Cannon, "History of the 27th Regiment Ala. Volunteer Infantry C.S.A.," undated, 27th Alabama File, ADAH, 5–6.

24. Wallace, *An Autobiography*, 1:369–370.

25. Simon and Marszalek, *The Papers of Ulysses S. Grant*, 4:155.

26. Wallace, *An Autobiography*, 1:369–370; George C. Kindelsperyer Diary, February 6, 1862, FDR; Chris Wolfram to mother, February 12, 1862, Christian A. Wolfram Letters, IHS; Frank Watters to sister, February 11, 1862, Walter Letters, FHS.

27. Isaac Pugh to wife, February 10, 1862, Issac C. Pugh Papers, UCR; Lew Wallace to wife, February 7, 1862, Lew Wallace Papers, IHS.

28. A. J. Williams, "A Union Boy at Donelson," December 15, 1898, *National Tribune*; E. W. Herman Diary, February 7, 1862, 7th Iowa File, SNMP; George C. Kindelsperyer Diary, February 7, 1862, FDR; Charles Cochran to mother, February 11, 1862, Mark A. Chapman Collection, UWY; William Reed to Star and Chronicle, February 10, 1862, William Reed Letters, 8th Missouri File, SNMP.

29. James Drish to wife, February 11, 1862, James F. Drish Papers, ALPL; Ira Merchant to Henry Yates, February 26, 1862, Ira Merchant Letter, ALPL; William Lyon to James Garfield, March 12, 1863, Fort Heiman and Vicinity Folder, FDV; "Condensed Letters," August 13, 1885, *National Tribune*; H. B. Hillen to Joseph Gilney, February 10, 1862, H. B. Hillen Letter, UA.

30. Wallace, *An Autobiography*, 1:369–372.

31. James Bailey to wife, February 6, 1862, Bailey Family Papers, TSLA, copy in FDC and 49th Tennessee File, FDR.

32. *OR*, 1, 7:129; Ambrose, *History of the Seventh Regiment Illinois Volunteer Infantry*, 27; Force, *From Fort Henry to Corinth*, 31; Thomas Miller to Benjamin Newton,

February 10, 1862, Thomas F. Miller Letters, ALPL; Hackemer, *To Rescue My Native Land*, 143.

33. *OR*, 1, 7:130; Reed, *Campaigns and Battles*, 15; George D. Carrington Diary, February 6, 1862, CHM; Milton Rood to father, February 9, 1862, Milton Rood Letters, SHSI.

34. *OR*, 1, 7:129, 219; I. P. Rumsey to father, February 7, 1862, I. P. Rumsey Papers, NL; George D. Carrington Diary, February 6, 1862, CHM; Milton Rood to father, February 9, 1862, Milton Rood Letters, SHSI.

35. *OR*, 1, 7:129–130; David Poak to sister, February 8, 1862, David W. Poak Papers, NC; Wallace, *Life and Letters*, 155.

36. *OR*, 1, 7:129–130; W. H. L. Wallace to Anne, February 7, 1862, Wallace-Dickey Papers, ALPL.

37. Ben H. Bounds Civil War Memoir, undated, 4th Mississippi File, FDR, 3, copy in 4th Mississippi File, VICK.

Chapter 6. "A Good Day's Work"

1. Alexander Simplot Diary, WHS, 24, copy in Alexander Simplot Diary, FDV; Andrew Foote to wife, February 6, 1862, Mississippi River 1861–1862, RG 45, A-5, NARA, copy in FDC; R. N. Stembel to James Eads, November 19, 1863, James B. Eads Collection, MHS; Lew Wallace to wife, February 5, 1862, Lew Wallace Papers, IHS.

2. Andrew Foote to wife, February 6, 1862, Mississippi River 1861–1862, RG 45, A-5, NARA; Smith, *The USS Carondelet*, 64; Joiner, *Mr. Lincoln's Brown Water Navy*, 26; R. N. Stembel to James Eads, November 19, 1863, James B. Eads Collection, MHS.

3. *OR*, 1, 7:133–134, 151.

4. Ibid., 122; Walke, "The Gun-Boats at Belmont and Fort Henry," 1:362–363.

5. *OR*, 1, 7:122; *ORN*, 1, 22:315; Edward M. Galligan Diary, February 6, 1862, MTHS.

6. *OR*, 1, 7:122; Taylor, "The Defense of Fort Henry," 1:370; Walke, *Naval Scenes*, 61–62; Edward M. Galligan Diary, February 6, 1862, MTHS.

7. Richardson, *The Secret Service*, 215; Walke, *Naval Scenes*, 62.

8. *OR*, 1, 7:134, 141, 151; Wallace, *An Autobiography,* 1:369–370; Walke, "The Gun-Boats at Belmont and Fort Henry," 1:363; Taylor, "The Defense of Fort Henry," 1:370.

9. *OR*, 1, 7:134, 141, 146, 151; Walke, "The Gun-Boats at Belmont and Fort Henry," 1:363.

10. *OR*, 1, 7:134, 141, 146, 151; Walke, "The Gun-Boats at Belmont and Fort Henry," 1:363.

11. *OR*, 1, 7:134, 141.

12. Ibid., 134, 141, 151.

13. Ibid., 141.

14. *ORN*, 1, 22:540–541.

15. *OR*, 1, 7:141, 151.

16. Walke, *Naval Scenes*, 65–66; *OR*, 1, 7:122–123; *ORN*, 1, 22:537, 540; *OR*, 1, 52, 1:207; Edward M. Galligan Diary, February 6, 1862, MTHS.

17. Walke, *Naval Scenes*, 62–63; USS *Essex* Muster Roll, 1862, RG 217, E UD292, Western Gunboat Flotilla Muster, Pay, and Receipt Rolls, 1862, NARA; Pension Application Papers, August 15, 1884, USS *Essex* File, and December 1, 1886, USS *Pittsburg* File, both in RG 92, E 1403 Water Transportation, NARA; Walke, "The Gun-Boats at Belmont and Fort Henry," 1:364; Edward M. Galligan Diary, February 6, 1862, MTHS.

18. Edward M. Galligan Diary, February 6, 1862, MTHS.

19. *OR*, 1, 7:123; *ORN*, 1, 22:541, 543; Walke, "The Gun-Boats at Belmont and Fort Henry," 1:363–365; Andrew Foote to wife, February 6, 1862, Mississippi River 1861–1862, RG 45, A-5, NARA; USS *Cincinnati* Muster Roll, 1862, RG 217, E UD292, Western Gunboat Flotilla Muster, Pay, and Receipt Rolls, 1862, NARA.

20. *OR*, 1, 7:123; *ORN*, 1, 22:541, 543; Walke, "The Gun-Boats at Belmont and Fort Henry," 1:363–365.

21. *ORN*, 1, 22:541, 545.

22. Ibid., 541–542.

23. *OR*, 1, 7:134, 141, 146; Powhaten Ellis to mother, February 11, 1862, Munford-Ellis Family Papers, DU.

24. *OR*, 1, 7:141, 152.

25. Ibid., 141, 146, 151.

26. Ibid., 134, 141–142, 151.

27. Ibid., 146–147, 152; Walke, "The Gun-Boats at Belmont and Fort Henry," 1:367; Taylor, "The Defense of Fort Henry," 1:371; *Donelson Campaign Sources*, 115; "From Clarksville, Tennessee," Charleston *Courier*, February 11, 1862.

28. Andrew Foote to wife, February 6, 1862, Mississippi River 1861–1862, RG 45, A-5, NARA.

29. Walke, *Naval Scenes*, 57; Andrew Foote to wife, February 6, 1862, Mississippi River 1861–1862, RG 45, A-5, NARA.

30. *OR*, 1, 7:123, 142; Taylor, "The Defense of Fort Henry," 1:371; Andrew Foote to wife, February 6, 1862, Mississippi River 1861–1862, RG 45, A-5, NARA; R. N. Stembel to James Eads, November 19, 1863, James B. Eads Collection, MHS.

31. Lanza and Taylor, *Source Book*, 454; Raab, *Confederate General Lloyd Tilghman*, 86; S. H. Batton to wife, February 7, 1862, FDV; Dabney Stuart Wier Diary, February 11, 1862, Mississippi Volunteers File, FDR; Unsigned Fragmentary Notes on the Capture of Fort Henry, undated, Civil War Collection, MHS; John Wood to wife, February 10, 1862, Hester Family Papers, MSU.

32. Taylor, "The Defense of Fort Henry," 1:372; Lanza and Taylor, *Source Book*, 454–455; John E. Smith to Aimee, February 8, 1862, 45th Illinois File, FDR; *Biographical Directory*, 1348; Charles Smith to wife, February 7, 1862, Letter Extracts, Charles F. Smith Papers, USMA.

33. Powhaten Ellis to mother, February 11, 1862, Munford-Ellis Family Papers, DU.

34. Walke, "The Gun-Boats at Belmont and Fort Henry," 1:364.

35. Richard L. McClung Diary, undated, UTA, 5; Cannon, *Inside of Rebeldom*, 13; J. P. Cannon, "History of the 27th Regiment Ala. Volunteer Infantry C.S.A.," undated, 27th Alabama File, ADAH, 6.

36. David Poak to sister, February 8, 1862, David W. Poak Papers, NC.

37. *OR*, 1, 7:129, 134, 147; J. W. Head to Gideon Pillow, February 6, 1862, Western Department, Telegrams Received and Sent, 1861–1862, RG 109, E 101, NARA; William H. Kinkade Diary, February 6, 1862, ALPL; Stowell, "'We Will Fight for Our Flag,'" 213; Richard L. McClung Diary, undated, UTA, 6; Joseph Brigham to mother, February 6, 1862, Brigham Family Papers, TSLA, copy in FDC and 50th Tennessee File, FDR; Cannon, *Inside of Rebeldom*, 13.

38. *OR*, 1, 7:129, 134, 147; J. W. Head to Gideon Pillow, February 6, 1862, Western Department, Telegrams Received and Sent, 1861–1862, RG 109, E 101, NARA; Andrew Jackson Campbell Diary, February 7, 1862, UTA; Cannon, *Inside of Rebeldom*, 13; Ben H. Bounds Civil War Memoir, undated, 4th Mississippi File, FDR, 3; William H. Kinkade Diary, February 6, 1862, ALPL; Stowell, "'We Will Fight for Our Flag,'" 213; Richard L. McClung Diary, undated, UTA, 6; Joseph Brigham to mother, February 6, 1862, Brigham Family Papers, TSLA, copy in FDC; Griffin Stanton Diary, February 6, 1862, UMEM.

39. *OR*, 1, 7:129, 134, 147; J. W. Head to Gideon Pillow, February 6, 1862, Western Department, Telegrams Received and Sent, 1861–1862, RG 109, E 101, NARA; Andrew Jackson Campbell Diary, February 7, 1862, UTA; Cannon, *Inside of Rebeldom*, 13; James Bailey to wife, February 2, 1862, 49th Tennessee File, FDR; Ben H. Bounds Civil War Memoir, undated, 4th Mississippi File, FDR, 3; William H. Kinkade Diary, February 6, 1862, ALPL; Stowell, "'We Will Fight for Our Flag,'" 213; Richard L. McClung Diary, undated, UTA, 6; Joseph Brigham to mother, February 6, 1862, Brigham Family Papers, TSLA, copy in FDC; Griffin Stanton Diary, February 6, 1862, UMEM.

40. *OR*, 1, 7:129–130, 220; George D. Carrington Diary, February 6, 1862, CHM; John White to cousin, February 9, 1862, John H. White Letters, ALPL, copy in FDC and Goldman Collection, USAMHI; Thomas Miller to Benjamin Newton, February 10, 1862, Thomas F. Miller Letters, ALPL; James Stewart Diary, February 6, 1862, UMC.

41. W. H. L. Wallace to Anne, February 7, 1862, Wallace-Dickey Papers, ALPL; *OR*, 1, 7:129–130, 220; Walke, "The Gun-Boats at Belmont and Fort Henry," 1:367; Wallace, *An Autobiography*, 1:376; John White to cousin, February 9, 1862, John H. White Letters, ALPL; George D. Carrington Diary, February 6, 1862, CHM; Hiram Scofield Diary, February 8, 1862, Hiram Scofield Papers, NL; I. P. Rumsey to father, February 7, 1862, I. P. Rumsey Papers, NL; Jacob Lauman to unknown, February 8, 1862, Jabob G. Lauman Papers, CHM.

42. *OR*, 1, 7:129–130, 220; "Peter Wilson in the Civil War," 262; David Poak to sister, February 8, 1862, David W. Poak Papers, NC; Walke, "The Gun-Boats at Belmont and Fort Henry," 1:367; John White to cousin, February 9, 1862, John H. White Letters, ALPL; George D. Carrington Diary, February 6, 1862, CHM; Hiram Scofield Diary, February 8, 1862, Hiram Scofield Papers, NL; Jacob Lauman to unknown, February 8, 1862, Jacob G. Lauman Papers, CHM; W. B. O'Neill to brother, February 10, 1862, 14th Iowa

File, FDR; Thomas Miller to Benjamin Newton, February 10, 1862, Thomas F. Miller Letters, ALPL; Charles Kroff Diary, February 6, 1862, Sheery Marie Cress Collection, UO; James Parrott to wife, February 3, 1862, James C. Parrott Papers, SHSI.

43. David Poak to sister, February 8, 1862, David W. Poak Papers, NC; Walke, *Naval Scenes*, 58.

44. *OR*, 1, 7:123; Walke, "The Gun-Boats at Belmont and Fort Henry," 1:367; Simon and Marszalek, *The Papers of Ulysses S. Grant*, 4:163; Richardson, *The Secret Service*, 217.

45. *OR*, 1, 7:129–130, 544; Kiper, *Major General John Alexander McClernand*, 72; John McClernand to Andrew Foote, February 7, 1862, Harwood Family Papers, SU, copies in LC; Andrew Foote to wife, February 6, 1862, Mississippi River 1861–1862, RG 45, A-5, NARA; Adolph Engelman to Mina, February 12, 1862, Engelmann-Kircher Family Papers, ALPL.

46. W. H. L. Wallace to Anne, February 7, 1862, Wallace-Dickey Papers, ALPL.

47. *OR*, 1, 7:125.

48. Andrew Foote to wife, February 6, 1862, Mississippi River 1861–1862, RG 45, A-5, NARA; *OR*, 1, 7:124, 590; Henry Halleck to Don Carlos Buell, February 7, 1862, Don Carlos Buell Papers, RG 94, E 159, NARA; Abram Keller to Miss, February 14, 1862, Dumville Family Correspondence, ALPL.

49. *OR*, 1, 7:136, 147; George Cullum to Henry Halleck, February 16, 1862, Henry W. Halleck Papers, LC; Richard L. McClung Diary, undated, UTA, 6.

50. *OR*, 1, 7:124.

CHAPTER 7. "THE ENTERING WEDGE TO ALL OUR SUBSEQUENT SUCCESSES"

1. *The Congressional Globe: Containing the Debates and Proceedings of the Second Session of the Thirty-Seventh Congress*, 707, 717.

2. *ORN*, 1, 22:545–547, 549; Milligan, *From the Fresh-Water Navy*, 25–26; Elihu Puckett to wife, February 15, 1862, Watters-Curtis Family Papers, FHS.

3. Frank Watters to sister, February 11, 1862, Walter Letters, FHS; *ORN*, 1, 22:546–547; Nevins, *Diary of the Civil War*, 205; Untitled Article, February 12, 1862, Monroe (Wisconsin) *Sentinel*; "A Grand Excursion," Evansville *Daily Journal*, February 12, 1862.

4. *OR*, 1, 7:123, 125; Lunsford Yandell Diary, February 11, 1862, Yandell Family Papers, FHS; David Poak to sister, February 8, 1862, David W. Poak Papers, NC; Henry Russell to unknown, February 10, 1862, Henry H. Russell Letter, FHS.

5. E. H. Dailey to mother, February 11, 1862, 4th Illinois Cavalry File, FDR; *OR*, 1, 7:120, 124; *ORN*, 1, 22:547; Walke, *Naval Scenes*, 67; I. P. Rumsey to father, February 11, 1862, I. P. Rumsey Papers, NL; John N. Ferguson Diary, February 7, 1862, LC; Unknown to sister, February 9, 1862, Robert H. Caldwell Papers, BGSU; Samuel Kirkwood to William Shaw, February 11, 1862, William T. Shaw Papers, SHSI; Lew Wallace to wife, February 9, 1862, Lew Wallace Papers, IHS.

6. *OR*, 1, 7:130–131; Lunsford Yandell Diary, February 7, 1862, Yandell Family Pa-

pers, FHS; Jones, *A Rebel War Clerk's Diary*, 1:95; J. H. Long to Sir, February 8, 1862, J. H. Long Letter, MU.

7. *OR*, 1, 7:861; *ORN*, 1, 22:548; Charles Christensen to friends, February 21, 1862, Charles Christensen Letter, UT; Ben West Diary, February 8, 1862, 12th Illinois File, FDR; William F. Willey Diary, February 9, 1862, OHS.

8. *OR*, 1, 7:131.

9. Ibid., 124.

10. Ibid., 120, 125.

11. Ibid., 125.

12. Ibid., 591, 593, 599.

13. Ibid., 591, 594–595, 605; Cooling, "The Reliable First Team," 51.

14. *OR*, 1, 7:594–595, 597, 605; George W. Cullum to Henry Halleck, February 7 and 9, 1862, George W. Cullum Letters, ALPL.

15. *OR*, 1, 7:604.

16. *ORN*, 1, 22: 545–546, 548, 577, 592; *OR*, 1, 7:598; William L. Jurney to Ry, February 12, 1862, 2nd Iowa File, FDR; Edward M. Galligan Diary, February 6–7, 1862, MTHS; "Services of Francis Le Chevallier during Rebellion between the North and South," 1887, Francis Le Chevalier Papers, UCB.

17. *ORN*, 1, 22:571–574.

18. Ibid., 510.

19. *OR*, 1, 7:123, 591.

20. Lunsford Yandell Diary, February 7, 1862, Yandell Family Papers, FHS.

21. *OR*, 1, 7:153–155.

22. Smith, *The Timberclads in the Civil War*, 226–240.

23. *OR*, 1, 7:153; "Capture of Fort Henry—Frolic of the Lincoln Gunboats," February 10, 1862, M. J. Solomons Scrapbook, DU.

24. *OR*, 1, 7:153–154; Gideon Pillow to W. W. Mackall, February 7, 1862, Western Department, Telegrams Received and Sent, 1861–1862, RG 109, E 101, NARA; Lunsford Yandell Diary, February 8, 1862, Yandell Family Papers, FHS; Powhaten Ellis to mother, February 11, 1862, Munford-Ellis Family Papers, DU.

25. *OR*, 1, 7:153–154, 864; *ORN*, 1, 22:821; "Federals on the Tennessee," February 10, 1862, Memphis *Avalanche*; Slagle, *Ironclad Captain*, 165.

26. *OR*, 1, 7:154; "Steamboats Destroyed," February 14, 1862, Clarksville *Chronicle*.

27. *ORN*, 1, 22:574–575; Walke, "The Western Flotilla," 1:430; Smith, *The USS Carondelet*, 69.

28. *OR*, 1, 10, 1:85.

29. *OR*, 1, 7: 153–156; unsigned, undated memoir in U.S.S. *Tyler* File, SNMP.

30. *OR*, 1, 7:154; Prize Application Documents, February 21, 1884, USS *Tyler* File, RG 92, E 1403 Water Transportation, NARA.

31. *OR*, 1, 7:154; *ORN*, 1, 22:821.

32. *OR*, 1, 7: 153–156; unsigned, undated memoir in U.S.S. *Tyler* File, SNMP.

33. *OR*, 1, 7:135, 155, 157, 888–889; *ORN*, 1, 22:579, 822; Operator to Albert Sidney Johnston, February 7, 1862, Western Department, Telegrams Received and Sent, 1861–1862, RG 109, E 101, NARA.

34. *OR*, 1, 7:155.

35. Ibid., 155.

36. Ibid., 155–156; John Wilcox to wife, February 12, 1862, John S. Wilcox Papers, ALPL, copy in FDC.

37. *OR*, 1, 7:156; John Wilcox to wife, February 12, 1862, John S. Wilcox Papers, ALPL; B to wife, February 17, 1862, 25th Kentucky File, FDR.

38. *OR*, 1, 7:155; *ORN*, 1, 22:570–571, 583; Slagle, *Ironclad Captain*, 172.

39. *OR*, 1, 7: 155–156; *ORN*, 1, 22:570; unsigned, undated memoir in U.S.S. *Tyler* File, SNMP.

40. James Fentress to wife, February 9, 1862, Talbot-Fentress Family Papers, TSLA; *ORN*, 1, 22:578–579; "Capture of Fort Henry—Frolic of the Lincoln Gunboats," February 10, 1862, M. J. Solomons Scrapbook, DU.

41. *OR*, 1, 7:861, 864, 867, 871–872; *ORN*, 1, 22:820; Albert Sidney Johnston to Mayor of Florence, Alabama, undated, Letters and Telegrams Sent, October 1861–April 1862, RG 109, Chapter 2, Volume 218, NARA; "Capture of Fort Henry—Frolic of the Lincoln Gunboats," February 10, 1862, M. J. Solomons Scrapbook, DU.

42. *OR*, 1, 7:861–862; Roman, *The Military Operations*, 1:218–223; Robert Cartmell Diary, February 15–16, 1862, Robert H. Cartmell Papers, TSLA.

43. *OR*, 1, 7:131.

44. Ibid., 865; *ORN*, 1, 22:823.

45. *OR*, 1, 7:131.

46. Ibid., 861–862; *ORN*, 1, 22:823; Mary E. Van Meter Diary, February 10–20, 1862, UK; "Notes of Reference," March 4, 1862, RG 109, E 116, NARA; Jim Roberts to wife, February 21 and March 7, 1862, Roberts Family Papers, UVA.

47. *OR*, 1, 7:869.

48. Ibid., 135; Connelly and Jones, *The Politics of Command*, 97.

49. *OR*, 1, 7:872.

50. Smith, *Shiloh*, 25–26.

51. *OR*, 1, 6:823; Albert Sidney Johnston to Mansfield Lovell, February 10 and 12, 1862, Letters and Telegrams Sent, October 1861–April 1862, RG 109, Chapter 2, Volume 218, NARA.

52. *OR*, 1, 7: 863, 867, 878; *OR*, 1, 6:827; Hess, *The Civil War in the West*, 39.

53. *OR*, 1, 6:825, 890; E. John Ellis, "A Retrospect," 1865, E. John Ellis Diary, LSU, 18.

54. *OR*, 1, 6:823.

55. Ibid., 824–826.

56. Ibid., 894.

57. I. P. Rumsey to father, February 7, 1862, I. P. Rumsey Papers, NL; Wallace, *An Autobiography*, 1:375; Andrew Foote to wife, February 6, 1862, Mississippi River 1861–1862, RG 45, A-5, NARA; Jesse Cox Diary, February 19, 1862, TSLA; R. N. Stembel to James Eads, November 19, 1863, James B. Eads Collection, MHS.

58. Andrew Davis to wife, February 21, 1862, Andrew F. Davis Papers, UI.

59. *OR*, 1, 7:259.

60. Ibid., 125, 591; *ORN*, 1, 22:549.

61. Phoebe Cross to sister, February 2, 1862, Phoebe Cross Letter, UT.

CHAPTER 8. "I THINK WE CAN TAKE IT; AT ALL EVENTS, WE CAN TRY"

1. *OR*, 1, 7:124.

2. Ibid., 595.

3. Ibid., 259.

4. For contemporary views, see William D. T. Travis Sketches, ALPL.

5. *OR*, 1, 7:393, 869; "Capture of Fort Henry—Frolic of the Lincoln Gunboats," February 10, 1862, M. J. Solomons Scrapbook, DU; John Murphey to friend, January 25, 1862, Farmer Family Papers, TSLA, copy in FDC and Martha Farmer Anthony Papers, TSLA; James Hallums to sister, February 2, 1862, Land between the Lakes Project Research Papers, TSLA, copy in FDC; F. E. Willey to friend, December 12, 1862, 49th Tennessee File, FDR.

6. *OR*, 1, 7:393, 869; Reuben Ross Journal, March 1862, Ross Family Papers, TSLA, copy in FDC.

7. *OR*, 1, 7:870; Gideon Pillow to unknown, February 6, 1862, Gideon Pillow Papers, RG 109, E 132, NARA.

8. *OR*, 1, 7:870.

9. Ibid., 870–871; W. A. Rorer to Susan, January 31, 1862, W. A. Rorer Letters, DU, copies in MDAH; Gideon Pillow to unknown, February 9, 1862, John B. Floyd Papers, RG 109, E 119, NARA.

10. Simon and Marszalek, *The Papers of Ulysses S. Grant*, 4:165, 175; Lew Wallace to wife, February 11, 1862, Lew Wallace Papers, IHS; Jacob Lauman to unknown, February 8, 1862, Jabob G. Lauman Papers, CHM; Abram J. Vanauken Diary, February 8, 1862, ALPL; William Wilson Diary, February 9, ALPL; E. C. Sackett to family, February 8, 1862, Sackett Family Letters, ALPL; Abiel M. Barker Diary, February 11, 1862, 32nd Illinois File, FDR; James Drish to wife, February 11, 1862, James F. Drish Papers, ALPL; Albert Rhodes Diary, February 17, 1862, NSHS; Charles Cochran to mother, February 11, 1862, Mark A. Chapman Collection, UWY.

11. Richardson, *A Personal History*, 217–218; Alexander Simplot Diary, WHS, 27, copy in Alexander Simplot Diary, FDV; Wallace, "The Capture of Fort Donelson," 1:404–405; Wallace, *An Autobiography*, 1:375–377; Daniel H. Brush Diary, February 15, 1862, ALPL.

12. *OR*, 1, 7:596; U. S. Grant to George Cullum, February 8, 1862, George W. Cullum Papers, USMA.

13. *OR*, 1, 7:598–601, 603; Stowell, "'We Will Fight For Our Flag,'" 214.

14. *OR*, 1, 7:120; *ORN*, 1, 22:577–578, 582; "Services of George W. Cullum, US Army from July 1, 1833 to November 1, 1864," George W. Cullum Papers, RG 94, E 159, NARA.

15. *OR*, 1, 7:598, 600; *ORN*, 1, 22:315, 550, 579, 584, 604; Andrew Foote to wife, February 6, 1862, Mississippi River 1861–1862, RG 45, A-5, NARA.

16. Eads, "Recollections of Foote and the Gunboats," 1:343–345; "To the Editors of the Independent," March 6, 1862, New York *Independent*; Milligan, *From the Fresh-Water Navy*, 24; Montgomery Meigs to Andrew Foote, February 12, 1862, Montgomery C. Meigs Papers, CHM.

17. *OR*, 1, 7:598, 600; *ORN*, 1, 22:315, 550, 579, 584, 604; Andrew Foote to wife, February 6, 1862, Mississippi River 1861–1862, RG 45, A-5, NARA. For the *Pittsburg*, see USS *Pittsburg* Paymaster's Ledger, 1862, VT.

18. *ORN*, 1, 22:579, 582–583–584; Walke, "The Western Flotilla," 1:430; Walke, *Naval Scenes*, 68.

19. *ORN*, 1, 22:592; "Services of Francis Le Chevallier during Rebellion between the North and South," 1887, Francis Le Chevalier Papers, UCB; Edward M. Galligan Diary, February 8, 1862, MTHS; USS *Cincinnati* and *Essex* Muster Rolls, 1862, RG 217, E UD292, Western Gunboat Flotilla Muster, Pay, and Receipt Rolls, 1862, NARA.

20. *OR*, 1, 7:596–597, 605; Fletcher, *The History of Company A*, 30–31; Thomas K. Mitchell Diary, February 11, 1862, 4th Illinois Cavalry File, FDR; James Powell to Charles Smith, March 25, 1862, Charles F. Smith Papers, USMA; James Thompson to wife, February 9, 1862, Thompson Family Papers, UAZ.

21. *OR*, 1, 7:261; Powhaten Ellis to mother, February 11, 1862, Munford-Ellis Family Papers, DU; Andrew Jackson Campbell Diary, February 7, 1862, UTA; James Coghill to wife, February 8, 1862, James Coghill Letters, UMOC; George W. Dillon Diary, February 8, 1862, 18th Tennessee File, FDR.

22. *OR*, 1, 7:261; Powhaten Ellis to mother, February 11, 1862, Munford-Ellis Family Papers, DU; Andrew Jackson Campbell Diary, February 7, 1862, UTA; James Coghill to wife, February 8, 1862, James Coghill Letters, UMC.

23. *OR*, 1, 7:135, 366.

24. *OR*, 1, 7:358; Cummings, *Yankee Quaker*, 185, 188; Wesley Smith Dorris Diary, January 19, 1862, UT; Milton Haynes to Lloyd Tilghman, January 19, 1862, Lloyd Tilghman Papers, MOC.

25. *OR*, 1, 7:276, 358; Cummings, *Yankee Quaker*, 188; W. W. Mackall to Bushrod Johnson, February 6, 1862, Bushrod Johnson Papers, RG 109, E 123, NARA; John M. Porter Memoirs, undated, Civil War Collection, TSLA, 14, copy in FDC and ECU; James Coghill to wife, February 8, 1862, James Coghill Letters, UMC.

26. *OR*, 1, 7:358; Clarence Johnson Article, September 8, 1933, Kentucky Library and Museum Papers, WKU; George Adams to wife, February 8, 1862, George Wiley Adams Letters, Civil War Collection, TSLA, copy in FDC.

27. Connelly, *Army of the Heartland*, 114; *OR*, 1, 7:262, 278, 870; Charles E. Taylor Diary, February 9, 1862, LSU, copy in CH.

28. *OR*, 1, 7:278, 870–871.

29. Ibid., 346, 865; Cooling, *Forts Henry and Donelson*, 132; Gower and Allen, *Pen and Sword*, 589; Nathaniel Cheairs Account, May 3, 1862, John C. Brown Autograph Book, Civil War Collection, TSLA, copy in FDC.

30. *OR*, 1, 7:272, 328, 870–871; Connelly, *Army of the Heartland*, 114–116. For more on Floyd, see Pinnegar, *Brand of Infamy*.

31. *OR*, 1, 7:329; Clarence Johnson Article, September 8, 1933, Kentucky Library and Museum Papers, WKU.

32. *OR*, 1, 7:316, 319.

33. Ibid., 329, 351, 871; Pinnegar, *Brand of Infamy*, 129; Jobe, "Forts Henry and

Donelson," 25; Hughes and Stonesifer, *The Life and Wars of Gideon J. Pillow*, 216–217; Thomas Dabney Wier Diary, February 12, 1862, UVA.

34. *ORN*, 1, 22:821; *OR*, 1, 7:868; Hughes and Stonesifer, *The Life and Wars of Gideon J. Pillow*, 214.

35. *OR*, 1, 7:865; Richard L. McClung Diary, undated, UTA, 6.

36. *OR*, 1, 7:161; Simon and Marszalek, *The Papers of Ulysses S. Grant*, 4:165, 175.

37. *OR*, 1, 7:161.

38. Ibid., 162, 383.

39. Ibid., 601, 606, 609; Grant, *Personal Memoirs*, 1:244–245.

40. *OR*, 1, 7:601, 606, 609, 619; Grant, *Personal Memoirs*, 1:244–245; Wallace, *An Autobiography*, 1:378; Stephens, *Shadow of Shiloh*, 42–43, 48; Simon and Marszalek, *The Papers of Ulysses S. Grant*, 4:180, 188, 211; General Field Order No. 9, February 10, 1862, Mason Brayman Papers, CHM; General Field Order No. 11, February 11, 1862, Mason Brayman Papers, CHM; Jasper Kidwell to mother, February 18, 1862, Ross-Kidwell Family Papers, IHS; John Hardin to father, February 17, 1862, John J. Hardin Letter, IHS; Henry Halleck to George Cullum, February 7 and 13, 1862, Henry W. Halleck Collection, Civil War Collection, MHS; Lew Wallace to wife, February 11 and 19, 1862, Lew Wallace Papers, IHS; Eugene Marshall, "Narrative of the Civil War, 1861–1862," undated, Eugene Marshall Papers, MNHS, 4; William T. Sherman to Gilbert A. Pierce, February 18, 1862, Rosemonde E. and Emile Kuntz Collection, TU; George Cullum to U. S. Grant, February 15, 1862, George W. Cullum Papers, USMA.

41. *OR*, 1, 7:601, 606, 609, 619; Grant, *Personal Memoirs*, 1:244–245; Simon and Marszalek, *The Papers of Ulysses S. Grant*, 4:180, 188, 211; William T. Sherman to Gilbert A. Pierce, February 18, 1862, Rosemonde E. and Emile Kuntz Collection, TU.

42. *OR*, 1, 7:601; I. P. Rumsey to father, February 7, 1862, I. P. Rumsey Papers, NL; Hackemer, *To Rescue My Native Land*, 144.

43. *OR*, 1, 7:605; Samuel Kennedy Cox Diary, February 11, 1862, 17th Kentucky File, FDR, copy in SNMP; Lew Wallace to unknown, February 13, 1862, Absalom H. Markland Papers, LC; David M. Claggett Diary, February 9, 1862, ALPL, copy in WKU, CHCH, and 17th Kentucky File, FDR; William Wilson Diary, February 9, 1862, ALPL; Thomas L. Hoffman Diary, February 12, 1862, SHSI; John M. Thayer, "At Fort Donelson," April 21, 1898, *National Tribune*; I. N. Prince to sister, February 25, 1862, J. N. Prince Letter, FDA.

44. *OR*, 1, 7:161–162, 170, 183, 192; I. P. Rumsey to father, February 7, 1862, I. P. Rumsey Papers, NL; Milo W. Brady Diary, February 11, 1862, 45th Illinois File, FDR; George D. Carrington Diary, February 11, 1862, CHM; E. S. Henline to friend, February 18, 1862, E. S. Henline Letters, 8th Illinois File, SNMP; Charles Tompkins to wife, February 1862, Charles B. Tompkins Papers, DU.

45. *OR*, 1, 7:161–162, 170, 183, 192; E. S. Henline to friend, February 18, 1862, E. S. Henline Letters, 8th Illinois File, SNMP; I. P. Rumsey to father, February 7, 1862, I. P. Rumsey Papers, NL; Milo W. Brady Diary, February 11, 1862, 45th Illinois File, FDR; Charles Tompkins to wife, February 1862, Charles B. Tompkins Papers, DU; George D. Carrington Diary, February 11, 1862, CHM.

46. Hicks, "Fort Donelson," 4; William H. Kinkade Diary, February 12, 1862, ALPL; Adolph Engelmann to Mina, February 10, 1862, Engelmann-Kircher Family Papers, ALPL; Nelson Wood to father, February 12, 1862, Hess Collection, USAMHI; James Drish to wife, February 11, 1862, James F. Drish Papers, ALPL; Charles Kroff Diary, February 12, 1862, Sheery Marie Cress Collection, UO.

47. *OR*, 1, 7:183, 192–193, 383; E. S. Henline to friend, February 18, 1862, E. S. Henline Letters, 8th Illinois File, SNMP; Dietrich Smith to Carrie, February 20, 1862, Dietrich C. Smith Papers, ALPL; Griffin Stanton Diary, February 12, 1862, UMEM; Channing Richards Diary, February 12, 1862, FHS.

48. Stickles, *Simon Bolivar Buckner*, 137; Connelly, *Army of the Heartland*, 113; Gott, *Where the South Lost the War*, 155.

49. *OR*, 1, 7:171, 351; Thomas Miller to Benjamin Newton, February 18, 1862, Thomas F. Miller Letters, ALPL; Selden Spencer, "Reminiscences of the Battle of Fort Donelson," undated, Civil War Collection, MHS; David Cornwell Memoir, undated, CWD, USAMHI, 60.

50. Catton, *Grant Moves South*, 153, 161; Brinton, *Personal Memoirs*, 115; *OR*, 1, 7:159, 171; James Butterfield to unknown, February 19, 1862, James A. B. Butterfield Correspondence, ALPL.

51. Charles Smith to wife, January 21 and 30, 1862, Letter Extracts, Charles F. Smith Papers, USMA; *OR*, 1, 7:215, 220; *OR*, 1, 52, 1:12; Wallace, "The Capture of Fort Donelson," 1:407; Addison Sleeth Memoir, undated, ISL, 9.

52. *OR*, 1, 7:171–172, 184, 188, 191, 193, 211; Wallace, "The Capture of Fort Donelson," 1:406, 408; George Durfee to uncle, February 17, 1862, George S. Durfee Letters, UIL; Charles Tompkins to wife, February 1862, Charles B. Tompkins Papers, DU.

53. *OR*, 1, 7:171–172, 184, 188, 191, 193, 211; John M. Porter Memoirs, undated, Civil War Collection, TSLA, 15, copy in FDC; Wallace, "The Capture of Fort Donelson," 1:406, 408; George Durfee to uncle, February 17, 1862, George S. Durfee Letters, UIL.

54. *OR*, 1, 7:171–172, 184, 188, 191, 193, 211; Wallace, "The Capture of Fort Donelson," 1:406, 408; I. P. Rumsey to family, February 16, 1862, I. P. Rumsey Papers, NL; George Durfee to uncle, February 17, 1862, George S. Durfee Letters, UIL; E. S. Henline to friend, February 18, 1862, E. S. Henline Letters, 8th Illinois File, SNMP.

55. "First Battle Experience-Fort Donelson," 501; S. C. Mitchell, "Recollections of a Private," October 15, 1887, Pulaski *Citizen*, copy in 3rd Tennessee File, FDR, 63; Marcus L. Henry Reminiscences, 1862, MSU.

56. Brinton, *Personal Memoirs*, 115.

57. Ferrell, *Holding the Line*, 16, original Flavel C. Barber Diary is in IU.

58. *ORN*, 1, 22:587; Walke, "The Western Flotilla," 1:431.

59. *OR*, 1, 7:398; Reuben Ross Journal, March 1862, Ross Family Papers, TSLA, copy in FDC.

60. *OR*, 1, 7:398.

61. Ibid., 159, 172, 190–191, 220, 223, 231.

62. "Fort Donelson," June 5, 1891, 56th Virginia File, FDR.

CHAPTER 9. "PRETTY WELL TESTED THE STRENGTH OF OUR DEFENSIVE LINE"

1. *OR*, 1, 7:262; *Donelson Campaign Sources*, 130. Many of the Tennessee sketches in the supplement are from Lindsley, *The Military Annals of Tennessee*.

2. *OR*, 1, 7:416.

3. Ibid., 277, 338, 370; Cooling, "A Virginian at Fort Donelson," 178, original journal in John Henry Guy Diary, VHS; Henry Bronson to Ella, February 14, 1862, J. H. Bronson Collection, NSHS; Robert Hughes Diary, February 13, 1862, Robert Morton Hughes Papers, ODU. For more on the 36th Virginia, see Scott, *36th Virginia Infantry*.

4. *OR*, 1, 7:267, 330; Clarence Johnson Article, September 8, 1933, Kentucky Library and Museum Papers, WKU; Albert Sidney Johnston to John Floyd, February 11, 1862, John B. Floyd Papers, DU.

5. Marcus L. Henry Reminiscences, 1862, MSU. For a revisionist biography of Floyd, see Pinnegar, *Brand of Infamy*.

6. Lanza and Taylor, *Fort Henry and Fort Donelson Campaigns*, 647.

7. Gott, *Where the South Lost the War*, 157.

8. Cooling, "A Virginian at Fort Donelson," 179.

9. "Fort Donelson," June 5, 1891, 56th Virginia File, FDR; James George to wife, January 18 and 22, 1862, James Z. George Papers, MDAH; Hughes and Stonesifer, *The Life and Wars of Gideon J. Pillow*, 213.

10. *OR*, 1, 7:267.

11. Ibid., 278, 389, 391, 393–394, 398, 409; James Hallums to sister, February 2, 1862, Land between the Lakes Project Research Papers, TSLA, copy in FDC; Reuben Ross Journal, March 1862, Ross Family Papers, TSLA, copy in FDC.

12. *OR*, 1, 7:389, 394, 410.

13. Ibid., 261, 279, 377, 394, 868; George Hamman Diary, February 20, 1862, ALPL.

14. *OR*, 1, 7:261, 279, 407; Wallace, "The Capture of Fort Donelson," 1:398.

15. S. C. Mitchell, "Recollections of a Private," October 15, 1887, Pulaski *Citizen*; J. T. Williamson, "Notes about the War (1861–1865)," undated, 3rd Tennessee File, FDR; *OR*, 1, 7:359; Marcus L. Henry Reminiscences, 1862, MSU; Timothy McNamara Diary, February 12, 1862, MDAH.

16. *OR*, 1, 7: 267, 279 329, 350; Nathaniel Cheairs Account, May 3, 1862, John C. Brown Autograph Book, Civil War Collection, TSLA, copy in FDC; Marcus L. Henry Reminiscences, 1862, MSU.

17. S. C. Mitchell, "Recollections of a Private," October 15, 1887, Pulaski *Citizen*; *OR*, 1, 7:279, 368; Thomas Miller to Benjamin Newton, February 18, 1862, Thomas F. Miller Letters, ALPL; James Coghill to wife, January 1862, James Lindsay Coghill Papers, VHS.

18. "Fort Donelson," June 5, 1891, 56th Virginia File, FDR. See also T. D. J., "Fort Donelson," 372–373.

19. Charles Tompkins to wife, February 1862, Charles B. Tompkins Papers, DU.

20. *ORN*, 1, 22:592; *OR*, 1, 7:280; John M. Porter Memoirs, undated, Civil War Collection, TSLA, 13, copy in FDC.

21. *ORN*, 1, 22:588, 594.

22. Ibid., 588; *OR*, 1, 7:389, 398.

23. *OR*, 1, 7:389, 393, 396, 398.

24. *ORN*, 1, 22:588; Walke, "The Western Flotilla," 1:431.

25. *OR*, 1, 7:389, 398.

26. Ibid., 389, 394, 396; Reuben Ross Journal, March 1862, Ross Family Papers, TSLA, copy in FDC.

27. *OR*, 1, 7:389, 398, 411; Reuben Ross Journal, March 1862, Ross Family Papers, TSLA, copy in FDC; Samuel R. Simpson Diary, November 10, 1861, TSLA.

28. *ORN*, 1, 22:588, 595; U. S. Grant to Henry Walke, February 13, 1862, WS.

29. *OR*, 1, 7:389–390, 398; H. L. Bedford Memoir, 1883, UT, 12. See also Bedford, "Fight between the Batteries and Gunboats at Fort Donelson," 165–173.

30. Grant, *Personal Memoirs*, 246; Badeau, *Military History of Ulysses S. Grant*, 1:39; Cooling, "The Reliable First Team," 52; Simon and Marszalek, *The Papers of Ulysses S. Grant*, 4:201.

31. *OR*, 1, 7:341–342, 347, 352; Selden Spencer, "Reminiscences of the Battle of Fort Donelson," undated, Civil War Collection, MHS; John Wood to wife, February 10, 1862, Hester Family Papers, MSU. For a modern treatment of Smith's operation on the Union left, see Bearss, "The Iowans at Fort Donelson: General C. F. Smith's Attack on the Confederate Right February 12–16, 1862, Part I," 241–268; and Bearss, "The Iowans at Fort Donelson: General C. F. Smith's Attack on the Confederate Right February 12–16, 1862, Part II," 321–343.

32. Welsh, *Medical Histories of Confederate Generals*, 79; Thomas Dabney Wier Diary, February 13 and 14, 1862, UVA; William L. McKay Diary, undated, Civil War Collection, TSLA, copy in FDC; M. E. Drake to A. J. Jones, March 26, 1862, Abraham G. Jones Papers, ECU; Selden Spencer, "Reminiscences of the Battle of Fort Donelson," undated, Civil War Collection, MHS.

33. Selden Spencer, "Reminiscences of the Battle of Fort Donelson," undated, Civil War Collection, MHS.

34. *OR*, 1, 52, 1:7–8; *OR*, 1, 7:227.

35. *OR*, 1, 52, 1:8.

36. Ibid., 9–10; *OR*, 1, 7:227; James Parrott to wife, February 18, 1862, James C. Parrott Papers, SHSI.

37. *OR*, 1, 52, 1:9–10; *OR*, 1, 7:227; Martin V. Miller to sister, February 24, 1862, WS.

38. *OR*, 1, 52, 1:10; *OR*, 1, 7:227–228; Thompson, *History of the Orphan Brigade*, 64.

39. *OR*, 1, 52, 1:10; *OR*, 1, 7:231; "Peter Wilson in the Civil War," 265, 272, 275; Kiner, *One Year's Soldiering*, 24–27.

40. *OR*, 1, 52, 1:10; *OR*, 1, 7:231.

41. *OR*, 1, 7:343; F. M. Ingram to Wayne, February 26, 1862, F. M. Ingram Letter, FDA.

42. *OR*, 1, 52, 1:8, 10; *OR*, 1, 7:227–228, 232; "Peter Wilson in the Civil War," 265, 275.

43. *OR*, 1, 52, 1:8, 10; *OR*, 1, 7:227–228, 232.

44. Kiper, *Major General John Alexander McClernand*, 76.

45. *OR*, 1, 7:159, 172, 188; Grant, *Personal Memoirs*, 1:246; Kiper, *Major General John Alexander McClernand*, 79; John McClernand to U. S. Grant, February 13, 1862, Mason Brayman Papers, CHM.

46. *OR*, 1, 7:267, 367; "Fort Donelson," November 1, 1883, *National Tribune*; Aaron Hollow Statement, November 6, 1963, Aaron/Erin Hollow Folder, FDV.

47. *OR*, 1, 7:360, 367; Andrew Jackson Campbell Diary, February 13, 1862, UTA.

48. *OR*, 1, 7:193, 203, 205, 208, 212; Kiper, *Major General John Alexander McClernand*, 76; General Field Order No. 10, February 10, 1862, Mason Brayman Papers, CHM.

49. *OR*, 1, 7:205; Force, *From Fort Henry to Corinth*, 42; Richard L. McClung Diary, undated, UTA, 7.

50. *OR*, 1, 7:360, 367–368; Richard L. McClung Diary, undated, UTA, 7.

51. *OR*, 1, 7:204–205, 212.

52. *OR*, 1, 7:212–214.

53. *OR*, 1, 7:212–214; Richard Oglesby to Isham Haynie, August 19, 1895, Isham N. Haynie Papers, ALPL.

54. *OR*, 1, 7:204, 213; "Report of 17th Ill. Reg.," February 1862, William R. Morrison Papers, ALPL, copy in FDC.

55. *OR*, 1, 7:213; Charles Tompkins to wife, February 1862, Charles B. Tompkins Papers, DU.

56. *OR*, 1, 7:204, 347, 368; Selden Spencer, "Reminiscences of the Battle of Fort Donelson," undated, Civil War Collection, MHS.

57. *OR*, 1, 7:360, 367–368; Andrew Jackson Campbell Diary, February 13, 1862, UTA.

58. *OR*, 1, 7:194, 204, 206, 213; Crummer, *With Grant at Fort Donelson*, 27; Adair, *Historical Sketch of the Forty-Fifth Illinois Regiment*, 4; John E. Smith to Aimee, March 6, 1862 45th Illinois File, FDR.

59. *OR*, 1, 7:204.

60. *OR*, 1, 7:206, 213–214, 368; George O. Smith, "Brief History of the 17th Regiment of Illinois Volunteer Infantry," 1913, ALPL, 2; Ferrell, *Holding the Line*, 19; Selden Spencer, "Reminiscences of the Battle of Fort Donelson," undated, Civil War Collection, MHS.

61. *OR*, 1, 7:172, 191, 193–194, 215; Ezra Taylor to G. S. Hubbard, March 16, 1862, Ezra Taylor Papers, CHM; Selden Spencer, "Reminiscences of the Battle of Fort Donelson," undated, Civil War Collection, MHS; Dan Young to Vance, February 21, 1862, John Vance Powers Papers, NJHS.

62. *OR*, 1, 7:173, 194, 206, 276–277, 338, 347; Samuel Barrett to unknown, February 18, 1862, Samuel Eddy Barrett Papers, CHM; George D. Carrington Diary, February 13, 1862, CHM; Selden Spencer, "Reminiscences of the Battle of Fort Donelson," undated, Civil War Collection, MHS.

63. *OR*, 1, 7:262, 330; Samuel Barrett to unknown, February 18, 1862, Samuel Eddy Barrett Papers, CHM.

64. Lowry, "A Fort Donelson Prisoner of War," 334; *OR*, 1, 7:174, 613; M. A. Ryan, "Experiences of a Confederate Soldier in Camp and Prison in the Civil War," undated, M. A. Ryan Memoir, MDAH, copy in 8th Mississippi File, FDR. For a concise collection of weather quotations, see Weather During Fort Donelson Battle Folder, FDV; Charles Tompkins to wife, February 1862, Charles B. Tompkins Papers, DU; Thomas L. Hoffman Diary, February 14, 1862, SHSI.

65. *OR*, 1, 52, 1:8; *OR*, 1, 7:190; E. S. Henline to friend, February 18, 1862, E. S. Henline Letters, 8th Illinois File, SNMP; Charles Sackett to mother, February 20, 1862, Charles O. Sackett Papers, SHSI; Wallace, "The Capture of Fort Donelson," 1:415; Samuel Barrett to unknown, February 18, 1862, Samuel Eddy Barrett Papers, CHM; James Parrott to wife, February 18, 1862, James C. Parrott Papers, SHSI.

66. Martin V. Miller to sister, February 24, 1862, WS; McAuley, "Fort Donelson and Its Surrender," 71; John R. Palmer, "The Field of Donelson," April 11, 1901, *National Tribune*; *OR*, 1, 7:220, 224; "Peter Wilson in the Civil War," 264; Wallace, "The Capture of Fort Donelson," 1:410; Cunningham, *Doctors in Gray*, 171; George D. Carrington Diary, February 14, 1862, CHM; William H. Kinkade Diary, February 15, 1862, ALPL; Reed, *Campaigns and Battles*, 16; William Wilder, "Reminiscences of the Civil War," 1903, William F. Wilder Papers, LC, 9; Henry Parcel to parents, February 20, 1862, Henry E. Parcel Correspondence, ALPL; Frank Reed to mother, February 17, 1862, 12th Iowa File, FDR; James Butterfield to unknown, February 19, 1862, James A. B. Butterfield Correspondence, ALPL; Daniel H. Brush Diary, February 15, 1862, ALPL; Milton Rood to father, February 17 and 20, 1862, Milton Rood Letters, SHSI; Chris Wolfram to mother, February 17, 1862, Christian A. Wolfram Letters, IHS; Gott, *Where the South Lost the War*, 147.

67. *OR*, 1, 7:185, 201, 214; Addison Sleeth Memoir, undated, ISL, 11.

68. George D. Carrington Diary, February 13, 1862, CHM; Dietrich Smith to Carrie, February 20, 1862, Dietrich C. Smith Papers, ALPL; Reed, *Campaigns and Battles*, 18; David Cornwell Memoir, undated, CWD, USAMHI, 60.

69. John E. Smith to Aimee, February 17, 1862 45th Illinois File, FDR.

70. *OR*, 1, 7: 343, 355, 368–369, 379; Smith, *James Z. George*, 50; M. F. Baxter, "My Services in the Confederate Army from April 1861 to May 22, 1865," undated, Marion Francis Baxter Papers, MDAH, 2–3; George W. Dillon Diary, February 14, 1862, 18th Tennessee File, FDR; Timothy McNamara Diary, February 14, 1862, MDAH; Thomas Dabney Wier Diary, February 14, 1862, UVA; Marcus L. Henry Reminiscences, 1862, MSU; Selden Spencer, "Reminiscences of the Battle of Fort Donelson," undated, Civil War Collection, MHS. See also Spencer, "Diary Account of Fort Donelson," 282–285. For more on Jackson's artillery, see Bohannon, *The Giles, Allegheny and Jackson Artillery*.

71. *OR*, 1, 7:262, 398–399; Marcus L. Henry Reminiscences, 1862, MSU; Reuben Ross Journal, March 1862, Ross Family Papers, TSLA, copy in FDC.

72. Samuel Barrett to unknown, February 18, 1862, Samuel Eddy Barrett Papers, CHM; Marcus L. Henry Reminiscences, 1862, MSU; *OR*, 1, 7:267–268, 279–280.

73. *OR*, 1, 7:267–268, 279–280.

CHAPTER 10. "YOU ARE NOT AT FORT HENRY"

1. *OR*, 1, 7:188; J. H. Rowett to brother, February 20, 1862, J. H. Rowett Letter, FDA; Henry H. Baltzell Diary, February 13, 1862, ALPL.

2. *OR*, 1, 7:174, 185, 188, 201, 221; Hiram Scofield Diary, February 14, 1862, Hiram Scofield Papers, NL.

3. *OR*, 1, 7:396; S. C. Mitchell, "Recollections of a Private," October 15, 1887, Pulaski *Citizen*.

4. *OR*, 1, 7:209.

5. Ibid., 268, 343.

6. Ibid., 399; H. L. Bedford Memoir, 1883, UT, 14.

7. *OR*, 1, 7:268, 343, 369; Charles Lutz to brother, February 21, 1862, Charles H. Lutz Papers, CWD, USAMHI; V. H. Stevens to uncle, February 28, 1862, Howard and Victor Stevens Papers, Coco Collection, HCWRT, USAMHI; Thompson, *History of the Orphan Brigade*, 75; John Jarvis to M. J. Kirkpatrick, March 1, 1862, John Douglass Jarvis Letter, FHS.

8. B. F. Boring, "From Cairo to Donelson," March 15, 1894, *National Tribune*; Barker, *Military History*, 9; Samuel R. Simpson Diary, February 14, 1862, TSLA; Hubert, *History of the Fiftieth Regiment*, 67, 77–78; A. F. Gilbert Memoir, 1928, Jill Knight Garrett Collection, TSLA, copy in 17th Illinois File, FDR; Marcus L. Henry Reminiscences, 1862, MSU.

9. *ORN*, 1, 22:592; *OR*, 1, 7:613; Jobe, "Forts Henry and Donelson," 43; Oliphant M. Todd Diary, February 13–14, 1862, LC; Eric Bergland Diary, February 12, 1862, RBHPC.

10. Wallace, "The Capture of Fort Donelson," 1:409; Abram Keller to Miss, February 14, 1862, Dumville Family Correspondence, ALPL; Adolph Engelman to Mina, February 12, 1862, Engelmann-Kircher Family Papers, ALPL; Henry Bronson to Ella, February 14, 1862, J. H. Bronson Collection, NSHS; Chris Wolfram to mother, February 17, 1862, Christian A. Wolfram Letters, IHS. Also claimed to have been left were the 32nd and 43rd Illinois and 52nd Indiana, as well as the Curtis Horse, or 5th Iowa Cavalry; John Hardin to father, February 17, 1862, John J. Hardin Letter, IHS; Eugene Marshall Diary, February 14 and 16, 1862, Eugene Marshall Papers, DU; Eugene Marshall, "Narrative of the Civil War, 1861–1862," undated, Eugene Marshall papers, MNHS, 4; Unknown to mother, February 25, 1862, Emily D. Sherwood Family Correspondence, LSU.

11. Simon and Marszalek, *The Papers of Ulysses S. Grant*, 4:198; Wallace, *An Autobiography*, 1:380, 383–389; Wallace, "The Capture of Fort Donelson," 1:409; Alexander Simplot Diary, WHS, 28, copy in Alexander Simplot Diary, FDV; Phillip Shaw Diary, February 14, 1862, 32nd Illinois File, SNMP and FDR.

12. *OR*, 1, 7:229, 236; Bela St. John Diary, February 10–14, 1862, Bela T. St. John Papers, LC; David W. Stratton Diary, February 12, 1862, VCPL, copy in STRI; Daniel P. Donnell to mother, February 1862, 2nd Iowa File, FDR and FDA; Eric Bergland Diary, February 12, 1862, RBHPC; Frank Fee to brother, February 19, 1862, Frank Fee Let-

ters, IHS; Edwin Hubbard to Nellie, February 20, 1862, Edwin Hubbard Letters, WHS; Samuel Kennedy Cox Diary, February 14, 1862, 17th Kentucky File, FDR; James Nelson Shepherd Diary, February 12, 1862, ISL.

13. *OR*, 1, 7:236, 252; Wallace, *An Autobiography*, 1:393, 395.

14. *OR*, 1, 7:174–175, 185, 194–195, 201; John McClernand to Richard Oglesby, February 14, 1862, Richard J. Oglesby Papers, ALPL.

15. *OR*, 1, 7:221; *OR*, 1, 52, 1:8.

16. *OR*, 1, 7:208–209.

17. Catton, *Grant Moves South*, 159; M. A. Ryan, "Experiences of a Confederate Soldier in Camp and Prison in the Civil War," undated, M. A. Ryan Memoir, MDAH.

18. *ORN*, 1, 22:585; Grant, *Personal Memoirs*, 1:248; Walke, "The Western Flotilla," 1:433.

19. *OR*, 1, 7:399; Reuben Ross Journal, March 1862, Ross Family Papers, TSLA, copy in FDC. See also "River Batteries at Fort Donelson," 393–400.

20. *OR*, 1, 7:395; *ORN*, 1, 22:585; Walke, "The Western Flotilla," 1:433; Slagle, *Ironclad Captain*, 176.

21. *ORN*, 1, 22:585, 591–592; Walke, "The Western Flotilla," 1:433.

22. *OR*, 1, 7:280, 393, 395, 401; Wesley Smith Dorris Diary, February 14, 1862, UT.

23. *ORN*, 1, 22:585; *OR*, 1, 7:280–281, 395–396; Wesley Smith Dorris Diary, February 14, 1862, UT; Walke, "The Western Flotilla," 1:434.

24. *ORN*, 1, 22:585; *OR*, 1, 7:395; Andrew Foote to Gideon Welles, February 15, 1862, Andrew H. Foote Papers, LC.

25. *ORN*, 1, 22:585, 593.

26. Ibid., 585; *OR*, 1, 7:395.

27. *ORN*, 1, 22:592–594.

28. Ibid., 592–594; *OR*, 1, 7:400.

29. *ORN*, 1, 22:586, 591; *OR*, 1, 7:396; Walke, "The Western Flotilla," 1:433–435.

30. *OR*, 1, 7:263, 396; John A. McClernand to John A. Logan, January 8, 1862, John A. Logan Papers, LC.

31. *OR*, 1, 7:281, 395–396; Reuben Ross Journal, March 1862, Ross Family Papers, TSLA, copy in FDC.

32. *ORN*, 1, 22:586; Walke, "The Western Flotilla," 1:434; Hoppin, *Life of Andrew Hull Foote*, 228–230.

33. *ORN*, 1, 22:586; *OR*, 1, 7:175.

34. Hoppin, *Life of Andrew Hull Foote*, 230; *ORN*, 1, 22:586, 591, 593.

35. *OR*, 1, 7:281, 384, 391, 395, 400, 408; *Donelson Campaign Sources*, 140; Marcus L. Henry Reminiscences, 1862, MSU; "A Confederate Private at Fort Donelson, 1862," 478; George D. Carrington Diary, February 14, 1862, CHM; David Bodenhamer, "The Battle of Fort Donelson," undated, Civil War Collection, TSLA, copy in FDC; Wesley Smith Dorris Diary, February 14, 1862, UT.

36. *OR*, 1, 7:281, 384, 391, 395, 400, 408; Cooling, "A Virginian at Fort Donelson," 180.

37. *ORN*, 1, 22:586, 593; Walke, "The Western Flotilla," 1:436.

38. Merrill, "Capt. Andrew Hull Foote and the Civil War on Tennessee Waters," 88;

Cooling, "The Forging of Joint Army-Navy Operations," 103; H. L. Bedford Memoir, 1883, UT, 18–19.

39. *ORN*, 1, 22:589; Grant, *Personal Memoirs*, 1:249; Wallace, *An Autobiography*, 1:394; George D. Carrington Diary, February 14, 1862, CHM; Samuel Kennedy Cox Diary, February 14, 1862, 17th Kentucky File, SNMP; Charles Tompkins to wife, February 1862, Charles B. Tompkins Papers, DU; Simon and Marszalek, *The Papers of Ulysses S. Grant*, 4:211, 213.

40. *OR*, 1, 7:262.

41. Ibid., 262–263, 268; Wilson, *The Confederate Soldier*, 45. For the attention paid to ammunition, see "Order Book. Quarter Masters Department Gen. Floyd's Brigade C. S. Army. From Feby 10th 1862 to," 1862, FDR.

42. *OR*, 1, 7:159, 175; *OR*, 1, 52, 1:8; Gott, *Where the South Lost the War*, 184.

43. *OR*, 1, 7:268, 384.

44. Ibid., 268.

45. Ibid., 276–277, 330.

46. Ibid., 338, 379, 384; Gower and Allen, *Pen and Sword*, 591; R. I. Hill Diary, February 14, 1862, 3rd Mississippi File, FDR; Cooling, "A Virginian at Fort Donelson," 180; Robert Hughes Diary, February 14, 1862, Robert Morton Hughes Papers, ODU.

47. *OR*, 1, 7:315, 330, 338, 379, 384; Robert Hughes Diary, February 14, 1862, Robert Morton Hughes Papers, ODU.

48. Hughes and Stonesifer, *The Life and Wars of Gideon J. Pillow*, 222.

49. *OR*, 1, 7:206–207.

50. Ibid., 265, 281, 286.

51. Ibid., 268, 360, 369.

52. Ibid., 268, 282, 331.

53. Ibid., 277, 338, 360, 371, 384.

54. Ibid., 286, 361, 372–373; Cummings, *Yankee Quaker*, 190; Lawrence, *Unrevised History*, 287; Marcus L. Henry Reminiscences, 1862, MSU.

55. *OR*, 1, 7:377; *Donelson Campaign Sources*, 120.

56. *OR*, 1, 7:331, 343, 347.

57. Ibid., 331, 344, 377; George W. Dillon Diary, February 15, 1862, 18th Tennessee File, FDR; Selden Spencer, "Reminiscences of the Battle of Fort Donelson," undated, Civil War Collection, MHS.

58. *OR*, 1, 7:174, 215, 218; S. C. Nelson to editor, February 28, 1862, 41st Illinois File, FDR.

59. *OR*, 1, 7: 338–339, 347.

60. Wallace, "The Capture of Fort Donelson," 1:415.

CHAPTER 11. "NOT GENERALLY HAVING AN IDEA THAT A BIG FIGHT WAS ON HAND"

1. *OR*, 1, 7:175, 223–224, 237; William Henderson to family, February 17, 1862, William L. Henderson Letters, SHSI; William S. Hillyer to John McClernand, February

15, 1862, Mason Brayman Papers, CHM; Edmund McLaury to sister, February 21, 1862, Edmund McLaury Letters, SHSI; Samuel Kennedy Cox Diary, February 15, 1862, 17th Kentucky File, SNMP; George D. Carrington Diary, February 15, 1862, CHM.

2. *OR*, 1, 7:175, 223–224, 237.

3. Ibid., 199, 223–224, 229, 237; Wallace, *An Autobiography*, 1:397; George D. Carrington Diary, February 15, 1862, CHM; "Capt. A. Schwartz. Memorandum of Battle. Ft. Donelson Feby 15, 1862," Mason Brayman Papers, LS, copy in FDR.

4. *OR*, 1, 7:393; Marcus L. Henry Reminiscences, 1862, MSU.

5. Bailey, "Escape from Fort Donelson," 64; Francis Baxter Biography, undated, Francis Marion Baxter Papers, CWTI, USAMHI.

6. *OR*, 1, 7:614, 619.

7. Grant, *Personal Memoirs*, 1:250.

8. Smith, *Shiloh*, 90–93.

9. Grant, *Personal Memoirs*, 1:250.

10. *ORN*, 1, 22:594; *OR*, 1, 7:160; *Donelson Campaign Sources*, 173; Henry Dwight memoir, undated, Henry Otis Dwight Papers, OHS.

11. *ORN*, 1, 22:588; Grant, *Personal Memoirs*, 1:249–250; Badeau, *Military History*, 1:44.

12. *OR*, 1, 7:408.

13. Ibid., 286, 339.

14. *OR*, 1, 7:215, 339; Wilson, *The Confederate Soldier*, 45.

15. *OR*, 1, 7:339.

16. Ibid., 339.

17. Ibid., 176, 339, 380; "Genl. McClernand Memorandum of Battle, Ft. Donelson, 15 Feb 1862," Mason Brayman Papers, LS; Thomas K. Mitchell Diary, February 15, 1862, 4th Illinois Cavalry File, FDR; S. C. Nelson to editor, February 28, 1862, 41st Illinois File, FDR; James Powell to Charles Smith, March 25, 1862, Charles F. Smith Papers, USMA.

18. *OR*, 1, 7:186, 216–218; *OR*, 1, 52, 1:12; Chetlain, *Recollections*, 86; Timothy McNamara Diary, February 15, 1862, MDAH; S. C. Nelson to editor, February 28, 1862, 41st Illinois File, FDR; R. H. McFadden to sir, February 16, 1862, 41st Illinois File, FDR.

19. *OR*, 1, 7:339; Mason Brayman Diary, February 15, 1862, Bailhache-Brayman Family Papers, ALPL.

20. *OR*, 1, 7:339.

21. B. F. Boring, "From Cairo to Donelson," March 15, 1894, *National Tribune*; *OR*, 1, 7:176, 186, 189; George S. Durfee to uncle, February 17, 1862, George S. Durfee Letters, UIL; David Cornwell Memoir, undated, CWD, USAMHI, 61.

22. *OR*, 1, 7:282, 339.

23. Ibid., 380; M. F. Baxter, "My Services in the Confederate Army from April 1861 to May 22, 1865," undated, Marion Francis Baxter Papers, MDAH, 3; R. H. McFadden to sir, February 16, 1862, 41st Illinois File, FDR.

24. *OR*, 1, 7:276, 339–340; Davis, *51st Virginia Infantry*. For a short synopsis of the 20th Mississippi, see the sketch by Glover Roberts in W. T. Booth Collection, USM.

25. "Fort Donelson," June 5, 1891, 56th Virginia File, FDR; Hoge, *Sketch of Dabney Carr Harrison*, 48–49. For more on the 56th Virginia, see Young, *56th Virginia Infantry*.

26. *OR*, 1, 7:339, 371, 373, 376; Rietti, *Military Annals of Mississippi*, 18; Marcus L. Henry Reminiscences, 1862, MSU; "Obituary," undated, John Gregg Papers, CWD, USAMHI; P. D. Browne, "A Centennial Story of Moody's Company G," 1962, William Lewis Moody Papers, VHS; "A Centennial Story of Moody's Company G," Fairfield Texas *Recorder*, January 18, 1962; Selden Spencer, "Reminiscences of the Battle of Fort Donelson," undated, Civil War Collection, MHS; John H. Wilson Reminiscences, undated, MSU, 1–2; R. I. Hill Diary, February 15, 1862, 3rd Mississippi File, FDR. For more on the Kentuckians and their commander, see Wills, "A Kentucky Lyon Roars," 2:186–214.

27. *OR*, 1, 7:361, 384–385; Willis, *Arkansas Confederates in the Western Theater*, 133; Timothy McNamara Diary, February 15, 1862, MDAH.

28. Marcus L. Henry Reminiscences, 1862, MSU.

29. *OR*, 1, 7:278, 361; Thomas Burton Jones Memoir, undated, 8th Kentucky File, FDR.

30. *OR*, 1, 7:218, 277, 371; S. C. Nelson to editor, February 28, 1862, 41st Illinois File, FDR; R. H. McFadden to sir, February 16, 1862, 41st Illinois File, FDR.

31. *OR*, 1, 7:217, 263; *OR*, 1, 52, 1:12; Morrison, *A History of the Ninth Regiment*, 22–23.

32. *OR*, 1, 7:282, 339, 341, 372–373; Americus Langston Diary, February 13, 1862, 7th Texas File, FDR. For Clough, see Clough Family Papers, UTAR.

33. *OR*, 1, 7:216–218, 340, 362, 373–374; Ben West Diary, February 15, 1862, 12th Illinois File, FDR; Isaac C. Pugh Charges, January/February 1862, Charles F. Smith Papers, USMA.

34. *OR*, 1, 7:175–176; 340, 362, 372.

35. John Kerr to wife, undated and February 24, 1862, John D. Kerr Letters, 41st Illinois File, SNMP; R. H. McFadden to sir, February 16, 1862, 41st Illinois File, FDR; John Lautzenhiser Diary, February 15, 1862, 41st Illinois File, FDR.

36. *OR*, 1, 7:266, 340, 373–374.

37. Ibid., 282.

38. Marcus L. Henry Reminiscences, 1862, MSU.

39. Smith, *Shiloh*, 90–93.

40. Sword, *Shiloh*, viii; Marcus L. Henry Reminiscences, 1862, MSU; Ferguson, *Chancellorsville*, 172–195; Smith, *Shiloh*, 90–93.

41. Ferguson, *Chancellorsville*, 172–195; Smith, *Shiloh*, 90–93.

42. Daniel H. Brush Diary, February 15, 1862, ALPL.

CHAPTER 12. "THE WHOLE LINE JUST SEEMED TO MELT AWAY AND SCATTER"

1. *OR*, 1, 7:175–176.

2. Whittlesey, *War Memoranda*, 34.

3. *OR*, 1, 7:263, 282.

4. Ibid., 175–177, 237, 243; Cooling, "The Reliable First Team," 53; Wallace, *An*

Autobiography, 1:399–400; "Genl. McClernand Memorandum of Battle, Ft. Donelson, 15 Feb 1862" and "M. Brayman Memorandum of Battle Ft. Donelson 15 Feb 1862," both in Mason Brayman Papers, LS, copy in FDR.

5. James Butterfield to unknown, February 19, 1862, James A. B. Butterfield Correspondence, ALPL.

6. *OR*, 1, 7:185–186, 188, 190; Gott, *Where the South Lost the War*, 194; Dietrich Smith to Carrie, February 20, 1862, Dietrich C. Smith Papers, ALPL.

7. *OR*, 1, 7:175, 186, 190, 374, 376; George S. Durfee to uncle, February 17, 1862, George S. Durfee Letters, UIL; Unknown to brother, March 2, 1862, 29th Illinois Papers, Lowry Hinch Collection, USAMHI; David Cornwell Memoir, undated, CWD, USAMHI, 61.

8. Daniel H. Brush Diary, February 15, 1862, ALPL; David Cornwell Memoir, undated, CWD, USAMHI, 62.

9. *OR*, 1, 7:190.

10. *OR*, 1, 7:341; Marcus L. Henry Reminiscences, 1862, MSU. For more on the 50th Virginia, see Chapla, *50th Virginia Infantry*.

11. *OR*, 1, 7:176, 186; William S. Stephens to sister, February 21, 1862, 30th Illinois File, FDR.

12. *OR*, 1, 7:190; Michael Lawler Biography, undated, Michael K. Lawler Papers, ALPL; Daniel H. Brush Diary, February 15, 1862, ALPL.

13. *OR*, 1, 7:176–177, 189; Gould D. Molineaux Diary, February 15, 1862, AC; "Capt. A. Schwartz. Memorandum of Battle. Ft. Donelson Feby 15, 1862," Mason Brayman Papers, LS.

14. *OR*, 1, 7:186; William D. Foster to sister, February 21, 1862, 30th Illinois File, FDR; David Poak to sister, February 17, 1862, David W. Poak Papers, NC.

15. *OR*, 1, 7:189, 243.

16. Ibid., 175, 251; David M. Claggett Diary, February 14, 1862, ALPL; Albert Rhodes Diary, February 17, 1862, NSHS; George Harvey to Mattie, February 21, 1862, George Harvey Letters, 31st Indiana File, SNMP.

17. *OR*, 1, 7:243, 251; Albert Rhodes Diary, February 17, 1862, NSHS; David W. Stratton Diary, February 15, 1862, VCPL, copy in STRI and FDR.

18. *OR*, 1, 7:177, 186, 189, 244, 246; George S. Durfee to uncle, February 17, 1862, George S. Durfee Letters, UIL; Albert Rhodes Diary, February 17, 1862, NSHS; David Cornwell Memoir, undated, CWD, USAMHI, 62; Smith, *A History of the Thirty-First Regiment*, 12; Jesse Connelly Diary, February 18, 1862, IHS; David W. Stratton Diary, February 15, 1862, VCPL, copy in STRI; Samuel Kennedy Cox Diary, February 15, 1862, 17th Kentucky File, SNMP; Henry Schaphard Diary, February 15, 1862, 29th Illinois File, FDR; Charles Smith to John Osborn, March 13, 1862, Civil War Related Material, IHS.

19. *Donelson Campaign Sources*, 163; Jones, *Black Jack*, 126, 129; Dawson, *Life and Services*, 38; *OR*, 1, 7:186–187; George D. Carrington Diary, February 15, 1862, CHM; L. A. McCook to A. L. Ryland, May 14, 1862, McCook Family Papers, LC; M. B. Brown to John Logan, February 18, 1862, John A. Logan Papers, LC; Edwin C. Haynie Statement, August 1, 1895, Isham N. Haynie Papers, ALPL.

20. *OR*, 1, 7:243–244, 247–249, 361, 381; Samuel Kennedy Cox Diary, February 15, 1862, 17th Kentucky File, SNMP; "Sixth Annual Reunion of 44th Regt. Ind. Vols," undated, Thomas S. Lacy Papers, CWD, USAMHI; Lancelot C. Ewbank Diary, February 15, 1862, IHS; James Nelson Shepherd Diary, February 15, 1862, ISL.

21. *OR*, 1, 7:187, 244, 248, 251; Curtin Alexander Brasher Diary, February 14–15, 1862, FDR, copy in CHCH.

22. David Cornwell Memoir, undated, CWD, USAMHI, 63–65.

23. *OR*, 1, 7:276, 340; Richard L. McClung Diary, undated, UTA, 7; "Capt. A. Schwartz. Memorandum of Battle. Ft. Donelson Feby 15, 1862," Mason Brayman Papers, LS.

24. *OR*, 1, 7:186, 198, 340, 346; "Capt. A. Schwartz. Memorandum of Battle. Ft. Donelson Feby 15, 1862," Mason Brayman Papers, LS; Thomas Burton Jones Memoir, undated, 8th Kentucky File, FDR.

25. George D. Carrington Diary, February 15, 1862, CHM.

26. Wallace, *Life and Letters*, 160.

27. *OR*, 1, 7:199, 201, 207.

28. William Tibbets to parents, March 2, 1862 (mislabeled 1861), William H. Tibbets Letters, ALPL, copy in FDC.

29. *OR*, 1, 7:263, 331, 347–348; J. K. Farris to wife, October 31, 1862, Civil War Collection, TSLA, copy in FDC; William L. McKay Diary Memoirs, undated, Civil War Collection, TSLA, copy in FDC; George Dillon Diary, undated, George W. Dillon Papers, TSLA, copy in FDC; Selden Spencer, "Reminiscences of the Battle of Fort Donelson," undated, Civil War Collection, MHS.

30. Selden Spencer, "Reminiscences of the Battle of Fort Donelson," undated, Civil War Collection, MHS.

31. *OR*, 1, 7:263, 331, 347–348; J. K. Farris to wife, October 31, 1862, Civil War Collection, TSLA, copy in FDC; William L. McKay Diary Memoirs, undated, Civil War Collection, TSLA, copy in FDC; George Dillon Diary, undated, George W. Dillon Papers, TSLA, copy in FDC; Selden Spencer, "Reminiscences of the Battle of Fort Donelson," undated, Civil War Collection, MHS.

32. *OR*, 1, 7:195, 199, 201, 331, 345, 348, 350, 352; Lawrence, *Unrevised History*, 289–290; Smith, *The Mississippi Secession Convention*, 177; J. K. Farris to wife, October 31, 1862, Civil War Collection, TSLA, copy in FDC; Thomas Dabney Wier Diary, February 15, 1862, UVA.

33. Selden Spencer, "Reminiscences of the Battle of Fort Donelson," undated, Civil War Collection, MHS.

34. *OR*, 1, 7:195, 199, 201, 331, 345, 348, 350, 352; Thomas Dabney Wier Diary, February 15, 1862, UVA, copy in FDR; William L. McKay Diary, undated, Civil War Collection, TSLA, copy in FDC; V. H. Stevens to uncle, February 28, 1862, Howard and Victor Stevens Papers, Coco Collection, HCWRT, USAMHI.

35. *Donelson Campaign Sources*, 143. See also Riddell, "Western Campaign," 316–323, and "Western Campaign," Richmond *Dispatch*, February 10, 1895.

36. *OR*, 1, 7:331–332, 348, 350, 352, 356; William Tibbets to parents, March 2, 1862 (mislabeled 1861), William H. Tibbets Letters, ALPL; Thomas H. Deavenport Diary,

February 15, 1862, Civil War Collection, TSLA, copy in FDC; David Bodenhamer, "The Battle of Fort Donelson," undated, Civil War Collection, TSLA, copy in FDC.

37. *OR*, 1, 7:352–353; George Dillon Diary, undated, George W. Dillon Papers, TSLA, copy in FDC.

38. *OR*, 1, 7:178, 195, 199, 201–202, 207–208, 348, 350, 353; Henry Uptmer Memoir, undated, 11th Illinois File, FDR.

39. *OR*, 1, 7:178, 195, 197, 199, 201–202, 207, 348, 350, 353, 356, 369; James T. Mackey Diary, February 5, 1862, MOC; William L. McKay Diary Memoirs, undated, Civil War Collection, TSLA, copy in FDC.

40. *OR*, 1, 7:343–344; Thompson, *History of the Orphan Brigade*, 66–67; Marcus L. Henry Reminiscences, 1862, MSU.

41. *OR*, 1, 7:195–196.

42. Ibid., 196, 199; W. H. L. Wallace to Anne, February 7, 1862, Wallace-Dickey Papers, ALPL; I. P. Rumsey to family, February 16, 1862, I. P. Rumsey Papers, NL; George D. Carrington Diary, February 15, 1862, CHM; Charles Lutz to brother, February 21, 1862, Charles H. Lutz Papers, CWD, USAMHI. For more on Ransom and the 11th Illinois, see Huffstodt, *Hard Dying Men*.

43. *OR*, 1, 7:196, 201–202, 207; Henry Weston to Mary, April 27, 1862, Henry S. Weston Papers, CWD, USAMHI.

44. *OR*, 1, 7:200, 208, 385; W. H. L. Wallace to Anne, February 17, 1862, Wallace-Dickey Papers, ALPL; George D. Carrington Diary, February 15, 1862, CHM; "The Sad Side of the Picture," February 17, 1862, M. J. Solomons Scrapbook, DU.

45. *OR*, 1, 7:200, 208, 210, 385; Jordan and Pryor, *The Campaigns of Lieut.-Gen. N. B. Forrest*, 81–84; Marcus L. Henry Reminiscences, 1862, MSU; *Donelson Campaign Sources*, 164; Timothy Blaisdell to sister, February 21, 1862, Timothy M. Blaisdell Paper, CWTI, USAMHI.

46. Duncan, *Recollections of Thomas D. Duncan*, 29–30.

47. W. H. L. Wallace to Anne, February 17, 1862, Wallace-Dickey Papers, ALPL; John E. Smith to Aimee, March 6, 1862 45th Illinois File, FDR.

48. *OR*, 1, 7:168, 197, 199, 201, 344; Frederick Eugene Ransom Order Book, undated, ALPL.

49. *OR*, 1, 7:200, 208, 385; George D. Carrington Diary, February 15, 1862, CHM; "The Sad Side of the Picture," February 17, 1862, M. J. Solomons Scrapbook, DU.

50. *OR*, 1, 7:200, 208, 385; "The Sad Side of the Picture," February 17, 1862, M. J. Solomons Scrapbook, DU.

51. *OR*, 1, 7:340; Marcus L. Henry Reminiscences, 1862, MSU.

CHAPTER 13. "UP TO THIS PERIOD THE SUCCESS WAS COMPLETE"

1. *OR*, 1, 7:624; Symonds, *Lincoln and His Admirals*, 119–120; George McClellan to Abraham Lincoln, February 16, 1862, Abraham Lincoln Papers, LC; Abraham Lincoln to Henry Halleck, February 16, 1862, Henry W. Halleck Papers, LC.

2. Wilson, *The Confederate Soldier*, 45.

3. *OR*, 1, 52, 1:8.

4. Wallace, "The Capture of Fort Donelson," 1:417.

5. *OR*, 1, 7:237, 252. For more on Rawlins, see Wilson, *The Life of John A. Rawlins*.

6. *OR*, 1, 7:237; Wallace, "The Capture of Fort Donelson," 1:417, 420; Wallace, *Life and Letters*, 160; Wallace, *An Autobiography*, 1:403–405; J. C. Powell to Charles Smith, February 1, 1862, Charles F. Smith Papers, USMA.

7. Edwin Hubbard to Nellie, February 20, 1862, Edwin Hubbard Letters, WHS; Jonathan Matter to cousin, January 17, 1862, Jonathan Matter Papers, Winey Collection, US-AMHI; Jonathan Blair to wife, February 20, 1862, Jonathan Blair Letter, ALPL, copy in 46th Illinois File, FDR; John Davis to Jackson, March 8, 1862, 46th Illinois File, FDR.

8. Kimbell, *History of Battery 'A,'* 38; Wallace, *An Autobiography*, 1:405–406; Frank B. Smith to friend, March 17, 1862, Sam House Letters, MU; Ezra Taylor to G. S. Hubbard, March 16, 1862, Ezra Taylor Papers, CHM; Henry Parcel to parents, February 20, 1862, Henry E. Parcel Correspondence, ALPL; William Bigbee to friend, February 28, 1862, Francis M. Brainerd Letters, IHS; *OR*, 1, 7:179, 210–211, 216, 238, 252; George Sawin to wife, February 20, 1862, George Sawin Papers, CHM; John D. St. John to parents, March 26, 1862, Bela T. St. John Papers, LC; Wood, *History of the 20th O.V.V.I.*, 41–43; Hess, *The Union Soldier in Battle*, 16; Cluett, *History of the 57th Regiment*, 8; John Stephens to wife, February 17, 1862, 76th Ohio File, FDR; R. W. Burt, "Fort Donelson," September 13, 1906, *National Tribune*; William Reed to *Star and Chronicle*, February 16, 1862, William Reed Letters, 8th Missouri File, SNMP; William F. Willey Diary, February 15, 1862, OHS. For the 1st Nebraska, see Cooling, "The First Nebraska Infantry Regiment," 131–146; Joseph LeBrant Diary, February 1862, Joseph LeBrant Papers, CWD, USAMHI.

9. *OR*, 1, 7:179, 216, 233, 238, 244–245, 252; George Sawin to wife, February 20, 1862, George Sawin Papers, CHM; John D. St. John to parents, March 26, 1862, Bela T. St. John Papers, LC; John Stephens to wife, February 17, 1862, 76th Ohio File, FDR; Lew Wallace to wife, February 19, 1862, Lew Wallace Papers, IHS.

10. *OR*, 1, 7:179, 216, 233, 238, 244–245, 252; George Sawin to wife, February 20, 1862, George Sawin Papers, CHM; John D. St. John to parents, March 26, 1862, Bela T. St. John Papers, LC; Cluett, *History of the 57th Regiment Illinois*, 8; Charles Kroff Diary, February 15, 1862, Sheery Marie Cress Collection, UO; John Stephens to wife, February 17, 1862, 76th Ohio File, FDR; Lew Wallace to wife, February 19, 1862, Lew Wallace Papers, IHS; William Reed to *Star and Chronicle*, February 16, 1862, William Reed Letters, 8th Missouri File, SNMP.

11. James S. Fogle to brother, February 25, 1862, 11th Indiana File, FDR; I. N. Prince to sister, February 22 and 25, 1862, J. N. Prince Letter, FDA.

12. D. P. Grier to Anna, February 20, 1862, Grier Family Papers, MHS; David Monlux to Jonathon Monlux, undated, David Monlux Letters, Civil War Collection, MHS; B to wife, February 17, 1862, 25th Kentucky File, FDR.

13. *OR*, 1, 7:242; Jones, *Black Jack*, 127; George D. Carrington Diary, February 15, 1862, CHM; J. K. Farris to wife, October 31, 1862, Civil War Collection, TSLA, copy in

FDC; Marcus L. Henry Reminiscences, 1862, MSU; Joseph Skipworth to family, February 24, 1862, Joseph Skipworth Papers, SIU.

14. *OR*, 1, 7:178–179, 187, 210; Wallace, *Life and Letters*, 163; Ezra Taylor to G. S. Hubbard, March 16, 1862, Ezra Taylor Papers, CHM; Samuel Barrett to unknown, February 18, 1862, Samuel Eddy Barrett Papers, CHM; *OR*, 1, 7:179, 210–211; Kimbell, *History of Battery 'A,'* 38; Wallace, *An Autobiography*, 1:405–406; Frank B. Smith to friend, March 17, 1862, Sam House Letters, MU; Henry Parcel to parents, February 20, 1862, Henry E. Parcel Correspondence, ALPL.

15. *OR*, 1, 7:179, 210–211, 216; Kimbell, *History of Battery 'A,'* 38; Wallace, *An Autobiography*, 1:405–406; Frank B. Smith to friend, March 17, 1862, Sam House Letters, MU; Ezra Taylor to G. S. Hubbard, March 16, 1862, Ezra Taylor Papers, CHM; Henry Parcel to parents, February 20, 1862, Henry E. Parcel Correspondence, ALPL; Joseph W. Johnson Recollections, undated, Joseph W. Johnson Collection, NSHS; Selden Spencer, "Reminiscences of the Battle of Fort Donelson," undated, Civil War Collection, MHS.

16. *OR*, 1, 7:282, 332, 345.

17. *OR*, 1, 7:282, 332, 345; Ferrell, *Holding the Line*, 23; *Donelson Campaign Sources*, 165; Lawrence, *Unrevised History*, 291; Wallace, *An Autobiography*, 1:408; Samuel Barrett to unknown, February 18, 1862, Samuel Eddy Barrett Papers, CHM; Joseph W. Johnson Recollections, undated, Joseph W. Johnson Collection, NSHS; Selden Spencer, "Reminiscences of the Battle of Fort Donelson," undated, Civil War Collection, MHS.

18. *Donelson Campaign Sources*, 143; Cooling, "A Virginian at Fort Donelson," 182; Daniel, *Cannoneers in Gray*, 19. For more on the Goochland artillery, see Weaver, *Goochland Light, Goochland Turner & Mountain Artillery*.

19. *OR*, 1, 7:207, 332, 348, 352–353; Calvin J. Clack, "History of Company A 3rd Tenn Regt, Infantry," undated, Civil War Collection, TSLA, copy in FDC; Ferrell, *Holding the Line*, 26–27; George W. Dillon Diary, February 15, 1862, 18th Tennessee File, FDR; Thomas H. Deavenport Diary, February 15, 1862, Civil War Collection, TSLA, copy in FDC; Nathaniel Cheairs Account, May 3, 1862, John C. Brown Autograph Book, Civil War Collection, TSLA, copy in FDC; J. T. Williamson, "Notes about the War (1861–1865)," undated, 3rd Tennessee File, FDR; David Bodenhamer, "The Battle of Fort Donelson," undated, Civil War Collection, TSLA, copy in FDC; Andrew Jackson Campbell Diary, February 15, 1862, UTA. For the 41st Tennessee, see Simpson, *Reminiscences of the 41st Tennessee*.

20. *OR*, 1, 7:178, 195, 197, 199, 201–202, 207, 252–253, 341, 348, 350, 353, 356, 369; James T. Mackey Diary, February 5, 1862, MOC; Samuel Barrett to unknown, February 18, 1862, Samuel Eddy Barrett Papers, CHM; Daniel Goodman to Hanah, February 23, 1862, Edwin R. Capron Collection, NSHS; I. N. Prince to sister, February 25, 1862, J. N. Prince Letter, FDA.

21. *OR*, 1, 7:178, 195, 197, 199, 201–202, 207, 252–253, 341, 348, 350, 353, 356, 369; James T. Mackey Diary, February 5, 1862, MCHS; William L. McKay Diary Memoirs, undated, Civil War Collection, TSLA, copy in FDC; Samuel Barrett to unknown, February 18, 1862, Samuel Eddy Barrett Papers, CHM; Daniel Goodman to Hanah, February 23, 1862, Edwin R. Capron Collection, NSHS; David Bodenhamer, "The Battle of

Fort Donelson," undated, Civil War Collection, TSLA, copy in FDC; Ferrell, *Holding the Line*, 27; R. I. Hill Diary, February 15, 1862, 3rd Mississippi File, FDR.

22. *OR*, 1, 7:282–283, 341; Thomas Dabney Wier Diary, February 15, 1862, UVA; George Dillon Diary, undated, George W. Dillon Papers, TSLA, copy in FDC; Ferrell, *Holding the Line*, 28; Charles Kroff Diary, February 15, 1862, Sheery Marie Cress Collection, UO.

23. *OR*, 1, 7:341, 374, 376; Marcus L. Henry Reminiscences, 1862, MSU.

24. *OR*, 1, 7:245, 250; Selden Spencer, "Reminiscences of the Battle of Fort Donelson," undated, Civil War Collection, MHS; M. A. Ryan, "Experience of a Confederate Soldier in Camp and Prison in the Civil War," undated, MSU, 1–2, also in M. A. Ryan Papers, CWTI, USAMHI; Marcus L. Henry Reminiscences, 1862, MSU.

25. Andrew Jackson Campbell Diary, February 15, 1862, UTA; Marcus L. Henry Reminiscences, 1862, MSU.

26. Cooling, "A Virginian at Fort Donelson," 183; Marcus L. Henry Reminiscences, 1862, MSU.

27. Marcus L. Henry Reminiscences, 1862, MSU.

28. *OR*, 1, 7:263, 283, 332; Robert Hughes Diary, February 15, 1862, Robert Morton Hughes Papers, ODU.

29. *OR*, 1, 7:283, 332.

30. Ibid., 332–333.

31. *OR*, 1, 7:269, 344; Hughes and Stonesifer, *The Life and Wars of Gideon J. Pillow*, 230.

32. *OR*, 1, 7:361; "Sketch of Lieutenant-General N. B. Forrest," 294.

33. *OR*, 1, 7:353–354, 357, 385; Hughes and Stonesifer, *The Life and Wars of Gideon J. Pillow*, 231; Nathaniel Cheairs Account, May 3, 1862, John C. Brown Autograph Book, Civil War Collection, TSLA, copy in FDC.

34. Ferrell, *Holding the Line*, 28.

35. *OR*, 1, 7:283; Nathaniel Cheairs Account, undated, Figuers Collection, TSLA, copy in FDC; P. O. Avery, "Donelson and Henry," September 8, 1887, *National Tribune*; George D. Mosgrove, "Fort Donelson," September 18, 1902, *National Tribune*; Cooling, "A Virginian at Fort Donelson," 187; Selden Spencer, "Reminiscences of the Battle of Fort Donelson," undated, Civil War Collection, MHS.

36. *OR*, 1, 7:265–266, 315, 365, 387; Hughes and Stonesifer, *The Life and Wars of Gideon J. Pillow*, 224.

37. *OR*, 1, 7:266; Wallace, "The Capture of Fort Donelson," 1:418–419; S. C. Mitchell, "Recollections of a Private," October 15, 1887, Pulaski *Citizen*.

38. Stickles, *Simon Bolivar Buckner*, 143–144; Williams, *Grant Rises in the West*, 247.

39. H. L. Bedford Memoir, 1883, UT, 4.

40. Grant, *Personal Memoirs*, 1:241.

CHAPTER 14. "THE ONE WHO ATTACKS FIRST NOW WILL BE VICTORIOUS"

1. *OR*, 1, 7:159; Wallace, *An Autobiography*, 1:410–411; Grant, *Personal Memoirs*, 1:251–252; David Cornwell Memoir, undated, CWD, USAMHI, 62; Wallace, "The Cap-

ture of Fort Donelson," 1:422; Woodworth, *Nothing but Victory*, 119; Simpson, *Ulysses S. Grant*, 115; William Dennis to brother, February 16, 1862, Ellen Waddle McCoy Papers, SEMO.

2. *OR*, 1, 7:159; Grant, *Personal Memoirs*, 1:251–252; David Cornwell Memoir, undated, CWD, USAMHI, 62; William Dennis to brother, February 16, 1862, Ellen Waddle McCoy Papers, SEMO.

3. *OR*, 1, 7:159; Grant, *Personal Memoirs*, 1:251–252; Wallace, "The Capture of Fort Donelson," 1:422; Wallace, *An Autobiography*, 1:412.

4. Grant, *Personal Memoirs*, 1:252; Wallace, "The Capture of Fort Donelson," 1:422; Wallace, *An Autobiography*, 1:412; Fuller, *The Generalship of Ulysses S. Grant*, 89–90.

5. *OR*, 1, 7:179; Grant, *Personal Memoirs*, 1:252; Smith, "Operations before Fort Donelson," 40; "M. Brayman Memorandum of Battle Ft. Donelson 15 Feb 1862," Mason Brayman Papers, LS.

6. *ORN*, 1, 22:588; *OR*, 1, 7:618.

7. *ORN*, 1, 22:588; Walke, "The Western Flotilla," 1:436–437; Smith, *The Timberclads in the Civil War*, 251; Spot Fontaine Terrell Diary, February 15, 1862, MU.

8. *ORN*, 1, 22:589.

9. Simon and Marszalek, *The Papers of Ulysses S. Grant*, 4:211, 213.

10. *OR*, 1, 7:216–217.

11. Ibid., 180.

12. Ibid., 180, 187, 190, 200, 238, 252; Wallace, *An Autobiography*, 1:412.

13. *OR*, 1, 7:180, 211; George O. Smith, "Brief History of the 17th Regiment of Illinois Volunteer Infantry," 1913, ALPL, 3.

14. *OR*, 1, 7:233, 240, 381; Wallace, "The Capture of Fort Donelson," 1:422–424; Wallace, *An Autobiography*, 1:414.

15. *OR*, 1, 7:233, 240, 381; Timothy McNamara Diary, February 15, 1862, MDAH; Charles Kroff Diary, February 15, 1862, Sheery Marie Cress Collection, UO.

16. *OR*, 1, 7:233–236, 238–239; Wallace, "The Capture of Fort Donelson," 1:424; George C. Kindelsperyer Diary, February 15, 1862, FDR.

17. *OR*, 1, 7:238, 245.

18. *OR*, 1, 7:239, 245, 247, 249; Samuel Kennedy Cox Diary, February 15, 1862, 17th Kentucky File, SNMP.

19. *OR*, 1, 7:361–362.

20. Ibid., 239, 245, 247, 249, 381; Rerick, *The Forty-Fourth Indiana*, 39; Lancelot C. Ewbank Diary, February 15, 1862, IHS.

21. *Donelson Campaign Sources*, 166; Churchill, "Wounded at Fort Donelson," 152–153.

22. *OR*, 1, 7:239, 245, 247, 249, 269; Wallace, *An Autobiography*, 1:422–423; Charles Kroff Diary, February 15, 1862, Sheery Marie Cress Collection, UO; William Reed to *Star and Chronicle*, February 16, 1862, William Reed Letters, 8th Missouri File, SNMP; Cooling, "A Virginian at Fort Donelson," 184.

23. *OR*, 1, 7:239, 245, 247, 249, 269; D. P. Grier to Anna, February 20, 1862, Grier Family Papers, MHS; Wallace, *An Autobiography*, 1:422–423; David Poak to sister, February 17, 1862, David W. Poak Papers, NC.

24. Grant, *Personal Memoirs*, 1:252.

25. *OR*, 1, 52, 1:8; *OR*, 1, 7:221; Jacob Lauman to wife, February 17, 1862, Jabob G. Lauman Papers, CHM; James Parrott to wife, February 18, 1862, James C. Parrott Papers, SHSI.

26. *OR*, 1, 52, 1:8, 10; *OR*, 1, 7:229; Grant, *Personal Memoirs*, 1:253; John N. Ferguson Diary, February 14, 1862, LC; Twombly, *The Second Iowa Infantry*, 15, copy in 2nd Iowa File, FDR; Charles Smith to unknown, February 19, 1862, Charles F. Smith Papers, USMA; Charles C. Cloutman Diary, February 13, 1862, SHSI; Thomas Newsham Account, undated, Charles F. Smith Papers, USMA; "The Siege of Donelson," February 26, 1862, Ottumwa *Courier*; Silas Shearer to unknown, June 22, 1862, Silas I. Shearer Papers, SHSI; William Holden to father, February 21, 1862, William C. Holden Letter, SHSI. For Smith's staff and orderlies, see General Orders 8, February 21, 1862, Charles Smith Letterbook, Charles F. Smith Papers, USMA.

27. *OR*, 1, 7:378; *Donelson Campaign Sources*, 120; James Samuel Jones Diary, February 15, 1862, 30th Tennessee File, FDR.

28. *OR*, 1, 52, 1:8, 10; *OR*, 1, 7:230; Brinton, *Personal Memoirs*, 121; "Peter Wilson in the Civil War," 266, 269; Daniel P. Donnell to mother, February 1862, 2nd Iowa File, FDR; Charles Smith to wife, February 17, 1862, Letter Excerpts, Charles F. Smith Papers, USMA.

29. *OR*, 1, 52, 1:8, 10; *OR*, 1, 7:230; Twombly, *The Second Iowa Infantry*, 15–17; Wallace, "The Capture of Fort Donelson," 1:423; John N. Ferguson Diary, February 14, 1862, LC; Daniel P. Donnell to mother, February 1862, 2nd Iowa File, FDR and FDA; James Weaver to wife, February 19, 1862, James B. Weaver Papers, UI; William Holden to father, February 21, 1862, William C. Holden Letter, FDA and SHSI.

30. *OR*, 1, 7:230; Greenwalt, *A Charge at Fort Donelson*, 13–14; James Weaver to wife, February 19, 1862, James B. Weaver Papers, UI.

31. Frank Reed to sister, February 24, 1862, 12th Iowa File, FDR; Daniel P. Donnell to mother, February 1862, 2nd Iowa File, FDR; "The Post of Honor: Second Iowa Volunteers," 154–155.

32. *OR*, 1, 7:229; Wallace, "The Capture of Fort Donelson," 1:423; Welsh, *Medical Histories of Union Generals*, 308; Charles Smith to Fanny, February 26, 1862, Charles F. Smith Papers, USMA; Charles Smith to wife, February 17, 1862, Letter Excerpts, Charles F. Smith Papers, USMA; Thomas Newsham Account, undated, Charles F. Smith Papers, USMA; Jacob Lauman to brother, February 19, 1862, Jacob G. Lauman Papers, CHM; James Butterfield to unknown, February 19, 1862, James A. B. Butterfield Correspondence, ALPL; Smith, "Operations before Fort Donelson," 40; James Parrott to wife, February 21, 1862, James C. Parrott Papers, SHSI; "Peter Wilson in the Civil War," 273; E. W. Herman Diary, February 15, 1862, 7th Iowa File, SNMP.

33. *OR*, 1, 7:229; James Parrott to wife, February 21, 1862, James C. Parrott Papers, SHSI; "Peter Wilson in the Civil War," 273; E. W. Herman Diary, February 15, 1862, 7th Iowa File, SNMP.

34. *OR*, 1, 7:230, 333, 346, 348–349, 370–371, 374; James Weaver to wife, February 19, 1862, James B. Weaver Papers, UI; Marcus L. Henry Reminiscences, 1862, MSU.

35. Edwin Hubbard to Nellie, February 20, 1862, Edwin Hubbard Letters, WHS.

36. *OR*, 1, 7:294, 333, 344–345, 349–351, 354, 370–371, 378, 392, 401; Thompson, *History of the Orphan Brigade*, 67–68; *Donelson Campaign Sources*, 120, 132–133; Bushrod Castleman to Peyton, February 19, 1862, Boyer-Castleman Family Papers, FHS; Wesley Smith Dorris Diary, February 15, 1862, UT; Selden Spencer, "Reminiscences of the Battle of Fort Donelson," undated, Civil War Collection, MHS.

37. *OR*, 1, 7:294, 333, 344–345, 349–351, 354, 370–371, 378, 392, 401; *Donelson Campaign Sources*, 120, 132–133; Bushrod Castleman to Peyton, February 19, 1862, Boyer-Castleman Family Papers, FHS; Nathaniel Cheairs Account, May 3, 1862, John C. Brown Autograph Book, Civil War Collection, TSLA, copy in FDC; Wesley Smith Dorris Diary, February 15, 1862, UT; Selden Spencer, "Reminiscences of the Battle of Fort Donelson," undated, Civil War Collection, MHS.

38. Andrew Jackson Campbell Diary, February 15, 1862, UTA; Lawrence, *Unrevised History*, 292; E. W. Herman Diary, February 15, 1862, 7th Iowa File, SNMP; "Narrative," Macon *Telegraph*, February 22, 1862; "14th Mississippi at Fort Donelson," Paulding *Eastern Clarion*, May 5, 1862.

39. *OR*, 1, 52, 1:8, 10, 13; *OR*, 1, 7:163, 226, 228–230, 232; Foster, *War Stories for My Grandchildren*, 41–42; Smith, *History of the Seventh Iowa*, 39–40; John N. Ferguson Diary, February 15, 1862, LC; James Parrott to wife, February 18, 1862, James C. Parrott Papers, SHSI; Thomas L. Hoffman Diary, February 15, 1862, SHSI.

40. *OR*, 1, 7:221; Hubert, *History of the Fiftieth Regiment Illinois*, 67–70.

41. *Eighth Reunion of the 12th Iowa Vet. Vol. Infantry*, 6; Milton Rood to father, February 17, 1862, Milton Rood Letters, SHSI; "Autobiography of Clarissa Emily Gear Hobbs," 1912, SHSI, 47. For more on Henderson, see Smith, "The Politics of Battlefield Preservation," 293–320.

42. *OR*, 1, 52, 1:9, 13; *OR*, 1, 7: 226; "Fort Donelson," *Southern Bivouac*, 345; Smith, "Operations before Fort Donelson," 42; James Weaver to wife, February 19, 1862, James B. Weaver Papers, UI; James Parrott to wife, February 18, 1862, James C. Parrott Papers, SHSI; Charles Sackett to mother, February 20, 1862, Charles O. Sackett Papers, SHSI, copy in FDR.

43. *OR*, 1, 7:283, 333; James C. Cook Diary, February 15, 1862, OHS, copy in 50th Tennessee File, FDR.

44. *OR*, 1, 7:180, 246, 249.

45. Ibid., 180; Wallace, "The Capture of Fort Donelson," 1:425.

46. *OR*, 1, 7:180, 239.

47. Ibid., 224; James S. Fogle Diary, February 15, 1862, 11th Indiana File, SNMP.

CHAPTER 15. "WE GOT THE PLACE"

1. Douglas Hapeman Diary, February 15, 1862, ALPL.

2. *OR*, 1, 7:234; Marcus L. Henry Reminiscences, 1862, MSU.

3. *OR*, 1, 7:283, 385.

4. Ibid., 187, 233, 239.

5. Ibid., 160, 222, 246, 250; *OR*, 1, 52, 1:10.

6. *OR*, 1, 7:283, 344; Robert Farquharson to Andrew Buchanan, July 18, 1862, Buchanan and McClellan Family Papers, UNC; Andrew Jackson Campbell Diary, February 14, 1862, UTA; Selden Spencer, "Reminiscences of the Battle of Fort Donelson," undated, Civil War Collection, MHS.

7. *OR*, 1, 7:365; Hughes and Stonesifer, *The Life and Wars of Gideon J. Pillow*, 232.

8. *OR*, 1, 7:318, 333, 345, 349, 357, 362, 366, 370, 407; Timothy McNamara Diary, February 16, 1862, MDAH; Andrew Jackson Campbell Diary, February 16, 1862, UTA; Marcus L. Henry Reminiscences, 1862, MSU.

9. *OR*, 1, 7:287, 299, 333, 385–386.

10. Ibid., 287, 333, 386; "Notes from conversation with Mr. Ed Walter on October 12, 1959 and August 7, 1963," Fort Donelson Aftermath, FDV.

11. *OR*, 1, 7:269, 283, 287, 334.

12. Ibid., 273, 283, 298, 334.

13. Ibid., 288, 298, 334; Grant, *Personal Memoirs*, 1:253–254; Wallace, "The Capture of Fort Donelson," 1:401.

14. *OR*, 1, 7:284, 288, 327, 334–335; Smith, "Operations before Fort Donelson," 43.

15. *OR*, 1, 7:284, 288, 300, 327, 334–335.

16. Ibid., 349.

17. Ibid., 264, 284, 302–303, 306; Jeremy Gilmer to wife, February 22, 1862, Jeremy F. Gilmer Papers, UNC.

18. *OR*, 1, 7:270, 362–363, 414.

19. Ibid., 293, 381–382, 415; *Donelson Campaign Sources*, 127, 146; Gott, *Where the South Lost the War*, 251; J. K. Farris to wife, October 31, 1862, Civil War Collection, TSLA, copy in FDC; Hugh to Father, March 10, 1862, Hugh Letter, FDA; Jack L. Dickinson, ed., "The Civil War Diary of James Conrad Peters, Sgt., Company 'B' 30th Battalion Va. Sharpshooters CSA," 30th Battalion Virginia Sharpshooters File, FDR; Rufus James Woolwine Diary, February 16, 1862, VHS; Robert Snead to wife, February 24, 1862, Robert Winn Snead Papers, VHS.

20. *OR*, 1, 7:378–379.

21. Ibid., 295, 386–387; Jordan and Pryor, *The Campaigns of Lieut.-Gen. N. B. Forrest*, 92; Francis Terry Leak Diary, December 22, 1861, UNC; "Notes from conversation with Mr. Ed Walter on October 12, 1959 and August 7, 1963," Fort Donelson Aftermath, FDV; Frank Gurley memoir, undated, Frank B. Gurley Papers, CWD, USAMHI.

22. *OR*, 1, 7:364–365, 386, 407, 415; Rowland and Howell, *Military History of Mississippi*, 159; F. H. Hunter to parents, March 2, 1862, 6th Arkansas File, FDR; "Notes from conversation with Mr. Ed Walter on October 12, 1959 and August 7, 1963," Fort Donelson Aftermath, FDV.

23. *OR*, 1, 7:160–161, 362–363; *Donelson Campaign Sources*, 129; Simon Buckner Order, February 16, 1862, Copy of Simon B. Buckner's Orders Arrangements for Surrender, FDV; Simon Buckner to Bushrod Johnson, February 16, 1862, Bushrod Johnson Papers, RG 109, E 123, NARA.

24. Smith, "Operations before Fort Donelson," 40–42; "Peter Wilson in the Civil War," 269; Nathaniel Cheairs Account, undated, Figuers Collection, TSLA, copy in FDC; James Parrott to wife, February 18, 1862, James C. Parrott Papers, SHSI.

25. *Donelson Campaign Sources*, 174; Cooling, "The Reliable First Team," 55; *OR*, 1, 7:160–161, 335; Simon B. Buckner, Jr., to W. E. Brooks, February 7, 1936, WS; Ulysses S. Grant to Simon Buckner, February 16, 1862, William S. Hillyer Papers, UVA and Ulysses S. Grant Papers, USMA; Simon Buckner to Grant, February 16, 1862, Simon Bolivar Buckner Papers, DU.

26. *OR*, 1, 7:161, 335; Simon Buckner to Ulysses S. Grant, February 16, 1862, Simon Bolivar Buckner Letter, UTA.

27. Connelly, *Army of the Heartland*, 124; *OR*, 1, 7:349, 354, 407, 409; Nathaniel Cheairs Account, undated, Figuers Collection, TSLA, copy in FDC; Thomas H. Deavenport Diary, February 16, 1862, Civil War Collection, TSLA, copy in FDC; Timothy McNamara Diary, February 16, 1862, MDAH; Francis Marion Baxter to Rit, undated, Francis Marion Baxter Papers, MDAH; Robert Farquharson to Andrew Buchanan, July 18, 1862, Buchanan and McClellan Family Papers, UNC; Rietti, *Military Annals of Mississippi*, 48.

28. Thomas H. Deavenport Diary, February 16, 1862, Civil War Collection, TSLA, copy in FDC; *OR*, 1, 7:381; "The Part Taken by Bolivar County in the Civil War Especially the McGehee Rifles," undated, 20th Mississippi Infantry Regiment Papers, MDAH; Thorne Hall to family, February 20, 1862, FDR; Smith, *James Z. George*, 53; Rowland and Howell, *Military History of Mississippi*, 159; Marcus L. Henry Reminiscences, 1862, MSU; Jacob Lauman to brother, February 19, 1862, Jacob G. Lauman Papers, CHM; William Wilder, "Reminiscences of the Civil War," 1903, William F. Wilder Papers, LC, 8; Harley Wayne to wife, February 18, 1862, Harley Wayne Correspondence, ALPL, copy in 15th Illinois File, FDR; Thomas Dabney Wier Diary, February 15, 1862, UVA; William L. McKay Diary Memoirs, undated, Civil War Collection, TSLA, copy in FDC; Andrew Jackson Campbell Diary, February 16, 1862, UTA.

29. *OR*, 1, 52, 1:10; James Weaver to wife, February 19, 1862, James B. Weaver Papers, UI; William Wilder, "Reminiscences of the Civil War," 1903, William F. Wilder Papers, LC, 7; Simon Eccles to James Henry, February 25, 1862, Simon F. Eccles Papers, NC.

30. *OR*, 1, 7:239, 246, 253; Wallace, *An Autobiography*, 1:427–428; William Wilder, "Reminiscences of the Civil War," 1903, William F. Wilder Papers, LC, 8; David M. Claggett Diary, February 16, 1862, ALPL.

31. *ORN*, 1, 22:590; Wallace, "The Capture of Fort Donelson," 1:428; Stephens, *Shadow of Shiloh*, 59; Lew Wallace to wife, February 17, 1862, Lew Wallace Papers, IHS.

32. Charles Kroff Diary, February 165, 1862, Sheery Marie Cress Collection, UO; Marcus L. Henry Reminiscences, 1862, MSU; F. C. Cromwell Journal, February 16, 1862, 12th Iowa File, FDR; James S. Fogle to brother, February 25, 1862, 11th Indiana File, BCHS, copies in ISL and FDR; V. H. Stevens to uncle, February 28, 1862, Howard and Victor Stevens Papers, Coco Collection, HCWRT, USAMHI.

33. Wallace, *Life and Letters*, 162–163; George Sawin to wife, February 20, 1862, George Sawin Papers, CHM; George L. Childres Diary, February 16, 1862, ALPL; Richard L. McClung Diary, undated, UTA, 9.

34. *OR*, 1, 7:180, 189–190, 196, 222, 225, 230; Wallace, *Life and Letters*, 163; I. P. Rumsey Memoir, undated, I. P, Rumsey Papers, NL; Samuel Barrett to unknown, February 18, 1862, Samuel Eddy Barrett Papers, CHM; James Butterfield to unknown, February 19, 1862, James A. B. Butterfield Correspondence, ALPL.

35. *OR*, 1, 7:180, 189–190, 196, 222, 225, 230; Hiram Scofield Diary, February 16, 1862, Hiram Scofield Papers, NL; I. P. Rumsey to family, February 16, 1862, I. P. Rumsey Papers, NL; Jacob Lauman to brother, February 19, 1862, Jacob G. Lauman Papers, CHM; John M. Porter Memoirs, undated, Civil War Collection, TSLA, 20, copy in FDC; Channing Richards Diary, February 16, 1862, FHS; Daniel P. Donnell to mother, February 1862, 2nd Iowa File, FDR and FDA; James A. Black Diary, February 16, 1862, ALPL; Abram J. Vanauken Diary, February 16, 1862, ALPL; Daniel H. Brush Diary, February 15, 1862, ALPL; James Weaver to wife, February 19, 1862, James B. Weaver Papers, UI.

36. *ORN*, 1, 22:588–589; I. P. Rumsey to family, February 16, 1862, I. P. Rumsey Papers, NL; James A. Black Diary, February 16, 1862, ALPL.

37. Smith, "Operations before Fort Donelson," 43; Nathaniel Cheairs Account and Statement, undated, Figuers Collection, TSLA, copy in FDC.

38. Simpson, *Ulysses S. Grant*, 118; "A Thrilling Episode," July 1, 1870, Columbia *Herald*, copy in 3rd Tennessee File, FDR; Simon B. Buckner, Jr., to W. E. Brooks, February 7, 1936, WS; Stephens, *Shadow of Shiloh*, 59; Grant, *Personal Memoirs*, 1:256–257; Stickles, *Simon Bolivar Buckner*, 171; Clarence Johnson Article, September 8, 1933, Kentucky Library and Museum Papers, WKU; Young, *Around the World*, 470; Smith, "Operations before Fort Donelson," 43; John M. Porter Memoirs, undated, Civil War Collection, TSLA, 20, copy in FDC.

39. Simon B. Buckner, Jr., to W. E. Brooks, February 7, 1936, WS; Marcus L. Henry Reminiscences, 1862, MSU; Field Order 17, February 16, 1862, John A. McClernand Papers, ALPL.

40. *OR*, 1, 7:196, 216; George Sawin to wife, February 20, 1862, George Sawin Papers, CHM; Francis Bateman to Parent, February 23, 1862, Francis Marion Bateman Papers, LC; Manning Force to James, February 16, 1862, Peter Force Papers, LC; John McClernand to Leonard Ross, February 16, 1862, John A. McClernand Papers, ALPL.

41. W. H. L. Wallace to Anne, February 17, 1862, Wallace-Dickey Papers, ALPL; Jacob Lauman to brother, February 19, 1862, Jabob G. Lauman Papers, CHM; Levi Stewart to sister, February 18, 1862, Levi Stewart Letters, ALPL, copy in 49th Illinois File, FDR; Samuel Morre to John Drake, February 23, 1862, Drake Family Papers, SHSI.

42. *OR*, 1, 7:197–198, 200, 202; Wallace, *An Autobiography*, 1:421; George D. Carrington Diary, February 16, 1862, CHM.

43. Charles Tompkins to wife, February 1862, Charles B. Tompkins Papers, DU; Henry H. Baltzell Memoir, 1916, ALPL, 9; *OR*, 1, 7:234, 242–243; "A Confederate Officer Relates a Story of Bravery of Iowa Soldiers at Fort Donelson," undated, SHSI;

Brinton, *Personal Memoirs*, 124–126; Newberry, *A Visit to Fort Donelson, Tenn.*; Wardner, "Reminiscences of a Surgeon," 3:181; John Burggraf to family, February 21, 1862, John G. Burggraf Letters, WU.

44. *OR*, 1, 7:241–242, 637–638; "Record of Services," undated, Logan H. N. Salyer Papers, CWD, USAMHI; Hugh to father, March 10, 1862, Hugh Letter, FDA; "Civil War Vet Survives to Help Found Local Bank," 1984, John P. Brownlow Papers, CWD, USAMHI. For more, see Adams, *Doctors in Blue*, 79–81; George Cullum to Dr. Franklin, February 18, 1862, George W. Cullum Papers, USMA.

45. A. F. Gilbert Memoir, 1928, Jill Knight Garrett Collection, TSLA.

46. *OR*, 1, 7:336–337, 363, 638; "An Incident in the Rebellion," March 24, 1862, Aaron Goodrich Letter to H. C. Lockhart Folder, FDV; Henry Kepcha to brother, November 1, 1862, 41st Illinois File, FDR; Benjamin Best to wife, February 18, 1862, Benjamin F. Best Papers, ALPL; E. H. Dailey to mother, February 22, 1862, 4th Illinois Cavalry File, FDR; Jonathan Blair to wife, February 20, 1862, Jonathan Blair Letter, ALPL; William L. McKay Diary, undated, Civil War Collection, TSLA, copy in FDC; Andrew Jackson Campbell Diary, February 16, 1862, UTA; Ferrell, *Holding the Line*, 34.

47. Dabney Stuart Wier Diary, February 16, 1862, Mississippi Volunteers File, FDR; Alexander Simplot Diary, WHS, 31–32, copy in Alexander Simplot Diary, FDV; Horace Lurton to mother, February 17, 1862, Horace Harmon Lurton Papers, LC, copy in TSLA; *Donelson Campaign Sources*, 14; James Weaver to wife, February 19, 1862, James B. Weaver Papers, UI. For Simplot's drawings, see Alexander Simplot Civil War Drawings, TSLA. See also Simplot, "General Grant and the Incident at Dover," 83–84.

48. Thomas Dabney Wier Diary, February 17, 1862, UVA.

49. *OR*, 1, 7:159; Grant, *Personal Memoirs*, 1:257–258; M. A. Ryan, "Experiences of a Confederate Soldier in Camp and Prison in the Civil War," undated, M. A. Ryan Memoir, MDAH; Timothy McNamara Diary, February 18, 1862, MDAH.

50. William L. McKay Diary Memoirs, undated, Civil War Collection, TSLA, copy in FDC; Thomas H. Deavenport Diary, February 16, 1862, Civil War Collection, TSLA; W. H. L. Wallace to Anne, February 17, 1862, Wallace-Dickey Papers, ALPL; M. A. Ryan, "Experiences of a Confederate Soldier in Camp and Prison in the Civil War," undated, M. A. Ryan Memoir, MDAH; John Lautzenhiser Diary, February 16, 1862, 41st Illinois File, FDR; Timothy McNamara Diary, February 26, 1862, MDAH; Thomas Dabney Wier Diary, February 21 and 23, 1862, UVA; Andrew Jackson Campbell Diary, February 19–20, 1862, UTA; Charles E. Taylor Diary, February 21–23, 1862, LSU; S. C. Mitchell, "Recollections of a Private," October 15, 1887, Pulaski *Citizen*.

51. Daniel, *Soldiering in the Army of Tennessee*, 93; Robert Farquharson to Andrew Buchanan, July 18, 1862, Buchanan and McClellan Family Papers, UNC; Ben H. Bounds Civil War Memoir, undated, 4th Mississippi File, FDR, 4; Jacob Lauman to brother, February 19, 1862, Jabob G. Lauman Papers, CHM; S. C. Mitchell, "Recollections of a Private," October 15, 1887, Pulaski *Citizen*; Harley Wayne to wife, February 18, 1862, Harley Wayne Correspondence, ALPL; "Peter Wilson in the Civil War," 274; Nye, "Jake Donelson A 'Cocky' Rebel"?; William H. Kinkade Diary, February 16, 1862, ALPL; Rob-

ert Kepner to sister, February 17 (mislabeled 7), 1862, Mead Family Papers, UI; "An Incident in the Rebellion," March 24, 1862, Aaron Goodrich Letter to H. C. Lockhart Folder, FDV; John Kinney to parents, February 17, 1862, Kinney Family Papers, OU.

52. *OR*, 1, 7:159; Grant, *Personal Memoirs*, 1:257–258; William L. McKay Diary Memoirs, undated, Civil War Collection, TSLA, copy in FDC; S. C. Mitchell, "Recollections of a Private," October 15, 1887, Pulaski *Citizen*; "Fort Donelson to Camp Morton," 33; M. A. Ryan, "Experiences of a Confederate Soldier in Camp and Prison in the Civil War," undated, M. A. Ryan Memoir, MDAH; Timothy McNamara Diary, February 26, 1862, MDAH; Thomas Dabney Wier Diary, February 21 and 23, 1862, UVA; Andrew Jackson Campbell Diary, February 19–20, 1862, UTA; Charles E. Taylor Diary, February 21–23, 1862, LSU.

53. Charles Tompkins to wife, February 1862, Charles B. Tompkins Papers, DU; W. H. L. Wallace to Anne, February 17, 1862, Wallace-Dickey Papers, ALPL; Hiram Scofield Diary, February 18, 1862, Hiram Scofield Papers, NL; George D. Carrington Diary, February 17–18, 1862, CHM; Richard L. McClung Diary, undated, UTA, 9; George S. Durfee to uncle, February 17, 1862, George S. Durfee Letters, UIL; Luther Cowan to Harriet, February 19, 1862, Luther Howard Cowan Papers, TSLA, copy in FDC; Samuel Keplar to companion, February 19, 1862, 58th Ohio File, FDR; Sylvester Lett to father, February 20, 1862, 11th Indiana File, FDR; "A Rebel Atrocity," Fremont *Journal*, February 28, 1862.

54. *OR*, 1, 7:626, 638; George D. Carrington Diary, February 16, 1862, CHM; George Dillon Diary, undated, George W. Dillon Papers, TSLA, copy in FDC.

Chapter 16. "The Trophies of War Are Immense"

1. *ORN*, 1, 22:584; Walke, "The Western Flotilla," 1:437; Baron Proctor to John, February 17, 1862, Baron Proctor Letter, DC.

2. George Cullum to Henry Halleck, February 17, 1862, George W. Cullum Papers, USMA; *ORN*, 1, 22:584; Aldrich, "How the Iowa Legislature Celebrated the Capture of Fort Donelson," 215–219, copy in Iowa Legislature Celebrates Capture by Aldrich, FDV; "The Great Victory on the Cumberland," February 19, 1862, Janesville *Daily Gazette*.

3. Alexander Simplot Diary, WHS, 31, copy in Alexander Simplot Diary, FDV; Stephen Patterson to Jefferson Patterson, March 3, 1862, Patterson Family Papers, WSU; "To the Editors of the Independent," March 6, 1862, New York *Independent*; Thomas Butler Gunn Diary, February 17, 1862, MHS; William E. Potter Diary, February 17, 1862, PU; Randall Cooke to daughter, February 17, 1862, Alexander K. Hall Family Papers, ADAH; Sallie Barksdale to Sandy, March 3, 1862, Alexander Brown Papers, DU; G. Hobart Taylor Diary, 1862, TAM; Robert Caldwell to mother, February 20, 1862, Robert H. Caldwell Papers, BGSU; William McKinney to cousin, February 19, 1862, Wallace Family Papers, WSU. For a large collection of newspaper accounts, see *Donelson Campaign Sources*, 49–102; Mungo Murray Diary, February 21, 1862, Mungo P. Murray Papers, CWTI, USAMHI.

4. Nevins, *Diary of the Civil War*, 207–208.

5. G. Crawfoot and N. M. Crawfoot to family, March 29, 1862, Hill/Morgan Family Papers, BGSU; "From Fort Donelson," Clarksville *News Chronicle*, February 14, 1862; M. E. Drake to A. J. Jones, March 26, 1862, Abraham G. Jones Papers, ECU; Catherine Broun Diary, February 17–23, 1862, RU and UNC; Nat Jewell to Mrs. Sam White, February 16, 1862, White Family Letters, DU. For many reactions around the United States, see the Lucy Wood Butler Papers, Stephen T. Andrews Letters, and Sam M. Fleming Collection, all in UNC; W. J. Davis to Alexander Robertson, February 18, 1862, A. T. Robertson Family Papers, TSLA, William Neal McGrew Diary, February 7, 15, and 17, 1862, TSLA.

6. Ruston Maury to Ann, March 5, 1862, Maury Family Papers, CWM; Richardson, *A Compilation of the Messages and Papers of the Confederacy*, 2:193–194, 197–199, 202–206, copy in Effects of Victory at Donelson/Henry Foreign Courts/J. D. Richardson Folder, FDV.

7. Charles Tompkins to wife, February 21, 1862, Charles B. Tompkins Papers, DU; George D. Carrington Diary, February 16, 1862, CHM; David M. Claggett Diary, February 17, 1862, ALPL; Lew Wallace to wife, February 19, 1862, Lew Wallace Papers, IHS; Thomas Bell to Cornelius Bell, June 4, 1862, Thomas Bell Letter, FDA; Robert Kepner to sisters, February 26, 1862, Robert M. Kepner Letter, UT.

8. Garrett Smith Ainsworth Diary, February 15 and 16, 1862, USM; F. C. Cromwell Journal, February 6, 1862, 12th Iowa File, FDR; William L. Henderson Journal, February 19, 1862, UI; Moses McCoid to Helen, February 12, 1862, Moses A. McCoid Papers, HL; J. M. S. to sister, February 25, 1862, 57th Illinois File, FDR; David Baker to sister, February 16, 1862, David Baker Letter, FDA; George Hamman Diary, February 16–17, 1862, ALPL; Payson Shumway to wife, February 22, 1862, Z. Payson Shumway Papers, ALPL; Harvey Bruce to mother, February 18, 1862, Bruce Family Papers, ALPL.

9. Hiram Scofield Diary, February 20, 1862, Hiram Scofield Papers, NL; Ben West Diary, February 20, 1862, 12th Illinois File, FDR; James Butterfield to unknown, February 19, 1862, James A. B. Butterfield Correspondence, ALPL; "The Excursion to Fort Donelson," Evansville *Daily Journal*, February 22, 1862; James Parrott to wife, March 2, 1862, James C. Parrott Papers, SHSI; Alonzo Eaton to brother, February 28, 1862, 2nd Iowa File, FDR; Richard Burt to wife, February 16, 1862, Richard Burt Letters, UMC; Manning Force to unknown, February 21, 1862, Manning F. Force Papers, UWS, copies in LC; P. Bishop, Jr., to father, March 1, 1862, P. Bishop, Jr., Carondelet Folder, FDV; Eugene Marshall Diary, February 21, 1862, Eugene Marshall Papers, DU.

10. Samuel May to father, February 26, 1862, Samuel May Letters, 68th Ohio File, SNMP; Benjamin Boring to Will, March 29, 1862, Benjamin Boring Letters, VCPL; David Poak to sister, February 17, 1862, David W. Poak Papers, NC; James Jones to unknown, March 1862, James H. Jones Letters, IHS.

11. Francis Bateman to Parent, February 23, 1862, Francis Marion Bateman Papers, LC; Jacob Lauman to brother, February 22, 1862, Jacob G. Lauman Papers, CHM; William Bullard to father, February 27, 1862, William N. Bullard Papers, CWD, USAMHI; Henry Weston to Mary, April 27, 1862, Henry S. Weston Papers, CWD, USAMHI; James Shepherd to friend, March 5, 1862, James Nelson Shepherd Correspondence, ISL.

12. "Written in 1903," 1903, Joseph W. Westbrook Papers, CWD, USAMHI; Regimental Order No. 55, February 27, 1862, 17th Illinois Records, ALPL; *OR*, 1, 7:364–365, 625; Eugene Marshall Diary, February 17, 1862, Eugene Marshall Papers, DU; "Gen. Bushrod Johnson—A Sketch of His Life," March 4, 1862, Nashville *Times*.

13. *OR*, 1, 7:625–626, 633–634; Jacob Lauman to unknown, February 17, 1862, Jacob G. Lauman Papers, CHM; Wallace, *An Autobiography*, 1:434; 32nd Illinois Consolidated Provision Return, March 1–5, 1862, ALPL.

14. Hackemer, *To Rescue My Native Land*, 149; Milo W. Brady Diary, February 22, 1862, 45th Illinois File, FDR; Edward M. Galligan Diary, February 22, 1862, MTHS.

15. Mary and B. H. Suddarth to children, March 28, 1862, Account of Fort Henry and Fort Donelson Battles Suddarth Folder, FDV; I. P. Rumsey to father, February 11, 1862, I. P. Rumsey Papers, NL.

16. *OR*, 1, 7:162; "Peter Wilson in the Civil War," 267; B. West to Lizzie, January 27, 1862, 12th Illinois File, FDR.

17. Dabney Stuart Wier Diary, February 10, 1862, Mississippi Volunteers File, FDR; Alexander Simplot Diary, WHS, 31, copy in Alexander Simplot Diary, FDV; James S. Fogle to brother, February 25, 1862, 11th Indiana File, FDR; Oliver Bridgford to wife, February 24, 1862, 45th Illinois File, FDR; George Sawin to wife, February 20, 1862, George Sawin Papers, CHM.

18. *ORN*, 1, 22: 797; *OR*, 1, 7:551, 579, 619.

19. Charles Cowell Diary, January 25, 1862, Cowell Collection, USAMHI; *OR*, 1, 7:71.

20. *OR*, 1, 7:595–596; James Thompson to wife, February 9, 1862, Thompson Family Papers, UAZ.

21. Thorne Hall to family, February 20, 1862, FDR; Simon and Marszalek, *The Papers of Ulysses S. Grant*, 4:177; Eugene Marshall Diary, February 19, 1862, Eugene Marshall Papers, DU; "Peter Wilson in the Civil War," 264; Charles Cochran to mother, February 11, 1862, Mark A. Chapman Collection, UWY; John Kinney to parents, February 17, 1862, Kinney Family Papers, OU.

22. *OR*, 1, 7:604; Thomas K. Mitchell Diary, February 4, 14, and 17, 1862, 4th Illinois Cavalry File, FDR.

23. *ORN*, 1, 22:457; *OR*, 1, 7:560, 595–596; Milton Rood to father, January 29, 1862, Milton Rood Letters, SHSI; Frank Whipple to mother, March 16, 1862, 11th Illinois File, FDR.

24. Louisa Boyd to Charles Smith, January 31, 1862, Charles F. Smith Papers, USMA; Lanza and Taylor, *Source Book*, 542–545; Edmond James Vinson Daybook, November 8, 1861–January 3, 1862, TSLA; *OR*, 1, 7:638; Thomas K. Mitchell Diary, February 18, 1862, 4th Illinois Cavalry File, FDR; John N. Ferguson Diary, February 13, 1862, LC.

25. "Death of H. C. Buckner," Richmond *Daily Dispatch*, January 8, 1862; Crummer, *With Grant at Fort Donelson*, 17; Cooling, *Forts Henry and Donelson*, 122; B. F. Boring, "From Cairo to Donelson," March 15, 1894, *National Tribune*.

26. Wilson, *The Confederate Soldier*, 48–57; Bela St. John Diary, February 19, 1862, Bela T. St. John Papers, LC.

27. *OR*, 1, 7:181.

28. Ibid., 255–256, 259, 303, 878–881; Samuel W. Ferguson Memoirs, 1902, Samuel W. Ferguson Papers, LSU.

29. *OR*, 1, 7:880, 883; *ORN*, 1, 22:824; Lunsford Yandell Diary, February 17, 1862, Yandell Family Papers, FHS; T. G. Pollock to father, February 19, 1862, Thomas G. Pollock Papers, UVA.

30. "A Brief History of Two Weeks of the War in Tennessee," February 23, 1862, Nashville *Times*; Cynthia Carter, "Recollections of the War," 1899, Pope-Carter Family Papers, DU, copy in FDC, 3.

31. Jesse Cox Diary, February 21, 1862, TSLA; John Lindsley Diary, February 16 and 17, 1862, Lindsley Family Papers, TSLA; O'Bryan Diary, February 16, 1862, Joseph Branch O'Bryan Papers, TSLA; S. W. MacGowan to cousin, February 17, 1862, Walter King Hoover Collection, TSLA. See also February 20, 1862, F. N. Walker Diary, and February 22, 1862, Robert Skipwith Diary, CWM; Eleanor Stuart to friends, February 21, 1862, Stuart Family Papers, VHS.

32. James Brown to Sarah, February 18, 1862, James J. Brown Papers, ALPL; David Monlux to Jonathon Monlux, undated, David Monlux Letters, Civil War Collection, MHS; Robert Price to father, March 15, 1862, Robert J. Price Letters, IHS; Cooling, "A Virginian at Fort Donelson," 189; George, *History*, 20; George Cullum to Henry Halleck, February 17, 1862, George W. Cullum Papers, USMA.

33. *OR*, 1, 7:386; Isham Harris to Albert Sidney Johnston, February 17, 1862, Western Department, Telegrams Received and Sent, 1861–1862, RG 109, E 101, NARA; Special Orders No. 30, February 15, 1862, Special Orders Western Department, October 1861–March 1862, RG 109, Chapter 2, Volume 220, NARA; Robert Cartmell Diary, February 15–16, 1862, Robert H. Cartmell Papers, TSLA; John Lindsley Diary, February 15, 1862, Lindsley Family Papers, TSLA.

34. Davis, *Jefferson Davis*, 398; Jones, *A Rebel War Clerk's Diary*, 1:96; Liberty Nixon Diary, undated, Liberty Independence Nixon Papers, AU; Thomas Goree to mother, February 21, 1862, Goree Family Papers, SHSU; Crist, *The Papers of Jefferson Davis*, 8:53. For more on the "reluctant rebels" that joined in the spring of 1862, see Noe, *Reluctant Rebels*.

35. John Nicolay to wife, February 17, 1862, John Nicolay Papers, LC, copy in Fort Donelson Account Folder, FDV; *OR*, 1, 52, 1:211; A. S. Baxter to Stephen Hurlbut, February 24, 1862, Mortimer Leggett Collection, UCSB.

36. Guyer, "The Journal and Letters of Corporal William O. Gulick," 266–267; I. P. Rumsey to family, February 16, 1862, I. P. Rumsey Papers, NL; John Brown to wife, February 24, 1862, John Brown, Jr., Collection, KHS; Myron Comstock to Verness Williams, February 21, 1862, Myron M. Comstock Letter, UT.

37. "Latest News," February 17, 1862, Cairo *Gazette*, copy in Civil War Collection, MHS; John Trotter to children, February 17, 1862, Maury Artillery File, FDR; Mrs. John A. Logan, "News From Donelson," May 31, 1888, *National Tribune*. For several news accounts, see Moore, *The Rebellion Record*, 4:170–187; George Turner to parents, February 25, 1862, George Turner Letters, PPL; Ted Barclay to sister, February 19, 1862, Ted

Barclay Letter, WLU; Wallace, *Life and Letters*, 157; Logan, *Reminiscences of a Soldier's Wife*, 123; Beale, *The Diary of Edward Bates*, 232–233; Donald, *Lincoln*, 336–337.

38. "State of Maine," March 19, 1862, Logan U. Reavis Papers, CHM; Wallace, *Life and Letters*, 168; Stephens, *Shadow of Shiloh*, 60; Lew Wallace to wife, February 19, 1862, Lew Wallace Papers, IHS; *OR*, 1, 7:628, 636–637; James Parrott to wife, February 21, 1862, James C. Parrott Papers, SHSI; J. F. Stuart to James Tuttle, February 24, 1862, James M. Tuttle Papers, SHSI; *Donelson Campaign Sources*, 14–17; Lorenzo Thomas to Charles Smith, February 24, 1862, Charles F. Smith Papers, USMA; General Orders 8, February 21, 1862, Charles Smith Letterbook, Charles F. Smith Papers, USMA; Charles Smith to wife, February 18 and 19, 1862, Letter Excerpts, Charles F. Smith Papers, USMA.

39. John E. Smith to Aimee, March 6, 1862 45th Illinois File, FDR; Simon and Marszalek, *The Papers of Ulysses S. Grant*, 4:229; *OR*, 1, 7:638; Seth Phelps to Ulysses S. Grant, February 22, 1862, Seth Ledyard Phelps Papers, MHS; Henry Crosby to Charles Smith, March 2, 1862, and Delany Eckels to Smith, February 25, 1862, Seth Phelps to Charles Smith, March 28, 1862, and James Grimes to Smith, February 24, 1862, all in Charles F. Smith Papers, USMA.

40. James Parrott to wife, February 21, 1862, James C. Parrott Papers, SHSI; E. W. Herman Diary, February 16, 1862, 7th Iowa File, SNMP; *OR*, 1, 7:629; Ulysses S. Grant to A. F. Goodman, March 15, 1862, William P. Palmer Collection, WRHS; Woodworth, *Nothing but Victory*, 119.

41. Stone, *Praise for Victory*; *ORN*, 1, 22:598; Woodworth, "Earned on the Field of Battle," 35; L. K. Shaffney to Julia Patterson, March 1, 1862, Patterson Family Papers, WSU; James S. Fogle to brother, February 25, 1862, 11th Indiana File, FDR; "A Reminisce of Fort Donelson," February 12, 1873, George C. Pope Papers, IHS.

42. John McClernand to Abraham Lincoln, February 18 and 27, 1862, Abraham Lincoln Papers, LC; *OR*, 1, 7:170, 180; Wallace, *An Autobiography*, 1:409; Plummer, *Lincoln's Rail-Splitter*, 72.

43. Ezra Taylor to G. S. Hubbard, March 16, 1862, Ezra Taylor Papers, CHM; John E. Smith to Aimee, March 6, 1862 45th Illinois File, FDR; "Peter Wilson in the Civil War," 273.

44. P. Bishop, Jr., to father, March 1, 1862, P. Bishop, Jr., Carondelet Folder, FDV.

45. Lanza and Taylor, *Source Book*, 354; Grant, *Personal Memoirs*, 1:260–261.

46. *OR*, 1, 7:628, 636–637; Schenker, "The Grant-Halleck-Smith Affair," 11–12; St. Louis citizens to Henry Halleck, February 28, 1862, Henry W. Halleck Papers, USMA.

47. *OR*, 1, 7:625; Sydenham Moore to wife, March 5, 1862, Sydenham Moore Family Papers, ADAH.

48. John Champenois to wife, March 28, 1862, John Franklin Champenois Family Papers, UTA; Isaac Beauchamp to wife, March 9, 1862, Isaac Beauchamp Letters, MOC; *ORN*, 1, 22:823; *OR*, 1, 7:264; Stevenson, *Thirteen Months in the Rebel Army*, 120; "After the Fall of Fort Donelson," 289–291.

49. Uffelman, Kanervo, Smith, and Williams, *The Diary of Nannie Haskins Williams*, 2; Henry H. Baltzell Memoir, 1916, ALPL, 9; John Nick Barker Diary, February 19 and 22, 1862, TSLA; Grant, *Personal Memoirs*, 1:258, 262; Villard, *Memoirs of Henry Vil-*

lard, 1:225–226; Clark, *The Notorious "Bull" Nelson*, 86–87; *ORN*, 1, 22:315, 587; *OR*, 1, 7:633, 638; John Spencer to brother, March 13, 1862, Spencer Family Papers, CWD, USAMHI.

50. A. B. Rush to Lizzie, February 20, 1862, A. B. Rush Letters, SHSI; Jesse Cox Diary, February 25, 1862, TSLA.

51. John Wilder to wife, February 23, 1862, John T. Wilder Papers, UTC; Schuyler P. Coe to mother, March 2, 1862, 1st Regiment Illinois Light Artillery File, FDR; William Eames to wife, February 25, 1862, William M. Eames Papers, TSLA; Robert Hughes Diary, February 17, 1862, Robert Morton Hughes Papers, ODU; Channing Richards Diary, February 28, 1862, FHS; "Employment Rolls and Nonpayment Rolls of Negroes Employed in the Defense of Nashville, Tennessee, 1862–1863," TSLA; I. M. Kirby to aunt, March 10, 1862, Isaac M. Kirby Letter, WKU.

52. *OR*, 1, 7:896; Williams, *P. G. T. Beauregard*, 118–121.

53. James Pope to mother, February 24, 1862, Pope-Carter Family Papers, DU, copy in FDC; Gustavus A. Henry et al. to Jefferson Davis, March 8, 1862, Gustavus A. Henry Papers, TSLA, copy in FDC; "The Demand for the Removal of Gen. A. S. Johnston," April 1, 1862, Nashville *Morning Bulletin*; Roland, *Albert Sidney Johnston*, 286–287, 290–291, 294.

54. *OR*, 1, 7:257, 260–261, 880.

55. *OR*, 1, 10, 2:24.

56. Hedley, *Marching through Georgia*, 37; "Camp Correspondence," March 20, 1862, Carlinville *Free Democrat*, copy in 32nd Illinois File, FDR.

EPILOGUE

1. Hugh to Father, March 10, 1862, Hugh Letter, FDA; Robert Price to father, March 15, 1862, Robert J. Price Letters, IHS; John E. Smith to Aimee, March 6, 1862 45th Illinois File, FDR.

2. S. E. Fiske to children, March 26, 1862, DeWitt Family Papers, TSLA; "Tabular Statement of Regiments, Commanders, Casualties, and Escapees at Fort Donelson, Feb. 16, 1862," Army of Tennessee Records, TSLA; Johnston, *The Life of Gen. Albert Sidney Johnston*, 478; *OR*, 1, 7:159, 167; Grant, *Personal Memoirs*, 1:257–258; Eliza Lucy Irion Neilson Journal, undated, Irion-Neilson Family Papers, MDAH, 21; J. Peeler to Dunbar Rowland, November 21, 1908, 4th Mississippi Infantry Papers, MDAH; "The Battle of Fort Donelson," 1864, Elizabeth Frances Bartlett Boyd Notebook, MDAH, 16; Clarke, *Diary of the War for Separation*, 83; Gott, *Where the South Lost the War*, 262–263; John A. Dougherty Diary, February 15, 1862, LSU.

3. Dietrich Smith to Carrie, February 20, 1862, Dietrich C. Smith Papers, ALPL; Henrietta Geisberg to friend, March 13, 1862, Anthony J. Baurdick Papers, EU; Charles Floyd to Turner, July 6, 1862, Charles H. Floyd Letters, ALPL; Robert Woodall Memo, December 27, 1862, 31st Indiana File, FDR.

4. George Smith Diary, March 21, 1862, UK.

5. Charles Smith to John Osborn, March 13, 1862, Civil War Related Material, IHS; Cyrus Hines to "General," February 22, 1862, Cyrus C. Hines Letter, IHS; William Austin to John Sargent, February 21, 1862, William H. Austin Letters, ALPL; William Tebbets to sister, March 2, 1862, William H. Tebbets Letters, ALPL; John Kerr to wife, February 20, 1862, John D. Kerr Correspondence, ALPL; Thomas Miller to Benjamin Newton, February 18, 1862, Thomas F. Miller Letters, ALPL; John D. St. John to parents, March 26, 1862, Bela T. St. John Papers, LC.

6. A. F. Gilbert Memoir, 1928, Jill Knight Garrett Collection, TSLA.

7. James Maroney to J. D. Graham, February 24, 1862, Myers-Burrage-Graham Papers, CWM; B. C. to sister, February 19, 1862, Boyer-Castleman Family Papers, FHS.

8. Henry N. Peters to family, April 23, 1862, Peters Family Papers, UAR; Nathaniel Cheairs to daughter, April 25, 1862, Cheairs-Hughes Family Papers, TSLA; William Wier to "Doc," May 6, 1862, Wier Family Letters, MSU; Thomas E. Wilson to A. J. Weissinger, May 13, 1862, Wiessinger Family Papers, MSU; Mary Durham to J. Z. George, July 9, 1862, James Z. George Papers, MDAH; *OR*, 1, 7:372; Hylan Lyons to wife, March 15 and 30, 1862, Hylan B. Lyons Papers, MU; William P. Halliday to Mrs. R. W. Hanson, February 19, 1862, Roger W. Hanson Papers, UK. See also the James Knox Polk Lewis Diary, TSLA.

9. John Hardin to father, February 17, 1862, John J. Hardin Letter, IHS; Sherman, *Memoirs*, 1875, 1:221; *OR*, 1, 7:136; Simon Buckner to Editors, *Louisville Journal*, March 4, 1862, Simon Bolivar Buckner Papers, HL; Allardice, *Confederate Colonels*, 121.

10. M. A. Ryan, "Experiences of a Confederate Soldier in Camp and Prison in the Civil War," undated, M. A. Ryan Memoir, MDAH; G. W. Giles to Shoog, October 5, 1862, G. W. Giles Letters, LSU.

11. Joseph Hall to Mary, February 21, 1862, Arthur Van Horn Family Papers, LC; Simon Eccles to James Henry, February 25, 1862, Simon F. Eccles Papers, NC; H. C. Brinkman to Sister, February 23, 1862, Henry C. Brinkman Papers, CIN; Oliver Bridgford to wife, February 21, 1862, Oliver Bridgford Letters, 45th Illinois File, SNMP; Moses Owne to mother, February 18, 1862, Moses Owen Letter, UT; John Burggraf to family, February 26, 1862, John G. Burggraf Letters, WU; B to wife, February 17, 1862, 25th Kentucky File, FDR.

12. Andrew Davis Diary, February 17, 1862, UI; Thomas Sterns to wife, April 5, 1862, Sterns Family Papers, UI; Andrew Davis to wife, February 9, 1862, Andrew F. Davis Papers, UI.

13. William Tibbets to parents, March 2, 1862 (mislabeled 1861), William H. Tibbets Letters, ALPL; Daniel Goodman to Hanah, February 23, 1862, Edwin R. Capron Collection, NSHS; James Parrott to wife, February 21, 1862, James C. Parrott Papers, SHSI; Charles James to brother, March 28, 1862, Durgin Family Papers, VHS; Daniel Horn to wife, March 5, 1862, Daniel Horn Papers, HL; Edward Fulton to mother, February 22, 1862, Edward A. Fulton Letters, UD; H. D. Munson to Willia, February 22, 1862, William O. Munson Letters, UAR.

14. Crummer, *With Grant at Fort Donelson*, 47.

15. Edward M. Galligan Diary, February 23, 1862, MTHS; Russel to friend, February 22, 1862, Ezra Greene Letters, FHS.

16. *OR*, 1, 7:629; Lorenzo Thomas to Henry Halleck, March 10, 1862, Ulysses S. Grant Papers, RG 94, E 159, NARA.

17. William Parkinson to James, March 25, 1862, William M. Parkinson Letters, EU; General Orders No. 22, April 28, 1862, Charles F. Smith Papers, RG 94, E 159, NARA.

18. *OR*, 1, 7:379; W. W. Mackall to John Floyd, February 25, 1862, John B. Floyd Papers, RG 109, E 119, NARA.

19. *OR*, 1, 7:254, 274, 401; Jeremy Gilmer to wife, February 22, 1862, Jeremy F. Gilmer Papers, UNC; John Floyd to Simon Buckner, August 15, 1862, John B. Floyd Papers, RG 109, E 119, NARA; "Resolutions Creating the Committee," undated, FDA.

20. *OR*, 1, 7:325; Gideon Pillow to George Randolph, May 15, 1862, Gideon Pillow to William Hardee, February 20, 1862, and Pillow to Editor of *Memphis Avalanche*, February 27, 1862, Gideon Pillow Papers, RG 109, E 132, NARA.

21. Selden Spencer, "Reminiscences of the Battle of Fort Donelson," undated, Civil War Collection, MHS; *Floyd's Retreat from Fort Donelson: With a Running Description of the Battle* (Cincinnati: A. C. Peters & Bro., 1862), UVA, original also in FDA; W. A. Rorer to Susan, April 22, 1863, W. A. Rorer Letters, DU, copies in MDAH; J. P. Jackson to sir, April 22, 1862, Camp Chase Papers, VHS; Casey to Joey, February 17, 1862, Joseph S. Williams Letters, DU; John W. Tuttle Diary, March 18, 1862, UK, 68.

22. John Floyd to Simon Buckner, August 15, 1862, John B. Floyd Papers, RG 109, E 119, NARA; *OR*, 1, 7:383; Nathaniel Cheairs Account, May 3, 1862, John C. Brown Autograph Book, Civil War Collection, TSLA, copy in FDC; Robert Farquharson to Andrew Buchanan, July 18, 1862, Buchanan and McClellan Family Papers, UNC.

23. Wallace, *An Autobiography*, 1:365; T. G. Pollock to father, February 19, 1862, Thomas G. Pollock Papers, UVA; Peter Sheaff to brothers, April 13, 1862, Charles Raymond Sheaff Papers, UCB; Henry R. Pippitt Diary, January 17, 1865, UT; Albright Koehler Diary, April 10, 1862, ALPL; Oliver Boardman to Henry, March 12, 1862, Oliver Boardman Correspondence, UI; Turner S. Bailey Diary, March 10, 1862, UI.

24. "Lt. Charles F. Humphreys Fort Donelson Ordnance Account Book, 1864–1865," TSLA; "Leaves From Diary of Z. C. Patten Tell of Civil War Days," April 9, 1930, Chattanooga *News*, copy in Stickley Collection, TSLA; Charles Alley Diary, February 3, 1863, 2nd Iowa File, FDR; Elmer Everett Diary and Letters, February 1863, FDA; E. S. Cooper Letter, February 14, 1863, FDA; Samuel Patton to Nellie, February 5, 1863, Patton Family Papers, FHS; W. L. Kemp to mother, February 10, 1863, Scott Family Papers, UMOC; Henry Gilbert Diary, February 4, 1863, UMC; George H. Palmer Diary, undated, ALPL, 5; James Moore to Montgomery Meigs, October 28, 1864, Moore Family Papers, ALPL.

25. Finding Aid, undated, George W. Frost Papers, RU; "Notes from Conversation with Mr. Ed Walter on October 12, 1959 and August 7, 1963," Fort Donelson Aftermath, FDV; Charles Grobe, "The Battle of Fort Donelson, a Musical Description," 1862, FDA; Peterson, *Administrative History*; Riggins, *A History of Fort Donelson National Military Park Tennessee*.

26. Ulysses S. Grant to sir, January 3, 1877, Charles F. Smith Papers, UMC.

27. Simon B. Buckner, Jr., to W. E. Brooks, February 7, 1936, WS.

BIBLIOGRAPHY

Abbreviations

AC	Augustana College
ADAH	Alabama Department of Archives and History
AHC	Atlanta History Center
ALPL	Abraham Lincoln Presidential Library
AU	Auburn University
BCHS	Bartholomew County Historical Society
BGSU	Bowling Green State University
CH	Carter House
CHCH	Chickamauga and Chattanooga National Military Park
CHM	Chicago History Museum
CIN	Cincinnati Historical Society
CWD	Civil War Documents Collection
CWM	College of William and Mary
CWTI	Civil War Times Illustrated Collection
DC	Dartmouth College
DU	Duke University
ECU	East Carolina University
EU	Emory University
FDA	Fort Donelson Archives
FDC	Fort Donelson Cooling Papers
FDR	Fort Donelson Regimental Files
FDV	Fort Donelson Vertical Files
FHS	Filson Historical Society
HCWRT	Harrisburg Civil War Roundtable Collection
HL	Huntington Library
IHS	Indiana Historical Society
ISL	Indiana State Library
IU	Indiana University
KHS	Kansas Historical Society

LC	Library of Congress
LS	Lincoln Shrine
LSU	Louisiana State University
LTU	Louisiana Tech University
MDAH	Mississippi Department of Archives and History
MHS	Missouri Historical Society
MNHS	Minnesota Historical Society
MOC	Museum of the Confederacy
MOLLUS	*Military Order of the Loyal Legion of the United States*
MSU	Mississippi State University
MTHS	Montana Historical Society
MU	Murray State University
NARA	National Archives and Records Administration
NC	Navarro College
NJHS	New Jersey Historical Society
NL	Newberry Library
NSHS	Nebraska State Historical Society
ODU	Old Dominion University
OHS	Ohio Historical Society
OR	*War of the Rebellion: A Compilation of the Official Records of the Union and Confederate Armies.* Washington, DC: US Government Printing Office, 1880–1901.
ORN	*The Official Records of the Union and Confederate Navies in the War of the Rebellion*, 30 vols. Washington, DC: US Government Printing Office, 1894–1922.
OU	Ohio University
PPL	Providence Public Library
PU	Princeton University
RU	Rice University
RBHPC	Rutherford B. Hayes Presidential Center
SCPL	Stewart County Public Library
SEMO	Southeast Missouri State University
SHSI	State Historical Society of Iowa
SHSU	Sam Houston State University
SIU	Southern Illinois University
SNMP	Shiloh National Military Park
STRI	Stones River National Battlefield
SU	Stanford University
TAM	Texas A & M University
TSLA	Tennessee State Library and Archives
TU	Tulane University
UA	University of Alabama
UAR	University of Arkansas

UAZ	University of Arizona
UCB	University of California Berkeley
UCR	University of California Riverside
UCSB	University of California Santa Barbara
UD	University of Delaware
UI	University of Iowa
UIL	University of Illinois
UK	University of Kentucky
UMC	University of Michigan, Clements Library
UMEM	University of Memphis
UMOC	University of Missouri Columbia
UNC	University of North Carolina
UO	University of Oklahoma
USAMHI	United States Army Military History Institute
USM	University of Southern Mississippi
USMA	United States Military Academy
UT	University of Tennessee
UTA	University of Texas at Austin
UTAR	University of Texas at Arlington
UTC	University of Tennessee at Chattanooga
UVA	University of Virginia
UWS	University of Washington
UWY	University of Wyoming
VCPL	Vigo County Public Library
VHS	Virginia Historical Society
VICK	Vicksburg National Military Park
VT	Virginia Tech University
WHS	Wisconsin Historical Society
WKU	Western Kentucky University
WLU	Washington and Lee University
WRHS	Western Reserve Historical Society
WS	Wiley Sword Collection
WSU	Wright State University
WU	Willamette University

Manuscripts

Abraham Lincoln Presidential Library, Springfield, Illinois
    17th Illinois Records
    32nd Illinois Consolidated Provision Return
    William H. Austin Letters
    Bailhache-Brayman Family Papers

Henry H. Baltzell Memoir
Thomas Barnett Papers
Benjamin F. Best Papers
James A. Black Diary
Jonathan Blair Letter
James J. Brown Papers
Bruce Family Papers
Daniel H. Brush Diary
James A. B. Butterfield Correspondence
George L. Childres Diary
David M. Claggett Diary
George W. Cullum Letters
James F. Drish Papers
Dumville Family Correspondence
Engelmann-Kircher Family Papers
Charles H. Floyd Letters
George Hamman Diary
Douglas Hapeman Diary
Isham N. Haynie Papers
John D. Kerr Correspondence
William H. Kinkade Diary
Albright Koehler Diary
Michael K. Lawler Papers
John A. McClernand Papers
Ira Merchant Letter
Thomas F. Miller Letters
Moore Family Papers
William R. Morrison Papers
Richard J. Oglesby Papers
George H. Palmer Diary
Henry E. Parcel Correspondence
Frederick Eugene Ransom Order Book
Sackett Family Letters
Z. Payson Shumway Papers
Dietrich C. Smith Papers
George O. Smith, "Brief History of the 17th Regiment of Illinois Volunteer Infantry"
Levi Stewart Letters
William H. Tibbets Letters
William D. T. Travis Sketches
Abram J. Vanauken Diary
Wallace-Dickey Family Papers
Harley Wayne Correspondence
John H. White Letters

John S. Wilcox Papers

William Wilson Diary

Alabama Department of Archives and History, Montgomery, Alabama

27th Alabama File

J. P. Cannon, "History of the 27th Regiment Ala. Volunteer Infantry C.S.A."

Alexander K. Hall Family Papers

Sydenham Moore Family Papers

Governor John G. Shorter Administrative Files

Atlanta History Center, Atlanta, Georgia

David G. Godwin Letters

Auburn University, Auburn, Alabama

Liberty Independence Nixon Papers

Augustana College, Rock Island, Illinois

Gould D. Molineaux Diary

Bartholomew County Historical Society, Columbus, Indiana

James S. Fogle Letters

Bowling Green State University, Bowling Green, Ohio

Robert H. Caldwell Papers

Hill/Morgan Family Papers

Carter House, Franklin, Tennessee

Charles E. Taylor Diary

Chicago History Museum, Chicago, Illinois

Samuel Eddy Barrett Papers

Mason Brayman Papers

George D. Carrington Diary

Jabob G. Lauman Papers

Montgomery C. Meigs Papers

G. W. Paris Papers

Logan U. Reavis Papers

George Sawin Papers

Ezra Taylor Papers

Martin R. Wallace Papers

Chicago Public Library, Chicago, Illinois

John H. Roe Letter

Chickamauga and Chattanooga National Military Park, Fort Oglethorpe, Georgia

Curtin Alexander Brasher Diary

David M. Claggett Diary, 17th Kentucky File

Christopher Newport University, Newport News, Virginia

Seth Ledyard Phelps Papers

Cincinnati Historical Society, Cincinnati, Ohio

Henry C. Brinkman Papers

College of William and Mary, Williamsburg, Virginia

Maury Family Papers

Myers-Burrage-Graham Papers
Robert Skipwith Diary
F. N. Walker Diary
Dartmouth College, Hanover, New Hampshire
Baron Proctor Letter
Duke University, Durham, North Carolina
Alexander Brown Papers
Simon Bolivar Buckner Papers
John B. Floyd Papers
Eugene Marshall Papers
Munford-Ellis Family Papers
Pope-Carter Family Papers
W. A. Rorer Letters
M. J. Solomons Scrapbook
Charles B. Tompkins Papers
White Family Letters
Joseph S. Williams Letters
East Carolina University, Greenville, North Carolina
Abraham G. Jones Papers
John M. Porter Memoirs
Emory University, Atlanta, Georgia
Anthony J. Baurdick Papers
William M. Parkinson Letters
Filson Historical Society, Louisville, Kentucky
Boyer-Castleman Family Papers
Don Carlos Buell Papers
"Fort Donelson, Tennessee"
Ezra Greene Letters
Patton Family Papers
Channing Richards Diary
Henry H. Russell Letter
Walter Letters
Watters-Curtis Family Papers
Yandell Family Papers
Fort Donelson National Battlefield Archives, Dover, Tennessee
David Baker Letter
Edwin C. Bearss Maps
Thomas Bell Letter
E. S. Cooper Letter
Daniel P. Donnell Letter
Elmer Everett Diary and Letters
Floyd's Retreat from Fort Donelson: With a Running Description of the Battle
Charles Grobe, "The Battle of Fort Donelson, A Musical Description"

William C. Holden Letter
Hugh Letter
F. M. Ingram Letter
John Douglass Jarvis Letter
J. N. Prince Letter
"Resolutions Creating the Committee"
J. A. B. Rogers Letter
J. H. Rowett
W. C. Stewart Letters
Fort Donelson National Battlefield Regimental Files, Dover, Tennessee
Charles Alley Diary, 2nd Iowa File
B Letter, 25th Kentucky File
James Bailey Letters, 49th Tennessee File
Abiel M. Barker Diary, 32nd Illinois File
Jonathan Blair Letter, 46th Illinois File
Ben H. Bounds Civil War Memoir, 4th Mississippi File
Milo W. Brady Diary, 45th Illinois File
Curtin Alexander Brasher Diary
Oliver Bridgford Letter, 45th Illinois File
Joseph Brigham Letters, 50th Tennessee File
Thomas B. Brumbaugh, "A Letter to Fort Donelson"
"Camp Correspondence," 32nd Illinois File
"Capt. A. Schwartz. Memorandum of Battle. Ft. Donelson Feby 15, 1862"
David M. Claggett Diary, 17th Kentucky File
David Clark Letter, 30th Tennessee File
Schuyler P. Coe Letter, 1st Regiment Illinois Light Artillery File
James C. Cook Diary, 50th Tennessee File
Samuel Kennedy Cox Diary, 17th Kentucky File
F. C. Cromwell Journal, 12th Iowa File
E. H. Dailey Letter, 4th Illinois Cavalry File
John Davis Letter, 46th Illinois File
Jack L. Dickinson, ed., "The Civil War Diary of James Conrad Peters, Sgt.,
    Company 'B'
        30th Battalion Va. Sharpshooters CSA," 30th Battalion Virginia
            Sharpshooters File
George W. Dillon Diary, 18th Tennessee File
Daniel P. Donnell Letter, 2nd Iowa File
Alonzo Eaton Letter, 2nd Iowa File
James S. Fogle Letters, 11th Indiana File
"Fort Donelson," 56th Virginia File
William D. Foster Letter, 30th Illinois File
"Genl. McClernand Memorandum of Battle, Ft. Donelson, 15 Feb 1862"
A. F. Gilbert Memoir, 17th Illinois File

Thorne Hall Letter

E. W. Herman Diary, 7th Iowa File

R. I. Hill Diary, 3rd Mississippi File

John T. Hodges Letter, 49th Tennessee File

F. H. Hunter Letter, 6th Arkansas File

J. M. S. Letter, 57th Illinois File

James Samuel Jones Diary, 30th Tennessee File

Thomas Burton Jones Memoir, 8th Kentucky File

William L. Jurney Letter, 2nd Iowa File

Henry Kepcha Letter, 41st Illinois File

Samuel Keplar Letter, 58th Ohio File

George C. Kindelsperyer Diary

Americus Langston Diary, 7th Texas File

John Lautzenhiser Diary, 41st Illinois File

Sylvester Lett Letter, 11th Indiana File

R. H. McFadden Letter, 41st Illinois File

S. C. Mitchell, "Recollections of a Private," 3rd Tennessee File

Thomas K. Mitchell Diary, 4th Illinois Cavalry File

S. C. Nelson Letter, 41st Illinois File

W. B. O'Neill Letter, 14th Iowa File

Order Book. Quarter Masters Department Gen. Floyd's Brigade C. S. Army.
    From Feby 10th 1862

Frank Reed Letter, 12th Iowa File

M. A. Ryan Memoir, 8th Mississippi File

Charles Sackett Letters

Henry Schaphard Diary, 29th Illinois File

Phillip Shaw Diary, 32nd Illinois File

John E. Smith Letters, 45th Illinois File

John Stephens Letter, 76th Ohio File

William S. Stephens Letter, 30th Illinois File

Levi Stewart Letter, 49th Illinois File

David W. Stratton Diary

"A Thrilling Episode," 3rd Tennessee File

John Trotter Letter, Maury Artillery File

Henry Uptmer Memoir, 11th Illinois File

J. W. Wall Letter, 49th Tennessee File

Harley Wayne Correspondence, 15th Illinois File

Ben West Diary, 12th Illinois File

B. West Letter, 12th Illinois File

Frank Whipple Letter, 11th Illinois File

Dabney Stuart Wier Diary, Mississippi Volunteers File

F. E. Willey Letter, 49th Tennessee File

J. T. Williamson, "Notes about the War (1861–1865)," 3rd Tennessee File

Robert Woodall Memo, 31st Indiana File

Fort Donelson National Battlefield Vertical File, Dover, Tennessee

Aaron/Erin Hollow

Account of Fort Henry and Fort Donelson Battles Suddarth

S. H. Batton Letters

P. Bishop, Jr., Carondelet Folder

Benjamin F. Cooling Papers

Copy of Simon B. Buckner's Orders Arrangements for Surrender

Dover Weekly Intelligencer 1859 Newspaper Dover Hotel Info

Effects of Victory at Donelson/Henry Foreign Courts/J. D. Richardson

Fort Donelson Account

Fort Donelson Aftermath

Fort Heiman and Vicinity

Fort Henry Newspaper Accounts

Aaron Goodrich Letter to H. C. Lockhart

Iowa Legislature Celebrates Capture by Aldrich

Newspaper Clippings on Fort Donelson and Dover

Alexander Simplot Diary

Weather during Fort Donelson Battle

Western Rivers/Steamboats/Twin Rivers

Huntington Library, San Marino, California

Simon Bolivar Buckner Papers

Daniel Horn Papers

Moses A. McCoid Papers

Indiana Historical Society, Indianapolis, Indiana

Francis M. Brainerd Letters

Civil War Related Material

Jesse Connelly Diary

Lancelot C. Ewbank Diary

Frank Fee Letters

John J. Hardin Letter

Cyrus C. Hines Letter

James H. Jones Letters

George C. Pope Papers

Robert J. Price Letters

Ross-Kidwell Family Papers

Lew Wallace Papers

Christian A. Wolfram Letters

Indiana State Library, Indianapolis, Indiana

Jesse Connelly Diary

James S. Fogle Letters

James Nelson Shepherd Diary
Addison Sleeth Memoir
Indiana University, Bloomington, Indiana
Flavel C. Barber Diary
Kansas Historical Society, Topeka, Kansas
John Brown, Jr., Collection
Library of Congress, Washington, DC
Francis Marion Bateman Papers
John N. Ferguson Diary
Andrew H. Foote Papers
Manning F. Force Papers
Peter Force Papers
Henry W. Halleck Papers
Roger W. Hanson Papers
Harwood Family Papers
Abraham Lincoln Papers
John A. Logan Papers
Horace Harmon Lurton Papers
Absalom H. Markland Papers
McCook Family Papers
John Nicolay Papers
Bela T. St. John Papers
Oliphant M. Todd Diary
Arthur Van Horn Family Papers
William F. Wilder Papers
Lincoln Shrine, Redlands, California
Mason Brayman Papers
Louisiana State University, Baton Rouge, Louisiana
John A. Dougherty Diary
E. John Ellis Diary
Samuel W. Ferguson Papers
G. W. Giles Letters
Emily D. Sherwood Family Correspondence
Charles E. Taylor Diary
Louisiana Tech University, Ruston, Louisiana
Seamans Family Papers
Charles E. Taylor Diary
Minnesota Historical Society, St. Paul, Minnesota
Eugene Marshall Papers
Mississippi Department of Archives and History, Jackson, Mississippi
4th Mississippi Infantry Papers
20th Mississippi Infantry Regiment Papers
Marion Francis Baxter Papers

Elizabeth Frances Bartlett Boyd Notebook
James Z. George Papers
Gilliam-Chason Family Letters
Irion-Neilson Family Papers
Timothy McNamara Diary
John T. Megee Papers
Eliza Barry Ricks Papers
W. A. Rorer Letters
M. A. Ryan Memoir
Mississippi State University, Starkville, Mississippi
Marcus L. Henry Reminiscences
Hester Family Papers
Wier Family Letters
Wiessinger Family Papers
John H. Wilson Reminiscences
Missouri Historical Society, St. Louis, Missouri
Civil War Collection
Henry W. Halleck Collection
"Latest News," February 17, 1862, Cairo *Gazette*
David Monlux Letters
Selden Spencer, "Reminiscences of the Battle of Fort Donelson"
Unsigned Fragmentary Notes on the Capture of Fort Henry
James B. Eads Collection
Grier Family Papers
Thomas Butler Gunn Diary
Seth Ledyard Phelps Papers
Montana Historical Society, Helena, Montana
Edward M. Galligan Diary
Murray State University, Murray, Kentucky
Sam House Letters
J. H. Long Letter
Hylan B. Lyons Papers
Spot Fontaine Terrell Diary
Museum of the Confederacy, Richmond, Virginia
Isaac Beauchamp Letters
James T. Mackey Diary
Lloyd Tilghman Papers
National Archives and Records Administration, Washington, DC
RG 45—Naval Records Collection of the Office of Naval Records and Library
A-5—Andrew Foote Letters
RG 92—Records of the Office of the Quartermaster General
E 1403 Water Transportation
USS *Conestoga* File

        USS *Essex* File
        USS *Pittsburg* File
        USS *Tyler* File
    RG 94—Records of the Adjutant General's Office
        E 159—Generals' Papers
            Don Carlos Buell Papers
            George W. Cullum Papers
            Ulysses S. Grant Papers
            Henry W. Halleck Papers
            John A. McClernand Papers
            Charles F. Smith Papers
            Lew Wallace Papers
    RG 109—War Department Collection of Confederate Records
        E 101—Western Department, Telegrams Received and Sent, 1861–1862
        E 103—Correspondence of the Eastern Department and the Army of the
            Mississippi, 1861–1862
        E 116—P. G. T. Beauregard Papers
        E 119—John B. Floyd Papers
        E 123—Bushrod Johnson Papers
        E 132—Gideon Pillow Papers
        Chapter 2, Volume 217—Letters and Telegrams Sent, September 1861–
            April 1862
        Chapter 2, Volume 218—Letters and Telegrams Sent, October 1861–
            April 1862
        Chapter 2, Volume 220—Special Orders Western Department, October 1861–
            March 1862
    RG 217—Records of the Accounting Officers of the Department of the Treasury
        E UD292—Western Gunboat Flotilla Muster, Pay, and Receipt Rolls, 1862
            USS *Cincinnati* Muster Roll, 1862
            USS *Essex* Muster Roll, 1862
Navarro College, Corsicana, Texas
    Simon F. Eccles Papers
    David W. Poak Papers
Nebraska State Historical Society, Lincoln, Nebraska
    J. H. Bronson Collection
    Edwin R. Capron Collection
    Joseph W. Johnson Collection
    Albert Rhodes Diary
Newberry Library, Chicago, Illinois
    I. P. Rumsey Papers
    Hiram Scofield Papers
New Jersey Historical Society, Newark, New Jersey
    John Vance Powers Papers

Ohio Historical Society, Columbus, Ohio
    James C. Cook Diary
    Henry Otis Dwight Papers
    William F. Willey Diary
Ohio University, Athens, Ohio
    Kinney Family Papers
Old Dominion University, Norfolk, Virginia
    Robert Morton Hughes Papers
Princeton University, Princeton, New Jersey
    William E. Potter Diary
Providence Public Library, Providence, Rhode Island
    George Turner Letters
Rice University, Houston, Texas
    Catherine Broun Diary
    George W. Frost Papers
Rutherford B. Hayes Presidential Center, Fremont, Ohio
    Eric Bergland Diary, February 12, 1862
Sam Houston State University, Huntsville, Texas
    Goree Family Papers
Shiloh National Military Park, Shiloh, Tennessee
    Oliver Bridgford Letters, 45th Illinois File
    Samuel Kennedy Cox Diary, 17th Kentucky File
    James S. Fogle Diary, 11th Indiana File
    George Harvey Letters, 31st Indiana File
    E. S. Henline Letters, 8th Illinois File
    E. W. Herman Diary, 7th Iowa File
    Samuel Kennedy Cox Diary, 17th Kentucky File
    John D. Kerr Letters, 41st Illinois File
    Samuel May Letters, 68th Ohio File
    Memoir, U.S.S. *Tyler* File
    William Reed Letters, 8th Missouri File
    Phillip Shaw Diary, 32nd Illinois File
Southeast Missouri State University, Cape Girardeau, Missouri
    Ellen Waddle McCoy Papers
Southern Illinois University, Carbondale, Illinois
    Joseph Skipworth Papers
Stanford University, Stanford, California
    Harwood Family Papers
State Historical Society of Iowa, Des Moines, Iowa
    "Autobiography of Clarissa Emily Gear Hobbs"
    Charles C. Cloutman Diary
    "A Confederate Officer Relates a Story of Bravery Of Iowa Soldiers at Fort
        Donelson"

Drake Family Papers
William L. Henderson Letters
E. W. Herman Diary, 7th Iowa File
Thomas L. Hoffman Diary
William C. Holden Letter
Edmund McLaury Letters
Milton Rood Letters
A. B. Rush Letters
Garrett Schreurs Diary
William T. Shaw Papers
Silas I. Shearer Papers
James M. Tuttle Papers
Voltaire P. Twombly Papers
Willaim W. Warner Papers
State Historical Society of Iowa, Iowa City, Iowa
James C. Parrott Papers
Stewart County Public Library, Dover, Tennessee
John Franklin Locke Diary
Iris Hopkins McClain, "A History of Stewart County, Tennessee"
Stones River National Battlefield, Murfreesboro, Tennessee
David W. Stratton Diary
Tennessee State Library and Archives, Nashville, Tennessee
Martha Farmer Anthony Papers
Army of Tennessee Records
Bailey Family Papers
John Nick Barker Diary
Brigham Family Papers
Robert H. Cartmell Papers
Cheairs-Hughes Family Papers
Civil War Collection
    George Wiley Adams Letters
    David Bodenhamer, "The Battle of Fort Donelson"
    John C. Brown Autograph Book
    Calvin J. Clack, "History of Company A 3rd Tenn Regt, Infantry"
    Thomas H. Deavenport Diary
    J. K. Farris Letters
    Henry Halleck Letter
    William L. McKay Diary
    John M. Porter Memoirs
Confederate Military and Financial Board Papers
Luther Howard Cowan Papers
Jesse Cox Diary
DeWitt Family Papers

George W. Dillon Papers
William M. Eames Papers
Elam Family Papers
"Employment Rolls and Nonpayment Rolls of Negroes Employed in the Defense of
    Nashville, Tennessee, 1862–1863"
Farmer Family Papers
Figuers Collection
    Nathaniel Cheairs Account
Isham G. Harris Papers
Gustavus A. Henry Papers
Walter King Hoover Collection
Land between the Lakes Project Research Papers
Lindsley Family Papers
"Lt. Charles F. Humphreys Fort Donelson Ordnance Account Book, 1864–1865"
Jill Knight Garrett Collection
    A. F. Gilbert Memoir
James Knox Polk Lewis Diary
William Neal McGrew Diary
Joseph Branch O'Bryan Papers
A. T. Robertson Family Papers
Ross Family Papers
Alexander Simplot Civil War Drawings
Samuel R. Simpson Diary
Rutledge Smith Papers
Stickley Collection
Talbot-Fentress Family Papers
"Tennessee River from Paducah, Ky. To Florence, Ala." Edmond James Vinson
    Daybook
Texas A & M University, College Station, Texas
    G. Hobart Taylor Diary
Tulane University, New Orleans, Louisiana
    Rosemonde E. and Emile Kuntz Collection
United States Army Military History Institute, Carlisle, Pennsylvania
    Civil War Documents Collection—CWD
        John P. Brownlow Papers
        William N. Bullard Papers
        David Cornwell Memoir
        John Gregg Papers
        Frank B. Gurley Papers
        Thomas S. Lacy Papers
        Joseph LeBrant Papers
        Mark P. Lowrey Papers
        Charles H. Lutz Papers

Logan H. N. Salyer Papers
Spencer Family Papers
Joseph W. Westbrook Papers
Henry S. Weston Papers
Civil War Times Illustrated Collection—CWTI
Francis Marion Baxter Papers
Timothy M. Blaisdell Paper
Mungo P. Murray Papers
M. A. Ryan Papers
Cowell Collection
Charles Cowell Diary
Goldman Collection
John H. White Letters
Harrisburg Civil War Round Table Collection
Coco Collection
Howard and Victor Stevens Papers
Hess Collection
Nelson Wood Letter
Lowry Hinch Collection
7th Illinois Cavalry Papers
29th Illinois Papers
Frank B. Smith Papers
Winey Collection
Jonathan Matter Papers
United States Military Academy, West Point, New York
George W. Cullum Papers
Ulysses S. Grant Papers
Henry W. Halleck Papers
Charles F. Smith Papers
University of Alabama, Tuscaloosa, Alabama
H. B. Hillen Letter
University of Arizona, Tucson, Arizona
Thompson Family Papers
University of Arkansas, Fayetteville, Arkansas
William O. Munson Letters
Peters Family Papers
University of California Berkeley, Berkeley, California
Francis Le Chevalier Papers
Charles Raymond Sheaff Papers
University of California Riverside, Riverside, California
Issac C. Pugh Papers
University of California Santa Barbara, Santa Barbara, California
Mortimer Leggett Collection

University of Delaware, Newark, Delaware
    Edward A. Fulton Letters
University of Illinois, Champaign, Illinois
    George S. Durfee Letters
University of Iowa, Iowa City, Iowa
    Turner S. Bailey Diary
    Oliver Boardman Correspondence
    Andrew F. Davis Papers
    William L. Henderson Journal
    Mead Family Papers
    Sterns Family Papers
    James B. Weaver Papers
University of Kentucky, Lexington, Kentucky
    Roger W. Hanson Papers
    George Smith Diary
    John W. Tuttle Diary
    Mary E. Van Meter Diary
University of Memphis, Memphis, Tennessee
    Griffin Stanton Diary
    "Tennessee River from Paducah, Ky. To Florence, Ala."
University of Michigan Clements Library, Ann Arbor, Michigan
    Henry Gilbert Diary
    Charles F. Smith Papers
    James Stewart Diary
University of Missouri Columbia, Columbia, Missouri
    Richard Burt Letters
    James Coghill Letters
    Scott Family Papers
University of North Carolina, Chapel Hill, North Carolina
    Stephen T. Andrews Letters
    Catherine Broun Diary
    Buchanan and McClellan Family Papers
    Lucy Wood Butler Papers
    Sam M. Fleming Collection
    Jeremy F. Gilmer Papers
    Francis Terry Leak Diary
University of Oklahoma, Norman, Oklahoma
    Sheery Marie Cress Collection
        Charles Kroff Diary
University of Southern Mississippi, Hattiesburg, Mississippi
    Garrett Smith Ainsworth Diary
    W. T. Booth Collection

University of Tennessee, Knoxville, Tennessee
    H. L. Bedford Memoir
    Charles Christensen Letter
    Myron M. Comstock Letter
    Phoebe Cross Letter
    Wesley Smith Dorris Diary
    J. P. Hollowell Letter
    Robert M. Kepner Letter
    Moses Owen Letter
    Henry R. Pippitt Diary
University of Tennessee at Chattanooga, Chattanooga, Tennessee
    John T. Wilder Papers
University of Texas at Arlington, Arlington, Texas
    Clough Family Papers
University of Texas at Austin, Austin, Texas
    Simon Bolivar Buckner Letter
    Andrew Jackson Campbell Diary
    John Franklin Champenois Family Papers
    Richard L. McClung Diary
University of Virginia, Charlottesville, Virginia
    Floyd's Retreat from Fort Donelson: With a Running Description of the Battle
    William S. Hillyer Papers
    Thomas G. Pollock Papers
    Roberts Family Papers
    Thomas Dabney Wier Diary
University of Washington, Seattle, Washington
    Manning F. Force Papers
University of Wyoming, Laramie, Wyoming
    Mark A. Chapman Collection
Vicksburg National Military Park, Vicksburg, Mississippi
    Ben H. Bounds Civil War Memoir, 4th Mississippi File
Vigo County Public Library, Terre Haute, Indiana
    Benjamin Boring Letters
    David W. Stratton Diary
Virginia Historical Society, Richmond, Virginia
    Camp Chase Papers
    James Lindsay Coghill Papers
    Durgin Family Papers
    John Henry Guy Diary
    William Lewis Moody Papers
    Robert Winn Snead Papers
    Stuart Family Papers
    Rufus James Woolwine Diary

Virginia Tech University, Blacksburg, Virginia
    USS *Pittsburg* Paymaster's Ledger, 1862
Washington and Lee University, Lexington, Virginia
    Ted Barclay Letter
Western Kentucky University, Bowling Green, Kentucky
    David M. Claggett Diary
    Kentucky Library and Museum Papers
        Clarence L. Johnson, "The Story of Forts Henry and Donelson"
    Isaac M. Kirby Letter
Western Reserve Historical Society, Cleveland, Ohio
    William P. Palmer Collection
Wiley Sword Collection, Suwanee, Georgia
    Simon B. Buckner, Jr., Letter
    U. S. Grant Letter
    Martin V. Miller Letter
Willamette University, Salem, Oregon
    John G. Burggraf Letters
Wisconsin Historical Society, Madison, Wisconsin
    Edwin Hubbard Letters
    Alexander Simplot Diary
Wright State University, Dayton, Ohio
    Patterson Family Papers
    Wallace Family Papers

Newspapers
Cairo City *Gazette*
Carlinville *Free Democrat*
Charleston *Courier*
Chattanooga *News*
Clarksville *Chronicle*
Clarksville *News Chronicle*
Clarksville *Weekly Chronicle*
Columbia *Herald*
Dover *Weekly Intelligencer*
Evansville *Daily Journal*
Fairfield (Texas) *Recorder*
Fremont *Journal*
Janesville *Daily Gazette*
Macon *Telegraph*
Memphis *Avalanche*
Monroe (Wisconsin) *Sentinel*
Nashville *Evening Bulletin*

Nashville *Morning Bulletin*
Nashville *Times*
Nashville *Union and American*
New York *Independent*
Ottumwa *Courier*
Paulding *Eastern Clarion*
Pulaski *Citizen*
Richmond *Daily Dispatch*
Richmond *Dispatch*
Syracuse *Herald*

PUBLISHED PRIMARY AND SECONDARY SOURCES

Adair, John M. *Historical Sketch of the Forty-Fifth Illinois Regiment, with a Complete List of the Officers and Privates and an Individual Record of Each Man in the Regiment*. Lanark, IL: Carroll County Gazette Print, 1869.

Adams, George Worthington. *Doctors in Blue: The Medical History of the Union Army in the Civil War*. New York: H. Schuman, 1952.

"After the Fall of Fort Donelson." *Confederate Veteran* 4, no. 9 (September 1896): 289–291.

Aldrich, Charles. "How the Iowa Legislature Celebrated the Capture of Fort Donelson." *Iowa Historical Record* 8 (January 1892): 215–221.

Allardice, Bruce S. *Confederate Colonels: A Biographical Register*. Columbia: University of Missouri Press, 2008.

Ambrose, D. Leib. *History of the Seventh Regiment Illinois Volunteer Infantry, From Its First Muster into the U.S. Service, April 25, 1861, to its Final Muster Out, July 9, 1865*. Springfield: Illinois Journal Company, 1868.

Avery, P. O. "Donelson and Henry." September 8, 1887, *National Tribune*.

———. *History of the Fourth Illinois Cavalry Regiment*. Humboldt, NE: Enterprise, 1903.

Badeau, Adam. *Military History of Ulysses S. Grant, from April, 1861, to April, 1865*. 2 vols. New York: D. Appleton, 1881.

Bailey, L. J. "Escape from Fort Donelson." *Confederate Veteran* 23, no. 2 (February 1915): 64.

Barker, Lorenzo A. *Military History (Michigan Boys) Company "D" 66th Illinois: Birge's Western Sharpshooters in the Civil War, 1861–1865*. Np: np, 1905.

Beale, Howard K., ed. *The Diary of Edward Bates, 1859–1866*. Washington, DC: Government Printing Office, 1933.

Bearss, Edwin C. "The Fall of Fort Henry." *West Tennessee Historical Society Papers* 17 (1963): 85–107.

———. *Hardluck Ironclad: The Sinking and Salvage of the Cairo*. Rev. ed. Baton Rouge: Louisiana State University Press, 1980.

———. "The Iowans at Fort Donelson: General C. F. Smith's Attack on the Confederate Right February 12–16, 1862, Part I." *Annals of Iowa* 36, no. 4 (Spring 1962): 241–268.

———. "The Iowans at Fort Donelson: General C. F. Smith's Attack on the Confederate Right February 12–16, 1862, Part II." *Annals of Iowa* 36, no. 5 (Summer 1962): 321–343.

Bedford, H. L. "Fight between the Batteries and Gunboats at Fort Donelson." *Southern Historical Society Papers* 13 (1885): 165–173.

Biographical Directory of the United States Congress. Washington, DC: Government Printing Office, 2005.

Black, Robert C., III. *The Railroads of the Confederacy.* Chapel Hill: University of North Carolina Press, 1952.

Bohannon, Keith S. *The Giles, Allegheny and Jackson Artillery.* Lynchburg, VA: H. E. Howard, 1991.

Boring, B. F. "From Cairo to Donelson." March 15, 1894, *National Tribune.*

Brinton, John H. *Personal Memoirs of John H. Brinton Major and Surgeon U.S.V. 1861–1865.* New York: Nealer Publishing, 1914.

Bruce, George A. "The Donelson Campaign." *Campaigns in Kentucky and Tennessee, Including the Battle of Chickamauga, 1862–1864.* Boston: Cadet Armory, 1908.

Brumbaugh, Thomas B. "A Letter to Fort Donelson." *Manuscripts* 36, no. 1 (Winter 1984): 31–35.

Burns, Ken. *The Civil War.* Walpole, NH: Florentine Films, 1990.

Burt, R. W. "Fort Donelson." September 13, 1906, *National Tribune.*

Cannon, J. P. *Inside of Rebeldom: The Daily Life of a Private in the Confederate Army.* Washington, DC: National Tribune, 1900.

Catton, Bruce. *Grant Moves South.* Boston: Little, Brown, 1960.

Chaffin, Tom. *Pathfinder: John Charles Fremont and the Course of American Empire.* New York: Hill and Wang, 2002.

Chapla, John D. *50th Virginia Infantry.* Lynchburg, VA: H. E. Howard, 1997.

Chetlain, Augustus L. *Recollections of Seventy Years.* Galena, IL: Gazette Publishing, 1899.

Churchill, James O. "Wounded at Fort Donelson." In *War Papers and Personal Reminiscences, 1861–1865.* St. Louis: Becktold, 1892.

Clark, Donald A. *The Notorious "Bull" Nelson: Murdered Civil War General.* Carbondale: Southern Illinois University Press, 2011.

Clarke, H. C. *Diary of the War for Separation, a Daily Chronicle of the Principal Events and History of the Present Revolution, to Which Is Added Notes and Descriptions of All the Great Battles, Including Walker's Narrative of the Battle of Shiloh.* Augusta: Steam Press of Chronicle and Sentinel, 1862.

Cluett, William W. *History of the 57th Regiment Illinois Volunteer Infantry, from Muster in, Dec. 26, 1861, to Muster Out, July 7, 1865.* Princeton: T. P. Streeter, Printer, 1886.

"Condensed Letters." August 13, 1885, *National Tribune.*

"A Confederate Private at Fort Donelson, 1862." *American Historical Review* 31, no. 3 (April 1926): 477–484.

The Congressional Globe: Containing the Debates and Proceedings of the Second Session of the Thirty-Seventh Congress. Washington, DC: Congressional Globe Office, 1862.

Connelly, Thomas L. *Army of the Heartland: The Army of Tennessee, 1861–1862*. Baton Rouge: Louisiana State University Press, 1967.

Connelly, Thomas L., and Archer Jones. *The Politics of Command: Factions and Ideas in Confederate Strategy*. Baton Rouge: Louisiana State University Press, 1973.

Cooling, Benjamin Franklin, ed. "The First Nebraska Infantry Regiment and the Battle of Fort Donelson." *Nebraska History* 45, no. 2 (June 1964): 131–146.

———. "The Forging of Joint Army-Navy Operations: Andrew H. Foote and Grant." In *Grant's Lieutenants: From Cairo to Vicksburg*, edited by Steven E. Woodworth. Lawrence: University Press of Kansas, 2001.

———. *Fort Donelson's Legacy: War and Society in Kentucky and Tennessee, 1862–1863*. Knoxville: University of Tennessee Press, 1997.

———. *Forts Henry and Donelson: The Key to the Confederate Heartland*. Knoxville: University of Tennessee Press, 1987.

———. "The Reliable First Team: Grant and Charles Ferguson Smith." In *Grant's Lieutenants: From Cairo to Vicksburg*, edited by Steven E. Woodworth. Lawrence: University Press of Kansas, 2001.

———. *To the Battles of Franklin and Nashville and Beyond: Stabilization and Reconstruction in Tennessee and Kentucky, 1864–1866*. Knoxville: University of Tennessee Press, 2011.

———. "A Virginian at Fort Donelson: Excerpts from the Prison Journal of John Henry Guy." *Tennessee Historical Quarterly* 27, no. 2 (Summer 1968): 176–190.

Crist, Lynda Lasswell, ed. *The Papers of Jefferson Davis*. 11 vols. to date. Baton Rouge: Louisiana State University Press, 1971–2008.

Croffut, W. A., ed. *Fifty Years in Camp and Field: Diary of Major-General Ethan Allen Hitchcock, U.S.A.* New York: G. P. Putnam's Sons, 1909.

Cross, C. Wallace. *Cry Havoc: A History of the 49th Tennessee Volunteer Infantry Regiment 1861–1865*. Franklin, TN: Hillsboro Press, 2004.

Crummer, Wilbur F. *With Grant at Fort Donelson, Shiloh and Vicksburg, and an Appreciation of General U.S. Grant*. Oak Park, IL: E.C. Crummer, 1915.

Cummings, Charles M. *Yankee Quaker, Confederate General: The Curious Career of Bushrod Rust Johnson*. Columbus, OH: General's Books, 1993.

Cunningham, H. H. *Doctors in Gray: The Confederate Medical Service*. Baton Rouge: Louisiana State University Press, 1958.

Cunningham, O. Edward. *Shiloh and the Western Campaign of 1862*. Edited by Gary D. Joiner and Timothy B. Smith. New York: Savas Beatie, 2007.

Daniel, Larry J. *Cannoneers in Gray: The Field Artillery of the Army of Tennessee*. Rev. ed. Tuscaloosa: University of Alabama Press, 2005.

———. *Days of Glory: The Army of the Cumberland, 1861–1865*. Baton Rouge: Louisiana State University Press, 2004.

———. *Soldiering in the Army of Tennessee: A Portrait of Life in a Confederate Army*. Chapel Hill: University of North Carolina Press, 1991.

Davis, George B., Leslie J. Perry, and Joseph W. Kirkley. *Atlas to Accompany the Official Records of the Union and Confederate Armies*. Washington: Government Printing Office, 1891–1895.

Davis, James A. *51st Virginia Infantry*. Lynchburg, VA: H. E. Howard, 1984.

Davis, Reuben. *Recollections of Mississippi and Mississippians*. Boston: Houghton, Mifflin, 1890.

Davis, William C. *Jefferson Davis: The Man and His Hour, a Biography*. New York: Harper Collins, 1991.

Dawson, George F. *Life and Services of Gen. John A. Logan as Soldier and Statesman*. Washington, DC: National Tribune, 1884.

Donald, David Herbert. *Lincoln*. New York: Simon and Shuster, 1995.

Donelson Campaign Sources Supplementing Volume 7 of the Official Records of the Union and Confederate Armies in the War of the Rebellion. Fort Leavenworth: Army Service Schools Press, 1912.

Duncan, Thomas D. *Recollections of Thomas D. Duncan*. Nashville: McQuiddy Printing, 1922.

Eads, James B. "Recollections of Foote and the Gunboats." In *Battles and Leaders of the Civil War*, 1:338–346. New York: Century, 1884–1887.

Eighth Reunion of the 12th Iowa Vet. Vol. Infantry. Fayette: Reporter Publishing House, nd.

Eisterhold, John A. "Fort Heiman: Forgotten Fortress." *West Tennessee Historical Society Papers* 28 (1974): 43–54.

Elliott, Sam Davis. *Isham G. Harris of Tennessee: Confederate Governor and United States Senator*. Baton Rouge: Louisiana State University Press, 2010.

———. *Soldier of Tennessee: General Alexander P. Stewart and the Civil War in the West*. Baton Rouge: Louisiana State University Press, 1999.

Engle, Stephen D. *Don Carlos Buell: Most Promising of All*. Chapel Hill: University of North Carolina Press, 1999.

———. *Struggle for the Heartland: The Campaign from Fort Henry to Corinth*. Lincoln: University of Nebraska Press, 2001.

———. " 'Thank God, He Has Rescued His Character': Albert Sidney Johnston, Southern Hamlet of the Confederacy." In *Leaders of the Lost Cause: New Perspectives on the Confederate High Command*, edited by Gary W. Gallagher and Joseph T. Glatthaar, 133–163. Mechanicsburg, PA: Stackpole Books, 2004.

Eubank, Damon K. *In the Shadow of the Patriarch: The John J. Crittenden Family in War and Peace*. Macon: Mercer University Press, 2009.

Ferguson, Ernest B. *Chancellorsville 1863: The Souls of the Brave*. New York: Knopf, 1993.

Ferrell, Robert H., ed. *Holding the Line: The Third Tennessee Infantry 1861–1864*. Kent, OH: Kent State University Press, 1994.

"First Battle Experience-Fort Donelson." *Confederate Veteran* 14, no. 11 (November 1906): 500–501.

Fletcher, Samuel H. *The History of Company A, Second Illinois Cavalry*. Np: np, nd.

Floyd's Retreat from Fort Donelson: With a Running Description of the Battle. Cincinnati: A. C. Peters & Bro., 1862.

Foote, John A. "Notes on the Life of Admiral Foote." In *Battles and Leaders of the Civil War*, 1:347. New York: Century, 1884–1887.

Force, Manning F. *From Fort Henry to Corinth*. New York: Charles Scribner's Sons, 1881.

"Fort Donelson." *Southern Bivouac* 1, nos. 9 and 10 (May and June 1883): 344–346.

"Fort Donelson." October 18, 1883, *National Tribune*.

"Fort Donelson." October 25, 1883, *National Tribune*.

"Fort Donelson." November 1, 1883, *National Tribune*.

"Fort Donelson to Camp Morton." *Confederate Veteran* 5, no. 1 (January 1897): 33.

Foster, John Watson. *War Stories for My Grandchildren*. Washington, DC: Riverside Press Cambridge, 1918.

Fuller, J. F. C. *The Generalship of Ulysses S. Grant*. Bloomington: Indiana University Press, 1958.

Gallagher, Gary W., and Joseph T. Glatthaar, eds. *Leaders of the Lost Cause: New Perspectives on the Confederate High Command*. Mechanicsburg, PA: Stackpole Books, 2004.

George, Henry. *History of the 3d, 7th, 8th and 12th Kentucky C.S.A.* Louisville: C. T. Dearing Printing, 1911.

Gibson, Charles Dana, and E. Kay Gibson. *Assault and Logistics: Union Army Coastal and River Operations, 1861–1866*. Camden, ME: Ensign Press, 1995.

Girardi, Robert I. "Leonidas Polk and the Fate of Kentucky in 1861." In *Confederate Generals in the Western Theater: Essays on America's Civil War,* edited by Lawrence L. Hewitt and Arthur W. Bergeron, Jr., 3 vols. Knoxville: University of Tennessee Press, 2011.

The Goodspeed Histories of Montgomery, Robertson, Humphries, Stewart, Dickson, Cheatham, Houston Counties of Tennessee. Columbia: Woodward and Stinson Printing, 1972.

Gott, Kendall G. *Where the South Lost the War: An Analysis of the Fort Henry-Fort Donelson Campaign, February 1862*. Mechanicsburg, PA: Stackpole Books, 2003.

Gower, Hershel, and Jack Allen, eds. *Pen and Sword: The Life and Journals of Randal W. McGavock*. Nashville: Tennessee Historical Commission, 1959.

Grant, U. S. *Personal Memoirs of U.S. Grant*. 2 vols. New York: Charles L. Webster, 1885.

Greenwalt, John G. *A Charge at Fort Donelson, February 15, 1862*. Np: np, 1902.

Guyer, Max Hendricks, ed. "The Journal and Letters of Corporal William O. Gulick." *Iowa Journal of History and Politics* 28, no. 2 (April 1930): 194–267.

Hackemer, Kurt H., ed. *To Rescue My Native Land: The Civil War Letters of William T. Shepherd, First Illinois Light Artillery*. Knoxville: University of Tennessee Press, 2005.

Hafendorfer, Kenneth A. *Mill Springs: Campaign and Battle of Mill Springs, Kentucky*. Louisville: KH Press, 2001.

Hamilton, James J. *The Battle of Fort Donelson*. South Brunswick: Thomas Yoseloff, 1968.

Hattaway, Herman, and Archer Jones. *How the North Won: A Military History of the Civil War*. Urbana: University of Illinois Press, 1983.

Hedley, F. Y. *Marching through Georgia: Pen-Pictures of Every-Day Life in General Sherman's Army, from the Beginning of the Atlanta Campaign until the Closing of the War*. Chicago: Donohue, Henneberry, 1890.

Hess, Earl J. *The Civil War in the West: Victory and Defeat from the Appalachians to the Mississippi*. Chapel Hill: University of North Carolina Press, 2012.

———. *The Union Soldier in Battle: Enduring the Ordeal of Combat*. Lawrence: University Press of Kansas, 1997.

"He Was at Fort Heiman." February 23, 1899, *National Tribune*.

Hewitt, Lawrence L., and Arthur W. Bergeron, Jr., eds. *Confederate Generals in the Western Theater: Essays on America's Civil War*. 3 vols. Knoxville: University of Tennessee Press, 2010.

Hicks, Henry G. "Fort Donelson." *MOLLUS*. Np: np, 1896.

Hoge, William J. *Sketch of Dabney Carr Harrison, Minister of the Gospel and Captain in the Army of the Confederate States of America*. Richmond: Presbyterian Committee of Publication of the Confederate States, 1862.

Hoppin, James Mason. *Life of Andrew Hull Foote, Rear-Admiral United States Navy*. New York: Harper and Brothers, 1874.

Hubert, Charles F. *History of the Fiftieth Regiment Illinois Volunteer Infantry in the War of the Union*. Kansas City: Western Veteran Publishing, 1894.

Huffstodt, Jim. *Hard Dying Men: The Story of General W. H. L. Wallace, General T. E. G. Ransom, and Their "Old Eleventh" Illinois Infantry in the American Civil War, 1861–1865*. Westminster, MD: Heritage Books, 2007.

Hughes, Nathaniel Cheairs, Jr. *The Battle of Belmont: Grant Strikes South*. Chapel Hill: University of North Carolina Press, 1991.

Hughes, Nathaniel C., and Roy P. Stonesifer, Jr. *The Life and Wars of Gideon J. Pillow*. Chapel Hill: University of North Carolina Press, 2001.

Hurst, Jack. *Men of Fire: Grant, Forrest, and the Campaign That Decided the Civil War*. New York: Basic Books, 2008.

Jobe, James. "Forts Henry and Donelson." *Blue and Gray Magazine* 28, no. 4 (2011): 6–27, 43–50.

Johnson, Leland R. *Engineers of the Twin Rivers: A History of the Nashville District Corps of Engineers, United States Army*. Nashville: United States Army Engineer District, 1978.

Johnson, Robert E. *Rear Admiral John Rogers, 1812–1882*. Annapolis: Naval Institute Press, 1967.

Johnston, William Preston. *The Life of Gen. Albert Sidney Johnston: His Service in the Armies of the United States, the Republic of Texas, and the Confederate States*. New York: D. Appleton, 1879.

Joiner, Gary D. *Mr. Lincoln's Brown Water Navy: The Mississippi Squadron*. New York: Rowman and Littlefield, 2007.

Jones, Archer. *Civil War Command and Strategy: The Process of Victory and Defeat*. New York: Free Press, 1992.

Jones, J. B. *A Rebel War Clerk's Diary: At the Confederate States Capital*. 2 vols. Edited by James I. Robertson, Jr. Lawrence: University Press of Kansas, 2015.

Jones, James Pickett. *Black Jack: John A. Logan and Southern Illinois in the Civil War Era*. Carbondale: Southern Illinois University Press, 1995.

Jordan, Thomas, and J. P. Pryor. *The Campaigns of Lieut.-Gen. N. B. Forrest and of Forrest's Cavalry, with Portraits, Maps, and Illustrations*. New Orleans: Blelock, 1868.

Kennedy, Joseph C. G. *Agriculture of the United States in 1860: Compiled from the Original Returns of the Eighth Census under the Direction of the Secretary of the Interior*. Washington: Government Printing Office, 1864.

———. *Population of the United States in 1860: Compiled from the Original Returns of the Eighth Census under the Direction of the Secretary of the Interior*. Washington: Government Printing Office, 1864.

Kimbell, Charles B. *History of Battery "A" First Illinois Light Artillery Volunteers*. Chicago: Cushing Printing, 1899.

Kiner, F. F. *One Year's Soldiering, Embracing the Battles of Fort Donelson and Shiloh*. Lancaster: E. H. Thomas, 1863.

Kiper, Richard L. *Major General John Alexander McClernand: Politician in Uniform*. Kent, OH: Kent State University Press, 1999.

Lanza, Conrad H., and Theodore B. Taylor. *Fort Henry and Fort Donelson Campaigns, February, 1862. Source Book*. Fort Leavenworth, KS: General Service Schools Press, 1923.

Lawrence, Betty, ed. *Unrevised History of the War for Southern Independence*. Meridian: T. U. Lawrence, 1995.

Lindsley, John Berrien. *The Military Annals of Tennessee*. Nashville: J. M. Lindsley, 1886.

Link, Newell Anderson. "An Inquiry into the Early County Court Records of Stewart County, Tennessee." MA Thesis, Middle Tennessee State College, 1952.

Logan, Mrs. John A. "News from Donelson." May 31, 1888, *National Tribune*.

———. *Reminiscences of a Soldier's Wife: An Autobiography*. New York: Scribner's, 1913.

Longacre, Edward G. *The Early Morning of War: Bull Run, 1861*. Norman: University of Oklahoma Press, 2014.

Lowry, J. T. "A Fort Donelson Prisoner of War." *Confederate Veteran* 18, no. 7 (July 1910): 334–335.

Magdeburg, F. H. "The Capture of Fort Donelson." In *War Papers Read before the Commandery of the State of Wisconsin, MOLLUS*, 284–295. Milwaukee: Burdick & Allen, 1903.

Manufactures of the United States in 1860: Compiled from the Original Returns of the Eighth Census under the Direction of the Secretary of the Interior. Washington: Government Printing Office, 1865.

Marszalek, John F. *Commander of All Lincoln's Armies: A Life of General Henry W. Halleck*. Cambridge, MA: Harvard University Press, 2004.

———. *Lincoln and the Military*. Carbondale: Southern Illinois University Press, 2014.

———. *Sherman: A Soldier's Passion for Order*. New York: Free Press, 1993.

Mattingly, Nancy Ann, ed. *I Marched with Sherman: Civil War Memoirs of the 20th Illinois Volunteer Infantry*. Lincoln, NE: iUniverse.com, 2000.

McAuley, John T. "Fort Donelson and Its Surrender." *Military Essays and Recollections*. Chicago: A. C. McLurg, 1891.

McPherson, James M. *Abraham Lincoln and the Second American Revolution*. New York: Oxford University Press, 1991.

———. *Battle Cry of Freedom: The Civil War Era*. New York: Oxford University Press, 1988.

Merrill, James M. "Capt. Andrew Hull Foote and the Civil War on Tennessee Waters." *Tennessee Historical Quarterly* 30, no. 1 (Spring 1970): 83–93.

Millett, Allen R., Peter Maslowski, and William B. Feis. *For the Common Defense: A Military History of the United States from 1607–2012*. New York: Free Press, 2012.

Milligan, John D., ed. *From the Fresh-Water Navy: 1861–1864: The Letters of Acting Master's Mate Henry R. Browne and Acting Ensign Symmes E. Browne*. Annapolis: United States Naval Institute, 1970.

Moore, Frank, ed. *The Rebellion Record: A Diary of American Events, with Documents, Narratives Illustrative Incidents, Poetry, etc.* 11 vols. New York: D. Vann Nostrand, 1861–1868.

Morrison, Marion. *A History of the Ninth Regiment Illinois Volunteer Infantry*. Monmouth, IL: John S. Clark, Printer, 1864.

Mosgrove, George D. "Fort Donelson." September 18, 1902, *National Tribune*.

Nevins, Allen, ed. *Diary of the Civil War*. New York: Macmillan, 1962.

Newberry, J. S. *A Visit to Fort Donelson, Tenn., for the Relief of the Wounded of Feb'y 15, 1862: A Letter*. New York: United States Sanitary Commission, 1862.

Niven, John. *Gideon Welles: Lincoln's Secretary of the Navy*. New York: Oxford University Press, 1973.

Noe, Kenneth W. *Reluctant Rebels: The Confederates Who Joined the Army after 1861*. Chapel Hill: University of North Carolina Press, 2010.

Nye, W. S. "Jake Donelson A 'Cocky' Rebel." *Civil War Times Illustrated* 1, no. 11 (April 1962): 51.

The Official Records of the Union and Confederate Navies in the War of the Rebellion. 30 vols. Washington, DC: Government Printing Office, 1894–1922.

Palmer, John R. "The Field of Donelson." April 11, 1901, *National Tribune*.

Paludan, Phillip Shaw. *The Presidency of Abraham Lincoln*. Lawrence: University Press of Kansas, 1994.

Panhorst, Michael W. " 'The First of Our Hundred Battle Monuments': Civil War Battlefield Monuments Built by Active-Duty Soldiers During the Civil War." *Southern Cultures* 20, no. 4 (Winter 2014): 22–43.

Parks, Joseph H. *General Leonidas Polk, C.S.A.: The Fighting Bishop*. Baton Rouge: Louisiana State University Press, 1962.

Peterson, Gloria. *Administrative History: Fort Donelson National Military Park, Dover, Tennessee*. Washington, DC: National Park Service, 1968.

"Peter Wilson in the Civil War." *Iowa Journal of History and Politics* 40, no. 3 (July 1942): 261–320.

Pinnegar, Charles. *Brand of Infamy: A Biography of John Buchanan Floyd*. Westport, CT: Greenwood, 2002.

Piston, William Garrett, and Richard W. Hatcher. *Wilson's Creek: The Second Battle of the Civil War and the Men Who Fought It*. Chapel Hill: University of North Carolina Press, 2000.

Plummer, Mark A. *Lincoln's Rail-Splitter: Governor Richard J. Oglseby*. Urbana: University of Illinois Press, 2001.

"The Post of Honor: Second Iowa Volunteers." *The Soldiers' Casket* 1, no. 1 (January 1865): 154–155.

Raab, James W. *Confederate General Lloyd Tilghman: A Biography*. Jefferson, NC: McFarland, 2006.

Reed, David W. *Campaigns and Battles of the Twelfth Regiment Iowa Veteran Volunteer Infantry from Its Organization, September, 1861, to Muster Out, January 20, 1866*. Np: np, 1903.

Rerick, John H. *The Forty-Fourth Indiana Volunteer Infantry: History of Its Services in the War of the Rebellion and a Personal Record of Its Members*. LaGrange, IN: np, 1880.

Richardson, Albert D. *A Personal History of Ulysses S. Grant*. Hartford, CT: American Publishing, 1868.

———. *The Secret Service, the Field, the Dungeon, and the Escape*. Hartford, CT: American Publishing, 1865.

Richardson, James D. *A Compilation of the Messages and Papers of the Confederacy, Including the Diplomatic Correspondence 1861–1865*. 2 vols. Nashville: United States Publishing, 1906.

Riddell, Thomas J. "Western Campaign." *Southern Historical Society Papers* 22 (1894): 316–323.

Rietti, John C. *Military Annals of Mississippi: Military Organizations Which Entered the Service of the Confederate States of America from the State of Mississippi*. Spartanburg, SC: Reprint Company, 1976.

Riggins, Van L. *A History of Fort Donelson National Military Park Tennessee*. Washington, DC: NPS, 1958.

"River Batteries at Fort Donelson." *Confederate Veteran* 4, no. 11 (November 1896): 393–400.

Roland, Charles P. "Albert Sidney Johnston and the Defense of the Confederate West." In *Confederate Generals in the Western Theater: Essays on America's Civil War*, edited by Lawrence L. Hewitt and Arthur W. Bergeron, Jr., 3 vols. Knoxville: University of Tennessee Press, 2010.

———. *Albert Sidney Johnston: Soldier of Three Republics*. Austin: University of Texas Press, 1964.

Roman, Alfred. *The Military Operations of General Beauregard in the War between the States, 1861–1865: Including a Brief Personal Sketch of His Services in the War with Mexico, 1846–8*. 2 vols. New York: Harper and Brothers, 1883.

Rowland, Dunbar, and H. Grady Howell, Jr. *Military History of Mississippi: 1803–1898,*

Including a Listing of All Known Mississippi Confederate Military Units. Madison, MS: Chickasaw Bayou Press, 2003.

Schenker, Carl R., Jr. "The Grant-Halleck-Smith Affair." *North and South* 12, no. 1 (February 2010): 11–12.

Scott, J. L. *36th Virginia Infantry.* Lynchburg, VA: H. E. Howard, 1987.

Sears, Stephen W. *George B. McClellan: The Young Napoleon.* New York: Ticknor and Fields, 1988.

Sherman, William T. *Memoirs of General William T. Sherman: Written by Himself.* 2 vols. New York: D. Appleton, 1875.

Simon, John Y., and John F. Marszalek, eds. *The Papers of Ulysses S. Grant.* 31 vols. to date. Carbondale: Southern Illinois University Press, 1967–present.

Simplot, Alex. "General Grant and the Incident at Dover." *Wisconsin Magazine of History* 44 (Winter 1960–1961): 83–84.

Simpson, Brooks D. *The Civil War in the East: Struggle, Stalemate, and Victory.* Lincoln, NE: Potomac Books, 2013.

———. *Ulysses S. Grant: Triumph over Adversity, 1822–1865.* Boston: Houghton Mifflin, 2000.

Simpson, John A., ed. *Reminiscences of the 41st Tennessee: The Civil War in the West.* Shippensburg, PA: White Mane, 2001.

"Sketch of Lieutenant-General N. B. Forrest." *Southern Bivouac* 2, no. 7 (March 1884): 289–298.

Slagle, Jay. *Ironclad Captain: Seth Ledyard Phelps & the U.S. Navy, 1841–1864.* Kent: Kent State University Press, 1996.

Smith, H. I. *History of the Seventh Iowa Veteran Volunteer Infantry during the Civil War.* Mason City, IA: R. Hitchcock Printer, Binder, 1903.

Smith, John Thomas. *A History of the Thirty-First Regiment of Indiana Volunteer Infantry in the War of the Rebellion.* Cincinnati: Western Methodist Book Concern, 1900.

Smith, Myron J. *The Timberclads in the Civil War: The Lexington, Conestoga and Tyler on the Western Waters.* Jefferson, NC: McFarland, 2008.

———. *The USS Carondelet: A Civil War Ironclad on Western Waters.* Jefferson, NC: McFarland, 2010.

Smith, Timothy B. *James Z. George: Mississippi's Great Commoner.* Jackson: University Press of Mississippi, 2012.

———. *Mississippi in the Civil War: The Home Front.* Jackson: University Press of Mississippi, 2010.

———. *The Mississippi Secession Convention: Delegates and Deliberations in Politics and War, 1861–1865.* Jackson: University Press of Mississippi, 2014.

———. "The Politics of Battlefield Preservation: David B. Henderson and the National Military Parks." *Annals of Iowa* 66, nos. 3 and 4 (Summer/Fall 2007): 293–320.

———. *Shiloh: Conquer or Perish.* Lawrence: University Press of Kansas, 2014.

Smith, William F. "Operations before Fort Donelson." *Magazine of American History* 15, no. 1 (January 1886): 40.

Spencer, Selden. "Diary Account of Fort Donelson." *Confederate Veteran* 5, no. 6 (June 1897): 282–285.

Stephens, Gail. *Shadow of Shiloh: Major General Lew Wallace in the Civil War*. Indianapolis: Indiana Historical Society Press, 2010.

Stevenson, William G. *Thirteen Months in the Rebel Army: Being a Narrative of Personal Adventures in the Infantry, Ordinance, Cavalry, Courier, and Hospital Services*. New York: A. S. Barnes & Burr, 1862.

Stewart County Heritage, Dover, Tennessee. 2 vols. Dallas: Taylor Publishing, 1980.

Stickles, Arndt M. *Simon Bolivar Buckner: Borderland Knight*. Chapel Hill: University of North Carolina Press, 1940.

Stone, A. L. *Praise for Victory: A Sermon, Preached in Park Street Church, Boston, February 23, 1862*. Boston: Press of T. R. Marvin & Son, 1862.

Stowell, Daniel W., ed. " 'We Will Fight for Our Flag': The Civil War Letters of Thomas Barnett, Ninth Illinois Volunteer Infantry." *Journal of Illinois History* 3 (Autumn 2000): 201–222.

Sword, Wiley. *Shiloh: Bloody April*. Rev. ed. Dayton, OH: Morningside, 2001.

Symonds, Craig L. *Lincoln and His Admirals*. New York: Oxford University Press, 2008.

T. D. J. "Fort Donelson." *Southern Historical Society Papers* 18 (1890): 372–373.

Taylor, Jesse. "The Defense of Fort Henry." In *Battles and Leaders of the Civil War*, 1:368–372. New York: Century, 1884–1887.

Thayer, John M. "At Fort Donelson." April 21, 1898, *National Tribune*.

Thompson, Ed. Porter. *History of the First Kentucky Brigade*. Cincinnati: Caxton, 1868.

———. *History of the Orphan Brigade*. Louisville: Lewis N. Thompson, 1898.

Tucker, Spencer C. *Andrew Foote: Civil War Admiral on Western Waters*. Annapolis: Naval Institute Press, 2000.

———. *Unconditional Surrender: The Capture of Forts Henry and Donelson*. Abilene: State House Press, 2001.

Twombly, Voltaire P. *The Second Iowa Infantry at Fort Donelson, February 15, 1862*. Des Moines: Plain Talk Printing House, 1901.

Uffelman, Minoa D., Ellen Kanervo, Phyllis Smith, and Eleanor Williams, eds. *The Diary of Nannie Haskins Williams: A Southern Woman's Story of Rebellion and Reconstruction, 1863–1890*. Knoxville: University of Tennessee Press, 2014.

Villard, Henry. *Memoirs of Henry Villard: Journalist and Financier, 1835–1900*. 2 vols. Boston: Houghton, Mifflin, 1904.

Walke, Henry. "The Gun-Boats at Belmont and Fort Henry." In *Battles and Leaders of the Civil War*, 1:358–367. New York: Century, 1884–1887.

———. *Naval Scenes and Reminiscences of the Civil War in the United States, on the Southern and Western Waters during the Years 1861, 1862 and 1863*. New York: F. R. Reed, 1877.

———. "The Western Flotilla at Fort Donelson, Island Number Ten, Fort Pillow and Memphis." In *Battles and Leaders of the Civil War*, 1:430–452. New York: Century, 1884–1887.

Wallace, Isabel. *Life and Letters of General W. H. L. Wallace*. Carbondale: Southern Illinois University Press, 2000.

Wallace, Lew. "The Capture of Fort Donelson." In *Battles and Leaders of the Civil War*, 1:398–428. New York: Century, 1884–1887.

———. *Lew Wallace: An Autobiography*, 2 vols. New York: Harper and Brothers, 1906.

Wardner, Horace. "Reminiscences of a Surgeon." In *Military Essays and Recollections: Papers Read before the Commandery of the State of Illinois, MOLLUS*, 3:173–191. Chicago: Dial Press, 1899.

War of the Rebellion: A Compilation of the Official Records of the Union and Confederate Armies. Washington, DC: US Government Printing Office, 1880–1901.

Weaver, Jeffrey C. *Goochland Light, Goochland Turner & Mountain Artillery*. Lynchburg, VA: H. E. Howard, 1994.

Welsh, Jack D. *Medical Histories of Confederate Generals*. Kent: Kent State University Press, 1995.

———. *Medical Histories of Union Generals*. Kent: Kent State University Press, 1996.

Whittlesey, Charles. *War Memoranda: Cheat River to the Tennessee 1861–1862*. Cleveland: William W. Williams, 1884.

Williams, A. J. "A Union Boy at Donelson." December 15, 1898, *National Tribune*.

Williams, Kenneth P. *Grant Rises in the West: The First Year, 1861–1862*. Lincoln: University of Nebraska Press, 1997.

Williams, T. Harry. *Lincoln and His Generals*. New York: Knopf, 1952.

———. *P. G. T. Beauregard: Napoleon in Gray*. Baton Rouge: Louisiana State University Press, 1954.

Willis, James. *Arkansas Confederates in the Western Theater*. Dayton, OH: Morningside, 1998.

Wills, Brian Steel. "A Kentucky Lyon Roars: Hylan B. Lyon in the Civil War." In *Confederate Generals in the Western Theater: Essays on America's Civil War*, edited by Lawrence L. Hewitt and Arthur W. Bergeron, Jr., 2:186–214. Knoxville: University of Tennessee Press, 2010.

Wilson, James H. *The Life of John A. Rawlins*. New York: Neale Publishing, 1916.

Wilson, LeGrand J. *The Confederate Soldier*. Memphis: Memphis State University Press, 1973.

Wood, D. W. *History of the 20th O.V.V.I. Regiment and Proceedings of the First Reunion at Mt. Vernon, Ohio, April 6, 1876*. Columbus, OH: Paul and Thrall, Book and Job Printers, 1876.

Woodworth, Steven E., ed. *Civil War Generals in Defeat*. Lawrence: University Press of Kansas, 1999.

———. *Decision in the Heartland: The Civil War in the West*. Westport, CT: Praeger, 2008.

———. "Earned on the Field of Battle: William H. L. Wallace." In *Grant's Lieutenants: From Cairo to Vicksburg*, edited by Steven E. Woodworth. Lawrence: University Press of Kansas, 2001.

———. *Jefferson Davis and His Generals: The Failure of Confederate Command in the West*. Lawrence: University Press of Kansas, 1990.

———. *Nothing but Victory: The Army of the Tennessee, 1861–1865*. New York: Knopf, 2005.

———. "When Merit Was Not Enough: Albert Sidney Johnston and Confederate Defeat in the West, 1862." In *Civil War Generals in Defeat*, edited by Steven E. Woodworth. Lawrence: University Press of Kansas, 1999.

Young, John Russell. *Around the World with General Grant*. 2 vols. New York: Subscription Book Department, 1879.

Young, William, and Patricia Young. *56th Virginia Infantry*. Lynchburg, VA: H. E. Howard, 1991.

INDEX